The Miegunyah Press

The general series of the
Miegunyah Volumes
was made possible by the
Miegunyah Fund
established by bequests
under the wills of
Sir Russell and Lady Grimwade.

'Miegunyah' was the home of
Mab and Russell Grimwade
from 1911 to 1955.

the constant gardener

the constant
gardener

Written and photographed by
Holly Kerr Forsyth

THE
MIEGUNYAH
PRESS

THE MIEGUNYAH PRESS
An imprint of Melbourne University
Publishing Ltd
187 Grattan Street, Carlton,
Victoria 3053, Australia
mup-info@unimelb.edu.au
www.mup.com.au

First published 2007
Paperback edition published 2008
Text and photographs
© Holly Kerr Forsyth 2007
Design and typography
© Melbourne University Publishing Ltd 2008

Designed by Pfisterer + Freeman
Typeset in Adobe Garamond Pro
Printed by Australian Book Connection

National Library of Australia
Cataloguing-in-Publication entry:

Forsyth, Holly Kerr, 1953–

The constant gardener / Holly Kerr
Forsyth.

9780522855401 (pbk.)

Includes index.
Bibliography.

Gardening—Australia.

635

Previous pages:
Page ii: Welcome to my world,
Wychwood, Tasmania.
Pages iv–v: *Magnolia denudata*.

Right: The David Austin rose
'Belle Story'.

Following page:
Page ix: *Hosta tokudama*
'Aureonebulosa'.

Contents

Acknowledgements

There are so many people who have helped bring this book about. All those mentioned throughout *The Constant Gardener* have generously allowed me to photograph and write about their gardens, and have shared their knowledge, and their love of horticulture, with me. So many have provided generous hospitality, most particularly my friends Sue and Ian Home.

My thanks also go to long-suffering friends who not only suggested walks in the park, but who read some of the chapters to ensure that I was making sense of the myriad topics that confront gardeners every day.

Others, including Chris Guppy, from the University of New England, Jeff Rohrlach, MD of AgroBest Australia Pty Ltd, Judy Horton of Yates, hellebore breeders John and Corrie Dudley, rare bulb grower Marcus Harvey, China expert Peter Valder, Bob and Derrilie Cherry of Paradise Plants and rosarian David Ruston kindly read relevant chapters. Needless to say, any mistakes that have somehow found their way into the book are all my own work!

I am indeed fortunate that Louise Adler, Chief Executive Officer at Melbourne University Publishing, embraced the idea of this book with such enthusiasm; again I am grateful for Tracy O'Shaughnessy's vision and insight, to Eugenie Baulch and to the entire team at MUP. My thanks to editors Sally Moss and Judy Brookes for their care in picking up any omissions or inconsistencies, and to Hamish Freeman for his wonderful design.

And, as always, my husband Ross and daughters Olivia (a wonderful cook, who re-tested all the recipes) and Camilla, and my sons Angus and Tom, deserve the greatest thanks for coping with a mother who is at her computer at most unsociable hours or travelling the globe in pursuit of her horticultural obsession.

Introduction

The American wilderness explorer and environmentalist John Muir wrote in 1901, 'Everybody needs beauty as well as bread, places to play and pray in, where nature may heal and cheer and give strength to body and soul alike.' Gardeners know this.

It is a trueism that the simplest things make us happiest. Think, for instance, of the utter bliss of holding your sleeping child in your arms. Or the satisfaction of sharing a cup of perfect coffee and a good chat with a friend who wants nothing more from you than the pleasure of your company. Standing in your garden—no matter how small—in the soft, early morning light in those first days of summer, the scent of anticipation hovering in the air, is another perfect pleasure. The garden is surely one of life's happy places: it provides joy, a creative outlet and great exercise—and helps us to put daily vicissitudes in perspective.

The Iranians understand the importance of gardens, which have been depicted in the decorative arts and represented in literature over many thousands of years, forming an integral part of their culture. From the earliest times, Persian gardens were created as the earthly representations, or reflections, of Paradise, an idea that became central to many cultures and religions throughout later centuries. Water, earth and trees are all considered sacred in pre-Islamic and Islamic culture; beauty, reflecting light, deflects evil.

The Constant Gardener is a collection of thoughts and musings about the garden and other topics that have moved me and inspired me; concerned me, even. The book describes how to prune a rose, build a stone wall or identify a garden pest. And, of course, it includes my favourite plants: how to grow them, how to use them. These are the species with which I have fallen in love over the past dozen or more years, when I have seen them thriving, in any one of the thousand gardens that I have visited to write about and to photograph.

Making a garden is one of the greatest of the arts—and one of the most difficult, for a garden does not stand still and, certainly, does not always grow according to plan. I hope this book will help you gain enormous pleasure from your garden as you create your own Paradise. I hope you will dip into it as you sit with a cup of tea, keep it by your bed for companionable night-time reading and, of course, take it into the garden as you tackle those essential garden chores.

As the Greek historian Xenophon wrote of the Persian king Cyrus in 399 BC, 'The Great King … in all the districts he resides in and visits … takes care that there are "paradises" … full of all the good and beautiful things that the soil will produce.' For, as many have noted, it is not just trees, flowers and vegetables that are raised in a garden; it is also the human spirit.

Opposite: A border at Wychwood, Tasmania. *Above*: Water rills are central to Persian gardens: here, Bagh-*e* Fin, Kashan.

The Meaning of It All

PART ONE

The Seasons

Among the reasons many of us are passionate about gardening is that it links us to the earth. We are, at the very least, bystanders watching creation take place. We witness the magic of nature that each season brings, from bright green tips pushing through the earth to buds unfurling into exquisite flowers; from autumnal colour to dormancy or death. Whichever part of this diverse country we live in, each season brings its own scent, distinct character and idiosyncratic beauty, then wanes in deference to the next. Gardening fulfils and inspires us, as it connects us with the most basic components of nature: life (in this case, from bare soil), death and then re-birth. In essence, we are in touch with the seasons, the natural cycle of events.

Although often chilly and gloomy, winter is a calm time, when the bones of the garden become clear and there is time for reading—and dreaming. Expectation builds towards spring, which is most enjoyed for its vigour and endless menu of delicious scents. Summer then provides a green backdrop to the brilliant, tropical colours of flowering cannas, hibiscus and frangipani. The tapestry of fiery colours in autumn adds excitement to a season that might otherwise be wistful as we once again approach the shorter, colder days of winter.

Tip: You might mark the seasonal change in temperature with a tapestry hedge. A choice of different hedging species will bring something visually fascinating with each season: a technicolour mix in autumn; the bones of dormancy—and often colourful berries and beautiful bark—in winter; and a fresh green dress when spring scampers in.

Winter

It is great to be alive on those winter mornings when, in cool to cold climates, a glorious, clear dawn light illuminates a crisp frost sculptured on everything from leaves and branches to fences and paving. The days are shorter and there is less time for working in the garden, but surely nothing lifts the spirits more than gardening on those clear, blue-sky, mid-winter days that we can experience in this country. It is in this season, when much of the garden can appear naked, that its structure becomes more evident. Hedges, standards and topiary, as well as berries, bark, twisted trunks, and walls and paving, take on additional *gravitas*.

Careful selection of plants for the winter garden can provide more than structure: the bare branches of wintersweet (*Chimonanthus praecox*), for example, are covered in highly scented, cream to pale yellow flowers throughout the coldest months. Many more plants bear a mass of winter berries, treasured as they brighten any gloom.

Winter is also, of course, a time to plant, following notes made a season or two earlier, to fill gaps or augment different colour schemes to brighten borders.

Opposite: Winter frost illuminates a sprig of Japanese box. *Previous page*: The blowsy blooms of the peony signal summer.

My winter garden is dominated by the strange forms of bare-branched frangipanis, which were planted when the house was built early last century. Excitement soon builds, however, as the beloved magnolias begin to perform in early spring.

Trees for winter bark

While most gardeners focus on fruit, flowers and foliage when drawing up a plant list, the changing colours, textures and patterns on the trunks of many trees have a unique beauty. These are often the bonus in the winter garden, when the trees are bare and there is less to intrigue. Many trees are prized for their bark alone, in particular the myrtles and crepe myrtles, some of the birches and several of the rhododendrons. Plane trees, liquidambars, gordonias, many of our eucalypts and some of the deciduous conifers also have lovely bark when you find the time to stop and stroke. Here are some further suggestions:

- *Acer griseum*: Discovered in 1901 in China by the plant hunter Ernest Wilson, the peeling, coloured bark of the paperbark maple, and its deep scarlet leaves in autumn, ensures it a place in many gardens.
- *Azara microphylla*: The fast-growing, evergreen vanilla tree from South America has colourful bark and frond-like, tough leaves. Its tiny yellow flowers have a vanilla fragrance.
- *Camellia yunnanensis*: From southern China, this large shrub to small tree has lovely reddish bark (which you can almost rub off) and lovely single white flowers.
- *Luma apiculata*: The cinnamon bark myrtle grows to a medium-sized tree, with the bonus of flaking, cinnamon-coloured bark and aromatic leaves. Its tiny white flowers bloom against fine dark green foliage during summer.
- *Prunus serrula*: Among the most arresting of trees, the birch-bark or Tibetan cherry boasts a ruby-red, striated trunk. The Manchurian cherry (*P. maackii*), a tall-growing tree from Korea, also has glowing red bark. The white spring flowers are followed by tiny black fruit.

Spring

You know how it is. The sweet scent of jasmine is carried on a late-winter breeze and you declare that this sometimes miscreant plant is your favourite. You cannot suppress the excitement at the approach of spring and the knowledge that the cold days of winter are numbered: the fat buds of wisteria start to unfurl to reveal those elegant, scented racemes in one of nature's magic shows. Wisteria tops your must-have list, and you are reminded that spring is your favourite season.

Have you ever watched Solomon's seal (*Polygonatum* spp.) develop over several spring days, from the fat, fresh-green flower-head emerging from a finely striped, papery sheath that pushes through the crumbly, dark soil to a finale of white, bell-like flowers (each decorated with a green rim), hanging delicately on a fine, arching wand? It's a profound experience.

There are about 30 species in this genus, native to the temperate regions of the northern hemisphere, where they thrive on the moist, humus-rich forest floor. The most commonly grown in gardens in this country is *P.* × *hybridum,* which looks marvellous multiplying behind a mass of hostas. It is particularly suited to woodland plantings and dappled shade.

One of the loveliest trees for the spring garden is the judas tree (*Cercis siliquastrum),* which flowers with clouds of pink blossom in September and October. The smaller growing *C. canadensis* 'Forest Pansy' is native to the USA and features red, heart-shaped leaves that appear on bare stems after a display of hot-pink flowers. I saw it a few years ago in a Melbourne garden, underplanted with black tulips, which were backed by a wide ribbon of *Helleborus argutifolius,* displaying dark pewter-coloured foliage. Recently released by the United States National Arboretum is 'Don Egolf,' a new compact *C. chinensis* cultivar, which produces masses of rose-purple flowers.

Manchurian pear (*Pyrus ussuriensis*), with its mass of white blossom in spring (and its blazing autumn colour) is another tree with year-round value. An avenue—or even just one specimen tree—of *P. calleryana* 'Bradford', planted to provide autumn colour and spring blossom, looks stunning in a cool-climate garden. This cultivar colours late and holds its leaves for many months. *P. calleryana* 'Chanticleer' has lovely autumn colours and spring blossom, and does not split in high winds like the more common *P. ussuriensis*. (Another favourite, the weeping silver pear [*P. salicifolia*], doesn't have autumn colour, but with its grey-green, soft, lanceolate foliage, is often used as a focal point at the end of a walk—instead of, for instance, a piece of sculpture.)

Summer

You might think that no season could surpass spring for anticipation and the joy of watching the garden come to life. But then the pure scent of gardenia washes over the garden, warning you that Christmas is close. The screeching of brilliant lorikeets soon alerts you to heavy, honey-rich trusses of yellow, red or pink blossom on the eucalypts and you wonder at the beauty of our native plants. The flamboyance of roses and lavenders also heralds summer. Finally, the bare branches of the frangipani, that prehistoric-looking member of the Apocynaceae family, display their summer plumage in yellow, cream and white, and in pinks and reds, apricots and orange.

You then decide that *summer* must be the most voluptuous season of the year, with the promise of swimming, bare feet and easy living.

The true test of a garden is whether it still looks good in the hottest month of February, when the fullness of the season is on the wane, and plants and their owners are exhausted by the heat and humidity. The gradual transition from the bleached-out tones of summer to the richness of autumn dawns as something of a relief.

Autumn

'Season of mists and mellow fruitfulness …' Is it because words such as these in Keats's 'Ode to Autumn' often seem to reflect upon autumn's fleeting beauty, that some of us feel slightly sad when nature starts to lose pace—when leaves turn and fall, and there is the prospect of cold mornings and nights ahead?

Autumn is a wonderful time, though—comfortable, rather than full of the frenetic activity of

1. The autumn garden is on fire with colour.
2. The winter blooms of *Helleborus niger* look like fresh snow on a burgundy carpet of fallen leaves.
3. Frost outlines the leaves of *Acer palmatum* var. *dissectum*.
4. Late winter brings the excitement of bulbs.
5. If it's spring, the rhododendron will be in bloom.

spring. 'Autumn is a second spring, when every leaf is a flower.' The author and philosopher, Albert Camus, put a positive spin on a season that many find somewhat melancholy. Others relish the promise of the bounty from the garden that accompanies autumn or the prospect of some gentle exercise when raking up fallen leaves.

Late afternoon walks are in soft light, through gently bracing air, sometimes scented with the smoke curling from wood fires. Peering across fences and through banks of trees and shrubs reveals gardens that were secret in summer, but now show the devotion of generations of gardeners who have loved them. In many old and beautiful gardens, the ground is covered with thick carpets of curling, crunchy leaves from exotic trees, splattered with dashes of oranges, reds and yellows. Massive trees, now almost bare, provide great strength and structure.

The straw colours of the decorative prairie grasses are starting to turn caramel, cream and bronze. Some among us may breathe a long sigh of relief that the relentless growth in the garden will abate for a few months and the watering and weeding of summer might end, providing time for those satisfying winter chores of cutting back, tidying up and putting the garden to bed under a winter blanket of mulch.

And, as the mountain areas around the country put on a kaleidoscope of fiery colours, autumn is a time of wonder and awe.

Tip: You don't have to own a cold-climate garden to enjoy the colours of autumn: numerous gardens in mountain areas are open in April and May. As well as at Mount Wilson, many on the Southern Highlands of New South Wales are open; in the hills behind Adelaide the trees colour beautifully at this time of year. Bright, in northern Victoria, attracts thousands of visitors, who also come to enjoy its autumn fireworks show.

Trees for autumn colour

- *Acer* spp.: The maples provide some of the best autumn colours of all: first come the fiery red colours of the North American maples, *Acer rubrum* and *A. saccharum*, followed by the deep scarlet of the paperbark maple (*A. griseum*). With parentage of the *saccharinum* (the silver maple) and *rubrum* species, the hardy and heat-tolerant *A. × freemanii* 'Autumn Blaze' gives amazing autumn colours. The trident maple (*A. buergerianum*) grows to about 9 m and is native to China and Korea. The Norway maple (*A. platanoides* 'Crimson King') has deep purple foliage in spring that turns orange in autumn: it reaches some 15 m after 20 to 30 years.

  The filigreed leaves of the Japanese maple (*A. palmatum*), particularly those of the Dissectum Group, flutter in autumn breezes, providing essential contrasts in texture and captivating light and shadow play. A particular favourite is *A. palmatum* 'Osakazuki' with its vivid scarlet foliage.

  A. pentaphyllum, a beautiful maple that is now rare in the wilds of its native Schezuan province in China, puts on a late autumn performance and is also spectacular on sunny days in very early winter. It grows well in Melbourne and comes into leaf, belatedly, in November.
- *Betula* spp.: Many of the birches feature butter-yellow leaves in autumn. There is the cherry birch (*Betula lenta*), as well as *B. alleghaniensis* (syn. *B. lutea*) and *B. papyrifera*: both of the latter have the bonus of beautiful bark.
- *Enkianthus*: These beautiful but temperamental, delicate mountain shrubs of some dozen species are treasures to covet. There is *Enkianthus cernuus* var. *rubens*, with its red, fringed flowers and brilliant red autumn colour, as well as the easier-to-grow *E. campanulatus*, with leaves of dull purple, scarlet and gold during autumn. *E. perulatus*, native to Japan, has small cascades of white flowers and delicate leaves that turn bright red in autumn.
- *Fraxinus angustifolia* 'Raywood': One of the most arresting of the autumn-colouring trees is the

Tip: Don't burn off those autumn leaves; mow over leaves to break them up, before they are raked for mulch.

claret ash, which turns deep burgundy and teams well with an underplanting of azaleas.

- *Halesia monticola*: The mountain silverbell is a graceful tree of the North American woodlands, where it can grow to some 15 m; its leaves turn yellow, pink and red at the first sign of the cooler months.
- *Liriodendron tulipifera*: The tulip tree is prized for its rich butter-yellow leaves in autumn. (Its distinctive pale green flowers in summer are another gift.)
- *Nyssa* spp.: Among the most spectacular trees for autumn colour in the cool-climate garden are the tupelos. There is the rare *Nyssa sinensis* from China; a small tree with an open habit, it sports very red juvenile foliage and later puts on a magnificent autumn show—several nurseries in Australia stock it. It is also worth searching for the more common but also beautiful *N. sylvatica*, which is native to Canada, North America and south to Mexico.
- *Oxydendrum arboreum*: The North American sorrel tree grows to about 8 m and in autumn turns into a mass of red, yellow and purple leaves.
- *Parrotia persica*: If you garden in a cold climate, you must have at least one specimen of the Persian witch-hazel, a small, spreading tree, which reaches about 4 m. Its yellows, golds and oranges also arrive early, sometimes starting to colour in late summer.
- *Sapium sebiferum*: For a small garden, the Chinese tallow tree, from the warmer parts of China and Japan, will provide (even in frost-free climates with limited chilling hours), the excitement of autumn yellows, reds and oranges without outgrowing its welcome. It is particularly popular in Sydney as a trouble-free street tree.

World famous

In the Yarra Ranges, about 70 km north-east of Melbourne, there are reminders of a bygone era when Melbourne families escaped the shimmering summer heat of the city to enjoy the clear, restorative mountain air, holidaying for weeks in one of the area's 100 gracious guest houses. From the 1880s to the 1940s, the area (with its associated villages of Strathvea, Healesville, Toolangi and Marysville) was billed as a 'World-famed Tourist Resort'. Guests travelled by steam train to Healesville, where they were met by horse-drawn drays, which transported them up the winding mountain roads to the guest houses; quite a trip, no doubt. Today the area is reached by a road that climbs through soaring forests of mountain ash shading centuries-old tree ferns. The principal streets of Healesville are lined with 100 deciduous, exotic trees, planted in 1897 to celebrate Queen Victoria's Diamond Jubilee. In 1913, the visit of the Duchess of York was commemorated in Queen's Park by the planting of oak trees from acorns collected from William the Conqueror's oak trees at Windsor Castle.

Autumn leaves

Leaves change colour in Autumn in response to a complex set of factors, from the genetic make up of the particular species, the rainfall and hours of sunlight it receives, the temperatures in autumn (when the plant stores sugars and available nutrients) to the various compounds in the leaves of different plants.

LANDSCAPE: THE GENIUS OF THE PLACE

Landscape

'First follow nature,' wrote the English essayist and poet Alexander Pope in 1711, in his *Essay on Criticism*. In 1731 he advised his patron Lord Burlington to honour the 'Genius of the Place'—location and landscape should dictate the garden created thereon.

Pope's words resonate, almost 300 years later and 28,000 km away, with those in this country contemplating the meaning of gardens in the twenty-first century. You can't help agreeing with the words of Horace Walpole, who wrote in 1772, '... the noblest lawn in the world fenced by half the horizon ...'. And consider also the eighteenth-century landscapes created by Lancelot 'Capability' Brown, who placed copses of trees to frame rolling hills in a vision of the Arcadian dream.

What manner of footprint should we be leaving upon the land? Over the decades conservationists, garden designers and environmental writers have implored us to touch the landscape with the lightest of hands. And yet, blocks of the Australian countryside are being snapped up by city dwellers, many of whom immediately mark out their territory with straight, regimented lines of Leyland cypress, so that any sense of place or appreciation of the surrounding landscape is blocked out and the dialect—the vernacular—of an area is lost.

Landscape is the collision of art and nature and the best gardens are, perhaps, those imbued with

A view into trees

At a house in East Ivanhoe, Melbourne, the tones of a mugga ironbark (*Eucalyptus sideroxylon*) with its black, furrowed bark prescribed the dark-stained western red cedar used for the verandah. A highlight window—a strip of glass running high up across the length of a wall—allows you to look out into the canopy of existing mature angophoras. The effect can be a sensation of floating, or of being in a tree house. And the result is that the surrounding landscape is captured, becoming part of the garden space. Neighbours' trees encroach and there is no clear definition between one building and those next door.

Tip: The challenge for the gardener lies in capturing and maintaining a view while protecting the introduced plants from the oft-accompanying winds. And this is how I like my jacarandas: I love them, but even more so, if they are planted in someone else's backyard. I'll have them in my borrowed landscape, thank you!

a strong personality. So, how, as we create our own personal paradise, do we overlay our gardens with a strong sense of ownership, while at the same time respecting its *genius loci*? A sense of place is a somewhat elusive thing—in some gardens it is the result of years of happy neglect or a carefully nurtured sense of insouciance; in others it comes from meticulously maintained hedges and borders. When you experience it, when you feel it, you will immediately recognise its magic. It is a feeling of well-being that remains with you, playing with your memory, urging you to return.

Many of Australia's best country gardens owe their presence, not just to the garden's design and planting, but to their situation. Many are blessed with that sought-after accoutrement—a stunning view.

Previous page: The Western Australian wildflower, *Schoenia cassineana*.

1. Walkers make the summer
   pilgrimage to Mount
   Kosciuszko, in the alpine
   country of New South Wales.
2. Dawn lights summer fields.
3. A quintessential Australian
   country scene: at Milgadarra,
   on the south-west slopes and
   plains of New South Wales.

1. The designer Edna Walling wanted trees to frame views of the surrounding landscape: here, Markdale, on the Southern Tablelands of New South Wales.
2. The wonderful view across Kawau Bay at The Saltings, in the North Island of New Zealand.

Gardening on the edge

Wide landscapes are part of our cultural imagination, carved perhaps from our earliest pioneering days when spaces were vast and hearts needed to be larger. Even those of us who haven't seen Uluru, or the Breakaways near Coober Pedy, are informed by their extraordinary size.

Everything about the landscape around Lake Eyre is big. The spaces are grand: the characters more so. You can stay at nearby William Creek (where the solar-powered telephone cost more than $1.6 million) in cabins, in the tented city, or in the pub. The person-alities will remain with you long after you've brushed the red sand and dust from your swag. Everything is larger than life: when city folk drop in, stories are told of how the locals fly their planes to the William Creek pub each night for a cool ale and park their planes on the dirt strip out the front (which is, in fact, the main road between Lake Eyre and Coober).

Anna Creek Station is a few hours' drive away. With 24,000 square kilometres (that's 3 million ha) of salt pan, lakes, rivulets and saltbush in the South Australian desert, Anna Creek is the world's largest cattle station. It could only just fit into the state of Texas and extends from the dingo fence (just north of Coober) to Lake Eyre.

You can fly for more than two hours and not leave Anna Creek Station air space. This is frontier country, and it is gardening on the edge. Through trial and error, the salty water and sandy soil now offer up a garden at Anna Creek. Most drought-tolerant species and those that thrive in dry coastal areas cope well in this environment.

Days can reach 50 degrees Celsius in summer, but winter nights can be freezing and spring brings frosts.

Not many Australians live in such climates, but gardeners in other parts of our country can learn from the gardening lessons demonstrated in this remote and challenging area. You can see what survives and thrives here in the following plant palette:

GROUND COVERS

The silver, carpet-forming convolvulus, *Convolvulus althaeoides*, and the white-flowering bush convolvulus or bush morning glory (*C. cneorum*) grow well here, along with the ground-covering, fleshy pigface (*Carpobrotus* spp.), which sports large, daisy-like flowers in November. The blue-flowering *Plumbago* 'Royal Cape' also thrives as a ground cover.

CLIMBERS

The red bougainvillea 'Mrs Butt' and purple-flowering *Bougainvillea glabra* 'Magnifica' grow well, as well as the potato vine and native wisteria, *Hardenbergia violacea*.

SHRUBS

The native *Eremophila* and a collection of grevilleas excel here, as do the oleanders.

TREES

The paperbarks (*Melaleuca* spp.) and Flinders wattle (*Acacia iteaphylla*) grow with the local coolibah (*Eucalyptus microtheca*).

The deciduous white cedar (*Melia azedarach*), with its lilac flowers, and the pepper tree (*Schinus molle* var. *areira*), with its panicles of red berries, love the dry conditions.

Landscape design is a partnership—ideally equal—between people and place. Part of the brilliance of a great country garden lies in the way it folds seamlessly into the surrounding countryside; it does not appear to be constructed. Perhaps a few plantings of exotic trees on the far side of a lake will lead to the indigenous plants that are part of the surrounding bush, surreptitiously enticing the landscape into the garden.

The Japanese have a word for it—*shakkei*, or borrowed landscape. It is the view and plantings, which belong to someone else, but which you can enjoy from the comfort of your own garden. It is the borrowed landscape that is so often crucial to the atmosphere of a garden; that contributes inescapably to the 'genius of the place'. Whether you garden in a confined space or on extensive hectares in the countryside, you will want to bring the surrounding environment into your garden picture.

It may be the trees in a neighbouring garden that make your city garden appear larger than it is or a park across the road that creates an essential sense of space, and tricks your sense of scale.

The designer Kath Carr and her mentor, Edna Walling, were masters at bringing the countryside into the constructed garden; at ensuring that nature collided with art. They would plant, at the

edges of a garden picture, those native trees that might be found in the paddocks beyond, placing them just as if a bird, or the wind, had dropped the seed.

Today, Melbourne architects Reno Rizzo and Christopher Hansson of Inarc Architects consider the outside environment when first looking at any project. They don't design spaces that are introverted; they want clients to look out, whether during the daytime or at night.

The firm creates houses with wide gallery halls, spaces cantilevered into tree canopies, and large amounts of glass that extend their houses into the garden which, in turn, becomes part of the overall design. Stained western red cedar, recycled blackbutt, rough-hewn bluestone, sawn Tasmanian sandstone and pigmented concrete make up the palette of materials that interpret and reflect the landscape that is integral to each project.

ENVIRONMENTAL CONCERNS

Environmental Concerns

Writers, geographers, landscapers and environmentalists have long argued the value of leaving the lightest possible footprint on the land. The nurseryman and landscape gardener Thomas Shepherd, who arrived in Sydney in 1826, admonished the landowners for denuding the land of its 'luxuriant verdure' and ruining its 'prospect'. Edna Walling advised her readers to 'Leave as little of yourself as possible ...', and environmentalist Tim Flannery asked in his 2002 Australia Day address, 'If we can see no beauty in Australian natives ... do we really have a truly sustainable future adapted to Australian conditions?' Such thinkers have implored us to turn to nature as the best guide and teacher of all.

The human footprint

No-one can have missed the widespread concern, mounting during the past decade, over our environment. As gardeners across Australia struggle to create and maintain their gardens in the midst of drought, global warming and increasing salinity, environmental responsibility becomes an unavoidable component of garden-making and good 'garden-keeping'. Many gardeners around the country are contributing to the efforts to preserve the planet.

Water issues

Even in periods of extended drought, at times some of our cities endure almost cyclonic weather.

Green is cool

Green surroundings cool houses: for example, a wisteria-covered pergola provides protection from the western sun; a large tree can reduce the temperature of an iron roof by 30 degrees Celsius; or vine-covered steel frames, erected beside a building, act as environmentally friendly air-conditioning.

Torrential rain—from 100 to 300 mm over one 24-hour period—can fall. Megalitres of clean water then run from roofs and down the gutters: drains clogged with leaves and litter can't cope. Roads flood, causing traffic chaos. The water is eventually lost into stormwater drains and escapes to sea.

Yet Australia has been in drought in almost every decade since the landing of the first fleet in 1788. Water is piped from struggling river systems and dams to cities that refuse to acknowledge a solution.

We can't force the heavens to rain, and certainly not on clear, blue-sky days; but when it does, common sense dictates that we catch what falls. The National Water Commission's *Australian Water Resources 2005 Report* tells of an uncoordinated approach to water management throughout the country, along with little or no harvesting of surface water.

Apathy seems a condition central to the water problem.

The quick fix is the ever-more onerous restrictions being placed upon gardeners, but papering over the chasms in our water management policy by targeting gardeners is not the solution to a drama instigated by European settlement. There are many reasons against looking to gardens as a panacea to the problem.

Opposite: The rare *Chamelaucium* spp. *gingin*.

Insights into sustainable living

Julie and John Eldridge's property at Red Hill on the Mornington Peninsula (just an hour from Melbourne's CBD) is a property with a difference: it has been designed and is maintained with sustainability principles foremost in mind. Their mud-brick house, built a decade ago, sits in the midst of their highly productive garden, which is based on strict permaculture practices.

Immediately outside the kitchen lies an expanse of herbs and vegetables, growing with ground covers of purple convolvulus, evening primrose, nutmeg-scented geranium and baby's tears.

The Eldridges grow more than two dozen different fruit trees to the west of the house, from pear, crab-apple and quince to olives and feijoa (the pineapple guava). A generous fruit cage protects the soft fruit and, connected to a purpose-built mud-brick chook house, provides the Rhode Island Red and Bard Plymouth Rock chooks with five-star accommodation. The Eldridges harvest some fruit from the trees that are not netted and share the rest with the birds. As you would expect in such a garden, they do not use chemicals to control pests, such as pear and cherry slug. Chinese geese and Muscovy ducks take care of the snails and slugs.

The adjacent kitchen garden has been created within a huge rectangular frame, netted against rabbits and heavily mulched with paper and compost. Irrigation is provided by weeping hoses made from recycled tyres placed under the mulch.

Central to the success of this living tapestry is its compost bin—a large, green plastic bin, which sits on top of the septic tank, recently converted (after permission from the local council) to a worm farm. As part of what was called a 'retro-fit', a kilo of special composting worms was placed in the septic tank, along with a constant supply of newspaper, coloured paper and magazines, cardboard, vegetable waste and garden prunings. Rose cuttings and undesirables such as plastics, masking tape and the plastic windows of envelopes don't go in. The base of the tank now resembles a humus-rich forest floor. A pipe aerates the system and a pump moves the treated and purified water to a reln drain further down in the garden, where other micro-organisms are also at work, aerating the soil.

Any excess rain water not used for the house is collected for later use in the garden as well.

The Eldridges are also careful with the products they use in their house and garden. They choose natural soaps and environment-friendly detergents that do not contain phosphorus and other chemicals.

One of the many clever innovations on this property is a living wall of vines: a thick screen of the red-flowered *Kennedia rubicunda* in partnership with the wonga vine (*Pandorea pandorana*) grows on wires attached to the metre-wide eves on the western side of the house. The living wall not only protects the house from the onslaught of the western sun, but from wind and rain.

The creation of beautiful surroundings enhances quality of life in countless ways, and the community benefits. To paraphrase my pin-up boy, the psychologist Karl Gustav Jung, 'The reduction of life to the mere factual, and the loss of the spiritual: that is the cause of all mental illness'. The mental health value of gardening is well known to those who practise garden-making. A major theme of the advice offered by the Mental Health Council of Australia, the peak national non-government organisation representing the mental health sector, goes under the leitmotif of 'ABC: Act, Belong, Commit'. The Council's website acknowledges the importance of creativity along with keeping active—physically, socially and mentally. Anyone who has worked or walked in a garden, watched plants grow or spent hours dreaming of creating a cool, calming oasis of beauty will attest to the emotional benefits of gardening.

You may not be able to afford a mansion on the harbour, a house on acreage or in a glamorous suburb, but each of us can create an enchanting retreat, a happy place, with plants.

Opposite: John and Julie Eldridge's sustainable garden.

Picture an ugly fence, rendered sweet-smelling by a clothing of star jasmine. Picture a small balcony housing pots of ever-changing bulbs and summer-fruiting tomatoes. Picture a tiny back garden, enlarged by an inexpensive mirror set at one end to reflect simple hedges, providing the effect of a series of secret spaces. Picture mean streets and hard, hot city pavements softened by trees like the white cedar, *Melia azedarach*.

Finding solutions to the water crisis

So, let's look at a couple of factors that would contribute to a solution to the water crisis. These are not the only answers, but an essential part of a multi-faceted, long-overdue response to it.

Apart from fixing leaking pipes and dripping taps, we must harvest public-space water run-off. Tank installation should be mandatory; make them more accessible to householders with serious subsidies. In existing houses, roof water can be harvested in 1000-litre tanks or inexpensive 200-litre food drums in narrow spaces or small gardens. New houses should be designed to incorporate large tanks of more than 20,000 litres, so that reliance on mains' water is greatly reduced.

It seems that political correctness might finally have sent us mad. I hear that a major city council in the country's hot north is filling in the magnificent fountains in its public squares in a bid to save water. Save it in other ways, you might well suggest, as the therapeutic value of the sound and sight of water must surely outweigh the amount of water lost by evaporation or spillage.

Water needs to be much more expensive, allowing the public choice over where it allocates funds. It takes 4 litres of water to make one of beer. It's a matter of choice: I choose not to drink beer, because I want to water my garden. So, forgo the beer, I say, and settle for water.

Wetlands

Wetlands, and the wildlife they attract, have a unique magic. If you are lucky enough to live near a public park that has lakes and waterways, or in areas where billabongs form after rain as if by some mystic force, the bird song that wakes you each dawn or the evening cacophony of croaking frogs will hold a special place in your heart.

Wetlands are one of the most productive and important ecosystems in the world. But due to urban expansion and the demands of agriculture upon resources, including land and water, Australia's wetlands are now severely endangered. Some 50 per cent of wetlands on private land have been lost, including large areas of freshwater meadows and marshes.

Weeds—garden escapes

'Whether gardeners grow Australian or foreign plants matters less than whether they grow invasive or benign plants.'
2005 Report, World Wildlife Fund

Many of the plants we now call weeds once graced our gardens. They have enjoyed our climate so much and become so comfortable in this country that they have jumped the garden fence to escape into bush- and farmland. These 'garden escapes' have made themselves so unwelcome, in fact, that they have been declared environmental weeds, noxious weeds, or agricultural weeds. Such weeds are a serious threat to the environment and our forest and agricultural industries. They include many plant species, from the pretty purple-flowering Paterson's Curse and the tenacious lantana to that thug, the radiata pine.

We can blame the first governor of the colony of New South Wales, Arthur Phillip, for the introduction of the poisonous lantana, now declared noxious in most states, as it invades forests and pastures via its scrambling, prickly canes and easily transported berries.

And that gloriously scented bulb, the freesia, which reminds many of us of childhood gardens—it hails from South Africa, along with many others, including watsonias, the cape daisy and the arum lily—was collected by the earliest settlers as their ships stopped at Cape Town on the voyage between England and the colonies. These introduced plants liked the climate of Western Australia so much that they quickly became weeds. Many of the worst environmental weeds are still for sale.

Did you know that 70 per cent of Australia's weeds in agriculture and in the natural ecosystem emanated from the 25,000-odd species of garden plants that have been introduced over the past two centuries? And that 40 per cent of the weeds most damaging to the pastoral industry have escaped from gardens, costing Australian agriculture some $4 billion annually? A 2005 report, commissioned by the conservation organisation World Wildlife Fund (WWF) and prepared by scientists from the CSIRO, makes frightening reading (*see* www.wwf.org.au).

The WWF report notes that nurseries are still selling 33 per cent of the emerging weeds in grazing industries, 20 per cent of the weeds impacting on rare or threatened native plant species, 25 per cent of the Weeds of National Significance and 25 per cent of the weeds on the World's Worst Invasive Alien Species list. Among the national dangers still on sale are periwinkle, fountain grass, gazania and Japanese honeysuckle.

It's not just exotic plants that damage the environment. The list of the top 10 invasive garden plants available for sale in southern Western Australia includes four native species. Many of our acacias, some eucalypts and the pittosporums are invasive in certain conditions.

There are 721 plants on the National List of Invasive and Potentially Invasive Garden Plants (*see* Weeds Australia's website at www.weeds.org. au). Space prevents the inclusion of all of them, so I will discuss just a few below.

• *Ailanthus altissima*: Tree of heaven or Chinese sumac grows to about 12 m and has a dense crown of mid-green pinnate leaves. Native to China, where it is valued as a street tree able to withstand pollution, it is a prolific seeder. If its roots are damaged or disturbed, it will send up suckers, spreading quickly to form an impenetrable thicket. It also produces toxins that prevent the establishment of other species and

Opposite: In Wendy Van Dok's garden, grey water supports a flourishing border.

Recycling water

Wendy Van Dok, a landscape designer specialising in water-efficient gardens, advises that harvesting grey water takes place in four stages. The first step is to intercept the water from the drains outside the laundry or bathroom via a diverter, which then allows excess grey water to be sent back to the sewer when the soil is saturated. The second step is to filter the water by placing a sock, at source, over the washing-machine hose or by a simple strainer in the drain. Step three is to transport the water by hose from the drain to the section of the garden you wish to irrigate. The water is distributed throughout the garden by an 'ag' pipe laid sub-surface, roughly in parallel sections, sloping at a 2 per cent slope away from an end that is exposed among the plant material. To water, the hose leading from the diverter is inserted into the exposed end of the ag pipe,

so the water can filter deep down among the roots. A cap can also be used over the exposed end of the ag pipe to prevent it clogging with soil or leaves.

In relevant sections of the garden, a segment of underground storm-water pipe can be replaced with ag pipe, so that the grey water (which would normally flow into the storm-water drain and out into the ocean) actually seeps into the garden bed. Any excess still runs back into the drain.

Kitchen water has a high grease content, so needs to be filtered before being used on the garden. Van Dok does not advise using grey water from the dishwasher, as detergents used are often caustic. Use liquid detergents in washing-machines, as these usually contain less sodium. Look for low-salinity, neutral pH and low-phosphorus products.

Salinity and its management

Bound up with questions of care for the environment, water conservation and a discussion of sustainable gardening comes the challenge of dealing with salinity, which afflicts many parts of Australia (*see also* Water-wise Gardening).

In the New South Wales country town of Wagga Wagga, some five hours' drive south-west of Sydney, the council has been addressing the serious problem of salinity for several years. In the early 1990s inspectors noticed that an inordinate number of homes in one area of the town were suffering rising damp, and roads were collapsing. Then, in 1994, evidence of salinity appeared at the local showground in the form of a massive pan of white salt. This indicated rising groundwater: salty water was being brought to the surface, drying and leaving the tell-tale crystals. Certain areas of the ground were constantly damp.

Council immediately sank bores to ascertain the cause. They discovered that, due to the removal of vegetation, run-off into old-fashioned rubble pits from the increasing number of houses and over-watering of gardens, had caused the water table to rise—in some suburbs to just beneath the surface.

With the co-operation of the local community, and the help and financial support of local and government bodies, the Council devised and implemented a management plan. A booklet, 'Water Wise and Salt Tolerant Plants' was made available and a waterwise category was introduced into the local garden competition to encourage residents to design and install gardens of minimum work and drought-tolerant plants.

Visitors from around the world now take part in Wagga's salinity tour, which includes Emblen Park, where salt-tolerant species are demonstrated. Council has encouraged householders to change their attitude to lawn, which uses 90 per cent of water used in the average garden. Shallow-rooted grasses have been replaced with low ground covers, and nature strips have been planted with well-mulched shrubs.

Reforestation is an important part of the plan, with hundreds of thousands of trees planted in surrounding rural areas. And the response of residents seems to indicate that the message is hitting home: they recognise that they must change the general culture of urban living, that water is a precious resource that can be dangerous if used incorrectly (*see* Seaside Gardening).

'Woofers' is an acronym for the international organisation 'Willing Workers On Organic Farms'. Travellers stay on a property for two nights and work three or four hours a day in exchange for board (*see* www.wwoof.com.au).

---

its aggressive root system can damage pipes and foundations.

- *Anredera cordifolia*: Madeira vine is indigenous to South America. This fleshy climber (with stems extending for some 20 m) flowers in fragrant, white, drooping spikes from summer to autumn. It is now widespread in coastal areas of New South Wales and Queensland. It spreads by water and via seed, aerial tubers, and underground, and invades rainforest by smothering small trees and shrubs. It is also salt tolerant, as it has been found scrambling over salt-water mangroves.

- *Chrysanthemoides monilifera* subsp. *rotundata*: Bitou bush is another traveller from South Africa and arrived here as seeds contained in the released ballast water of ships entering Australian river ports. It forms an impenetrable, glossy-leaved mass that covers sand dunes, choking out native vegetation. With yellow daisy-like flowers for most of the year and juicy fruits attractive to birds, it spreads easily.

- *Echium plantagineum*: Paterson's Curse (also known to honey producers as Salvation Jane) is a European native and is among the first species

to flower after the winter months. It is that pretty purple blanket you see covering hillsides throughout rural Australia. Don't be deceived, however: its lengthy taproot makes it a tough competitor in pastures. It quickly spreads, its large basal rosette smothering nutritious pasture grasses and poisoning horses, pigs and sheep. The prolific seeds persist in the soil for up to a decade. It has now naturalised throughout Australia—across 33 million ha—and costs Australian farmers $30 million annually.

• *Lantana camara*: Common lantana was originally from South America. It is a rambling shrub with prickly stems that invades disturbed sites, taking over from native vegetation in bushland. It is particularly rampant in warmer, wetter parts of the country and is poisonous to stock.

• *Lilium formosanum*: The Taiwan lily is among my favourite weeds. Native to Asia, it decorates roadsides around eastern Australia in summer, surviving in the poor soil and reaching almost 2 m tall. It blooms with highly scented, statuesque, white, lemon-throated trumpet flowers and is a prolific seeder.

Above: In the Botanic Gardens in Wagga Wagga, New South Wales.

1. The guest cottage overlooks a calm waterway at Peach Flat.
2. *Callistemon sieberi.*

Wetland restoration entices migrating Japanese snipe

In the foothills of the Snowy Range, 10 km north of the Central Gippsland town of Briagolong, lie 4 ha of wetlands that horticulturalists Michèle Adler and Rod McMillan are restoring as a community project. The intention is to put people back in touch with nature and to right the imbalance created through frenetic lives, often in confined spaces in busy cities.

Set within their evocatively named 110 ha property, Peach Flat, the wetlands are being created on river flats which, in a previous life, had been drained for cattle grazing. When Rod and Michèle bought the site in 2000, they found drainage channels a metre deep, and degraded land in need of restoration. Today the area has been redesigned to increase water catchment; islands have been installed to attract birds and animals, and plantings of indigenous and endemic flora carried out.

After a feasibility study to assess the site's soil and topography, the water table and water quality, a survey of existing flora and fauna was carried out, and a design for the project created. This led to the establishment of a consortium, which includes Landcare Australia, Watermark (Standards Australia Limited) and the local Wellington Shire. Despite the drought, the wetlands created during Stage 1 attracted wood ducks, and later lapwings, snipe, Pacific herons and Pacific black duck. The Japanese snipe now visit during their annual migration from Siberia.

Around the wetland plantings of the local, long-lived blackwood (*Acacia melanoxylon*), particularly important as habitat, have been increased. And without grazing competition, many indigenous plants are returning: the black wattle (*A. mearnsii*) is an excellent habitat for sugar gliders; the tall spike-rush (*Eleocharis sphacelata*) provides cover for water birds; and the native grass, *Poa labillardieri*, flowers with lilac spikes above grey-green, narrow leaves and provides important ground cover. The indigenous species on the islands provide essential winter-roosting spots.

The Peach Flat and Community Wetland Project has generated interest from local professional, commercial and community groups, which have helped revegetate the site and record its fauna.

The wetlands can be observed at any time by a trail that hugs the boundary of the property adjacent to Marathon Road. There are also plans to construct hides and open an interpretive and environment centre. The project will form an essential link with wetlands on the nearby plains to provide a staging post for birds during their seasonal migration.

One of the happiest sounds in the garden is the croak of the pobblebonk frogs at dusk.

The wetland site adjoins an existing lake and garden developed by Rod and Michèle as part of their 'Land for Wildlife' property, in which introduced plants blend harmoniously with indigenous species. The garden close to the house is the more detailed and formal; semi-circles of Chinese elm provide shade, much needed in the heat of summer, and hedges of box encase beds of the tough and drought-tolerant native *Eriostemon myoporoides* and the aromatic mint bush *Prostanthera incisa*. Punctuation points of clipped *Westringia glabra* subtly direct visitors along paths and walkways. Plantings of native *Grevillea* 'Red Hooks' and *Callistemon sieberi* blur the lines between the natural bush and the constructed garden.

Rogue rhododendron

Australia is not the only country in which once-valued garden species have become a problem. The rocky islands in the jewel-like Bantry Bay off Ireland's wild and romantic south-west coast are covered by the introduced *Rhododendron ponticum*. A spectacular sight, it flowers deep purple throughout summer, but outcompetes the indigenous conifer and understory species by smothering them.

• *Mimosa pudica*: Sensitive plant, humble plant or touch-me-not is a dense ground cover native to Brazil and has become a problem in the north of Australia, as the seeds remain viable for many years. It bears small, round pink flowers in summer and the stems and petioles are prickly. When touched, the leaves droop.

• *Nassella* spp.: Some of the much-promoted xero-phytic grasses are highly invasive. This genus, for instance, is a close relative of the dreaded serrated tussock, and is still for sale in some nurseries.

• *Pinus radiata*: The dreadful radiata pine (origin-ally from California) is common in plantations and shelterbelts. If you have ever been unlucky enough to have a neighbour plant a double row of them on your boundary, you would know they drop limbs with the slightest wind, self-seed mercilessly and rob the soil of nutrients.

• *Schinus molle* var. *areira*: The elegant, drought-tolerant pepper tree from South America (which lines many stately homestead drives and often provides welcome shade on country lawns) has naturalised throughout South Australia, Victoria and the Northern Territory, earning it a place on the 'don't plant' list. Its graceful, drooping leaves support clusters of creamy flowers in late spring to early summer, which turn to pink berries that are dispersed by birds.

• *Spathodea campanulata*: The evergreen African tulip tree, which provides welcome shade along the main street of Port Douglas and flowers up until Easter is, however, something of a nuisance in tropical climates. It grows to 10 m and flowers vermilion on shiny, emerald-green leaves across a broad dome. It loves the wet tropics, from north-ern New South Wales to Far North Queensland.

Every reader will have a pet plant on their 'must not grow' list. Some, such as the mock orange (*Murraya paniculata*), which is a nuisance in subtropical parts of Australia are much loved and well behaved in the southern states. Plant breeders are also helping gardeners by developing sterile cultivars of our favourite plants. We all need to contribute to the safe-keeping of our environment.

Above: Periwinkle. *Opposite*: A sense of place, Jugiong, NSW.

Winegrower conserves and restores wetland

Banrock Station Wine and Wetland Centre lies in the heart of South Australia's Riverland region, at the junction of Banrock Creek and the Murray River. Since 1992, 900 ha of mallee woodlands, floodplains and wetlands on the 1750 ha vineyard estate have been part of an extensive program of rejuvenation initiated by Wetland Care Australia.

The plan at Banrock is to replicate nature—in other words, to replicate the era before the Murray River was regulated (first for paddle steamers and then for irrigation) by a series of weirs, which prevented essential flooding and caused the water-table to rise. Some 90,000 megalitres of water per day is needed to replenish the river floodplain forests and flush away salt residues.

Twenty years ago the area was barren from overgrazing, but after more than a decade without sheep farming in the area, many remnant indigenous ground-layer species have regenerated in the area: the dense green ground cover of the salt-tolerant samphire, along with lignum (*Muehlenbeckia florulenta*), native flowers like the tiny poached egg daisy and pigface (*Disphyma australe*), and sedges and native grasses provide habitat for wildlife once more.

With the help of hundreds of school children, like those from Blackforest Primary School who first visited from Adelaide in 1998, thousands of trees and shrubs have been planted: black box (*Eucalyptus largiflorens*), river red gum (*Eucalyptus camaldulensis*), seven

different indigenous mallee species, the local saltbush (*Atriplex nummularia*), bluebush, acacias and hopbush. One of the goals is to create a corridor of native vegetation from one side of the property to the other through which wildlife can travel. Nothing is nursed: survival relies on the meagre annual rainfall.

An 800 m boardwalk, complete with bird hides and story centres, leads you into the restored main lagoon, among yellow-billed spoonbill, black swans, pelicans, Pacific black and white-eyed ducks, and blue-winged shovellers, many of which had not been seen at the site for years.

Another crucial victory for conservation has been the eradication of most of the European carp from the Banrock wetlands. The mature female carp breeds two to three times a year and can lay more than one million eggs at a time. The carp suck up and spit out mud; the turbidity created prevents sunlight reaching aquatic plants. The carp also uproot and destroy plants as they feed.

Banrock Station enjoys 12.5 km of river frontage. Responsible irrigation for the vineyards and cropping is a priority. State-of-the-art computers, assessing weather conditions and soil moisture, control the irrigation. Since 1996 Landcare Australia has received in excess of $660,000 from the sale of Banrock wines in Australia—the seed funding for 18 new wetland restoration projects around the country. And there is more work planned.

Plants I Love

PART TWO

AGAPANTHUS

Agapanthus

It is impossible to ignore these flamboyant exotics in summer, when they bloom for months in great swathes, most often in a stunning blue. They are so generous and easy to please that it is difficult not to love them. Many a country garden has been saved by agapanthus, as they flower year after year regardless of the weather—and they cope with the salt winds that often assault coastal gardens.

Native to southern Africa, and a member of the onion family (Alliaceae) the clump-forming agapanthus—sometimes called lily of the Nile—thrives throughout most of Australia. They assert themselves by slowly spreading their roots underground, as well as via copious seeds dispersed by wind, water and wildlife.

In recent years it has become somewhat unacceptable to hail the agapanthus, largely due to the reputation of just one of the group's members: the blue *Agapanthus praecox* subsp. *orientalis*. We've become aware of the damage often caused to our environment by 'garden escapes'—exotic plants that are so comfortable in our climate that they 'jump the garden fence'—and this is one example. Freesias, watsonias, the cape daisy and the agapanthus were among the plants collected by early British settlers when their ships rested at Cape Town on the way to the Antipodes. All have enjoyed the Australian climate so much that they have spread into the bush, choking out many of our native plants.

However, we do not have to continue to eschew this hardy trouper: nurserymen have developed a large range of agapanthus cultivars, many sterile—but all with rosettes of jewel-like blooms that cannot ever become garden thugs. Among the new varieties are tall, or dwarf, cultivars, some that die down over winter, along with others in a range of blues and in pinks and white.

♥ My favourites

- *Agapanthus* 'Black Pantha', also known as 'Dutch Blue Giant', has deep blue-black flowers on 2 m stems and is perfect for the rear of a garden border.
- *Agapanthus* 'Purple Cloud', growing to over 1 m with deep blue to purple flowers, is also known as 'Wavy Navy'.

STERILE

- *Agapanthus praecox* 'Albo Roseus' (sometimes sold as 'Strawberries and Cream') holds soft pink flowers on 40 cm stems.
- *Agapanthus praecox* 'Plenus' grows to almost 60 cm and flowers in a very dark blue, double bloom.

DECIDUOUS/HERBACEOUS

- *Agapanthus inapertus* 'Inky Tears' has pendulous inky-blue flowers and grows to about 20 cm.
- *Agapanthus* 'Laurie's Inky' grows to 75 cm and blooms with pendulous, dark blue flowers on stems that are stained purple at the base.
- *Agapanthus campanulatus* 'Alba' has white flowers with claret tips, held on 1 m stems.
- *Agapanthus* 'Zella Thomas' has deep blue flowers, can reach 1 m and has virtually no seed.

MINIATURE

Miniature forms of agapanthus are particularly

Opposite: The jewel-like blooms of agapanthus unfurl in summer. *Previous page*: *Helleborus lividus*.

1. *Agapanthus* 'Bressingham Blue'.
2. *Agapanthus* 'Black Pantha'.
3. *Agapanthus praecox* subsp. *orientalis*.

useful for growing as an edging, to spill over a gravel drive, or into a courtyard.

These miniature cultivars are bred from the efficient *A. praecox* species, so take care to cut off seed-heads once the flowers are spent.

Slender-foliaged, variegated

- *Agapanthus* 'Bressingham Blue', with mid-blue flowers, and more delicate, slender foliage, grows to about 40 cm.
- *Agapanthus* 'Tinkerbell' is sought for its variegated leaf, although it doesn't flower as prolifically as some varieties. It has small blue flowers and grows to about 40 cm.
- *Agapanthus* 'Snow Flake', a dwarf form reaching to 50 cm, has sturdy white flowers.
- *Agapanthus* 'Peter Pan' is also called 'Midnight Bell' and has blue flowers and slender foliage. It grows to just 17 cm.

❀ Requirements

Agapanthus will cope with half shade but they flower better in full sun. They seem to thrive on neglect, surviving drought, although they can also benefit from moist soil and water-preserving mulch.

❧ Care

If you have inherited a garden with summer-saving stands of agapanthus remember to remove flower-heads as soon as they start to fade so that they don't go to seed and escape to where they will not be welcome. New plants from seed will often revert to the parent plant, so propagate by division, after flowering, or in winter for spring growth and blooms.

APPLES AND CRAB-APPLES

Apples
AND CRAB-APPLES

There is surely nothing more delicious than a crisp apple picked from the tree in your own garden, the early morning dew still frosting its rosy—or new-green—skin. The apple is a member of my favourite genus—*Malus* (part of that most diverse of families, the rose family, Rosaceae)—and is a genus containing some 30 species of fruiting, deciduous apple and crab-apple trees.

The genus *Malus* can be divided into two groups: the larger eating apple cultivars that mostly belong to one species, and the balance of species that produce the smaller, very decorative and mostly edible crab-apples.

The eating apple and its cultivars

Apples are native to the temperate-to-cold central regions of Asia and will grow in a range of soils. In order to bear fruit, most need between 750 and 1000 hours of chilling each winter—that is, hours during which the temperature drops to less than 4 degrees Celsius—although a few do well in temperate and warm temperate climates.

> **Tip:** You can trick the tree into thinking these temperatures have been reached by manually defoliating it! This leads to a hormone change in the plant that causes flowering (*see* Care).

There are thousands of cultivars of the eating apple, *Malus pumila*, some dating back hundreds of years. The fruit ranges in size from approximately 4 to 9 cm in diameter, produced on a medium-sized tree. By choosing a good range of varieties you can enjoy crisp, new-season apples from December through autumn and into early winter.

The fun starts just after Christmas with the first of the apples, 'Delicious'; then come 'Gravenstein'

and 'Gala', full flavoured and long keeping, in January. In late March to May you can enjoy 'Pink Lady'; 'Mutsu' is among the last to mature and is a large, green apple, with the sweetest, most perfumed juice.

♥ My favourite eating apples

- *Malus pumila* (now established through DNA research to be the species from which the eating apples are derived, rather than *Malus × domestica*) is a lovely, spreading tree with soft green, downy leaves from which white-blushed-with pink blossom emerges in spring. As most varieties of *M. pumila* are not self-fertile you will usually need to plant nearby a different cultivar that flowers at the same time.

NEW AND WARM TEMPERATE TO HUMIDITY TOLERANT

- 'Ballerina': suitable for warm-temperate and humid climates, with green-skinned, mid-sized fruit. Originally bred for intensive orchard production, these slim-growing trees have found a place in small gardens.

EARLY RIPENING

- 'Delicious': a dense, sweet apple that tolerates slightly fewer chilling hours.

Opposite: The delicate blossom of *Malus ioensis*.

- 'Gravenstein': an old variety that dates to seventeenth-century Europe. Crisp and juicy, it is delicious for eating straight from the tree or for using in cooking.

MID-SEASON RIPENING

- 'Pink Lady' has a creamy, sweet flesh and is picked during autumn.

LATE RIPENING

- 'Cox's Orange Pippin': grown since about 1825, this apple bears small, strongly flavoured, sweet, orange to red fruit suitable for dessert cooking.
- 'Golden Delicious': a crisp, honey-flavoured, golden-skinned apple, often used as a pollinator. It can be used as an eating apple or in cooking.
- 'Granny Smith' was bred in the late nineteenth century in Sydney and is named after Mrs Anne Smith. Most often used as a cooking apple, it has a sharp flavour and crisp, white flesh.
- 'Mutsu': a very scented, crunchy, juicy, green-blushed-yellow-skinned apple.

For small spaces

In my warm temperate Sydney garden I have two 'Ballerina' apples planted as sentinels at each end of the long, narrow strip that is my vegetable garden. I love the soft pink blooms each spring and the green apples that hang on this compact, neat tree from December, ripening ready for picking by March. Growing to about 5 metres high—but I keep mine pruned lower, for ease of netting and handling—both 'Maypole' and 'Ballerina' are perfect for city courtyards as they take up little space and can be tucked into corners. It is hard to resist picking them, but they will continue to ripen until, in mid-autumn, the stalk comes away with gentle twisting.

The crab-apple—species and cultivars

The garden in my next life is going to feature crab-apples, to me the most elegant of the genus. Crab-apples are mostly small to medium-sized trees that hail from the cold and cool-temperate regions of the world, from Russia to Northern America, most requiring chilly winters to set fruit. Most are easy-care: disease resistant and requiring little pruning. Trees for all seasons, they are deservedly among the most prized of the ornamental trees.

Crab-apples produce fragrant, delicate blossom in spring, soft green leaves that progress to brilliant autumn foliage, and a colour parade of bright fruits that are less than 5 centimetres in diameter. There are some 900 species and varieties of crab-apple—so, once again, choice is the gardener's dilemma.

♥ My favourite crab-apples

EARLY FLOWERING

- *Malus × purpurea* 'Aldenhamensis', an erect tree with bronze leaves, is an early-flowering variety with wine-red flowers and purple fruit.
- *Malus baccata*, the Siberian crab-apple, and its cultivars are among the most disease-resistant and the earliest to flower after winter, producing pink buds that open to fragrant white blossom, followed by small fruits.

EARLY FLOWERING AND WARM CLIMATE-TOLERANT

- *Malus floribunda*, also one of the first crab-apples to flower in spring, produces an abundance of hot-pink buds that open to a softer pink to cream. It copes in warmer, more temperate climates, with fewer chilling hours than usual.

Tip: Underplant *M. floribunda* with bluebells or hellebores, or with the ground-covering bugle flower *Ajuga reptans*.

Opposite: An avenue of *Malus floribunda* at Foxglove Spires in the New South Wales town of Tilba Tilba.

DECORATIVE

- *Malus* 'Elise Rathke' is decorated in autumn with large Granny Smith-like crab-apples, which colour pink and green and are delicious when stewed.
- *Malus ioensis*, perhaps the most elegant of all the crab-apples, has downy, apple-green leaves that emerge at the end of winter, to be followed by dark pink flower buds that unfurl into refined, shell-pink blossoms. A neat, small tree, perfect for a small garden, it grows quite well in warm temperate regions away from the coast. *M. ioensis* is easily recognised by its layered branches that descend to the ground in beautiful horizontal sweeps—if you are one who likes to 'lift' the crown of your trees to easily mow underneath, do choose a different tree.
- *Malus* × *purpurea* 'Eleyi' has arresting purple leaves, crimson flowers and red fruit.
- *Malus trilobata* is an unusual species that has a maple-like leaf, brilliant red autumn colouring, and large white flowers in spring.

DISEASE RESISTANT

- *Malus* × *purpurea* 'Lemoinei', with deep red flowers, is more disease resistant than other varieties of this species.

SCENTED

- *Malus angustifolia* and *M. bracteata* are very fragrant.
- *Malus coronaria*, the American crab-apple, is noted for its scented blossom, although the fruit is bitter.

Tarte tatin (serves 6–8)

My daughter Olivia has perfected the recipe for the best tarte tatin—that delicious French invention— I have tasted. Crucial to this somewhat decadent dessert is the caramelly, slightly chewy base that drips down the hot, halved apples that are baked to a tender texture under the buttery, flaky pastry.

Filling

8 to 10 medium-sized apples ('Golden Delicious' or mid winter 'Braeburn' are best); peeled, cored and halved

Caramel topping

75 g unsalted butter, softened (not melted)

175 g castor sugar

Pastry

Quantity of butter crust pastry, or commercial puff pastry, rolled to fit pan

Method

Pre-heat oven to 220°C.

Spread softened butter over base of a round, heavy-based, 20 cm (8 in) cast-iron pan (not one with a removable base, as it will leak). Sprinkle over sugar. Place apples, cut side up, over butter mixture. (Remember you turn this tart upside-down when cooked.) Place pan directly over low heat so butter and sugar melt slowly together (about 10 minutes; do not attempt to stir). When the sugar crystals have melted, increase heat slightly to caramelise the sugar. This will take an extra 20 to 25 minutes. To prevent apples sticking, gently move, or shake,

pan from time to time. You may have to move pan around on heat to ensure that all sections of the caramel turn golden. Watch to ensure apples and sugar do not burn.

When the caramel is a deep golden colour (up to 35 minutes in total), remove pan from heat. Place pastry over the top and tuck inside the pan, folding the edge over (this will form a delicious thick, crisp edge when cooked). Pierce with fork to let air out while cooking, to prevent pastry becoming soggy.

Bake for approximately 20 to 30 minutes, until pastry is cooked. Remove from oven; cool just slightly in tin. (You can prepare up to a few hours in advance and simply top with pastry, and bake, as you sit down for the meal.)

To serve: turn onto plate (take great care not to burn yourself with any of the caramel as you up-end the tart). Serve luke-warm or cool, with clotted cream or best quality vanilla ice-cream.

Serve this delicious tarte tatin as the perfect end to Sunday lunch in autumn or winter, perhaps after a cheese course of a piquant blue such as gorgonzola, served with walnuts and fresh-picked salad greens.

SMALL-GROWING VARIETIES, OR TWO-TONED FRUIT

- *Malus* 'Golden Hornet' bears white to pink blossom followed by yellow fruit in autumn.
- *Malus* 'Gorgeous' has soft pink flowers in spring and maintains rich, deep green foliage throughout summer, turning yellow in autumn. It bears clusters of crimson-red apples throughout autumn and into winter.
- *Malus* 'John Downie' has both red and yellow-toned fruit throughout autumn. The fruit is suitable for both preserving and eating.
- *Malus* 'Serenade' and *M.* 'Shaker Gold' have two-toned fruits that progress from lemon to gold to copper; the colours are most vivid in the colder areas.

TALL-GROWING VARIETIES

- *Malus spectabilis* reaches some 8 m in height and has red buds which open pink, to be followed by yellow fruits.
- *Malus spectabilis* 'Riversii', bred in the United Kingdom, has the largest flowers of all the crab-apples.

Planting

If you have the garden space, plant smaller varieties of crab-apple—such as 'Golden Hornet'—in a copse of up to 15 trees. These small trees have a slightly pendulous habit and produce a cloud of white to pink blossom early in spring. The flowers are followed by masses of uniform yellow fruit in autumn which persist on the tree after leaf fall. Team this crab-apple with the reliable 'John Downie'; it is also suitable for a small garden.

Plant fragrant varieties where the prevailing winds will carry the spring scent to the house.

Requirements

Apart from their chilling requirements, apples and crab-apples are among the easiest of the fruit trees to grow. Grow in a sunny, sheltered spot, if possible; they favour rich, free-draining slightly acid soil. Fertilise, water and mulch well after pruning and after fruiting.

Care

Plant trees in the dormant season. Prune during winter, although you can cut out crossing branches, or branches that are in the way, at any time. Branches that cross are unsightly and can, if they rub and become damaged, allow disease to enter the tree.

Not all crab-apples are edible, although most can be used for a jelly—which is delicious, if time consuming, to make (*see* Fruit—quince).

BAMBOOS

Bamboos

You may have noticed stands of bamboo flourishing in late Victorian or Edwardian gardens around the country, reflecting a fascination in the early twentieth century with all things Oriental. Houses of the era featured treasures brought back from trips to Japan, and decorative woodwork, often painted vermilion, reflected the fashion for Chinoiserie. And, as a fond reminder of Eastern mysticism, bamboo was planted in gardens.

Bamboos are members of the grass family Poaceae, and part of the subfamily Bambusoideae, made up of about 70 genera and more than a thousand species. They occur naturally throughout the colder parts of Asia and South America; some hail from Africa and North America, and a handful are native to the Australian tropics.

Bamboos have enjoyed the warm parts of Australia to such an extent that they have earned a reputation as something of a garden nightmare. Unfortunately, as a result, the many safe and suitable species have been much maligned and excluded from planting lists.

Whether you want a weeping bamboo, a giant, or a miniature, shrub-like plant—or even a species that can be used as a grass—it is essential to ascertain whether the bamboo you love is clump forming (pachymorphic) or running (leptomorphic). The clumping species, which come from the tropics, are non-invasive and hence not a problem; the runner species, which come from cold, frosted and snowy, climates, do present a problem in Australia unless confined in strong pots.

The canes, known as culms, grow quickly in their annual, two-month, growing season in late spring—up to 400 mm a day—when all growth and leaves are achieved. The plant then doesn't change throughout the year.

❤ My favourites

The different sizes, colours, patterns and markings on the upright canes of bamboos make them a highly decorative and effective addition to the garden, and there is a species suitable for every situation, whether for a small city courtyard or a large country garden.

Strong
Due to its high silica content, bamboo provides one of the strongest of all woods. And, in ancient China, the sheath on bamboo was used to make shoes.

SMALL

- *Shibataea kumasasa*, or Fortune-Inviting Bamboo, is a runner, so it needs to be contained in a strong pot. It has feathery, delicate foliage and complements evergreen shrubs like azaleas and camellias.

TALL

- *Bambusa textilis* var. *gracilis*, the evocatively named Slender Weavers' Bamboo, a narrow bamboo, is a clumping species which reaches some 8 m in height and is ideal for hiding buildings.

Opposite: The invasive black bamboo, *Phyllostachys nigra*.

- *Bambusa vulgaris* 'Vittata', the clumping Painted Bamboo, has golden stems with fine, green, vertical stripes, and reaches 12 to 15 m in height, with canes of 10 cm in diameter. It is suitable only for very large gardens.
- *Dendrocalamopsis oldhamii*, or Boisterous Giant Timber, is among the tallest of the bamboos. It is clumping and grows to 15 m. It can, however, be grown indoors if kept trimmed.

BLACK

- *Bambusa lako*, or 'Timor Black', is popular, black-stemmed and clump forming.
- *Phyllostachys nigra*, is a running, invasive bamboo, which must be grown in an impermeable concrete container.
- *Sinobambusa tootsik*, or Temple Grass, is a running invasive, which must be scrupulously contained.

POPULAR

Create vibrant colour schemes

Imagine the golden-stemmed *Bambusa multiplex* 'Alphonse Karr' teamed with the burgundy-stemmed gingers and the purple phormiums, complementary in form and colour. Create something dramatic by combining the vivid purple, red or orange-leaved cannas with the tropical look of bananas, *Musa* spp., and listen for the beat of jungle drums.

- *Drepanostachyum falcatum*, the Blue Bamboo, is among the most popular in Australia. It is a clumping forest bamboo from Nepal and copes with light shade or full sun.
- *Schizostachyum*, the Murray Island Bamboo, is a very pretty, delicate bamboo with paper-thin stems.

Isolation or integration?

While bamboos are most often used in splendid isolation, the clumping varieties can be safely and effectively integrated with other plants (*see* Hedges).

EDIBLE

- *Phyllostachys aurea* has edible shoots (but take care: it is a runner).

HEDGES

Many bamboos make excellent hedges.
- *Pogonatherum paniceum*, Malay Pigmy Grass, makes an excellent informal hedge and can be woven through borders and shrubberies to add essential structure and form.
- *Bambusa textilis* var. *gracilis* clumps without spreading more than 15 cm a year and can be clipped to form a hedge (*see* Tall, page 39).

❊ Requirements

Bamboos are easy to cultivate and are drought tolerant and hardy once established. They need food and water in late spring and summer, however, when they send up their new shoots. Don't over-water those you are cultivating in pots, but don't allow pots to dry out, or the plant will shed its leaves.

❧ Care

If you find yourself host to a bamboo making itself at home in your garden—for example, the robust *Phyllostachys aurea*—apart from digging it up (the shoots are edible), you can cut it off at ground level and paint the ends with a glyphosate, then repeat. And repeat again!

Bamboos drop their leaves throughout the year. Canes can last up to five years. Thin out clumps, preferably in spring, by removing older or dead culms, to encourage fresh new growth. Use sharp secateurs or long-handled loppers to cut flush with the ground.

1. *Dendrocalamopsis oldhamii*, Boisterous Giant Timber, photographed at Mr Bamboo, in Sydney.
2. *Pogonatherum paniceum*, Malay Pigmy Grass.
3. Tiger grass, *Thysanolaena maxima*.
4. *Drepanostachyum falcatum*, the Blue Bamboo.

Colonial times

Bamboos were also popular with colonial gardeners. A stand of giant bamboo—transplanted from Sydney's Vaucluse House, home to the pioneering Wentworth family—has been planted at the rear of the newly restored Experiment Farm Cottage, at Parramatta, New South Wales.

Experiment Farm was home to James Ruse, a farmer from Cornwall, who had been convicted of break and enter and who arrived at Farm Cove with the other 1100 convicts and officers of the First Fleet in January 1788. Ruse was lent a hectare of land some 18 kilometres to the west, at Parramatta, as the Governor, Arthur Phillip, sought desperately to make the struggling colony self-sufficient. The experiment was successful and by early 1791 the emancipated Ruse and his new wife, Elizabeth Perry, no longer needed to rely on government rations: his hard work was rewarded with Australia's first land grant, of 15 ha.

The property was purchased in 1793 by the surgeon John Harris, who, in the 1830s, built the Indian bungalow that you see today. Experiment Farm Cottage was bought by the National Trust (New South Wales) in 1962 and, in 2001, with Commonwealth government assistance, the Trust and Parramatta Council re-created the lost nineteenth-century landscape that had surrounded the house, reclaiming the garden from the subdivision and housing development of the 1920s. The property now forms part of an important historic precinct—often called the cradle of the nation—which includes nearby Hambledon Cottage and Elizabeth Farm, built by John and Elizabeth Macarthur.

BOUGAINVILLEAS

Bougainvilleas

Bougainvilleas are big, brash and beautiful. There are 14 main species in the genus, all from the tropical areas of South America.

Until recently, this genus had never been on my 'must-have' list—they were too big, too bright, too brassy and brash. In recent years, perhaps because they have endured endless months of drought, they have staged such a welcome performance in many of our towns and cities that only the most hard-hearted among us could remain unmoved. They seem so full of the joy of living that it is impossible not to admire their flamboyance.

In the temperate and warm climates throughout Australia bougainvilleas are decorating houses, clothing fences and pergolas, brightening highway verges and romping up trees. They usually remain deceptively plain for months, but by early summer—when the jacarandas, along with school and university exams, are in full swing—they burst into a kaleidoscope of intense colour, fabulous in any combination. Their flamenco shades conjure up images of easy days spent swimming through clear green water and dinners outdoors during balmy, scented evenings.

In warmer and tropical climates there is a bonus: bougainvilleas are likely to spot-flower all year. The flowers of this plant are, in fact, insignificant, very small white or cream trumpets held inside showy bracts that are like pieces of vibrantly coloured tissue held together by whimsy.

Despite the bougainvillea's festive appearance, beware, as its boughs are typically armed with frightening spines that help the plant to scramble up anything that provides a path towards the sun.

♥ My favourites

MOST COMMON

- *Bougainvillea glabra* and *B. spectabilis*, two of the most common species, have given rise to dozens of hybrids in a paintbox of fiery colours, including the following:
- *Bougainvillea glabra* 'Magnifica' is cerise.
- *Bougainvillea* 'Apple Blossom' is white.
- *Bougainvillea* 'African Sunset' starts off peach and deepens as it ages.
- *Bougainvillea* 'Barbara Karst' is a 'real red'.
- *Bougainvillea* 'Killie Campbell' is a hot pink.
- *Bougainvillea* 'Lady Mary Baring' is gold.
- *Bougainvillea* 'Mr Buck' has softer pink shades.
- *Bougainvillea* 'Mrs Butt' is very vigorous and flowers an intense cerise.
- *Bougainvillea* 'Scarlet O'Hara' is a clear red fading to orange.
- *Bougainvillea* 'Tropicana Gold' combines fruit-salad reds, pinks and oranges.

SMALL GROWING

- The *Bougainvillea* 'Bambino' series are Australian-bred and suitable for more restricted spaces. They make excellent hedges as they reach only about 4 m.
- *Bougainvillea* 'Bilas' has red flowers.
- *Bougainvillea* 'Arora' blooms in pink through to creams.
- *Bougainvillea* 'Miski' is orange.
- *Bougainvillea* 'Zuki' has purple flowers.

Opposite: The brilliant colours of the bougainvillea shout 'summer'.

even plant multiple colours to secure the bank of a dam in frost-free climates, just as I have seen wisteria used successfully in one country garden.

❀ Requirements

Bougainvilleas love heat, of course, and flower best in warm climates or warm areas of the garden, and

1. *Bougainvillea* 'Inca Gold'.
2. A bougainvillea romps through a jacaranda in late November.
3. A façade in Rome is enlivened with a cascade of bougainvillea.

❧ Planting

Many neighbourhoods in the warm-climate states of Australia boast hedges of pink, apricot or red oleander backed with a loosely clipped, informal, second hedge of deep burgundy bougainvillea; jacarandas arch gracefully above, shading the scene with a brilliant blue canopy. *Bougainvillea* 'Mrs Butt' flowers an intense cerise, in counterpoint, perhaps, to the soft pink and white colours of *Rosa* 'Pierre de Ronsard', which scrambles through a thick blanket of creamy Chinese star jasmine. *Bougainvillea* 'Scarlet O'Hara', clear red fading to orange, might tumble down a retaining wall of large rocks behind a mass planting of *Canna* 'Tropicana', and 'Bengal Tiger', with their brilliant, striped foliage, flowering in fiery reds, yellows and oranges.

Use any of the bougainvilleas, espaliered along traditional horizontally stretched wires, or in a fan shape, on walls; let them cascade over unsightly fences; grow them in pots, urns or hanging baskets; allow them to drip from window boxes. You could

under stress. Don't overdo the fertiliser of liquid potash, as this will produce abundant foliage but no flowers, and don't fret about watering as they dislike wet feet. And they prefer a free-draining soil.

❦ Care

Do cut off any of the strident, thug-like, shoots that reach for the sky. Restrict root growth to keep plants under control. The general rule for pruning is after flowering, to maintain desired size; they flower the following season on the new growth produced.

As bougainvilleas don't use suckers to attach themselves to walls—which they love as they store heat—they are not likely to damage point work.

Tip: Why not plant the Bambino series all together, for the hottest hedge you are ever likely to see!

Bromeliads

What do you plant in a dark, inaccessible side passage—a narrow path, perhaps—between two inner suburban houses, an area of the garden that you would rather forget, but which is visible from your house? What requires little water, little soil and minimum light, yet offers dramatic form and foliage patterns? What flowers for weeks, or months, with razzamatazz and in a range of dazzling colours?

The answer is bromeliads, a large group of plants that were once a well-kept horticultural secret. Bromeliads hail from the American continents and are widespread from the state of Virginia through to the very tip of Argentina. Their versatility and toughness make them well worth incorporating in most frost-free gardens. They display marvellous contrasts in foliage colour, texture and shape and, each spring, send up spires of long-lived colourful flowers.

Sadly, many species are becoming lost due to the destruction of their natural habitat through logging or changes in land usage. It is up to us to prevent them becoming extinct by appreciating their always flamboyant, sometimes eccentric, charms.

♥ My favourites

The bromeliad group includes the epiphytic *Billbergia*, *Guzmania* and *Tillandsia* genera; the flamboyant *Aechmea*, *Vriesea*, *Neoregelia* and *Nidularium* genera; and the best known of all, the pineapple, *Ananas comosus*, which took Europe by storm in the fifteenth century.

Many bromeliads are epiphytes (they live on air, needing little or no soil), although some are terrestrial. Many, such as the tillandsias and the billbergias, can be strapped onto trees or attached to driftwood, or will scramble across rocks. The flowers of the various genera vary greatly, from showy clusters to tall and brilliantly coloured spikes, to insignificant or almost non-existent.

TILLANDSIA

Silvery, scented, candelabra branches.
- *Tillandsia argentea*, as its name suggests, has silvery tufts; it looks wonderful mounted on rock or on a weathered wooden garden seat.
- *Tillandsia cyanea*, strongly scented, is coveted for its heady fragrance of cloves.
- *Tillandsia* 'Fatal Attraction' grows like a beautiful candelabra on branches or in hanging baskets.

Mystery

One of the best known of the *Tillandsia* genus is Spanish moss (*Tillandsia usneoides*), which hangs like dripping cobwebs from tree trunks, most notably from giant magnolias in the grounds of old mansions in the deep south of North America. You can also see it at Isola Madre, a garden that covers one of several islands that float in the blue waters of Lake Maggiore, among the largest of the Italian lakes, and owned by the Borromeo family of bankers since the fifteenth century.

Opposite: The hybrid 'Sheer Joy'.

- *Tillandsia recurvata*, tiny and exquisite, settles into the folds and forks of trees.
- *Tillandsia usneoides*, the well-known, delicate Spanish moss, can cascade from trees.

VRIESEA

Closely related to the tillandsias but much more flamboyant is the *Vriesea* genus of some 250 species, native to Central and South America.
- *Vriesea carinata*, the lobster-claw bromeliad, flowers with a flattened spike in brilliant colours.
- *Vriesea splendens* bears a red or orange sword-like flower.
- *Vriesea imperialis*, the giant bromeliad, is perfect for teaming with many of the gingers.

NIDULARIUM

The *Nidularium* genus, comprising 46 species, hails from the tropical rainforests of Brazil. This genus, suited to small gardens and courtyards, will grow in a minimum of soil and needs only a light misting on hot summer days. The members of this genus are valued for their pretty flowers because they do well in poorly lit areas and last for months.
- *Nidularium innocentii* has dark green leaves with pink or maroon markings. Cultivars, from small-growing to exotically marked, are available.

For the frogs

Nidularium takes its name from the Greek word *nidulus*, which means 'little nest', as its flower nestles in the rosette, or cup, formed by the brightly coloured leaves. The cups catch the rainwater and in the Amazon are so large the frogs lay their eggs in the water collected there.

- *Nidularium purpureum* is a small-growing species with velvety, purple leaves.
- *Nidularium* 'Ruby Lee' has rich red foliage.

Planting

Bromeliads are particularly effective when teamed with tropical and subtropical foliage; the key to using them effectively lies in respecting their often-strident foliage shape and structure, for there is nothing discreet about these plants. Use them with other bold plantings; don't try to mix them with too-refined perennials. They are a natural companion to anthuriums with their regal, waxy flowers; to calatheas with their fascinating leaf forms and markings; to cordylines or phormiums in all their brilliant colours, and to the lush elephants' ears (*Alocasia* spp.). Set them off against a loose hedge of the tropical vireya rhododendron 'Flamenco Dancer' or back them with a mass of begonias or bergenias, with their heart-shaped leaves.

Requirements

These plants do need good drainage and will die if water collects and sits around their roots. They also dislike midday sun, but the more intense the colour, the more sun they will tolerate. The coarser-leaved bromeliads, like some of the stemless *Vriesea* genus, can take more sun, the softer-leaved less sun, and none like frost. They will reside happily in steamy bathrooms, atriums, conservatories and window boxes.

Care

Bromeliads are easygoing providing they do not become waterlogged and—in most cases—as long as they receive some protection from full sun. They can be grown in potting or orchid mix, do not need fertilising and rarely need watering.

A bromeliad bible

In his book *Bromeliads for the Contemporary Garden*, New Zealand commercial grower Andrew Steen discusses his long-time passion for this large group of plants. As he points out, the foliage of these plants comes in many different and exciting shapes, developed in response to horticultural needs and environments, 'from needle thin to broad and flat, symmetrical or bizarre, soft to spiky'. Steen's book, with its detailed descriptions and 300 excellent colour photographs, is the first affordable work on these plants. Such specialist works were, until recently, only in the domain of the botanist or collector.

1. *Neoregilea* 'Correlaoujii'.
2. *Neoregilea* 'Prince of Darkness'.

BULBS

Bulbs

Among the many joys to be found in making a garden is the anticipation of the changes in light, colour and scent that each season brings. Planning for the gardening months ahead is almost as enjoyable as the result. Each year, each season brings a cache of bulb catalogues, which provides a good excuse to settle down with a pot of tea and indulge in some 'dream time'.

Then, year round, the letterboxes of garden lovers across the country bulge with exciting packages that will flower, somewhat miraculously, a few seasons later. Surely there is nothing more exciting to a gardener than watching the fresh green tips of a hidden treasure emerge from seemingly unforgiving soil, to astound us all, yet again, that so much scented beauty can erupt from so inauspicious a source.

In some climates, such as hot and sweaty Sydney and Brisbane, you might be forced to accept that some bulbs must be treated as annuals, as they will not flower well in a second year. But the many joys that buying, planting and watching flowering bulbs brings to a gardener is surely worth such a yearly indulgence.

Gardeners use the term *bulb* not only for true bulbs but also for corms, rhizomes and tubers—any plant that stores its nourishment, and its memory, in a swollen system, most often planted beneath the ground.

The true bulb is a perfect, complete package, consisting of a short stem emerging from several fleshy scales, or leaves, that are wrapped around the flower bud, which is already formed. The food for the following year's flowers, formed as the leaves die down, is stored in the bulb; among these are tulips, daffodils and lilies.

Corms—crocuses and gladioli—are similar to true bulbs but are squat and solid, rather than made up of scales.

Rhizomes—trilliums and irises—are thick, swollen storage stems, which are usually planted on the soil surface, and from which the leaves emerge.

Tubers are irregularly shaped, underground stems, among them begonias and cyclamens.

❧ Planting

Be bold with bulbs. They are most effective when planted massed, either in borders, or in generous drifts under trees. For a natural look, throw them out in handfuls, in the shadow of the canopy—as you would cast, say, poultry feed or pelletised fertiliser. Create a different look each year by adding, or changing, wide ribbons of flowering bulbs to a perennial border or clumps of changing varieties to a basic matrix, or grid.

Choose bulbs to create a wild meadow, instead of persevering with ruinously expensive quantities of wildflower seed which will, in any case, fight a losing battle against our tough grasses and long growing season. For an easy-care meadow, plant low-growing bulbs on the perimeters of a grassed area and along the edges of a wide, swooping, mown central path; add taller varieties towards the middle. And plant a mix of early-, mid- and late-season bulbs to keep the 'meadow' flowering for months. Bluebells, which some gardeners eschew as weeds, will multiply wonderfully and flower till the end of November. Then, a monthly rough cut with the mower blades as high as

Opposite: *Hemerocallis* hybrid.

possible will do until Easter, when the fresh shoots will again emerge (*see* Meadow Gardens).

In a small garden mass plantings remain the most pleasing. Or plant in pots, in multiple layers, for an extraordinary show of scented flamboyance, and to bring inside when they are at their best.

♥ My favourites— a seasonal selection

AUTUMN-FLOWERING

Autumn is the season of falling leaves and, perhaps, trepidation over the cold months ahead. Cheer yourself up with some autumn-flowering bulbs, which will have started emerging from their covering of mulch by mid-summer.

Amaryllis

This genus should not be confused with *Hippeastrum*, which it once included but which is now a separate subgenus.

- *Amaryllis belladonna* are commonly called belladonna lilies—or, somewhat outrageously, naked ladies, because the long flower spikes erupt from the soil in early autumn, before the leaves appear. Native to the Cape Province, they will flower in sun or, particularly in warm temperate climates, in shade. For the best blooms, plant the bulb exposed above the soil and leave undisturbed for years: they love being crowded. They like it hot and dry in summer when the top section of the bulb can bake in the sun. They are most often pink, but the new variety, 'Hathor', is cream with pale yellow at its throat and is delicately scented; 'Cape Town' is crimson and 'Spectabilis' is pale pink with white markings.

Colchicum

The flowers of the autumn crocus emerge pink, lilac or white from the soil before the leaves appear. Most of the 45-odd species need frosty winters to bloom well, although some, from Mediterranean regions, like hot and dry summers; some also flower well into spring.

- *Colchicum autumnale*, the meadow saffron, which is native to Europe, is a lilac-pink, while the cultivar 'Album' produces a mass of white blooms.
- *Colchicum speciosum* is native to Iran and surrounding regions. Pink flowered, it is one of the most beautiful and easiest to grow.

Autumn crocus

Rare-bulb grower Marcus Harvey loves the autumn-flowering species, *Colchicum speciosum*. 'It has some of the largest flowers; it's tough, it's versatile and—one big plus—it has narrow, neat, erect leaves, a much tidier proposition than many of the others. It has a white-flowered form, much coveted by bulb growers,' he says.

- *Colchicum kesselringii* is spring flowering and has crisp, white flowers with a mahogany mid-stripe.

Crinum

Similar to amaryllis, the crinum lily flowers from a large bulb, which likes to be planted with its neck above the soil, so that it, too, can bask in the sun.

- *Crinum moorei*, from South Africa, is quite cold hardy and flowers in lush white or pink trumpet-shaped flowers in late summer and early autumn.
- *Crinum pedunculatum*, the swamp lily, is native to eastern Australia and flowers with a mass of white starry flowers on a long neck which emerges from a base of wide, strappy leaves.

Cyclamen

Cyclamen are tubers that sit on or just beneath the soil surface and flower with delicate, downward-facing flowers comprising five recurved petals which emerge from a swathe of beautifully marked, heart-shaped leaves. And, they don't just flower in autumn: with 20 species in the genus, it is possible to have a cyclamen flowering almost every month of the year.

- *Cyclamen hederifolium* is among the easiest of the cyclamens to grow, flowering for many months from March onwards.
- *Cyclamen graecum*, next to flower, produces an

1. *Cyclamen hederifolium* carpets the ground for months.
2. A swathe of *Crocus vernus* under an ancient oak.
3. *Fritillaria pontica*.

explosion of tightly packed blooms and is happy in full sun and dry conditions. It, too, flowers for many months.

- *Cyclamen coum*, native to Turkey and Lebanon, blooms next, through autumn and into winter, from among its beautiful marbled leaves.
- *Cyclamen cyprium* 'Elizabeth Strangman'—flowering in late autumn through to winter—has dark leaves with exquisite white spotting.
- *Cyclamen repandum*, with its curled petals and exquisite marbled, ivy-shaped leaves, performs in spring.
- *Cyclamen libanoticum* blooms next, with its large shell-pink flowers tending to float, according to Marcus Harvey, 'like exotic butterflies over handsomely marked, heart-shaped leaves'.
- *Cyclamen pseudibericum* flowers a little later, with richly coloured carmine blooms that you could mistake for those of an over-sized *C. coum*, except that its glossy leaves have distinctly scalloped margins.
- *Cyclamen purpurascens*, a scented cyclamen, with large, glossy green leaves which are purple on the underside, is the last to flower.

Although cyclamen don't like to be disturbed, you can divide the tubers to propagate. The usual method of propagation, however, is from seed, although germination can be slow and erratic, and 9 to 15 months are needed to produce full-sized plants. Seeds should be stratified—steeped in quite hot water mixed with a little detergent for two or three days—and planted in autumn.

Eucharis

These elegant bulbs, commonly called the eucharist lily, are native to South America. Their scented, white flowers, borne in clutches of four on long stems and looking a little like daffodils, emerge from glossy green foliage in early autumn. Frost tender, they enjoy humus-rich, moist soils in a shady spot.

Lycoris

Spider lilies flower in autumn in a range of colours, from tangerine to yellow.

- *Lycoris aurea*, the golden spider lily, is native to China and Japan and grows to some 60 cm. It bears rays of 8 cm wide deep yellow flowers.

Tip: The golden spider lily, *Lycoris aurea*, looks fabulous, planted by the hundreds, lighting up a dark woodland, or, perhaps, illuminating a stand of deep green conifers.

Nerine

Very similar in looks to lycoris, nerines—also sometimes called spider lilies—flower in hot pink, pale pink or red; and, for those who like a more restrained palette, in pure white. Plant them in well-drained soil in a sunny spot and don't over-water in summer.

Zephyranthes candida

By late summer, the white-flowering autumn crocus, sometimes called the storm lily, *Zephyranthes candida*, will have sent up a carpet of slim green foliage, a perfect edge to a drive or a garden border. Masses of white flowers resembling large stars bloom in autumn, welcome at a time when much of the garden seems to be shutting down for winter.

WINTER-FLOWERING

Crocus

One of my many enduring memories from an annual marketing meeting I used to attend each February at Epernay, in the Champagne district of France, is of swathes of Dutch crocus pushing through the frost-covered, rock-hard, inhospitable-looking grey earth. From the first meeting there, back in the 1970s, it was striking how the new season was so clearly marked by emerging plants. Another winter, while visiting London's Kew Gardens, I was again captivated by a mass of delicately striped blue and white crocus spreading like a glittering carpet beneath ancient oaks. That species, *Crocus vernus*, flowers in early winter in a range of scented colours, but my favourite remains the blue, often sold here as the variety 'Remembrance'. 'Pickwick' is a white and purple–blue striped variety, while 'Jeanne d'Arc' is white.

There are about 80 species of crocus, which is related to the iris family, native to temperate Asia, North Africa and Europe. They flower in white, pale blue, purple–blue and yellow, from early autumn to late winter in cold climates. Plant in full sun or semi-shade, in well-drained soil that is kept moist when the bulbs are actively growing.

• *Crocus sativus* is one of the most valuable of the crocus species, with its pretty lilac flowers in early winter. The slender red stigmas of this crocus provide the costly spice saffron, which imparts a delicate fragrance as well as a rich golden colour to many of the world's cuisines. It is also used for medicinal purposes.

Galanthus

The true snowdrop, or galanthus, belongs to a genus of almost 20 species that flourish in cold climates. Among these treasures, which are released by the growers in very limited numbers— you may have to beg for more than one or two— is my favourite, *Galanthus nivalis* 'Flore Pleno', which is double and delicately marked with green spots. The larger flowered *G. elwesii*, from Turkey and the Balkans, flowers from distinctive blue–grey leaves.

Leucojum

After a recent taxonomic makeover there are now just two species remaining in this genus, *Leucojum aestivum* and *L. vernum*. Native to North Africa and the Mediterranean, the snowflake is perhaps the poor cousin of the more refined—and more pernickety—galanthus but it is most welcome to those who garden in warm temperate climates as it doesn't need frosty nights to flower. It blooms in August, when its nodding white bells appear, along with the paperwhite narcissus and early daffodils.

Muscari

The grape hyacinth is an easy and generous addition to the late winter and early spring border, and looks wonderful massing out towards the front of a border. Native to Mediterranean regions and western Asia, the brilliant blue of *Muscari armeniacum* looks gorgeous, picked and placed in a shallow bowl with sprigs of the scented pink and burgundy flowers of *Daphne odora*.

SPRING-FLOWERING

Plant spring-flowering bulbs in massive drifts, if you have the space, or in clumps in garden beds. Leave them undisturbed for years; they prefer not to be watered in summer, when they are dormant. Catalogues for spring-flowering bulbs start arriving in late January, so, while in summer it is difficult to imagine our gardens several seasons ahead, it will be necessary to rouse ourselves from the lethargy of the hot summer holidays to do a little planning!

Convallaria majalis

This most elegant of white flowering lilies, lily of the valley, is sought after for bridal bouquets— but it is not always easy to grow. A tiny rhizome, it enjoys cold climates and rich soils, and likes to be left undisturbed to naturalise in the shade.

> **Tip:** If you too have no luck with the covetable lily of the valley (*Convallaria majalis*) try planting a brick nearby; it loves the warmth that the brick attracts and holds. A bulb grower in the Victorian goldmining town of Castlemaine provided that tip!

Fritillaria

These European and Middle Eastern bulbs are not the easiest to grow but are a fascinating genus of about 200 species of daintily marked and richly coloured blooms.

• *Fritillaria acmopetala*, with its delicate, nodding, green and purple bell-like flowers, is found in the cedar forests of Lebanon, Cyprus, Syria and Turkey. It likes cold winters and dry, warm summers.

• *Fritillaria meleagris*, the chequerboard fritillary,

also known as the snakeshead fritillary, bears a fascinating pattern of maroon and white checks on its bell-like bloom. It is the quintessential meadow bulb of the northern hemisphere. It is, in fact, quite easy to grow in the colder parts of this country, but is perhaps a little too precious to relegate to the meadow garden, where it would have to compete with our tough grasses.

A precious place

In the English county of Wiltshire a full-time guard is assigned to look after the health and safety of the meadow near the village of Cricklade, as garden tourists emerge from winter hibernation to marvel at the new season's offerings.

- *Fritillaria camschatcensis*, the Black Sarana, is the last to flower, with black to purple bells on 45 cm high stems. It hails from the moist subalpine meadows of Alaska and Asia.
- *Fritillaria imperialis*, the crown fritillary, the tallest of the genus and the easiest to grow, is native to northern Iran, southern Turkey, Afghanistan and Pakistan. Its pendant clusters of yellow, orange or red bell-shaped blooms hang from the top of stems which can reach 1.5 m. It also likes cold winters and dry, warm summers.

Native to Iran

Several species of fritillary, including huge populations of *Fritillaria imperialis*, are found in Iran, also one of the epicentres of the bulbous and rhizomatous iris. Eremurus, anemones, bluebells, muscari and some species of crocus are also native to Iran.

Tip: *Gladiolus tristis* is extremely elegant, and looks wonderful planted with bearded iris, if your climate is not humid, and with daylilies, if you are in a warm temperate to subtropical area. Or set it against a background of the arching canes of philadelphus, deutzia or may.

Gladioli

Don't be deterred from designing with this genus by your memories of the antics of Barry Humphries' alter ego, Edna Everage, waving gladioli about to mock the middle class! There are many species within this large genus that are delicate, and definitely desirable. Those in the know speak of 'species gladioli' when they want to refer to those with elegant, arching fronds from which small, often fragile, funnel-shaped flowers emerge.
- *Gladiolus carneus* flowers in gently arching spires of pink, white or mauve.
- *Gladiolus tristis* carries large cream, white or pale-yellow blooms on stems up to 60 cm long; the flowers are fragrant in the evening.
- *Gladiolus tristis* 'The Bride' is white flowered.

Hyacinthoides

The common bluebell is a favourite with many, as it seems to grow anywhere, earning it the opprobrium of some smart gardeners.
- *Hyacinthoides hispanica*, the Spanish bluebell, grows easily, and multiplies generously, in most climates in Australia, flowering in scented blue to lilac spikes. Add them to your meadow garden for quick effect, or plant under a tunnel of fruit trees.
- *Hyacinthoides non-scripta* is the English bluebell. Like its cousin it bears fragrant blue bells on stems that reach about 30 cm.

Hyacinthus

Who can resist buying a few—well, maybe more than a few—of these gorgeous, highly scented spring beauties each year? In warm to temperate

climates the flowers become smaller as they reappear in successive seasons. Justify such indulgence by thinking of the gorgeous scent that emanates from the thick spikes of spring blooms, which emerge in a range of colours. Plant them under deciduous trees so that they can receive winter sun to encourage flowering: they don't like wet feet in summer, so plant where they can remain dry.
• *Hyacinthus orientalis* is one of three species in a genus that is native to regions ranging from Asia to the Mediterranean. A heavily scented, thick spike of tiny blooms is held atop a sturdy stem.

Iris
This group of bulbous and rhizomatous plants is complicated—and so gorgeous that it has been honoured with its own chapter later in this section.

Ixia
The African corn lily is a genus of 50 cormous plants from the regions of South Africa that receive winter rain. Plant them under trees so that the vibrant star-like flowers that are held on wiry stems are not bleached by bright light.
• *Ixia viridiflora* flowers in a fascinating duck-egg blue. You can identify the true *viridiflora* by a black spot on the flower.
• *Ixia maculata* flowers with a mass of pink and burgundy star-like flowers on long, wand-like stems. Try them massed to create a meadow effect, perhaps under a flowering cherry.

Moraea
The African answer to the iris, this genus, a member of the Iradiceae family, is made up of some 120 species, but only a few are found in cultivation. They love a place in the sun.
• *Moraea aristata*, the Peacock Iris, blooms in white, with a deep blue peacock eye. It is happy in many parts of this country and will naturalise even under pine trees, ground usually so inhospitable that nothing will grow in it.
• *Moraea loubseri*, flowering in Australia in September, is a lilac bloom with a deep blue to black centre.

A rare treasure
Moraea loubseri, almost unknown in the wild, has been propagated at Kirstenbosch—the botanic gardens in Cape Town—and disseminated throughout the horticultural world.

Narcissus
Colloquially known as daffodils, this is a large genus of easy-to-grow bulbs that flower for months from late winter. The varieties, bred from the 50-or-so wild species, have been grouped into 12 divisions by an international convention among horticulturalists. In Division 1 are the trumpet daffodils, the most important group; Division 2 comprises the large cupped daffodils, while Division 4 contains the double-flowered daffodils. Division 8 contains the multi-headed, or tazetta, daffodils, and Division 11a the split corona daffodils, where the cup, or corona, is divided and curls back against the petals. They are all beautiful and fascinating, and many are scented.

The most important consideration for gardeners who do not live in areas of cold winters is when each variety blooms. In coastal Sydney and further north choose early-flowering varieties; for temperate areas you can enjoy also mid-flowering varieties, and for cooler areas, where spring arrives later, the late-flowering varieties.
• The miniature daffodil, 'Tête à Tête', which flowers towards the end of winter, does well in warm temperate climates, as does the vampish 'Jetfire' with her swept-back petals and orange cup. These belong to Division 6, set up to house the progeny of *Narcissus cyclamineus*, the most distinctive of all daffodils, native to Portugal but lost to cultivation for over 200 years. After it was rediscovered, it was, according to Marcus Harvey, used repeatedly in breeding. 'As the name suggests it has the very upswept or sweptback petals that suggest the poor little thing has had a very great shock or taken a fast ride on a motorbike, or both.' The miniature 'Titania', white with a delicate yellow cup, is also early.

• Early flowering varieties such as the 'King Alfred' type from Division 1, and the multi-headed forms hailing from the Mediterranean regions, will also reward those in warm climates. Try 'Grand Soleil d'Or', which blooms in July and is butter-yellow with an orange cup, and the cream, very scented 'Erlicheer'.

• The mid-flowering 'Summer Rain', 'Serendipity', and 'Secret Love' are also suitable for warmer climates. The later flowering daffodils, particularly some of the spectacular doubles, are susceptible to 'blasting', a disappointing problem resulting from warm and dry conditions that causes the developing flower to die at the bud stage.

• *Narcissus papyraceus*, the 'Paperwhite', once thought of as a cultivar from Division 8, is now classed as a separate species and grows wild in the western Mediterranean. This highly scented, cluster-flowered bulb is among the first to bloom in June, and in China is grown in pots to celebrate the new year. Another species also native to the Mediterranean, the hoop petticoat, *N. bulbocodium*, flowers in bright yellow with an extended trumpet and almost invisible petals.

Scilla

Sometimes called squills but more often also called bluebells, this easygoing genus contains some 90 species, native to Europe, Asia and Africa.

• *Scilla peruviana*, the Peruvian hyacinth, is native to Europe and North Africa and flowers in short, dense clusters of jacaranda-blue flowers from late spring through summer.

• *Scilla vincentina* will cope with warm temperate to humid climates if planted in part shade so that the roots are kept cool.

• *Scilla verna* flowers with a cluster of white starry blooms.

Tulipa

Tulips really are an indulgence—except, perhaps, in the coldest of climates in this country. The thousands of cultivars that most of us think of as tulips are mostly derived from *Tulipa gesneriana*—

not, in fact, one species, but the collective name for a group of old cultivars.

Devotees who garden in temperate or warm temperate climates will chill them in the crisper of the refrigerator for six weeks to copy the hours of cold that they would receive in northern hemisphere gardens. However, unless you are prepared to lift them each year (storing them carefully so that the mice won't find them), you may have to resort to an annual purchase if you feel your spring will not be spring without them. In cold climates in Australia you can leave them in the ground from year to year—but the flowers will usually become smaller with each season. However, the smaller growing but large-flowered rock garden tulips, such as *Tulipa greigii*, *T. fosteriana* and *T. kaufmanniana*, can remain in the ground for many years without any such loss. Try *T. greigii* 'Red Riding Hood', 'Toronto' or 'Cape Cod'; and *T. kaufmanniana* 'The First' or 'Ancilla'.

Then again, half the fun is poring over the catalogues that arrive each season; ordering; then unpacking the boxes so full of promise as they arrive in the post!

SUMMER-FLOWERING

Summer is the time when hot colours in the garden are called for: fragile tones will just look insipid under clear, blue skies. Many of the South African bulbs, which love the climate in this country, flower throughout summer: if they do not become nuisances in your climate, they are the answer to no-fuss garden-making.

Allium

Members of the onion family, the alliums—a genus of some 700 species—are useful, often tough bulbs, although again some of the large-flowered species, such as the stunning *Allium giganteum*, need a cold climate to do well. Easier to grow, and almost as effective as some of the more coveted species, are the well-known chives.

• *Allium giganteum* flowers with huge heads of cerise stars on 2 m stalks.

• *Allium christophii*, the star of Persia, carries

1. The tiny 'Tête à Tête' narcissus.
2. The seeds of *Clivia miniata*.
3. The coveted lemon-flowering clivia.

1. The tulip 'Salmon Parrot'.
2. 'Queen of the Night'.
3. 'Renown'.
4. The easy-to-grow *Scilla peruviana*.
5. The autumn-flowering nerine 'Fothergilla Major'.

large spherical maroon heads on spikes that are 60 cm tall.

- *Allium* 'Globemaster', with its huge, densely packed spheres of lilac-purple florets, flowers for weeks. This cultivar is a favourite of Marcus Harvey, who writes, 'Large bulbs, blooms the size of a baby's head and flower power to burn'.
- *Allium schoenoprasum*, chives, which grow to some 25 cm in clumps of fine, highly flavoured, cylindrical leaves, are very easy to cultivate. They enjoy a sunny spot in a variety of soils, and will flower with small, edible, lilac-coloured heads throughout summer.
- *Allium tuberosum*, or garlic chives, bear smart, round, white heads throughout summer, from leaves and stalks reaching 30 cm.

Babiana

These South African cormous plants are similar in appearance to their compatriots, sparaxis and watsonias, so they look appropriate when planted together, either in an informal border or in a wild meadow. There are more than 50 species in the genus, but the most common is *Babiana stricta*, from which many hybrids in a range of colours have been derived. Easy to grow in warm temperate and cool climates, they like full sun and rich, well-drained soil.

Cardiocrinum

A genus of just three species from the cool parts of eastern Asia, these are usually very expensive plants and seem difficult to flower—but when they do bloom, they are stunning. That's just as well, because they are also monocarpic: the plant dies after it flowers.

- *Cardiocrinum giganteum*, the giant Himalayan lily, flowers from the offsets produced once the plant has died after flowering. Bearing multiple white, scented trumpet flowers held on 4 m stems which emerge from glossy, heart-shaped leaves, it is a sight to behold. I have seen these plants flowering among a small woodland of carefully pruned *Arbutus unedo*, the strawberry tree. They emerged, tall and erect, with their dark green leaves, from a carpet of leaf litter, to tone perfectly with the mottled cinnamon-coloured bark and forest-green leaves of the arbutus.

Clivia

A while ago, a friend requested a recommendation for a ground cover suitable for her south-facing garden, which receives just a few hours of dappled sunlight each day. Among the few plants that would respond well to this challenge is the clivia, the Kaffir lily. Do not underestimate this tough trouper, which will do well in dry shade, often under large trees, where most other plants might struggle to give you foliage, let alone to flower. Clivias like being left undisturbed, and do not need much water: wet feet will cause them to rot. They need good drainage so will thrive in a scoria mixture. Provide shelter in frost-prone areas, perhaps under awnings, which will also keep them dry. And, they tolerate hot afternoon sun. They do not need fertiliser, although they will thank you for an annual application of a foliar feed.

The must-have cream to yellow variety—once firmly in the domain of the plant collector only—is now much more reasonably priced. A mass of the orange-flowering clivia, with their deep green leaves, can look terrific, too.

Named for Lady Clive, the Duchess of Northumberland, in whose greenhouse *Clivia nobilis* first flowered in the United Kingdom, the four species in the genus produce strappy green leaves from short rhizomes with thick fleshy roots.

The plump seeds of the orange clivia turn a brilliant red as they mature, while those of the cream flower turn a bright yellow. These can be simply pressed into seed raising mix to create pups, or let them seed where they fall, then divide up the new plants.

Crocosmia

This is a genus of seven species from South Africa; sword-like leaves emerge from underground corms, and spires of brightly coloured flowers appear during summer. Requiring little water, they can be a godsend, but they can multiply in a determined fashion, so watch that they do not become a nuisance.

• *Crocosmia × crocosmiiflora*, from South Africa, is a great plant for warm-climate gardens, sending up spires of flowers to add drama to summer borders. 'Lucifer' is fire engine red, while 'Bressingham Blaze'—which can make itself too much at home, however—is orange.

Dierama

Dierama spp., Angel's fishing rod, are related to the iris family and are indigenous to tropical Africa and south Africa. They flower with delicate, bell-like pendulous flowers on tall, waving stems.

Eucomis

The pineapple lily, *Eucomis comosa*, is often seen in old country gardens and survives frosty climates as well as coastal environments. It is a great addition to the summer garden, performing when most bulbs are still preparing for their late winter or spring display.

• Underplant summer-flowering trees like crepe myrtle with the new *E. comosa* 'Sparkling Burgundy', whose fascinating pink to burgundy coloured spires made up of dozens of tiny, star-like flowers, held high on rich red stems, flower at the same time as the crepe myrtle kicks up her lilac, pink and cerise skirts.

Galtonia

These are frost-hardy bulbs from South Africa. The most common of the four species in the genus is *Galtonia candicans*, which sends up a long spike on which dozens of pendant-like white bells hang. Galtonias like a sunny spot in well-drained soil and look terrific as a background to a swathe of the summer-flowering daylily, *Hemerocallis* spp.

Hemerocallis

The daylilies are easygoing, tough, waterwise plants, flowering year after year in a wonderful range of colours and in a wide variety of climates. All parts of the daylily are edible, being rich in vitamins (particularly vitamins A and C) and high in protein.

Daylilies grow from tubers, which can be added raw to salads: they have a rich nutty flavour. The stalks are similar to asparagus.

Hippeastrum

The 'hippies', once part of the genus *Amaryllis*, are greatly loved but also a little difficult to compartmentalise. Do we class them as bulbs, or lilies; tropical plants, or a genus for warm temperate gardens? Whatever, they will survive light frosts, and for all this, and for their good looks, have been afforded the honour of a chapter of their own later in this section.

Hymenocallis

From Central and South America, these lovely, large white, trumpet-shaped blooms, held atop tall, thick green stems, appear from late summer to autumn. Plant bulbs in semi-shade in well-drained soil—but don't allow them to dry out.

Lilium

While some of the best known of the lilies are bulbs, I have put them in a section all on their own (*see* Lilies).

Rhodohypoxis

From the mountains in South Africa, these tuberous plants, mostly *Rhodohypoxis baurii*, flower with a mass of white or pink blooms from clumps of soft, grass-like foliage. While they are alpine plants they will also flower in warm temperate and humid climates.

❀ Requirements

In colder areas, most bulbs can remain in the ground to flower from season to season. In warm areas, plant bulbs deep and keep them well mulched. Most bulbs need full sun to flower well, and most require moisture in the season in which they flower. Too much water during their dormant season will in most cases rot the bulb.

❦ Care

Refrigerate hyacinths and tulips for six to eight weeks before planting to trick the bulbs into thinking they are in frozen soil, and to convert the starch to sugar. If you lift tulips, store them in paper bags until the following January, before chilling.

Remove spent flowers and seed-heads of bulbs, not only for good looks but also so that the plant puts its energy into prolonged flowering and food manufacture for the following season.

Don't cut off the leaves immediately after flowering; bulbous plants need the dying leaves to build up food, which will be stored in the bulb for the following year's flowering. I like to hide the untidy, dying leaves of my spring bulbs by scattering among them seeds of an annual such as nasturtium or Virginian stock—what you choose will depend upon your climate. The fast-growing and short-lived annuals do a great job of hiding the spent leaves of the bulbs. And many will self-seed to return the following year.

Fertilise—but don't over-fertilise—after flowering with blood and bone to assist food manufacture, and again as new growth is emerging. Over-fertilising will promote leaf growth over flowers.

Growers

There are bulb growers in each state, many in the cold, mountain areas of Victoria and Tasmania. Some grow rare treasures, releasing only limited stock, sure to tempt the treasure hunter in each of us. Others supply a vast range of scented bulbs in quantity.

Hancock's Daffodils is a small, family-run farm that has been growing and breeding bulbs for Australian gardens since 1917 and is now owned by Christine and Will Ashburner. Their spring catalogue offers about a thousand cultivars of daffodil as well as a paintbox of other genus, from the tiny, brilliant blue grape hyacinths of the *Muscari* spp. to the must-have giant sea squill, *Urginea maritima*. There is something for everyone, whether you live in a city on the coastal fringe or you garden on country acres in a cold climate. Bulbs can be purchased at Hancocks Bulbs, 2 Jacksons Hill Road, Menzies Creek, Victoria 3159, from mid-February through March. You can also visit when the daffodils are blooming, from late August to late September, 11am to 4pm. Telephone 03 9754 3328, visit www.daffodilbulbs.com.au or write for a brochure. Catalogues are posted free of charge until the end of March each year; bulbs are mailed until early April.

Another excellent bulb farm, Blue Dandenongs, Victoria, can be contacted on 03 9751 9555 or admin@bluebulbs.com.au

Garry and Sue Reid raise over 1800 rare bulbs at their property near Wodonga in north-east Victoria, specialising in botanical treasures that will thrive in their hot and dry climate. Many are native to South Africa, the south-west of the United States, South America and the Mediterranean. Those that will also thrive in more humid, coastal climates, such as the early flowering *Narcissus*, *Sparaxis*, and the hostas, are raised in shade houses. The Reids can be reached at 02 6027 1514.

Twice each year Marcus Harvey releases his catalogue of rare treasures, exquisitely illustrated by Susan Jarick's delicate watercolours. In one summer catalogue he offered *Fritillaria obliqua*, the black Greek fritillary. It is now rare in the wild, its habitat having been bulldozed to provide for the burgeoning suburbs of Athens. In 2002 Marcus carefully collected seed at the only known site near Cape Marathon. His seasonal catalogue offering the rare plants that he grows at his nursery, Hill View Rare Bulbs, will send your imagination trekking through snowy mountain passes in the Himalayas or to the high forests of China. He notes that collectors will find 'the Holy Grail of bulbs, novices will be able to cut their teeth on the slightly less exotic, and all gardeners will find no-fuss additions to the nooks and crannies laid bare by winter's reign'. Email Marcus Harvey on hillview@tasmail.com or telephone 03 6224 0770.

Van Diemen Quality Bulbs are at 363 Table Cape Road, Wynyard, Tasmania 7325. Visit www.vdqbulbs.com.au or telephone 03 6442 2012.

CAMELLIAS

Camellias

There are certain plants that, for most of us, typify each month of the year and trumpet the changing seasons; the camellia is one. Flowering in Australia from late summer and early autumn right through until spring, the camellia has been in cultivation in China at least since 500 BC. As summer ends, the appearance of its flowers assures us that, in the midst of the tragedy and mayhem that seem part of life around the globe, beauty and good are determined to flourish.

Members of the Tea family (Theaceae), camellias must be the most versatile of plants, and the most generous. City and country gardens around the nation are alight with this friendly flower for months, often when there is not much flowering in the garden.

Camellias don't usually have a perfume, but they do have an earthy scent that is reminiscent of much-loved, old gardens. It is a fragrance that promises endless excitement and surprise in gardens created over years of ownership by passionate horticulturalists who have not been able to resist, let alone choose between, the myriad of camellia treasures on offer.

Camellias thrive in a range of climates, from steamy subtropical to temperate and colder areas. They happily submit to a great range of uses and are particularly handy in small city gardens where they will allow themselves to be clipped and twisted to hide a structure or boundary. They are prized for their flowers as symbols of refinement and beauty, the seeds for oil for cosmetics, and the leaves of the *Camellia sinensis* for tea.

❤ My favourites

The variety among the three main species of camellia—*sasanqua*, *japonica* and *reticulata*—is vast, offering a camellia for every purpose and position. It is impossible to name your favourite camellia: it could be 'Cho Cho San', pale pink and oh, so refined; or the peony-like, peach-coloured 'Easter Morn'. Use camellias as a feature tree, as a hedge, or as a 'coat hanger' for climbers; espalier them along an otherwise unattractive fence, or mass-plant them to contain an unstable bank.

Flowering starts around March with the likes of that most useful of camellias, *C. sasanqua* 'Setsugekka'—a glorious white with a flamboyant yellow centre. After the last sasanquas come the japonicas, usually by May; then the big, bossy reticulatas flower right up until summer is almost upon us.

SASANQUAS

Early flowering
- *Camellia sasanqua* 'Sestugekka' is white with a yellow centre and makes an excellent hedge.
- *Camellia sasanqua* 'Weroona' bears large, semi-double blooms of pink and white.

Tip: Keep sasanqua camellias compact—and the leaves small—by clipping them twice yearly. You can clip camellias into a cloud or wave pattern, effective along a driveway that leads into a large country garden. This less formal look gives you 'cheating time' if you are prone to prune less often than you should.

Opposite: *Camellia sasanqua* 'Setsugekka'.

1. *Camellia reticulata*
   'Crimson Robe'.
2. Camellias flourish in
   the Cassidy garden.
3. *Camellia japonica*
   'Hickaroo Jongi'.
4. *Camellia sasanqua*
   'Mine-no-yuki'.

Small-leaved sasanquas, which originate in southern Japan, make an excellent, moderately fast-growing, dense hedge.

- *Camellia sasanqua* 'Beatrice Emily' has loose, cream flowers edged in pink.
- *Camellia sasanqua* 'Jennifer Susan' has an upright growth habit and hot pink to salmon-coloured, semi-double flowers.
- *Camellia sasanqua* 'Mine-no-yuki', sometimes evocatively called 'Snow on the Ridge', has loose cream flowers.
- *Camellia sasanqua* 'Paradise Blush', from the Paradise series bred by Bob Cherry at Paradise Plants just north of Sydney, also makes an excellent hedge.
- *Camellia sasanqua* 'Pure Silk' has pink buds that open to semi-double white flowers with plum on the reverse of the petals.
- *Camellia sasanqua* 'Star above Star' is a generous and easy-to-grow camellia, which becomes a cloud of pink and white each April.

Espalier
- *Camellia sasanqua* 'Setsugekka' has masses of fluted white flowers on long and subtle limbs and is particularly successful espaliered; prune after flowering to train new growth along the wires (*see* Pruning).

Tip: The sasanqua species is easy to espalier, to cover a bagged wall or an inauspicious boundary. Fade out the fence by painting it green, then tension galvanised wires and plant your camellias about 60 cm apart. After flowering, prune and twist the flexible branches along the wires.

Ground covers
- *Camellia* 'Baby Bear': the dainty, elegant flowers are the palest pink. With a dense habit, it is used for bonsai.
- *Camellia sasanqua* 'Marge Miller' has mid-pink blooms and a cascading habit.

Tip: Plant ground-covering camellias along the top of a retaining wall and allow them to cascade down. (Also an effective use of wisteria, by the way.)

Plant ground-covering camellias lying down to achieve the fastest growth.

High edging—low growing
- *Camellia sasanqua* 'Little Liane', a compact, low-growing bush, flowers prolifically, with white blooms.
- *Camellia sasanqua* 'Paradise Petite', flowers in a soft pink.

Tip: The low-growing cultivars, which reach about 1 m, are good as edgers, or as a layer sandwiched between an even lower hedge and a higher backing hedge.

Use camellia hedges as 'coat hangers' to support climbing nasturtium or clematis: in early summer the large flowers of *Clematis jackmanii* against the camellia's dark green, glossy foliage, look fabulous. The climbers add glamour to the camellia's beautiful shiny leaves when the flowering is finished. The hybrid fuchsias like the same conditions as the camellias and their wandy growth twisted through the camellia looks out of this world. If you live in a cold climate, grow the flame-red climbing nasturtium (*Tropaeolum speciosum*) through camellias. And if red is a little bright for your taste, you could substitute the climbing yellow heart vine (*Dicentra scandens*) which has mid-green leaves and pendulous yellow flowers.

You can thread *Camellia sasanqua* through a hedge of a different genus. Wrap the white-flowering 'Mine-no-yuki' around a simple column to create a striking punctuation point at the end of a walk, or weave it into itself to make a hedge.

JAPONICAS

The japonica camellias, with larger leaves than the sasanquas, hail from Japan, Korea and China, and also make beautiful, dense hedges, particularly if pruned from the word *go*. Varieties for use in gardens have been bred for more than 300 years.

> Tip: To create a stilt hedge, rub off the lower shoots of young plants to develop a canopy to clip; this can then be under-planted with colour-coordinated, lower-growing species. Clipped to a sharp wedge, this treatment is extremely effective in a courtyard garden or a formal, very structured space, or against a low wall.
>
> 'Brushfield's Yellow' lines the drive to Japan's Imperial Palace and forms a great hedge, lighting up wintry skies with its yellow blooms.
>
> Think of camellias planted with a stilt hedge of well-clipped *Cupressus torulosa* or × *Cupressocyparus* 'Leighton Green'.

Hedges

- *Camellia japonica* makes a stunning medium-height stilt hedge.
- *Camellia japonica* 'Onetia Holland' has round, peony-like flowers and vigorous, compact growth.
- *Camellia japonica* 'Lovelight' has large white flowers.
- *Camellia japonica* 'White Nun' also has large white flowers.
- *Camellia japonica* 'Brushfield's Yellow' is Australian-bred and bears yellow flowers.

Espalier, fan or wall shrub

- *Camellia japonica* 'Tinsie' is a spectacular single-flowered red bloom with pink central boss.
- *Camellia japonica* 'Lady Loch' is an elegant pale pink bloom with deeper pink veining.

Visual impact

- *Camellia japonica* 'Dixie Knight Supreme' is reminiscent of thick cream splashed with strawberry jam.
- *Camellia japonica* 'Drama Girl' flowers in salmon pink.
- *Camellia japonica* 'Fred Sander' is deep red.
- *Camellia japonica* 'Jessie Burgess' is a beautiful salmon pink.
- *Camellia japonica* 'Lady de Saumarez', a sport of 'Fred Sander', blooms prolifically in a stunning deep pink.
- *Camellia japonica* 'Nuccio's Gem' is perhaps the most perfectly formed of all the camellias, with waxy, white petals.
- *Camellia japonica* 'Thompsonii' is fascinating as it seems to change its appearance each year: streaked with several shades of pink against a soft pink background, it can also be splashed with crushed raspberry blotches. It is a cheery sight throughout the winter months.

Pink splashed

Camellia japonica 'Thompsonii', of unknown parentage, was first noted in the 1890s at Camden Park, the Sydney garden of the Macarthur family, where many Australian camellias were developed.

> Tip: Use the variegated *Camellia japonica* 'Benten' to illuminate a dark area in the garden, or use it clipped into tripods or orbs to mark the exit from a shaded woodland.

Also revered are the japonica higo camellias, which were greatly admired by the Japanese samurai, the warrior noblemen of ancient Japan—and, to higo devotees today, the one true camellia. They are a single-flowered group within the japonica species.

Opposite: Eryldene.

Camellia gardens for reference

One of the most comprehensive and important collections of camellias in Australia can be found on Sydney's North Shore, at Eryldene, and includes 50 different species and more than 400 cultivated varieties. The collection was compiled by camellia expert Professor EG Waterhouse; his two books on the subject, illustrated with exquisite watercolours by Paul Jones, are now collectors' items (*see also* Garden Buildings).

The earliest camellia to bloom at Eryldene, the *Camellia sasanqua* 'Weroona', grows beside The Temple in the front garden. The rare yellow *C. chrysantha* (syn. *C. nitidissima*) flowers in June. There is the flamboyant reticulata cultivar 'Crimson Robe', which has given birth to so many of the large-flowered varieties and which was developed from the specimens first found in the temple gardens in Yunnan province and introduced to the west in the early nineteenth century. Bringing the flowering season to a close, this magnificent species, with its deep green, large leaves, can be frost tender; while Yunnan province is mountainous, it also straddles the Tropic of Cancer.

You can also see camellias at Camden Park, the second house built for John and Elizabeth Macarthur (who had arrived in the colony with the second fleet on 28 June 1790), which remains a busy family home. Designed by the architect John Verge and completed in 1835, the extensive gardens are attributed to John and Elizabeth's fifth son William (1800–1882). He was a politician, a botanist and a nurseryman, a member of the colony's intellectual elite, and in correspondence with centres of learning throughout the world and at the centre of a worldwide horticultural exchange. William travelled extensively, collecting a wide range of exotic plants, and, in the manner of leading English families, sponsored plant hunters like the explorer and naturalist Ludwig Leichhardt.

Among the rare plants in the garden is *C. japonica* 'Anemoniflora', first taken to England from China in 1806 and thought to be the oldest camellia in Australia. The extensive collections of camellias in the Lower Garden are being restored, including the glorious *C. japonica* 'Thomsonii'. Visit on the open weekend in September each year.

Isola Madre, in the blue waters of Lake Maggiore in northern Italy, is perhaps most famous for its collection of more than 800 different camellias, some of which are more than 150 years old. The banks of the salmon-pink, large-flowered *C. japonica* 'Drama Girl', the peony-form 'Tomorrow' and the pink and red striped 'Tomorrow's Dawn', are simply breathtaking. Others are severely clipped to form narrow hedges, which soften extensive stone walls; others are pruned to create walkways. Visit from September to December.

• *Camellia japonica higo* 'Yamato-nishiki' has elegant pink, white and marbled flowers on the same plant and boasts some 200 stamens in the centre of a flat, single bloom.

RETICULATAS

This large-leaved species is native to the Yunnan province in the south-west of China, so it thrives in the similar, temperate climate of some parts of Australia. The voluptuous plants had been cultivated for centuries in China, and made their way to England in 1820 via a Captain Rawes of the East India Company. The upright 'retics' are the most obvious choice as a feature tree, growing to several metres in height and supporting large, flamboyant blooms.

As trees
Camellia reticulata 'Crimson Robe', blooming in a rich cerise, was bred by Harry and Peg Cassidy at their garden at Harrietville in northern Victoria. 'The retics are great in landscaping,' Harry says. 'They become big trees.'

Early flowering
• *Camellia reticulata* 'Juban' has smaller, delicate flowers in the palest blush pink.

Other species
• *Camellia hiemalis* 'Sparkling Burgundy' is among the first to flower, at the end of March.
• *Camellia oleifera* hails from southern China. Its seeds are pressed for oil, which is used for cooking and to make cosmetics.
• *Camellia tsaii*, the Temple Camellia, has an elegant, willowy growth form, a delicate fragrance and small, nodding flowers.

Precious
The Temple Camellia was once so treasured by the Chinese that it formed part of their economy.

Plant hunters
It was, of course, the plant hunters of the nineteenth century who brought the western world the camellia, collecting seed and specimens in wild and dangerous country. The most intrepid, and the most successful, must have been George Forrest who, in July 1905, had based himself at the French Catholic Mission at Tzekou, 3000 metres up in Yunnan province at the point where China, India and Tibet meet. He escaped a terrible death at the hands of furious Tibetan lamas only through feats of daring, ingenuity and great determination that would make Harrison Ford look pedestrian. As he finally escaped, climbing to 7000 metres in mountainous Yunnan, he could still record 'Up and up we climbed, cutting our way through miles of rhododendrons, tramping over alps literally clothed with primulas, gentians, saxifrages, lilies etc., for these unknown hillsides are a veritable botanists' paradise.' Plant lovers today will sympathise with such passion.

• *Camellia yunnanensis* is a delightfully perfumed species, with white flowers with a central boss of yellow stamens, and stunning cinnamon-coloured bark.
• *Camellia saluenensis* flowers with a single, deep pink flower; from south west China, this species was crossed with *C. japonica* to raise *Camellia × williamsii* cultivars such as 'Donation' and 'Anticipation'.
• *Camellia × williamsii* cultivars are particularly

Did you know?
Did you know the camellia is named in honour of the Jesuit Georg Josef Kamel, who worked in the Philippines early in the eighteenth century? Or, that *Camellia reticulata* is the floral emblem of Yunnan province?

long flowering in a colder climate. 'Donation' produces semi-double, pink blooms for months. 'Anticipation' is a New Zealand-bred camellia, flowering with a peony-form bloom in a deep pink. 'EG Waterhouse', bred by Professor Waterhouse, bears a perfectly formed fuchsia-pink flower.

Planting

Don't mix japonica camellias with sasanquas, as they are not the same in form and shape. Use japonica cultivars and hybrids to extend the flowering season.

Requirements

Camellias, like rhododendrons, magnolias and daphnes, are acid-loving plants. They will appreciate you tipping out the teapot under them. Do not espalier camellias on a new wall; the lime in the render or point work is not to their liking. Mulch with aged lucerne mixed with compost and aged cow manure; poultry manure is too alkaline.

Care

If buds are developing in clusters on japonica and reticulata camellias, remove some buds so that just one is left to produce larger flowers.

Inspiration

Camellias have always inspired artists, from creators of the delicate silk and china paintings of the Orient to our own botanical artists determined to capture both their strength and delicacy, along with the luminescence of their petals. *Camellia japonica* 'Nuccio's Gem' must surely be the camellia that inspired the artist Paul Jones; the flower is formal, its petals perfectly imbricated, its texture like the complexion of some renowned beauty in literature. It is the ultimate flower to adorn the jacket lapel or evening shirt.

Experts debate whether the camellia should be pruned, apart from the removal of any crossing branches. Harry Cassidy believes the plant should only be pruned to achieve the ideal camellia shape—that which would allow a small bird to fly straight through.

You can prune camellias hard, however, even into old wood if necessary—although you may want to do this over a two-year period to ensure that shock to the plant is not too great. Of course, to again reduce the impact of pruning, do so after flowering; and, as always, then fertilise, water well and mulch.

Above: A crisp frost outlines the blooms of *Camellia japonica* 'Debutante'.

CLEMATIS

Clematis

Clematis are for those among us who cannot visit a nursery without filling the boot of the car with plants that have no designated place in our gardens. They are for all gardeners who spend winters dreaming over catalogues of rare treasures that they just should not covet. Among the most versatile and useful of plants, clematis are somewhat under-utilised in this country, however, perhaps because of their reputation for being fussy about their environment and growing conditions.

Clematis is an enormous genus from the Ranunculaceae family. It includes over 200 species and more than a thousand cultivars. Most are native to the northern hemisphere and can be broken up into several groups of species, each of which has its own cultural idiosyncrasies and requirements. The different groups take a bit of sorting out, and, just to confuse us further, do not always fit neatly into the various categories. But, with the choice available, you need never let a tree go to waste again, nor a vertical space remain bare (*see also* Vertical Surfaces).

Main species and groups, origins, cultural attributes and care

The main clematis classes include the Viticella, Evergreen, Atragene, Montana, Florida, Texensis, Integrifolia, Heracleifolia and Recta groups.

VITICELLA

The Viticella group, from southern Europe and Turkey, is perhaps the easiest of all to grow, particularly in a more humid climate. It is often recommended for novice clematis devotees. The flowers range from small and bell-shaped to open flat, or double. Late flowering (in autumn), these clematis enjoy being hard pruned in mid-winter, and then will flower together with your climbing roses towards summer.

• *Clematis patens*, part of the Viticella group, is native to China and Korea. The large-flowered hybrids bred from *C. patens* are too flamboyant for some, but in terms of pizzazz they are surely unsurpassed. There is nothing subtle about these blooms: some are the size of dinner plates.

EVERGREEN

• *Clematis aristata*, evergreen and native to Australia, also tolerates humid climates.
• *Clematis paniculata*, native to New Zealand and intolerant of humidity, flowers in trusses of white stars. A low retaining wall or the risers of a flight of steps can be effectively decorated with this evergreen. Or enjoy it shimmering from the fine leaves of a silver birch through which you have allowed it to clamber.
• *Clematis armandii* is native to southern China; among the best is the scented 'Apple Blossom' variety. Prune immediately after flowering as this species flowers on the previous season's ripened wood.
• *Clematis cirrhosa*, from southern Europe, blooms in autumn and winter with masses of nodding, bell-like flowers. It requires a sunny, free-draining position and is dormant in summer, sometimes losing its leaves.

ATRAGENE

The Atragene group is spring flowering and includes *Clematis alpina*, *C. koreana* and *C. macropetala*

Opposite: *Clematis texensis* 'Gravetye Beauty'.

and their hybrids. These clematis are all frost hardy but require a free-draining position. The Atragene group of clematis does not need the rich growing conditions or deep planting that the large-flowered cultivars require, and plants can be pruned immediately after flowering.

MONTANA

The Montana group, from the Himalayas, China and Tibet, is relatively easy to grow, and vigorous. Plants bear prolifically with pale pink to white blooms, many vanilla-scented. The Montana species flower on the previous season's wood, so you need to prune as soon as you can bear to part with the fluffy seed-heads that follow the late spring-to-summer flowers.

FLORIDA

The free-flowering Florida group, also from China, will not withstand heavy frosts but is happy growing in pots.

TEXENSIS

The rare *Clematis texensis*, from the state of Texas in the United States, has tiny, tulip-like flowers in late summer. Among my favourite is the burgundy-coloured *C. texensis* 'Gravetye Beauty', named after Gravetye Manor, William Robinson's home in the south of England. It likes the cold.

INTEGRIFOLIA

The Integrifolia group is non-climbing and herbaceous but will scramble over low shrubs in perennial borders where it teams naturally with other members of the Ranunculaceae family, including columbines, delphiniums, hellebores and the feathery thalictrums. Or, let these clematis cascade down banks or form ground covers. They will break your heart, however, if you try to grow them in a humid climate, as by early summer the leaves will be ruined by mildew.

HERACLEIFOLIA

The Heracleifolia group, somewhat similar to Integrifolia, are woody-stemmed, herbaceous clematis that should be pruned in spring, after the risk of frost has passed.

RECTA

The herbaceous species from the Recta group are scented, producing masses of star-like flowers, attracting bees and butterflies to the garden. You could also grow them in pots to be popped into the border—Gertrude Jekyll style—when they are at their best. If left in the pot after flowering, they can be cut back and stored out of sight.

Planting

Traditionally used to cover a trellis or a pergola, clematis add sparkle to a plain hedge or form an exciting and unusual ground cover. Roses and clematis go together particularly well: the clematis will hide the less-than-perfect bare legs of climbing roses. Try the velvet-red *Clematis* 'Niobe' with the dusky shades of *Rosa* 'Souvenir de la Malmaison'.

The double white flowers of *C.* 'Duchess of Edinburgh' are luscious with the rich creams of the 'Iceberg' or 'Lamarque' roses that you may

have planted to scramble through a hedge of conifers such as *Cupressus torulosa* or × *Cupressocyparis* 'Leighton Green'.

Cover an arbour with passionfruit and team with the red and purple *Clematis* 'Fireworks'; or with *C.* 'Miss Bateman', which blooms white with purple stamens to match the passionfruit flower.

The endlessly flowering *C.* 'Gipsy Queen' is particularly good value. Another favourite is 'Twilight', which starts flowering at Christmas and keeps going till May. Grow it through a hedge of the trouble-free rugosa roses; the clematis will start to flower in a soft mauve-to-pink above *Rosa rugosa* 'Rosarie de l'Hay' and will continue as the deep red hips of the rose develop towards winter.

Think of the hot pink *C.* 'Red Corona' flowering in spring with a once-only rose like the glorious 'Mme Gregoire Staechelin', or the double, purple *C.* 'Vyvyan Pennell' toning with blue-flowering wisterias. And try the lavender-blue *C.* 'William Kennett' with wisterias. Combine the repeat-flowering modern climbing *Rosa* 'Bantry Bay' with the deeper pink gorgeous *R.* 'Titian' and add a pale pink clematis. The possibilities are endless.

❀ Requirements

Clematis grow towards the sun, but keep their roots cool by cutting a square of shade cloth with a hole in the centre and an opening in one side: place this over the root area. Cover with mulch to disguise the cloth.

🌿 Care

Clematis love a limey soil, but I have found they also grow well in rich, acidic soils. When planting, dig a very large hole. Add plenty of well-rotted compost. Plant with three sets of nodes under the ground, so that the plant will shoot strongly.

1. The exuberance of clematis and alliums at Broughton Castle, Oxfordshire, England.
2. *Clematis* 'Niobe'.
3. *Clematis jackmannii*.

DAHLIAS

Dahlias

With their rather formal and rigid flower shape, dahlias have been out of favour for years, thought by some to be keeping company with bad taste. Popular between the two world wars—when they joined Hybrid Tea roses, carnations and gladioli to grace garden beds cut into front lawns of couch or buffalo— dahlias could never be accused of being dull, nor discreet, flowering as they do in the richest of hues, from cerise and purple to yellow and orange. Lauded by one early twentieth-century Australian garden writer as 'The King of the Autumn', they bloom in a wide variety of forms: some are single-flowered, some perfectly round, others like pompoms. Some are cactus-formed, some are star-shaped; others resemble peonies. New, more relaxed cultivars like the single, clear-red 'Bishop of Llandaff' and 'Yellow Hammer' have given dahlias another chance at horticultural respectability.

The dahlia is a genus of about 30 species and is a member of the daisy, or Asteraceae, family, although most of the modern hybrid varieties have been bred from just three dahlia species: *coccinea*, *pinnata* and *hortensis*. The genus is native to Mexico, where it is the national flower, and to Central America. In Australia, dahlias do best in areas that do not suffer from long and humid summers.

The many cultivars have been sorted into 10 main groups, according to the shape, size and form of the flowers.

❤ My favourites, by group

- Group 1: the single-flowered dahlias. This group includes the so-smart 'Yellow Hammer', with a disc of yellow anthers and stamens at its centre.
- Group 2: anemone-flowered. With an outer row of florets, sometimes curving in towards a densely packed, raised centre in the same colour, this group contains the orange to pink 'Miss Saigon'.
- Group 3: collared, or collarette. These hybrids have an outer row of eight rounded florets, with a central row—or collar—of short florets, often

in a different colour. The yellow 'Clair de Lune' is in this group.
- Group 4: waterlily. This group, which includes 'Fascination', with its deep pink flowers and dark foliage, features double rows of florets and resembles the flower of the waterlily.
- Group 5: decorative. The flowers in this group, including the orange 'Golden Ballade', are distinguished by very double flower-heads and no visible central disc.
- Group 6: ball-flowered. As their name suggests, this group has perfectly spherical blooms—some can be up to 15 cm across—and includes the deep purple 'Black Pearl'.
- Group 7: pompom-flowered. With flower-heads up to 5 cm across, and shaped like spherical pompoms, this rather formal-looking group includes the creamy-coloured 'White Aster'.
- Group 8: cactus-flowered. There is no central disc to the somewhat spikey, ragged flowers in this group, which includes 'Border Princess'.
- Group 9: semi-cactus-flowered. The flowers in this group are a little softer than those of Group 8; the petals are broader at the base and softly in-curved. 'Salmon Keen' is in this group.

Opposite: The dahlia 'Linda'.

• Group 10: miscellaneous. This group is a collection of small groups of disparate flower shapes—often new cultivars of single or semi double-flowered dahlias—and includes 'Bishop of Llandaff', with its stunning dark foliage, and the orange 'Tally Ho'.

Planting

While some people may think that perennial borders are politically incorrect in these times of global warming and climate change, dahlias are among several good doers becoming increasingly recognised as garden saviours. Team *Dahlia* 'Fire Mountain' (with its double, pure-red, flowers and black foliage) with the tough, fire engine red *Crocosmia* 'Lucifer', also at its flamboyant best in high summer; then temper these hot colours with bronze fennel.

The much underestimated bergamots (*Monarda* spp.) will provide a suitable companion to dahlias,

coloured foliage, can perform magnificently.

So, when many of the stars of the summer garden have retreated with heat exhaustion, you may be grateful for the dahlia, which, dressed in garish garb, will bring its bling to your garden, laughing loudly at those who obey the rules.

Care and requirements

Dahlias can be grown from seedlings, cuttings or tubers. Plant tubers—which will guarantee your chosen variety—in rich soil at a depth of about 8 cm, and in a sunny sheltered position, in spring, for summer flowering. Dahlias are heavy feeders, so prepare the soil by adding aged manure a fortnight before planting. Apply more fertiliser when plants reach about 30 cm, and, for show-class results, apply a high-potassium liquid fertiliser every two weeks after buds form.

For the best flowering leave your dahlia plants undisturbed. In areas of heavy frost, however, you

1. A border of dahlias lights up autumn skies.
2. 'Shirley's Pride'.
3. 'Tally Ho'.
4. Dahlia, Group 10 cultivar.
5. 'Meadow Lea'.

as will the easy-to-please—if you don't have to contend with humidity—sedums.

Anchor the yellow and orange section of your garden with the daisy-like *Bidens triplinervia*, the tall coneflower (*Rudbeckia* spp.) and the no-care yellow-flowering daylilies. Against this canvas the majestic, yellow-flowering mulleins (*Verbascum* spp.) and the apricot *Dahlia* 'Heat Wave' and 'Tally Ho', with its orange blooms above green to pewter

might lift tubers after the plants have died down in autumn or after the first frost blackens the foliage. These tubers should be stored in sawdust, out of sun and away from damp and rodents.

When dividing tubers, make sure you have at least one 'eye' present to ensure new growth. You can also propagate by taking cuttings of new sections that shoot from the tuber; these will flower that same season.

Eucalypts

There is surely no plant that speaks of Australia more eloquently than the eucalypt. This genus of more than 700 species is emblematic of this country, and the sight of those glaucous, grey-green, sickle-shaped leaves, and their distinctive scent, will remind you of home, no matter where in the world you encounter it. If the vocabulary of roses, perennial borders and exotic trees with wide, deep green leaves speaks of the determination of early settlers to domesticate and tame a land wild and foreign to their sensibilities, the vernacular of Australia is most clearly imprinted by one genus: *Eucalyptus*.

Eucalypts grow in a wide range of climates and are now cultivated in many different countries. But most—except for a few species from New Guinea and South-East Asia—are endemic to Australia.

The eucalypts are glorious trees, in the right place. That means, most often, in their natural habitat, or in a paddock providing shade for cattle resting, chewing laconically and surrounded by shimmering summer grasses. If you live on country acres you can freely indulge your admiration for this genus: you might choose whatever species grows naturally in your area to plant towards the perimeter of your garden, bringing the landscape into the constructed garden.

While they range in size and form from the multi-stemmed mallee or mid-sized shrubs to massive forest trees, most eucalypts can grow too big for the average suburban garden. Their use can create conflict with neighbours, cause problems with drains, and ruin paving as they annually shed bark, branches and leaves.

Don't panic, though, if you love the eucalypt with its flamboyant blossom and the birdlife it attracts. There are small-growing, grafted varieties now available for those of us who garden in small city spaces.

No book—not even one of several hundred pages—could discuss every eucalypt that flourishes in this country, especially if it also intended to mention a rose or two, a lemon tree, spring bulbs and more than a few much-loved and useful perennials. So, sadly there is only room here to discuss a few of the best.

❤ My favourites

THE SMALL-GROWING CULTIVARS

Stan Henry, a Queensland nuseryman, has been experimenting since 1956 with dwarf varieties of eucalypts to indulge those of us who adore the blossom and want to attract native birds, and bees, but don't garden in grand expanses.

Henry's decades of experimentation led him to a successful cross between *Corymbia ptychocarpa* (syn. *Eucalyptus ptychocarpa*)—native to the top end of the Northern Territory and used as a street tree in Cairns, its large clusters of winter flowers varying in colour from white to pink to red—and the rough-barked *Corymbia ficifolia*, from the south of Western Australia. The result—from a selection of some 200 plants—is the 'Summer Series': *Eucalyptus* 'Summer Red', which boasts a large head of red blossom, and *E.* 'Summer Beauty', with generous trusses of soft pink flowers with strong apricot overtones.

The breeding program is continuing: there are more cultivars in the pipeline, some still being

Opposite: A clutch of the gorgeous 'Summer Series' eucalypt blossom.

evaluated. Recently released are 'Summer Snow', with pink buds that open to a bright white; and 'Summer Glory', a lilac pink. Each variety is a little different; each has its own special features.

Planting and care

The small eucalypts reach about 5 m, making them suitable for the average-sized garden through-out much of Australia. They are perfect for court-yards, happy in large pots, and could make an attractive informal hedge if pruned regularly—although you would not want to remove those glorious flowers, which are followed by decorative gumnuts. All varieties, all frost hardy, are now graf-ted by licensed nurseries onto the rootstock most suitable for the area in which they are to be sold.

Tip: Nurseryman Tony Hoopman, of Toowoomba Wildflowers, advises treating smaller growing eucalypt hybrids as a grafted fruit tree. 'So, look after them until they are settled in, [providing] extra water in summer,' he says. 'They should be pruned after flowering, in early autumn, and before the seed pods have developed to prevent energy being expended on seed production rather than the formation of good, winter-colouring foliage.'

BLUE GUMS

These eucalypts feature bark that sheds in long strips (and that sometimes accumulates in a collar at the base) to leave a smooth, mottled and beautifully coloured trunk.

- *Eucalyptus saligna*, the Sydney blue gum, sheds its bark each December in great, weeping, leathery strips to reveal a smooth, brilliantly coloured bark. It flowers with a mass of white honey-filled flowers in summer: you can identify it easily by the 'Mercedes wheel' that appears at the top of the gumnuts that follow!
- *Eucalyptus leucoxlyon*, the South Australian blue gum, is a small to medium-sized tree with a straight, single trunk and smooth creamy bark shed in flakes. It flowers—from lime-green buds held on long peduncles—with glorious clusters of cream, white or red blossom in late autumn to spring.
- *Eucalyptus globulus*, the tall Tasmanian blue gum, has sessile buds, distinguished by their warty appearance, which develop into gumnuts covered in an attractive white powdery film. The creamy flowers appear from spring through to early summer and are the floral emblem of Tasmania.

SCRIBBLY GUMS

These are identified by the distinctive squiggly, wiggly, scribble patterns, made by insects, on their smooth grey trunks. There are only a few varieties where the pattern becomes the most pronounced feature of the tree; two commonly affected include *Eucalyptus haemastoma* and *E. racemosa*.

- *Eucalyptus racemosa* is a medium-sized tree native to the east coast of Australia, from south of Sydney into southern Queensland and to the west of Sydney into the Blue Mountains.
- *Eucalyptus haemastoma* is a medium-sized broad-leaved tree native to a small area of bushland from Lake Macquarie to Sydney and flowering with small cream to yellow flowers in spring and summer.

STRINGYBARKS

These are, as their name suggests, distinguished by their trunks of rough brown fibrous and stringy bark. Most are classed in the Capillulus section of the genus (with obvious radiating hairs from leaves and stems) and the seeds are almost sessile, brown to black, and held in tight round clusters of three, five or seven.

- *Eucalyptus baxteri*, the brown stringybark, comes from the south-eastern section of New South Wales, across southern Victoria and into South Australia and Kangaroo Island.

THE ARGYLE APPLE

- *Eucalyptus cinerea*, the Argyle apple, has soft grey leaves and, with or without its tightly packed

1. The silver princess, *Eucalyptus caesia*.
2. *Eucalyptus macrocarpa*.
3. *Eucalyptus pachyphylla*.
4. In the wrong place: a tall tree in a small space.

flowers, is prized by florists for arrangements. It is part of the very large Maidenaria section of the genus, with flower filaments inflexed in the bud.

> Tip: *E. cinerea* is coppiced by some growers for an annual crop of the distinctive round juvenile leaves.

THE MANNA GUM

- *Eucalyptus viminalis* subsp. *viminalis*, the Manna or ribbon gum, is native to a large area, from the Northern Tablelands of New South Wales to the coast south of Sydney and on through the southern half of Victoria and into the eastern half of Tasmania.
- *Eucalyptus viminalis* subsp. *pryoriana*, the Gippsland Manna gum, is endemic to a small area east of Melbourne, and is loved by koalas.

MALLEE

- *Eucalyptus caesia* 'Silver Princess', a weeping eucalypt, is distinguished by its powdery white and silver stems which bear gorgeous large gum-nuts. It is greatly loved by honeyeaters and parrots. From the wheat belt of Western Australia, it resents summer humidity. Like many Australian native plants this eucalypt can sulk if its demands—of particular soil and climatic conditions—are not met, and I have rarely seen it looking happy outside its natural environment.
- *Eucalyptus pachyphylla:* the glorious yellow blossom of the red bud mallee appears from late winter to summer, bursting from large-ribbed buds, which turn a deep pink before they split to reveal a mass of perfectly arranged butter-yellow stamens. Native to central Australia, this is a drought-tolerant species that grows to some 6 m with a single trunk, or multiple trunks, decorated with peeling grey bark.
- *Eucalyptus pyriformis,* the pear-fruited mallee, is another gorgeous spreading tree from Western Australia, distinguished by large yellow blossom that bursts from ribbed, pear-shaped buds in late winter, followed by pear-shaped fruits.

- *Eucalyptus macrocarpa* has stunning steel-grey leaves and exceptionally large and attractive flat-topped woody fruit. Large buds split to reveal a mass of showy pink to red stamens that can measure 8 cm across.

IRONBARKS

These are eucalypts with a hard, often furrowed bark.
- *Eucalyptus sideroxylon* 'Rosea', the pink-flowering mugga ironbark, is distinguished by hard, burnt-black, furrowed bark and clouds of gorgeous pink blossom in winter and spring. Growing to some 30 m, it is only for large gardens. The garden designer Kath Carr always included this stunning tree in her landscape plans.

THE MOST BEAUTIFUL AND MAJESTIC

- *Eucalyptus pauciflora* subsp. *niphophila*, the snow gum, is among the most beautiful of all the eucalypts. It is native to the high country of the Snowy Mountains where it stands bravely in copses, bending in the face of freezing winds. In winter its smooth bark takes on greens and browns, caramel and red, glowing in the light of the setting sun and reflected in tracts of freshly fallen snow.
- *Eucalyptus marginata*, the majestic Western Australian jarrah, grows to some 40 m, often as a natural mono species in the forests to the south of the state. The honey-filled cream flowers are held in clusters and appear in spring.
- *Eucalyptus rubida*, the candlebark, has creamy bark that can turn pink and red in winter. They are arresting when planted in a large garden as a series of copses—one a group of seven, the next of three, the next of five—tying the entire scene together.

BLOODWOODS AND GHOST GUMS

The corymbias are a group of over 110 species known as bloodwoods and ghost gums that have recently been split off from the genus *Eucalyptus* into their own genus.
- Rough barked, the bloodwoods heal any wounds with a reddish brown sap, hence the common name. Likewise, the ghost gum derives its common

name from its ethereal smooth white to grey bark; some species shed their bark in patches or strips.

· *Corymbia calophylla*, the majestic Western Australian marri, reaches 36 m in the forests to the south of the state. It was among the trees that broke the hearts, and the backs, of early settlers who needed to clear the land before crops could be planted and houses built. Its summer flowers are white and followed by large, urn-shaped capsules.

· *Corymbia citriodora*, the lemon-scented gum, native to Queensland, is among the most beautiful and ghostly of this group of trees and will tolerate a wide range of climates. With its smooth white trunks it marks out the long drive of one of Australia's best country gardens. It can also look ethereal planted in a copse in a mulch of light-coloured gravel.

> **Tip:** You can identify *C. citriodora* by its 'wrinkly armpits', the folds and wrinkles that appear in the undersides where the branches join the trunk!

· *Corymbia maculata*, the spotted gum, grows to around 30 m and is native to the coasts of eastern Australia. It sheds its bark to reveal spots in grey and green, and flowers in winter in clusters of creamy white flowers.

❀ Requirements

Most eucalypts drain the soil of nutrients and moisture, making understorey planting a challenge. In any case, a mulch of eucalypt leaves, devoid of planting, looks simple—and natural.

❧ Care

Prune eucalypts from when young to create well-shaped trees. The dwarf varieties will enjoy a light trim over the entire tree after flowering; or, if necessary, cut back hard during winter to three or four branches.

Hot colours

Many houses over recent summers would have featured arrangements of flowering gum in gorgeous combinations of luminescent orange, hot pink and bright red. During a recent December we had guests from chilly Europe at our place and felt a somewhat xenophobic urge to put on a more Australian Christmas than in previous years. So, before serving a lunch of prawns, pavlova and passionfruit, we hit the flower markets to scoop up armfuls of the brilliantly coloured, fluffy blossom of several new cultivars of dwarf eucalypts.

The genus *Corymbia* can be susceptible, particularly in more humid climates, or where air circulation is poor, to a species of the fungus *Ramularia*, or blight, identified by a mass of closely clustered spots on the leaves. It looks a little like a spreading rust, and in severe cases the leaves appear to have turned black. Spray with copper oxychloride at the rate of 2 grams per litre of water. Or, buy a commercial, ready-mixed leaf curl copper fungicide or fungus fighter. Trees often grow out of this problem.

Prevention is better than cure: keep trees healthy with deep watering, regular fertilising and generous mulching. Fertilise after pruning, and after flowering, with a low-phosphorus plant food such as slow-release granules specially formulated for native plants. Apply to watered ground and always water in well.

An icon

Eucalyptus camaldulensis, the river red gum, was eulogised by the landscape painters of the nineteenth and early twentieth centuries and immortalised in the shimmery paintings of the South Australian artist Hans Heysen.

FERNS

Ferns

Ferns conjure up all sorts of evocative images, among them visions of intrepid Victorian plant hunters risking their lives in exotic locations to transport botanical prizes back to garden owners endlessly hungry for the rare and unusual. They speak of steamy tropical locations and dangerous jungles; and remind us of elegant days past, of palm courts and of shaded courtyards in the Far East.

Ferns are ancient plants: some date back to the Devonian era, about 400 million years ago; others were found 350 million years ago, in the Carboniferous period. They range from tall-growing tree ferns to low-growing, delicate ground covers and enjoy a range of climates, surviving in a variety of soils.

Planted in dense, verdant swathes, they are the ultimate tapestry plant. With their bright green foliage they look beautiful with white-flowering bulbs such as galanthus (snowdrops), and, if you live in a climate where they will flourish, *Convallaria majalis* (lily of the valley) with her brilliant green, hosta-like leaves. Ferns flash their undersides, which might be brown and speckled with spores, or silver, reflecting light and illuminating the gloom of the rainforest conditions that they love. Most love the damp, humus-rich conditions of the forest floor; others are content in dry shade.

So, if your garden is starved of light and you despair of creating a pleasing botanical oasis, consider a garden of ferns to create a cool, private enclave for quiet contemplation.

♥ My favourites

ADIANTUM

There are over 200 species in this genus, the best known being the common maidenhair fern, *Adiantum aethiopicum*. With its clouds of feathery fronds, it is tougher than its delicate appearance would suggest. It loves humus-rich, moist soil and misty conditions: you will often see it growing happily in pots in bathrooms—but it doesn't like wet feet.

ASPLENIUM

Asplenium, commonly called spleenworts, are from a diverse genus of 700 species that are found in all corners of the globe. Its members therefore have differing cultivation requirements.

• *Asplenium australasicum*, the bird's nest fern, native to Australia and the South Pacific, has thick, shiny, bright green leaves that grow—sometimes to 2 m long—from a central base, or 'nest'. It is frost tender and likes humid conditions.

• *Asplenium nidus*, a similar species that enjoys warmer conditions, grows in rock crevices and in trees in the tropical rainforest. If given a shaded position this fern will thrive on very little care and survive with little water.

• *Asplenium bulbiferum*, commonly known as 'Hen and Chickens', is native throughout much of Australia and New Zealand and is a more fragile-looking fern, similar to the maidenhair fern.

> **Tip:** Shallow-rooted ferns are happy to be moved about the garden from time to time. An occasional boost with a weak solution of Seasol will help settle in relocated plants.

Opposite: The delicate fronds of *Adiantum aethiopicum*.

• *Asplenium scolopendrium*, the hart's tongue fern, is native to the United Kingdom and Europe, to Asia and North America. This species is most suited to growing outdoors in cold climates. It has long, undivided, strap-like upright fronds.

BLECHNUM

The water ferns, or fish-bone ferns, comprise more than 200 species and are found in temperate, as well as tropical, parts of the world, most often in the southern hemisphere. Most of these easy-to-please ferns have small stems and fish-bone looking foliage that grows from a central point.
• *Blechnum nudum*, the fishbone water fern, is native to the mainland of south-eastern Australia and to Tasmania. It likes damp conditions and thrives in the shade, although it also likes full sun—it can be a nuisance, making itself too much at home in shady parts of a garden.

DOODIA

The *Doodia* genus, the rasp ferns, contains 11 species of small-growing ferns, native to the Pacific, Australia and New Zealand. Some are similar to the maidenhairs, some to the fish-bone ferns.

OSMUNDA REGALIS

The gorgeous royal fern, *Osmunda regalis*, is aptly named as it is so elegant. A deciduous fern, it looks delicate; yet it must be as tough as boots, as it is native to the United Kingdom and Europe, where it withstands punishing winters, after which it erupts in fresh pink shoots in summer. Keep it damp; in Ireland it grows in great golden swathes in boggy areas.

PTERIS

Pteris spp., the brake fern, is a genus of deciduous and semi-deciduous ferns from the damp gullies of subtropical and tropical rainforests. Not surprisingly, these ferns love water during their growing period, and dappled light. Of the 250 species known, about eight are native to Australia. They have long fronds, each with a central rib, and opposite leaflets.

POLYSTICHUM

The shield ferns are very pretty ferns, distributed from tropical parts of the country to sub-Antarctic regions.
• *Polystichum proliferum*, from south-eastern Australia, reaches about 1 m. Easygoing, it provides an interesting mid-layer understorey in a shade garden.
• *Polystichum setiferum* is native to Europe and has elegant, horizontal leaflets, held on upright fronds.

> **Tip:** Plant the *Polystichum* ferns so that the cinnamon colouring of the new croziers can be appreciated as they unfurl.

THE TREE FERNS

The two genera commonly called tree ferns—Cyathea and Dicksonia—are tall growing, mostly from the humid tropical and subtropical, frost-free regions of the world. An umbrella-like crown of lacy, weeping fronds emanates from a central bud at the end of a stem, which can reach up to 15–20 m in the right conditions. The stem is a complicated system of tissues which conduct nutrients and is often covered in brown, fibrous, aerial roots. Tree ferns love rainforest conditions of misted, dappled light and moist, humus-rich soils.

Cyathea

A large genus of some six thousand species, spread throughout subtropical and tropical, frost-free regions of the world, most cyatheas have a single stem, which grows to as tall as 15 m and is topped off with a crown of fronds. Most of the fronds have scales at their base, which can be prickly to touch and, once removed, will leave scars on the trunk. These tree ferns can be easily transplanted.
• *Cyathea australis*, the rough tree fern, flourishes in the basalt soils of Mount Wilson in the Blue Mountains, west of Sydney, where stands of it are reminiscent of a corps of long-legged ballerinas! Native to the east coast of Australia, this

1. A shady corner in Mary and Steve Lukezic's Benalla garden, *Rambling Rose*.
2. The fronds of *Asplenium bulbiferum* unfurl.
3. The tree fern *Dicksonia antarctica*.
4. Maidenhair ferns cover the damp walls at Villa d'Este, at Tivoli, near Rome.

The *Fern Garden*

There is a small, somewhat secret place to one side of the Sculpture Garden at the Australian National Gallery in Canberra. It is quite hard to find, but once you do discover it, you will probably want to sit alone in the cool, dark shade, in peaceful and restorative contemplation.

Alternatively, you can look down on the *Fern Garden*, created by artist Fiona Hall, through a picture window in the gallery. There, you can read about the genesis and the soul of this living sculpture.

The *Fern Garden* is an arrangement of *Dicksonia antarctica*, local to the area, which grow from the mountain ranges that cut through the eastern side of Australia from Queensland down to Tasmania. The juxtaposition of art and nature appealed to Fiona Hall. 'In a garden there is continual upkeep; things lose their leaves. The ferns get new fronds in spring and autumn, they then die, so inevitably you are not going to have it looking like a museum exhibit.'

'I was asked if I would like to do a garden in the gallery grounds,' says Fiona. 'For me it was a dream come true. And I think it was brave of them, as I have no background in horticulture.'

graceful tree fern holds its long, mid-green, slightly weeping fronds on a slim brown-to-black trunk. In the deep volcanic soils and under the protection of old-growth forests, these dramatic and elegant ferns reach towards the light, growing to some 15 m in height. They coexist happily with exotic species, looking somehow appropriate as they provide protection for azaleas and rhododendrons.

- *Cyathea cooperi*, the scaly tree fern, or coin spot tree fern, reaches 6 to 8 m in humid conditions. It makes a stunning, shady canopy for light-shy plants such as the yellow-flowering clivea.

- *Cyathea medullaris*, the New Zealand black tree fern, reaches up to 15 m in height, with fronds up to 6 m long. The black trunks are typically covered in black frond scars. It likes dappled shade and water and is a heavy feeder.
- *Cyathea rebeccae* is the tree fern of the wet tropics.

Dicksonia

The Dicksonia, or soft tree fern, genus comprises 30 species spread throughout diverse regions, from Malaysia to Australia and New Zealand. They are mostly frost hardy, at least to some extent, but they like protection from the wind, and humus-rich, moist soil. Native to south-eastern Australia, they are slow growing, although they will reach 15 m in height in the right conditions. They are hardier than the species in the *Cyathea* genus.

- *Dicksonia antarctica* can withstand frost to minus 10 degrees Celsius and will tolerate overhead sun.

🌿 Care

Tree ferns love a teaspoon of sugar, placed once a month at their head in the centre of the fronds. And water down the neck of the plant—this assumes, of course, that your tree fern has not grown too tall!

Ballast

Tree ferns made their way from Australia to the United Kingdom as ballast on ships and are now adorning large gardens in Cornwall that bask in the warm influence of the Gulf Stream. There, at Trebah Garden, they are planted down a ravine that ends on the beach at the mouth of the Helford River, where American tanks and lorries were loaded onto waiting landing craft for the D-Day invasion of Normandy in 1944. A hectare of the Tasmanian tree fern *Dicksonia antarctica* clings to the valley sides, providing a filigree canopy for a huge mass of blue 'Lace Cap' hydrangea and the prehistoric-looking *Gunnera manicata*.

Opposite: Just south of Rome, the glorious Ninfa.

Ninfa

About an hour south of Rome, in the shadow of the towering Lepini Mountains and the Etruscan hill city of Sermoneta, lies the wild and romantic garden of Ninfa. Once a thriving town of churches, a crenellated castle, town hall, houses, bakeries and blacksmiths, all within double city walls, Ninfa dates at least to the first century, when the Roman official and writer Pliny the Younger recorded a visit to the temple of the Nymphs, which gave the town its name.

Built on the edge of a fast-flowing river, Ninfa was acquired in 1297 by the aristocratic Pietro Caetani. In 1382 the town was destroyed when the family opposed the Pope in the religious struggles of the time, and any townspeople who survived fled. Ninfa lay deserted and crumbling for hundreds of years.

Then, almost a century ago, members of the Caetani family reclaimed their lands and set about stabilising the ruins—some of which were still decorated with the remains of Byzantine frescoes. They replenished the gardens and rejuvenated the waterways. Today there is no surface that does not support cascades of roses, wisteria and jasmine, which drip down the mellow walls and romp up stately trees.

There are collections of dogwoods, maples and viburnums; ancient cypress soar towards the light, playing host to wild roses like *Rosa filipes*, which tumbles like a wedding veil of fine netting, flowering in white clusters against the deep green pine needles. A stone bridge from Roman times, which crosses the Ninfa River, is festooned with long purple racemes of *Wisteria floribunda* 'Macrobotrys' in May and is ablaze with roses by June.

You wander around a bend in the river, which is edged with swathes of *Iris laevigata*, flowering blue in May, and with *Gunnera manicata*, the giant rhubarb that erupts from frozen earth each spring, to come across a grove of the bamboo, *Phyllostachys sulphurea* 'Viridis', its jade-green glistening spires forming a cool cathedral. Massing at its feet are the sparkling, fresh green leaves of *Asplenium scolopendrium* (the hart's tongue fern), reflected in a still pool that has formed there.

In the dark days of World War II the Caetani family held open house for collections of friends: artists, writers, diplomats, politicians and travellers, many of whom left written records of the gardens. It is easy to imagine that the sometimes-troubled guests might have found some peace in this shady grove.

GERANIUMS AND PELARGONIUMS

Geraniums

AND PELARGONIUMS

Summer gardens in Italy and France each year feature clouds of brilliantly coloured geraniums: they cascade down ochre-washed walls from window boxes, they drip from urns set on walls or beside swimming pools; they hang from baskets and tumble down dry banks as a ground cover. These plants, correctly known as pelargoniums, belong to the family Geraniaceae. Along with the real *Geranium*, the very useful genus *Pelargonium* consists of almost 300 species, most endemic to South Africa and its neighbour Namibia, although some are native to south-west Asia, Australia and New Zealand.

The genus *Geranium*, like pelargoniums, consists again of some 300 species—of perennials, biennials and even annuals. Sometimes called cranesbills, geraniums make up a large and widely used genus, greatly loved by gardeners from England to the United States to Australia.

The genus *Erodium* comprises about 60 species, mostly native to the Mediterranean region, with a few found in Africa and Australia.

The three genera bear masses of small, simple and charming five-petalled flowers in a range of colours from white and cream to lilac and pink to red and purple.

Geraniums

Sometimes colloquially called 'species geraniums' by gardeners in the know, cranesbills are among the easiest and least fussy of plants. While they perhaps flower most generously in the cooler regions of Australia, they cope well with humid and warm temperate climates. Their five-petalled, symmetrical flowers bloom in a range of blues, purples and pinks above a mass of interestingly lobed and dissected leaves. While they may not flower as vigorously in the hot and sticky Sydney climate as they will, for instance, on the Southern Highlands of New South Wales, they deserve a place in every garden, if only for their foliage and their ability to cover the ground in a soothing, green tapestry.

The tallest of the cranesbills—*Geranium maderense*, native to Madeira—reaches about 1.5 m. It copes with a range of temperatures—from frosts down to minus 1 degree Celsius, as well as with humidity; and, perhaps most useful of all, it also tolerates dry summers. This species looks wonderful planted in multiples, to weave in wide ribbons through the garden. With its burgundy stems, it tones perfectly with the tall burgundy-leaved cannas, and, flowering with clouds of pink to purple blooms through summer, with many of the salvias, or with the smaller growing cranesbills. Team with the ground covering *G. phaeum* for its intense burgundy flowers.

❤ Favourite border plants and ground covers

- *Geranium phaeum*: deep burgundy flowers.
- *Geranium* 'Johnson's Blue': among the best of the true-blue flowering cranesbills, growing to some 50 cm.
- *Geranium* × *magnificum*: vigorous, grows to about 60 cm in height and bears a mass of deep blue flowers throughout summer.

Opposite: Pelargoniums cascade from grand urns at Villa Reale, Lucca.

- *Geranium pratense*, the meadow cranesbill: hails from across Europe into China but is perfectly content in a range of climates.
- *Geranium macrorrhizum* 'Ingwersen's Variety': a low-growing cultivar with a mass of delicate, pink to lilac flowers.
- *Geranium renardii* grows to around 30 cm in height and masses out quickly with bright green, rough leaves, and white flowers marked with fascinating purple stripes.
- *Geranium* 'Brookside' will flower for months over spring and summer in most gardens.
- *Geranium traversii* 'Seaspray': one of the most effective varieties for coastal gardens, from New Zealand and the Chatham Islands and growing to just 15 cm.

Planting

Geranium maderense would look effective also planted against a backbone of the undemanding *Loropetalum chinense* 'China Pink', with its pendulous, fragrant, pink-fringed flowers; the tough berberis; or any of the smokebush, with their burgundy and brown leaves. The burgundy-leaved *Heuchera* 'Palace Purple' makes an effective companion in a cool climate—and the whole picture would look even more exciting set off with violet-painted wooden tripods covered with the lilac-flowered *Clematis* 'Kathleen Dunford' or the burgundy *C.* 'Niobe'.

In cool climates mix the cranesbills with clumps of the architectural onion *Allium cristophii*, with *A. giganteum,* and with that stunning purple-flowering poppy 'Patty's Plum', then back the picture with clouds of old-fashioned floribunda or David Austin roses. In a blue-based border

> **Tip:** Choose a selection of *Geranium* species to fill various positions in the garden, from the tall to the mid-size to the small.

employing a palette of violets and lavenders, *Geranium × magnificum*, which is covered for months with small, true-blue flowers, complements an edging of *G.* 'Johnson's Blue'. They all team perfectly with the blue-flowered echiums.

Requirements

Most cranesbills are frost hardy; grow them in sun or half sun and moist, rich soils. Prune back after flowering to keep tidy and prevent them from becoming sparse and thin.

Care

Geraniums (and pelargoniums) can suffer from rust—millions of spores that spread infection. Get to this problem when you first notice it, for, as with most problems in the garden, that old saying 'a stitch in time saves nine' is pertinent here. First, destroy any affected leaves, or cut away

and destroy affected sections of the plant. Then spray with PestOil (*see* Pests and Diseases).

My way of dealing with pests and diseases in the garden, however, is to choose a different plant. Perhaps the ideal approach to gardening into the twenty-first century is to create gardens of species—whether exotic or native—that are suited to their environment.

2

1. A rich border of *Geranium* × *magnificum* and berberis.
2. Pelargoniums cascade to the water's edge at the Hotel Cipriani in Venice.
3. At 'The Scented Rose', in Tasmania, a shed is clothed in pelargoniums.

3

Pelargoniums

For easy gardening in warm and not-too-humid climates there is hardly a better choice than the tough and generous pelargonium, sometimes called storksbills. They come in several forms, as perennials and shrubs, or as climbers and scramblers, suited to all styles of garden, from formal to cottage. The leaves can be small and neat with a jagged edge, or broad and toothed, scalloped or dissected. Some have smooth, fleshy leaves, some are covered in fine hairs, some are scented. Pelargoniums flower in a range of colours, from lilacs to pinks, cerise and reds, as well as white; some are double. With modern breeding, the hybrids are countless.

Tip: Use the shrubby pelargoniums in frost-free gardens as a loose hedge, a backbone, or part of a border, along with other warm-climate show-ponies such as the burgundy-leaved cannas, the brightly coloured salvias and black mondo grass.

Apart from being an excellent choice for hanging baskets and window boxes—which will best display their heart-shaped leaves—the scrambling ivy-leaved pelargonium hybrids will quickly cover a fence.

Planting

In the hot and dry conditions of South Australia the ivy-leaved pelargoniums look marvellous scrambling up telephone poles. Mix the different colours in the same groups together: the lilacs with the pinks, with, perhaps, a red to add a highlight. Let the palest of them weave through a covering of Chinese star jasmine—or, perhaps, the pink and white rose 'Pierre de Ronsard'.

For colonial gardens

Geraniums—*Pelargonium* spp.—considered a hothouse treasure in the United Kingdom, were collected by our earliest settlers in the eighteenth and nineteenth centuries as their ships rested at the Cape of Good Hope on the way to the new colonies. Initially causing great excitement, this genus proved so robust growing in the mild conditions of New South Wales that they quickly became commonplace and a symbol of the working man's garden.

Requirements

Pelaragoniums will cope with only the lightest of frosts: in Europe they are used as annuals and brought into a hothouse for winter; in milder climates, they are covered during the cold months.

Care

Pelaragoniums like well-drained soil and won't tolerate over-watering. Cut off spent flowers and fertilise with an all-purpose liquid fertiliser annually. Prune these hardy plants to keep tidy and prevent the shrubby species from becoming leggy, and they will flower for months. Propagate by simply breaking off a piece and placing it directly into the ground or a pot.

Erodiums

This least known member of the Geraniaceae family, closely related to geraniums and pelargoniums, is found in the rocky, dry soils and cool regions of Europe and South America, as well as in Asia and Australia. With small flowers similar to species geraniums, erodiums, sometimes known as heronsbills, are more usually grown by specialist collectors in rockeries. In cool climates they can be useful as ground covers, particularly in poor soils.

Gingers

Gingers are part of the rather complicated family Zingiberaceae, which is made up of several different genera, many of which answer to the common name of ginger. You could describe them all as architectural—but perhaps you would be doing them a disservice, for they are exotic rather than structured or rigid.

Gingers are wonderful garden plants, great for massing; they are fascinating, diverse, deliciously scented—and many are edible. Many are native to South-East Asia, the Pacific and South America, but, despite the common belief that they are tender tropical plants, there are numerous species that are hardy in the colder climates of the southern states of Australia.

There are, in fact, nearly two thousand genera and species within the family, including the edible ginger, *Zingiber officinale*; the spice cardamom, *Elleteria cardamomum*; and the gorgeous torch ginger, *Etlingera elatior*.

❤ My favourites

ALPINIA

The ornamental gingers, the alpinias—easy-going, disease free and cold tolerant—cope well with the humid Sydney climate, and do well even further south in more temperate climates. Native to Asia and the Pacific, they grow from rhizomes to form large clumps.
• *Alpinia zerumbet*, the elegant shell ginger, blooms with drooping sprays of waxy, cream and pink buds that open to yellow-throated flowers.
• *Alpinia galanga*, the Thai ginger generally known as galangal, is prized for its thick rhizome, which can be grated or dried to create a delicious and very distinctive spice that is crucial to many Thai dishes.

COSTUS

The spiral gingers, the genus *Costus*, comprise some 150 species from throughout the wet tropics. Clump-forming, they provide a very effective ground cover: they have medicinal and agricultural uses, too. Available in both large-growing and dwarf species, many have flowers that are edible, adding glamour to summer salads.
• *Costus speciosus* has beautifully coloured stems and pale, apple-green, zebra-striped leaves, with cobra-like flower-heads in white, bright red or pale yellow.
• *Costus* 'Barbados', from South America and the West Indies, is a brilliant red.

HEDYCHIUM

The Hedychiums, the ginger lilies, are the most scented genus in the family, and are native to southern Asia. They grow from rhizomes and form clumps, which can reach 3 m.

Many uses

The stems of *Costus* spp. are used in many different ways: they are pounded and used as matting in Asia, and in parts of South America the juice is extracted from the stem to cure eye diseases. In Africa the stems are hung over doors to ward off evil spirits.

Previous page: The blue ginger, *Dichorisandra thyrsiflora*.

- *Hedychium coronarium*, bearing a very fragrant white lily, is from India and is used for making perfume.
- *Hedychium gardnerianum*, a shorter species native to the Himalayas, is one of the most cold tolerant of the gingers. Its spikes of pale yellow scented flowers appear in late summer. In humid and many coastal areas, however, it has become something of a weed.
- *Hedychium greenii* has a burgundy-backed leaf.

> **Tip:** *Hedychium greenii* teams well with cannas and other pink and red-coloured foliage plants.

- *Hedychium coccineum*, from China, India, Sri Lanka and Thailand, has a lovely red flower and is softly scented.

HELICONIAS

The crab-claw gingers, *Heliconia* spp., are native to tropical America, Asia and the Pacific. Although they belong to a different family, the Heliconias are members of the taxonomic group Zingiberales, so are closely related to the gingers. As they are used in similar ways, in similar conditions, I have included them in this chapter.

> **Tip:** The vibrantly coloured Heliconias, whch can be 'too much' in a more subtle southern climate, work beautifully in the strong light of northern Australia.

Spectacular

- *Heliconia angusta* 'Red Christmas' bears dazzling, red blooms in winter.
- *Heliconia caribaea*: both the 'Purpurea' and 'Gold' flower for much of the year.
- *Heliconia* 'Fire Flash' bears a mass of orange flowers held high over many months.

- *Heliconia angusta* 'Orange Christmas' and 'Yellow Christmas' bear upright spires of red or yellow bracts in summer.
- *Heliconia rostrata*, commonly called 'Hanging Parrot's Beak', with its pendulous cascade of colourful bracts, is a spectacular addition to the warm-climate garden.

Fragrant jewel chicken (serves 6)

This wonderfully aromatic chicken is delicious served with rice noodles and dry-roasted, crushed peanuts.

Ingredients

2 kg diced chicken thigh meat
1 tbs olive oil
1 tbs butter
800 ml coconut milk
4 coriander roots, chopped finely
3 fresh, small red chillies, diced
(remove seeds if you wish to remove heat)
5 g fresh galangal, diced, or 1 tbs dried
7 fresh kaffir lime leaves
juice of 3 limes
finely grated rind of 1 lime
2 tbs fish sauce
1–2 tbs palm sugar
tiny pinch salt
1 bunch fresh coriander leaves, chopped
Few leaves basil, chopped

Method

In a heavy-bottomed pan, saute chicken meat in olive oil and butter, to seal; set aside. In same pan, bring to boil all other ingredients except coriander and basil leaves. Add chicken pieces and simmer 30 minutes, until chicken is cooked. Stir in chopped coriander and basil, and serve, topped with crushed peanuts and with boiled or steamed rice, or rice noodles.

Tip: You can use banks of heliconias to separate areas of the garden, just as you might employ a hedge or a screen.

Mass planting

- *Heliconia stricta* 'Dwarf Jamaican', from South America, bears orange bracts that emerge from red-ribbed foliage.
- *Heliconia psittacorum* 'Sassy': the rainbow-coloured parrot flowers emerge from lance-like leaves that reach to 1 m.
- *Heliconia psittacorum* 'Andromeda' bears prolific bright orange flowers with green tips.

Tip: Team heliconias with the multi-coloured cordylines, with the blue ginger *Dichorisandra thyrsiflora* and with plantings of miniature cannas. For a calmer look, or for your tapestry garden, try *Heliconia indica* 'Rubra', which, while it has flowers that are insignificant, boasts wonderful foliage.

ZINGIBER

- The genus *Zingiber* comprises some 100 species, most of which are frost tender, enjoying heat and humidity.

Ornamental

- *Zingiber spectabile*, the golden beehive, has stunning flowers with heads of waxy, yellow bracts.

Edible

- *Zingiber officinale*, the edible ginger that we all know, loves warm climates. Plant in spring for summer flowers of white spikes. You know the root is ready to harvest when the leaves die down in autumn.

OTHER GINGERS

- *Etlingera elatior*, the torch ginger, is native to tropical Asia and is among the most stunning plants you will find anywhere in the world. The gorgeous flower is statuesque and delicate at the same time. The flowers erupt from the underground rhizomes and bloom among the ginger-like stems, which can reach 3 m. The red waxy bracts are arranged around a head of imbricated petals, which each seem to be outlined in a fine pink line. The torch ginger likes well-drained but rich soil and flourishes in sun or part shade. Dead-head constantly for continuous blooming.
- *Dichorisandra thyrsiflora*, the blue ginger, included here because of its similarity to members of the ginger family, grows in a range of frost-free climates and flowers in late summer through autumn with brilliant blue spires that stand erect from glossy green leaves.

❀ Requirements

Gingers like well-drained, rich soil and regular watering from spring through summer and autumn.

❦ Care

Don't water in winter. Gingers that flower terminally must have the spent stems cut down to ground level as they flower only once per stem.

Tip: *Zingiber spectabile* looks fabulous in front of a hedge of hibiscus, cordylines or crotons.

1. *Heliconia rostrata.*
2. *Heliconia bihai.*

HELLEBORES

Hellebores

If, in the depths of winter and the midst of drought, survival of the fittest has become your gardening motto, you might have fallen for the genus *Helleborus*, a member of the Ranunculaceae family. It is time to salute these useful, and beautiful, plants that seem oblivious to appalling weather, and are tough and forgiving, but somewhat under-appreciated.

English breeder Elizabeth Strangman, in her definitive book on the genus, *The Gardener's Guide to Growing Hellebores*, explains their magic as, 'Nature's gift to gardeners in the dismal months … when the weather is cold and discouraging and spring seems a long way ahead'.

In Europe often called the Christmas rose, in Australia the winter rose, the hellebore is the quiet achiever of the plant world. If you are into horticultural conspicuous consumption, she is not for you. She is no drama queen, and you need to seek out her modest blooms. But the charms of the hellebore are many, from the form of the daintily held flowers to their colours and petal shape. Some blooms are pointed, some distinctly rounded; take time to appreciate their delicate colourings and superb markings in an amazing range of colours, from dazzling white to pink to black-purple. Some are intricately marked with speckles or splotches, some are double. Some have jagged leaves, some are deeply veined or netted; some foliage is the deepest forest green, some blue to steel grey. In the case of most species, the leaves grow flush with the ground and are stemless, but in a few species, known as caulescent hellebores, the leaves are held on fleshy stems.

Hellebores hail from Britain to the Balkans, from Turkey and into Russia and China, but there is a species suited to almost every corner of this country. The deciduous species are extremely frost and cold hardy. In regions where high rainfall and humid summers mean that many garden stars are the victims of unrequited love, the hellebore, with her subtle differences, her clever leaf veining and her elegant flowers, has what it takes to infatuate the collector and plant hunter. And, they flower when there is not much else around. There is much to love about the humble hellebore!

♥ My favourites

HELLEBORUS X HYBRIDUS

The promiscuity of this species is what makes it so exciting, for the offspring bear widely differing markings and colours! And *Helleborus × hybridus* and its hybrids will happily multiply, forming clumps that reach up to 60 cm in height, in anything but the poorest soil. Like all hellebores they love the frost, but *H. × hybridus* cope with hot summers and winter rains that would rot some of the fussier species.

- *Helleborus × hybridus* 'Mrs Betty Ranicar', named for a much-loved Tasmanian gardener, is a double white. If you have any from the original garden, treasure them, as those grown from seed do not always come true.
- *Helleborus × hybridus* 'Pluto' bears an almost-black bloom.

CAULESCENTS

The caulescent species—with an obvious stem rising from the ground—and their hybrids stand the best chance of survival in the humidity of northern coastal regions.

Opposite: *Helleborus × hybridus*.

- *Helleborus argutifolius* has impressive serrated leaves and flowers early in spring, with large sprays of yellow-green flowers that hold on until the following winter.
- *Helleborus foetidus*, sometimes called the stinking hellebore, with deeply cut foliage of forest-green, flowers in late winter with a chandelier of small green bells which last for weeks.
- *Helleborus foetidus* 'Wester Flisk' holds its clusters of flowers on red stems that reach about 60 cm.
- *Helleborus lividus* bears bowl-shaped cream flowers among green to blue leaves, and likes the damp.
- *Helleborus* × *sternii* 'Boughton Beauty' features jagged, blue-green, toothed leaves and pale green to pink flowers.
- *Helleborus* × *ericsmithii* will cope with extreme drought.

DECIDUOUS

- *Helleborus viridis* has the palest lime-green flowers, which emerge before the new leaves.
- *Helleborus torquatus*: rare and greatly prized by collectors, the cerise blooms emerge just before its mid-green foliage.
- *Helleborus purpurascens* reaches about 30 cm and flowers pink to grey.

Planting

- *Helleborus foetidus* 'Wester Flisk' looks great grown in a swathe through the garden, perhaps as a ribbon, weaving through a border. It tolerates dry shade, making it a great companion for *Euphorbia amygdaloides* var. *robbiae*.
- *Helleborus* × *ballardiae*, with stunning pewter-coloured foliage, enjoys full sun in cool-climate gardens, but in warmer areas grows well in shade, particularly in a southerly position.
- *Helleborus niger* needs steady moisture and a cold climate. Plant it under trees that colour in autumn—such as *Liquidambar styraciflua*—so that the dazzling white flowers that emerge in mid-winter appear like freshly fallen snow on a tapestry carpet of glistening burgundy leaves.

Hellebore heaven

Among the new treasures offered by Corrie and John Dudley, whose Elizabeth Town nursery in Tasmania's north is close to heaven for hellebore lovers, is the double white 'Aglaia'. They also offer 'Scorned Woman', a double red 'so sumptuous', says John, 'that it will stop traffic'. *Helleborus* 'Thalia' is a formally shaped double pink with maroon spotting, while 'Isobel Wilcox' is a large double pink with all-over red spotting.

Requirements

The experts advise that hellebores prefer an alkaline soil, but this genus cannot be too fussy as its species thrive in warm temperate coastal climates and in sandy soils and also form impressive carpets in the acidic, basalt soil enjoyed by some of the frosty mountain areas of New South Wales.

Care

Fertilise hellebores with lime in summer, when the flower buds are forming, and water in well. Propagation by division, which will ensure that each offspring replicates its parent, is simple and best done at the end of summer. Lift to divide and replant.

Seeds of all species and cultivars are stratified (to simulate autumn conditions) upon harvesting at 22 degrees Celsius for a minimum of 42 and a maximum of 152 days. Gather seeds fresh and never allow them to dry out: stratify in a mix of moistened coir (coconut fibre) and vermiculite for a period of not less than 50 days. They are then ready to sow in a free-draining medium to germinate naturally in an isolated part of the garden. And if you want to keep some of your special × hybridus cultivars true, you must prevent others nearby from seeding by removing spent flowers.

Cut off most of the old leaves of hellebores so that the emerging flowers are fully appreciated.

1. *Helleborus* 'Nancy Ballard'.
2. *Helleborus lividus*.
3. The hellebore walk at Moidart, on the Southern Highlands of New South Wales.
4. *Helleborus niger*.
5. *Helleborus* 'Mrs Betty Ranicar'.

Great Fosters

The glorious parterre garden at Great Fosters at Egham in Surrey, close to Heathrow airport (once known as Great Forresters and part of the Royal Windsor Old Forest, playground of kings and queens, incorporating a Tudor pile used by Henry VIII as a hunting lodge) has been restored. Clipped yews and box hedges, which had almost overgrown the interconnecting grass paths a little more than a decade ago, were cut right back to the hard wood, allowing them to regrow dense, from the base. An intricate pattern now constrains lavenders, catmint, sage and alliums. Like all parterre and knot gardens, it is best appreciated from the castellated tower of the house or from a high window and is connected to the sunken rose garden, across one arm of the moat that surrounds the property, by a wisteria-swathed bridge. It has taken more than a decade, but these wonderful gardens have now been returned to their pre-war elegance and beauty, and, along with the house, are listed by English Heritage.

Above: At Great Fosters, thought to have once been a hunting lodge for Henry VIII.

Mazes in different dress

In late 1998, Adrian Fisher, a maze designer renowned in the United Kingdom and the United States, was commissioned to create a maze from corn at the Enchanted Maze, the first such maze in the southern hemisphere. One hundred thousand corn seedlings were planted over an area of nearly 2 ha: by April 1999 it had been seen by some 25,000 visitors.

Australian artist Marion Borgelt was then commissioned to create the Year 2000 maze, comprising 55 rings, each 12 m in diameter. The circles were open in places and closed in others to create the puzzle. The entire design was bordered by 17,000 annuals: marigolds and petunias in gold, orange, red and purple. Since then a different designer has created a Maize Maze each year.

Thirty thousand kilometres away, near the medieval market town of Figeac, in the Lot region in the south-west of France, is a maze of roses created by Australians Pixie and Don Lowe, in the grounds of the twelfth-century Château de Saint-Dau.

'Le Labyrinthe des Roses' was planted with more than a thousand climbing roses, both old and modern, and repeat-flowering roses selected for perfume and arranged by colour and historic significance. The maze takes the form of three enormous, interlocking circles in the shape of Tudor roses. Along more than 2 km of pathways lined with impenetrable walls of blooms visitors find storyboards telling of the provenance and story of roses, their place in history and art, as well as practical details about their cultivation and care. The complicated planting plan took more than two years to become a reality, and roses were sourced from three local nurseries and ordered six months in advance of planting.

Now the fairytale castle towers above a maze traced by roses, an extraordinary sight when they first burst into bloom in late May. While the peak season at the maze is early summer, when the scent of thousands of blooms fills the air, the selection of repeat-flowering varieties and the addition of hundreds of clematis ensure that the garden is never without a bloom.

Above: At Naumkeag, a garden designed by the Boston landscape architect, Fletcher Steele.

Parterres and knot gardens

Designed to replicate the intricate embroidery fashionable in medieval times as well as the finely detailed designs of Persian carpets, knot gardens are created by laying out hedging plants of different foliage shapes, textures and colours in clipped patterns. In the earliest designs, knot gardens were quite functional: arranged as they were to keep medicinal and culinary herbs and perennials separate. Later patterns became more intricate, housing annual, flowering plants, or designed as elegant swirls drawn in varieties of box and set against a background of gravel.

You can have great fun planning and plotting your knot garden. Use graph paper, tracing paper or butter paper to draw your shapes to scale. Mark out the areas that will use the different types of box (or other plants) by colouring the sections with different coloured pencils. Keep a note of which colours relate to which species. This will also provide you with a guide when you are ready to plant out.

The two boxes, English and Japanese (*Buxus sempervirens* and *B. microphylla* var. *japonica*), look good together. The faster growing Japanese box is lighter in colour; the denser, slower-growing, darker green English box can be kept cut lower. Your knot garden can be as complicated as your energy will allow; create fancy 'over and under' designs by weaving the variegated box into your design. If you don't want too much maintenance, a more simple parterre of a mass of box can be clipped as much or as little as you like. But, as with all hedging, regular clipping will create the most intricate, and most formal, result (see Hedges).

You can also use several other plants to create the basic pattern of your knot garden: santolina, westringia, lavender and lonicera are just a few. Remember that the slower growing the species you choose, the more finely detailed the resulting knot garden or the more simple parterre.

In the south-west of France

At 'Le Labyrinthe des Roses' thousands of bearded iris are planted at the feet of the roses to add perfume and colour in May and June. Clematis of different cultivars and species, which tone or contrast with the roses, have been selected to extend the flowering season from May to October. *Rosa* 'Gold Bunny' contrasts with the purple *Clematis* 'Ville de Lyon'; the hot pink trusses of *R.* 'Dorothy Perkins' tone with *C.* 'Gypsy Queen', while the deep pink, scented rose 'Etoile de Hollande' looks superb climbing through the softer *R.* 'Pink Cloud' and the modern French climber *R.* 'Pierre de Ronsard'.

Above: The Palazzo Ruspoli, north of Rome, is one of the best-preserved maze gardens in Italy, planted in 1612 for Ottavia Orsini Marescotti.

MEADOW GARDENS

Hippeastrums

Almost two decades ago a friend gave me a small box of seeds. The woody flakes, truffle-black, were from her mother's large country garden in a cold region of western New South Wales. I scattered them either side of our front steps in the city and, I must confess, forgot about them. A year or so later thick, strappy mid-green leaves appeared, and another year on, three plump flower-heads, held aloft on a hollow spike, pushed up from the soil and unfurled to reveal fleshy petals the colour of crushed strawberries and whipped cream. They were *Hippeastrum*, once part of the genus *Amaryllis*, the spectacular tropical lilies that are native to South America.

As the flamboyant flowers died off, the drama continued, through scenes of senescence and decay, to be followed by lime-green, bulbous seed-heads, which eventually dried and split to further scatter hundreds of seeds the size of five cent pieces. In the years since, I have shared the annual harvest with friends and clients, and many a country garden now boasts these beauties, resplendent each summer, often either side of their front gate.

Hippeastrums, while most comfortable in a warm climate, cope well in chillier areas, as long as late frosts are not a constant threat. And they love being pot-bound, so gardeners in marginal climates can grow them inside to be popped into a border, complete with plastic pot, when in flower. You will find them blooming in brilliant colours, in pots, in the flower shops, ready to decorate the Christmas table, and in gardens from early summer.

Multiple blooms, each of which can be up to 50 cm in diameter, crown a long stem. They flower in a range of reds, pinks and whites and can be splotched or splashed, or licked with cream. There are more than 80 species and many more hybrids, many developed by Dutch nurserymen.

♥ My favourites

DWARF AND LOW-GROWING CULTIVARS

- *Hippeastrum* 'Apple Blossom' bears cream to white flowers delicately striped with hot pink.

MID- TO TALL-GROWING CULTIVARS

- *Hippeastrum* 'Belinda' is a complex mix of reds, reminiscent of a box of crayons—all wonderfully mashed together!
- *Hippeastrum* 'Christmas Gift' is white.
- *Hippeastrum* 'Desert Dawn' is a clear red.
- *Hippeastrum* 'Kalahari' is a cherry red.
- *Hippeastrum* 'Red Lion' is deep red.

Tip: The low-growing *Hippeastrum* 'Apple Blossom' looks great at the front of a garden bed, perhaps teamed with the pewter-foliaged, blue-flowering *Ajuga reptans* and edged with black mondo grass, or toning with the white-flowering *Cerastium tomentosum* ('Snow in Summer').

Opposite: The soft pink shades of 'Apple Blossom'.

✿ Planting

Back the red hippeastrums—'Belinda', 'Desert Dawn', 'Kalahari' and 'Red Lion'—with a clear red Hybrid Tea rose such as the heavily scented 'Mr Lincoln'. In Queensland I have seen entire borders of different cultivars and diverse hues of hippeastrum, although I prefer them as accent plants or in swathes against a cool green background. And I think of them as tulips for those who garden in warm temperate to tropical climates.

✿ Requirements

It is said that hippeastrums prefer a rich but well-drained soil, but they will also thrive in poor, sandy soil.

✿ Care

Don't bury the bulb; plant it with the tip just above soil level. And don't over-water as the bulbs will rot. Snails love them and will quickly decimate young flower buds and strip leaves, so offer early protection.

1. From a friend's country garden.
2. A border of hippeastrums.
3. The black seeds of the hippeastrum.

Irises

The iris has a place in many cultures. The flower has fascinated philosophers, politicians, painters and poets—and gardeners—throughout history. It is the flower of kings and queens and is revered by artists, eulogised by writers, employed by cooks and chemists.

There are some 300 species growing throughout the northern hemisphere: no true iris is native to south of the equator. They are divided mainly into rhizomatous and bulbous types.

Rhizomatous irises have sword-like leaves and are divided into three main groups: bearded (with a tuft of hairs on the three lower petals); beardless (including the water iris, *Iris ensata*, Louisiana and Pacific Coast iris, and Spuria and Siberian iris); and Evansia irises, which have a raised crest, instead of a beard, on the lower three petals. Most rhizomatous irises are very frost hardy and do not like summer moisture.

Bearded irises, mostly hybrids of *I. germanica*, are extremely friendly plants in drought: they don't need a lot of water and are dormant over summer. Don't despair, though, if your climate doesn't allow you these jewel-like blooms. Those who live in humid, coastal climates will have greater success with Evansia irises. These, unlike the bearded iris, like woodland conditions and summer rain—but then, that now seems to be an unpredictable phenomenon.

Bulbous irises, divided into three main groups—the Juno, Reticulata and Xiphium irises—like moisture during the growing period, but prefer dryness during summer, when they are dormant. The Xiphium irises have given rise to hybrids including the English, Spanish and Dutch irises.

❤ My favourites

RHIZOMATOUS

- *Iris confusa*, the fascinating bamboo-stemmed iris, is used in Yunnan, China, as a medicinal plant. It has lovely bamboo-like stems and lilac to white butterfly-like flowers.
- *Iris cristata*, the woodland Evansia iris from the south-east of the United States, masses out into attractive, low-growing clumps of leaves from which white or pale lilac flowers emerge.
- *Iris ensata* (syn. *I. kaempferi*), the Japanese flag iris, is the gorgeous creature of the revered Japanese temple gardens and its blooming in spring is greeted with euphoria in Japan. These are a beardless, rhizomatous iris that flowers in large, flat, purple or blue blooms in spring and early summer. They like rich, acid soil, and

Tradition

In *The Iliad*, Homer depicted the iris as the messenger of the gods. Hera, wife of Zeus, an intermediary between heaven and earth, was also responsible for leading the souls of dead women to the Elysian Fields. A Greek tradition, in her honour, is to plant iris alongside the graves of women. The shape of the flower represents the Trinity to Christians; in the Far East, especially in Japan, the iris is attendant to ceremony and tradition. It has been cultivated in China for centuries, the subject of reverent literature and art.

Opposite: The bearded iris 'Queen of Elegance'.

moisture in summer. My favourite is the blue and white striped 'Geisha Gown'.

- *Iris germanica*, the best known of the bearded irises, has a delicate scent that is a sure harbinger of summer. This species is significant for its six petals, the first three of which are known as the standards and grow upright. The three outer petals, the falls, flare out and downwards, while the beard, in the centre of each fall, guides insects towards the pollen. *I. germanica* is among the parents of the flamboyant bearded hybrids, which are so popular in Australia. They are a perfect accompaniment to roses and the colour combinations are endless.
- *Iris japonica*, from the Evansia group, is not the most stunning of the irises but it's useful for gardeners who do not enjoy frosty winters. It is probably easiest to grow in warm climates, as you would expect of this native of southern China and of parts of Japan. *I. japonica* quickly masses out, with the help of runners, with sprays of softly waving, mid-green foliage from which wiry spires erupt and which hold several small blue butterfly flowers in late winter and spring.
- The Louisiana hybrids are rhizomatous beardless irises, with *Iris fulva* and *I. brevicaulis* among their parents. They flower with flat, open blooms in a range of colours, from white to yellow to cerise, lilac and purple. They are swamp or water irises, so they need plenty of water year-round and enjoy a sunny position.
- The water iris *Iris pseudacorus*, a beardless iris from Europe, flowers with yellow blooms in early spring. It loves the boggy edges of dams or lakes, in full sun.
- *Iris pumila* is a beautiful, small rhizomatous bearded iris that flowers in purple from 15 cm high foliage. It is perfect for the edge of a border in frosty climates.
- *Iris unguicularis* (syn. *I. stylosa*), the Algerian iris, is a beardless iris, which bears blue, white or purple flowers with a very faint scent in winter. This small-growing iris likes dry conditions and is perfectly happy in poor soil. It masses out beautifully in cold climates.
- *Neomarica gracilis*, the Apostle's iris, native to Mexico and Brazil, loves tropical and subtropical regions, where it multiplies quickly. Plants bear scented white and lilac blooms in late spring to summer. They like part shade and moist, humus-rich soil.

Planting for colour

Copper-toned bearded irises such as 'Rustler' or the reliable 'Copatonic' look stunning flowering with the apricot roses 'Just Joey' and 'Apricot Nectar' or coffee-coloured roses such as 'Julia's Rose'.

Pink-toned bearded irises such as the pink 'Vanity' and the burgundy-coloured 'Battle Hymn' team well with the once-only pink and salmon rose 'Albertine', mixed with 'Climbing Peace'. Team the remontant rose 'Pinkie' with the pale pink iris 'Barga Girl' and the shell-pink rose 'New Dawn'.

You might want to shock with contrary colours: team the rich cerise-flowering rose 'Bantry Bay', the deep red 'Chrysler Imperial' (one of the most fragrant of all roses), the intense 'Paul's Scarlet' and the clear-red, single 'Altissimo' with the blue-flowering iris 'Louisa's Song', purple with light lilac top, and the pale lilac iris 'Queen of Elegance'.

Other blue and purple irises are 'Sooner Serenade', a very dark purple, and 'Skylab' which is two toned with velvet falls.

Consider these purple irises: pale lilac 'Queen of Elegance', the deep lilac 'Maroubra' and 'Lady Charm', a deep black-purple. 'Around Midnight' and 'Black Tie Affair' are almost black.

BULBOUS

- *Iris xiphium*, from the western Mediterranean, is important as the parent of most of the Spanish and Dutch hybrid irises. The spring flowers, in blues and mauves and occasionally in yellow or white, are borne above narrow, lance-like leaves. They are more suitable for temperate climates than some of the flamboyant, rhizomatous irises.

1. A border of blue iris.
2. 'Battle Hymn'.
3. 'Dance Man'.
4. 'An Evening in Paris'.
5. 'Supreme Sultan'.
6. 'Flare'.
7. 'Heather Blush'.

Below: A swathe of iris at Hesket House, Victoria.

A garden in Tasmania

At Culzean, a 10 ha garden in northern Tasmania, a 1.5 ha lake is landscaped with a variety of irises, among them *Iris pseudacorus, I. ensata, I. louisiana* and *I. sibirica*.

Sited near the charming village of Westbury, which boasts the state's only original village green, Culzean (pron. *Cullaine*) is a grand park-like garden designed around a wonderful collection of exotic trees, now mature. Apart from a collection of magnolias, there is a *Catalpa bignonioides* 'Aurea' and there are oaks, copper beeches, silver birches and several atlantic cedars, *Cedrus atlantica* 'Glauca'. In the woodland you wander through massed bluebells, rhododendron and iris, extraordinary in October, and, in November, past massed plantings of mollis azaleas. There are clumps of foxgloves and sheaths of the so-friendly Solomon's Seal, *Polygonatum × hybridum*.

Every way the visitor turns, dense plantings give way to peaceful vistas. At the bottom of the garden, by the river and beyond a mass of blue hydrangeas, you look back, across the lake, on self-sown plantings of red valerian toning with the bronze tones of the foliage of the water lilies. The towering trees are reflected in the still waters of the lake.

❀ Requirements

Winter is the time to prepare the soil to receive the cultivars you will have chosen from all those colourful catalogues. Successful growers of bearded iris know that you should plant them where the sun can burn and the frost can bite. Whoever coined this useful homily was speaking of the rhizome—the root of the iris—which should be planted not beneath the soil but level with it, where it can bask in summer sun and enjoy winter frosts.

🌿 Care

Bearded irises need lifting and dividing every few years to ensure continued flowering. Cut off the leaves to ease the lifting of the clump with a sturdy garden fork. Divide clumps with a sharp knife or spade, discarding old, dried-out or rotted rhizomes. Trim roots slightly and replant.

Pick bearded iris flowers while still in bud; you can snap off each bloom as it is spent, providing up to a fortnight of flowering. If transport is necessary carry the stems, in bud, wrapped lightly in very slightly damp newspaper. The blooms can stain if crushed: in Egyptian and Roman times the iris was used to provide dyes.

Tip: For those of us who live in a sweaty climate that prevents bearded irises flowering, try this: pour a bag of party ice onto the rhizomes a couple of times each winter to trick them into thinking they are growing in the frosty environment they love.

LILIES

Lilies

Magnificent liliums, found growing naturally across the cool temperate to cold regions of Asia and into North America, have been cultivated for centuries. A genus of about a hundred species, liliums have enjoyed an honoured position in various cultures, signifying purity and mysticism. Most flower in summer, bearing scented trumpets on long stems on which grass-like, or broad and glossy, leaves are arranged.

♥ My favourites

- *Lilium auratum*, flowering close to Christmas in an array of scented, flamboyant, cultivars, is revered in its home country of Japan, where it is called the golden ray lily. It is easy to imagine the sensation it caused in the United Kingdom when it first appeared there in the late nineteenth century.
- *Lilium candidum*, the Madonna lily, blooms with multiple pure-white, scented trumpets. It loves sunshine.
- *Lilium longiflorum* bears up to eight pure-white, fragrant trumpets on a long, erect stalk.
- *Lilium martagon*, the Turks Cap lily, is a collector's item with its rich, burgundy-coloured, flung-back petals that form nodding flowers. It loves a cool climate.
- *Lilium lancifolium*, the orange tiger lily, native to Japan and eastern China, will cope with warm temperate climates where winters are cold. It loves rich, acidic soils and is one of the easiest of the lilies to grow. It happily forms lots of bulbs on and just above the soil.
- *Lilium formosanum*, the very pretty but invasive Taiwan lily, and dubbed our November lily, flowers on tall spikes in summer and into autumn along the edges of highways in the eastern states (*see* Weeds).

- *Lilium regale* bears yellow-throated, white, trumpet-like flowers which are preceded by long pink buds appearing in generous whorls on stalks up to 2 m long.

🌿 Planting

Lilies look best planted in generous swathes, so that their distinctive scent can fill the air.

❀ Requirements

Most lily bulbs are planted beneath the ground. All like well-drained soil and cool roots, although they will flower best in a sunny position. Some will cope better with humid climates than others. They are best suited to a cool climate and humus-rich soil; in humid areas they will need to be treated as annuals.

🌿 Care

Plant the fat bulbs just below the surface and mulch well, particularly as the flower stalks are emerging. They also respond well to liquid feeds. The snails love them, so give them protection!

Previous page: Lily buds unfurl to signal the arrival of summer.

1. *Lilium auratum* 'Stargazer'.
2. *Lilium longiflorum*.
3. *Lilium auratum* 'Nippon'.

A childhood memory

I fell in love with lilies many years ago when, during my childhood, my family used to holiday at Mount Tamborine, in the hinterland behind Queensland's Gold Coast. They were holidays of scent and colour: I remember so well the distinctive smell of the deep red basalt soil, and of the cream-rich milk that used to be sold in a billycan from the back of the farmer's little covered truck.

I also remember the fragrance of the gorgeous gardens that surrounded the house where we spent each of those holidays. That house—it was called 'Mistover'—clung to the edge of the escarpment at the village of Eagle Heights and overlooked a long ribbon of dense tropical rainforest—of tallow-woods (*Eucalyptus microcorys*), Australian cedars, hoop pines, firewheel trees, Queensland kauri pines and soaring Bangalow palms.

We would wake in the mornings among swirling mists, and each evening on dusk black swarms of fruit bats would fly along the length of that rainforest, from south to north, a mass that took more than an hour to pass by. I never wondered where they were going; I simply

thought how exotic they looked. My mother loved them too, for they reminded her of an altogether easier life in Ceylon, where she had lived for more than twenty years after her marriage to my father, until that country achieved its independence and became Sri Lanka.

As I looked out beyond the canopy of the rainforest, the lights of the Gold Coast would flicker to life, becoming an exciting, glittering heaven on earth.

Mistover's gardens cascaded down the escarpment towards the rainforest and were arranged in rock-edged terraces. They were bursting with brilliant orange tiger lilies (*Lilium lancifolium*) that would flower for months over summer. Although orange is not my favourite colour, I adored those brilliant, brash blooms, with their dipping heads of recurved, cerise-spotted petals. They were planted with a mass of curry plant, *Helichrysum italicum*, so you can imagine the heady fragrances that would hang in the air over those steamy Queensland Christmas holidays.

MAGNOLIAS

Magnolias

There can be no more cheering sight in mid-winter than the large shell-pink, goblet-shaped flowers of *Magnolia × soulangeana*. Each year in late June, when the earliest of the magnolias unfurl their pink and cream flowers, held on a tracery of black-grey branches against a clear, intensely blue winter sky, I am, yet again, taken by surprise at the absolute perfection of the simplest things in life.

In the garden next to mine an old magnolia limbers up for weeks for this annual performance, the expectation tantalising and teasing those who pass by. The buds, held aloft on contorted branches, get fatter and fatter, and the first scented, aristocratic flower then emerges.

The magnolia has been cultivated in China, where its beautiful flowers symbolise purity, for more than 1500 years. The genus was introduced to the western world in 1687, when *Magnolia virginiana* was sent to the Bishop of London from North America by the missionary–botanist John Bannister. And since Sir Joseph Banks introduced the first Asiatic magnolias—*M. denudata* and *M. liliiflora* from eastern China and Japan—a century later, the pure sensuality of the genus has captivated the horticultural world.

Plant hunters, dispatched from Britain in the eighteenth century to search for botanical trophies for the great houses, risked terrible deaths throughout China, the Himalayas and Tibet in their quest for the exotic and rare that exemplified the mysteries hidden behind closed borders. Among the most intrepid was Ernest 'Chinese' Wilson who wrote that magnolias were the 'Aristocrats of ancient lineage, possessed of many superlative qualities ... They have the largest flowers ... no other genus can boast so many excellences. Their free-flowering character and great beauty of blossom and foliage are equalled by the ease with which they many be cultivated.'

Magnolias are trees of such presence that you need just one in a garden to create instant impact.

There are more than 80 species and dozens of cultivated varieties to ponder over, however, so there is a magnolia for every size of garden, for any use, and for all climates.

♥ My favourites
EARLY-SEASON FLOWERING

- *Magnolia × soulangeana*—a cross between *M. denudata* and *M. liliiflora*—with its striking form and generous flowering, is a good choice if you have room for only one tree. The cultivar 'Alexandrina' has white goblet-shaped flowers stained purple at their base and 'Brozzonii' produces the largest flowers of this group. Other wonderful soulangeana cultivars are the crimson 'Lennei' and the white 'Lennei Alba.'
- *Magnolia denudata*—formerly known as *M. heptapeta*—native to China and cultivated there for more than a thousand years, displays its scented, mid-sized, creamy blooms in early-to-mid-August. But for weeks before this, its white buds emerge slowly from brown sheaths which are covered in fine hairs that catch the morning light or, when covered in frost, create wonderful winter pictures.

Opposite: The winter buds of *Magnolia denudata*.

1. *Magnolia liliiflora*.
2. *Magnolia liliiflora* 'Nigra'.
3. *Magnolia × soulangeana* 'Lennei'.
4. *Magnolia × soulangeana*.

LATE-SEASON FLOWERING

- *Magnolia delavayi*, the large-leaved evergreen species, was discovered in 1886 by Father Jean-Marie Delavay (1834–1895), after whom it is named, in China's Yunnan province, where it is now used as a street tree. Growing wild in the Woolliang mountain range, south of Kunming in Yunnan, *M. delavayi* is decorated with gorgeous flower buds, which have a beautiful pink blush and which open to blooms that range from pink to cream to pale green from late summer through autumn.

SMALL GROWING

- *Magnolia stellata* 'Rosea', a pink form of the star magnolia which bears its flowers at the end of exotic twisted branches from mid-winter to late spring, and *M. liliiflora*, at 5 m, are suitable for smaller gardens.
- If it's just one tree you want as a stunning piece of garden sculpture, *M. stellata* 'Rubra' sports a mass of delicate pink blooms set against a contorted trunk that becomes blackened with age—but then, who could possibly confine their choice to just one species?
- *Magnolia sieboldii*, while boasting a relatively unimpressive form, produces white blooms of exquisite, fragile beauty. For those who like to search for the unusual, *M.* 'Elizabeth', named in 1978 for Elizabeth Stolz, director of the Brooklyn Botanic Garden, is a pyramid-shaped tree with pale lemon-coloured flowers with pink stamens.
- Don't ignore the michelias, closely related to the magnolia, and with wonderfully scented flowers. There is the well-known, small-growing *Michelia figo*, with small purple to pink blooms, great for hedges; *M.* 'Emerald Green' is also a small tree. The glorious *M. doltsopa* 'Silver Cloud' is a larger tree and flowers with large cream flowers.

LARGE GROWING

- *Magnolia campbellii*, flowering mid to late season, and perhaps the most coveted of all, is suitable for large gardens in cool climates. This extraordinary tree, occurring naturally from south-west China to Nepal and growing to some

30 m, takes up to 20 years to display its huge goblet-shaped blooms: the impatient among us might search out the more vigorous varieties, such as *M. campbellii* 'Charles Raffill', which flowers after just a few years. *M. campbellii* var. *mollicamata*, which flowers with a paler bloom from elegant, elongated buds, was introduced to the western world by the plant hunter Frank Kingdon-Ward when he sent seed to Kew

Early plantings

Among the first of the magnolias to be planted in Australia must have been at Woolmers, the estate of Thomas Archer, who arrived in Van Diemen's Land in 1813. His great grand-daughter, Dorothy Halkerston (1889–1971), recalled: 'We went to live at 'Woolmers' when I was three … From the outside the house was a dignified Georgian design, with a noble porch and circular steps leading up to the front door. Two wide lawns lay in front, planted with trees and divided by a gravel driveway leading from the big iron entrance gates. … Up one side of the house grew an old magnolia, and to this day the scent of those creamy cups brings my childhood back in a series of vivid memories.'

Camden Park

Among the trees to be replanted at Camden Park is a *Magnolia* × *soulangeana* 'Soulange-Bodin' propagated from a specimen planted in the Old Orchard (now part of the Elizabeth Macarthur Agricultural Institute), which is thought to be the oldest in Australia. William Macarthur's notes indicate that the magnolia was planted in about 1844, probably purchased by him from Loddiges' Nursery in London.

1. In the heart of the magnolia.
2. *Magnolia grandiflora*.
3. *Magnolia grandiflora* 'Little Gem'.

Gardens in 1914. You can see one of these special trees, which will flower at a much younger age than the species, in Melbourne's Royal Botanic Gardens; it was collected on the Gaoligongshan range on the border between China and Myanmar (Burma).

• *Magnolia macrophylla*, or the big-leaf magnolia, has leaves more than 1 m long, with a fascinating silver underside. I saw it for the first time in a collector's garden of botanical treasures on an island in Lake Maggiore in the north of Italy, where, in April and May, it is alight with heavily perfumed flowers, each 40 cm in diameter, along with banks of azaleas, a collection of rhododendrons and walkways covered in wisteria. While rare, you can still find this species in Australia.

• *Magnolia grandiflora*, among the tall-growing, large-flowered, warm-climate magnolias, has wondrous large, bowl-shaped, waxy, white flowers. If you don't have the space for this monster, which grows to more than 20 m, with a spread as wide, its smaller cousin 'Little Gem' has a similar flower with the same delicious lemony scent but won't grow much taller than 4 m. It is a quick grower, excellent for shading a courtyard, for cultivating in large pots (with its charcoal-green leaves which have brown fuzzy undersides, it looks so-smart in black ceramic pots), or for clipping into a thick hedge; it is tolerant of city pollution. The impressive espaliers you often see on houses in English gardens are most often of the intensely fragrant *M. grandiflora* 'Exmouth'.

🌿 Planting

Magnolias are trees of such presence that great things can be achieved with just one, or with several. In a much-photographed Russell Page (1906–1985) garden on Long Island, a simple elliptical pool is approached by way of a path that curves gently down several terraces. While the copses on either side of the path are of dogwood, the same stunning effect could be achieved with magnolias. For impact, just one species of magnolia would be used—perhaps *M. × soulangeana*—because of its arching form. If you are an incorrigible collector, however, there are many cultivars of this early-flowering species that will look good together while satisfying the plant hunter in you.

❀ Requirements

Magnolias love well-drained acid soil, rich in organic matter, but will also cope with sandy, alkaline soils.

🌿 Care

Magnolias are easy to grow and relatively pest free. The time to move deciduous magnolias is mid-winter, when the big nurseries also sell the bare-rooted trees. Prune only in order to remove any crossing or congested branches and to maintain the desired shape. I like to prune my magnolias by cutting any surplus branches, when in bud, to decorate the house.

Orchids

Almost any time of the year is orchid time. This enormous and diverse plant group of some 900 genera and more than 30,000 species flowers throughout much of Australia for up to nine months of the year in an extraordinary range of shapes and colours. Different orchid forms—ephiphytic, lithophytes and terrestrial—can be found naturally on all continents except Antarctica.

Many of the 190-odd genera of orchids native to Australia occur naturally as epiphytes, growing harmlessly upon other plants. Most native orchids occur in the wetter fringes of the country, and, unlike their more pernickety, foreign cousins, the Australian species seem to thrive on neglect.

❤ My favourites

CIRRHOPETALUM

- *Cirrhopetalum fascinator* (also called *Mastigion fascinator*) is a species of orchid native to Vietnam, prized for its exotic markings and distinctive shape. It features thread-like tails hanging from purple-spotted blooms.

COELOGYNE

Members of this genus (pronounced *see-lodginee*) form pseudobulbs linked by rhizomes; the leaves emerge from the top of each pseudobulb. Native to Asia, many from the Himalayas, they prefer cooler weather but can also thrive in warmer climates, where they flower in late winter.

- *Coelogyne cristata* produces, in late winter, gorgeous arching branches of delicate, milk-white flowers with yellow and gold throats. When brought indoors, they will fill a room with scent.

CYMBIDIUM

Among the more temperamental orchids are cymbidiums, comprising about 50 species found naturally in Japan, throughout Asia, to Australia. Both terrestrial and epiphytic, they produce long, strappy leaves from pseudobulbs and sprays of brightly coloured flowers from mid-winter to spring, although modern breeding has extended the flowering season.

Cymbidiums love the morning sun. On advice from nurseryman Colin McLaughlin, I moved a large pot of several that had not flowered for some five years to a spot on a terrace that received several hours of early-morning sun each day. By the following February, a couple of months after the move, they had sent up a dozen spikes which unfurled to a collection of purple, pink and yellow blooms.

- *Cymbidium canaliculatum*, native to tropical Queensland and into northern New South Wales, is drought tolerant and flowers with green to yellow blooms which smell of coconut.

DENDROBIUM

Flowering in spring, the dendrobiums, many of them native to Australia, are a large and diverse genus. They are among the easiest orchids to grow: almost in defiance of neglect they survive, forgotten, until they push up spikes of delicately scented, intricately marked blooms, to brighten winter days and herald spring.

The primary demands made by dendrobiums are sunshine, particularly in the morning, and excellent drainage. Grow them in blue metal, or

Opposite: The spidery blooms of a *Miltassia* hybrid.

orchid mix, and, if you remember, fertilise once every three months to promote flowering. Some are deciduous and need a good soaking to burst into flower, but most enjoy a drought; they thrive, pot bound, on almost no water, a situation that replicates their natural habitat of cracks and pockets in trees. And they love hollow logs.

• *Dendrobium kingianum*, *D. curvicaule*, the robust *D. tarberi* (native to the Lamington National Park behind Queensland's Gold Coast) and *D. tetragonum* are among the easiest to grow.
• *Dendrobium curvicaule* (syn. *D. speciosum* subsp. *curvicaule*), the rock lily, native to north-eastern Australia, flowers in frost-free climates in late winter and spring, with cascades of scented cream and yellow flowers.
• *Dendrobium kingianum* var. *album* sends up an arching mass of scented, delicate white bells each spring.
• *Dendrobium speciosum*, the glorious king orchid, is native to New South Wales and flowers with huge trusses of scented pale yellow blooms.
• *Dendrobium tarberi*, native to frost-free parts of north-eastern Australia, flowers with scented white and cream trusses that are up to 50 mm long.
• *Dendrobium tetragonum* flowers in exotic, spidery blooms that vary in colour from cream to yellow and green, to brown.

EPIDENDRUM

This large genus of about a thousand species hails from the southern United States, Mexico and Central and South America. Most species have slim, reed-like stems and are lithophytes or epiphytes.
• *Epidendrum ibaguense*, the crucifix orchid, is easygoing, demanding only full sun to flower with spherical heads in a range of vivid colours. I love to see them in trees, surreptitiously held in place with fine blackbird netting.

ONCIDIUM

The easy-to-please dancing ladies of the genus *Oncidium*, from South America, comprise over 650 species, most with a pseudobulb that likes to be crowded and 'mounded up' to ensure good drainage. Oncidiums love the sun and are happy in potting mix or garden soil, given plenty of mulch and water. They usually flower—often with a prominent 'lip'—in arching wands of scented yellow and brown blossom.
• *Oncidium discolor Broomfieldii* bears wands of scented pale yellow blossom.

PAPHIOPEDILUM

You will find many species of the fascinating slipper orchid growing wild in the remote mountain areas of Sabah and North Borneo. Others are native to southern China, New Guinea and the Solomon Islands. The genus, coveted by collectors, flowers in brilliant colours, boasts truly extraordinary markings and is distinguished by a lip or 'pouch', a modification to collect food and moisture. Paphiopedilums often grow through leaf litter carpeting the forest floor; some cling to rock faces, others thrive in the rainforest canopy. In cultivation they are best grown pot bound, in a bark-based compost. They enjoy shade, and misting in the warmer months.

PHAIUS

The tall-growing flowering swamp orchids are native to Africa, the Indian subcontinent, Asia and Australia. They flower on tall spikes from spring to summer.
• *Phaius tankervilleae*, the well-known nun's orchid from India, Sri Lanka, China and Australia, flowers in summer with cream to brown flowers on 12 cm spikes.

PHALAEONOPSIS

Everyone's favourite orchid, the moth orchid is a fragile beauty, but a primadonna, and needs more tender care, and a little more shade, than most. The 60-odd species are native to the tropical rainforest of Asia, New Guinea and northern Australia, and most are epiphytes; cool stone walls provide a perfect microclimate. To encourage flowering, feed from February with flower-inducing fertiliser; when flowering is finished, after summer, use a growth fertiliser.

Opposite: A *Dendrobium* hybrid.

1. The soft stem *Dendrobium* flourishing on a leopard tree in a Queensland garden.
2. A stone trough of *Pleione* hybrids at Elizabeth Town nursery, in northern Tasmania.

RESTREPIA

The 40-odd species of this miniature genus are commonly known as the 'cockroach orchid'— somewhat unfairly as they bear exquisite markings. Single-leaved and with just a single, elliptical bloom, these epiphytes are native to South America and tolerate a wide range of climates, as long as they receive plenty of water in light and airy conditions.

• *Restrepia antennifera*, from Columbia, Venezuela and Equador, blooms in a rich yellow, pink or cerise and is covered in leopard-like red spots or in fine stripes.

At Wonga-Belle Gardens

You can see orchids in their natural warm temperate to tropical environment in Far North Queensland. There, jungle-covered mountains crash down into endless kilometres of coconut palm-fringed coastline, to be met by opal-toned, blue and green waters that lap sweeping white sands. There are also gardens, flowering with the flamboyant torch gingers, in both red and white; shell gingers scent the morning and the evening air; the rare jade vine is a mass of dripping, brilliant green pea-flowers; and orchids flutter like many-coloured butterflies.

At Wonga-Belle Tropical Gardens and Nursery, just north of Wonga Beach, 30 minutes from Port Douglas, on the Captain Cook Highway, a large collection of orchids thrives.

According to nurseryman Colin McLaughlin orchids don't deserve their reputation for being difficult. 'The misconception with orchids is that they are hard to grow. They're not,' he insists. 'But people look after them too much. They give them too much water, or they give them too much shade. And grow orchids that are best suited to your climate; don't try to grow tropical orchids in cooler climates. They are well worth any effort.'

SPATHOGLOTTIS

Covering the moist floor of forests in Asia, the Pacific Islands and Australia, spathoglottis enjoy plenty of mulch and water, as well as an all-round fertiliser twice a year.

• *Spathoglottis plicata*, the ground orchid, is native to South-East Asia, Australia and the Pacific Islands. This easy-to-grow orchid, which flowers with a small pink bloom on the end of a wiry stem emerging from pleated leaves, has naturalised through the Hawaiian Islands.

VANDA

The *Vanda* orchids love growing in full sun. The vast range of epiphytic vandas—flowering for much of the year in colours from pinks, purples and cerise to apricots, and in shapes from big and broad to small and delicate—like their aerial roots in the ground and protected with a cover of compost. You can cut them when they get too tall; replant the top half, or tie to trees or tree stumps.

Planting

Grow orchids, as a collection, in pots, or strap them to trees, using pieces of black netting. The king orchids look best strapped to rocks, or tucked into crevices, preferably in a position where their arching spires can be best appreciated.

Requirements

Orchids love the early morning sun and to flower well they need a couple of hours of sun each day. If using orchids as indoor plants, place them outside after flowering, under a deciduous tree, rather than in direct sun. To prevent fungal infection, keep water off the leaves.

Care

Orchids like to be root bound, so only repot, in orchid-growing media, every two years. Water once a week and drain; don't leave them standing in a saucer. If growing in the garden, try to replicate the conditions in which they are found in nature.

PALMS

Palms

Palms are often elegant and topped with delicate, feathery foliage, often regal and stately, flowering with long plumes of pale flowers which are followed by brilliantly coloured fruit. Others bear crimped and pleated foliage; some are multi-stemmed and others produce fronds almost flush with the ground. Yet palms are not on the top of the must-have list for every gardener. They are sometimes given a bad press due to inappropriate use in garden design, and some have fallen out of favour due to their tendency to become weeds. But among the 4000-odd species, there is one suited to almost every garden situation, and, while most are native to hot and humid regions, some will thrive in a range of climates. Palms cannot be surpassed, surely, for imparting a luscious, tropical or exotic atmosphere.

Towards Australia's Top End, at Palm Cove, about an hour's drive north of Cairns in Queensland, great drifts of coconut palms (*Cocos nucifera*) lean laconically towards the clear water and the sweep of sparkling white sand that curves into the mountains to the south, and, to the north, into an ocean that seems to stretch forever. Nothing typifies the tropics more than this palm: add a full, bloated moon hanging heavy above the water, framed by those gently waving fronds, and the scene is picture-postcard perfect.

Perhaps it is because palms are reminiscent of a luxurious life in the tropics of the Far East that they were so popular in Victorian times. You can still find late-nineteenth-century country homesteads in Australia that are visible from 'miles around' because of the palms planted to alert long-ago travellers that journey's end was close. Today, the right palm in the correct place—discreetly lit at night—can create a magical, enchanted, easy-care garden that will provide hours of peace and pleasure without too much hard work.

♥ My favourites

FEATHER FOLIAGE

- *Archontophoenix alexandrae*, the frost-tender and fast-growing Alexander palm and one of six species of the *Archontophoenix* genus, is native to the tropical and subtropical rainforests of north-eastern Australia—especially the Queensland coast. In the wetter areas it forms dense clumps. The flowers emerge from beneath a silvery collar on the trunk just below the crown of fronds, and are followed by red fruit.
- *Archontophoenix cunninghamiana*, the Bangalow palm, is native to southern Queensland and northern New South Wales. It grows to almost 20 m and can be differentiated from the Alexander palm by its slightly more drooping fronds and pale lilac, pendulous flower spikes.

> **Tip:** *Archontophoenix alexandrae* is suited to container planting and for courtyards, with its slender, elegant trunk and shallow roots needing little space. It is fast growing, and, as it sheds its beautifully feathered fronds cleanly, it is relatively low maintenance.

Opposite: *Chamaerops humilis*, photographed on the shores of the Mediterranean.

FEATHER FOLIAGE WITH FOLDED LEAFLETS

The Phoenix, or date, palms belong to the Arecaceae family and comprise almost 20 species of mostly single-stemmed palms, found on Crete and the Canary Islands, and in North Africa, the Middle East and Asia. They have long leaves that droop from a central rib. Take care when clearing away old fronds: the lower leaflet on each frond is a sharp spine that can cause serious injury. The flamboyant panicles of flowers are followed by wonderful cascades of yellow, orange, red or black fruit.

- *Phoenix canariensis*, the Canary Island date palm, grows to some 21 m and develops a thick trunk featuring the scars of old leaf bases. It bears delicious fruits.
- *Phoenix dactylifera*: nothing speaks more eloquently of the mystery of the Middle East and North Africa than this date palm; it has been cultivated there for some 5000 years.
- *Phoenix roebelenii*, the clumping pygmy date palm, native to China and Laos, reaches about 3 m, making it popular for small gardens and as an indoor plant.
- *Caryota mitis*, the fishtail palm, is the most widely grown of the *Caryota* genus, which is native to Sri Lanka and tropical Asia, to China, and to the north of Australia. The fishtail palm grows to 6 m, flowers with masses of perfumed, cream flowers and has softly crimped triangular leaves.

Tip: *Caryota mitis* is suitable for the sunny, western side of a house in a subtropical to tropical climate.

- *Cyrtostachys renda*, the lipstick or sealing wax palm, is native to Indonesia and Malaysia; the distinctive red leaf bases are therefore most brilliant in the warmest of our climates. It grows as a series of slender trunks, each with a crown of fronds decorated with brilliant red sheaths. Remove some of leaves to alleviate stress, and divide crowded clumps, in spring or early summer, into smaller clumps.

Tip: Very slow growers, the *Cyrtostachys* species love warmth and water.

- *Dypsis lutescens*, the golden cane palm, bears feathery, evocative fronds. Found on the beachfront along the east coast of its native Madagascar, and popular in Australia as a landscaping palm, it forms clumps of yellow-green stems topped with recurved fronds that glint yellow to orange in the sun. It tolerates dry seasons and loves full sun.

LARGE, PLEATED LEAVES

- *Licuala grandis*, the elegant ruffled fan palm, bears cylindrical, pleated leaves that are somewhat like huge elliptical dinner plates. Its trunk reaches about 1.5 m, so it makes an excellent mid-border plant for massing in a warm temperate to tropical climate. One of about 100 species that occur naturally in wet areas from Southern China to India, and down to northeastern Australia, it is happy in sun or filtered light but dislikes wind.

FAN- OR PALM-SHAPED

- *Bismarckia nobilis*, a single-species genus from Madagascar, develops large fan-shaped silver-to-grey foliage, an unusual colouration that can be at odds with the bright light of the tropics. Slow growing, this palm will eventually reach some 15 m. It thrives in tropical and subtropical climates that have a dry season: it will cope with cooler climates if planted in a sunny, well-drained spot.

Tip: Plant *Bismarckia nobilis* in a swathe, perhaps as the background to the lipstick palms and some of the gorgeous tropical frangipanis—but you will need a large space to do justice to this combination.

Opposite: The silver grey fans of *Bismarckia nobilis*.

- *Chamaerops humilis*, the Mediterranean fan palm, is the only palm species native to Europe. It also grows in North Africa on the slopes of the Atlas and Rif Mountains. It appears as a clump, is happy in warm temperate climates and bears its perfumed yellow flowers in late spring.

SLENDER

- *Hydriastele wendlandiana*, the slender, clumping Florence Falls palm, is native to the monsoonal rainforest in the Northern Territory. It is a shade-loving palm, made up of two or three slender stems topped with fronds of short, flat leaves and stunning sprays of red berries. As each plant grows to some 20 m, it is sought after as a plant for a large tropical garden.
- *Rhopalostylis baueri*, the native Norfolk Island palm, features slender trunks that can reach up to 15 m, topped with tufts of pinnately divided, deep green fronds above a sheath from which sprays of flowers emanate, to be followed by red fruits. It favours temperate forest conditions, filtered light and deep, moist soil.

STATELY STREET TREE

- *Roystonea regia*, the stately Royal Palm, grows to some 25 m. It is among 10 species of the *Roystonea* genus, most native to the Caribbean Islands, and enjoys tropical conditions.
- *Roystonea elata*, the Florida Royal Palm, with a smooth grey trunk, is often planted as a street tree, or in large gardens, so that its majestic form—up to 30 m in height—can be fully appreciated.

COLD TOLERANT

- *Chamaedorea elegans* is perhaps the most popular palm of all for growing indoors—hence its common name, the parlour palm. Single stemmed and growing to around 2 m, with deep

1. A Canary Island date palm (*Phoenix canariensis*) at Yering Station in Victoria's Yarra Valley.
2. The rare Chilean wine palm (*Jubaea chilensis*) grows in the Geelong Botanic Gardens.

green fronds and pale lemon flowers in panicles, it is indigenous to the high rainforests of southern Mexico and Guatemala, but also does well in warm temperate climates.

- *Rhopalostylis sapida*, the Nikau or Chatham Island palm, is the world's most southerly palm, found in the coastal and rainforest areas of New Zealand and its surrounding islands. Reaching up to 10 m in height, it bears distinctive, upright frond arrangements, each up to 2.5 m long, and is sometimes dubbed 'the feather duster palm'. The Mauri word *nikau* means 'many leaves on the same stalk'.
- *Trachycarpus fortunei*, the Chinese windmill palm is at home in the subtropics, but also must be one of the most cold-tolerant palms in the world.

Frost hardy

'I got the surprise of my life a few years ago, walking near the Scottish border, where I saw it growing beautifully in a front garden,' garden designer Tim Hays says of *Trachycarpus fortunei*. This palm is farmed in southern China, where the fibre is used to make bedding, string, clothing, mats, and brooms.

SALT TOLERANT

- *Wodyetia bifurcata*, the once-rare, very pretty Foxtail Palm, is indigenous to a minute section of north-eastern Queensland. Elegant, arching fronds are made up of leaflets that radiate from all sides of the central leaf stalk. Like many of the date palms, it is useful for coastal plantings as it tolerates salt. It's also drought tolerant, although it grows faster with moisture. Clusters of pale lemon to green flowers are produced beneath the crown shaft, and the large fruits turn orange and red as they ripen.

OTHER FAVOURITES

- *Livistona australis*, the Australian cabbage palm, among 30 species in this genus, bears a tough, rather sharp, array of leaves that grows atop a trunk that reaches some 3 m.
- *Rhapis humilis*, the slender lady palm, native to southern China, is an elegant palm that rarely exceeds 2 m in height.

Tip: *Rhapis humilis* makes an excellent pot plant and also thrives in a shaded, southerly courtyard or narrow passage, creating a soothing, feathery, dappled effect of light and shadow. Team these palms with the white-flowering *Spathiphyllum* sp. for a cooling green-and-white effect.

- *Mauritiella aculeata*, the rare ghost palm, native to the Amazonian regions of Bolivia, Peru, Brazil and Venezuela, features palmate leaves with silver undersides.

Botanical Ark

Mauritiella aculeata can be seen at Alan and Susan Carle's 15 ha private botanical gardens, Botanical Ark, set at the head of the beautiful Whyanbeel Valley, a 30 minute drive north of Port Douglas in Queensland. The Carles raised their specimen from seed collected in Peru. 'At night there is a white powdery glow under them,' says Alan. 'The underside of the leaf is silver and it also looks wonderful up-lit.'

Tip: Now plantation grown, there was once a vigorous black market trade in the seed for this palm—which, I have been told, has hallucinogenic effects.

Care

Cocos palms are invasive in the Sydney region, their prolific seeds being spread by bats, birds and wind. Check the following website if unsure when making your choice: www.weeds.org.au

PEONIES

Peonies

Peonies, surely one of the most beautiful and most evocative of all garden plants, are demanding about the conditions in which they grow and, sadly, will not thrive in any but the colder parts of the country. If your garden is situated in any of the mountain areas of New South Wales, Victoria or Tasmania, or in the colder inland cities, however, you can happily indulge your love of these voluptuous exhibitionists.

It is easy to understand the craving for the peony. Cultivated for centuries in China, where it is considered a symbol of both masculinity and brightness, the peony is often referred to as the King of Flowers. It features in literature and graces porcelain, paintings, textiles and lacquer work, expressing delicacy and strength. The ethereal blooms represent elegance, purity and breeding.

Roman times

The healing powers of the peony were detailed by Pliny the Elder (24–79 AD), the leading Roman authority on science during the first century AD. It is thought the peony was introduced to England by the Romans.

❤ My favourites

There are more than 30 species of deciduous perennials and shrubs in the genus—mostly found throughout Asia and into the states of the former Soviet Union, although a few are indigenous to North America—and thousands of named cultivated varieties. They bloom in colours ranging from scarlet to cerise to pale pink, and from cream to white and yellow, and even in almost black. Flowers can be single to very double, and are described by breeders as anemone-type,

crown-type or bomb-type, often with ruffled petals. Leaves differ between species; some are divided into many segments and lobes.

Most peonies need a cold winter—during which the herbaceous species die back to the ground—to initiate the flower buds. This is the time to add a rich manure and mulch, and then watch in wonder while fat red shoots unfurl as the frosts clear and long stems develop rose-like flowers by early summer. It is easy to understand why these gorgeous plants have become a magnificent obsession for some!

TREE PEONIES

Although they do better in cold climates, the deciduous Chinese tree peony is more likely than the herbaceous peony to grow successfully in the temperate to warm climates in Australia. The tree peony—which is really a shrub—has woody stems that might reach 3 m in height. It produces enormous, flamboyant, often double heads each spring. While originally from China, tree peonies have also been cultivated in Japan for more than 1500 years.

- *Paeonia delavayi* is among the easier of the tree peonies to grow: it reaches some 2 m, has mid-green, deeply dissected foliage and bears single, velvety, deep red flowers with a rich gold centre in spring.
- *Paeonia suffruticosa*, the Moutan, from northern China west to Bhutan, grows to almost 2 m and

Opposite: *Paeonia suffruticosa* 'Etienne de France'.

1. *Paeonia lactiflora* 'White Wings'.
2. *Paeonia* 'Madame Edouard Doriat'.

bears white, cream, pink or red, often double blooms that are sometimes scented.
- *Paeonia rockii*, a stunning peony, blooms white with a maroon splash at the base of each petal.
- *Paeonia suffruticosa* 'Etienne de France' bears a luscious pink, very double, blowsy bloom.
- *Paeonia lutea*, the yellow tree peony, was discovered in western China in the late nineteenth century, and bears single, bright yellow flowers with an orange centre, held on stunning mid-green, saw-toothed leaves.

HERBACEOUS PEONIES

Many of the best-loved herbaceous peonies, which die back to the ground at the end of summer, are hybrids of the Chinese species *Paeonia lactiflora* and bear wonderful, often scented, often very double blooms on handsome foliage.

White flowering
- *Peonia lactiflora* 'White Wings' bears, needless to say, a pure-white bloom.
- *Peonia lactiflora* 'Kelway's Glorious', bred by the English nursery Kelway, is a luscious, scented, double bloom in a cream to blush pink.
- *Peonia lactiflora* 'Yan Fei Chu Yu'. bears a beautiful cream to white, very double bloom.

Pink flowering
- *Paeonia lactiflora* 'Moonstone' is very double, with the softest blush imaginable.
- *Paeonia lactiflora* 'President Franklin D Roosevelt' has a clear, deep pink, double bloom.

A peony farm
At Romswood, a peony farm near the town of Woodend on the western side of Mount Macedon in Victoria, some 16,000 blooms, from 50 different varieties, bloom in November, an extraordinary, restorative sight. 'They have had healing qualities in China for many centuries, where they use the corms in medications,' explains owner Jan White.

- *Paeonia lactiflora* 'Sarah Bernhardt' is one of the best known and has rose-pink, double, scented blooms.
- *Paeonia officinalis*, the European herbaceous peony, grows to approximately 60 cm and bears single or double pink-to-red blooms from spring to summer.
- *Paeonia officinalis* 'Rubra Plena' is very popular, bearing deep red to cerise, very double, ruffled flowers.

Planting

Arrange the red *Paeonia officinalis* against a background of a late-flowering hot-pink rhododendron. Add a further backdrop of the black to purple foliage of the smokebush *Cotinus coggygria* 'Grace' and a few of the lighter pink herbaceous peonies: 'Kelway's Scented Rose', 'Albert Crousse', or the deeper pink 'June Rose', perhaps, for extra excitement (*see* Colour, to tempt you even further).

Requirements

Peonies are long-lived, trouble-free, not too thirsty and rarely attract pests. They like full sun to light shade and well-drained, rich soil. They are heavy feeders, enjoying a dose of a low-nitrogen, high-phosphorus and potassium fertiliser in autumn and again just after flowering. Mulch well.

Care

Peonies don't like to be moved, so choose your planting position carefully.

To establish tree peonies dig a large hole 1 m square x 1 m deep and fill it with good soil, compost and manure that has been aged for at least two years. Place stones in the bottom to ensure perfect drainage. Plant the roots about 10 cm deeper than they were when you bought them, so that they will sucker and send up shoots. Do not allow them to dry out during the first couple of years; after that, leave them be. They are susceptible to frost damage while buds are forming.

RHODODENDRONS

Rhododendrons

Rhododendrons are among my favourite plants, not because I think they make particularly attractive trees, nor because I admire their foliage. It is the flowers that I love, not least because of the ease with which they can be picked, while still in bud, and transported, and because of the fun you can have with combining colours in the garden and in a vase. They are often deliciously, delicately, scented, and they bloom in either brilliant colours or gentle shades for months, from the end of one summer to the beginning of the next.

Part of the allure of rhododendrons is the mystery attached to the exotic places in which they occur naturally—from northern China to the Himalayas and to Japan. Some of the most glorious are found in Papua New Guinea; others are native to North America.

The genus, part of the Ericaceae family, includes over a thousand species, most evergreen, divided into various subgenera according to physical characteristics. Like most plants, they grow best in Australia in areas that mirror the conditions experienced in the regions where they grow wild. They are happiest in this country in the cool mountain areas behind our coastal cities, where many of the gardens in which they have found a home are named after mountain outposts on the Indian subcontinent or after treacherous and inaccessible Himalayan passes.

Rhododendrons range in size and habit from massive trees reaching 20 m, with huge leaves and waxy, usually bell-like flowers, to epiphytes that cling to the sides of mist-shrouded mountain ravines, and to tiny, ground-hugging species suited to rockeries or garden understorey.

♥ My favourites

VIREYAS

Most rhododendrons are suited to a woodland setting in a cool temperate to cold climate, but the *Vireya* subgenus flourishes in warm temperate to tropical climates, and will tolerate coastal sites. They will also grow in cold climates but hate frost. Vireyas, some of which are poisonous, flower in bright colours and many are wonderfully scented.

- *Rhododendron tuba*, one of the loveliest vireyas, bears distinctive, long, tubular trusses of scented pale pink flowers growing from elegant, rounded leaves. It grows wild in New Guinea, where it reaches 5 m.

SCENTED

With the exception of some of the vireya rhododendrons, the scented species flower in the colour range cream to lemon to blush pink.

- *Rhododendron decorum*, which can reach up to 6 m in the wild, flowers from an early age with highly scented cream to pale pink, funnel-shaped blooms.
- *Rhododendron falconeri*, native to the Himalayas, has beautiful, deep green foliage supporting large trusses of fragrant, pale yellow flowers and attractive, flaking bark.
- *Rhododendron* 'Fragrantissimum', one of the loveliest and easiest to grow, is a hybrid with a divine scent that emanates from a mass of clotted-cream flowers.
- *Rhododendron lindleyi* has cream-blushed-pink, lemon-scented blooms: this often epiphytic species reaches just over 4 m in its native habitat, among rocks in the Himalayas.

Opposite: Rhododendron 'Loderi group'.

Rose tree
Rhododendron is a Greek-based word meaning 'rose tree'.

- Rhododendrons from the Loderi group are greatly coveted for their perfume and are a cross between *R. griffithianum* and *R. fortunei*, the latter being one of the first of the genus to be introduced to the west from its native eastern China.

DECIDUOUS AND SCENTED

- *Rhododendron arborescens*, native to North America, is a deciduous species with scented flowers.

LARGE

- *Rhododendron griffithianum*, reaching up to 18 m in the wild in the Himalayas but much less in cultivation, bears highly scented blooms in cream to pink in late spring.

Plant hunting
Many of the tales of the plant hunters of the eighteenth and nineteenth centuries feature rhododendrons, further adding to their intrigue. Philip Short's account of the adventures of the plant hunters, *In Pursuit of Plants*—detailing vampire bats and plants used by cannibals to accompany a meal of human flesh—tells how George Forrest braved the wrath of Buddhist monks in far north-western China to bring the western world some 260 species of rhododendron.

Joseph Hooker trekked through the precarious gorges in the Himalayas, where, at 3000 metres, 'a most noble white rhododendron, truly enormous and delicious lemon-scented blossoms strewed the ground'. He was perhaps describing *Rhododendron nuttallii* or maybe the glorious *R. lindleyi*.

- *Rhododendron magnificum*, the largest growing of the genus, reaches 18 m in its native habitat of China and north-eastern Myanmar. It bears long, funnel-shaped, crimson flowers.
- *Rhododendron nuttallii*: surely the most fabulous of all the rhododendron, and native to western China, Myanmar and northern India, this evergreen tree, which grows to over 10 m, bears trusses of creamy wax-like, heavily lemon-scented blooms splashed yellow at the throat.
- *Rhododendron nuttallii* 'Stead's Best', with very fragrant white flowers, is a cross between *R. lindleyi* and *R. nuttallii*.
- *Rhododendron sinogrande*, growing to approximately 15 m in its native New Guinea, has the largest blooms and massive, leathery, downturned leaves, from which candles of cream flowers stand erect.

MID-SIZED

- *Rhododendron cinnabarinum* has blue-green, cinnamon-scented, rounded foliage and red-to-orange, bell-shaped flowers. It grows to about 3 m in cultivation.
- *Rhododendron lutescens*, with delicate, funnel-shaped, pale lemon blooms, has a rather informal, untidy habit and can be cut back hard after flowering. Native to western China, it grows to about 6 m and is prized for its grey brown, flaking bark and its flush of bronze leaves in spring.
- *Rhododendron niveum*, with its extraordinary smoky-purple flowers, is now very rare in the wild, where it occurs at above 2500 m. It was introduced to the rest of the world from the eastern Himalayas by Hooker in 1849.
- *Rhododendron yakushimanum* has a thick velvet-like coating—known as indumentum—on the underside of its leaves, protecting the plant from the cold and from sap-sucking insects. It is a medium-sized, compact, slow-growing species: in the 1930s just two plants were sent to England from the Japanese island of Yakushima. It bears a dome of pale pink flowers.
- *Rhododendron yakushimanum* 'Grumpy' bears soft pink to apricot blooms.

1. *Rhododendron arborescens*.
2. The hybrid rhododendron 'Helene Schiffner'.
3. *Vireya* rhododendron 'George Budgens'.
4. *Rhododendron facetum*.

In an Irish garden

Like much of Ireland, its south-west corner, County Cork, is washed by the warm Gulf Stream, making it possible to create large gardens of tender treasures sought from the British colonial outposts by eighteenth- and nineteenth-century plant hunters and their sponsors. If you drive west from the city of Cork you can reach Bantry Bay, the world's deepest harbour, by the wild and beautiful Pass of Keimaneigh, descending precariously between the mountains that run between Ballangarry and Ballylicky on the coast. Follow the road to the fishing village of Glengarriff, set on one of the countless inlets that slice into the rocky shore and backed by deep green, pine-covered mountains that seem to reach into the sea.

The 15 ha Garinish Island, the site of Ilnacullin garden, rests in this sheltered bay, winking jewel-like in the summer sun. Ilnacullin was the magnificent obsession of John Annan Bryce, a Belfast-born Member of Parliament who bought the exposed, rocky island in 1910 from the British War Office. There, with some help from Harold Peto, the English architect and landscaper (and an annual rainfall of some 1850 mm or 73 inches), Annan Bryce created a renowned garden of rare plants from all over the world.

Annan Bryce made his fortune from Russia's oil and teak, and lost it during the 1917 revolution; as a result, a two-room cottage was built instead of the Peto design for a grand, seven-storey residence. In 1923, encouraged by friends, Annan Bryce decided to open his gardens to the public to supplement his budget. He died later that year and his widow, Violet, continued the garden, which was gifted to the Irish people when her son Roland died in 1953.

Among Annan Bryce's earliest plantings at Ilnacullin were shelter belts of Scots pine, creating a microclimate and protection from the Atlantic winds. Soil was brought from the mainland to lay over the existing grey shale, although a feature was made of the many granite rocks that emerge throughout the garden. The deep pink rose 'American Pillar' scrambles over a large, weather-beaten rock; meticulously pruned, this rose becomes one mass of colour in late June to mid-July. Another rock is covered in a mix of the cerise-to-blue flowering climber *Rosa* 'Veilchenblau' along with 'Chaplin's Pink' and the deep pink, thornless 'Zephirine Drouhin'.

It is the vast collection of rhododendrons for which Ilnacullin is most famous, however, and mid-May is the time to see them at their best. The rhododendrons are followed by wisteria draping itself over the mellow stone pavilion that is the centrepiece of the Italian Garden. The mountains of County Cork and Kerry, which provide such a sense of place to this garden, erupt in the background.

The extraordinary scent of *Rhododendron arborescens*, native to the United States, fills this garden. The large-leafed *R. sinogrande*, from New Guinea, grows almost to its natural 15 m, providing protection for the Himalayan *R. thomsonii*, with its marvellous peeling bark. There is also the heavily scented hybrid *R.* 'Lady Alice Fitzwilliam', with pale pink to cream flowers that are marked with yellow.

From the Italian Garden you climb weathered stone steps to the Temple of the Winds, which frames spectacular views of the Sugar Loaf and Hungry Hill mountains, part of the rugged and romantic Caha Mountains. From there, a glade of rhododendrons leads to the Martello Tower, one of many such fortifications built around the Irish coast in the early nineteenth century to guard against a feared Napoleonic invasion and from where the best vistas across the water to surrounding islands and into the Walled Garden can be gained.

Today more than 100,000 visitors enjoy Ilnacullin annually, but the garden still imparts the romantic, private and secluded feeling that must have filled Annan Bryce and his wife with such excitement and passion.

SMALL

- *Rhododendron impeditum* is among the smallest of the genus. Bearing violet flowers, it grows wild as a heathland plant in the foothills of the Himalayas.
- *Rhododendron pachysanthum* reaches just 1 m, making it ideal for massing along the edge of a garden bed; its dominant feature is the stunning silvery indumentum on the reverse of its leaves.
- *Rhododendron williamsianum*, reaching about 1.5 m in height, and native to western China, is an evergreen shrub that bears delicate, bell-shaped pale pink blooms. After the flowers fade, a wonderful flush of polished new leaves appears. It is a difficult species to source.

HEAT AND SUN TOLERANT

- *Rhododendron maddenii* is one of the few species that is happy in the sun. It has rough brown, flaking bark and fragrant lemon-coloured flowers.

Planting

If I had hectares in which to play I would plant a swathe of the yellow *Rhododendron luteum* (also known as the pontic azalea), borrowing from the azalea dell at Chatsworth, that extraordinary garden in Derbyshire, England. Many of the treasures collected throughout the subcontinent by eighteenth-century plant hunters continue to thrive in this wonderful 50 ha garden. Chatsworth's azalea dell is a sight that leaves you gasping in late May, when its distinctive scent fills the air. Then, months later, with the approach of autumn, the leaves turn to bronze and gold, as if on fire.

You'll also love the brilliant red-flowering rhododendron varieties teamed with red-foliaged plants like the smokebush, *Cotinus coggygria* 'Purpureus',

'Royal Purple' or 'Grace', and with *Hydrangea quercifolia*, with its russet leaves. Experiment with the deep red *Rhododendron facetum* to offset a planting of the pink and teale-foliaged *Phormium* 'Tricolor'. The red-flowered rhododendron 'Earl of Athlone' looks stunning together with the silver-pink 'Countess of Athlone'; try also the brilliant-red 'Bulstrode Park' with the silver-to-mauve cultivar 'Admiral Piet Hein'. The blackest of the reds flower on 'Bow Tie' and 'Red Crystal'. Any of these combinations look stunning arranged together in a vase (*see* Colour).

Requirements

All rhododendron love moist but well-drained, acid soil, enriched with organic matter and well mulched with old straw, lucerne or pine needles. Ensure adequate ventilation and provide winter sun but summer shade.

Prune rhododendrons regularly to encourage and maintain desired shape—whether a dense bush, or an open tree—taking care, of course, not to compromise flowering.

Care

One rhododendron that has become a problem in the northern hemisphere is *Rhododendron ponticum*, which has become a 'garden escape'—a plant that has 'jumped the garden fence', making itself so much at home that it seriously threatens the environment. You will see this plant covering islands in Bantry Bay, in the south-west of Ireland, as your boat takes you out to Ilnacullin garden. This purple-flowering rhodie looks rather picturesque and pretty, to be sure, but it is smothering the indigenous conifers growing across these rocky islands.

ROSES

Roses

Hundreds of thousands of words have been written about the rose—that symbol of perfection—by poets, historians, horticulturalists, botanists and other experts. Often, though, the descriptions of old roses and the provenance of the roses that we know and love today can be confusing. After all, the breeding and development of plants in the wild was frequently spontaneous and random, and no garden writer or photographer was present taking notes, so sometimes boundaries are blurred.

Here is a simple and brief history of the development of the rose: it is a fascinating story and invaluable in understanding their care. This chapter details the different species, groups and relationships: it is followed by a further chapter on their attributes, uses, requirements and care and by a celebration of great rose gardens.

Early history

The growing and breeding of roses for decorative, useful and cultural purposes dates back thousands of years. Wild roses have always played an important part in Chinese art and have been recorded in Chinese gardens for some 3000 years. Roses have been used for creating essences and fragrances in Sumerian Iran since around 2000 BC. In AD 77 the Roman writer and scientist Pliny noted many disorders that could be treated with rose preparations.

Roses are central to Greek mythology: the tears of the goddess of love, Aphrodite, were said to have mixed with the blood of her wounded lover, Adonis, to create the rose. The Romans believed the rose sprang from the blood of Venus. Since such times roses continue to be valued for their health-giving properties; they are depicted in art and in literature, in music, and in all religions and cultures.

Some 150 distinct species, or wild roses, are known, and these have given rise to countless more recognisable groups and cultivated varieties.

Wild roses, all native to the northern hemisphere—most from Iran, Afghanistan, the western parts of China and the southern countries of the former USSR—include those truly wild as well as those that may not be pure species but, rather, natural crosses. They were typically to be found growing at the edge of woodlands, where they used their thorns to scramble up trees and over other shrubs.

Roses bloom in a vast range of colours and hues, in different forms, with different growth habits, and with a variety of perfumes—some subtle, some rich, some exotic and others elegant.

Before we can appreciate the Old, or Heritage, roses that developed over the centuries—finishing, of course, with the Modern roses, including the Hybrid Tea and cluster-flowered Floribunda roses—we need to go back in botanical history to examine the species roses, or the roses that occurred in the wild. Some of these can still be found in their natural habitat, while many are still available and are greatly loved for use in our gardens. Some have given rise to the different classes of roses, by chance and through deliberate breeding.

Opposite: The golden rose 'Lady Hillingdon'.

Old roses

1. 'Souvenir de la Malmaison'.
2. 'Baronne Henriette de Snoy'.
3. 'Madame Isaac Pereire'.
4. 'Schneezwerg'.
5. 'Queen of Denmark'.
6. *Rosa rugosa* 'Scabrosa'.
7. 'Mme Hardy'.
8. 'Duchesse de Buccleugh'.

The Wild roses— a species guide by origin

SOME OLD SPECIES

- *Rosa gallica*, *R. × damascena* and *R. rubiginosa* are wild roses that have been grown throughout Europe for centuries and have given rise to many of the classes of Old roses described below.
- *Rosa gallica*, native to central and southern Europe, is an upright shrub of about a metre, with slim stems clothed in tiny prickles. It suckers prolifically and bears pink flowers, which are followed by red hips.
- *Rosa × damascena* is thought to be a naturally occurring cross between *R. gallica* and *R. phoenicea*, a wild, sprawling species very different from *R. gallica*.

EUROPE, AFRICA AND ASIA

- *Rosa canina*, the Dog Rose or Briar Rose, is often used as an understock for rambling roses. (This is the rose you may have seen naturalised through the hills areas of South Australia.)
- *Rosa spinossissima* (syn. *R. pimpinellifolia*), the Burnet Rose, or Scotch Rose, is a frost-resistant, small, neat, very thorny bush that bears small, single, scented flowers.
- *Rosa × dupontii*, which the New Zealand rosarian Nancy Steen called 'The Snow Bush', is a vigorous climber with apple-green leaves, loved for its trusses of large, single, white flowers. It is probably a cross between *R. moschata* and *R. gallica*.

CHINA

- *Rosa hugonis*, also called the Golden Rose of China, was sent to Britain from China in 1899.
- *Rosa primula*, similar to *R. hugonis*, and known as the incense rose for the scent of its fern-like foliage, flowers in a paler, more gentle lemon.
- *Rosa laevigata* was not discovered in America, as is often thought, but rather in China. It became naturalised after being taken to America, because it layered wherever a shoot touched the ground. It is now the national flower of Georgia and is often the first flower of the rose season. It can be used as hedging (*see* Hedges).

- The incredibly popular *Rosa* 'Wedding Day', with its huge trusses of white blossom, was bred in the United Kingdom by crossing the two Chinese species *R. longicuspis* (also known as *R. mulliganii*, and which many readers will have seen covering an arbour in the white garden at Sissinghurst) and *R. moyesii*, which was introduced to the west in 1903. *Rosa moyesii* has clear-red flowers and huge rosehips.

NORTHERN CHINA

Rosa bracteata, the Macartney Rose, was first sent to Britain in 1792 by Lord Macartney's embassy in Peking. This rose, which bears serious thorns, has wonderful rich foliage and large, fragrant, cream flowers. It loves warm climates, so much so that it can be a pest.

CENTRAL CHINA

- *Rosa banksiae* var. *normalis*, the single white banksia rose, is found growing wild in central China. The double white form was taken from China to Kew Gardens by the plant hunter William Kerr in 1807.
- *Rosa banksiae Lutea*, the double yellow form, was particularly loved by our early settlers.

WESTERN CHINA

- *Rosa chinensis*, from the remote mountains of western China, is one of the species that is very important in the development of the Modern rose.
- *Rosa filipes* is a rampant, rambling climber. It has given rise to the clone 'Kiftsgate', which smothers structures in the garden of the same name in the Cotswold village of Chipping Camden, in England, and was so named in 1951 by the noted English rosarian Graham Thomas.

SOUTHERN CHINA

- The huge *Rosa gigantea*, a parent of the Tea roses, which bears the largest blooms of all the rose species, is native to Myanmar and southern China.

THE HIMALAYAS

- *Rosa brunonii*, the Himalayan Musk rose, arrived in Europe in 1822 from the Himalayas. It is a rampant climber with long, elegant, grey-green foliage and great trusses of white blooms.

JAPAN

- *Rosa multiflora* was introduced to Europe from Japan in 1862. It has clusters of open white blossom with delicate yellow stamens and is important as the parent of many ramblers, some of the dwarf Polyanthas and, through the latter, the cluster-flowered Floribundas.
- *Rosa rugosa* is native to Japan, where it is a coastal plant, and to China. Today there are hundreds of varieties bred for use in the garden. To my mind they are not for the flower border but, rather, make wonderful hedges as they are easy to maintain, cope with some neglect and are tolerant of a range of conditions.

> **Tip:** Among the most useful of the wild roses are the Rugosas. These are tough, easy to care for and tolerant of a range of soils. They flower for months with single or double blooms, in a range of colours, that are followed by stunning rosehips—from which you can make an excellent jelly or tea that is rich in vitamin C.

THE MIDDLE EAST

- *Rosa foetida*, with single, acid-yellow flowers, and its offspring, the very double *R. foetida persiana*, are native to the Middle East and have contributed a great deal to our Modern yellow roses.
- *Rosa hemisphaerica*, sulphur-yellow and very double, is a good choice for dry climates that mimic conditions in its native Iran.

The Old roses

Old roses are those established before the introduction to the west of the repeat-flowering China roses at the end of the eighteenth century. They are the result of deliberate or spontaneous crossing and breeding of the species roses introduced above.

Within these Old roses are several classes: Gallica, Damask, Alba, Centifolia and Moss. Their shrub form is often relaxed and informal; the buds are charming but relatively insignificant, and open to a luscious flower of many different forms, mainly in pinks and cerise. Only a couple bloom yellow and there are just a few whites. The main disadvantage of these Old roses is that they flower only once each season.

Gallicas

Rosa gallica has given rise to the Gallicas developed for the garden, and has contributed also to the classes we call Damasks, Albas, Centifolias and Moss roses. *Rosa gallica* was used by English, French and Dutch breeders to develop different varieties, which became known as the Gallicas, flowering in deeper pinks, with some striped and marbled. The leaves of the Gallicas are often rough in texture and dark green, oval and pointed at the tip. Their small, pointed buds are beautifully encased in the long, pointed sections of the green sepals. They are not fussy about their growing conditions.

The oldest cultivated form of *Rosa gallica* is 'Officinalis', or the 'Apothecary's Rose', featured as a symbol in the English War of the Roses, when it was known as the 'Red Rose of Lancaster'. It is thought to have first appeared in the town of Provins, south-east of Paris, where it was used in perfume production; it was also used for medicinal purposes. It bears semi-double, crimson blooms with yellow anthers and a rich fragrance.

Some of the favourite varieties bred from *Rosa gallica* include the following:
- 'Belle de Crécy', bred in 1848, is reliable and free flowering.
- 'Charles de Mills' is a large-flowered luscious carmine, opening to a rich, flat bloom.
- 'Duchesse de Buccleugh', so elegant, was bred in France in 1846, and bears a magenta bloom which opens flat with the distinctive green 'eye'.

Damasks

The second class among these Old roses and also found in ancient history, the Damask is thought to have been grown by the Persians and taken to France by the Crusaders in the Middle Ages. The Damask Rose, *Rosa × damascena*, is probably a naturally occurring cross between *R. gallica* and *R. phoenicea*. Damask roses are usually thorny, growing to about 2 m in height, sprawling in habit, with grey-green pointed leaves that are downy on the underside. The very fragrant flowers are usually a clear pink, with no purple, and the hips, when they appear, are long and thin.

THE AUTUMN DAMASK

This ancient class of rose is the only repeat-flowering Old rose. The Autumn Damask plays an important part in our history of the rose, as it was to contribute to the development of the Portland rose and, through this, to repeat flowering in other rose groups. A very prickly shrub, the Autumn Damask *R. × damascena* var. *semperflorens* is distinguished by its leaves, which surround the flowers.

The following are among the important cultivated Damask varieties:
• 'Ispahan', appearing in cultivation before 1832, flowers for weeks in early spring with large, voluptuous, rich-pink, wonderfully scented blooms.
• 'Kazanlik', also known as *Rosa × damascena* 'Trigintipetala', is one of the roses grown at Kazanlik in Bulgaria for the production of attar of roses.
• 'Mme Hardy', one of the loveliest of the Damasks, bears flat white flowers with the typical green 'eye'. It was bred in 1832 by Monsieur Hardy, who was in charge of the rose collection at Empress Josephine's garden, Malmaison, today on the outskirts of Paris.
• 'Omar Khayyam', was bred in about 1893, supposedly from a seed collected from the rose on Omar Khayyam's grave at Nashipur in Iran.

Albas

This group of roses, which was grown in ancient times and used for medicinal purposes, was probably brought to Britain by the Romans. Experts agree—judging from the flowers, form and rosehips—that the albas are the result of a natural cross between *Rosa × damascena* and the Dog rose, *R. canina*, or a species very closely related to the Dog rose. This is a small but important group, often reaching more than 2 m in height, with grey-green foliage and superbly scented white to pale pink flowers. They are tough and forgiving and among the easiest of the Old roses to grow, coping with difficult conditions and even tolerating half-shade.

A few of the best include the following:
• 'Alba Semi-Plena', flowering with large clotted-cream blooms on attractive foliage, is also cultivated at Kazanlik in Bulgaria for attar of roses.
• 'Félicité Parmentier' is very beautiful, bearing a very quartered, pale pink bloom on pale leaves.

Centifolias

Not as ancient as the three classes already discussed, it is thought that the Centifolias evolved over a century, from the beginning of the 1600s, probably as a cross or a series of crosses between several species, including *Rosa gallica*, *R. phoenicea*, *R. moschata* and *R. canina*, resulting in what came to be classed as this separate species, or class, *R. × centifolia*. The shrub is relaxed, with large, round, serrated leaves; the flowers are many-petalled and were popular as subjects for Dutch flower painters.

'Centifolia', also known as the 'Old Cabbage Rose', with very double, pink, cabbage-like blooms on arching stems, is among the most coveted and most beautiful in this class. 'Fantin Latour', with blush-pink, very double blooms, is also extremely popular in gardens today: it is thought to have ancestors other than *R. × centifolia*—perhaps *R. chinensis*. It grows to about 2 m and was named after the French flower painter Henri Fantin Latour.

Moss roses

This class has developed from the Centifolias and, because of a genetic fault, or sport, has developed a most attractive, moss-like 'fuzz' on the green sepals that encase the flower buds. It is not known when or where this natural sport occurred, but a Moss rose is thought to have existed in France in the first part of the seventeenth century. It was first listed in an English catalogue in 1724. Most of the varieties of Moss roses were bred during just two decades, between 1850 and 1870, and hence some show signs of China rose genetics being present. One of the loveliest of the Moss roses is the tall-growing, double white to shell-pink 'Comtesse de Murinais', bred in France in 1843.

The China roses and later groups

China roses

The next, and crucial, part of the rose story occurs towards the end of the eighteenth century, during a time of much travel and discourse between East and West, and when traders were transporting plants from China back to Europe. As we know, thousands of plant genera and tens of thousands of species are native to China, as are at least a hundred wild, or species, roses. Some of these had crossed, or hybridised, before Europeans took them back to the west. The resulting roses are known as the China roses, and they are the bridge between the East and the West, between the Old roses and the new, Modern roses.

The most important characteristic of these China roses was that they flowered repeatedly throughout the growing season, a characteristic itself unusual in nature. Most species roses flower in the second season, on a long shoot that did not flower the previous year—that is, on second-year wood. In the case of the first China rose a mutation caused each stem—even the new shoots—to produce flowers. This was noticed (it is thought in the Sichuan province) and the plant was propagated, producing a class, or group, known as China roses.

The China roses—which are more open and twiggy than other roses, with smooth foliage often

tinged with pink or red, and few thorns—arrived in the west as four varieties. These were 'Slater's Crimson China', which arrived in Britain in 1792; 'Parson's Pink China (also called 'Old Blush China'), which arrived in 1793; 'Hume's Blush China', arriving in 1809; and 'Park's Yellow Tea Scented China', which arrived in Britain in 1824 (and is thought to have been a cross between a China rose and *Rosa gigantea*), which bears the largest blooms of all the rose species.

While the species and classes from the Middle East and Central Europe already discussed were more glamorous, and more popular than these earliest four China roses, soon hybridising with the European roses took place, resulting in a great variety of new roses. Some of these still displayed the characteristics of the Old, European roses, while the characteristics of the China rose were more obvious in others.

Portlands

This group is thought to contain some China rose genes—probably 'Slater's Crimson China', which imparted its rich red colour—along with Gallica and Autumn Damask genes. The Portlands are small, neat shrubs and, though repeat flowering, retain the look of truly Old roses. By 1848 there were 84 varieties growing at Kew Gardens in London, among them 'Comte de Chambord', bred in France in 1860 and bearing a very full, very fragrant, deep pink bloom.

Bourbons

The Bourbon roses—named for the Ile de Bourbon, now called Reunion, a small island in the Indian Ocean—soon took over from the Portland roses. While their flowers still display the characteristics of the Old roses, the Bourbons represent the first step towards the Modern roses that we call Hybrid Teas. It is thought that a natural cross occurred between the Autumn Damask rose and the China rose 'Old Blush China' when farmers on the island planted the two together as hedges. Seed was gathered from

Hybrid Teas

1. 'Vol de Nuit'.
2. 'Bengali'.
3. 'Apricot Nectar'.
4. 'Century Two'.
5. 'Antique'.
6. 'Bob Wooley'.
7. 'Violet Carson'.
8. 'Duet'.

Modern roses

1. 'Nevada'.
2. 'Pierre de Ronsard'.
3. 'Ballerina'.
4. 'Papa Meilland'.

this early, spontaneous, cross; and from this the glorious Bourbon roses, with their luscious globe-like, highly perfumed blooms, were developed. The blooms and the bush are still 'Old rose' in appearance, but the foliage and stems look more like the modern, Hybrid Teas. As a bonus, the Bourbons are usually repeat flowering.

Among the best are the following:

- 'Honorine de Brabant', a pale pink rose, is among the loveliest of the Bourbons.
- 'Souvenir de la Malmaison' bears a luscious, heavily quartered pale pink bloom, which can, however, suffer from black spot in misty climates.
- 'Madame Isaac Pereire' flowers in a sumptuous deep carmine, with one of the richest scents of all roses.
- 'Boule de Neige', bred in 1867 in France, has few thorns and a fragrant, pure-white flower.

Noisettes

There were several other Old-style roses being developed as breeding, hand in hand with chance, marched inexorably towards the birth of the Hybrid Teas. The Noisettes were the result of a cross, in the United States in 1802, between the species rose, *Rosa moschata* and the China rose 'Old Blush China' (formerly 'Parson's Pink China').

Among the lovliest, 'Lamarque', with her gorgeous blooms the colour of clotted cream, is a repeat-flowering, very popular, climbing rose.

Hybrid perpetuals

The leadup to the breeding of the Modern rose continued with the development of the Hybrid Perpetual rose. It is impossible to be absolute about the origins of the Hybrid Perpetuals, which are thought to be a combination of several different roses in an attempt to breed a reliable, repeat-flowering plant.

Teas

The Tea roses represent by far the most exciting development in the story of the rose—to my mind at least—as the Tea rose is a parent of the modern Hybrid Tea. Originally classified as Tea Scented China roses, the Tea rose is the result of cross between two of the original four China Roses ('Hume's Blush China' and 'Park's Yellow Tea Scented China') with various of the Bourbon and Noisette roses. Success came first in 1835 with a rose bred in England and named 'Adam', bearing a large, double, buff to apricot coloured bloom. It is a vigorous bush rose, or forms a low-growing climber.

The gorgeous blooms of the Teas enjoy a range of scents, including that of a freshly opened packet of China tea, as described by the English rosarian Graham Thomas.

CLIMBING TEAS

With parents in the southern part of China, the old Tea roses—particularly the climbing Teas—are the roses with which gardeners in the more humid parts of the country will succeed. Sydney rosarian Roger Mann advises that the shell-pink, richly quartered climbing Tea 'Devoniensis' is one of the best. 'As a class, the Teas are the outstanding performers in humidity, along with the Chinas and at least some of the Noisettes,' he says. 'They were born, after all, in the subtropical climate of the south of China, so our muggy summers don't faze them, nor lay them low with black spot like so many modern roses, which have a strong infusion of blood from that high-desert plant *Rosa foetida*. Ditto the banksians and *R. laevigata*, though they probably aren't what most people are thinking of when they ask for roses.'

Some of the best:

- 'Marie Van Houtte' is a beautiful, very double, pink to pale yellow climbing Tea rose that doesn't mind humidity.
- 'Lady Hillingdon' bears elegant golden blooms that hang down on red stems.

HYBRID TEAS

As I have explained, the Tea rose is one of the parents of the Hybrid Teas, the first of which, 'Victor Verdier', was bred in France and introduced in 1859. Anything earlier should, therefore, be classed as an Old rose, or a Heritage rose, although the much-loved Australian rosarian David Ruston believes that cutoff point is too early, choosing to categorise roses that appeared before 1940 as an Old rose. You see, in plant breeding, and where natural crossing as well as hybridisation occurs, there are no absolutes!

English rosarian and breeder David Austin writes, 'Although we refer to them as Modern roses to differentiate them from the Old roses, the Hybrid Teas have now been with us for a long time'. While it is generally accepted by garden historians that the first Hybrid Tea appeared in 1859, it was Guillot's breeding of 'La France' in 1870 that firmly secured the place of the Hybrid Teas on the rose family tree.

And it was the first breeder of Hybrid Teas in Great Britain in around 1879, the farmer Henry Bennett, who first used the term and who—with French rosarian John Sisley—introduced a more systematic method of rose breeding. Until then, the process had been somewhat hit and miss.

The Hybrid Teas are the result of a cross between the Hybrid Perpetuals (which provided hardiness, large flower size and vigour, deep colours and strong scent) and the Tea roses (which contributed remontency and thick, shiny, large petals and beautiful flower buds that have a high, pointed centre). The bushes are upright, with none of the romance and softness of the Old roses.

The loveliest of the older Hybrid Teas include the so-elegant pink 'Mme Abel Chatenay', which covers the fence at Ruston Roses in the Riverland of South Australia (*see* Rose Gardens). Raised in France in 1895, she is a cross between the Tea rose 'Dr Grill' and the first Hybrid Tea, 'Victor Verdier'.

'White Wings' is an early single-flowered Hybrid Tea. With its dark green foliage and chocolate-coloured anthers, it remains as popular today as when it was introduced in the United States in 1947.

NEW HYBRID TEAS

The new Hybrid Tea roses include, in the whites, 'Elina'—a perfectly shaped, very scented cream

rose with very long stems. Also try 'Silver Jubilee' and 'Anna Pavlova'.

Among the apricots try 'Joyfulness', which has copper-salmon flowers and a very long stem, excellent for picking. Favourites include the very hardy 'Apricot Nectar', which teams well with almost anything else in a garden. 'Leaping Salmon', also known as 'Emmanuelle', was bred in the United Kingdom in 1986. She is scented, repeat-flowering and a glorious, unusual salmon pink.

Among the reds, you can choose from the marvellously scented, large-flowered 'Mister Lincoln'; the medium-red 'Miriana' a large-flowered Hybrid Tea bred in France in 1981; and the deep red 'Peter Frankenfeld'. Try the repeat-flowering, very fragrant 'Mary Delahunty' and the double, very scented and disease-resistant 'Mary Donaldson'. Among the pinks choose 'Paul Neyron'.

A rose nursery

William Macarthur, eighth child of Elizabeth and John, travelled extensively, sponsored plant hunters and explorers, and collected a wide range of exotic plants. William's original 'List of Plants Cultivated at Camden' for 1843, 1845, 1850 and 1857, held at the house today, details over 3000 plants cultivated in the Lower Garden. He offered for sale more than 70 varieties of roses, including the yellow banksia rose, one of the original plantings of which still blooms at Camden Park.

Types, uses and care

Surely those early mornings in spring must be the very best time in the garden. There is just the faintest hint of summer in the air: the cold edge has gone, but there is no humidity. The scent of wisteria and jasmine hovers in the stillness just after dawn, when the only sounds are the just-woken birds. And, it's nearly rose time again.

Mid-winter may be a time when you want to be

indoors, in front of a fire with your books, ignoring that last sad rose bloom clinging to a straggling, almost bare, branch. That's the time, however, to prune the roses that you already have, and to choose those you want to plant before the first sign of warm weather. Winter is also the best and most economical time to buy roses, when they are sold bare-rooted.

It is impossible to name one's favourite rose: ask any expert and they will answer, 'The one I saw last'. This equivocation is easy to understand as there are so many with a rich, so-rose scent, so many in a glorious array of rich—or gentle—colours and so many different forms. There is a rose for every part of the garden, and for every use.

Ground covers

As well as providing effective, low-maintenance ground covers, many roses are perfect for growing down banks and hiding unattractive retaining walls. Councils love them as garden strips down the centre of roads, along highways or as plantings to soften footpaths, perhaps cascading from planter boxes. Many of the climbing roses can be used most effectively in this way.
- 'Raubritter', a pink, cupped rose bred in Germany by Kordes, looks enchanting cascading down a bank or a terrace.
- 'Ralph's Creeper' is a very remontant, semi-single red rose with a pale cream on the reverse of the petals.

The Flower Carpet roses have been on the market in Australia for some 15 years and have sold in the millions—for good reason. They are tough, disease resistant and easy-care, while at the same time providing good-looking ground covers:
- 'White Meidiland', covered in clotted-cream double blooms from rich blue-green leaves, is attractive and tough.
- 'Red Meidiland' and 'Scarlet Meidiland' (a newer cultivar) are bold red.

CARE
Give ground-covering roses a position in full sun, a regular fertiliser and an annual hair cut with hedge trimmers. They will reward with thousands of blooms, for months.

Climbers or scramblers

Use climbing roses to retain banks, in the same way as you would use ground covers. They will clothe arbours, romp up trees to extend interest over many months, and cover fences. Grow two or more together over tripods and obelisks, to add structure, height and scale to the smallest of gardens.

COLOUR
Apricots, soft yellows and white
- 'Mermaid'—very thorny and very fragrant—is a vigorous, pale yellow rose, evergreen in warmer climates. A great show-off, it will happily cover a sunny wall.
- 'Meg', a soft apricot-coloured modern climbing rose, also looks marvellous carefully trained to decorate a mellow brick wall.
- 'Céline Forrestier', a soft-lemon, double rose, looks luscious with the white rose 'Francis E Lester' or the very perfumed white rose 'Rambling Rector'. Indulge in mass plantings of these beautiful roses, all together, for maximum effect.

Tip: Imagine this: the palest of pink wisteria flowers in long trusses with the first clotted cream to blush-pink blooms of *Rosa* 'Devoniensis' and the pink flowers of *R.* 'New Dawn'. Together they cover a lychgate that is painted in nine-tenths white semi-gloss to which one-tenth Taubmans pink 'Bedarra' has been added.

Pinks and reds
So many of the pink climbers are among the most elegant of roses: think of 'Reine Victoria'; and the camellia-like 'Louise Odier', which flowers in a stronger pink. 'Blossomtime', with her deep pink, elongated buds that open to elegant shell-pink blooms, looks stunning planted with the red blooms of the remontant, Old rambling rose

Climbing roses

1. 'Mermaid'.
2. 'Reine des Violettes' flowers at Woodbridge, near Auckland, on New Zealand's North Island.
3. The once-only flowering 'Albertine'.
4. In Deb Weir's beautiful Adelaide garden, the tennis court is clothed in 'Pierre de Ronsard'.
5. 'Altissimo'.

'Bloomfield Courage'. And you must have, somewhere, somehow, the glorious pink 'Mme Grégoire Staechelin'; she is among the most beautiful of all roses, although she is only once-flowering.

OVER FENCES

Climbing roses are traditionally used to clothe tennis court fences. Two excellent choices are the shell-pink 'Phyllis Bide', which is hardly ever without a flower, and the pink and white 'Pierre de Ronsard'.

Other lovely pink climbers include 'Renae' and 'Shot Silk'; the strident colours of the Polyantha 'Pinkie', which is always covered in blooms, are toned down by a companion planting of 'Dainty Bess'. Try the deep red 'Charles Mallerin' with the pale pink, voluptuous climbing 'Souvenir de la Malmaison'. Cover a country barbed-wire fence with the vigorous 'Edna Walling' rose, with her trusses of pink blooms, but do make sure you buy the real thing: there are some inferior impostors about!

IN TREES

The rose you might choose to grow through a tree will depend a little on the tree. Roses growing through fruit trees look romantic, but you need to select a thornless rose, to allow you to prune the tree for easy management—including, if you don't wish to donate all your produce to marauding wildlife, to net it at fruiting time. Consider the Bourbon *Rosa* 'Zéphirine Drouhin', with loose, very scented, hot-pink blooms; or her offspring, 'Kathleen Harrop', which also flowers from early summer almost to winter, for your apple trees, for instance. *Rosa* 'Crepuscule', with her soft apricot blooms that continue to appear until well into autumn, is perfect with the walnut (*Juglans regia*), which colours to a glorious butter-yellow in autumn. The lovely cream to white 'Madame Plantier', good also as a pillar rose, has few thorns. If you don't need to prune the rose, but can allow her to romp away completely uninhibited, you could choose the once-flowering but spectacular 'Albertine'; remember, though, that she has lethal, hooked thorns. She is a vigorous climber, perfect for leaving to climb a large tree.

The apricot to pink-flushed-lemon 'Souvenir de Madame Leonie Viennot' looks wonderful scrambling through a silver birch (*Betula pendula*), where the leaves have a lemon tone. The copper-yellow Tea rose 'Climbing Lady Hillingdon' and the paler lemon climbing Tea 'Sombreuil' look marvellous together; 'Veilchenblau', also known as the blue rambler rose, is fascinating contrasting with yellows or toning with pinks and cerise.

HEDGES

Almost any rose can be used to make a charming hedge. If you don't want to create a good deal of additional work for yourself, though, you might consider selecting roses that can be 'taken to' with the hedge trimmers. Cut back ruthlessly straight after flowering. A rose hedge looks particularly good backed with a butterfly-attracting, delicately scented buddleia—and both enjoy the same conditions and treatment in terms of watering, fertilising and pruning.

Timing is all

At Melbourne's Flemington Racecourse, the famous roses are timed to be at their best for Melbourne Cup Day. Bordering the lawns that flow down to the track, and mirroring a hedge of 'Crépuscule', are hedges in more toffee tones: there is 'Brass Band' and 'Pure Poetry', both Floribundas. Scrambling along the fence is 'Joyfulness'. Hedges in other sections of the garden— either dividing spaces or lining paths and driveways—include the ever-popular 'Ferdy', 'Bonica' and the shell-pink, very elegant 'Flamingo'. There are also hedges of the tiny, apricot to honey-coloured Polyantha rose 'Perle d'Or' (often mistaken for its pinker cousin, 'Cecile Brunner', as is the taller 'Bloomfield Abundance'). The tiny pink rose 'Chips Apple Blossom' and the miniature rose 'Little White Pet' both form an effective hedge or edge to a border.

Planting

The French-bred 'Manou Meilland' and her parent, 'Baronne de Rothschild' (with the same cerise petals with silver undersides) look stunning planted together as a hedge. The Floribunda rose 'Summer Breeze', a lovely dusty pink, is a good choice for cooler, misty climates: it flowers non-stop and doesn't get some of the mildew problems that you might expect in such climates. Some of the Hybrid Teas make an excellent formal hedge: you won't see one much smarter than 'Just Joey' and 'Apricot Nectar' planted together and edged, perhaps, with a caramel to apricot-flowering bearded iris.

❧ Requirements

The best time to buy roses is in winter, when the major growers sell them bare-rooted. Order from catalogues, well in advance. Most often, when sourcing your roses from nurseries and growers, you will be purchasing grafted plants, so it's important to select plants grafted to understock suited to your climate. Each state grafts onto different understocks: South Australia uses 'Dr Huey' or *Rosa* 'Indica Major', which suits an alkaline soil; Western Australia grafts onto *fortuneana* understock, the most vigorous stock for sandy conditions; the eastern coastal areas, with their often-acid soils, use the thornless *R. multiflora*, which is also used for Melbourne gardens. West of the Great Dividing Range, however, 'Dr Huey' and 'Indica Major' are more suitable. Most of the Tea roses are easily grown on their own roots.

✿ Care

While roses love clay, they also demand good drainage; you might improve heavy clay by adding gypsum and mulch (*see* Soil). Some gardeners build up garden beds to ensure perfect drainage.

Keep up good garden-keeping practices with correct watering and fertilising. A deep water once each week is better than lots of quick, shallow watering. It is said that roses do not like competition from other plants and purists suggest keeping the ground bare of other plants, perhaps

In a South Australian garden

Rosarian David Ruston advises: 'In the hot Australian climate bury the graft; do not get sun scald on the bud union.' This will result in a better root system and in several shoots growing from below the ground level, but from above the graft, so that they anchor the bush—a single stem will move with the wind. And, in bushfire areas roses that were planted below ground level will shoot again after fire. But do watch for any understock, which you will recognise as it is completely different from the grafted stock.

creating your rose garden in a separate part of the garden, to be viewed only when in full flower. That is not my preference, however, and I love to see a hedge of lavender in glorious, purple flower around roses, with iris, the perfect partner, planted

Food for roses

At Flemington Racecourse the roses receive a solid feed with 'Grow Better'—a pelletised organic fertiliser made up of nitrogen-rich poultry, and other, manures, along with seaweed and kelp—in early September. This is followed by a nitrogen-phosphorus-potassium liquid fertiliser at half-strength twice as often as recommended—sometimes as often as three times a week—which is sprayed on until it runs off. Some is absorbed through the leaves and some taken up through the soil. Varieties that need a 'push' to ensure that they bloom when expected also receive 'Charlie Carp' fertiliser, watered on weekly through the growing months, when the plants are in full leaf. A feed of solid food is applied again in January.

beneath the bushes. I have great fun teaming up bearded iris with the different roses in contrasting and toning shades.

Pruning

First ascertain whether your roses flower on new (that is, current season's) growth or on last year's growth, as you do not want to prune off shoots that are about to flower. When you do prune, cut above a bud, or 'eye'.

Begin by removing any diseased or damaged wood, right back to a healthy joint. Remove any crossing branches that might rub on others, creating wounds that will encourage disease. Remove old wood to ensure the continuing development of the shape you want, to encourage a succession of young and healthy shoots, and to create an open structure that will allow air to circulate.

Don't prune too early if you live in a frost-prone climate as you do not want the plant to shoot too soon, when there is a risk of damage to young, fresh growth.

Weigh down the 'arms' of standard roses with rocks to encourage each branch to grow downwards, rather than horizontally, and promote greater flowering.

After pruning comes feeding, then deep watering and mulching. One rosarian applies sheep manure, blood and bone and pelletised chook manure, in that order, at a rate each of two handfuls per square metre, added immediately after the roses are pruned. The gardens are then mulched heavily to cap in any disease. One spray with lime sulphur is applied immediately, and after two weeks a spray of copper oxychloride is followed by white oil for scale problems.

Propagation

I will not go into the technical details of budding onto selected rootstocks as that is a job for professionals, but many roses strike easily from cuttings.

Malcolm Rogers, who, with his wife Lorna, has a wonderful rose garden in Renmark, South Australia, keeps cuttings for propagation while pruning. Thirty centimetre long pieces the thickness of a pencil are placed straight in the ground, in a trench into which aged manure has been dug. No propagating mixture or hormone is used, but the cuttings are not allowed to dry out. After 12 months they can be planted in their final place and fertilised with blood and bone. 'You get beautiful root systems and you never get a sucker,' Malcolm says, of roses grown on their own roots.

Above: Clever rose supports at Castle Howard, in England's north.

SALVIAS

Salvias

Most of us think of sage as the herb used to flavour food or to make a thera-peutic tea—or as that somewhat strident red-flowering species you might see in a public park. But *Salvia officinalis*, a member of the mint family, has almost a thousand offspring, siblings and cousins that flower in a wide range of colours from pale pink to magenta and red, through true-blue, purple and lilac to yellow, amber and umber. Salvias—named by the Roman scientist and natural historian Pliny the Elder—are incredibly good-natured plants, hard working and uncomplaining, adjusting to the toughest of conditions without too much fuss.

Salvias come from most parts of the world, with over half of them native to the Americas. So, no matter where you live in this diverse country, there will be a salvia suited to your conditions; they are easy to grow and very rewarding. Many flower for months in glorious colours; they have varied leaf textures and a variety of growth habits.

The flexibility and wide colour range of the salvias mean that they can be very successfully incorporated into perennial borders—in both formal designs and cottage gardens. So, if you fancy yourself a modern-day Gertrude Jekyll but live in a climate that in no way matches that of the south of England, salvias could be your salvation.

Most salvias bear tubular flowers held high above leaves that emanate from square stalks in whorls or clusters, found on shrubby, usually ever-green, often straggly and somewhat untidy plants. The foliage varies in texture from smooth to velvety, and in colour from deep to olive green to red-tinged and to grey. Some have scented foliage, making them very pleasant to work amidst.

Take care when choosing salvias, though, as some, such as the bog sage (*Salvia uliginosa*) can be invasive. While this will become a problem in rich soils, it might be a godsend if you garden in conditions where many plants struggle.

♥ My favourites

HUMID AND COASTAL CLIMATES

- *Salvia involucrata × karwinskii* is a quick-growing shrub, bearing pink flowers in winter to late spring.
- *Salvia leucantha*, Mexican bush sage, is native to the tropical forests of central and eastern Mexico and reaches over 1 m. It has mid-green to grey leaves that are paler on the underside and white and lilac flowers throughout summer.
- *Salvia microphylla* 'Margaret Arnold' flowers in a cyclamen pink.
- *Salvia microphylla* 'Huntington' is red flowering, a hardy trouper that is widespread in Australia.

Tip: *Salvia splendens* 'Van Houttei', bred in Holland, was named for the Belgian nurseryman Louis Benoit Van Houtte.

- *Salvia splendens* is native to Brazil and was first described in 1822; it flowers in scarlet spikes and is happiest in areas of high humidity.
- *Salvia splendens* 'Van Houttei' has saw-toothed leaves and long, dark, cerise to red flowers in autumn.

Opposite: *Salvia* 'Costa Rica Blue'.

SUN AND SHADE

- *Salvia chiapensis* is a versatile plant with shiny foliage and sprays of cerise flowers year-round. It likes the sun but will also perform in dense shade and reaches about 80 cm.
- *Salvia buchananii* is a similar plant to *S. chiapensis* but has smoother foliage and larger, gorgeous flowers.

FROST TENDER

- *Salvia madrensis*, which hails from the Sierra Madre in Mexico, needs some protection from frost but holds its butter-yellow flowers from autumn to spring. It grows to 2 m and can be slashed a few times during the growing season to reduce its height.

LESS HUMID CLIMATES, AND FROST HARDY

- *Salvia forsskaolii*, from the Himalayas, is fully hardy. The foliage of this salvia is very wide at the base; it boasts masses of 1 m-tall spikes of mauve flowers.
- The greggii varieties are not recommended for humid climates, in which they become woody. They are suited to cool southern gardens and to dryer inland climates. They are frost- and heat-resistant and enjoy a long flowering period.
- *Salvia greggii* 'Lara', named for the granddaughter of salvia grower Sue Templeton, has a cream and pink bi-coloured flower.

BLUE FLOWERING

- *Salvia guaranitica* 'Costa Rica Blue' grows to less than 1 m.
- *Salvia* 'Black and Blue' also grows to less than 1 m, making it suitable for smaller gardens.
- *Salvia discolor* grows to 1 m, has leaves that are olive green on top and grey underneath, and very dark, navy-blue flowers.
- *Salvia melissodora*, which reaches 2 m, bears very scented lavender-blue flowers.

- *Salvia patens* and *S. azurea* are both lovely blues, but are a little too easy to grow in mild climates.
- *Salvia chamaedryoides* likes cool and dry conditions.

Planting

The grey to silver leaved *Artemisia* 'Valerie Finnis' and *A.* 'Powis Castle' are 'garden musts', tying together different spaces in the garden and different blocks of plants, including salvias, and thus creating a cohesive whole. The striking blue-flowering *Salvia* 'Indigo Spires' and *S.* 'Black Night', planted at the back of any border, look fantastic with fat blue spires of delphiniums that reach skywards, and, a little further forward, with a mass of a mid-blue flowering bearded iris: add just a few of the palest blue *Iris* 'Silverado'. Related to the salvias, the aromatic *Agastache rugosa*, from China and Japan, grows to over 1 m and flowers in lilac to pink spikes. (With its volatile oil and aniseed-flavoured and scented leaves, it is used in Chinese medicine.) Froth up the border with cleome and sprinkle the delicate-looking but tough Queen Anne's lace at the very back of the entire scene. Grow soft-coloured poppies, which provide seeds for neighbours who might walk past and admire the garden.

Requirements

Salvias grow best in light, well-drained soil in full sun. Many dislike frost, although the herbaceous species will cope with cold weather.

Care

Cut back after their summer flowering to encourage blooms into autumn, and to promote a dense habit. Propagate easily, in spring and summer, by root cuttings, or by cuttings taken as you prune.

WISTERIAS

Wisterias

Too gorgeous, too fragrant and too useful. Wisterias. Surely the most glorious plants of all, wisterias deserve a section all of their own, although they are, of course, climbers (*see* Climbers). I know what you are thinking: I said this about daphne, about gardenias, and about that rich-red, impossibly richly scented old Bourbon rose 'Madame Isaac Pereire'. The fact is, all plants are wonderful, but some are even more so than others! And each favourite can convey memories of particular times of the year.

Perhaps nothing promises warm weather more than the wisteria stirring from its winter dormancy. As the wisteria flower buds swell towards the end of winter—getting fatter as each day warms—and the lime-green leaves start to unfurl, you know the cold months will soon be over. Then, for two weeks in September or October—depending upon the climate in which you garden—you are treated to an orgy of indescribable scent from voluptuous racemes of pea flowers in a range of lilacs and purples, pinks, white and creams.

This deciduous twiner is a genus comprising about 10 species, native to China, Japan, Korea and North America. If you look carefully you will notice that the stems of the Japanese wisteria, *Wisteria floribunda*, which was introduced to the west in 1830, twine clockwise, while those of the more vigorous Chinese wisteria, *W. sinensis*, twine anti-clockwise. *Wisteria brachybotrys* (syn. *W. venusta*) is an early-flowering species, with white blooms that have yellow markings.

Wisterias are frost hardy, but if you garden in areas that suffer from severe spring frosts you will find the flower buds burnt in unlucky seasons. The late-flowering American species, *W. macrostachya*, a slender, vigorous climber that twines anti-clockwise, may be a wiser choice for gardens in our coldest climates. There are countless covetable cultivars of wisteria available, each suitable for different conditions and applications.

♥ My favourites

EARLY FLOWERING AND HIGHLY SCENTED

- *Wisteria brachybotrys* 'Murasaki Kapitan' (also known as 'Blue Velvet') bears short, fat lilac racemes and is the first to flower.
- *Wisteria floribunda* 'Lawrence' flowers with a beautiful, pale blue raceme 50 cm long and comprising almost 200 individual, heavily scented florets in each raceme.
- *Wisteria floribunda* 'Geisha', a vigorous, upright plant, flowers in light blue with a narrow raceme up to 40 cm long.
- *Wisteria sinensis* 'Jako' flowers early in spring with richly scented, white racemes.

BLUE

- *Wisteria floribunda* 'Royal Purple' is recommended for container growing and flourishes in most climates. It flowers when young, will re-flower in summer, and has a good dark colour.

Tip: I love a few varieties of wisteria planted together in a pot for a luscious mix of colours and an extended flowering period—but choose the stronger ceramic over terracotta containers.

Previous page: The 'darling buds' of spring.

- *Wisteria sinensis* 'Blue Pacific' is not too vigorous, so is also suitable for pots.
- *Wisteria sinensis* 'Amethyst' also is not too vigorous.

PINK

- The *Wisteria brachybotrys* cultivars spot flower in summer, when the florets have pink tones.
- *Wisteria floribunda* 'Honbeni', also known as 'Rosea', has a lavender-pink flower with a yellow blotch.
- *Wisteria brachybotrys* 'Showa-beni', also called 'Pink Chiffon', is an early-flowering cultivar in a cold climate. It blooms with a short raceme of true-pink bud that opens to blush-pink florets.

LATE FLOWERING

- *Wisteria macrostachya* flowers in late November, so the flowers may escape damage from all but the most brutal of late frosts. It flowers with heavy, 30 cm long racemes which have a honey smell and a good dark blue colour.
- *Wisteria floribunda* 'Macrobotrys' produces extra-ordinary, metre-long, lilac and purple racemes.

> **Tip:** *Wisteria floribunda* and cultivars look extraordinary dripping from a bridge or from a pergola, where their long racemes can be best displayed and appreciated.

- *Wisteria sinensis* 'Black Dragon' produces double dark purple flowers and looks particularly effective when planted with a lilac, earlier flowering wisteria. Such a combination will also extend the flowering period.

> **Tip:** Cover a long walkway in *Wisteria floribunda* 'Royal Purple' and with yellow or clotted-cream flowering David Austin climbing roses, a breathtaking sight in October when its scented, deep blue racemes mingle with the quartered blooms of the roses.

Planting

Wisteria can be used in myriad ways, apart from the most obvious use of forming a scented roof to a pergola. A tree wisteria is an option for a small garden: use a piece of wood as the upright, with two struts nailed across the top. Prune the wisteria to create a head about 1 m high and 1.5 m across: once a strong trunk is formed you can cut away the support. And, for that large and happy band of gardeners who are completely undisciplined and cannot bring themselves to choose, one solution is to plant your wisterias on poles.

> **Tip:** Plant multiples of the one cultivar to drip down, or stabilise, a bank or to cover an unsightly retaining wall or, in the country, a dam wall. Just five plants, after about eight years, will cover about 25 m.

You can grow wisteria along a wire fence: you might choose several different cultivars to ensure weeks of flowers. Centre each plant between two fence posts and prune so that each develops only one stem, growing almost as a self-supporting standard. The 'leads' are kept trimmed to 2 m either side, so that the varieties do not mix, and are attached to wires that thread through galvanised iron eyelets.

Wisteria grown with roses can look heavenly, but this combination is not for those who prefer their gardening to be low maintenance. But then some might call such a garden—along with such items as a weak, de-caf, skim-milk caffé latte—a 'why bother?'

Requirements

Wisterias are easy to grow, do not demand excessive water and flower when just a few years old.

Care

A word of warning about this beautiful but unruly

1. At Levens Hall, in England's Lake District.
2. *Wisteria brachybotrys* 'Murasaki Kapitan' grown on wires in the author's garden.
3. The long racemes of *Wisteria floribunda* 'Alba'.
4. Vita Sackville-West's planting of *Wisteria venusta* at Sissinghurst.

plant. Wisterias can sulk and they can misbehave. If you do not subject them to strict discipline they will cause no end of trouble. Do not allow wisterias to haul themselves up onto the house; the climbing parts can easily pull a structure away. A freestanding support is the safest way to enjoy wisteria. Or use rope to train wisteria up to a structure like a pergola. The rope then rots out and the wisteria is not pulling on the structure.

Hard-prune wisteria in late spring, straight after flowering, to create the overall shape required. Then tip-prune long suckers and tie them in the required position. Once you have the growth and cover you want, prune all new shoots to two or three leaves, thus encouraging the development of the good, fat flower spurs. All unwanted, untidy, long shoots can be gently pulled away as they appear, particularly over summer.

In winter you will simply be tidying up, pruning any long strands back to five fat buds.

For those who think all this sounds daunting, take heart: once the plant is mature the production of new shoots lessens annually and the task becomes much less time-consuming.

Feed wisteria only if they are in harsh conditions: a legume, they obtain most of their nitrogen from the sunlight. Too much nitrogen fertiliser will encourage foliage at the expense of flowers. Water well in the flowering season to extend the blossoming period.

There are two main reasons for wisteria not flowering: they are not planted in full sun (at least four hours per day are required) or they are pruned hard in winter, thus removing the flower buds. As well, be sure to buy vegetatively produced wisterias; any grown from seed may take years to flower.

Grouped Garden Elements

PART THREE

BORDERS

Borders

If you have travelled to the United Kingdom in June or July you've no doubt admired those virtuoso borders that move, seemingly without effort, from one theme and colourway to another as the spring finishes and the summer progresses. Such clever planting takes meticulous planning, and deep knowledge of plants and their habits. Success also depends upon a reliable rainfall as well as mountains of hard work, particularly in the growing season. It is a clever gardener who can keep plants looking happy, and perennial borders blooming, in this country, particularly in times of climate change. There are, however, plenty of hardy plants that, with a little planning and thought, will perform well in difficult Australian conditions, providing excitement and interest for months.

The traditional border is most often backed by a wall or a hedge and is often flanked by lawn. It is best viewed, perhaps, in its entirety, from across a wide expanse of grass. In large gardens, particularly those that surround the great English country houses, maintained today for the lucrative garden-visiting market, the double herbaceous border is the pinnacle of the art. Each of the two borders is a mirror of the other and is separated by a perfect grass path: it takes a small army of gardeners to keep it at its peak. Most of us do not have the space, or the means, to maintain such complicated schemes. Fortunately, there are lots of less demanding designs that can provide plenty of enjoyment.

Nevertheless, whether you are creating twin borders to form part of a grand design, or a smaller arrangement for a more relaxed section of a cottage garden, there are certain constraints that must be addressed. A border is a three-dimensional phenomenon: it is essential to think about the height, width and depth you want your chosen plants to reach, as well as their leaf shape and texture. The combinations of flower and foliage, volume, height and width, texture and tone are endless.

❤ My favourites

It is impossible to talk about borders without discussing colour (*see also* Colour).

GREY, SILVER, WHITE, CREAM, PALE YELLOW AND PALE PINK

Whatever themes or patterns you play with for your border, use grey and silver-leaved species to soften the different areas, to tie one section to the

A plantman's garden

Gravetye Manor, created by plantsman and writer William Robinson after he bought the Elizabethan manor in 1885, remains today a glorious garden of some 15 ha. Take tea on the north lawn, where Robinson, towards the end of his life, sat in his wheelchair to scatter bulbs into the deep perennial borders. These borders, which are at their peak from late June until the end of August, are filled with a luscious mix of dianthus, geraniums, artemisia, baby's breath and salvia, and with arching canes of soft pink, sweetly scented old-fashioned roses, all spilling over wide edgings of York stone laid down by Robinson.

Opposite: The summer blooms of *Persicaria bistorta*. *Previous page*: Succulents mean sustainable gardening.

1. The twin borders at Stevens-Coolidge Place, a perfectly preserved example of the American Colonial Revival movement, in North Andover, Massachusetts.
2. In a garden by Sue and Ian Home on Victoria's Mornington Peninsula, ribbons of grey stachys thread through summer borders.
3. The glorious border created by plantswoman Joan Arnold at Busker's End, Bowral, in New South Wales.
4. In Pat and Judy Bowley's garden at Wildes Meadow, on New South Wales' Southern Highlands.

next, and to create cohesion throughout the garden. Among the most successful of such planting schemes are those planned around a palette of greys, silver-whites, creams and the palest of pale lemons: many garden lovers will have seen such a scheme at Sissinghurst, that much-admired garden in Kent, in England, created by Vita Sackville-West and her husband Harold Nicolson.

Imagine the frothy white flowers of the tall-growing perennial Queen Anne's lace at the rear of a border that includes *Achillea* 'The Pearl': she has tiny, white, bobbly flowers—but she can make herself a little too much at home. Enhance the pastel shades with the delicate species gladioli—not the strident Edna Everage types—which flower in tones of pale pink and cream. In cool climates, team a mass of the pink toothbrush-like flowers of *Persicaria bistorta* with a large collection of species geranium, including the tiny pink *Geranium sanguineum* var. *striatum*, and *G. pratense* 'Mrs Kendell Clark' which flowers in a pale lilac with fine white stripes.

Use tripods supporting a variegated honeysuckle and the pink and white climbing rose 'Pierre de Ronsard' to add height. Add a favourite shrub rose—'Jacqueline du Pre', perhaps. She is very pretty, not a tantrum thrower, and bears pale pink blooms with pink stamens up to three times in a season. Jazz it all up with the rich carmine of the old Gallica rose 'Tuscany Superb'. Tie the entire scene together with the variegated lavender *Lavandula* × *intermedia* 'Walberton's Silver Edge', along with *L. stoechas* 'Rocky Road', flowering pale lilac and pink.

BE DARING—APRICOT, BROWN, CINNAMON, COPPER

You can have enormous fun with the apricot colours, to which I always add brown, just to be controversial. Think of the cinnamon-coloured roses—including everybody's favourite, the repeat-flowering Hybrid Tea 'Just Joey'—with a copper-coloured iris. And don't forget that often-sulky rose 'Julia's Rose': if you can grow her she provides the opportunity for great excitement in the garden. I love her with bearded iris such as 'Copatonic', or 'Supreme Sultan' with its brown 'falls'.

Virtuoso planting

One of the most exciting gardens in England is based on a series of borders and was created, over three decades, in the Cotswolds' village of Hidcote Boyce. The owner, who grew up at nearby Kiftsgate Court, one of England's best known and most admired open gardens, in the village of Chipping Camden, was taught by a mother who was a respected plantswoman.

Two massive teardrop-shaped beds, broken up by paving stones that create circles that house different colourways, form the basis of the half-hectare design. There is a yellow border, then a pink and then a blue. Reds create a theme that connects all the beds: there is the smoke bush (*Cotinus* spp.), the burgundy berberis and the purple-leaved Norway maple (*Acer platinoides*

'Crimson King'). There are standards of the pink-flowered *Indigofera decora*, underplanted with golden oregano, all offset with grey *Atriplex cinerea*.

A long, deep border on the warm south side of the house is dominated by the red-leaved plants which provide a rich canvas for those that flower in pinks and lilacs. At the front are clumps of *Allium cristophii* and *A. giganteum*, with their strident heads of bright pink, both happy with the more delicate *Erodium pelagoniiflorum* and *E. glandulosum*, cousins of the species geranium (*see* Geraniums). The colours give way to the blues and greys of *Linum* 'Alice Blue', *Agapanthus* 'Lilliput' and *Veronica* 'Ionian Skies'. The entire border is backed with the frothy mid-blue flowers of a ceanothus, which is espaliered against the house.

Coton Manor

Susie and Ian Pasley-Tyler's Northhampton-shire garden, Coton Manor, is 4 ha of what must be English perfection. There is something in this garden to fascinate virtually all year round. In spring and summer the cleverly planted terrace borders are full of interest. 'Each border comes into its own as the one above is slightly off its peak; they don't all peak at the same time,' explains Susie. The main border, which is backed by a holly hedge, comprises silvers, greys and yellows in early spring. In high summer there are lots of deep blues and scarlets, before the planting scheme reverts to whites for autumn.

TONE IT DOWN

The easy-to-please *Phygelius* 'Salmon Leap' looks good in such company and will tone down any clumps of red hot pokers that you may have added for a little drama. Edge all this with a wide ribbon of the clove-scented, pink to apricot *Dianthus* 'Mrs Sinkins' and team her silver foliage with black mondo grass. Imagine the large-flowered, honey-coloured climbing rose 'Meg' rambling in the background.

EXTRAORDINARY COLOUR

One of the most exciting bases for a border is the red, burgundy and purple colourway. Team a deep red bergamot with *Eupatorium maculatum* 'Gateway', with its froth of pink flowers and chocolate-coloured leaves, and with new treasures like *Berberis* 'Rose Glow', with its dark burgundy foliage which ages to rose pink. Back with the tall-growing, easygoing *Salvia* 'Black Knight' and an outrageous mass of the cerise, apricot and pink blooms of the rose 'Mutabilis'; nearby plant *Salvia* × *sylvestris* 'Ostfriesland' as well as *S.* 'Waverly', with its purple-tinged foliage. The generous and easy *Sedum* 'Autumn Joy' seems to thrive in a range of climates—but dislikes humidity. Artemisias such as the cultivars 'Powis Castle' and 'Valerie Finnis' will lighten the scene and weave it all together.

TIE TOGETHER WITH GRASSES

Grasses, including *Miscanthus sinensis* 'Gracillimus' with its caramel-coloured seed-heads, will pick up the burgundies and pink tones nearby: it is endlessly interesting with the sun filtering through it. (*See* Grasses.)

Maintenance and design

To help with maintenance, you might consider running a path behind your border, just in front of its backing wall. And think about edges to your border—for ease of maintenance and mowing, and for good looks. A wide, flat, stone mowing edge is traditional; a deep-spaded edge means more work for you. Consider, instead, allowing edging plants to spill over onto the lawn (*see* Edgings and Ground Covers).

I like to break up big borders with 'punctuation marks' of box balls, or domes or cones of yew or lillypilly, or with iron tripods covered in a slow-growing climber. This serves to simplify an expanse into workable sections, making each a little less daunting: you can repeat planting schemes, for a cohesive look, and maintain one section at a time.

In Australia, where growing seasons are long, and rainfall is irregular, you might augment perennials with easygoing spring and summer bulbs, with hardy lily species, and even, towards the rear of a border, with shrubs (*see* Shrubs, for plenty of choice). Choose easygoing perennials such as the salvias and the sedums; most importantly, be kind to yourself by planting species that love your growing conditions.

Opposite: A border in the Cotswold's village of Hidcote Boyce in England.

CLIMBERS

Climbers

If you have used every available space in your garden—horizontal, vertical and even elevated—to grow plants, chances are you have included plenty of climbers in your botanical repertoire.

Climbing plants must represent among the greatest value in the horticultural world. They can clothe unsightly garden boundaries and cover arbours to divide up space, preventing the garden from revealing its secrets too quickly. They can add height to the garden by covering tripods and obelisks, and grow through trees and shrubs or through hedges, to flower on when their host has finished blooming. They can create a cooling system; deciduous vines trained over a metal frame that stands alone beside a building will provide a living wall that becomes an environmentally sound air conditioner.

You can allow climbers like bougainvillea to drip from window boxes in a flamenco show of brilliant, clashing colours. Plant climbers in multiples of just one species to secure a bank or to cascade down a less-than-glamorous retaining wall: wisterias, and roses like the cream 'Heidesommer' and 'Raubritter' (a pink, cupped Hybrid Tea) look marvellous when used in this way. In coastal areas the Australian native *Hibbertia scandens* is used as a ground cover, and to stabilise sand dunes.

I was once asked for advice on a climber that would cover a large steel pergola that protects a barbecue area in the grounds of an apartment complex in a city that enjoys cold, frosty winters. Shade in summer was essential, along with light and warmth in winter. I suggested the soft apricot, almost thornless, remontant rose, 'Crépuscule', that I had also recommended for growing through a fruit tree in a different garden. It would look stunning growing with the golden climbing hop

(*Humulus lupulus* 'Aureus'), a fast-growing, deciduous climber.

But the combinations and possibilities for gardening with climbing plants are endless, so read on!

♥ My favourites

- *Bignonia capreolata* is a moderately frost-hardy climber often found in old country gardens in the New England area of New South Wales, around Armidale, Walcha and Tamworth. It is particularly helpful in autumn, when other flowering plants are getting ready to take a winter break. The late summer to autumn flowers are followed by pod-like fruit.
- *Campsis grandiflora*, the Chinese trumpet climber, is deciduous. It is not scented but its brilliant, deep apricot blooms look striking as they flower throughout summer and autumn against a grey or putty-coloured background.
- *Cissus rhombifolia*, grape ivy, with its diamond-shaped, coarsely toothed leaves, hails from tropical America and is a less vigorous species than the Australian native *C. antarctica*, the kangaroo vine. This twining climber is fantastic for providing dense shade as well as seclusion. It reaches about 4 m.
- The beautiful *Clytostoma callistegioides*, with its veined, lilac and cream, trumpet-shaped flowers in late spring and summer, is native to South America and was formerly included in the genus *Bignonia*. Water well in summer; provide sun to half shade, well-drained soil and good support.
- Carolina jessamine (*Gelsemium sempervirens*),

Opposite: The clematis 'Red Corona'.

1. The bright tones of the climbing hop *Humulus lupulus* 'Aureus'.
2. *Campsis grandiflora*.
3. *Mandevilla amabilis* 'Radiance'.
4. *Rosa laevigata*.
5. *Solandra maxima*.

from the southern states of the United States, flowers with scented yellow trumpets in spring. Take care: all parts of this plant are poisonous.

- Hoyas (*Hoya carnosa*) are gloriously scented, waxy flowered climbers that love being pot bound. Wonga-Belle gardens, at Wonga Beach in Far North Queensland, houses a range of the hoya vine, including the large-flowered, deep red *H. macgillivrayi*. Don't prune off spent flowers as they re-flower on the same flower spur.
- The golden climbing hop (*Humulus lupulus* 'Aureus') features bright, yellow to lime-green, toothed leaves which are divided into three to five lobes and hot-pink flowers like those of an ivy geranium. An invaluable deciduous plant as it provides dense mid-summer shade, it dies back in winter, ready to be cut down and tidied up. You can grow it up through another plant— anything that can survive its exuberance. It loves frost but will also grow in a warm climate. You could try growing it with a cerise-flowering rose like the much-loved thornless *Rosa* 'Zéphirine Drouhin'. This luminous twining climber also looks great on a rusted or 'antiqued' tripod, to light up a dark or dreary corner of the garden. It does take a little time to cut down and dispose of, so it's a bit of extra work. But then again, we don't want maintenance-free gardening, do we?
- The moonflower (*Ipomoea alba*) can be rampant, but its beautiful crepe-paper flowers are so heavily scented that it is hard to resist. It's quite easy to pull out.
- Jasmine is among the loveliest of all climbers. There are about 200 species of jasmine. While the common jasmine, *Jasminum polyanthum*, is thought of by many as a weed, it is almost the first plant to flower in spring. No matter where in the world I might encounter it, the scent of this jasmine will always transport me to a warm early-August day in Sydney, when fences, gates and banks across the harbour city are covered in this white and pink-flowered scrambler, herald-ing an end to winter. It's best to plant it where it can be well contained—ideally in a strong pot.
- Another favourite is the Chinese star jasmine (*Trachelospermum jasminoides*), which is also greatly loved by gardeners in frost-free climates. It covers walls and fences with its starry white flowers and fills the air with sweet scent in October and November. It is also an easygoing and generous plant to cover any retaining wall that may be of less-than-perfect beauty.

- Sweet peas (*Lathyrus* spp.) are among the loveliest of flowers, reminding many of us of a simpler time, when seeds and cuttings were exchanged by our mothers across the front fence, resulting in a garden style that was consistent from suburb to suburb and from decade to decade.

While St Patrick's Day may be an excuse for many to drink green beer and indulge in a very long lunch, many of us were brought up to believe that, in the southern hemisphere, the day on which the Irish honour the saint who banished the snake is the date by which you should have planted your sweet peas. However, it is now accepted that Anzac Day, in late April, is the final date by which they must go in—and that this later date is, in fact, preferable in more humid climates.

This fast-growing annual, aptly named *Lathyrus odoratus*, was first described by a Sicilian monk, Father Franciscus Cupani, in his book *Hortus Catholicus*, published in 1697. In 1699 Cupani sent seed to Dr Robert Uvedale, a botany-obsessed master at Enfield Grammar School in England, who was described as having 'the greatest and choicest collection of exotic greens … anywhere in the land'. Uvedale was part of the lively horticultural exchange taking place at the time between scholars, leading families and plant enthusiasts. According to historian Richard Bisgrove in his book *The English Garden*, Uvedale 'devoted so much attention to his collection of exotics that he was threatened with dismissal from his post'. We can all sympathise. Uvedale was so taken with the whimsical blooms that he popularised the sweet pea, and by the mid-eighteenth century there were pink, purple, white and bicolour forms available.

Sweet peas were 'all the rage' in Australian gardens early in the twentieth century, and by

1923 the horticultural company Yates was offering more than 100 different varieties. Father Cupani's original, small-flowered purple and maroon specimen can still be found in old country gardens, and seed has been passed on to Sydney's Botanic Gardens. As well, thanks to Yates, it is again available, marketed as 'Original', and enjoys that wonderful perfume that will transport you back to your childhood. 'Colorcade' is also a traditional favourite, with its mix of early-blooming, brightly coloured stems.

In association with New Zealand plant breeder Dr Keith Hammett, Yates has developed a selection of new varieties that concentrate on perfume. There is 'Your Highness' which is described as having a 'scent that is simply majestic'. There is 'Patricia Ann', with unusual flowers in mixed colours, each with fine veins of darker shading rippling through the petals; 'Pink Reflections' is highly perfumed and flowers in shades of pink in late winter and spring. 'Old Fashioned', with a particularly good perfume, flowers later, performing best in areas with a cooler spring.

Dwarf varieties 'Cupid', 'Bijou' and 'Potted Fragrance' work well as ground covers or tumbling from pots and window boxes. The baby of the group is 'Pixie Princess,' a mixed-colour variety that reaches just 22 cm in height. I adore the soft pink 'Lucy' mixed with the stronger pink 'Kiri Te Kanawa' and backed with the pure-white 'Elegance'.

- Mandevilla, often still called dipladenia—and also known as Brazilian jasmine—is a frost-tender climber that is quite restrained and spectacular mixed with another climber. Or grow several mandevilla, in varying shades of pink, together. Try *Mandevilla sanderi* 'Scarlet Pimpernel' with the soft-pink 'Wilma's Choice', 'Red Riding Hood' with the pale pink 'My Fair Lady', 'Crimson Fantasy' or 'White Fantasy'. The new 'Pink Fantasy Mini' tolerates cold better than some of the other cultivars. The new varieties in the Sun Parasol range include 'Tango Twirl', 'Parfait Passion' and 'Crimson Fantasy'.

M. × *amoena* 'Alice du Pont' grows up to 10 m and produces clusters of large deep apricot to cherry-coloured blooms. They all love being grown in pots and like good watering and regular feeding.

- The Chilean jasmine (*Mandevilla laxa*) produces glorious, scented, white blooms in summer.
- Add pizzazz to a plain pot or mark the changing of the seasons by covering walls in the five-lobed Virginia creeper (*Parthenocissus quinquefolia*) or Boston ivy (*P. tricuspidata*) both of which turn into a mass of brilliant red and orange leaves in autumn. They are easy to grow, frost hardy and demand no special attention. Most importantly they will not damage brickwork that is in good condition. Virginia creeper will also help to keep moisture out of walls.

I like to grow these creepers as a backdrop for other deciduous climbing plants, such as the climbing hydrangea (*H. petiolaris*) which also looks wonderful flowering white against a dark brick wall. In this way you extend the autumn colour and mix up the texture and form of the foliage.

- The evergreen, South African *Podranea ricasoliana* will cover a dividing trellis in its pink, frilled flowers, if in a warm, frost-free climate. Prune in winter after flowering, which lasts from spring to autumn.
- The Rangoon creeper, or red jasmine (*Quisqualis indica*) is a fabulous, very vigorous, evergreen creeper for tropical climates. The flowers are more fragrant at night and flower through summer, opening white and deepening to pink and then red.
- The vigorous golden chalice vine (*Solandra maxima*), also known as Hawaiian lily, is salt and wind tolerant and often seen adorning garages and sturdy fences around the country in coastal gardens in temperate to warm climates. It needs lots of space and strong support to show off its huge fragrant, golden, cup-like flowers, borne on woody stems in spring and summer.
- The potato vine (*Solanum jasminoides*) is an extremely fast-growing frost-hardy vine from Brazil that is covered in pale blue flowers from

Opposite: An antiqued iron gate is a perfect foil for *Rosa* 'Constance Spry', the first rose bred by the English breeder David Austin.

1. At Redding House, *Ficus pumila* is kept under control with regular clipping.
2. *Plumbago auriculata*.

late spring to early autumn. The cultivar 'Album' flowers white. It won't damage structures and can be cut back after blooming. *Solanum wendlandii*, with its huge big bunches of lavender flowers, is spectacular at the height of summer. I love to grow potato vines with the evergreen clematis.

• Stephanotis (*Stephanotis floribunda*), or Madagascan jasmine, is among the most beautiful of the climbers but is, for me at least, also among the most temperamental. It is not vigorous and rather prone to mildews if not growing in enough light, but the clusters of highly fragrant, bell-like flowers are so beautiful that, each year, I am seduced into buying another pot in full flower. With their purity and delicacy the blooms are greatly prized for bridal bouquets.

Grow in dappled sun—a protected northerly aspect is perfect—for flowers from spring to autumn. Tie back long straggly arms and prune for shape and control after flowering, when you should also fertilise, and, if growing in containers, repot.

• There can surely be no greater botanical show-off than the jade vine (*Strongylodon macrobotrys*) from the Philippines, which, despite its breath-taking star quality, is not a prima donna and which flowers from late July to November in the far north of Australia. The red-flowering species, the Flame of the Forest, from Madagascar, also grows at Wonga-Belle gardens, along with the pink species, indigenous to the Indonesian archipelago, through Papua New Guinea and into the Top End of Australia. The honey in the centre of the jade flower is a particular favourite of the male sunbird and also attracts the Cairns birdwing, the world's biggest butterfly. While the jade vine can suffer from nematode (*see* Pests and Diseases), the beauty of this treasure is worth any trouble, as long as you are gardening in a suitable climate.

- The fascinating snail vine (*Vigna caracalla*) looks particularly good wending its way through a tree—*Magnolia × soulangeana*, for instance. The pink and cerise-flowered magnolia is exciting when, in times of drought, it spot flowers to team with the purple and cream spiral racemes of the snail vine. It can become a bit rampant towards the end of summer—so prepare to get out the pruning equipment. It is not difficult to cut back as its stems are not particularly strong.
- The *Vitis* genus contains more than 60 species of shrubs and vines that use tendrils to clamber over pergolas and fences. Most are decorative, with only a few species providing edible fruit (most wine grapes are cultivars of *V. vinifera*). Grapevines provide cooling shade in summer, a canopy under which to enjoy long, laconic luncheons, and—in cold climates—glorious autumn colour before the heart-shaped leaves fall, allowing the sun to warm the house during winter. (*See also* Fruit.)

  The ornamental species most often grown include the Crimson Glory Vine (*V. coignetiae*), a rapid grower from Korea and Japan. Give it lots of room to spread and enjoy its red and orange leaves in autumn. *V. vinifera* 'Purpurea', with its gorgeous purple foliage, is also popular for covering pergolas.
- From India, *Thunbergia grandiflora*, with its glorious flat, orchid-like, drooping blue flowers, is a fast-growing, evergreen climber. Frost tender, it loves humidity.

Care

Sow sweet pea seed when soil temperatures are between 15 and 20 degrees and air temperatures are between 18 and 25 degrees. Sow in a well-watered trench, in sun and preferably north facing, in soil to which aged compost has been added. Some horticulturalists recommend adding lime to sweeten the soil, which should have a pH approaching neutral. Cover with seed-raising mix and try not to water again until seeds have emerged.

Good drainage is the key to successful propagation: water at the base of plants rather than on leaves.

Place small twigs beside plants to guide and support emerging sweet pea seedlings, and pinch back plants as they grow. In English gardens, prunings from hazel, or other trees, are saved to a make decorative upturned baskets as supports. Or create a support by tying three stakes into a teepee and wrapping with horizontal layers of string. As sweet pea buds won't open once picked, pick spikes that have some open blooms.

Mildew and aphids seem to be the major threat to the sweet pea, but both can be controlled with proprietary treatments. Grow the dwarf varieties in pots.

Requirements

The pruning of grapevines is similar to that for wisteria: prune each winter to provide shape and form or to remove the previous year's fruiting canes. New growth is tied in place and all inward-facing shoots are removed. All remaining canes are shortened to two or three buds. Throughout summer gently pull away rampant growth not needed to create the desired frame. (*See* Pruning.)

> **Tip**: Choose climbers that won't invade the mortar between bricks, and don't allow vigorous climbers to hoist themselves up on structures attached to the house. A free-standing structure is the safest way to enjoy strong growers like wisteria (*see also* Wisterias).
>
> Be wary of the small-leaved creeping fig (*Ficus pumila*) which can look stunning but must be kept clipped very hard and flush with the surface on which it is growing to retain the juvenile leaves. If you let the leaves become large and coarse the roots will get stronger and can do great damage.

Conifers

The plants generally referred to as conifers are a huge and diverse group of mostly evergreen trees, shrubs and ground covers contained within several families, more than 70 genera and thousands of species.

Conifers are found in all parts of the world and are recognised by their needle-like or scale-leaves. They range in size from the tiny alpine species to the prostrate junipers and the massive redwoods that are icons of the North American forests.

Widely used to form hedges and ground covers, conifers can also contain banks and slopes, or serve as sentinels, guarding entrances or focusing the eye and the attention. Some conifers make wonderful specimen trees in a large garden. Here then, chosen from a long list of species and cultivated varieties, are a number of favourites.

❤ My favourite specimen trees

AGATHIS

- *Agathis australis*, the New Zealand kauri, and that country's largest native tree, is the only one of the 13 species in the genus *Agathis*—also part of the Araucariaceae family—that will cope with frost.
- *Agathis robusta*, the frost-tender kauri pine, was greatly favoured by early landscapers in the Australian colonies as it was ideal for august plantings on grand country estates.

ARAUCARIA

This ancient genus of 19 species, mostly from the region around New Caledonia but also from Australia, New Guinea and South America, is part of the Araucariaceae family, along with the newly discovered Wollemi Pine. The following are among the best known and most often grown.

- *Araucaria bidwillii*, the bunya pine, is native to two plateaus in Queensland. It has sharp, 5 cm long, pointed leaves and was often planted in

old country gardens. The nuts are popular as bush tucker.

- *Araucaria cunninghamii*, the hoop pine, is native to coastal regions of eastern Australia, from mid New South Wales to Far North Queensland. This fast-growing but long-lived tree is distinguished by grey, horizontal bands, or hoops, on its trunk.
- *Araucaria heterophylla*, the Norfolk Island pine, grows to over 60 m on the cliffs and in the rainforests of Norfolk Island. It is greatly favoured in Australia for beach-front plantings but is also grown as an indoor pot plant.

CEDRUS

These majestic, beautifully shaped conifers—the true cedars—will grow well in warm temperate climates—and, of course, also love cold climates. As they grow to very large trees, be kind and plant them only if you have the space for them to stretch out their arms. They come from Cyprus, Turkey, north-west Africa, Syria, Lebanon and the Himalayas and have wonderful cones that are somewhat like tennis balls.

- *Cedrus atlantica* 'Glauca' has elegant blue-grey needle-like leaves.
- *Cedrus deodara*, the Himalayan deodar, hails from the region spanning Afghanistan to Nepal and grows to more than 60 m in the wild. In rich soil, and with good rainfall, it is fast growing; let its

Opposite: The swamp cypress thrives in Longstock Gardens in the south of England.

gorgeous, elegant branches weep down across the ground.

- *Cedrus libani*, the architectural 'cedar of Lebanon', was introduced into Britain before 1680, where, with judicious tree surgery, it makes an arresting feature in several large and well-known gardens.

CRYPTOMERIA

The Sugi, or Japanese cedar, a single-species genus, and its cultivars like rich soil and full sun.

- *Cryptomeria japonica*, the Japanese red cedar, a pyramidal, tall-growing conifer, takes on russet tones in autumn.

> **Tip:** Several dwarf varieties—such as *Cryptomeria japonica* 'Nana' and 'Elegans'—make handy corner posts or 'punctuation points' at the end of paths or can serve to break up borders.

GINKGO

Perhaps the strangest of all the conifers, and among the oldest, the ginkgo is in fact a fossil. *Ginkgo biloba*, the maidenhair tree, will grow to some 100 m in its favoured conditions: a cool climate, deep soils and plenty of water. In autumn its leaves turn a rich butter-yellow.

> **Tip:** The leaves of the ginkgo can be dried and added to other herbs, or used alone, to make a herbal tea.

JUNIPERUS

This genus, part of the Cupressaceae family, consists of about 60 species, all slow growing, long lived and relatively drought hardy. Some of the species are prized for their timber.

- *Juniperus chinensis* is native to China and Japan and varies in form and habit.
- *Juniperus chinensis* 'Blaauw' grows to just 1.5 m and is valued for its blue-grey foliage.
- *Juniperus chinensis* 'Spartan' is valued as a feature

tree or as a focal point at the end of a walk or a vista, as it has a columnar form and rich, dark green foliage.

- *Juniperus communis*, the common juniper, is native to the United Kingdom, Europe and North America, and grows to about 6 m in height. It produces green berries, which, when ripened to black, are used to flavour gin. There are many different cultivars to cover a range of different garden uses and situations.
- *Juniperus squamata*, the weeping juniper, has a central trunk and long limbs—some up to 8 m—falling from the crown, giving it the appearance of a tent or child's cubby house! Some of the cultivars form ground covers.

PICEA

The beautiful spruces, a genus of about 45 species, must be among the most elegant of the conifers. Members of the Pinaceae family and from cool climates and high altitudes in the northern hemisphere, the evergreen and slow-growing spruces like rich, acidic soil and good rainfall.

- *Picea abies*, the common spruce or Norway spruce, is your quintessential Christmas tree, although not one to be planted out into a suburban garden after the festive season, as it can reach 60 m.
- *Picea abies* 'Little Gem' is a small and slow-growing form of the Norway spruce.
- *Picea pungens* 'Glauca', the Colorado blue spruce, is slow growing, but the beautiful, conical shape it develops, with layers of horizontal arms with soft, blue-grey needles, make it worth waiting for; a must for any cold-climate garden.

PINUS

A large and very diverse genus incorporating more than 100 species, all native to the northern hemisphere, with only one occurring naturally

> **Tip:** *Picea pungens* 'Glauca' looks wonderful backing a planting of shrubs, including the smoke bush, with its burgundy-toned foliage (*see* Colour).

Grand perfection

Has the grand perfection of a tree ever moved you to tears? It's not often one is overwhelmed by even the most majestic of trees, although one might empathise with plants, speak to them (thank them, even) when they perform generously. At Isola Madre—a garden that covers one of several islands that float in the blue waters of Lake Maggiore, one of the largest of the Italian lakes—you'll see such a tree: a Kashmir cypress, *Cupressus cashmeriana*.

Isola Madre, owned by the Borromeo family of bankers since the fifteenth century, is an island of botanical treasures. It is the site of a family home, while the spectacular gardens on the nearby Borromean Isola Bella have always been used as a showpiece for entertaining.

Surrounded by mountains capped with snow for much of the year, Lake Maggiore is, to many, the most picturesque of these northern Italian lakes. It is a little less frenetic than its neighbour, Lake Como, but no less dramatic. Extending into Switzerland, Lake Maggiore has long been a holiday destination for Europeans, and grand gardens in the English landscape style became the fashion from the seventeenth century. There, just as in the United Kingdom, plant hunters were sponsored by leading families who received, in return, dividends in the form of seeds of the botanical bounty.

Isola Madre enjoys a climate several degrees milder than the gardens on the shore, just a 20-minute ferry ride away, and provides an amenable home to horticultural treasures from all over the world. The Kashmir cypress there is said to be the largest in Europe, towering to more than 30 m. More than two centuries old, the long, glaucous tendrils of this specimen weep softly to the ground. It stands in front of the palazzo, which, renovated into its present incarnation in the early sixteenth century by the architect Pellegrino Pellegrini, has been open to visitors since 1978.

I want to share with you the recipe for a delicious risotto that I was served at a restaurant on Isola Bella.

Risotto mantecato with baby shrimp and fava, or broad, beans (serves 6)

400 g peeled fava, or broad, beans

400 g shelled, uncooked, baby shrimp (or prawns) or a white boneless fish

2 cloves garlic, finely chopped

Extra-virgin olive oil

Finely chopped parsley

Dry white wine (about ½ a glass)

Salt and pepper

1 small onion, finely chopped

100 g butter

500 g Carnaroli rice

Fish stock (up to 500 ml)

Chicken and beef stock (up to 1 L)

40 g grated parmesan cheese

Method

Blanch the beans in boiling water; let them cool, then peel the exterior skin. Cook half of the cleaned, peeled beans in salted water. Keep the remaining beans aside. When the beans are well cooked, whip them with some of their cooking water so as to obtain an homogenous and smooth puree. Keep aside in a cool area.

In a copper pan, sauté the shelled shrimp, which have been previously sliced lengthwise (or the boneless fish) with finely chopped garlic, extra-virgin olive oil and parsley. Thin with some dry white wine, add a pinch of salt and set aside.

Sauté the onion with a knob of butter in a heavy saucepan; add the rice and toast lightly. Wet with some fish stock and bring to a boil. As the liquid is absorbed, add more stock, alternating between the fish and the chicken and beef stock, and stirring continuously. (Italian cooks say the rice should be 'calling out' for the stock!) When the rice is half cooked, add the sautéed seafood with its broth. Five minutes before the rice is ready, add the whole fava, or broad, beans that had been set aside.

When the rice is al dente, whisk in a knob of butter, some grated parmesan cheese and a drop of extra-virgin olive oil. Add some salt and pepper. Serve immediately, while it is still steaming, with a spoonful of the pureed beans.

south of the equator, the pines are mostly large trees, although several species are used in Japanese gardens, clipped to represent clouds and mountains.

- *Pinus bungeana*, the rare lacebark pine, was brought to Australia from central China in 1992 and can now be seen in the Royal Botanic Gardens, Melbourne.
- *Pinus cembroides*, native to Mexico, produces edible nuts that are high in protein.
- *Pinus pinaster*, the maritime pine, is found near the Mediterranean coast in France and Italy and has a distinctive, flat to gently rounded canopy. It likes sandy soil and frost-free climates. Resin is extracted from its trunk.
- *Pinus pinea*, the stone pine or umbrella pine, from which the delicious pine nut is gathered, is native to southern Europe. With its flat top and architectural form, it adds *gravitas* to any garden.
- *Pinus wallichiana*, the Bhutan pine, bears long needles that grow in clumps of five.

THUJA

- *Thuja plicata*, the western red cedar, is part of a genus of five species and a member of the Cupressaceae family. Growing to some 20 m, it is native to the west coast of North America and enjoys cool to warm temperate climates, plenty of moisture and deep, rich soils. It bears flattened sprays of mid- to dark green, tough leaflets which have a pineapple fragrance when crushed. It makes a beautiful specimen tree and is used as hedging, while its wood is prized for roofing and carpentry.

WOLLEMIA

- *Wollemia nobilis*, the only species in the third genus in the Araucariaceae family, will reach over 30 m in the right conditions. The juvenile leaves are soft and fern like, while the adult leaves are mid-green and stiff. It is native to warm temperate forests of the Wollemi National Park, 150 km north-west of Sydney, but will cope with an

1. A collection of conifers at Hillview at Exeter in the Southern Highlands of New South Wales.
2. A quiet corner at Thuya Gardens, in the village of Northeast Harbor, Maine, on the east coast of the United States of America.
3. The russet autumn tones of *Cryptomeria japonica*.
4. A beautiful specimen: a mature *Araucaria bidwillii*.
5. A lookout through stands of northern white cedar (*Thuya occidentalis*) at Thuya Gardens.
6. A glorious example of *Pinus palustris*.

- *Sequoia sempervirens*, the Californian redwood, native to the west coast of North America, can grow to over 110 m in just 20 years, making it suitable only for parks and extremely large gardens.

SEQUOIADENDRON

- *Sequoiadendron giganteum*, the wellingtonia or big tree, like the *Sequoia* a single-species genus, is native to North America and is suitable only for a very large garden that enjoys deep, rich soil.

extraordinary range of temperatures, from minus 5 degrees Celsius to a hot 45 degrees.

❧ Planting

I did not realise how beautiful, and how useful, conifers could be until travelling through Italy, with a landscaper's focus, a decade or so ago. I saw clearly then how the Renaissance palette of those three essential elements of good gardens—water,

A rare find

Wollemia nobilis was thought to be extinct until discovered by ranger David Noble in the Wollemi National Park, some 150 km north-west of Sydney, in 1994. The tale is as breathtaking as those of the plant hunters of the eighteenth century who risked their lives to bring us the botanical treasures that we take for granted today. The Wollemi pine is now available for purchase in pots, and becoming popular as Christmas trees, but, growing to over 36 m in its natural warm temperate environment, it is not for most backyards.

A 'living fossil'

Metasequoia glyptostroboides, lost to the world for some 800 years, was previously known only as fossil remains. It was found again in 1941, in China, another example of horticulture bringing together different worlds and different cultures.

stone and evergreens—could be put to wonderful effect in Australia.

These evocatively scented evergreens—for only a few conifers are deciduous—have many different applications in garden design. Conifers make wonderful specimen trees, or they can stand, dark and mysterious, as background to light-foliaged or variegated trees: such treatment was one of the signatures of the Danish-born Australian garden designer Paul Sorensen (1891–1983).

Deciduous conifers

There are just a handful of deciduous conifers, adding autumn colour and their distinct form to any landscape.

- *Metasequoia glyptostroides*, the dawn redwood, is a member of the Taxodiaceae family and the only species in the genus. It is a rapid grower in

Tip: Danish-born garden designer Paul Sorensen was famous in Australia for his painterly use of conifers such as the Bhutan cypress, *Cupressus torulosa*. These he would illuminate by 'a shaft of light' created by planting a silver elm, or a variegated tulip tree, in its foreground.

its preferred conditions: moist but well-drained, rich soils in temperate to cool climates.

- *Taxodium distichum*, the swamp cypress, is native to the swamps of Florida, where it rises from still waters in mysterious, dark copses. Its delicate, feathery leaves are an apple-green, turning to russet in autumn, before falling.
- *Taxodium ascendens* 'Nutans', the pond cypress, and a smaller cousin of *T. distichum*, grows to about 20 m, with branches becoming pendulous with age. It does not insist on growing in water, however, and will perform happily in damp parts of the garden.

Sentinels and punctuation points

- *Cupressus sempervirens*, the pencil pine, is the conifer you may have seen in the Italian countryside. It reaches up to 15 m and bears green cones which become red to brown. With a vigorous root system, care needs to be taken with its placement in the garden.
- *Cupressus sempervirens* 'Nitschke's Needle', smaller than the species, is useful for city gardens where it grows into upright green pillars, reflecting, perhaps, the lines of nearby office towers.
- *Juniperus communis* 'Compressa' is slow growing, becoming a column of 1 m.
- *Thuja occidentalis* 'Pyramidalis Compacta' grows to a deep green, compact column of up to 3 m.
- *Thuja occidentalis* 'Columna' is a fastigiate conifer: use it to direct a visitor along any particular path.

Ground covers

- *Juniperus conferta*, which loves sandy soils, is a prostrate conifer that can spread to almost 1 m.
- *Juniperus × media* (syn. × *pfitzeriana*) cultivars are often used as a ground cover in large areas in public places, as they are tough and fast growing, but, as they have a most unpleasant smell, it remains a mystery to me why any one of a number of more suitable species is not chosen instead!
- *Juniperus procumbens*, from western China, and its smaller growing cultivar 'Nana', form spreading, prostrate ground covers with soft, blue-green leaves.
- *Juniperus squamata* 'Blue Carpet', with its spreading form and blue-green foliage, can be used as a ground cover.

Hedges

- × *Cupressocyparis leylandii* 'Leighton Green', like all plants employed as hedging, needs to be clipped from day one to create a dense and pleasing wall of green. Many councils are considering banning the planting of this conifer, however, as it grows rapidly, blocking neighbours' views and light, and creating much discord. There have been thousands of court cases in Britain over its use!
- *Thuja occidentalis* 'Smaragd', with its fine emerald-green foliage, is better suited to the Australian climate than yew (*Taxus baccata*), popular as a hedging plant in northern hemisphere gardens.

Miniatures

You might showcase a collection of prostrate and miniature conifers such as the grafted junipers, which can look stunning when set into a wide stone terrace.

- *Juniperus squamata* 'Blue Star' is a neat, rounded conifer, reaching just half a metre in height and width.
- *Picea glauca* var. *albertiana* 'Conica': unlike the species, this cultivar grows to just over 3 m, forming a neat cone with soft, blue-green foliage.
- In Japanese gardens the Japanese black pine (*Pinus thunbergii*) and the Japanese red pine (*P. densiflora*), with their long, elegant needles, are often pruned and shaped to create layers of horizontal limbs.
- The dwarf mountain pine (*P. mugo*) is native to the mountain areas of Central Europe. While it can grow to 8 m it is often dwarfed by winds and is popular for use in bonsai.

✿ Care

Maintain healthy trees by keeping roots cool with a thick layer of mulch kept away from the trunk of the tree, where it could cause collar rot.

You should not hard-prune conifers: if you want to keep them dense, and to a certain height, little and often is the way to go.

The genius of the place

The sight of pencil pines will always bring to mind the Tuscan countryside, where they contribute so much to the 'Genius of the Place', in the words of the English essayist and poet Alexander Pope as written in a letter to his patron, Lord Burlington, in 1731. Nature and art collide successfully in this part of Italy, where the ridges of each rolling hill are emphasised by stands of *Cupressus sempervirens*, leading the eye into the distance and the mind to ponder what might lie beyond.

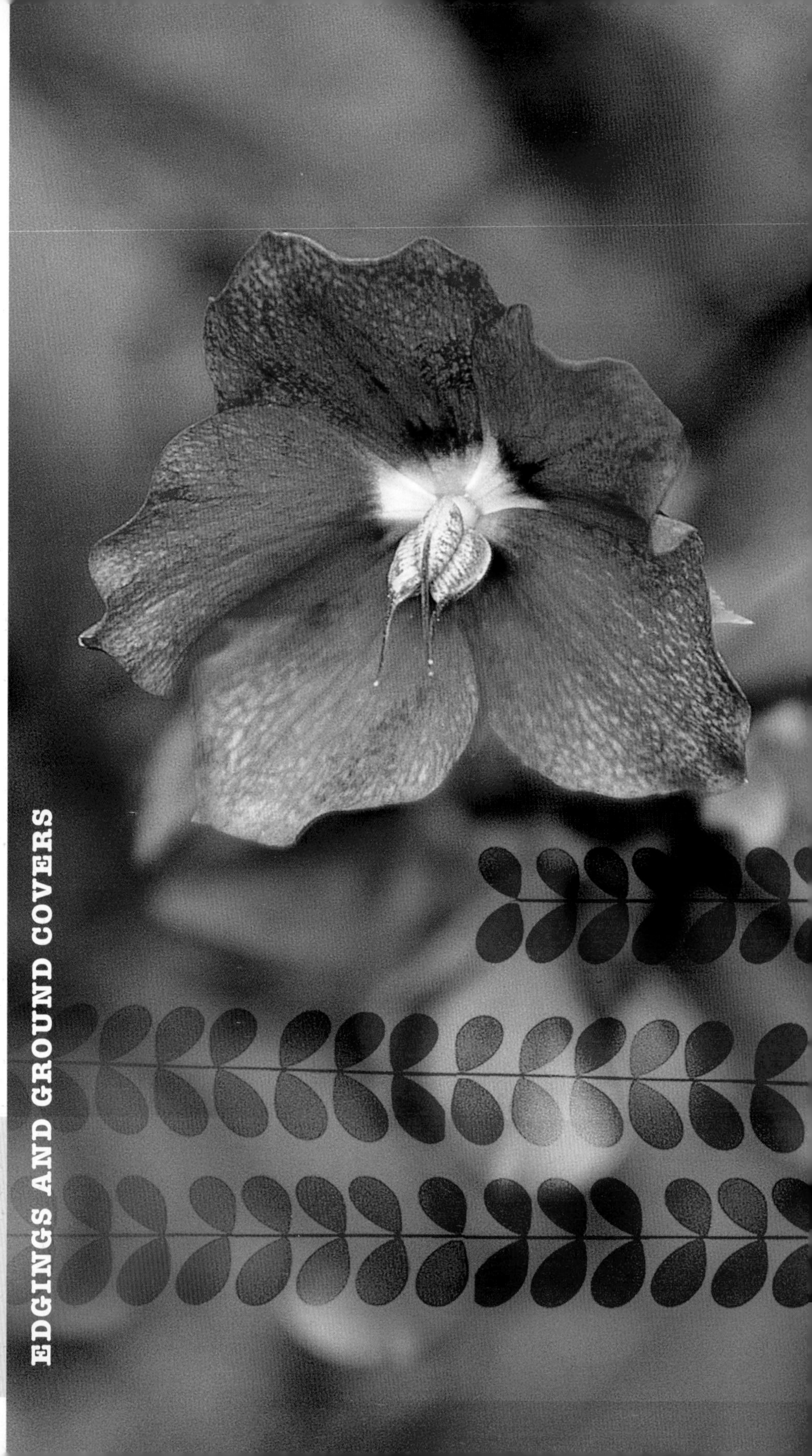

EDGINGS AND GROUND COVERS

Edgings

If you are the sort of gardener who insists on an immaculately neat garden, to you an edge will be a hard cement or brick barrier, preventing plants and soil from stepping out of line (*see* Hardscaping). The most restful garden, however, is often one that strikes a fine balance between being highly maintained—perhaps even strait-jacketed—and one that looks so relaxed that the innocent observer might assume (wrongly, of course) that it is maintenance free.

Some of the most pleasing garden vistas are created by allowing plants to make themselves at home, allowing the garden—as the writer Beatrice Bligh (1916–1973) put it—'to gain with age that priceless air of inevitability and nonchalance'. Some plants love spreading out, creating spontaneous edgings that look as if nature had placed them there. Make friends with these species: they will reduce your workload, allowing you to garden when the mood takes you, rather than finding yourself controlled by a demanding, high-maintenance garden.

❤ My favourite edgings

- Among the best of the edgers are the dwarf agapanthus, such as the white 'Snowball', the blue-flowering 'Peter Pan' and the variegated 'Tinkerbell'—all of them attractive and drought resistant. (*See* Agapanthus.)
- *Ajuga reptans*, the bugle flower, with its short spires of azure-blue flowers, when grown in semi-shade and with a certain amount of water, makes an excellent, spreading, edging plant (*see also* Borders).
- The matting *Dianthus*, such as 'Mrs Sinkins', make good edgers, with the bonus, in cool temperate to cold climates, of wonderfully fragrant, blush-pink blooms in spring. Even in hot and humid climates, where flowering is unlikely, the steel-grey foliage and matting habit are useful.

- Matting thyme and other herbs, such as wild strawberries, were popular with colonial gardeners in New South Wales in the earliest days of European settlement in Australia, a time when box (*Buxus* spp.) was hard to obtain; when box did arrive in the colony, it was expensive.
- *Liriope muscari* is a good alternative to mondo grass and has narrow, strappy leaves. Tough and waterwise, it is happy in sun or shade. 'Evergreen Giant' has dark green leaves, while 'Variegata' has green and gold striped leaves and blue to purple flowers. There is a smart white-flowering form, the variegated 'Monroe White', while the new 'Isabella' is a delicate pink with fine foliage.
- Ivy-leaved geraniums (*Pelargonium* spp.) also make a low-care edger in warm and dry climates. They will need ruthless cutting back, though, if you don't want them to scramble over the entire border.
- The tough-as-nails mondo grass (*Ophiopogon japonicus*) is an easy-to-grow edging plant, although in warm climates it can become a nuisance. It likes sun or shade and grows to about 20 cm high. I love the black form, *O. planiscapus* 'Nigrescens', when teamed with the hot-pink flowers of salvia and backed with euphorbias, with their lime-green flower-heads.

There are also good reasons for carefully considering the use of ground covers in your garden. Apart from looking smart and creating a cohesive

Opposite: A purple-flowering hellebore.

look, ground covers conserve moisture in the soil and suppress weeds. They can cascade down less-than-pretty retaining walls and hold banks together, all of which helps to reduce maintenance.

Ground covers of grasses (*see also* Grasses) create a contemporary, easy-maintenance feel, while forget-me-nots, violets, ajuga and erigeron contribute to a woodland design.

Your use of ground-covering plants is limited only by your imagination, as is the palette of species you can employ, so I will discuss here just a few of my favourites.

♥ My favourite ground covers

- Top of my list must be the Chinese star jasmine (*Trachelospermum jasminoides*) and its cousin *T. asiaticum*, which has smaller flowers and a more dense growth. Both are loved as climbers, in warm climates covering ugly fences and decorating railings and filling the suburbs with scent. Planted in multiples, they will quickly cover a difficult area or hold together a bank. They are not frost tolerant.
- Ivy—usually the common ivy, *Hedera helix*—needs to be considered with care, as it can become rampant, even damaging mortar in brick structures. However, it is an excellent choice for covering tough areas where grass will not grow. Some of the cultivars, such as the variegated, burgundy-leaved 'Atropurpurea' and the yellow-splashed 'Goldheart', will be less aggressive than the species.
- The beach bean (*Canavalia rosea*) from tropical and subtropical coastal regions of the world and with luscious, large leaves and pink, pea-like flowers, is a vigorous ground cover for sandy soils. It is used in the stabilisation of sand dunes.

1. A swathe of ground covers at Lanleigh on the Northern Tablelands of New South Wales.
2. *Asteriscus maritimus*.
3. The tough *Liriope muscari*.
4. The endangered *Encephalartos lebombonsis*.

- The white-flowered snow-in-summer (*Cerastium tomentosum*), with its soft, grey-green foliage, is a useful ground cover, particularly effective cascading over low rock walls. It teams well with the blue-flowered *Convolvulus sabatius*.
- The South African salt- and heat-loving succulent commonly known as pigface, *Lampranthus* spp., is a creeping ground cover that thrives in the harshest of conditions, including in the face of salt winds. The flowers, usually in hot colours, can be large or, in the case of *L. veredenbergensis*, tiny, held on a compact, small-leaved plant.
- The variegated aluminium plant, *Lamium maculatum* 'White Nancy', is a member of the mint family and is native to Europe, Asia and Africa. It is frost hardy and tough, isn't fussy about soil and loves the sun.
- The prostrate evergreen *Cotoneaster dammeri* has little white flowers in the spring and red berries in the autumn. *C. horizontalis* makes a stunning ground cover: its horizontal, flattened branches look particularly effective trained along a retaining wall. Its pink summer flowers are followed by a showy mass of red fruit and orange, red and pink autumn foliage.
- In cool climates allow *Cyclamen hederifolium* to sheet over the ground.
- Hellebores, particularly the most common, *Helleborus* × *hybridus*, quickly mass out to form a rich, easy-care carpet that flowers for months in reds, whites and pinks, in single and double blooms. And imagine a carpet of rich burgundy autumn leaves that have fallen from a liquidambar, brightened with emerging snow-white *H. niger* in mid-winter!
- *Hydrangea petiolaris* is not only a good climber but an effective ground cover, as you may have seen demonstrated at Kew Gardens in London.
- Many roses can be used effectively as ground covers. But when choosing from the several that work well in this way, think about how you will remove spent flowers to keep the display looking its best. You can't go past the Flower Carpet series for easy care and good looks: I love the 'White Meidiland' roses, with their restful, deep green leaves and quartered flowers, reminiscent of the old-fashioned Moss rose. (*See* Roses.)
- Massed periwinkle, *Vinca minor*, is a saviour in large gardens, particularly if water is an issue; and this small-flowered species is better behaved than the larger-flowered *V. major* which can, in certain conditions, run amok!
- The ground-covering moss *Scleranthus biflorus* hails from New Zealand. It masses out with a lime-green oval leaf and tiny white flowers but dislikes humidity.

♥ My favourite native ground covers

- The newly developed *Adenanthos* 'Green Carpet' is a low, prostrate, spreading ground cover. It has green deeply divided leaves along the stems that spread horizontally, and red flowers that attract birds. The species, with its pink to purple flowers for months from spring, occurs naturally from south of Perth almost to the south coast.
- The prostrate grevilleas will also quickly cover a bank. *Grevillea* 'Poorinda Royal Mantle' flowers with red toothbrush-like blooms and bronze foliage. Also think about *G.* 'Gingin Gem' and *G.* 'Bronze Rambler'.
- *Hibbertia scandens* is a yellow-flowering ground cover that will also thrive in salty, sandy coastal gardens.
- The Australian native *Myoporum parvifolium*, with starry white flowers, is a spreading, prostrate shrub that copes well with tough conditions.
- *Scaevola aemula*, the fan flower, forms a coarse-leaved, ground-hugging matt with blue flowers from early spring to late summer. Native to coastal areas, it copes with salt winds and light frosts. Use it also to cascade down a retaining wall. *Scaevola* 'Summer Time Blues' flowers for months in bright, mid-blue blooms.
- In shady areas the native violet, *Viola hederacea*, is a good choice, requiring little maintenance and quickly forming a dense green mat with lilac and white flowers.

FRUIT

Fruit

In my garden in the chilly Southern Highlands of New South Wales, a harvest luncheon held each Easter soon became a celebration of all good things produced in the garden. Lunch was based around what could be grown—from late tomatoes, picked and bottled a few months before, to the hazelnuts harvested that morning and tossed raw into the salad, which had come from the vegie garden. Pears always featured, as did baked quince, served with one of a variety of meats, and the apples from the 'long walk' were served sliced, with cheese, or were baked into an aromatic Tarte Tatin (*see* Apples).

Leonie Norrington's whimsical book *Tropical Food Gardens* is dedicated to her 'Grandma Eve', to whom you just have to warm. Norrington writes that her grandmother:

came to live in Darwin from New Guinea straight after the Second World War and grew food with a passion. She befriended the local Chinese market gardeners and swapped seeds and advice. She secreted plants out of government trials in her bra. She built food gardens around all the shacks and army camps she lived in, and until she died forced advice, cuttings and her passion for growing food on everyone she met.

A true gardener!

Such sharing is, of course, the essence of gardening, whether you are pressing posies of flowers upon friends, seeds and cuttings on neighbours, or vegetables and fruit on almost anyone who will accept them! Here are just a few of my favourites.

♥ My favourites

AVOCADOS

Persea americana, the tropical avocado, is a medium to large tree, fast growing and frost tender, with deep green leaves followed by large elliptical fruit throughout summer.

Requirements

Avocados like rich, well-drained soil and need plenty of water when the fruit is developing. While most cultivars are self-pollinating, growing two or more cultivars will ensure better cropping. Make sure you buy grafted trees, not those grown from seed, which may take years to fruit. Pick fruit when still hard and allow to ripen indoors.

Care

Avocado trees can suffer from powdery mildew. Counter by drilling several holes in the trunk so that a liquid phosphorus, applied with a large syringe, can be taken up over a period of three hours. Prune simply to shape, or to remove crossing branches.

BANANAS

The parent of most eating bananas is *Musa acuminata*, native to tropical Asia. The fruit is borne at the end of one of a series of fleshy stems, which dies after fruiting. Cut back the dead trunk and allow new stems to emerge from the base. Pick bunches when fruit is still green and hang in an airy spot to mature. Propagate by dividing the bulky corm beneath the soil.

CITRUS

The growing of citrus is hardly a new or unusual

topic, but surely every garden book—even a companion that does not aspire to be all-encompassing—will include the main species within this large group, not all of which are true members of the genus *Citrus*. The genus, which is part of the rue family, Rutaceae, and contains about 15 species, originated in South-East Asia and is found south to New Caledonia but has been cultivated in Europe since before the time of Christ.

If you have visited Italian or French gardens around the Mediterranean you will have seen citrus used in many different ways: as shady avenues, trained to cover metal arbours, or in Versailles-style wooden tubs or terracotta pots. In seventeenth and eighteenth-century Europe, orangeries—elaborately designed and heated glasshouses—were built to cultivate the exotic fruit. The French king Louis XIV is said to have cultivated lemon trees in solid-silver tubs at his palace at Versailles.

Cumquats

Introduced to the western world by the plant hunter Robert Fortune (1812–1880) from China, cumquats are very decorative and usually easy to grow, although they are frost tender. They can differ slightly in appearance from the oval Nagami (*Fortunella margarita*) to the round, Marumi (*Fortunella japonica*) but, for me, their best feature

is the wonderful scent of their winter blossom. In my garden small boys, and the sulphur-crested white cockatoos, love to pull off the glistening golden fruit, leaving them to create a squishy mess on the paving!

> **Tip:** Cumquat trees make elegant formal standards to decorate courtyards or to stand sentinel at entrances—and the fruit makes excellent marmalade.

Grapefruit

The grapefruit, *Citrus paradisi*, loves the warmer climates.
- *Citrus paradisi* 'Marsh Seedless' is perhaps the most popular variety.
- *Citrus paradisi* 'Ruby' has red-fleshed fruit.
- *Citrus paradisi* 'Thompson's Pink' also bears red-fleshed fruit.

Lemons

There are three main cultivars of lemon (*Citrus limon*) which, in general, prefers a warm southern Mediterranean-style climate with mild winters.
- *Citrus limon* 'Eureka' is almost thornless and bears fruit from spring through to autumn; it is the variety most often grown in warm coastal areas.

Preserved lemons

My recipe for preserved lemons originally comes from Stephanie Alexander: over the years I have added to it to make it mine. These salty, unique lemons can make the plainest cut of meat, or rice dishes or the simplest recipe, special. I must have given dozens of bottles away as presents over the past decade. Tie them up with ribbon and attach a hand-written card detailing your favourite recipe, and you will be a welcome guest!

	Method
Quantity of fresh lemons	Into clean, hot, glass jars pack quartered and
Bay leaves or Kaffir lime leaves	deseeded lemons, layered with the rock salt, the bay
Whole peppercorns	or lime leaves, a peppercorn or two, one or two
Whole cloves	cloves per jar, and a small cinnamon stick. Seal and
1 small stick cinnamon, per bottle	store for a month or two (will last for many more).
Rock salt	

- *Citrus limon* 'Lisbon' is a thorny variety bearing large and juicy fruit.
- *Citrus limon* 'Meyer' is thought to be a cross between an orange and a lemon. It is less acidic, tolerates cold and frost, and fruits with smooth, thin skin.
- *Citrus limon* 'Lots a Lemons' is a dwarf form of the 'Meyer' lemon and will reach about 1.5 m.

Limequats
- The limequat (× *Citrofortunella floridana*) is a cross between West Indian Lime and the cumquat *Fortunella* 'Marumi'. It is a small tree requiring less heat than other lime varieties, and bears heavy crops of small, oval, pale yellow fruit.
- *Citrofortunella floridana* 'Eustis' is a good substitute for the lemon or lime and excellent in a pot.

Limes
The lime (*Citrus aurantifolia*) fulfils one of my gardening yardsticks: anything you grow or own should be both useful and beautiful. The scented flowers of the lime are followed by delicious, aromatic, sour fruit that can be used in cooking and in drinks. For some varieties wait until the fruit turns yellow before picking: the flavour will be richer. They like warm temperate to tropical climates, a sunny spot, and, like all citrus, regular fertilising and watering.
- *Citrus aurantifolia*, the Tahitian lime, becomes a small, neat tree, reaching up to 3 m, and bears large, seedless, juicy fruit for much of the year.
- *Citrus australasica* 'Rainforest Pearl', a variety of the Australian finger lime, is a hardy small shrub which bears long, narrow sour fruit useful in Asian cooking.
- *Citrus hystrix*, the Kaffir lime, grows to under 2 m and is suitable, like most citrus, for growing in pots. Pick the leaves to use in Asian recipes.

Mandarins
Growing to up to 4 m tall, mandarins (× *Citrus reticulata*) will tolerate a wide range of climates.
- *Citrus* 'Ellendale', a mandarin and orange cross from Queensland, has very sweet fruit.

- *Citrus reticulata* 'Clementine' is cold tolerant.
- *Citrus* × *tangelo* 'Minneola' is very juicy and the easiest to peel.

Oranges
The orange (*Citrus sinensis*) grows to about 8 m, with glossy green leaves from which waxy white blossom gives out its heavenly scent in spring. Oranges like temperate and warm-temperate climates.
- *Citrus aurantium* is the sour 'Seville' orange best suited for making marmalade.
- *Citrus sinensis* 'Valencia' is frost hardy.
- *Citrus sinensis* 'Washington Navel' bears large, sweet, brilliant orange fruit throughout winter and, with its dense habit, is very suitable for hedging. 'Joppa' is your choice if you live in a tropical climate.
- *Citrus sinensis* 'Harvard Blood' and 'Arnold Blood' have exotic red flesh and a tangy flavour.

General requirements for citrus
To avoid thick skins and sour, dry fruit, water well at fruiting time. However, citrus hate being waterlogged, which will cause leaves to drop. Any uneven watering can cause fruit drop.

Care
If you can discipline yourself to do it, break off young fruit in the first three years to encourage a strong plant. Then thin out heavy crops to ensure better quality fruit.

For a good look—and to prevent fruit from being near the ground and for protection against disease—trim the base of the tree canopy.

Prune all citrus just to keep them in shape, cutting out any misshapen, crowding or crossing branches. As always, follow with fertilising (alternate between chicken manure and citrus food), watering and mulching.

Planting
All citrus make smart espaliers, although you need to keep them healthy, as this method of pruning will expose any less-than-perfect branches or leaves (*see* Pruning).

FIGS

Figs (*Ficus carica*) come into their own in late summer, when the shops are full of the rich, sweet fruit. Native to Turkey and western Asia, these small, deciduous trees are perfect for a courtyard in temperate and warm temperate climates.

• *Ficus carica* 'Black Mission' is the luscious black fig grown in California.
• *Ficus carica* 'Brown Turkey' has purple fruit and pink flesh.
• *Ficus carica* 'Smyrna' is, unlike most other varieties, not self-fertile.

Requirements

Figs enjoy a variety of soils and climates but do not like early winter frosts, and do not enjoy being allowed to dry out, which will cause the fruits to drop before maturity.

Care

Prune trees in winter, and propagate from the prunings. The non-edible figs are to be treated with great care as most have aggressive roots that will head for your drains.

> **Tip:** A favourite entrée, or supper dish, comprises a fresh, perfectly ripe fig, served with thinly sliced prosciutto and a slice of goat's cheese; top with a few walnut halves and a drizzle of your best olive oil. Serve on a bed of fresh baby spinach on a plain white plate. What could be easier, more healthy, or more delicious?

GRAPEVINES

Grown for millennia, both table and wine grapes are most often cultivars of *Vitis vinifera*, a species native to the warmer parts of Europe and the Mediterranean. It is frost hardy, although in marginal areas, such as the Champagne district of France (with an average temperature of just 10 degrees Celsius, the coldest wine-growing area in the world), late frosts at bud burst are an annual worry,

and in some years devastate a large percentage of the crop. Champagne is made with just three grape varieties: the white variety 'Chardonnay' and the black-skinned grapes 'Pinot Noir' and 'Pinot Meunier'.

Among the cultivars of table grapes are 'Albany Surprise'.

Requirements

All grapevines enjoy rich, well-drained soil and dry summers as humidity will encourage mildew problems. In many wine-growing areas, including in the sherry region of Spain, irrigation is outlawed, to concentrate sugars and flavour.

Care

Grapevines are often grafted onto *Vitis labrusca* rootstock, which is resistant to the root aphid *Phylloxera*, a scourge of grape-growing regions around the world.

LYCHEES

Redolent of the exotic places of the Far East, the scented fruit of the lychee can be eaten fresh, added to meat dishes or used in salads. The crusty, red outer skin is easily cracked to reveal the translucent creamy flesh.

• *Litchi chinensis*, a single-species genus from the warm south of China and South-East Asia, grows well in the heat and humidity of Queensland. It is an evergreen tree and reaches about 9 m, with a canopy of up to 4 m in diameter.

Care

Plant lychees where they will be sheltered from the wind and in deep soil, and fertilise and water regularly, easing off when the tree is fruiting.

MANGOES

Mangoes are the fruit of my childhood: our back garden on the Gold Coast had two large mango trees, to which I would escape to read a book, or simply to hide when household chores threatened. I never tired of eating that fragrant, deep yellow fruit, and we always stayed in bathing costumes to bite into the entire fruit, allowing the juice

1. Espaliered apple at Wychwood nursery in northern Tasmania.
2. Step over hedge of apple at Wychwood.

to drip down onto the grass. Everyone should experience that at least once in their life!

Requirements

The mango (*Mangifera indica*) likes a frost-free climate with summer rain. In Australia, growing them further south than Coffs Harbour, on the New South Wales coast, is marginal. The evergreen trees, which grow to some 24 m, are self-pollinating, and the tiny green flowers appear on stiff sprays. Fruit is sometimes borne only every second year.

Care

Apply a complete fertiliser to help prevent fruit dropping.

MORINDAS

I would love to be able to grow *Morinda citrifolia* in my garden, for friends swear that the expensive noni juice produced from the small tree, a member of the Rubiaceae family, assists with arthritis and all sorts of aches and pains. Variously called the Indian mulberry, the Tahitian noni or the great morinda, it is native to South-East Asia but has spread through India to the South Pacific. It is therefore unlikely to grow well in warm temperate climates, although it is said to tolerate a wide range of soils and to flower and fruit all year.

MULBERRIES

The taste and scent of a perfectly ripe mulberry (*Morus nigra*) also takes me back to my childhood, when we children would be invited by our elderly neighbours to help ourselves to the juicy red fruit from their mulberry tree. We would return home with clothes, hands and lips stained ruby red, and bearing clutches of leaves to feed our silkworms, which were in shoeboxes under the bed, strictly against the instructions of our mother. (We certainly reaped the silk from the cocoons spun by these creatures, although it is the white mulberry that is the traditional food source for silkworms in China and Iran.)

There are 10 species in this ancient genus, which originated in East Asia but was also culti-vated in ancient Islamic gardens and in Europe. Brought to England by the Romans—along with figs, peaches and almonds—the mulberry bears heart-shaped leaves with toothed margins. There are male and female catkins on the one tree, and it is the female flowers that form the mulberry. They like full sun in a frost-free climate and rich, well-drained soil. They take up to six years to bear fruit, so it is worth purchasing a well-established plant.

OLIVES

Australia's history with the table olive (*Olea europaea*) dates back to 1800, when the first tree was part of a consignment of plants sent out by Joseph Banks with George Suttor, a London market gardener. John Macarthur planted olives at his Elizabeth Farm at Parramatta in 1805, on his return from his first stint in exile in England, and Sydney's Botanic Gardens became a distribution centre in the 1820s.

Today there are about 8 million olive trees in Australia—Crete has 27 million trees—but we still produce only about 5 per cent of our needs. The industry worldwide is worth $20 billion annually. If you want to be part of the industry in Australia, there are almost 100 olive oil processing plants in this country at present.

The oil content of the olive can vary from 2 to 25 per cent; also, one variety of olive will produce very different oil from the next, and the same cultivar will produce different oil in a different environment. The leading commercially grown cultivar is 'Frantoio', an oil-specific Tuscan variety that grows well in Australian conditions. The Agricultural Research Institute can advise on choosing the right tree for different uses and conditions, and can assess fatty acid profiles and advise growers on nutrient values, but my picks for domestic growing are as follows.
- 'Manzanillo': this medium-sized olive is the most widely grown cultivar for the home garden. It is a heavy bearer, good for pickling and oil production, with a good flesh-to-pit ratio.
- 'Nab Tamri': a prolific producer giving a beautiful olive oil.

Planting

If you garden in a small space, grow olives in a pot, in full sun, for a Mediterranean look. If planting out, dig in lime if your soil is acidic, then add Dynamic Lifter and mulch heavily. Water trees for the first couple of years, before leaving them be. Most olive trees are self-fertile. However, commercial growers include different varieties for cross-pollination to increase yield, particularly for tough years.

Take care if you want olives for your city garden: the roots are shallow but can travel many metres looking for water. Farmers who have hedged olive trees as very effective windbreaks have found suckers emerging in the midst of wheat fields, and they will compete with the eucalypts in our native forests. The advice from the experts is this: in a small space, plant your olives in a good strong pot.

Requirements

Olives enjoy hot, dry summers and winter rain.

PASSIONFRUIT

This vigorous climber with glossy green, wrinkled leaves is greatly loved in Australia as the essential final touch to the pavlova, considered by many of us our national dessert!

There are some 400 species in the genus, but it is *Passiflora edulis* that is grown for its delicious fruit. The cultivars 'Nellie Kelly' and 'Panama Gold' produce fruit without the need for cross-pollination with another plant.
- *Passiflora edulis* 'Norfolk Island' is a strong grower.
- *Passiflora edulis* 'Nellie Kelly' is an Australian cultivar with a smaller leaf.

Pavlova (serves 6)

My mother's recipe for 'pav' is, I believe, the best and is still de rigueur *when we have overseas visitors, or when we are staying with friends overseas. I have spent many hours driving around foreign supermarkets and markets looking for passionfruit— essential, for any Aussie, to the flavour and enjoyment of this delicious dessert. I have to share with you mum's recipe, which, for me, has always been foolproof.*

4 eggs

Pinch salt

1 cup + 1 tbsp castor sugar

1 tsp vanilla essence

1 tbsp cornflour

3 tsp lemon juice or 1 tsp white vinegar

Method

Separate the eggs (which are at room temperature), ensuring that the bowl in which you will whip the egg whites is spotlessly clean and absolutely dry. Make sure that not a drop of the yolk is allowed to touch the egg whites. (Save the yolks for the torcilla, that sinfully rich pannacotta-type dessert that is classic to the sherry region of Spain.)

Whip egg whites, with a pinch of salt, until stiff, dry peaks form. Slowly add, a tablespoon at a time,

the cup of castor sugar. Whip until glossy peaks form. Add vanilla essence.

The next and very important step is to fold in the remaining 1 tbsp of sugar, into which you have folded the cornflour. Then gently fold in the lemon juice or vinegar.

Spread onto a baking tin on which you have placed baking paper lightly greased (use butter, not margarine). Place in the centre of the oven, pre-heated to 200°C. After 10 minutes turn the oven off and leave overnight. Do not open the oven until it is cold.

Top the pavlova with plenty of whipped cream and the essential passionfruit pulp. I also add sliced mango, or banana. Serve with very frozen, best quality vanilla ice-cream, and imagine you are in the tropics!

1. The fruit market in
   old Sorrento, Italy.
2. Olive trees shade a
   Mediterranean garden.
3. Grapevines pruned high
   at Ravello, Italy.

Requirements

Passionfruit vines need a place in the sun and plenty of space to spread their roots. They love a fertiliser that is high in phosphorus and potassium: apply from spring through summer and water regularly to ensure sweet fruit. They can take a year or more to bear fruit, which should be harvested when still smooth but eaten when the skin becomes wrinkled. Prune after fruiting to encourage new growth on which fruit is produced and to thin out the vine so that sunlight can reach as many of its parts as possible.

Care

Many passionfruit are grafted: watch for suckers appearing from the root stock below the graft. Remove suckers so that they don't take over and kill off your more precious cultivar.

Passionfruit

The common name 'passionfruit' is attributed to the significance early Christian missionaries gave the flower. To them, the 10 petals and the sepals represented the apostles at Christ's crucifixion and the halo of filaments around the centre looked like the crown of thorns.

PAW PAWS

Paw paws (*Carica papaya*) are a delicious, healthy fruit, conjuring up dreams of holidays consisting of hot sun, white sand and clear, aquamarine water—and these are the conditions they need to grow and fruit well! *Carica papaya* is a short-lived, soft-wooded tree native to Central and South America.

Requirements

Male and female flowers are usually borne on different trees, although self-fertile varieties have recently been bred. Trees bear for about five years, so you will need to sow a new a plant annually to keep up supply of this fragrant fruit.

Care

Grow in a sheltered spot; they like humid conditions and summer rain. Pick the fruit when it is green—but with just a little colour—to ripen indoors.

PEACHES

Peaches (*Prunus persica*) growing to about 8 m tall, and flowering in clouds of white or pink blossom, were first recorded in gardens in China, where they decorate screens, silk fabric and porcelain.

Requirements

Peaches like similar growing conditions and climates to the apple and the pear, and need high chilling hours to fruit well. The cultivar 'Texstar' is an early-fruiting variety that has a lower chilling requirement than most.

Planting

Stone fruit, including peaches, are a good choice for an espalier on a north-facing wall, which will warm up and store heat to assist fruit in ripening. Such treatment also allows for the management of fruit trees in a restricted space, and makes for ease of pruning and netting. (The fascinating Arthur Wall, in Hobart's Botanic Gardens, was built in 1829 under instruction from Governor Arthur, and was heated in order to grow espaliered exotic fruits.)

PEARS

If you garden in a suitable climate, a walk of fruiting pears (*Pyrus communis*) is a glorious sight in spring when the single white blossom covers the carefully pruned branches. In winter, when leaves have fallen, the newly pruned structure adds bones to any garden design. Then, in late summer and autumn, the pears hang in green, heavy, teardrops, to be picked, before fully ripe, for eating or cooking.

Pears are not self-pollinating, so you will need to plant several varieties for good cropping.
• *Pyrus communis* 'Beurré Bosc' is the gold to brown-skinned variety.

• *Pyrus communis* 'Bon Chrétien' is an ancient variety, a parent of 'Williams' and 'Packham's Triumph'.

Planting

Create a high, sturdy pear tunnel with a frame built of galvanised iron by the local blacksmith or builder. As always with garden structures, scale it up. You'll be planting the trees about 2.5 m apart, so place the uprights at that width. Have at least three horizontal struts included so that the arms of the pears can be well espaliered. The tunnel will meet overhead, so ensure that there are two or three longitudinal struts running the length of the tunnel.

Espaliered pears will need a summer prune to cut away shoots reaching for the sky in a most unattractive manner, and then a winter prune (*see also* Pruning).

Care

Pick pears when green, so they will ripen without becoming floury. They are ready to pick when a gentle twist is enough to pull the fruit from the tree.

When pruning fruit trees you must decide what you are trying to achieve, and must ascertain whether the tree fruits on the current season's wood or on old wood. Pears and apples, for instance, set fruit on two- to three-year-old wood, while most stone fruit trees require the previous season's wood. But home gardeners, who don't want, or need, massive crops of fruit, should prune off some of the wood. For the home garden an open vase shape is easy to maintain—and prune to ensure the tree is kept at a serviceable height.

PERSIMMONS

Among the most decorative of small trees, persimmons are also useful. The fruit of the frost-hardy Chinese species (*Diospyros kaki*) hang in glowing golden orbs throughout autumn. The non-astringent cultivar 'Fuyu' doesn't need a second tree for pollination, although the crop might be heavier with a second variety. The leaves turn a gorgeous orange and red in autumn in cold climates, but the tree copes with a range of climates.

Care

Prune wood that has borne fruit to allow new wood to bear the next crop.

PLUMS

Plums (*Prunus* × *domestica*) hail from north Asia and southern Russia, so they need cold winters to fruit well. You will also need at least two compatible varieties to enjoy fruit, as few are self-fertile and all benefit from cross-pollination. Choose varieties that flower at the same time. Reaching about 9 m, this is not a tree for a small garden. After the white blossom in spring the summer fruit can be golden, green, red or black, depending upon the variety.

• *Prunus* 'Elvins' is a non-fruiting, but decorative Australian cultivar of the cherry plum.
• Early-flowering varieties include 'Santa Rosa' and the blood plum 'Satsuma'; mid-season varieties include the delicious 'Angelina' and 'D'Agen', while late-season include 'Greengage' and 'Coe's Golden Drop'.

POMEGRANATES

The pomegranate (*Punica granatum*) produces, from summer through to autumn, extremely decorative rich red fruits that look marvellous as a still life on a table or side board. The apple-sized fruits are edible, however. Packed with red-black seeds in chambers divided by membranes, they are an ancient symbol of fertility. From the Mediterranean and the Middle East—they flower throughout Iran in April—they cope well with a range of climates. The tangerine-coloured flowers are followed by gorgeous red fruit borne on the current year's growth.

• Named varieties include 'Wonderful'.

QUINCES

With its scent that fills the house at Easter, the quince is almost my favourite fruit. April is the time of the year when the days are becoming shorter and that first, early-morning chill in the air has warned us that winter is coming. And it's the time of the year when the house is filled with the scent not of spring blossom but of autumn cooking. It's the time when 12 months of good garden-keeping reaps the rewards of orchards laden with produce; a time for meals based around what is ripe in the garden.

Bowls are overflowing with nuts picked from the garden, freezers are full of raspberries, apples are being poached. And my mother's heavy ceramic pot rests in a slow oven for hours, enclosing a bounty of quince slowly turning a deep, rich ruby-red.

Closely related to apples and pears, and also a member of the Rosaceae family, the quince—the lone species *Cydonia oblonga*—has been grown in Iraq, Iran and Turkey for thousands of years, although its name suggests it might also have been found in the Cretan city of Cydon, now Canea. A symbol of love and fertility for the ancient Greeks and Romans, the quince was believed by some historians to be the forbidden fruit in the Garden of Eden. It arrived in Britain in the thirteenth century, probably with the 10-year-old Eleanor of Castile, bride to Edward, son of Henry III, and was a luxury.

Often knobbly and scarred by birds, the fruit can, at best, be described as handsome, but a bowl of fresh quince will fill your house with the scent of apples, lemons and pears all mixed into one soothing aroma. Several different cultivars are suitable for Australia, from the low-growing 'Vranja'—suitable for smaller gardens and bearing white blossom followed by pear-shaped, fragrant, golden fruits, particularly good for cooking—to 'Smyrna' and 'Champion'.

Requirements

Frost resistant and deciduous, the quince loves cool climates and thrives in a variety of soils—but prefers moist, rich acidic soils. Trees grow to about 8 m, often in the most picturesque of shapes.

Plant young trees in early spring, in a sunny position. The large flowers, from white to rose-pink, must be about the prettiest in the garden, and just before winter the leaves turn a rich butter-yellow.

Commercial growers take out the top, for ease

Sue Home's quince jelly (makes 8–10 medium-sized jars)

6–8 large quinces
Muslin or jelly bag
Sugar

Method
Wipe quinces clean; chop roughly and place—skin, pips and all—in a large, non-reactive pot with cold water to just cover. Bring to a gentle boil and simmer until quinces are mushy.

If using a jelly bag (available at some specialty shops), place jelly bag in large basin and tip mixture into bag. Carefully suspend bag over basin to allow liquid to drip through for several hours or overnight. If using the old-fashioned double muslin tied between the four legs of an upended stool, the method is the same. Do NOT squeeze the bag as jelly may become cloudy.

In the same non-reactive pot, measure the resulting liquid and add sugar cup for cup. Stir over heat until sugar dissolves, then boil rapidly, skimming scum from the surface at regular intervals. Chill a small, flat plate and when the liquid is clear red, place a teaspoon of liquid onto the plate. Run a finger through the liquid and when it remains separate and does not run together, the jelly is ready to bottle.

Pour immediately into hot jars and seal. Serve with sourdough toast or scones, or the jelly may be used to baste a chicken as it roasts.

This recipe works well with the 'japonica quince' (the fruits of the japonica bush). Simply pick a kilo or two when they are a light gold colour and follow the instructions above. The flavour is quite distinct and equally delicious.

Tip: Easter is the time to buy quince, when they are heartbreakingly cheap. Carry home as many as you can, then pot roast them or turn them into jam or paste. My friend Sue Home makes a clear, jewel-like quince jelly, but I simply chop the fruit up roughly—skin, pips and all—and pack them into a heavy pot. Squeeze in about 6 lemons; add a litre of hot water in which an unseemly amount of sugar has been dissolved and leave in the slowest of ovens for 15 to 20 hours. (I use about 4 cups of sugar to 8 to 10 quinces, but you can use less.) Eat them hot with ice-cream, mash them into a paste, or top them with a cake batter and bake. Or lay them, with chopped and sautéed onions, beneath roasting lamb back straps or pork loin … yum! And these baked quinces keep, frozen, for months. Until the following Easter, in fact.

of management and care, but also to encourage a strong root system. The trees look marvellous, however, when left to stretch out their elegant branches, and are happy with minimal pruning.

Care

Quinces fruit after about five years. Once the flowers have finished in late spring, green fruits develop under the large leaves; the ripening fruit becomes so large that the branches bend under its weight. When the fruit, which is covered in a soft protective down, is ready to harvest it resembles glowing, yellow lanterns. In a year when a late frost has not hit the blossom, one tree can yield up to 50 kg of fruit.

Pear and cherry slug is the bane of apple, pear and quince growers in some climates. These nasty, slim, black, slimy slugs—the precursor to the sawfly—can defoliate the tree in summer and autumn and will eventually kill the tree. Spray with Bordeaux mix at blossom bud burst and then again at leaf fall. (*See also* Pests and Diseases.)

RASPBERRIES

The raspberry (*Rubus idaeus*), yet another member of the Rosaceae family, is native to Europe and north Asia, and flowers in spring and summer along prickly canes. There are several varieties available, which will provide fruit from early summer through to autumn.

Tip: The pruning of soft fruits like raspberries and blackberries (*Ribes nigrum*) is straightforward: each autumn, remove any canes that have fruited and tie in place fresh new canes to produce fruit in the following year. Depending upon the space you have available, tie canes along wires as a boundary, or in waves or spirals (*see* Design).

STRAWBERRIES

Rich, sweet, red strawberries (*Fragaria × ananassa*) are so easy to grow. Native to warm temperate climates, strawberries are creeping perennials that love sun and acid soil.

Apartment dwellers need not miss out: grow them in terracotta pots or wooden troughs—or even in heavy plastic bags. Courtyard owners can allow them to tumble over the edges of planter boxes.

Care

Plant virus-free plants from autumn to spring in a sunny spot in rich soil, water well and apply a liquid fertiliser each fortnight. Mulch well with straw to keep the fruit from being spoiled by ripening on bare soil.

The best way to eat a mango

With a sharp knife slice off each of the 'cheeks' of the mango, holding the fruit up on its end. Then criss-cross the flesh of each cheek into a lattice pattern, taking care not to cut through the skin. Turn the section inside out so that the flesh splays out in a series of cubes that are easy to eat (or scoop off with a spoon).

GRASSES

Grasses

'Gardens should send shivers up and down our spines,' said the American land-scaper James van Sweden at a garden design conference in Melbourne a few years ago. This begs the question, yet again, as to just what it is that makes a garden great.

A proponent of blending the uncultivated with the cultivated, van Sweden addressed the conundrum, discussing elements of scale and space. He advocated injecting a 'new energy' into garden design and eschewed what he called the 'boring lawn bureaucracy'.

The gardens van Sweden designs around the world employ vast blocks of plants—sedums, salvias and sages—and a selection of elegant-but-easy grasses, from the low-growing sedges, *Carex* spp., to the taller *Miscanthus* and *Calamagrostis*—to create what he describes as 'an alloy of naturalism and free spirit'.

♥ My favourites

CALAMAGROSTIS

The tall-growing reed grass, a member of the Poaceae family, is a genus of over 250 species.

• *Calamagrostis* x *acutiflora* 'Karl Foerster' reaches 1.7 m and flowers in summer with silky plumes. It is most effective when left to take on burnt umber colours for the winter garden.

CAREX

The clump-forming sedges are a genus of 1500 or so species of perennial grasses, many from East Asia and New Zealand. They like dry, rocky situations but will also grow well in damp soils.

• *Carex abula* 'Frosted Curls' has gorgeous long, weeping foliage that grows in silver to caramel curls.

• *Carex elata* 'Aurea', known better as Bowles' golden sedge, has yellow leaves with a golden margin. Like many sedges, it loves boggy areas.

MISCANTHUS

Another member of the Poaceae family, *Miscanthus* grow well in any soil, in full sun, occurring naturally from Africa to Asia. Some reach 3 m in height, and they flower in summer with soft brown plumes that colour wonderfully in autumn.

• *Miscanthus sinensis* is among the least invasive of the grasses.

• *Miscanthus sinensis* 'Zebrinus' is tall growing with gold stripes on the sword-like leaves.

MOLINIA

The moor grasses, a genus of a small handful of species and members of the Poaceae family, are slim grasses that that take on an incandescent beauty in autumn.

• *Molinia caerulea* is native to damp, acid soils in northern Asia and bears small purple spikes in summer.

PENNISETUM

The fountain grass forms clumps of soft foliage, from which gold or burgundy, brush-like plumes emerge in summer. It can be invasive.

• *Pennisetum setaceum* 'Rubrum', with burgundy foliage to 1.5 m and flowers with rose-pink fluffy plumes, is said, after rigorous testing, to be sterile.

Previous page: Miscanthus sinensis.

1. The tough, frost-hardy perennial grass *Hakonechloa macra*.
2. A matrix of repeated species in a Michael McCoy garden.
3. Tall grasses in counterpoint to a swathe of tangerine geum.

POA

A genus of some 500 species, these tough grasses are found throughout temperate climates. Hard wearing, they are often used in areas of high traffic, although some have become weeds. (*See* Weeds in the Garden.)

• *Poa mariesii* is a tough grass that attracts butterflies.

POGONATHERUM

• *Pogonatherum paniceum* 'Monica', the baby panda bamboo, comes from the rainforests of South-East Asia. It forms a tight clump that looks effective planted in swathes or swirls among gravel or stones.

STIPA

Grasses of the steppes, these feather grasses are happiest in dry conditions. Take care as they can form wide clumps which can be very difficult to remove.

• *Stipa gigantea*, deceptively delicate in appearance, grows into great clumps. It bears its silver to pink oat-like fluffy flowers, held on tall, tough stems, in summer.

✿ Planting

Grasses are indispensable in a natural, or free-form, garden, helping to achieve that look of insouciance, where the boundaries of the cultivated garden are 'frayed' so that the designed landscape blends naturally into its surrounding. This is a style also dubbed 'prairie planting'.

Happy in most soils, the ornamental grasses, with their rustic tones, look stunning mass-planted with the appropriate architecture. They can also be employed in the creation of wild meadows and borders created with a new-found freedom. Wash the garden canvas with wide rivers of just a handful of species; they are bold, beautiful and robust. When they have finished flowering, leave the seed-heads alone to turn gold and red: they look stunning silhouetted against a glowering winter sky. Or cut them back ruthlessly.

🍃 Care

Wide, floodplains of grasses look dramatic in gardens in the United Kingdom but are perhaps not so practical in parts of Australia where snakes are a concern.

Any grass can become invasive if it loves its environment. Hasten slowly as some grasses have not been fully tried. More than 100 grasses are listed on the weeds list. Check first on www.weeds.org.au and www.wwf.org.au.

The latest 'look'

Among the new wave of garden designers who promote the use of grasses are the American-based Piet Oudolf; James van Sweden; Henk Gerritsen; and Australia's Michael McCoy. Grasses, which create height without using too much lateral space, are featured in the gardens McCoy designs and are used in repeating chunks: in one large garden he used 800 *Miscanthus sinensis* 'Gracillimus', the tall, fine-leaved grass that is one of the decade's must-have species.

Designer brief: Michael McCoy

Melbourne garden designer and writer Michael McCoy is perhaps best known for his detailed knowledge and ingenious use of fascinating plant material. But, he insists, the mass a plant creates and its ability to fill a space are its most important qualities.

Resolving the tension between loving plants and respecting the rules of good design is the greatest challenge for any gardener. For a designer it is crucial. McCoy's solution is to employ a basic matrix of large blocks of plant material, which also allows for individual input from clients. The result is that there are multiples of each of the basic plants in flower at any one time. In November it might be the tangerine geum, in late summer *Sedum* 'Autumn Joy'; grasses play an important part in the garden story throughout autumn and winter. The plan is deceptively simple: within a simple matrix lies a great deal of detail.

In small spaces, McCoy advises using a couple of dominating elements—one superb tree, a piece of sculpture, or just one or two repeated perennials, to provide an impact. He likes plants that reach a reasonable height quickly, or he will install a vine-covered structure to create a sense of a green surround. Grasses, which create height without using too much lateral space, are a favourite. In courtyards, plants that provide seasonal dynamism and change are preferred over a predominance of hard landscaping. Changes in colour and texture

(in leaves and flowers) and in volume are vital.

A McCoy garden might include the tough *Sisyrinchium striatum*, with spires of cream flowers throughout summer, and *Stipa gigantea*, deceptively delicate in appearance, bearing its silver to pink, fluffy flowers at over 1 m. *Smyrnium perfoliatum*, a biennial, euphorbia-like, acid lime-green—stunning planted with the hot-pink dicentra—is another favourite. *Helleborus foetidus* 'Wester Flisk', with its deep red stems, is a useful woodland plant in a range of climates and *Epimedium perralderianum*, perfect for mass planting in the shade, takes on bronze to red tones in autumn and through winter.

Clients are provided with an easy-care regime for these low-maintenance gardens, although McCoy warns against confusing low maintenance with simple maintenance. 'Someone who is pushing a lawn mower will have a simple maintenance garden, but not a low maintenance garden,' he explains. McCoy's clients can use the brush cutter in late winter to cut the plantings to the ground. 'Rake it all off, mulch it and feed it and don't do a thing for the rest of the year,' he says.

McCoy insists that there is no real value in design for the sake of style or fashion—that the quality of design must be measured against the extent to which it matches the lifestyle of the owners. That sounds like good advice.

HEDGES

Hedges

Being a greedy gardener, I love hedges. I find the structure they provide calming; I adore the way they enclose, providing privacy, secrecy and expectation. I admire how they divide the garden into manageable sections, edging and defining, marking out space, and directing the garden visitor along discreetly planned garden routes. I love the colour of them—most often green upon green upon green. What I love most about hedges, though, is that they provide opportunities to add yet more species to the garden. Let me explain.

Hedges are central to any garden design, whatever its size. They are the bones of a large garden and are also crucial to a small garden, providing a backdrop for, perhaps, a small vignette of dramatic or complicated planting, thus creating the illusion of a much grander space. They provide screening from the street and its traffic, or perhaps from neighbouring properties. They dress a bare fence and dress up even the plainest of houses. For an über-elegant, structured look, go for the clean lines of double and triple hedges, clipped at varying heights. Different species will create hedges in varying shades of green.

Hedges, like stone walls, can be cultural mediators, providing information about their creators and about the history of the property they adorn. The 'laid' hedges that remain in Tasmania, for instance, speak of that state's colonial past and of the British settlers who established expansive colonial estates in the then Van Diemen's Land.

Traditional hedging materials range from conifers to mock orange to box and the deciduous plants, which produce a tapestry effect as they change colour and texture throughout each season. Gardeners in the United Kingdom love the tapestry hedge, effective in Australia in cold climates. By planting a selection of up to five species with complementary form, habit and horticultural needs but which turn, in autumn, to an array of leaf colour, a stunning hedge of constant interest can be created easily.

Beech most often forms the backbone of the English tapestry hedge. In Australia, hornbeam (*Carpinus betulus*) is easier to grow; or use an evergreen such as holly, well clipped of its berries, to stop it becoming a pest. Add myrtle (*Luma apiculata*); the red-leaved pittosporum; the green- or purple-leaved berberis; and the autumn-colouring maples.

Hedges of roses are extremely effective, and for ease of maintenance you can't beat the tough and easy-care rugosa roses; my current favourites are *Rosa rugosa alba*, with its large, white, fragile-looking flowers, and *R. rugosa* 'Agnes', with its clotted-cream, double blooms. Rugosas will cope with almost no water or fertiliser and reward you with constant blossom over summer and brilliant hips that hang on for weeks over autumn. Hard-prune annually or every second year. You'll find hedges of the tough, thorny Cherokee rose (*R. laevigata*) in outback Queensland, where it provides an effective stock barrier. Hedges of the spiny Osage orange (*Maclura pomifera*), which were used in a similar way, can still be found in some extant colonial gardens in Victoria.

In my back garden *R. banksiae lutea* bursts into bloom in August; its arching canes of pale lemon flowers weave through, and tone with, the fresh, lime-green leaves of a boundary hedge of mock orange, *Murraya paniculata*. The modern rose 'Heidesommer', which is covered in white blooms for most months of the year, also makes a great hedge.

Previous page: Camellia japonica 'Elegans Champagne'.

Hedges can provide the 'fusion food' of the horticultural world. A severely clipped hedge of a rich green conifer such as Bhutan cypress (*Cupressus torulosa*) looks wonderful with climbing 'Iceberg', 'Lamarque' or 'Devoniensis' roses scrambling through. The dark, severe background in counterpoint to the cream roses running riot is simply delicious: for even greater effect add a white clematis like 'Elizabeth'. Try also *Pandorea jasminoides* 'Lady Di'.

Hedges of once-flowering shrubs like camellia become 'coat hangers' for clematis and other climbing plants, ensuring colour and excitement when the hedge has finished flowering. The intense red flowers of the climbing nasturtium, *Tropaeolum speciosum*, look terrific winding through the large, dark, glossy leaves of *Camellia reticulata*—and you get months of drama. Or scatter a packet of the seeds of the common nasturtium and allow them to hoist themselves up on the lower branches. And if you have a hedge that is thinning out at the bottom (perhaps because, despite the best advice, you could not bear to prune it from its infancy) try planting some hardy climbers such as *Trachelospermum jasminoides* at its base. They will climb up through the 'leggy' lower branches, thickening up your screen and providing you with wonderful scent in spring.

The English enclosure laws of the eighteenth century, when farmers divided common grazing land into small plots for individual use, resulted in a patchwork of regionally idiosyncratic hedges being created throughout the United Kingdom. One of the most popular methods for enclosing stock was through the various forms of the 'laid' hedge. This involved cutting the base of the hedge three-quarters through and then bending it over to lie on the ground. The shoots that grew from the cut wood created a wide and impenetrable hedge.

There are various versions of the laid hedge: one method involves tying together bundles of the hedging plant material. You then cut into the stems close to the ground, without cutting through entirely. Lay the bundle down, into the field and at an angle, on top of the previous bundle. Work downhill, but bending the bunches backwards, uphill, and secure with stakes. Traditionally the stakes are linked together at the top with hazel or willow binders. It sounds complicated, but it creates an effective barrier that is also decorative, particularly in winter, when the tracery of the bare structure is visible.

For cold climates the slow-growing *Thuja occidentalis* 'Smaragd', a beautiful emerald-green in mid-summer turning to bronze in winter, is an excellent choice for a hedge in a formal garden.

I love a loose hedge of the thorny *Berberis thunbergii* 'Atropurpurea', planted with roses that flower in pink and white. For a tough and drought-resistant arrangement, back with the casual look of the scented buddleia (*Buddleja*

Tip: Some of us adore clipping—it gives us that immediate sense of achievement—but if you don't, you could create a 'wave hedge'. Just let the plants grow and 'wave' the cutting tool over the top in great sweeps: it doesn't have to be perfect.

To line a driveway

In a large country garden, I have lined the long, swooping drive with a loose hedge of dwarf oleander (*Nerium oleander*), flowering in apricot and white, inserting the occasional red-flowering cultivar to guard against any hint of tedium. The oleander is, of course, tough and drought resistant, and a trim with the electric shears after flowering is about all the maintenance that's required. The oleander will bend elegantly over the drive, which is edged with autumn crocus. Apart from 'finishing' the drive, the hedge invites further exploration of the scented treasures behind. You could also use a low-growing buddleia for the same effect.

spp.) or may (*Spiraea* spp.). Prune these, and other plants that grow in long canes, from the base, cutting out a few canes at a time and allowing the plant to maintain its natural arching form—and avoiding a woeful truncated appearance.

The slow-growing buxus is suitable for low hedging in the formal garden. Add severely clipped cones or tripods to create drama and connect the various areas; and variegated box (*Buxus sempervirens* 'Variegata') to lighten certain parts of the garden. Japanese box (*B. microphylla* var. *japonica*) is faster growing than common box, *B. sempervirens*. It is more waterwise and hardier, and it doesn't have the unpleasant smell of the other. It will tolerate full sun or semi-shade.

Or use the fast-growing *Lonicera nitida*, easily produced from cuttings, if you are in a hurry. If you are coping with salt-laden winds in a coastal garden, the sea box (*Alyxia buxifolia*) will be preferable to English box. The white-flowered *Escallonia* 'Iveyi' makes a fast-growing hedge that

lined with a hedge of 'Lorraine Lee' roses, the pink to apricot rose by Australian grower Alister Clark, also looks wonderful.

Hedges of perennials will create a less formal look, tying sections of the garden together, and will not cause too much pain if one plant dies, as an unsightly gap will not be too obvious. Try the grey palette of lavenders, which thrive in a dry climate. In misty mountain climates, the Russian sage (*Perovskia atriplicifolia*) is more successful, especially in combination with the greys and blues of the catmint, *Nepeta × faassenii*. *Westringia fruticosa* makes a successful hedge in a dry climate but requires frequent clipping from an early age if it is to become dense from the base, as does *Teucrium fruticans*, another grey-leaved plant that, with regular clipping, makes a great hedge.

In frost-free climates, and if you don't want your life ruled by the hedge trimmer, you can plant a loose hedge of the tall-growing canna with the deep red leaf; add a second layer of interest

clips well; it will create a micro-climate to protect treasures in a seaside garden.

Plumbago (*Plumbago auriculata*), a South African genus of more than a dozen species, can be used in the same way. It was introduced to Australia by the earliest settlers who sailed to the new colony via Capetown. Among the more recent cultivated varieties is the intense-blue 'Royal Cape', which is more tolerant of both drought and frost, as well as a white-flowered variety, 'Alba'. A drive

with the shorter ginger lily, *Hedychium greenii*, with its burgundy-backed leaf. Tropical gardens, with their strong colours, patterns and forms, benefit from the cool green backdrop of a hedge. Choose the Golden Penda (*Xanthostemon chrysanthus*), a Queensland rainforest tree with dark, shiny foliage and stunning yellow flowers, or the lemon-scented myrtle (*Backhousia citriodora*), the aromatic leaves of which make a refreshing tea and can be used in cooking.

1. Hedges of may (*Spiraea* spp.) flower in early spring.
2. Clipped perfection at Chateau Yering in Victoria's Yarra Valley.
3. Hedges divide the garden at Levens Hall into 'rooms'.
4. A camellia hedge, more than half a century old, protects a Federation house from a busy street.
5. A stilt hedge can be underplanted with several layers of plant material.
6. A parterre of clipped box in Sarah Thompson and Rod Kirsop's Sydney garden.

The 'laid' hedges at Old Wesleydale are of hawthorn.

But it is the stilt hedge that pleases the must-have-it-all side of my personality. A stilt hedge—a thick head of growth sitting atop a bare stem—divides the garden into compartments while allowing tantalising glimpses of what lies beyond. More importantly, it invites several layers of under-planting.

Any of the conifers makes an excellent stilt hedge. Buy them fully grown or create them cheaply yourself by purchasing young plants and rubbing off side shoots until the desired height is reached. The 'mop top' robinia also copes well with this treatment: underplant with drought-resistant viburnum, *Viburnum tinus* 'Lucidum', with its white flowers and red berries. Add a third layer of the heavily scented *Murraya paniculata* if you are not in an area where this plant has become a garden escape.

The Manchurian pear (*Pyrus ussuriensis*) also lends itself to the stilt hedge, and the smaller growing *Magnolia grandiflora* 'Little Gem' looks wonderful used in this way, with the bonus of gloriously scented, huge cream flowers for months over summer and autumn: underplant with low-growing sacred bamboo, *Nandina domestica* 'Nana'.

As with ground covers, the possibilities for growing hedges are limited only by your imagination!

♥ My favourites

- My top pick for hedging must be our own lilly-pillies—now all included in the genus *Syzygium*—with their soft form, dense growth habit and fresh pink tips on new growth. There are several possible choices, from *Syzygium australe*, with its dark glossy leaves and white flowers, to the small-growing 'Tiny Trev' to use instead of buxus; its bronze new growth teams well with a second hedge of the small-growing *Pittosporum tenuifolium* 'Tom Thumb' with its burgundy foliage. (*See also* Native Plants.)
- *Arbutus unedo*, the Irish strawberry tree, a beautiful tree with an interesting bark, also makes a deep-green, dense hedge. The cream to pink autumn flowers accompany the previous year's fruit, which make a delicious jelly.
- Think a little beyond the usual and perhaps create a loose hedge of the low, scrambling *Bougainvillea* 'Temple of Fire' to provide an annual flash of sunset colours in creams, oranges and pinks.
- The Natal plum, *Carissa macrocarpa*, from southern Africa, has small, round, glossy leaves and fragrant, white, star-like flowers. It copes with partial shade or full sun and with salty winds. It doesn't mind being grown in pots, is good for a loose hedge and is a better choice than gardenias in times of drought.
- Hornbeam (*Carpinus betulus*) is easier to grow in this country than beech, a classic hedging plant, and a favourite in large gardens in the northern hemisphere.
- Cotoneaster is on the weed list, but you can indulge in *Cotoneaster* 'Cornubia', with its big red berries and beautiful autumn colours, as it is sterile, so doesn't seed.
- The new dwarf eucalypt hybrid can make an unusual and effective hedge. Remove the leader—the central trunk—at about 2 m to encourage the plant to thicken up to form a hedge. (*See also* Eucalypts.)

The laid hedge

In northern Tasmania there's a secret, hidden valley so beautiful that, once you've found it, you may not want to leave. It runs from east to west, into the magnificent Western Tiers, and is sheltered from the north by a series of low mountains that are clothed in old-growth forest and steeped in indigenous history. And a quiet revolution is taking place there.

Antique dealer John Hawkins and his artist wife Robyn moved to the Chudleigh Valley a few years ago and set about renovating an historic property, at the same time reinstating some of the crafts introduced by the Europeans who had arrived in the area from 1829, but which had been lost over the past century.

Among these is the art of hedge laying, practised in the United Kingdom for more than a thousand years. Not only valuable as a windbreak, 'laid' hedges give shade, prevent erosion and provide habitat for wildlife. And, when properly maintained, they create an impenetrable barrier to contain stock.

John Hawkins wanted to renovate the hedges that divide the valley, creating a patchwork of green paddocks bound by ribbons of hawthorn that flower in spring in clouds of white blossom. Many of the hedges are more than 150 years old but had been allowed to grow untamed over the past few decades.

Each region in Britain employs a slightly different method of hedge laying, depending upon the type of animal being housed, plant material available, altitude and climate. There is the Midlands, or Bullock, style; the Yorkshire and Lancashire styles; the Welsh Border style; and the Brecon style. As with stonewalling, the region from which a settler had come could be identified by his method of hedge laying.

The hedges around Scott and Deborah Wilson's property, Old Wesleydale, along the Mole Creek Road at the village of Chudleigh, date from the early nineteenth century. Taught by Karl Leibsher, a Shropshire hedge layer brought by Hawkins to Tasmania over two winters, Scott has returned the hedges to working order by laying them in a Midlands style, traditionally used for restraining bullocks. This style includes a heavy binding along the top of the hedge, plaited from willow or hazel.

Traditional hedge laying involves, first, clearing away undergrowth and weeds, particularly from a hedge that has been neglected and allowed to grow tall. Untidy side branches are removed. A cut, known as a pleach, is made in the back of the trunk, leaving a 'hinge'; old-time hedgers recommend that this should be as thick as a lamb's tongue. In fact, the thickness will depend on the age and thickness of the stem or trunk—the pleacher—which should fall over unaided. If the hinge is too thick it will break; too thin and the sap will not flow.

A chainsaw or a traditional billhook—a tool that dates to medieval days when it was a weapon of war—is used for making this cut. Today specifically designed for hedge laying, the billhook comes in many different styles. Scott Wilson uses a Yorkshire billhook, 50 cm long, with a 35 cm long blade that is sharpened on both edges, one edge being a straight cut and the other incorporating a large hook.

Once the required cuts have been made, the pleachers are laid down along the line of the hedge in a diagonal pattern; stakes are driven through to stabilise the hedge, and the top is bound. Suckers will emanate from the cuts, and within a few years a dense hedge—which will remain impenetrable for the next half century—will have been created. The hedge is trimmed twice a year, in spring and in late summer. John Hawkins trims his finished hedges to 1.2 m high with a curved Japanese tea cutter, with one man on either side of the hedge.

Hedges that are beyond being renovated in this way can be first coppiced: cut them back to ankle height and allow them to sucker; within five years they can be laid in the traditional manner.

Similarly, to install a new hedge, plant saplings, five to a metre, in a staggered row. Within five years you will have a thick hedge that is ready to be laid. Several European species can be used—from oaks to English maples, crab-apples, hazel, beech and ash—which, although exotic, provide a home to myriad local fauna.

The result of all this planning and effort is a working hedge that looks spectacular when bare over winter and is a mass of blossom in spring, a fresh green in summer and a colourful tapestry in autumn.

The cypress hedge

The Leyland cypress (× *Cupressocyparis leylandii*) can make an excellent hedge if clipped religiously. But, in the United Kingdom many councils have outlawed this maligned conifer, over which there have been tens of thousands of court cases, a murder and a suicide. The problem comes when gardeners use it to block out neighbours, robbing them of their amenity.

- The New Zealand native *Griselinia littoralis*, the kapuka, clips well to a salt-tolerant hedge (*see also* Seaside Gardening).
- *Luma apiculata*, the myrtle, with its scented white flowers and good foliage, quickly forms a dense hedge.
- *Michelia figo*, related to the gorgeous magnolias, makes a wonderful hedge, with its smaller, glossy leaf and wine-coloured, heavily scented flowers in spring. It clips beautifully.
- Another New Zealand native, *Olearia paniculata*, the akiraho, makes a fast-growing, dense hedge if regularly clipped. With its bright green, wavy-edged leaves, it resembles a pittosporum. Wind and salt tolerant, it bears creamy, scented flowers in autumn.
- *Pittosporum tenuifolium* 'Sunburst' is a fast-growing cultivar that needs constant pruning and is not happy in very hot and humid areas. The slower growing *P.* 'Limelight' is a better choice for a hedge than the fine-leaved 'James Stirling', which also requires frequent pruning. The gold *P. tobira* also makes a very successful hedge and loves being clipped into mounds, tripods and obelisks.
- The cherry laurel (*Prunus laurocerasus*) is a great hedging plant for cool climates, with the added bonus of interesting cherry-like fruits that make a great jam. *P. lusitanica* is salt tolerant.
- The snowberry (*Symphoricarpos albus*) carries

striking white fruit in autumn. It suckers and forms a dense shrub, so makes a terrific informal and wild hedge for large gardens. If you are using it as a hedge you can take to it with the electric hedger, but to keep it as a romantic, arching shrub, cut out one cane at a time at its base.
- Try the drought-resistant *Viburnum tinus* 'Lucidum', and *V. plicatum* 'Newzam' creates a low-growing hedge.

Tip: problem hedges

The Japanese privet (*Ligustrum japonicum*) is popular for hedges—well clipped so that it doesn't flower to create seed that can be spread by wind or birds—but is on the CSIRO list of weeds. (But the fast-growing *L. vulgare* 'Tuscany' can safely create a low hedge.)

I am loath to recommend one of my favourite plants, the mock orange or orange jessamine (*Murraya paniculata*) as it can be a nuisance in subtropical climates—although there is nothing that will grow as well in some of the depleted, sandy Sydney soils.

Keep hedges of *Ficus benjamina* very well clipped to prevent their root system becoming aggressive; a stilt hedge of *F. hillii* creates a fast-growing screen but needs to be kept ruthlessly pruned to prevent the roots from searching for the nearest water source.

✿ Care

Clip hedges just after spring, once the new leaves emerge—but after flowering, of course. A light 'haircut' is given in mid-summer to keep plantings dense. Box is clipped after autumn and in spring, always when hot weather is over, to ensure that the newly trimmed plants don't burn.

Most hedges will benefit from being clipped to a shape that is slightly wider at the base to allow light and sun to reach all parts of the plant.

Herb Gardens

'The borage brought itself,' says one country gardener of this bright blue-flowered perennial herb, greatly loved by bees, that has made itself at home among her roses. 'I do love volunteers.'

'Sharing the love of gardening is so very therapeutic,' says another, a comment that perfectly articulates the philosophy by which many gardeners live. 'The key to happiness is being in touch with nature; being in the garden.'

Throughout the ages the idea of a secluded, inward-looking, fragrant garden has been synonymous with feelings of safety and peace. Enormous benefit is derived from quiet reflection in a scented garden, and herb gardens have soothed and delighted people for centuries.

Apart from effectively edging paths and garden beds, swathes of herbs make easy additions to flower borders, an essential part of a classic cottage garden design. Mass plantings of parsley provide an effective deep green rib that can snake through the front of a border of foliage; add plenty of the gently coloured sage with its soft, eau de nil foliage; or heat up a summer border with a mass of yellow-flowering thyme. Back with fennel to add height and a bronze cloud of delicate, feathery fronds.

Herbs also have their place in very manicured gardens where summers are hot and dry: severely clipped globes and tripods of teucrium, curry plant, lavender and rosemary add scale to gardens that rely on form and structure rather than colourful floral displays.

Herb gardens are also a natural-remedy medicine chest. In one kitchen garden that I've seen, over 180 different herbs are grown, divided into four large beds housing remedies for nervous and sleep disorders, for the immune system, for the skin, and for the digestive system. Within this layout are 28 smaller squares planted with a wide range of herbs for all ailments and uses. The herbs are all labelled and are grouped under various

The Rockies

In the foothills of Canada's Rocky Mountains—just 45 minutes west of the city of Calgary—the Black Foot Siksika, the Kootenay and the Stoney tribes have been using native plants for centuries. The spring bark of the balsam poplar tree (*Populus balsamifera*) is edible and contains a medicine; in spring the tree is tapped for its syrup. The trunk of the trembling aspen (*Populus tremuloides*) features a powder that prevents sunburn. Growing underneath is the wolf willow (*Elaeagnus commutata*), also known as the silverberry; its fragrant yellow flowers produce black seeds that are eaten in times of famine and are used to make necklaces. The Inuit people make a tea of cloudberry, wild spearmint, crowberry, and Labrador.

The needles of the majestic lodgepole pine (*Pinus contorta*), which clothes the lower mountain slopes in iconic, 30 m high stands, are used to make a tea that provides four times the vitamin C of limes. Its dominant understorey is the Canadian buffalo berry (*Shepherdia canadensis*), a favourite with both the grizzly and the black bear, as its seeds provide most of the calories for the 2 kg of weight that each must gain daily in summer!

Previous page: Sage: traditionally used with fish dishes.

1. Summer pots bursting with herbs.
2. Combinations of potted herbs make excellent presents.
3. Ginkgo leaves turn golden in autumn.

> **Tip:** Make ice cubes embedded with mint leaves to add to cool drinks in summer. They add a festive look to the simplest of summer drinks. I also love bowls created out of ice in which a selection of pretty flowers—from violets, to nasturtiums, and the bright green leaves of herbs like tarragon—have been trapped. (Use two bowls, the smaller inside the larger, to create the ice 'bowl'.) Summer salads of mango and prawns look particularly festive served this way.

uses, such as medicinal, beverage, aphrodisiac and sensory; and there's a 'tussie mussie' bed, which relates to the language of flowers.

In another large garden commercial herb beds are arranged as four concentric circles, the outer one with a radius of 12.5 m. In the central bed are six pear trees, underplanted with mint, spearmint and peppermint. Other circles house many varieties of eating apples.

Yet another garden comprises beds raised to allow for ease of weeding and so that people with disabilities can touch, smell and enjoy the herbs. Wide paths are of gravel.

Some medicinal plants

- *Agrimonia eupatoria*, agrimony, is a digestive herb cultivated for the liver. It can be dried, rubbed through a sieve to eliminate twigs, and used as a tea.

> **Tip:** Meadowsweet (*Filipendula ulmaria*) contains salicylic acid compounds of aspirin. It is used as a digestive herb, in particular for moderating the stomach's acid/alkaline balance and for easing nausea. It is said to be helpful for aching legs, rheumatism and arthritis. To make a tea from meadowsweet, infuse 1 to 2 teaspoons of the dry herb in a cup of boiling water for 10 to 15 minutes.

- *Aloysia triphylla*, lemon verbena, is a sprawling shrub that can grow up to 3 m in height but also requires severe pruning to keep it within the bounds of your herb patch or vegie garden. It bears pale lilac fluffy flowers in summer, and its leaves have the most delicious scent when brushed or crushed. Make a cleansing tea by immersing a few of the leaves in boiling water. Add lemon and honey. Or dry the leaves and add to sachets for the linen press.
- Grow the scented perennial French tarragon (*Artemisia dracunculus*) from cuttings. Among its various culinary uses, it is delicious roasted with chicken.
- *Centella asiatica*, pennywort, is used extensively throughout Asia as a medicinal herb to speed healing and in meditation.
- *Cymbopogon citratus*, lemon grass, is a tropical herb that likes to bask in the sun, with a long glass of water! Regular fertiliser will also ensure fat, succulent stalks.
- *Epilobium angustifolium*, the pink-flowered willow herb, is a spreading perennial that naturalises in burnt-out areas and it is now being used to treat prostate cancer. Take care, though, as it can become weedy.
- Among the trees that are said to have a medicinal or restorative use is *Ginkgo biloba*, the ginkgo or maidenhair tree. The leaves of this ancient tree, stunning in large gardens in a wide range of climates, turn butter-yellow in autumn, and are collected for adding to tea. Experiments are being conducted as to the benefits of ginkgo in the prevention and treatment of Alzheimer's Disease.
- *Hypericum perforatum*, St John's wort, has been used to boost the immune system and as an anti-depressant. Tests are being conducted on its use in the fight against HIV, viral hepatitis and chronic fatigue syndrome.
- The leaves of *Laurus nobilis*, the bay tree, are great in casseroles—and the plant makes an excellent hedge. It is said that bunches tied and hung in your pantry are a deterrent for the infuriating pantry moth—but, I must confess, this doesn't work for me!

Pesto (makes 2 cups)

A favourite in our household is pesto. It is made in great quantities in summer, when the vegetable garden is full of basil, and when this delicious herb is inexpensive to buy in bunches. It can be frozen, in small tubs (for it is rich and is used only in small quantities) to be used with pasta, on tiny pizzas, to be added to slow-baked tomatoes (also a favourite activity undertaken when tomatoes are in season), to be dolloped on risotto and on baked meats.

There are various recipes for pesto, but it is crucial, in my mind, that no other herb is added to the mix. And I always use two different cheeses: the best parmesan I can find, usually Reggiano, and provolone—or, for a more piquant pesto, pecorino. I crank up the garlic: but take care not to allow the garlic to overpower the basil.

6 cups basil leaves, fairly tightly packed, washed and dried (no stems)

5 cloves garlic, peeled, chopped and crushed

300 g pine nuts, very lightly toasted, to bring out the flavour (watch them carefully: they can suddenly burn)

120 g best parmesan, chopped

110 g provolone or pecorino, chopped

1.5 cups virgin olive oil

Method

Add all ingredients to blender, except olive oil. Drizzle this in slowly once other ingredients have started to blend. Add the oil in the quantity to your taste (I use about 1.5 cups).

- *Leonurus cardiaca*, the motherwort, with its attractive palmate leaves, is a diuretic.
- *Melissa officinalis*, lemon balm, is a gentle digestive that is easy to grow in flower borders.
- *Ocimum basilicum*, sweet basil, is a summer annual, which I always grow for as many of the warmer months as possible to add pizzazz to almost any salad or vegetable dish and to make the pesto that is a favourite of one of my sons. I make large quantities and freeze it in plastic tubs (see above for the recipe).
- *Ocimum tenuiflorum*, Thai or sacred basil, is said to reduce fever and inflammation.
- *Salvia sclarea*, clary sage, supposedly used by Achilles, is said to be a remedy for foot odour. It also aids digestion and calms nerves. *Salvia miltiorhiza*, red sage, is a bitter herb used as a mouthwash for inflamed gums or tonsillitis and can aid in circulation.
- *Stevia rebaudiana*, a herb from Paraguay, is a sugar substitute. About 200 times sweeter than sugar, it is important for diabetics.
- The flowers of the linden tree, *Tilia cordata*—often seen in large and small gardens in cool climates, planted to create a stilt hedge—provide a tea that is said to lower blood pressure and calm nerves. It is also said to improve digestion and act as a diuretic.
- *Trifolium pratense*, red clover leaf, is thought to be important in the natural treatment of some of the effects of menopause.
- *Valeriana officinalis*, valerian, is a nerve antidote and considered an excellent soil conditioner.

Planting and care

Herbs are sun lovers, but some, including the mints, peppermints, and parsley, will grow in the shade. Basil should be watered in the mornings; like most herbs, it doesn't like wet feet. It will die off after flowering, so pick the leaves constantly, and also plant over successive weeks for summer-long harvesting.

LAWNS

Lawns

I have been known to say that as long as my lawn is green I am happy, even if there is the odd—or more than just the odd—weed in it. However, such advice is hardly of use to those who dream of a sward of perfect, even, green lawn.

A lush, green lawn is a sign of garden health and, like most things worth having, takes a little effort to achieve and maintain. Correct mowing, aerating and fertilising are all part of a lawn maintenance program. After enduring months of being mown through summer, of being tramped upon, of drought or heavy downpours and less-than-perfect drainage due to thatch left by grass clippings and other debris, your lawn will be begging for some tender care to prepare it for an autumn and winter rest.

Top tips for a good-looking lawn

- Just like any plant, grass needs light, food and water to remain healthy and grow well. The annual activity of aerating is a simple matter of raking up any leaves or other material, or piercing the lawn with a garden fork. You can walk on it with those spikes that attach to your shoes, or can hire an aerating machine from a large hardware store if you are really keen. (Watch out for any irrigation system.) Distribute a fertiliser and water in well. (*See also* Soil, for a discussion of soil needs.)
- Top-dress lawns with a special topdressing soil, or sand, in early spring when new growth starts and in early summer. Don't apply too thickly, then level off, ensuring that the tips of the grass are visible.
- Specific lawn fertilisers are readily available: a slow-release organic conditioner is best, and is best applied in spring. Simply broadcast on a

damp lawn—preferably in the morning—in the quantities stipulated on the packet. Water in, as with all fertilisers.
- Take care not to cut the lawn too low—known as scalping—as this will expose soil and encourage weeds.
- Lawn pests include black beetle, which at the larval stage is the dreaded curl grub; treat with Yates's Baythroid, a low-toxin, synthetic pyrethroid that doesn't enter the food chain and is not harmful to earthworms and other useful soil organisms (*see* Pests and Diseases).
- Dog urine is high in nitrogen and so will cause burnt marks and patches on a lawn.
- Control weeds with a mix of fine dry sand, sulphate of iron and sulphate of ammonia. Spread this mix over broadleaf weeds and clovers—a handful per square metre. You can water after a couple of days.
- Return your mower clippings to the lawn, at the same time returning nitrogen and other nutrients

Tip: If you are plagued with onion grass (*Romulea* spp.) you will have to eradicate it completely before laying lawn or applying lawn seed. There are no short cuts: first spray off the onion grass with glyphosate. Wait for the onion grass to re-appear and re-apply glyphosate. You may need to repeat this process to be sure that you have killed off all the tiny bulbs.

Opposite: The native violet, *Viola hederacea*, is effective as a lawn substitute or ground cover.

1. Courtyard pavers are softened with native violets.
2. In Diana and Brian Snape's Melbourne garden, the ground hugging *Mazus pumilio*: it loves moist, fertile soils.
3. Thuya Gardens.
4. The moss-like Canberra grass, *Scleranthus biflorus*, enjoys a cool root system.

and reducing moisture loss. Mow before weeds have time to seed as these would also be distributed across the lawn.

- And try a combination of grass varieties, such as blue and green couch together, to suit your climate and other growing conditions.

♥ My favourite lawn grasses

Grasses fall into two categories: warm-climate grasses and those that will enjoy cool and cold climates.

WARM-CLIMATE GRASSES

These are perennial, running grasses that may brown off in winter. If you don't like that look oversow, in autumn, with a cool-climate grass for winter greening.

- Buffalo (*Stenotaphrum secundatum*): originally from the West Indies, and named for the ship that carried it to Australia, this is a good choice for a coastal lawn. It is hard working and hard wearing and will cope with some shade. New varieties of soft-leaf buffalo include 'Sir Walter' and 'ST91'. Only certain herbicides can be used on the soft-leaved buffalo, so check instructions carefully before applying.

- Green couch (*Cynodon dactylon*), also known as Bermuda grass, copes well with traffic. It has a thicker underground stem, which means that it can regenerate itself much more quickly. 'Santa Ana' is a variety bred in California, well suited to drought conditions, which can be mixed with kikuyu.

- Queensland blue couch (*Digitaria didactyla*) is native to East Africa and Madagascar, is very fine and has an attractive blue sheen.

- Kikuyu (*Pennisetum clandestinum*) requires no water, but remains green and thick in tough seasons, so is the choice for drought-resistant gardens. From East Africa and Kenya, this broad-leafed grass can be rampant, so edge garden beds in wood so that the 'whipper snipper' can keep recalcitrant runners in check.

COOL-CLIMATE GRASSES

- Bent, the 'putting green' grasses, *Agrostis tennuis* and *A. palustris*, are used to give a very soft lawn with a fine-textured finish. High maintenance, they are used in cool, humid climates.
- Chewings fescue (*Festuca rubra* var. *commutata*) is often combined with Kentucky blue to form a fine, deep green and dense lawn. Cut high under trees.
- Tall fescue (*Festuca arundinacea*) is tolerant of a wide range of conditions and provides an even sward from sun to shaded areas. It is a rapid grower and establishes a deep root system, making it a good choice to stabilise banks.
- Kentucky blue (*Poa pratensis*) is greatly loved in cold climates for its fine-leaved, luxurious growth and blue sheen. A creeping grass, it grows all year round and is used in parks and sports fields.
- Rye grasses, the annual *Lolium multiflorum*, and the perennial *L. perenne*, are used with other grasses. Soft and quick growing they do not mow evenly however, so are not used for 'bowling green finishes'. Often combined with Kentucky blue and Chewings fescue.

Planting

To lay a lawn, prepare the soil first: add organic matter to sandy soil and break clay soil down with sandy loam.

A smoothly raked, friable sandy loam is the best base upon which to lay turf. Roll turf out as soon as it is delivered. Lay rolls across any slope, rather than down it, and place strips edge to edge.

To sow seed, prepare the soil as described above. You might want to mix the fine, light seed with sand to aid distribution: scatter seed, on a calm day and in the early morning, as the weather warms in spring. Broadcast in two directions to ensure even cover; rake over lightly to aid even distribution and water lightly. Keep damp until germination. Ease off watering as the lawn grows stronger.

Non-grass lawns

There are several alternatives to lawn, which are most interesting and often more easygoing, requiring less maintenance, than grasses. They are often a better choice for shaded areas, and can soften stone steps and courtyards. So, if a velvet smooth sward of green lawn is not something you feel you must have, here are some alternatives that will nevertheless make sure your garden looks inviting.

- *Dichondra repens*, or kidney weed, forms a bright green, dense matt in a sunny position that is not subject to heavy traffic. It grows taller in shade, and copes with a light mow.
- Among the Australian native grasses, *Danthonia* spp., which grows to 25 cm, doesn't need cutting throughout summer.
- *Phyla nodiflora*, lippia, is an excellent, root-binding, flat grass substitute that has tiny white or pink flowers for much of the year, in sun or shade, and is salt tolerant.
- *Hemiandra pungens*, or snakebush, is related to native rosemary (*Westringia* spp.) and blooms with mauve or white flowers from prickly foliage. It forms mats up to 12 m in diameter in a sunny spot and in well-drained soil.
- *Scleranthus biflorus*, the prostrate, bright green Canberra grass, is a moss-like ground cover native to alpine areas of Australia, New Zealand and South America.
- *Soleirolia soleirolii*, also known as baby's tears (as is *Erigeron* spp.), forms a thick, lush cover of tiny bright green leaves. Native to the western Mediterranean and Italy, this is a creeping ground cover that loves shady, damp conditions. It answers to many other names, including Irish moss, Japanese moss and Corsican carpet. There is a gold version, *S. soleirolii* 'Aurea', which would look stunning lighting up gloomy areas.
- Any of the matting thymes, such as the lilac-flowering woolly thyme, *Thymus* 'Mauve', make excellent alternatives to lawn. Try a combination of a dozen different matting thymes for a glittering carpet effect.
- *See also* Edgings and Ground Covers for a discussion of prostrate grevillea, ajuga, periwinkle, native violets and snow in summer (*Cerastium tomentosum*), which also make excellent substitutes for grass.

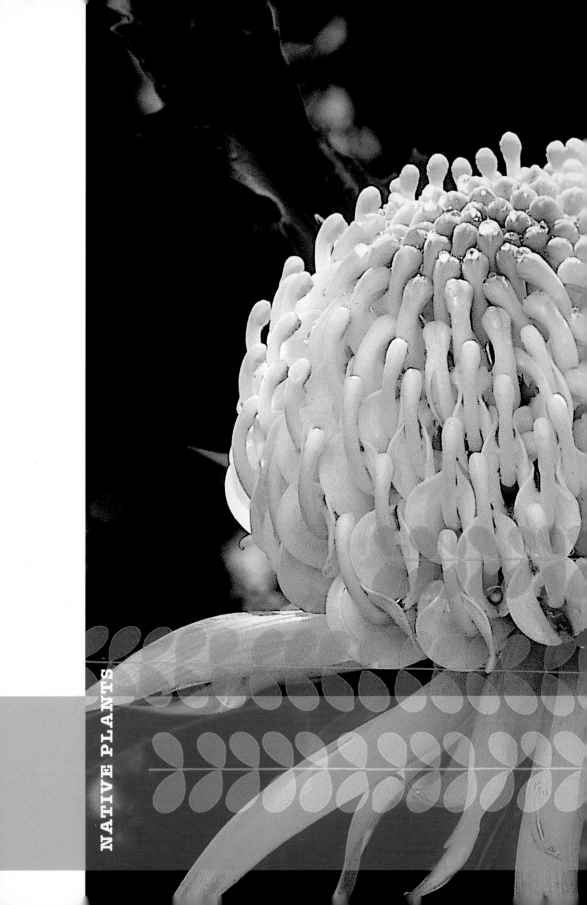

Native Plants

In the midst of continuing concern over climate change and the drought conditions accompanying it, the debate continues over whether we should be gardening with Australian trees or with exotics. Some city councils now demand a high proportion of native plant material in the mandatory landscape plan that must accompany a development application. Yet there is a discourse that argues that gardening is the manipulation of nature, the imposition of the will of humans upon their surroundings.

Since before the sweet chestnut (*Castanea sativa*) was introduced into Britain by the Romans more than a thousand years ago, plant hunters and obsessed gardeners alike have been trawling the world for botanical treasure to carry home. And lime trees (*Tilia × europaea*), now so much part of the English countryside, lining country lanes and grand avenues alike, were sent from Dutch nurseries in the seventeenth century.

The first settlers to this country bemoaned the khaki 'forest in rags' and yearned for the intense greens of home. Peter Cunningham, surgeon aboard five convict fleets between 1819 and 1828, wrote in *Two Years in New South Wales, Sydney*, his account of life in the young colony, that the gum tree provided 'no rustlings of the fast-falling leaves, nor burstings of the buds into life and loveliness in the spring'. Colonists did not need a psychologist to tell them that the mid- to dense greens can provide a sense of well-being.

In mountain areas like Victoria's Mount Macedon, where leading nineteenth-century families sought summer refuge—and close association with colonial power at leisure—collections of northern hemisphere trees underlined success. These giants now contribute strong bones to the garden after the fire of autumn foliage has lost its glow and when the dripping mists of winter arrive.

The Australian Horticultural Therapy Association has long understood the use of plants—touch, sight and smell—in areas such as anger management, in aged care and in healing from serious illness. There is an emotional benefit from observing the change in seasons: the rhythm of birth, growth, senescence, death and then rebirth, and an understanding that the seasons will, inevitably, come and go. This is most evident in deciduous trees.

Yet many native plants do change with the seasons: eucalypts do, but more subtly. The bark of the Sydney blue gum takes on vibrant colours in summer when it strips off in great leathery shards. The snow gum (*Eucalyptus niphophila*) flaunts its brilliant carmines, oranges and emeralds in winter. But anyone who has inherited a mature eucalypt in a city garden will attest to the fact that it sheds leaves all year and drops limbs with frightening regularity. It is for good reason that the eucalypt was dubbed the widow-maker.

Australian garden history confirms, however, that many European settlers, while at first finding native flora threatening and while they sought to domesticate and familiarise a scene they considered a wilderness, became captivated by their surroundings as their eye matured.

In a large country garden you might consider allowing the landscape to dictate design. Colours might reflect the summer tones of native grasses, or of the wide Australian sky; the plant palette could blend seamlessly with the forms and

Opposite: The rare white waratah.

textures of the indigenous vegetation. Plant trees endemic to the area—species that may have been swept away when earlier settlers created grazing land or cultivated crops—and thus recreate a habitat for native birds and animals.

❧ Planting

The leaves of many indigenous plants range from matt grey to olive-green; the combinations of tone, leaf form and texture are even more crucial than when using a European palette of brighter, more intense greens. Australian plants absorb light, rather than reflecting it to provide energy and vibrancy. Their flowers are more subtle; it takes time, care and skill to draw out and best display their discreet charms.

STEPS TO SUCCESS

Consider local indigenous plants

Observing what grows well in your area is the first step to success with indigenous plants, although this can also be misleading, as what grew naturally before suburbia took over is not always appropriate in cities of drains, paving and swimming pools. If you planted the broad-leaved paperbark (*Melaleuca quinquenervia*), stunning in the Lachlan swamp in Sydney's Centennial Park where it occurs naturally, in a garden in the nearby suburb of Randwick, you would soon suffer the problems created by the water-seeking roots. This paperbark, which is indigenous to Sydney's coastal swamps—and has become naturalised in Florida's Everglades—is not a suitable tree for a city garden.

As the geographer, the late George Seddon, pointed out in the prologue to Diana Snape's book, *The Australian Garden: Designing with Australian Plants*, not all 'native' plants suit every garden. 'Lemon-scented gums pushing into the foundations of valuable nineteenth-century terraces in their minute front yards in the inner suburbs of Sydney and Melbourne constitute bad gardening,' he writes. The silver princess (*Eucalyptus caesia*) endemic to the sands of Western Australia is just as exotic in an eastern state garden as the box hedge or iceberg rose, today so often ridiculed as emblematic of gardening's cultural cringe.

Plant needs and habits

An increase in horticultural knowledge has made it easier to garden successfully with indigenous plants than it was three decades ago, when lack of understanding of plant needs and habits gave 'native gardens' a bad name. There are many good reasons for designing with native plants, but if creating a maintenance-free garden is one of them, you will be disappointed. Do not think that a random selection of indigenous species, dotted about the lawn, or grouped together in a few island beds—and then left to fend for themselves—is going to give you an aesthetically pleasing, care-free oasis. Indigenous plants require their fair share of attention. Most are exacting about soil and climate; they must be pruned appropriately and at the right time, weeds must be kept in check, and mulching is still a golden rule.

Nature's design principles need to be observed. But the scent of milk and honey—and the sound of birdsong—will greet you as you arrive at any garden that employs a palette of well-chosen Australian native plants.

♥ My favourites

GROUND COVERS

- *Ajuga australis* is an effective ground cover, sending up spires of pink or lilac flowers; it seems tolerant of all conditions, except, perhaps, heavy frost.
- *Hardenbergia violacea*, the native wisteria, is a showy climber, or ground cover, and will cope with frosts, although heavy frosts may have the effect of a winter prune!

GRASSES

- *Lomandra* is a genus of 50 species of native grass-like plants related to the lilies and the grass trees. They are frost tender and tolerant of dry, poor soils, but will also thrive in swampy conditions.

LILIES

- *Blandfordia grandiflora*, those evocative red and yellow flowering Christmas bells, are native to southern Queensland and northern New South Wales.

CLIMBING PLANTS

- *Billardiera* spp. is a genus of nine species that flower with pendulous bells followed by elongated berries.
- *Billardiera longiflora* is a twiner that grows to some 3 m and bears cream, bell-like flowers, followed by flamboyant purple berries.
- *Clematis glycinoides* is an unusual climber bearing white flowers in spring. Evergreen, it is useful for covering walls.

> **Tip:** The leaves of *Clematis glycinoides* can be crushed and the aroma inhaled to alleviate the symptoms of headaches and colds.

- *Hibbertia* spp.: most of the 120-odd species of *Hibbertia* are native and will grow in any well-drained soil; they are perfect for coastal gardens.
- *Hibbertia scandens* can climb to 6 m and also forms an effective ground cover, often being employed to stabilise sand dunes.
- *Kennedia* is an Australian genus comprising 16 species of climbing or trailing plants that will quickly cover a fence or create a green, or living, wall. Most will survive light frost, love light soils, sun or shade and will tolerate drought conditions.
- *Kennedia nigricans*, the black and yellow coral pea, will cope with dry summers and wet winters.
- *Pandorea* spp.—once known as both *Bignonia* and *Tecoma*—comprises six species of twiners native to Australia and New Caledonia. Named after Pandora in Greek mythology, it features trumpet-shaped flowers in white to cream to blush-pink and cerise, among tough, ribbed leaves.

> **Tip:** The *Pandorea* climbing species demand a sunny position and sandy soils, love water and will tolerate light frosts. Cut back after flowering to prevent them becoming invasive.

The running postman

One of the earliest settlers in Western Australia, Georgiana Molloy—who, with her husband John, established settlements in the far south of the state—wrote home to England about the brilliant colours of the native ground cover *Kennedia rubicunda*, nicknamed 'the running postman' because of its red, pea-like flowers.

- *Pandorea jasminoides*, the bower vine, or native jasmine, flowers in trumpets of cerise or pink.
- *Pandorea jasminoides* 'Lady Di' has white flowers through summer, to extend the flowering time of other climbers.
- *Pandorea pandorana*, Wonga-Wonga vine, flowers in cream and white for just a few weeks in summer.
- *Sollya* is a Western Australian genus of just three species. *Sollya heterophylla*, reaching up to 2 m, bears delicate, nodding, bell-like blue flowers that are followed by navy-blue fruit.

ORCHIDS

Easy-to-grow native orchids such as the spectacular *Dendrobium speciosum* occur naturally, over a large area from Victoria to North Queensland, on exposed sandstone rock. For a detailed discussion of the vast range from which you can choose, *see* Orchids.

> **Tip:** Kangaroo paws like lots of sun and fertiliser in autumn. Cut right back to the ground after flowering to encourage fresh new growth, and divide in autumn.

1. The native rosemary, *Westringia fruticosa*.
2. Alpine daisies flower through January in the Snowy Mountains.
3. The rare black kangaroo paw, *Macropidia fuliginosa*.
4. The grass tree, *Xanthorrhoea australis*.
5. In the sands north of Perth, the blue-flowering *Lechenaultia biloba* is found with *Hibbertia hypericoides*.

PERENNIALS

- *Anigozanthos manglesii*, the red and green kangaroo paw, is the floral emblem of Western Australia but will grow in other parts of the country if the humidity is not too high and the soil is well drained and sandy.
- *Anigozanthos* 'Regal Claw' is a low-growing form with orange and red flowers.
- *Bracteantha viscosa*, once part of the *Helichrysum* genus and known generally as 'sticky daisy', is a great bird attractor.
- The *Dianella* genus, named after Diana, the ancient Roman goddess of hunting, contains about 30 species of clump-forming perennials, native to Australia, New Zealand and the Pacific Islands.
- *Dianella revoluta* is an easygoing lily that tolerates sun and shade, drought and wet soil. It bears beautiful sprays of tiny blue and yellow flowers in spring, followed by purple berries in late summer. You might choose it over agapanthus, which can become an environmental weed if not scrupulously dead-headed.
- *Wahlenbergia stricta*, part of a genus of 200 species, flowers with starry-blue flowers; it is greatly loved by the bees, important for pollination. Tall growing, it is native to the south of Australia and self-seeds freely in open woodland.

SMALL SHRUBS

Only four of the genus *Boronia* are not indigenous to Australia. The evergreen shrubs have fragrant leaves and scented, four-petalled flowers. They are tricky to grow, requiring cool roots in acid sandy soil and a sheltered position, and are often short lived. They occur naturally in the dry schlerophyll forests.

- *Boronia megastigma*, the brown boronia, is used for perfume.
- *Boronia molloyae*, which bears tiny bell-like cerise flowers, is the only plant named after Georgiana

Molloy, who was among the first settlers to arrive south of Perth in May 1830. She ameliorated her loneliness, and her grief after the loss of two children, by collecting seeds and plant specimens for Kew.
- *Boronia serrulata*, with pink flowers on a small upright shrub, is endemic to a small area around Sydney.

> **Tip:** *Xanthorrhoea* spp. look great grouped in threes, or in pots, or standing behind swathes of grey-leaved westringia or with any of the silver-leaved grevilleas. They love sandy soil, good drainage and heat.

XANTHORRHOEA

Could there be anything more evocative of Australia than the iconic grass tree, *Xanthorrhoea* spp.? Now classified as part of their own family, Xanthorrhaceae, the grass trees comprise some 30 species, found in a range of areas, from coastal heathlands to forests both wet and dry. The flowers and fruits were used by indigenous Australians as tinder, to make fire. With tufts of spiky leaves emerging from the apex of a woody stem,

> ## Childhood holidays
> On regular childhood holidays to O'Reilly's guesthouse in the Lamington National Park, we knew we had 'arrived' when the first grass tree was spotted, growing bent and gnarled, and often charred by bushfire, on the rocky slopes by the edge of the winding road, above the township of Canungra in the Gold Coast hinterland.

> **Tip:** *Boronia molloyae* would look beautiful foregrounding some of the medium and tall-growing grevilleas.

> **Tip:** Take care, when purchasing a grass tree for your garden, that your plant has the seal of approval from the National Parks, to ensure that it has not been harvested illegally.

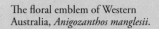
The floral emblem of Western Australia, *Anigozanthos manglesii*.

Floral emblems

I started thinking about the floral emblems of our States when I realised that the flamboyant *Anigozanthos manglesii*, the red and green kangaroo paw—named after the amateur botanist and plant hunter Captain James Mangles, who had in fact never been to the colonies—is the emblem of Western Australia. I felt rather cross that the choice had not been a species named for Georgiana Molloy, an early settler south of Perth, who collected the flora of the south of Western Australia for Mangles and centres of botanical learning in Britain in the early nineteenth century.

I started wondering about the stories behind the choices of floral emblem for Australia. Here is what I found out.

Acacia pycnantha, the golden wattle, a tall shrub reaching up to 8 m and native to the temperate parts of the country, was formally proclaimed our national floral emblem on 1 September 1988, the year of Australia's bicentenary. It flowers in panicles of bright yellow, scented, balls from late winter to mid-spring that emerge from sickle-shaped grey-green leaves.

Gossypium sturtianum, the Sturt's desert rose (so-named after the explorer Charles Sturt (1795–1869)), is the floral emblem of the Northern Territory. Part of the hibiscus family and a close cousin of the species that produces cotton, it is native to northern Australia and its beautiful hibiscus-like flowers comprise five overlapping mauve petals with a stunning burgundy centre.

After much discussion about various flora indigenous to the state, *Dendrobium phalaenopsis*, the Cooktown orchid, was declared the floral emblem of Queensland on 19 November 1959. It is an intense deep pink, similar in colour to the state's official colour—maroon.

Telopea speciosissima, the waratah, was proclaimed the floral emblem of New South Wales in 1962. This glorious, flamboyant native, found in the sandstone soils of the Blue Mountains, west of Sydney, flowers in brilliant crimson—and, rarely, white—in spring and early summer.

Wahlenbergia gloriosa, the royal bluebell, was announced as the floral emblem of the Australian Capital Territory on 26 May 1982.

The pink form of *Epacris impressa*, the common heath, was declared as Victoria's floral emblem in 1958. This shrub grows to about 1 m and is native to sandy slopes in south-eastern Australia. The pink tubular flowers appear from winter to spring.

Swainsona formosa, the Sturt's desert pea, native to the dry outback, was adopted as the floral emblem of South Australia on 23 November 1961, when it was known as *Clianthus formosus*. It is a trailing annual that bears large, bright red spring flowers with a distinctive black 'eye'.

The floral emblem of Tasmania is *Eucalyptus globulus*, a massive blue gum that can reach 70 m. The juvenile leaves are a silver-grey, becoming a deep green on maturity, and the cream flowers are rich in scent and nectar. It is a fast grower, planted throughout Tasmania for its timber.

Anigozanthos manglesii, the red and green kangaroo paw, was proclaimed the floral emblem of Western Australia on 9 November 1960. It is one of about 12 species of the genus *Anigozanthos* endemic to the south-west of Western Australia. The family Haemo-doraceae, to which it belongs, occurs in Australia, Papua New Guinea, South Africa and the Americas.

they are extremely slow growing, some having reached just 30 cm when up to a century old.
- *Xanthorrhoea australis*, the southern grass tree, grows on the dry hillsides in south-eastern Australia. Spears of fragrant white flowers emerge in spring once the plant is about 15 years old.

EDGERS, LOW-GROWING HEDGES AND HEDGES

There are many native plants that love being clipped to a hedge, providing a dense background against which you can showcase shrubs or small trees.
- *Isotoma axillaris* makes a good edging plant: prune it back hard so that it will thicken up.
- *Westringia fruticosa* makes a terrific, low-growing hedge, if clipped regularly; it seems less susceptible to humidity than most grey-leaved plants.

LILLYPILLIES

Members of the Myrtaceae family, these evergreen trees or shrubs, the *Syzygium*, *Acmena* and *Waterhousia* genera are considered by some botanists to belong to the genus *Syzygium*. They clip beautifully into dense, glossy green hedges and into topiary, or they make an excellent specimen tree. There is a variety to suit every climate, any aspect and any sized garden.

Lillypillies are at home in deep, rich soil but will tolerate a range of well-drained soils. They love the sun but will cope with shade. They have smooth leaves that, when young, take on a range of colours (bronze, pink, cerise and lime green); they have fluffy flowers and edible purple, blue or white fruits. Left to grow as trees, some will reach 8 m; at home in the rainforests of northern New South Wales and Queensland, *Syzygium luehmannii* will reach up to 30 m.

> **Tip:** Much loved by bush food devotees, the well-known lillypilly, the riberry (*Syzygium luehmannii*), can be made into jams and jellies and can be poached to use with cuts of meat such as lamb backstraps in much the same way as I have recommended for baked quince (*see* Fruit).

Pimple psyllid resistance
- *Syzygium australe* 'Aussie Southern' and 'Elegance' are happy in coastal situations.
- *Syzygium luehmannii*, and its cultivars are less prone to the lillypilly psyllid, a tiny native insect that causes little bumps on new growth (*see* Pests and Diseases). Cultivars include 'Royal Flame', 'Little Lucy' and 'Cascade'.
- *Syzygium paniculatum*, the east coast lillypilly, is also psyllid-resistant.

Small growing
- *Syzygium* 'Aussie Compact'.
- *Syzygium australe* 'Tiny Trev' is a dwarf form with small, tightly packed leaves; it makes a great small hedge or potted plant.

Cold tolerant
- *Acmena smithii* var. *minor* is psyllid-resistant and cold tolerant. New cultivars include 'Allyn Magic', 'Dusky', 'Hot Flush', 'Hedgemaster' and 'Minipilly'.
- *Waterhousia floribunda* has glossy green leaves and white or pink powder-puff flowers, followed by gorgeous red berries. More tolerant of cool climates, it is very popular for hedges in Melbourne.

SHRUBS AND SMALL TREES

Acacia

For many of us, wattles are synonymous with Australia—and, of course, the golden wattle (*Acacia pycnantha*) is our national floral emblem. Many optimistically associate their bright yellow blossom each July and August with the end of winter, although for some the blossom heralds the beginning of the hay fever season.

Acacia is a genus of more than 1200 mostly evergreen species, some 900 occurring naturally in Australia. They usually bloom with yellow or cream, pollen-filled heads or spikes of fluffy blossom that attract abundant bees. These are fast-growing but short-lived trees and shrubs often used as 'nurse plants' to protect slower growing, and perhaps more precious, trees.

- *Acacia baileyana*, the Cootamundra wattle, is perhaps the best known of the genus. There is a purple-leaved form, 'Purpurea', which is, however, a little more fussy.
- *Acacia decurrens*, the black wattle, grows quickly to 15 m and has fine, feathery leaves; it enjoys a warm temperate to cold climate and deep, moist soils.
- *Acacia leprosa*, the cinnamon wattle, is lemon-yellow. The blood-red form, produced by cuttings, is commercially known as 'Scarlet Blaze'. It was chanced upon in Sherbrooke Forest in 1995, on the eastern edge of Melbourne.
- *Acacia linifolia*, with soft grey-green foliage, is easy to team with a variety of exotic plants. Placed towards the boundary of a garden, it will draw the eye into the distance, creating a sense of space.
- *Acacia longifolia*, the Sydney golden wattle, occurs along the east coast of Australia and grows to about 5 m.

> **Tip:** *Acacia longifolia* makes a good first defence against salt winds, or an informal hedge in a coastal garden.

- *Acacia melanoxylon*, the blackwood, loves the deep, rich basalt soils of the Southern Highlands of New South Wales, where it blooms in spring with yellow fluffy orbs. Its wood is valued for cabinet-making.
- *Acacia paradoxa*, the hedge wattle, which enjoys a range of conditions, from coastal climates and soils to semi-arid regions, bears needle-like thorns. It provides a good habitat for small birds like wrens, robins and fantails, and can make an impenetrable hedge.

Agonis
- *Agonis flexuosa*, the Western Australian willow myrtle, or peppermint, is tough but elegant, often used as footpath plantings throughout Perth. It has aromatic weeping leaves and white flowers.

- *Agonis flexuosa* 'After Dark', the purple-leaved willow myrtle, can look stunning planted with the yellow rose 'Frülingsgold' and the apricot Hybrid Tea rose 'Apricot Nectar' but, like many purple-leaved varieties, does not grow as strongly as the species.

Banksia
Many of us remember, with a certain amount of trepidation, the big, bad banksia men of May Gibbs's *Snugglepot and Cuddlepie* books. Perhaps the banksia men are among the reasons that some gardeners have been slow to appreciate the beauty in Australia's indigenous flora!

Named after Sir Joseph Banks, who discovered the genus at Botany Bay when he accompanied Captain James Cook on the first voyage of discovery, in 1770, this is a genus of some 70 species of small trees and large shrubs. They prefer sandy, well-drained soils that are not too rich in nutrients and a position in the sun.

- *Banksia baxteri*, with its striking serrated leaves, is native to the far south of Western Australia and flowers with umber-coloured cylindrical heads.
- *Banksia coccinea*, also native to Western Australia, bears gorgeous red flowers from winter to summer.
- *Banksia ericifolia*, the heath banksia, with its flowers that appear like glowing umber candles, occurs naturally on the sandstone soils of the low mountain ranges along the east coast of Australia.
- *Banksia integrifolia*, the coast banksia, enjoys a wide distribution along the eastern coast of Australia and grows rapidly, flowering with cream to yellow spikes from late summer to early winter.
- *Banksia ornata* and *Banksia marginata*, native to Kangaroo Island, attract the beautiful yellow New Holland honey-eater.
- *Banksia serrata*, 'Old Man Banksia' (the banksia that frightened Gibbs's gumnut babies), is particularly confronting when the large cream to green flowers turn to seed and develop dark, woody 'eyes'. It grows along the east of the country, on sandstone ridges and sand dunes.

1. *Acacia decurrens*.
2. *Acacia baileyana*.
3. *Hakea buculenta* 'Red Hot Pokers'.
4. *Banksia coccinea*.
5. *Banksia hookeriana*.
6. *Grevillea* 'Robyn Gordon'.

Callistemon

Like most native plants, the bottlebrushes, *Callistemon* spp., are adored by native birds, particularly the rainbow lorikeets. Flowering for much of the year with brilliantly coloured red, pink or cream cylindrical spikes which feature long stamens, they look much more effective in groups or clusters, rather than one or two dotted about. Woody seed capsules, sessile to the branch, develop after the flowers fade. Like the genus *Melaleuca* to which they are related, some callistemons also feature a papery bark. They love full sun and hot climates and they will take hard pruning—and can even be hard-pruned into a hedge—although a light prune after flowering is preferable.

- *Callistemon citrinus*, or the scarlet bottlebrush, has given rise to many cultivars, including 'Reeves Pink', 'White Anzac' and 'Mauve Mist'. They look stunning combined with grevilleas, forming a border that will provide a haven to native birds.
- *Callistemon sieberi*, the river bottlebrush, grows on the banks of east coast streams; it is a small tree with grey-green leaves and silvery-pink new growth. The flower spikes are cream with pink tinges and appear from spring to autumn.
- *Callistemon viminalis*, the weeping bottlebrush, thrives in the coastal lowland areas of Queensland and into northern New South Wales, where it grows to 10 m. The small-growing callistemons, which also feature weeping foliage, include 'Captain Cook', the very dwarf 'Little John' and the new 'Mathew Flinders', which grows to less than 1 m in height and half that in width. Try *C.* 'Harkness', which grows to about 4.5 m and is easygoing and not too fussy about its growing conditions. The dwarf varieties are suitable for growing in pots.

Ceratopetalum

Ceratopetalum gummiferum, the New South Wales christmas bush, flowers, as you would expect, in December. What we think of as flowers are in fact the sepals; these enlarge and turn red and papery after the clusters of tiny cream flowers die off at the end of summer. The christmas bush dislikes frost and enjoys half sun and a light soil with excellent drainage.

> **Tip:** The red bracts of *Ceratopetalum gummiferum* look wonderful in a vase with the orange, pink or cerise blooms of the new small-growing cultivars of eucalypts.

Chamelaucium

Chamelaucium uncinatum, Geraldton wax, native to Western Australia and abundant in the town of Geraldton, north of Perth, flowers in a range of pinks and reds, hates frost, but enjoys sandy soils. There are plenty of new, grafted varieties available, but many suffer from root rot. Keep them all in shape with a light prune after flowering.

Grevilleas

Contrary to popular opinion, not all native plants look tough; there are many that are soft and gentle, with blue-green leaves and flowers in pastel shades. Grevilleas are one such group. This enormous genus of species and cultivated varieties, part of the Proteaceae family, provides a wide choice for all climates and styles of gardens.

Grevilleas are wonderful small trees for courtyards. As shrubs, they look great in copses or in borders. They team beautifully with dozens of other native species (and with some exotics) and flower in a vast range of sizes and colours. They grow in a variety of sizes and forms and their leaves range in colour from bright lime-green to soft grey to blue-green, and in shape from toothed to lobed. They also have a wide range of climate needs; many will not tolerate frost, and others are grafted onto *G. robusta* or *G. banksii*, making them tolerant of humidity.

Prune grevilleas from the base up to create a well-shaped small tree. Those that have been allowed to become leggy will recover from a hardprune in spring; water well and feed with a low-phosphorus fertiliser. The lower growing hybrids, like 'Robyn Gordon', 'Superb' and 'Ned Kelly', can be cut to 10 cm above the ground.

Gorgeous grevilleas

The fabulous Illawarra Grevillea Park, set in the shadow of the Bulli Pass, is located some one and a half hours south of Sydney. This 20 ha expanse of landscaped gardens and rainforest walks houses what must be about the largest collection of grevilleas in Australia. The park was the brainchild of local nurseryman and grevillea lover Ray Brown. 'Most of the non-hybrid stuff is wild-sourced,' he explains. 'We go out into the wild, collect seed, and document where they come from. About half the grevilleas in Australia are on the rare and endangered list.'

Even a quick stroll around the park will demonstrate the diversity of grevilleas and the myriad ways in which this large genus can be used in gardens. The popular low-growing Grevillea 'Robyn Gordon' masses at the front of the borders or at the base of a bank. The taller growing G. 'Sandra Gordon', G. 'Claire D' and G. 'Honey Gem' are useful for loose hedges or screens. It's a feast for both the garden lover and the birds. (See Useful Contact Details for more information.)

Large-growing hybrids such as 'Sandra Gordon', 'Moonlight' and 'Honey Gem' can be cut back to a metre or so above the ground. 'Scarlet Sprite' has a spreading form. Prune lightly from an early age to encourage thicker growth and increased flowering.

The prostrate grevilleas, such as G. 'Poorinda Royal Mantle', do not need any pruning. And the pink-flowered trailing grevillea, G. goodii, with soft blue leaves, is a ground cover that will cascade over walls or down banks.

Think about the many bird-attracting hybrids available, with soft, grey-green leaves and pastel-coloured flowers: 'Coconut Ice', 'Moonlight', 'Silver-eye Cream', 'Parfait Crème' and 'Misty Pink'.

- *Grevillea aquifolium*, the holly-leaved grevillea, is found in Victoria and South Australia and flowers with red toothbrush-like, nectar-filled flowers through spring and summer.

- *Grevillea banksii* is a subtropical, east-coast species that grows to almost 10 m and has grey-green, divided leaves. With its pretty pink flowerheads it has provided the genes for many of the beautiful large-flowered, soft-coloured hybrids.
- *Grevillea robusta*, the silky oak, a tall tree and not for small backyards, grows to some 30 m in its preferred coastal environments. It flowers in orange to umber flowers through summer and has soft grey foliage. It is prized for its beautiful timber.
- *Grevillea rosmarinifolia*, the smaller growing spider grevillea, is a dense, spreading shrub that loves the cool climate of south-eastern Australia. It flowers in gorgeous red, coiled flower-heads from winter to spring.

Leptospermum

The coastal tea tree, *Leptospermum* spp., a member of the Myrtaceae family, acquired its name when Captain Cook tried to make a tea for his crew from the leaves, which are aromatic when crushed, hoping it would protect the crew from scurvy. Most members of the genus are native to Australia, with a few species coming from New Zealand and Malaysia. They are mostly not tolerant of frost, growing on the sandy soils of coastal regions of the country. They bloom with five-petalled pink, cerise or cream flowers on elegant, weeping, wandy branches. The flowers are followed by sprays of woody capsules.

- *Leptospermum laevigatum*, the coastal tea tree, is native to the east coast of Australia, where it grows in the sand dunes and bears white flowers in spring and summer.
- *Leptospermum scoparium*, the New Zealand manuka, occurs also in the south of the Australian mainland and Tasmania and has given rise to myriad brightly flowering cultivars such as 'Ruby Glow' and 'Pink Pixie'.

TREES

Angophora

Closely related to the eucalypts, the angophoras, or apple gums, are beautiful, mostly tall, trees that cling to sandstone cliffs on the east coast.

1. The native wisteria (*Callerya megasperma*) found in Queensland and New South Wales.
2. *Melaleuca fulgens*.
3. *Leptospermum scoparium*, the New Zealand manuka.
4. The scented native frangipani.

• *Angophora costata*, the Sydney red gum or smooth-barked apple, has glaucous leaves on twisted branches that play host to swarms of sulphur-crested white cockatoos. It is easy to imagine that our earliest European settlers, as they sailed through Sydney Heads, might have looked in wonder upon these lovely trees as the early morning sun lit their glowing pink trunks.

Backhousia
• *Backhousia citriodora*: the glossy leaves of the lemon-scented myrtle have a distinctive lemon scent when crushed.
• *Backhousia myrtifolia*, one of the predominant species of the tropical rainforest, often plays host to native orchids.

Buckinghamia
• *Buckinghamia celsissima*, the gorgeous pearl tree, one of two species in the genus and a member of the Proteaceae family, is native to the coastal rainforests of northern Australia, but grows well down to Sydney, where it flowers with its racemes of creamy flowers in summer and autumn. These are followed by woody fruits.

Casuarina and Allocasuarina
The *Casuarina* and *Allocasuarina* genera, both commonly called the she-oak, belong to the Casuarinaceae family. The former is common in tropical and subtropical areas, while *Allocasuarina* are found in southern Australia.

The she-oaks have gently weeping, grey-green branchlets. Not much grows under these tall, fast-growing trees that love sandy coastal soils and are valued as shade trees.
• *Casuarina cunninghamiana* is the largest of the she-oaks, growing to some 30 m along river banks, where it is prized for its ability to prevent erosion.
• *Casuarina equisetifolia*, the beach she-oak, is found naturally on sandy shores along the east coast, and along the Indian Ocean.
• *Casuarina glauca* is an upright tree that grows to 10 m along creeks, estuaries and coastal parts of eastern Australia.

Tip: Copses of the ethereal *Allocasuarina torulosa* provide a home for the rare red-tailed glossy black cockatoo, which loves the seeds from the cones.

• *Allocasuarina torulosa*, the water-loving rose she-oak, has a corky trunk and long, weeping, pink-tinted fronds.

Cedars
• *Melia azedarach*, the white cedar, with pretty lilac flowers followed by berries that are poisonous to children but not to birds, is a street tree in many dry-climate Australian cities.
• *Polyscias murrayi*, the pencil cedar, is a member of a genus of around 150 species native to South-East Asia, the islands of the Pacific, and Africa, as well as to Australia. A palm-like tree that grows to about 24 m, it bears cream flowers in autumn, on pinnate leaves that can be over 1 m long.
• *Toona ciliata*, the Australian cedar (which used to be called *T. australis* and before that was included in the genus *Cedrela*), has beautiful fine-grained wood and is greatly prized for cabinet-making. It is a slow-growing tree native to the mountain slopes along the east coast of Australia. It likes good rainfall and deep, rich soils. It will break your heart, though, if you try to grow it in frost-prone areas.

Ceratopetalum apetalum
Ceratopetalum apetalum, the coachwood, is one of a genus of five species found along the east coast of Australia and its hinterland, and into New Guinea. You can identify the coachwood, which loves rainforest conditions, and grows to some 20 m, by the large, grey-green, mossy disks on its trunk. It is often multi-trunked, and has tough deep green leaves and small cream flowers.

Elaeocarpus
Elaeocarpus reticulatus, the blueberry ash, native to the east coast of Australia and among 200 species in the genus, is a relatively fast-growing

tree with fringed flowers in summer that are followed by blue berries. Trees of this species grow to about 9 m, are frost tender, and have shiny leathery leaves and racemes of white flowers in spring and summer.

Eucryphia lucida

Eucryphia lucida, the Tasmanian leatherwood, is familiar to many because of the highly scented, delicious honey that comes from its white flowers. These small trees are an important component of old-growth forests in Tasmania; they do not flower until over 70 years of age and produce most heavily at around two centuries. Once lost through logging, they will be difficult to replace.

Hymenosporum flavum

The single-species *Hymenosporum flavum*, the beautifully scented native frangipani, is covered in butter-yellow and white flowers each summer. It comes from the subtropical rainforests of northern Australia and New Guinea but grows happily south to Sydney. It likes moist, rich soils and is fast growing, up to 9 m.

Melaleuca

Melaleuca spp., the paperbarks, comprise a genus of more than 200 species of evergreen trees and shrubs. Most are native to Australia and many have cream to grey papery bark that can be peeled off in generous sheets. They are closely related to the bottlebrush; some species have similar flowers while others have blooms that resemble powder puffs. Some species produce honey. They like well-drained soil in full sun; prune from an early age to stop woody growth becoming untidy.

> **Tip:** The paperbark of the *Melaleuca* spp. can be used to wrap meats such as crocodile in some styles of bush cooking.

• *Melaleuca armillaris*, the bracelet honey myrtle, grows to about 8 m in coastal regions in south-eastern Australia. It has long, elegant, needle-like deep green leaves and bears cream flowers in spring and summer.
• *Melaleuca ericifolia*, the swamp paperbark, grows to 8 m in the swampy regions of south-eastern Australia.
• *Melaleuca fulgens* sports small lilac bottlebrushes, although there is also a red form and an orange form. From the dry regions of Western Australia, it is a popular garden tree.
• *Melaleuca incana*, the beautiful grey honey myrtle, has grey-green weeping foliage and cream to yellow flowers. It grows to about 3 m and is native to the southern part of Western Australia.
• *Melaleuca linariifolia*, the flax-leaved paperbark, is found at the edges of swamps and creeks in eastern Australia. It grows to about 6 m and has the idiosyncratic peeling cream papery bark.
• *Melaleuca linariifolia* 'Snowstorm' is a low-growing tree that blooms in summer in a mass of cream blossom.
• *Melaleuca quinquenervia*, at home in the swampy parts of the east coast of Australia, is also native to New Caledonia and New Guinea. Growing to some 15 m, and with roots that will seek out the nearest water source, the atmospheric broad-leaved paperbark is not a tree for the suburban backyard— nor, even, for the public footpath.

Stenocarpus sinuatus

Stenocarpus sinuatus, the firewheel tree, grows to some 30 m in its native habitat of the rainforests of coastal Queensland to New South Wales, although it will survive south to Melbourne. The firewheel tree likes full sun and rich, well-drained soil and bears orange to red wheel-like flowers in summer. You often see it planted as a street tree.

❀ Requirements and care

Native plants love blood and bone and dislike phosphorus. Spring is the best time to fertilise, at the rate of about a handful per square metre, onto damp soil and always well watered in afterwards. Or you can also use special native slow-release fertilisers.

Remove the cones of the banksia to promote better flowering the following year.

SHRUBS

Shrubs

In these days of sensible garden-making, where waterwise plants are afforded new respect and mulching has become a good habit—and when complicated perennial borders are most often seen in glossy garden books sent 'downunder' by English publishers—shrubs are again appreciated for their versatility and utility. They can be used to create a pleasing border or scented shrubbery of year-long interest, they can divide garden spaces into 'rooms' or they can create a superb hedge. Again, your choice of shrubs to plant will be dictated by your soil and climate. Choose what grows well in the parts of the world that are similar to where you garden.

♥ My favourites

ARDISIA

A genus of some 250 species of evergreen shrubs, *Ardisia* spp., native to almost every continent, thrive in the tropics and subtropics. Pots of the red-berried, compact holly-like coralberry (*Ardisia crenata*) were very popular with early settlers to the colonies. From Japan, China and the Himalayas, this species is also happy in temperate climates. In Australia it grows to about 2 m and produces layered branches of deep green, glossy foliage which bears star-like white flowers in spring and summer, followed by red berries.

BRUGMANSIA

This is one of my favourites, for the simple reason that it has fragrant flowers. Commonly known as angel's trumpet—somewhat ironic as the plant is highly toxic—and once included in the *Datura* genus, this plant, with its tall, woody stems, and large, pendulous trumpet-shaped flowers, makes a good addition to the rear of a shrubbery for a somewhat tropical look, or, if no small children are about, a feature tree in a courtyard.

Native to South America and members of the Solanaceae family, this small genus contains just five species, all of which are poisonous. The most commonly grown in Australia is *Brugmansia × candida*, which grows wild in Ecuador, flowering in summer, and is scented, particularly at night. The variety 'Grand Marnier' has smart apricot trumpet-like flowers. Brugmansias will tolerate a light frost and are content in a humid climate. Sandy soil is fine, although they also love a mulch of aged manure and compost.

CALLICARPA

Callicarpa, or beauty bush, is a genus of about 140 evergreen and deciduous shrubs and trees from tropical to warm temperate parts of the world. They bear rather unimpressive flowers on mid-green attractive leaves but are most prized for the richly coloured berries that grace the plant throughout autumn. They are not fussy about their growing conditions and can be pruned after the fruit has fallen. Among the most popular is the Japanese beauty bush, *Callicarpa japonica*, grown for its pink fruit and interesting seeds in autumn and because it looks wonderful arranged, with roses, in a vase. It grows to almost 2 m, so is useful for the back of a border, behind some of the small-growing lilacs or viburnums. It also looks wonderful with autumn-colouring shrubs such as *Hydrangea quercifolia*, with leaves that turn to a rich plum colour after summer.

Previous page: *Fuchsia* 'Lye's Unique'.

CEANOTHUS

Another really useful shrub, *Ceanothus* spp. is sometimes called Californian lilac, which is somewhat misleading as some members of the genus have no scent. It does, however, flower in a range of wonderful blues, from the deep blue *Ceanothus griseus* to the softer-blue and much-loved *C. arboreus* 'Trewithen Blue', which has large panicles of fragrant flowers.

Ceanothus arboreus 'Mist' flowers with ethereal grey-blue spikes; allow it to bloom with its clouds of fluffy flowers behind blue iris or tripods of blue or cerise-flowering clematis.

Ceanothus griseus var. *horizontalis* 'Yankee Point' is extremely useful for the front of a rockery or above a retaining wall as it is a low-growing variety that spreads to about 3 m in width.

All ceanothus are tolerant of frost and most soils. Tip-prune after flowering to create and maintain your desired shape.

COTINUS

Better known as smoke bush, for its hazy clouds of pink to red to burgundy plumes that flower in spring and early summer, this is the genus for all seasons, as the stunning, cerise and purple leaves produce a rich tapestry of colours in autumn.

Plant *Cotinus* species in front of all manner of autumn-colouring shrubs and trees, from the maples to the tupelos to the elderberry (*Sambucus* spp.), with its flattened heads of scented, cream flowers in summer. Use them in combination with magenta flowers, or with oranges, reds and yellows to tone them down. You can put them with sugary, icy pinks and whites to add depth and richness, but I love to team them with deep red flowering rhododendrons and with pink peonies for an over-indulgence of colour throughout the year.

Try the *Cotinus* species—including *Cotinus coggygria* 'Royal Purple' and 'Velvet Cloak'—with *Sambucus nigra* 'Guincho Purple', which also has black-purple leaves that turn bright crimson in autumn. This combination looks stunning underplanted with the yellow-toned hostas such as 'June' or the Japanese variegated grass *Hakonechloa*

macra 'Aureola'. *Cotinus obovatus* and *C.* 'Grace' are more subdued forms than the very intense 'Royal Purple'.

Cotinus all like a well-drained soil and a sunny position, although they are tolerant of most conditions, except humidity. They can be pruned in winter, when they are bare, but I just prune them as I need the flowers for the house (*see* Colour).

FUCHSIA

Many of you will have visited the beautiful Regency city of Bath, in the south-west of England, best known as home, for a while, to Jane Austen; famous for its Roman baths, and applauded for its lyric architecture. On my last visit, a few years ago, it was, however, the hanging baskets that adorned the city streets, suspended on chains of different lengths, from green-enamelled posts, that impressed me most. Among the cascading pelargoniums and the blossoming petunias that were packed into moss-lined wire baskets were an array of fuchsias, providing clouds of reds, pinks and purples, cerise and cream.

Fuchsias, first collected from the West Indies by the Franciscan monk Charles Plumier (after whom the frangipani genus *Plumeria* spp. is named), honours the sixteenth-century German physician and herbalist Professor Leonard Fuchs.

A member of the Onagraceae family, this large genus contains thousands of hybrids and cultivars of deciduous or evergreen shrubs—depending upon your climate—and flowers seemingly endlessly from early spring through summer and into autumn. Some are frost hardy, some are not, and most dislike very high temperatures. The flowers are tubular and often pendulous, suspended from whippy branches, and made up of four central petals—often brilliantly coloured—that are protected by four contrasting sepals emerging from a brightly coloured tube. They can be double, frilled and fancy, or single and discreet, most often in soft pinks, cerise or purple and often bicoloured, with wonderfully long stamens. Most are native to South and Central America, although four species are native to New Zealand and one hails from Tahiti.

1. *Fuchsia* 'Mrs Popple'.
2. The rich burgundies of the smoke bush (*Cotinus coggygria*) are a perfect foil for the cerise blooms of watsonias.
3. The apricot tones of *Brugmansia* 'Grand Marnier'.

- *Fuchsia* 'Leonora,' growing to about 75 cm, has soft-pink flowers and lends itself to being pruned and trained into a standard.
- 'Lady Thumb,' at 30 cm, is suitable for growing in pots; it is covered for months in tiny, semi-double flowers that have deep pink sepals protecting white petals.
- 'Lye's Unique' has elongated pink petals and elegant, curving white sepals.
- 'Voodoo' is a big, flamboyant, bloomer in purple and pink; while 'Mrs Popple' flowers with single, purple petals encased in scarlet sepals.

Planting

In the right conditions fuchsias make great informal hedges; plant them also in a long perennial and herbaceous border to add structure and a permanent 'backbone'. Group several cultivars together in a hanging basket and in-fill with annuals for maximum effect. Remember, though, that hanging baskets take dedication to keep looking good: three gardeners work full-time to keep those displays in the city of Bath at their peak.

You'll have greatest success with fuchsias if they are planted in an easterly aspect, where they can enjoy the early morning sun; avoid the baking, afternoon, western sun. Fuchsias enjoy part shade and cope with being placed on a verandah, under cover, where many other plants will develop mould and mildew problems in the less-than-perfect circulation. Keep them well watered, though.

Give them a good hard-prune in winter so they'll thicken up in spring. Take care in cold areas to prune when the risk of severe frost is past. Feed fuchsias with potash when flowering, and at other times with a high-nitrogen fertiliser, particularly important when grown in pots. An organic, water-soluble fertiliser like Seasol or Charlie Carp is suitable.

LAVATERA

There are several lavateras, or mallows—also known as the Australian hollyhock, and related to the hibiscus—that make great additions to shrubberies and borders. A genus of about 25 species, they are found from the Mediterranean to the Himalayas, Australia and North America. They will all cope with most soils but are relatively short-lived. The best known is probably *Lavatera* 'Barnsley', which is covered in soft-pink flowers for months during spring and summer. Cut back after flowering to stop the plant becoming straggly; propagate easily from cuttings.

LOROPETALUM

In my Sydney garden, the outstretched burgundy foliage of the fringe flower, *Loropetalum chinense f. rubrum* (often sold as 'Burgundy'), looks marvellous flowering a bright pink behind the low-growing rose 'Tuscany Superb', with its rich velvet-like cerise blooms. Add to the mix the hot-pink flowering *Salvia microphylla* 'Margaret Arnold'—which copes with humidity. She is offset by a planting of *S.* 'Black Knight' with its stunning lime-green leaves, and by a ground cover of lime hostas.

If I am feeling energetic I add in, each year, spring-flowering pink or burgundy tulips or cerise or blue hyacinths; the entire scene is edged with wide ribbons of black mondo grass.

At present there is just one species in this genus, which seems to be happy in the widest range of climates, from those of the frosty mountain regions to the hot dry summers of north-east Victoria, from the warm temperate to the subtropical. Propagate easily from cuttings in late summer.

MAHONIA

A genus comprising about 70 species, some of which are perfumed, mahonias burst into plumes of yellow flowers in spring and continue through to winter. The flowers are followed by purple or yellow fruit—depending upon the species—which are greatly loved by birds. Leaves are often whorls of spiny, sharp-edged leaflets which colour wonderfully in autumn. They are perhaps best planted as a swathe at the back of a wide shrubbery in a large garden, where their brilliant colours can be fully exposed. They also look stunning with a selection of the blue-flowered salvias. Prune to prevent growth becoming too straggly and pull away suckers to create new plants.

OLEANDER (*NERIUM OLEANDER*)

Described by one country gardener as the rhododendron of the desert, *Nerium oleander* is perhaps the ultimate sensible plant. Flowering throughout summer in a range of colours, from white through to apricot, pink and red, oleanders fulfil a number of garden needs. Evergreen shrubs and small trees, they can be put to various good uses in a wide range of climates. Perhaps most useful as an informal hedge or screen, they are also effective as an easy-to-please backdrop to a border of plants. They are fabulous as the first defence against the salt winds that torment a seaside garden.

Native to a huge area from the Mediterranean regions of Spain, Italy and France—where you'll see them tumbling from walls edging mountain roadsides, clinging to cliffs and lining river banks—to China and Japan in the east, they love the conditions in many parts of Australia.

Poison warning

Most members of the Apocynaceae family, which includes frangipani, golden trumpet vine (*Allamanda* spp.) and periwinkle, are extremely poisonous; all parts of the oleander are deadly. The milky sap will cause skin irritations, and there have been reports of people becoming fatally ill when using cuttings as kindling for a barbecue.

Oleanders look particularly good coppiced annually and growing in large wooden Versailles-style tubs. Either tone or contrast the colour of the container with that of the flower: think black tubs with white flowers or ochre pots with an apricot-flowering cultivar. If you are prepared to take the time, you can even train them into a

Above: The oleander, here *Nerium oleander* 'Hawaii', is effective as a screen or hedge.

Torcilla

12 egg yolks

1 cup castor sugar

1 tsp vanilla essence

600 ml pouring cream

Method

Beat egg yolks and sugar until thick and pale. Add vanilla essence and cream and mix until just combined. Place in a 20 cm diameter ceramic baking dish and bake uncovered, in a larger pan of water, at the lowest possible oven heat for about 6 hours. (I leave it in a very low oven during the day, then turn the heat off and leave it overnight.) The water in the bain marie should reach just halfway up the side of the ceramic dish: check during the cooking time to ensure the water does not completely evaporate. Serve with poached fruits such as figs or pears.

standard for use in tubs, to add interest and height to a small garden, or as a stilt hedge (*see* Hedges).

They are covered from spring to autumn in clusters of flowers, either single or double, in a selection of colours from white to apricot, pale pink, brilliant red and even yellow. The flowers are funnel-shaped and surrounded by a ring of petals, or corolla lobes, with characteristic, fringed throats at the centre of the bloom.

The smaller growing varieties, including the apricot to pink, double, *N. oleander* 'Mrs Roeding', make an excellent low hedge or border to a driveway. Edge with the tough liriope, or the grey-leaved, spreading *Dianthus* 'Mrs Sinkins', which flowers with pale pink, gloriously scented blooms in spring and summer. Try also the apricot *N. oleander* 'Hawaii', which grows to 2 m, along with 'Petite Salmon' and 'Petite Pink', 'Little Red' and 'Marrakesh', also a brilliant red.

Growing a little taller, to about 3 m, are the cerise-flowering 'Algiers' and the pure white 'Casablanca'. *Nerium oleander* 'Tangier' has clear-pink blooms; the larger growing 'Cherry Ripe' has deep pink flowers, while 'Isle of Capri', with pale yellow flowers, grows to about 4 m.

Oleanders can be erect in habit, or arching, particularly if cut back hard each year, a practice that is well tolerated as they flower on new wood. Take to them ruthlessly with the hedge trimmer to prevent them becoming leggy: the tougher the treatment, the better they flower. They demand little water—oleanders hate wet feet—are not fussy about the soil in which they are growing, and will tolerate light frosts. They need plenty of summer sun, however, to flower well. Propagate oleanders by cuttings, or by layering: peg a low-growing, rangy stem into the soil. Cover lightly and wait a year: cut away your new plant after roots have formed.

ZENOBIA

The single-species *Zenobia pulverulenta*, or dusty zenobia, is native to pine forests of the south-east of the United States. This frost-hardy shrub, grown for its wonderful, large, scented flowers rather like lily of the valley, loves cool, humus-rich, acid soil.

Spices

Spices, which have been important for centuries as magical and medicinal potions, in perfumes, in cooking, and even as poisons, conjure up images of exotic locations and great adventure.

The history of the spice trade is long and evocative, shrouded in drama and mystery. It is a tale of great danger and daring, adventure and exploration to unknown, distant places—and of great reward. Spices were used by the ancient Romans, whose cookbooks included many recipes that relied upon these aromatic and often therapeutic plants. The spice trade dates to the Middle Ages (700 AD – 1000 AD), when it was controlled by Muslim merchants; by the sixteenth century it had become the most important commercial enterprise in the old world—equivalent, perhaps, to the gold rush of nineteenth-century Australia or the search for oil today.

The voyages of the Venetian Marco Polo to China in the thirteenth century, of Vasco da Gama to India and of Christopher Columbus, both in the fifteenth century, and of Ferdinand Magellan in the early sixteenth century were searches for routes to facilitate the spice trade. Spices were perhaps the early version of fusion food as cultures of the East and the West were brought together—the Venetians, who dominated the sea routes and ports between 1200 and 1500, with the Chinese; the Portuguese with the Indonesians; and the British with the Indian and Ceylonese. Trade around the Spice Islands and along the so-called spice route was dominated by the Portuguese in the sixteenth century, by the Dutch in the next century and by the British in the eighteenth century.

Cinnamon was found only in Sri Lanka (then Ceylon), cassia in Myanmar and China; and nutmeg came from the Banda Islands, a location that was a closely guarded secret for many years. Cloves were found in just two of the Spice Islands—now known as the Maluku Islands, or the Moluccas—

part of the Indonesian archipelago, lying on the equator between Sulawesi and New Guinea. The spice trade became less valuable when Europeans were able to take seeds and plants back to their own colonies for production there. The provenance of the hot peppers is questionable; they are native to the tropical regions of America, but how and when they reached Asia, where they are crucial to the cuisine, is the subject of debate.

Spices are produced from the buds, seeds, berries and bark of the plant; the leafy parts become herbs. Crucial today as flavouring for a great range of cuisines from different parts of the world, spices should be kept in airtight jars, away from light and heat, to preserve their all-important aroma and flavour.

My mother was a great curry cook, learning as a young bride in Ceylon—now Sri Lanka—where she lived from her marriage at the age of 19 until 1957, when my parents settled in Queensland after Ceylon gained independence.

After that, Sunday lunch at our house was most often a curry, with an exciting selection of sambal (side dishes), always followed by a dessert of sherry trifle. The curry was hot, very hot (just as my father liked it) and sambal—of chopped onion and tomato, sliced banana dipped in shredded coconut, chopped mango in season and sliced cucumber—were served for their cooling effect as well as to contribute different flavours, colours and textures to the dish.

There was never any fruit, or vegetables, in the curry—simply meat. My father maintained that real curry, real *Ceylonese* curry, was made only of meat (although you can make a range of wonderful

Opposite: Spices in the bazaar in Esfahan, Iran.

curry dishes with vegetables). And Dad loved to see the occasional boyfriend who may have joined us for Sunday lunch enjoying my mother's curry: he felt that the real test of a man was how hot he could take his curry! I remember the trepidation I felt as friends, eager to please, would tell Dad how much they enjoyed hot curry, only to sit, struggling, with perspiration pouring down their faces. However, all that is another story! I have given you Mum's recipe for curry, below, as I often make it.

And these are the spices I use most often.

❤ My favourites

CAPSICUM

The capsicum is a genus of some 10 species from the tropical regions of America, including cayenne, bell, paprika and chilli peppers, as well as Tabasco pepper, playing an important role in adding the heat to a variety of cuisines from around the globe.

Small, inconspicuous flowers are followed by colourful, hollow fruits which vary in size, shape and colour—and in the strength of their heat. The smaller fruited species and varieties are usually the more concentrated and hotter in flavour.

Capsicum annum encompasses most of the varieties that we use in cooking; it comes in a variety of shapes, flavours and colours, from large to small, sweet to hot, and from green to yellow to purple and red.

The varieties are then sorted into several groups, according to fruit size and shape. The Longum group includes cayenne pepper and paprika pepper. The Conoides group includes the small-fruiting, hot chilli peppers.

Care

These annual plants make a colourful addition to the summer and autumn vegetable garden, needing well-drained but rich soil and regular summer watering. Sow seed or propagate from cuttings.

Capsicum frutescens, the Tabasco pepper, is a short-lived perennial, reaching up to 3 m. The small summer fruits are very hot.

CARDAMOM

A member of the ginger family, Zingiberaceae, *Elettaria cardamomum* is native to the East, from India to Sri Lanka and Malaysia. It is a shrub reaching some 3 m bearing purple and yellow flowers, followed by small fruits containing aromatic seeds which are dried and ground to produce the spice. Propagation is by seed or division of rhizomes.

With a unique flavour and fragrance, it is often used in curries. It is best used in very small amounts, as it can impart a slightly earthy tone. It also loses its fragrance and flavour quite quickly—so purchase in small quantities.

CINNAMON

Cinnamomum zeylanicum, part of the laurel family, is a tree native to Sri Lanka, growing to around 10 m in height. Its bark is dried to provide the spice.

CLOVES

Syzygium aromaticaum, the clove or Zanzibar lillypilly, is now a widely cultivated tree, although it is native to the Moluccas. It grows to about 15 m in warm climates and bears fragrant flowers. Cloves are the dried flower buds.

Saffron

In many cultures a symbol of affluence, saffron is the world's most valuable spice as so little is gathered from each plant: up to 100,000 flowers are needed to produce just 500 grams.

NUTMEG AND MACE

Myristica fragrans, a large evergreen tree native to the Moluccas, is two spices in one, obtained from a fruit that looks like a small, bright-red peach. Mace is the thin brown to red membrane surrounding the nutmeg kernel. The nut in the centre is grated to provide nutmeg.

SAFFRON

Crocus sativus is the most valuable species of the crocus genus, bearing pretty lilac flowers from autumn into early winter. The slender red stigmas provide saffron, which imparts a delicate fragrance, as well as a rich golden colour, to many of the world's cuisines.

TURMERIC

Curcuma domestica, the spice turmeric, is native to Malaysia. It is a member of the ginger family and is important in the cooking of curries and as a yellow colouring. The striking flowers emerge from bright orange rhizomes among large clumps of bright green canna-like leaves.

Turmeric grows best in fertile soils in tropical climates and needs to be well watered once the new leaves, which can reach 1m, appear. The rhizomes are harvested after the leaves have died down. It will cope with warm temperate climates.

Tip: If you buy the richly scented vanilla as the pod, rather than as the liquid extract, split it open to reveal the tiny seeds. Scrape out the seeds and mix with a little sugar before using to flavour desserts.

VANILLA

Vanilla planifolia, a climbing orchid, is native to Mexico, although it is now cultivated as a commercial crop in Madagascar, Papua New Guinea, Indonesia and India. Today we take this delicious spice for granted, although it was unknown to the world until some 500 years ago. The green fleshy pod which is harvested from the orchid has no flavour or aroma and must be cured over a three-month period by heating, which activates an enzyme that provides the flavour. The black pods are then left to dry further in the sun for a month.

Ruth's curry

I always use blade steak and cook it 'long and slow'—and at least the day before I intend to eat it.

2 kg blade steak
2 tbsp butter
1 tbsp canola or olive oil
2 onions, finely chopped
Several cloves of garlic, crushed
1–4 tsp cayenne pepper
(depending upon how hot you like it)
4 tsp fenugreek seeds
2 tsp mustard seeds
2 tsp each of ginger, tumeric, cinnamon
2 whole cloves
Pinch nutmeg

Method

Cut the steak into 2.5 cm cubes, removing fat or gristle (ask the butcher to do this).

In a heavy pan, melt a couple of tablespoons of butter and one of canola or olive oil. Add steak, a few cubes at a time, to brown, removing, and setting aside, after each group is browned.

Cook finely chopped onion and crushed garlic for a few minutes, until clear but not browned. Add, and cook on low heat for a good 5 minutes, the chosen spices. I always use cayenne pepper, fenugreek seeds, mustard seeds, ginger, turmeric, cinnamon, two whole cloves and a tiny pinch of nutmeg, but you should experiment, particularly with the amount of cayenne you choose to use. (You could, for instance, also use corinader or mixed spice.) Be careful to remove, before serving, the whole cloves, as they can add a bitter taste (and it is very unpleasant to bite on a clove!)

Return the meat to the pot with the cooked spices, stir for a few minutes; add a little water, or stock, as needed, and simmer on the lowest possible heat for an hour. (While we sometimes add a tin of tomatoes these days, my mother would never have approved of this, always saying that added fruit was not correct.) Cool the curry and refrigerate. The following day cook in an oven at 180°C for 30 minutes and serve, with boiled rice and a selection of sambal.

Sambal—or condiments—can include chopped cucumber mixed with yoghurt, to cool down a hot curry. Tomato and chopped onion was always served in our house, as were pappadams, mango chutney, banana, which was sliced and tossed in desiccated coconut and, of course, boiled rice. I like to serve chopped glace ginger, dry roasted cashews and sultanas. I always add a steamed vegetable dish, too. Eat with a spoon and fork.

Tip: Add cubed potato to the last half-hour of cooking if you think you have made the curry too hot. The potato takes up the heat: enjoy the potato as a vegetable curry, or discard.

Succulents

The huge range of species that comes under the general term *succulents* has become increasingly popular as Australian gardeners cope with watering restrictions and climate change. Succulents are fire-resistant, make excellent ground covers, require minimal weeding, staking, spraying or fertilising, do not shed their leaves and can grow in almost no soil; many are salt tolerant. I know: they sound too good to be true. So, in recognition of their importance, succulents have been given their own section, although they could also fit nicely into the chapters on Waterwise Gardens or Seaside Gardens.

Succulents are plants that store water from good seasons, to be used in times of drought or stress, and have developed to survive in arid or harsh environments. The term can be applied to a great range of genera, from aeoniums to agave and aloes, to bromeliads and cactus, echeverias, euphorbias, sempervivums and many other xerophytic plants—those that have adapted to grow under dry conditions. They are found in all regions and on all continents except Antarctica.

They come with a range of adaptations that allow them to cope with, even thrive in, difficult situations. Some store water in their base; others have leaves that are modified to present as little surface as possible to the sun. Some develop increased root-to-shoot ratios and some breathe only in the cool of the night. Others cope in toxic environments or extreme weather. Others have specialised mechanisms for redistributing salt away from growing areas or expelling it through specialised glands. Some have leaves adapted to cope with wind-carried salt or sand.

Their great variety of form, texture and colour and their ability to cope with dry shade, exposed hillsides, areas in rain shadow, rooftops, rockeries and containers make succulents incredibly useful in garden design. However, while they are the easiest of plants to care for, their form is not to everyone's taste: that somewhat questionable word *architectural* is sometimes the kindest adjective you might find to describe their often bizarre shapes.

A useful selection

AEONIUM

Among the most effective of the succulents are the aeoniums, native to the Canary Islands, the Mediterranean and north Africa.
- *Aeonium arboreum* 'Schwartzkopf', a purple-leaved variety, survives on almost no water and makes a great foil for more difficult colours such as orange and hot pink. Or, combine it with its lime-green cousins.
- *Aeonium arboreum*, lime green and less flamboyant, teams well with a mass of the tall-growing *Euphorbia characias*, which flowers for months in lime-green spikes with a maroon 'eye'.
- *Aeonium decorum* is easy to grow and provides drama without heartache.

AGAVE

The 'architectural' agaves hail from the Caribbean, Mexico and the West Indies; most have striking grey-green toothed leaves, and flower with dramatic spires.
- *Agave americana*, one of the most widely grown species, is stemless, with sword-like leaves emanating from a central point. The stunning yellow

Opposite: *Sedum* 'Ruby Glow'.

1. The orange blooms of *Aloe polyphylla*.
2. Giant pigface, *Carpobrotus acinaciformis*, stores water in its modified leaves.
3. At Larnach Castle, succulents and grasses are set against a brilliant blue pot.
4. *Kalanchoe thyrsifolia* 'Flapjacks'.
5. A waterwise mix of *Aeonium arboreum* and *A. a.* 'Schwartzkopf'.
6. *Echeveria elegans* quickly forms a dense mat, and thrives on little care.
7. Succulents look effective in charcoal-to-black pots; here, *Agave attenuata*.

flowers, atop a 6 m stem, take up to 10 years to appear.

• *Agave americana* 'Marginata' and 'Mediopicta' are both popular, with arresting yellow splashes on their leaves.

ALOE

Native to South Africa, Madagascar and the Arabian peninsula, the aloes are a varied genus of up to 300 species: some are trees, some are shrubs and others are stemless perennials. Like most succulents they like well-drained soil and hot climates.

• *Aloe plicatilis*, the twisted tree aloe, bears fan-like clusters of grey-green succulent leaves atop twisted fleshy trunks that grow to about 2 m.

• *Aloe polyphylla* is native to mountainous parts of Africa. This rare plant grows in stemless, sharply toothed rosettes, from which a series of brilliant red flower spikes erupt.

> Tip: You can see *Aloe polyphylla* in the South Seas Garden at Larnach Castle, on the Otago Peninsula, near Dunedin, on New Zealand's South Island.
> Combine *A. polyphylla* with some of the lower growing aloes and soften the look with sempervivums, which spread to form a dense matt of rosettes.

> ## In colonial gardens
> The orange flower spires of an early *Aloe* species grace the drive at Elizabeth Farm, and also at Camden Park, the second home Elizabeth and John Macarthur built in the new colony of New South Wales. These plants, along with many others, would have been collected by the earliest settlers as they rested at Capetown on the way to the new colony.

BEAUCARNEA

Beaucarnea recurvata, the ponytail palm, is a maintenance-free succulent, closely related to the

Yucca, with a palm-like appearance. The trunks, with their swollen, bulbous, sometimes corky appearance support long, strappy leaves and spires of pink or white flowers after a few years.

Requirements

Beaucarnea spp. like a warm, frost-free climate and dislike wet feet, particularly in winter.

COTYLEDON

The cotyledons, members of the Crassula family, are fast growing and easy to care for. There are nine species in this genus of succulent shrubs and sub-shrubs.

• *Cotyledon* 'Silver Ruffles' and *Cotyledon* 'Silver Waves' bear dramatic white to grey to silver wavy leaves.

• *Cotyledon macrantha* looks wonderful with any of the purple-foliaged succulents.

CRASSULA

This very varied genus of about 300 species comprises easy-to-grow and easy-to-propagate ground covers, perennials, shrubs and sub-shrubs.

• *Crassula arborescens*, the silver jade plant, is widely grown, spreading out to some 3 m, with blue-grey succulent foliage.

• *Crassula ovata*, an old-fashioned succulent, with bright green leaves and feathery flower-heads, is useful for forming thick edgings to dry-garden beds.

ECHEVERIA

Most of the 150 species of this genus hail from Mexico and have fleshy, smooth-edged or crimped leaves, most often in rosettes that sit just above the soil. They mass out to spill over the edges of rockeries and in summer send up flower spikes in umbers, oranges or acid yellows.

EUPHORBIA

This genus is another that is proving to be the gardener's saviour in times of low rainfall and water restrictions. The 2000-odd species of euphorbia occur in a wide range of climates, from the tropical, subtropical to dry parts of South Africa and its close neighbours to the dry Mediterranean countries, as well as in the snow-fed meadows of the Himalayan ranges. Some are trees, others are herbaceous perennials or ground covers and some are succulents with cactus-like forms.

Most euphorbias are extremely drought tolerant, and flower—in wonderful colours, from acid greens and yellows to oranges—for months, from the depths of winter until mid-summer. Best suited to the chorus, euphorbias were not created to be solo performers. Plant them in sinuous drifts that will provide a calm backdrop to the garden divas. All are good for massing out; some are best standing at the back of a border. Most are frost hardy: some cope better than others with humidity. The books tell you it is impossible to kill them—useful if you garden in difficult conditions.

- *Euphorbia amygdaloides*, the wood spurge, is native to Europe and Asia Minor and reaches to 1 m, providing height and structure in the garden. It has glossy, dark green leaves, and flowers from spring for some three months. The 'Purpurea' and 'Rubra' cultivars have splashes of colour in the lime-green bracts.
- *Euphorbia amygdaloides* var. *robbiae* is particularly useful as it thrives in dry shade under trees, seemingly blissfully unaware of competition from roots.

- *Euphorbia characias* subsp. *wulfenii* is frost hardy and sun loving, flowering early with acid-yellow heads atop blue-green leaves. It has a dense habit and has given rise to several cultivars, including 'Blue Wonder', 'Lambrook Gold', 'Burrow Silver' and 'Portuguese Velvet'.
- *Euphorbia dulcis* 'Chameleon' bears bronze to burgundy foliage and lime-green flower-heads.
- *Euphorbia* × *martini* is a beautiful offspring of *E. characias* and *E. amygdaloides*. It has red foliage on gorgeous red stems and lime-green bracts with dark red centres. It has a dense form, making it suitable for clipping, and, unlike some species, does not self-seed too much. It will survive humid climates better than most of the genus.

- *Euphorbia griffithii*, from the eastern Himalayas, likes summer moisture.
- *Euphorbia griffithii* 'Fireglow' has red flowers.
- *Euphorbia griffithii* 'Great Dixter' bears russet-coloured flowers.
- *Euphorbia myrsinites* is a low-growing, trailing, tough species that spreads across a 60 cm diameter; it looks particularly effective in rockeries or walled borders, where it can cascade over edges like an arrangement of cubes.
- *Euphorbia palustris* is a large-growing, dense shrub and is one of the few species of the genus that will grow well in damp soil.
- *Euphorbia pulcherrima*, the well-known poinsettia tree, is native to Mexico and reaches several metres in frost-free climates.
- *Euphorbia rigida*, a silver or blue-foliaged species, is more suited to dry climates, and copes with exposed coastal areas.
- *Euphorbia schillingii* and *E. sikkimensis* are not summer flowering and will cope with dry conditions.

1. *Euphorbia myrsinites*.
2. *Euphorbia cyparissus*.
3. *Sedum* 'Autumn Joy' gets more beautiful with age.

• *Euphorbia* 'Diamond Frost' has lime-green foliage and flowers in a froth of white blossom, most unusual for this genus. It grows to less than 50 cm tall and enjoys a sunny spot.

FURCRAEA

Very similar in looks, and closely related, to the agaves, *Furcraea* is a genus of 12 species of stemless perennial succulents.

> **Tip:** Line a path with the beautiful grey-leafed *Furcraea bedinghausii*, perhaps softened further with ribbons of lavender.

KALANCHOE

So easy to grow, these succulents are often used in city landscaping.
• *Kalanchoe pumila* has masses of pink flowers, grey leaves and a trailing habit. Plant a leaf to propagate more. As they tolerate dryness, they are particularly useful for growing in pots or window boxes where watering might be difficult.

SANSEVIERIA

Mother-in-law's tongue must be about my least favourite genus of plants, but I admit that some species can look stylish when planted en masse. Sansevierias cope well with shade but, if given half shade or sun, will flower with scented cream spikes at night. Beware, though, as this newly popular plant can become weedy and difficult to eradicate in subtropical climates.

SCHLUMBERGERA

Flowering for months in a range of colours, from pink to cerise to red, are the flamboyant zygo-cactus, more correctly called *Schlumbergera* spp. They look most effective cascading from baskets or pots, as they bloom from the tips of fleshy limbs. Give them morning sun in a frost-free climate.

SEDUM

The large *Sedum* genus comprises some 400 species. Many have interesting foliage and textures, good structure and strong lines and are invaluable in any garden, particularly as they love a hot and dry climate.
• *Sedum spectabile*, native to China and Korea, and its cultivars are among the most useful.
• *Sedum spectabile* 'Autumn Joy' copes well with drought—but not with humidity. For many gardeners, its foliage and fading winter flowers are more appealing than its hot-pink blooms—unless you are going for the lime-green and pink combination afforded by the euphorbias and sedums together.
• *Sedum* 'Chocolate Sauce' has lime-green foliage that ages to bronze. Leave flower-heads on the plant to add drama to the winter border.

SEMPERVIVUM

The sempervivums are a genus of about 40 species, most of which grow in symmetrical rosettes that spread out to form a dense mat. They are stunning in rock gardens, hugging the base of retaining walls (or growing in almost soil-free pockets in a wall) or in pots. They love a sunny spot in well-drained, gravelly soil.

✿ Requirements

Most succulents will cope with light frost but most do not like high humidity: look to their native habitat for tips on cultural preferences. Most require a well-drained soil but are not fussy about soil pH. They enjoy full sun, although some will cope with dry shade under trees.

✿ Care

Experienced coastal gardeners know that creating a microclimate is the first step to happiness over heartbreak. Plant a shelter belt of hardy, salt-and-wind-tolerant shrubs; then plant another, and even a third (*see* Hedges; Seaside Gardening). Then, you can choose succulent species from a more extensive plant list.

All succulents look effective with a mulch of pebbles and stones. Cut out old flower stems after they have died off, taking care to leave new growth.

Opposite top and bottom: South Seas Garden, Lanarch Castle.

South Seas Garden at Larnach Castle

The new South Seas Garden at Larnach Castle, set on the Otago Peninsula near Dunedin on New Zealand's south island, comprises plants that cope with the salt winds of its exposed site and that reflect the colours of the coastal landscape. Blue spires of the dramatic *Echium pininana*, along with the acid-yellow flowers of *Aeonium undulatum* usher you into this garden, which is arranged in terraced beds down a steep hillside. Dry stone walls, constructed from the local volcanic rock, pay tribute to the vernacular stone walling on the peninsula that, in turn, speaks of the Scottish heritage of the region. Stone seats, created as viewing points in the walls, are cushioned with *Azorella trifurcata*, from South America. A collection of succulents includes the endangered *Aloe polyphylla* with its dramatic, whirling growth pattern and orange flowers, growing alongside the emerald-green *Agave ferox*.

TREES

Trees

I think that I shall never see
A poem lovely as a tree
A tree whose hungry mouth is prest
Against the earth's sweet flowing breast
A tree that looks at God each day
And lifts her leafy arms to pray
A tree that may in summer wear
A nest of robins in her hair;
Upon whose bosom snow has lain;
Who intimately lives with rain.
Poems are made by fools like me,
But only God can make a tree.

This poem by the American writer Joyce Kilmer (1886–1918), a soldier killed in World War I, really says it all, doesn't it? It captures so well so much of what we love about gardening, about its transience, and its permanence, about its serendipity—and about the grandeur of the tree.

American Beauty is a film that every parent should see. It's about obsessions of all sorts, and dangers dressed in various costumes. There are many memorable lines in it. Perhaps not the seminal quip, but one that might resonate with many gardeners, is that made by the highly varnished Annette Bening character as her husband comments that the neighbours may have been unfriendly because she had cut down their tree. 'It was just as much our tree,' she protests. 'Those roots were on our side of the fence.'

Trees are beautiful creatures, but throughout the Australian suburbs plenty of problems are caused by trees that should be in the middle of a paddock and nowhere near a neighbour's fence line, a power line or a sewerage line, and certainly not in the middle of a neighbour's view. Inappropriate trees can also provide unwanted shade, crack foundations and poison soil.

Councils often refuse permission to remove inappropriate plantings, and it takes a new mortgage to hire a tree surgeon to make some trees safe. Our cities are full of tragic-looking street trees with their centres chopped out to allow for power lines and councils sometimes find themselves having to dig up footpaths to root-prune trees that are breaking up ratepayers' walls.

While many suburban councils require a landscape plan for a new development and can insist on suitable planting before approval is given, most councils will tell you that they don't have control over what is planted in an existing garden. If you are unlucky enough to have a beautiful view suddenly threatened by a newly planted row of × *Cupressocyparis leylandii*, or, heaven forbid, radiata pines, you may have no recourse, apart from praying that understanding and good manners might prevail on the part of your neighbours.

The point is this: Large trees in the appropriate environment, where they have space to grow as nature intended, are wonderful. Bad choices, usually made inadvertently—through ignorance on the part of authorities or advisers—are the stuff of nightmares. Obtaining information on recommended trees for your area can be extremely difficult. Given the potential for angst it would seem sensible for councils to maintain a set of recommendations for trees that are useful, aesthetic and responsible.

So what trees can you grow without being struck off your neighbours' party list? Do your research, choose carefully, and enjoy a mutually acceptable outcome!

❤ My favourites

- The low-growing and sculptural Japanese maples (*Acer palmatum* Dissectum Group) are a perfect choice for a city garden. (*See also* Seasons, Native Plants and Tropical for more choices.)
- *Albizia julibrissin*, the silk tree, has a glorious

Opposite: The crepe myrtle, *Lagerstreomia indica*.

spreading canopy with delicate feathery foliage reminiscent of the jacaranda. Two or three planted in proximity will eventually meet and form an umbrella over an entertainment area. Similar in appearance to the coveted tropical poinciana, this is the tree for you if you don't garden in hot and humid climates.

- *Alnus acuminata*, the evergreen alder, is a great tree for a country garden, but it grows a mile-a-minute so is not for a city plot. This tree can be wonderful if you have a large enough garden, or as a street tree. The water-loving *A. glutinosa*, the black alder, sporting tiny pine-cones and pink catkins in winter, thrives in a damp garden.
- *Alnus cordata*, the Italian alder, is a tall, columnar, elegant tree that grows to some 20 m in cool climates, although, as it is native to the south of Italy, it tolerates warm temperate conditions.
- *Melia azedarach*, the large-growing white cedar, is a fast-growing tree for a wide range of climates, from frost-prone to arid, and popular as a street tree. Its flowers are tiny star-like lilac blooms which are followed by poisonous berries. This tree copes well with drought conditions.
- The limes, by which I mean European limes, *Tilia* spp., are beautiful trees, in the northern hemisphere often seen as a pleached hedge (*see* Hedges). You can grow them well in this country in cool temperate climates. The rare weeping silver linden *Tilia* 'Petiolaris', with its fine, very dissected, green to silver foliage and cream flowers, is not found in the wild, but must be propagated by grafting. With their white undersides, the leaves look marvellous shimmering in the midday sun.

CORNUS

The dogwoods (*Cornus* spp.) are among the most glorious of the cool-climate trees. Mostly native to North America, dogwoods flower in showy bracts in white, cream and pink, followed by red or black berries, then brilliantly coloured autumn leaves. One of the most beautiful is *Cornus florida*, which grows to about 10 m.

There is a much-photographed garden on Long Island in the United States, designed by Russell Page (1906–1985) where a flight of steps swooping down to a stone-edged elliptical pool is flanked by an elegant avenue of dogwood (*C. kousa* var. *chinensis*), flowering white on outstretched, blackened branches.

Cornus controversa and *C. alternifolia*, with their elegant, layered branches, are perhaps the pick of all medium-sized trees for a cold to temperate climate. They all love plenty of moisture and well-mulched, rich, acid soil.

LAGERSTROEMIA

Come summer, the crepe myrtles will be dancing in their crumpled skirts of pinks, cerise, lilac and purple. A member of the Lythraceae family, along with the pomegranate and the cigar plant, the crepe myrtles (*Lagerstroemia* spp.) are a genus of more than 50 species of small trees native to Asia and some parts of Australia. You could say they are the lilacs for gardeners who cannot grow those gorgeous, scented, cold-climate treasures. Crepe myrtles are valued also for their twisted, smooth trunks, which are splashed with creams, greens and caramels; and for their autumn leaves, which turn orange and red.

It is mostly *Lagerstroemia indica* that you see flowering in suburban front gardens and on footpaths. Native to China, with an open spreading habit, this multi-stemmed species features large, blowsy panicles which are actually made up of a mass of tiny, crumpled flowers.

Tip: For young copses of trees I erect a shelter barrier of shade cloth across several star posts. This is erected in time for the windy season: for instance, in the Southern Highlands of New South Wales you know that high winds will hit in August and September. But filter the wind: take care when creating wind breaks of plant material or shade cloth not to create a tunnel for the wind or a barrier over which the wind can be dumped on the garden.

1. The pink euodia, *Tetradium daniellii*, grows in the mountain woodlands of China and Korea.
2. The bark of the crepe myrtle is beautifully marked.
3. The Chinese elm becomes a large tree.
4. The beauty of bark: here *Eucalyptus saligna* strips off in summer.
5. The leopard tree, *Caesalpinia ferrea*.

Most reach about 5 m, but small-growing variet-ies include the white 'Petite Snow' and 'Pixie White'. Among the taller growing varieties is 'Andre de Martis', a hot pink; 'Watermelon Red' (you guessed the colour); and *L. indica* 'Eavesii', which has lilac blooms. The tallest growing culti-vars include the deep red flowering 'Tuscarora', which grows to some 8 m. *Lagerstroemia subcostata* has beautiful bark, and its gorgeous autumn tones appear mid-winter. It waits until all the other horticultural performances are over before it says, 'Look at me'.

Crepe myrtles are easy to cultivate and are tolerant of most soils, even of depleted sandy soils. They can suffer from mildew in humid climates, although this doesn't seem to set them back at all. The small-growing 'Indian Summer' range—some grow to waist height, while other varieties will get to your shoulder—is said to be disease resistant.

I should confess to a prejudice: I hate to see crepe myrtles pruned; pruning seems to cut them off at the elbow and encourage unsightly knobbly knees. I do love hedges, am not at all averse to wielding pruning implements, and admit that many species that will naturally grow into lovely trees make excellent hedges—but I believe the crepe myrtle is not one of them.

With their interesting, patterned bark, and open form, they make a perfect tree to shade a courtyard or a small garden. I love to see them reaching over a picket fence, or over an informal hedge, perhaps of the 'wandy', scented buddleia, which has similar blooms in purples and lilacs; and the butterflies come running! Or plant crepe myrtles—several of each of a variety of the colours and tones—as a loose barrier or wind filter. Even from the near distance they look like a summer-flowering lilac.

JACARANDA

Native to the drier parts of tropical and sub-tropical South America, the genus *Jacaranda* con-tains some 50 evergreen and deciduous species, most with fern-like leaves which turn butter yellow before falling in late winter.

The most common, *Jacaranda mimosifolia*, although not indigenous to Australia, tells Austral-ians of almost every generation that exam time has well and truly arrived when the clusters of hanging, bell-like, lavender-blue flowers appear in late October and November. This jacaranda, also known as Brazilian rosewood, is perhaps my favourite tree, particularly if it is planted in someone else's backyard and is simply part of my borrowed landscape. You need a large garden to grow it well, to allow its elegant canopy to stretch out gracefully to its full width of some 15 m— and it can grow to almost 20 m in height. The gorgeous flowers fall to form a brilliant purple carpet, but then soften to a brown mush that can be dangerously slippery underfoot. Jacarandas are not suitable for small gardens, nor for courtyards, and will cause endless work if planted near a swimming pool. Their shallow but vigorous roots will travel to seek water, heading for water pipes, and can lift pavers and damage brickwork.

They make an arresting sight, however, when planted as avenues, or as specimen trees on lawns, in large spaces. The New South Wales town of Graf-ton is famous for its jacarandas; they love them in the Victorian river town of Mildura, and in Novem-ber people drive for hours to the nearby village of Monak, to view the mature jacarandas that line the main street. Jacarandas flower at the same time as the bougainvillea and the cerise bracts of this vigo-rous climber winding through the blue canopy form a kaleidoscope of intense colour, like so many can-can skirts flashing at summer. They flower partic-ularly well with summer rain to follow a dry winter.

Jacarandas thrive on a certain amount of neglect; the blue of the blooms is deeper when they are in somewhat stressed conditions and after a particularly dry and cold winter. They love plenty of water in summer and are fast growing in full sun, in well-drained, fertile soil, and in frost-free climates. Don't ruin their beautiful spreading form by lopping; they respond to pruning by sending shoots skywards. If you must prune, cut back to a fork in the tree. They can be propagated from seed in early spring, or from cuttings taken in summer.

Opposite: Jacarandas bloom in November at Michael and Cynthia Keenan's property, Tamlaght, near Mildura.

The white cedar, *Melia azedarach*, is used as a street tree in dry climates.

QUERCUS

The stately oaks (*Quercus* spp.), comprising some 600 species, are wonderful trees for very large gardens. From the northern hemisphere, with many slow growing and living to a great age, they produce wood that is highly prized for ship building, flooring and furniture.

- The English oak (*Quercus robur*) is, of course, the best known, eulogised in literature and in paintings of the English landscape school.
- The saw-tooth, or Japanese, oak (*Q. acutissima*) holds its attractive shiny leaves into winter, after they take on golden autumn colours.
- The pin oak (*Q. palustris*), with its distinctive, deeply lobed leaves, grows to a great height and is one of the best-colouring of the genus. The willow-leaf oak (*Q. phellos*), with its narrow, elegant leaves, also grows to some 30 m and colours wonderfully in autumn.

Planting and care

In some areas, an owner is not permitted to prune a tree more than 5 m in height or 3 m in canopy spread without council permission. Therefore it pays to note what horticultural problems you might be inheriting before you buy a property.

Advice on your rights and obligations as a tree-loving neighbour comes from the Law Society in your nearest capital city, which offers extremely helpful recorded information. Along with advice on friendly approaches to neighbours, there is information on mediation through the Community Justice Centre.

Buy trees young, in most cases. They will quickly catch up to a more established tree, and will have formed a much better, stronger root base than trees bought as more mature specimens.

There are differing opinions as to the importance and value of staking young trees. Some believe the tree is better left to develop its own strong root system, if necessary in the face of potentially damaging winds. I am not one who shares this opinion, as I cannot bear to see plants facing an onslaught of weather extremes. I use three or four stakes, either timber or galvanised iron star posts, and use a wide plastic strap, wide hessian ribbon or wire safely encased in tubing to tie two figures of eight around the tree trunk and the posts—one supporting the tree in one direction and the other supporting it in the opposite direction. Once the tree is established you can remove the stakes and ties.

(*See also* Magnolias; Eucalypts; Native Plants; Tropical.)

> **Tip:** *Paulownia fortunei*, a fast-growing species that has recently become popular as a plantation tree, is used for making musical instruments and furniture. Beware of planting it in a city garden, though, as it can sucker vigorously.

TROPICAL

Tropical

If you travel to Far North Queensland you'll find seas of brilliant blues and greens, jagged mountains that disappear among the clouds or crash onto sandy shores. A special fragrance—an exotic mix of ripe fruit and ginger flowers, with a base note of earthy scents from layers of fallen rainforest leaves—hovers in the air, and at night a huge moon hangs heavy in an inky sky, framed by softly waving palms.

Tropical plants remind you of holidays in such places, of endless days of sun, surf and sand, of dripping ice-cream, of mangoes eaten in your swimwear, and of lazy afternoon sleeps. In warm temperate, and warmer, climates you can re-create that relaxed and happy atmosphere with a selection of flamboyant plantings. With their can-can skirts in hot and happy colours, climbing plants like bougainvillea add to the summer holiday mood. (*See also* Climbers; Bougainvilleas.)

❤ My favourites

GROUND COVERS

Favourite ground covers for hot and humid climates include the tough, variegated liriope and the salt-tolerant, vermilion-flowered coral fountain, *Russelia equisetiformis*. The fern-like *Phyllanthus myrtifolius* is an extremely useful, drought-tolerant plant—fragile looking, but in fact tough.

Use dwarf mondo grass between stepping stones, or as edgings, along with a variegated grass-like *Acorus* spp. The fragrant *Gardenia radicans* makes an excellent ground cover or, clipped very tight, a 'step-over' hedge.

Most of the spiderworts, *Tradescantia* spp. (also known as *Rhoeo*), make excellent ground covers in subtropical and tropical climates. Many have variegated and very decorative foliage, although *T. fluminensis* is the weed sometimes called wandering jew. It's not difficult to pull out, however, so I don't regard it as much of a nuisance, and

'Variegata' has most attractive lime-green and white striped foliage. *Tradescantia pallida* 'Purple Heart' is the one I love for the tropical garden as it teams so well with the bright colours suited to the clear light of warm climates. Propagate it easily by breaking off a piece and placing it in the ground.

PERENNIALS

- The giant calla lily, or elephant's ear (*Alocasia macrorrhiza*) among 70 or so species of the genus, hails from South-East Asia. Generous, arrow-shaped green leaves are carried on 1 m stalks. It looks particularly effective when planted en masse. The flowers are like those of the arum lily and have a faint scent.

- Perfectly suited to their common name, the glorious flamingo flowers, *Anthurium scherzerianum*, are popular as houseplants but I love them with a mass planting of a low-growing soft palm like the lady palm (*Rhapis humilis*), in a shady courtyard. Anthuriums speak of the tropics, even in a temperate climate; they love humidity and moisture—but also demand good drainage—as well as morning sun.

- The cannas are must-haves for the tropical garden and are no longer the somewhat uninteresting plants that many of us remember from childhood gardens, where they would grow into huge, unattractive clumps. These days I love playing with the different canna cultivars, their brilliantly coloured leaves immediately adding a tropical flare to a temperate garden. The new cultivars,

Previous page: Frangipanis: the colour of summer.

with their brilliant leaf colourings and markings, look fabulous when planted with the blue gingers, with strelitzias, with the red to burgundy-leaved cordylines, and with frangipani.

- Try *Canna* 'Tropicana' with its paddle-like leaves splashed with red and orange. 'Bengal Tiger' is striped in greens, creams and yellow. Plant a swathe of the yellow-flowering daylily, 'Stella d'Oro', in front and perhaps edge with the variegated liriope. To encourage fresh foliage and stop cannas becoming too thick and impenetrable, cut them right back to the ground in winter.
- The gorgeous blue ginger (*Dichorisandra thrysiflora*) is not a ginger at all but a member of the Commelinaceae family, to which the tradescanias belong. Native to South America, this fleshy ginger-like perennial grows to about 1.5 m and bears stunning bright blue flowers through summer. It looks fabulous with some of the brilliantly coloured cannas. It is easily propagated with cuttings or divisions once flowering is over.
- The peace lily (*Spathiphyllum* spp.) is native to tropical America and some parts of the Far East but will grow happily in dappled shade in warm temperate climates where there is summer humidity. Then, it will flower for months with white spathes atop tall stems. Cut back untidy foliage to maintain a fresh, tropical look.
- If your climate is temperate to tropical, *Strelitzia reginae*, the bird of paradise, native to South Africa, is another good choice for a garden of colour and excitement, although its rather aggressive form will not be to everyone's taste. 'Mandela's Gold' is a softer yellow cultivar, and there is a pink now available: I can imagine it massed against a charcoal-painted background, with the occasional orange-flowering species thrown in for additional razzamatazz. Strelitzias are late winter- and spring-flowering and cope with hot afternoon sun. They don't demand much care, but prune off dead leaves and spent flowers to tidy them up.
- Native to South-East Asia, coleus (*Solenostemon scutellarioides*) are grown for their brilliantly coloured foliage which features an array of markings in reds, pinks, cerise, lime-green or yellow.

This fast-growing perennial looks most effective if planted en masse.

- I have tried to grow *Tacca integrifolia*, the bat plant—which I saw growing in great swathes in a garden in Port Douglas—in my Sydney garden without any success, so I am convinced it is a flower only suited to the tropics. The purple and white flowers are actually tiny, and the bracts that spread out behind give rise to the common name; it has long, drooping filaments that look like cat's whiskers. This species hails from southern China, South-East Asia and East India, while the exotic, black-flowering species, *T. chantrieri*, is extremely fussy about its growing conditions, liking hot, humid climates, rich, rainforest-type soils and excellent drainage.

SHRUBS

- The Chinese lanterns, *Abutilon × hybridum*, derived from hybridising several South American species, will flower for months in red, pink, white, yellow and oranges, in warm climates. They quickly add body to borders, or make a good, informal hedge in a seaside garden. They are happy to be chopped back regularly and love sun and plenty of water when flowering.
- The acalyphas, or cat's tails, are a very variable genus of some 400 species of perennials, shrubs and trees, most from the tropics of the Far East and tropical America. *Acalypha hispida*, with its gorgeous long, red, fluffy catkins, is native to East Asia and grows to around 4 m. *A. reptans* is sometimes seen cascading down retaining walls or banks and in hanging baskets as it grows to only 30 cm. *A.* 'Firestorm' is a shrub with wonderful red to pink foliage; use it as a hedge, or with other brightly coloured foliage plants in a shrubbery. Acalyphas are drought tolerant and will also grow in warm temperate climates.
- Hedges of oranges and reds look somehow appropriate—glamorous even—in the clear, brilliant light of the tropics and for this use there is probably no better plant than the croton, *Codiaeum* spp., a genus of about 15 species of evergreen shrubs grown mostly for their flamboyant foliage. They like plenty of water and food in the summer

growing season. *Codiaeum variegatum*, which comes in a range of brightly marked cultivars, can be clipped hard, perhaps to highlight the shape of a building or to create a line of defence in a coastal garden.

- You can create multiple hedges from the candy-coloured ixoras: try the larger leafed *Ixora* 'Malay Pink' planted behind a smaller *I.* 'Little Willy'. The ixoras are a genus of around 400 species of tropical shrubs. They have attractive glossy leaves and a great range of hybrids flower in reds, pinks, yellows, oranges and whites. They are frost tender and like well-drained, rich soil. They look wonderful planted with hibiscus and with pentas: go mad with colour!

- The gorgeous medinilla, with their pleated, leathery foliage, and cascades of pink flowers—a little like hanging bunches of small grapes—are not widely grown in Australia, as they like it hotter and more humid than the climate of most regions. From a genus of about 300 species of shrubs and climbers native to South-East Asia, some of which are epiphytic, *Medinilla speciosa* will grow in the full sun, unlike *M. magnifica*, which is native to the Philippines.

- *Pachystachys lutea*, golden candles, comes from the West Indies and tropical Central and South America. Plants can reach 2 m in height and form excellent hedges, or shrubbery, in frost-free climates. They flower with bright-yellow or orange bracts which sit proud of the bright green leaves like lit candles.

- From a genus of some 60 species native to tropical climates, the exotic and dramatic *Pseuderanthemum atropurpureum*, a member of the Acanthaceae family, is grown for its foliage, often burgundy and often patterned, splashed with pinks, creams and white. From Polynesia, it flowers with small white or pink blooms and is easily propagated with cuttings.

HIBISCUS

Nothing reminds me of my childhood more than hibiscus, which flourished in an array of calypso colours in my mother's garden. The furniture in our house was always decorated in a selection of the brilliantly coloured blooms as she sought to create the tropical feel of the house she and my father had in Colombo.

A genus of the Malvaceae family and comprising over 200 species, hibiscus are native to China, North America, tropical Africa and the countries along the Pacific. Most are evergreen but some are deciduous, with leaves that are mostly toothed or lobed. Flowers are comprised of five overlapping petals with a central column of fused stamens. They come in a range of colours that will have you remembering tropical sunsets, but they can also flower in discreet creams and whites, and fragile, pale pinks. They can be added to salads and in some cultures are used in traditional medicine.

Like many plants, hibiscus can be pruned to create a hedge, although they look more effective foregrounding a hedge in a tone that complements the green of their leaves. These gorgeous blooms are for all who want to dream of sun, sand and surf—not only for those of us who grew up to the sound of Elvis crooning *Blue Hawaii*.

- If you were asked to name just one species that conjured up images of the tropics it would surely be the best known of the genus, *Hibiscus rosa-sinensis*, a medium-sized shrub that has given birth to thousands of cultivated varieties. Flowers range in size from dainty to the size of generous dinner plates, and among the thousands of hybrids are the evocatively named 'Hawaiian Sunset', 'Surfrider', 'Blue Bayou' and 'California Girl'. The flowers can be single or double and in a range of colours from a pure white ('The Bride') to yellow, orange, hot pink ('Dorothy Brady') and vermilion.

- Native to China, *H. mutabilis*, the Rose of Sharon, flowers in single or double, peony-like blooms: it grows to about 2 m. The charming *H. schizopetalus*—coral hibiscus, also known as the fringed hibiscus—which is indigenous to East Africa, has delicate, lantern-like pendulous flowers with recurved, frilled petals. Place it so that you can look up at it above another plant—perhaps a swathe of coleus (*Solenostemon scutellarioides*) if you like lots of rich colour. Add a wide ribbon of red-flowering daylilies (*Hemerocallis* spp.).

1. *Tradescantia spathacea* is a good ground cover in warm climates.
2. The flamingo flowers are perfect for a tropical border.
3. *Canna* × *generalis*.
4. The hot colours of the canna look just right under clear summer skies.
5. The tropical tones of *Acalypha wilkesiana* Hybrid.
6. *Medinilla speciosa*.

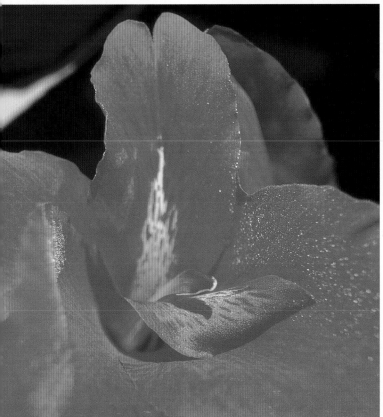

1. *Hibiscus rosa-sinensis* Hybrids: here, 'Tropicana'.
2. 'Kala Kaua'.
3. 'The Bride'.
4. 'Ruby Wedding'.
5. 'Evelyn Howard'.
6. 'Sun 'n' Surf'.
7. *Plumeria rubra*.
8. The fruit salad colours of a mature frangipani.

- *Hibiscus tiliaceus*, the sea hibiscus, growing naturally throughout the coastal regions of the Pacific and tropical Asia, can withstand salt winds. It forms a sprawling tree and looks effective planted en masse as a first defence against salt winds, and to provide protection to plants less tolerant of tough conditions. Its yellow flowers, which change to orange before falling, bloom among large heart-shaped leaves. Similar in form and flower, *H. diversifolius* is a tough native of the Top End, and is also able to with-stand salt winds. *Hibiscus coccineus*, swamp hibiscus, is native to the swamps of Georgia and Florida, and blooms with a distinctive, slim-petalled, coral-red flower resembling that of the bauhinia.
- If it's scent you must have, the species native to Hawaii, the white-flowering *H. arnottianus*, has a delicate fragrance: it grows wild in the mountainous parts of the island of Oahu. *Hibiscus* 'Snowqueen' has generous splashes of cream and white on emerald-green, matt leaves, making it a stunning addition to some planting schemes. Plant in multiples to show clearly your design hand, and underplant with Chinese star jasmine, that most useful of climbers, which you would use in this situation as a ground cover.
- *Hibiscus syriacus*, which is deciduous in cooler climates and will tolerate light frosts, flowers in paper-fine, single flowers in a range of pastel colours, from the white 'Diana' to blue-purple 'Blue Bird' and the cerise 'Woodbridge'. The single-species *Lagunaria patersonia*, the Norfolk Island 'hibiscus', has beautiful flowers but the seeds leave an awful mess and can also cause skin irritations.

TREES

Often growing to great heights, trees in the tropics need plenty of space to display their full brilliance.

- One of the most beautiful of all trees, *Amherstia nobilis* was sought after by plant hunters for hundreds of years. In 1853 the Duke of Devonshire, who sponsored these treasure-hunting expeditions throughout the subcontinent, sent a gardener to Burma (now Myanmar) just to obtain a specimen of *A. nobilis* for his great conservatory at Chatsworth in Derbyshire. Also known as the Pride of Burma, it bears clusters of head-turning coral and gold orchid-like flowers. It's difficult to propagate and grow; impossible if you don't live in a hot and humid climate. It was named for Lady Sarah Amherst, an amateur botanist and wife of the Governor General of India in the early nineteenth century. Now almost unknown in the wild, it is also difficult to grow in cultivation.
- The bauhinia, or orchid tree, flowers with butterfly-like blooms, in pink or cream, mostly in the tropics. It is used as street trees in some Queensland towns and there is a beautiful, mature specimen growing at Camden Park, in Sydney: it was planted as seed in the 1830s by the explorer Ludwig Leichhardt, who stayed at Camden Park with the Macarthur family on several occasions. Bauhinias have very distinctive leaves, made up of two broad leaflets, like the wings of a resting butterfly. Among the most often cultivated is the South African *Bauhinia galpinii*, which grows to about 4 m, and has a branching, spreading canopy.

- *Caesalpinia pulcherrima*, the peacock tree, is a close relative of the equally gorgeous poinciana and flowers with similar coral-red orchid-like flowers on soft green foliage. It is more a shrub than a tree for avenue or specimen planting, usually growing to about 3 m—although sometimes larger. The leopard tree, *C. ferrea*, is a much taller growing tree, native to Brazil and prized for its smooth bark, which is mottled with olive-green patches.
- The tropical *Cassia javanica*, also known as pink shower, or rainbow shower, grows to up to 20 m in humid climates and full sun. Native to South-East Asia, it makes an excellent, drought-tolerant street tree and provides summer shade for outdoor diners.
- The fast-growing *Peltophorum pterocarpum*, the yellow flame tree, is a member of the legume family and related to the cassia. Native to Indonesia, Malaysia and the northern-most part of Australia, it is extremely adaptable, growing on the edge of mangrove swamps. It can reach 15 m and flowers in fragrant yellow panicles in summer.
- Wider than it is high, the poinciana (*Delonix regia*) grows to around 10 m in height and 15 m in width, stretching out its elegant arms with their feathery, bright green foliage. One of the most beautiful of trees for the warm-climate garden, the poinciana loves warm summer rain and, well-drained soil and flowers from northern New South Wales to the tropics of Port Douglas and on, towards Broome. The flame-red, orchid-like flowers of the poinciana are one of the best sights of summer.
- If you don't garden in the tropics, you can achieve a similar effect with *Albizia julibrissin*, the silk tree (*see* Trees).
- From the Canary Islands the ancient, prehistoric-looking *Dracaena draco* is extremely hardy and drought tolerant. Its common name, dragon's blood tree, reflects the red resin that can seep from the trunk. It grows to about 10 m and is popular in beachside public plantings. The multi-stemmed trunk supports a head of stiff, spiky leaves that bear orange berries in summer. It can look terrific planted in a group with frangipani.
- The ornamental bananas—particularly the largest growing, the Abyssinian banana (*Ensete ventricosum*), which reaches some 5 m in five years, before it flowers and dies—are stunning as shady, lush plants for the background. The paddle-shaped, olive-green foliage of the banana features a hot-pink mid-rib. The genus of seven species is native to Asia and Africa: the cultivar 'Maurelii' has beautiful bright green leaves with burgundy undersides. The dwarf pink-flowering banana, *Musa velutina*, has tiny red, decorative bananas.
- *Tabebuia rosea*, the pink trumpet tree, a new introduction to Australian gardens—or at least to those in Queensland and the warmest parts of this country—is a native from tropical South America. It flowers with panicles of pink blossom, a little reminiscent of those of the crepe myrtle, from September to November. Take care: it is a fast-growing tree and I am not yet convinced that it may not become a problem.

FRANGIPANI (*PLUMERIA* SPP.)

The tough and beautiful frangipani, *Plumeria* spp., the sight and scent of summer, create dappled shade and a soothing, cooling play of light and shadow over a warm-climate garden. This genus houses eight species, mostly deciduous, and was named in honour of the seventeenth-century French botanist Charles Plumier. Originally from Central America, the trees can reach 10 m. The fragrant salver-form flowers, from 5 cm to 13 cm in diameter, appear in early summer at the end of somewhat bizarre, tortured, rubbery branches bearing tough, deeply veined mid-green leaves.

Frangipanis are extremely undemanding, requiring only a frost-free climate, well-drained soil and several hours of sun daily. In the West Indies and from southern Mexico to the Americas they occur naturally on hillsides in poor but well-drained soil, under a blazing sun. They also thrive in coastal gardens.

I fall in love with the frangipani all over again each year on my annual pilgrimage to the far north coast of New South Wales, when I find myself dreaming on scraps of paper of the garden I would enjoy if I lived in a hot and humid climate. Frangipanis, with their scent mixing that of apricot, peach, jasmine and honeysuckle, would take centre stage. They are indispensable to the tropical garden, but these jewels no doubt find their way into the treasure chests of those who garden in less-than-suitable climates.

• *Plumeria alba*, native to the West Indies, is the largest species, growing to some 14 m, with a canopy as wide; the leaves are more than 50 cm in length. *P. obtusa*, from Cuba and Jamaica, grows to some 8 m, is evergreen, and bears very white flowers, sometimes with pale yellow centres. The easiest to grow, and probably the most common in Australia, is the yellow and white flowering *P. rubra* var. *acutifolia*.

• The pink to carmine flowering species that is also seen often in Sydney's federation gardens, *P. rosea*, has gorgeous orange to yellow centres that conjure up dreams of tropical sunsets. *P. rubra* is fabulous, with crimson flowers on a broad canopy some 8 m high. *Plumeria* 'Golden Kiss' has large trusses of deep gold to apricot flowers.

• Also known as the temple tree, the pagoda tree and West Indian jasmine, frangipanis are very slow growing, so if you inherit a garden with these trees or shrubs already established, treasure them. They make wonderful features for courtyard gardens, can be planted in banks as an informal hedge or boundary, or can bend elegantly over a reflection pool. The dwarf cultivars are suited for growing in containers in climates where they need to be taken inside for winter protection. They become deciduous in a climate with a dry season; in warm temperate climates they lose their leaves in late March.

Planting and care

For gardeners in cooler climates who want to introduce some of the colours of the tropics, keep plants dry in the winter to avoid rot. Grow in a warm spot that receives winter sun, and some shade in summer.

Most hibiscus require full sun to flower well. They are happy in sandy, slightly acid soils, but most won't tolerate frost. Prune occasionally to maintain the desired shape. Hibiscus flowers only last a day when picked, and are better left out of water.

Frangipanis are easy to propagate. Take cuttings in late spring and summer, up to 30 cm in length, from branches that are not flowering. Leave in the sun for up to a week so that the cut end can dry out, forming a callous. Root in a well-drained pot of sand. The milky sap that seeps from cut branches, or when leaves are removed, is poisonous, and can damage eyes and cause skin irritations. In the cooler climates plant frangipani near a north-facing wall that will retain warmth. Fertilise with high-potassium products.

Plant bananas in a north-facing position and feed with compost and manure to which you have added a few handfuls of dolomite per square metre. They demand good drainage.

Tropical plants are heavy feeders: in the tropics soil gets leached easily, especially during the wet season. Fertilise quarterly, with nitrogen fertiliser, or with Dynamic Lifter.

Maintaining a Healthy Garden

PART FOUR

SOIL

Soil

Where should I start on the all-important subject of soil? I could be glib and say there are two types of soil: heavy clay or hungry sand. But that would be irresponsible, so I will discuss what you can find in between, as well.

Most of us know that the success of our garden depends largely upon the health of its soil. It is essential, then, to understand the soil you have and to provide it with anything it lacks. Soil is a living community and contains a zoo-full of micro-organisms and animals that rely for their nutrition upon the organic matter in or on the surface of the soil. Soil mineral particles are held together by hyphae (fine strands of fungus) and by secretions produced by countless micro-organisms. So, organic matter is the magic ingredient for improving soil structure and its ability to hold moisture and take up nutrients.

Soil types

The soil in my Sydney garden is sand; it seems to gobble up the manures and mulches that I lavish upon it and has taken almost two decades of tender care to improve. I pine for the volcanic soil, dark as chocolate cake, of a garden-past in the Southern Highlands of New South Wales: I used to proclaim to anyone who would listen that you could put a dead stick in that ground and it would grow. In fact, that foolhardy claim was probably responsible for many of my gardening follies. I thought you could grow anything at all in that beautiful, rich soil. But I digress.

At horticultural school we were instructed to perform somewhat tedious tests to ascertain various soil types and their texture. These involved moulding a handful of a particular soil—we never called it dirt—with a little moisture into a shape like a fat worm. If it was sticky, could be formed into a flat ribbon and did not break when bent, it was considered to be clay. It was called sandy if it was gritty and crumbled upon falling. In between these two extremes you will find loam and clay loam, both very desirable. Loam feels spongy, but not sandy, when the texture test is applied, and

clay loam will form an unbroken ribbon up to 80 mm long. In short, this ideal structure was indicated by a shape that remained firm and held together when dropped.

Most gardeners don't need to carry out such tests to determine what type of soil they have: it is obvious as you work it and water it. Clay, made up of very fine particles, is my favourite soil, as the soil 'colloids' found in clay-based soils are best at holding onto the different nutrients in an ionic bond known as the Cation Exchange Capacity (CEC). Clay is, therefore, the most naturally fertile, even though it may be slow to drain, and heavy and difficult to work until you take to it with gypsum, aged manures and thick layers of mulch, which break down and contribute to the soil's structure. Sandy soil, or sandy loam, will also thank you for manures, mulch, and—the best antidote of all—compost. You will need to apply these very regularly, for they seem to disappear in sand: years of such devotion will reward you with a rich loam—a delight to use.

Although you can send a soil sample to professional soil-testing services, you can determine the acidity or alkalinity of a soil with a home-testing soil kit, bought from your local nursery.

Opposite: *Gordonia axillaries*: like magnolias, camellias and rhododendrons, they like acid soil.
Previous page: *Hydrangea* 'Matilde Gutges'.

This kit will also indicate the balance of nitrogen (N), phosphorus (P) and potassium (K) in your soil, and you can fertilise accordingly.

Soil pH is the measure—from 1 to 14—of its acidity, neutrality or alkalinity. A pH below 7 indicates an acid soil, greatly loved by plants such as camellias, azaleas and magnolias. Pure water, on the other hand, has a neutral pH of 7. A pH above 7 is found in an alkaline soil, preferred by lavenders or broccoli, for example. Although it is difficult to turn an alkaline soil into an acid one, an acid soil can be made more alkaline by the addition of garden lime. Geology and climate are responsible for soil: acid rocks—sandstone and granite, its lava equivalent rhyolite, and others high in silica—along with a high rainfall, break down to produce acid soil. A low rainfall and calcium-rich rocks result in an alkaline soil. Basalt is the lava equivalent of dolerite and gabbro: all three are calcium and magnesium-rich and are described as basic rocks.

In fact, while a neutral pH is best for most plants, many will thrive in either type of soil; so it is more crucial that they receive regular and correct fertilising and watering.

A vast variety of activities is taking place beneath the soil in your garden, and a wide array of living organisms—from earthworms (your best friends) to woodlice, slugs and beetles—are breaking down large pieces of waste material into a form accessible to plants: you can aid the process by adding layers of organic matter, whether compost, mulch or leaf litter. And eschew the use of chemicals on the garden, out of consideration for the birds and insects, let alone the soil organisms. All parts of the soil are interdependent and the processes taking place in the topsoil and subsoil are integrated: by destroying one small element, you upset the complex natural balance and jeopardise the health of your soil.

Fertilisers

Just like us, plants need good growing conditions, with a nutrient-rich food supply and correct amounts of water, to be strong and healthy.

Happy plants are vigorous and even in colour. Malnourished plants will suffer stunted growth, are disease-prone, and will produce fewer flowers, deformed fruit, and mottled or discoloured foliage.

As I have said, plants find their food in the soil. Some elements, such as nitrogen, phosphorus and potassium, are required by many plants in large amounts for healthy growth. Others—known as trace elements—are required in minute quantities. We need to provide anything that is lacking. In addition, the pH of the soil has an important effect on its ability to access the nutrients in the soil. Acid soils can tie up phosphorus, while alkaline soils can prevent iron (and other trace elements) being released to plants. There is a great range of soil conditioners and organic fertilisers on the market—some based on seaweed, some on the environmental pest, European carp—as well as a wide range of prepared fertilisers formulated to specific plants: for example roses, citrus, orchids, tomatoes, camellias and azaleas, and native plants (many of which don't flower as well, if given too much phosphorus).

Little and often is the way to go with any fertiliser—advice that those of us who are time poor may find difficult to accept. Too much fertiliser can 'burn' leaves or kill the plant. Always dampen the soil before application and water well after.

Excellent fertilisers

AGED CHOOK MANURE

Poultry manure is another highly recommended organic product which, if spread thickly and topped with spoiled lucerne as a mulch, also helps suppress weeds and conserve water. You can layer this manure in your compost heap, too. And, of course, you can buy pelletised poultry manure to broadcast as you would blood and bone.

BLOOD AND BONE

This is an organic all-purpose fertiliser that you can either throw over the garden—and then water in—or apply in liquid form.

Opposite: A glorious border at Glebe Cottage, in New Zealand's South Island: the reward for improving your soil.

GREEN MANURE CROPS

Green manure is incredibly beneficial to your soil, if you have the room for it—although you can also apply this method to small garden beds that you are prepared to leave fallow, and free of ornamental plants or vegetables for a season. Green manure is a crop that is ploughed back into the soil while still green. Broadcast a quantity of seed—most often a legume crop such as alfalfa, lupins or clover at about 30 grams per square metre—at the right time (often autumn when the soil is still warm) on weed-free soil. When the crop is almost mature, but well before it starts to go to seed (usually in spring), turn it into the soil. The nitrogen-fixing bacteria that live in the root nodules of leguminous crops assist in breaking down the plants, adding structure to the soil.

HOME-MADE COMPOST

Your own sweet-scented, dark and crumbly compost is, of course, the best and cheapest of all soil conditioners and fertilisers—it adds to the structure and porosity of your soil and releases essential nutrients as it breaks down.

Making compost is not just kind to your garden and wallet; it is also kind to the environment. It

avoids increasing landfill and releasing CO_2 and other harmful gases, such as dioxin, into the air. The average Australian household produces 14 tonnes of green house gas emissions each year. Each Australian produces 2.25 kilograms of waste every day, making us one the world's largest waste producers.

There is almost nothing in the garden that can't be returned to it, and most of us hate to throw out food scraps, newspapers and garden prunings. But, for many of us, making compost is surrounded with mystery and intrigue. We all have horror stories of commercial compost bins that don't work—so sit idle—or compost heaps that become a sodden, smelly mess or, worse still, attract vermin and become home to other unpleasant creatures.

Making compost does not require a science degree, however. To achieve healthy and deliciously scented compost, there are just a few rules that should be followed.

The micro-organisms of compost bins and heaps need a balanced diet of the correct amount of moisture, warmth and air. They also need the 25 units of carbon (derived from woody carbohydrates) to every unit of nitrogen (from such things as lawn clippings and kitchen waste). This is known as the C:N ratio, and it should, after the carbon is burned off during the composting process, finish at a measurement of about 12:1. But that is almost more than you need to know for success—so, let's reduce the process to the basics.

Compost ingredients

Many readily available ingredients, such as grass clippings, leaves, vegetable kitchen scraps, even a wilted bunch of roses, can be usefully returned to the soil. Coffee grounds, eggshells, floor sweepings, paper and cardboard, hair and wood ash are also in. One kilogram of urea per cubic metre will add nitrogen to the heap. You can also add some soil, comfrey leaves, poultry manure, blood and bone or nettles as activators.

What to avoid

Certainly, avoid persistent weeds like flick weed and onion grass and don't add dairy products or meat scraps as they can bring maggots. Oils and fats are also best avoided, and obviously items like disposable nappies are out.

What can go wrong

Compost bins need to be large enough to generate enough heat—reaching at least 55 degrees Celsius—to break down materials and prevent pests like cockroaches breeding. Promote a neutral pH by adding a handful of lime or wood ash (a source of magnesium, calcium and potassium); this will also help deter nasties like cockroaches that prefer acidic conditions. Weeds, vegetable waste and seaweed will also help in this direction. And the good bacteria in compost heaps don't like acidity. Materials that are low in calcium include bark, ferns, straw, oak leaves and wood, so these won't help promote a neutral pH.

Pine needles, which are acidic, should not be added to compost heaps, but I love them as a scented, evocative mulch around acid-loving plants such as strawberries, rhododendrons, camellias or magnolias.

And compost bins need air. We want to promote aerobic composting; if there is not enough air in the bin or heap, the process becomes anaerobic, which is slower and also causes unpleasant odours. Straw, leaves, paper and cardboard provide essential structure—and that means air—to the heap. Don't add papers and magazines with coloured inks, however. And you will need to aerate your heap with a fork, or use a tumble bin with a handle that facilitates turning.

Structure

Compost bins can take many forms. You can buy them in black plastic, ready to assemble, or as metal bins on legs that can be turned. You can make them from hardwood: run horizontal planks between corner posts, with front sections that can be removed for ease of access and handling. Very simple bins can be made by running hessian, chicken wire lined with cardboard, or plastic around four-star posts (you would use these open-topped containers for garden prunings and lawn clippings—not for food scraps). Or, make a hay-bale

1. A clever composting area and worm farm at Redding House, Benalla.
2. A hay-bale compost bin.
3. Evidence of calcium deficiency in apples.
4. Iron deficiency in fruit trees.

bin by surrounding your composting material with a double stack of lucerne or hay-bales: plant pumpkins or trailing nasturtiums on the top of your hay 'walls'. Semi-permanent heaps and bins like these can be built on bare soil; expensive, wooden affairs should be constructed on concrete.

Leaves and other organic mulches can be tied into black plastic bags and stored out of sight until well composted or needed.

To discover the magic of compost, however, you'll need to embrace the golden rule: there is nothing instant about compost making. Patience is the most important ingredient of all (*see also* Community Gardens).

Liquid fertilisers

Seasol, produced by an Australian company from kelp, is an example of an organic liquid seaweed-based conditioner and tonic, and is one answer to the rehabilitation of sick plants. It is also used to ameliorate transplanting shock. It encourages a better root system, helps a plant cope with drought and frost and assists in the resistance to pests and diseases. The same company produces Powerfeed, a mixture of liquid fertiliser and Seasol.

LOW-PHOSPHORUS FERTILISERS

These are best for Australian native plants, and several companies make suitable, easy-to-use products.

Mushroom compost

This commercially produced compost is alkaline, so don't use it near acid-loving camellias, rhododendrons, azaleas and magnolias. Only add it to acid soil if you are growing plants like roses and certain vegetables that like alkaline conditions.

Nutrient deficiencies

When your plants are lacking in nutrients, there will be tell-tale signs:
• *Boron*, important for plant health, is needed in minute amounts in soil. A lack of this element, often a problem in the cultivation of beetroot, otherwise the easiest of vegetables to grow, results in stunted growth and woody beetroot, often with black spots on the skin. Apply Borax, dissolved at the rate of half a level teaspoon per 4.5 litres of water applied to 1 square metre; although an essential nutrient, Borax is extremely toxic if used in excess.
• *Calcium deficiency* appears most often in tomatoes and apples: the bottoms of tomatoes become brown and scaly, and brown pits form on the skin of apples, causing bruised patches in the flesh. Apply a foliar spray of calcium nitrate at the rate of 5 grams per litre of water. Alternatively, for a slow-release calcium that also assists with soil structure, dig in a thin sprinkling of garden lime around the plant.
• *Iron deficiency* manifests as yellow patches between the leaf veins, while the veins remain green. The problem often occurs in alkaline soil: lower the soil pH with iron chelates to create a more acidic soil.
• *Magnesium deficiency* presents as yellowing around the edges of a leaf, often with a triangle of green left in the centre of the leaf. In many vegetables the deficiency appears as a mottled yellow across the leaf. Spray the foliage with Epsom salts (magnesium sulphate) at the rate of 20 grams per litre of water. Repeat fortnightly until the problem is corrected.
• *Manganese deficiency* shows up as yellow patches between the veins. Apply a foliar spray of manganese sulphate at 1 gram per litre of water.
• *Nitrogen deficiency* produces pale yellow leaves and stunted growth. An application of sulphate of ammonia is the quick fix; blood and bone will provide a slower response.
• *Phosphorus deficiency* creates stunted growth and a purplish tinge to leaves. Apply superphosphate or blood and bone.
• *Potassium deficiency* produces leaves with a burnt yellow look, especially around the edges. The leaves of fruit trees turn cup-shaped. Apply sulphate of potash to the soil to correct levels.

MULCH

Mulch

One of the most satisfying garden jobs is tipping bags of collected autumn leaves onto the lawn and mowing over them. Then, rake them up, toss in a balanced fertiliser, and scatter them over your garden beds. Yum. Each to his own, I suppose. You can also add them to the compost heap or use them to create a no-dig, lazy person's vegetable garden.

If the leaves are decorative, like the rich red leaves of the liquidambar, you can leave them where they have fallen under trees as a natural mulch; they look wonderful when early-flowering plants such as *Helleborus niger* appear like pristine snowflakes through the winter carpet. And excitement builds when the new lime-green shoots of spring bulbs push through a russet mulch of spent leaves.

You know it's Friday in my city neighbourhood when those leaf blower vacuums crank up. A young mother I know believes they start their high-pitched whine the moment she puts her baby down to sleep.

It's not so much the noise that irritates, nor the fact that it is just as easy—and somehow more organic—to wield a picturesque broom. It's what then happens to the leaves that gets me stirred up.

Real gardeners don't use blower vacs. It seems that it is maintenance men—I refuse to call them gardeners—who, keen to get the job done quickly, will tidy a client's footpath by either blowing fallen leaves onto the neighbour's side or—a much greater sin—blowing them into the gutter. And what happens when it finally rains? The gutters clog and the drains flood, of course.

It's also the waste of a good mulch that makes my lips purse in disapproval. While fallen leaves may not be full of nutrients, as a garden mulch they can suppress weeds, add structure to the soil, protect the surface from sun and wind, and conserve moisture. Mulch helps to keep the soil temperature stable—for which your plants will say thank you.

In very cold areas where the soil freezes over winter, you may want to mulch in autumn, when the ground is still warm; some gardeners 'in the know' advise not to mulch until winter frosts are over, as a thick layer of organic matter in the depths of winter hugs heavy frost to the ground and can damage plant roots. Others say it is crucial to hold the mulch until after a good dose of rain; in a country as diverse as ours, you need to adjust advice to suit your local conditions. Some do it whenever they can obtain the spoiled lucerne, the rice husks or the harvest 'trash'—and others among us just have to mulch when the spare moment presents itself.

When applying mulch, it's best to ensure the soil is damp. Then add organic pellets (such as Dynamic Lifter) or blood and bone. Spread your chosen mulch at a depth of about 10 cm, although I always apply it more thickly.

Mulching materials

From among the many different materials you can use as mulch, my favourites are:

Soft mulches

I believe the best mulch is spoiled *lucerne*, which fixes essential nitrogen in the soil. Buy it in bales that are not too big to handle and apply it in thick

Previous page: The delicate pink and cream blooms of *Arisaema candidissimum* push through a mulch of lucerne.

biscuits, except where you have planted swathes of perennials or bulbs (when you will have to tease it out).

If you are lucky enough to get access to stables, shearing sheds or paddocks, you can help yourself to *manure* which, after being well aged, can be used to top-dress garden beds. You can, of course, also buy commercial composted cow manure in easy-to-handle bags. (As with all such products, as well as fresh manures and potting mixes, take care when handling; wear gloves and a face mask.)

Rice husks, which decompose slowly and release small amounts of nitrogen, potassium and phosphorus, make an excellent soil conditioner. There is also *coir, sugar cane* and *cotton trash*: although be careful to choose crops that have not been treated with pesticides. Bunnings recently released an excellent coir mulch in a small, easy-to-store block, which increases at least five-fold when dunked in a tub of water. There is also a coir block specifically for orchids, one for roses and for raising seeds. *Coco mulch* can also be purchased in blocks at nurseries. If you live near an essential oil factory or a winery, you may have access to inexpensive mulches of *herb trash* or *grape seed marc*.

Then, there are the *leaves* (mentioned above) and, of course, your own, home-made *compost* (perhaps the best mulch of all), which is also a wonderful fertiliser and soil conditioner (*see* Fertilisers, page 286).

Hard mulches

Difficult as it may be to believe, a mulch of *pebbles* or washed *stones* will reduce humidity; they also look decorative and conserve water, although (obviously) do not add nutrients to the soil. They appear particularly effective when accompanying plants that naturally occur in a rocky habitat; think of alpine communities of orchids, saxifrages, gentians, *Ranunculus*, auriculas and other tiny treasures that enjoy a scree bed.

The silver to grey plants of the Mediterranean, which demand good drainage, look most attractive with a mulch of pebbles. A surface dressing of pebbles also looks at home in a herb garden. And in a country garden in Victoria I saw a stunning woodland created from copses of lemon-scented gum (*Corymbia citriodora*) planted in threes, fives and sevens, their smooth trunks and glaucous leaves toning perfectly with a mulch of smooth cream and grey stones and pebbles. I've also admired silver-grey, rough-cut *gravel* used as a mulch around the bright green leaves of newly emerged hostas (this mulch also serves to deter snails, the scourge of hostas). A gravel mulch allows gardeners to work without tramping soil about and treading on the plants.

Take care if using *woodchip*. A mulched tree should not be used immediately on the garden. Compost the chips for about six to eight weeks, adding blood and bone and chicken manure to replace the nitrogen that will be used as the material breaks down. Be wary, too, of new eucalypt chips: observe how little grows under a stand of gums—the resins and oils that impart that delicious scent to the air are not conducive to growing much else. On the other hand, it is thought that composted eucalypt or camphor laurel mulch assists in the suppression of pathogens in the soil.

> **Tip:** Eucalypt chips—laid onto a well-compacted earthen path—make a soft and aromatic path, a perfect choice for a walk that meanders through a planting of native species.

PROPAGATION

Propagation

'One of the great pleasures in life is nurturing living things and watching them grow to maturity and reach their full potential.'—Angus Stewart, *Let's Propagate!*

'Plants for free' is the line that the call to propagate usually takes—and it's almost true. As Stewart points out in his book, the capacity for plants to regenerate from all sorts of bits and pieces—leaves, roots, stems, petals and, of course, seeds—is truly amazing.

Propagation by seed—of course, one of the most popular ways of creating new plants—is discussed under individual plant entries, so is not further addressed in this chapter. Vegetative plant propagation is both a science and an art. But don't be daunted; you don't have to be an expert to experience the exhilaration of success.

Propagation methods

There are several ways to create new plants from old, usually depending upon the plant material.

Division

The easiest method is by division, suitable for clumping perennials like kangaroo paw, clivias, agapanthus and bearded iris. This is done when flowering is finished and the plant is entering a growth cycle. Cut back the green leafy material above the ground prior to removing any damaged or old parts of the plant and to facilitate digging out the clump with a large fork. Then, divide the clump into several pieces, using a sharp, strong knife or spade. Replant the pieces or clumps and water in.

Tip cuttings

Propagation by tip cuttings is the best method for a wide range of woody plants, including camellias,

mock orange (*Murraya paniculata*), bay and box. Cuttings are ideally taken in mid- to late summer, as new growth starts to darken, but whenever you have the time is okay. I use what I prune, whenever I prune. Cuttings should be 10 to 15 cm long, with three or four sets of 'eyes' or nodes. Remove a third to a half of the lower leaves and scrape away a little of the outer layer at the base of each piece. Dip that end in a rooting hormone powder to assist the strike rate. Insert the piece (and including the tip isn't essential) into propagating mix and keep damp.

Offsets

Succulents like echeveria, sempervivum, aloes and agaves are particularly easy to propagate as they form offsets—often called pups—at the base of the plant. These can be separated and potted up, usually in summer when they are growing strongly.

Leaf cuttings

Fleshy plants like sedums, aeonium, echeveria and kalanchoe can also be propagated readily from leaf cuttings—usually in spring and summer. Place the base of a whole leaf into a coarse potting mix; a rooting hormone is not necessary. New plantlets will form along the cut surface.

Layering
AIR LAYERING

Air layering is simpler than it sounds and is most suited for plants that are difficult to strike from

Opposite: The luscious pink bloom of the rose 'Blossomtime'.

cuttings, such as some magnolias, rhododendrons, crab-apples and certain grevilleas. It is also useful for producing relatively large plants in quite a short time. Air layering involves cutting two rings through the bark of a slim branch that is still attached to the parent plant. Make a cut from ring to ring to peel off the bark; this is known as a girdle. (Clear away any shoots from where you are going to make the girdle.) Surround the girdle with a medium such as sawdust, coconut fibre or sphagnum peat moss and encase the whole in aluminium foil. Once roots are emerging from the foil, you can cut the stem from the parent plant and pot it up. The growing season—usually spring and summer—is the best time to propagate in this way.

SIMPLE LAYERING

Simple layering can be achieved if a branch or shoot is lying close to the ground. Just peg it down with a bent piece of wire (the layer) into the soil and leave it to strike roots. Scraping back some of the outer layer to expose the inner layer to the soil will assist the process. Cut off the new, rooted section a year or so later and pot up as usual.

Maintaining your cuttings

A polystyrene fruit box makes a perfect propagation container; or use the more portable 160 to 200 mm plastic pots. Use a sheet of glass or a plastic cover to increase humidity, and a shade cloth over the top for really hot days. Don't allow cuttings to dry out and keep them misted. You can buy heat trays and thermostat-controlled trays from garden companies, such as Diggers Club (www.diggers.com.au).

Damping off, or dieback, which causes stem rot and wilting, can be controlled by a systemic fungicide, such as Fongarid (*see* Pests and Diseases).

Always use a good-quality propagating or potting mix and wear a mask to prevent breathing in the medium.

Tip: Anti-transpirants are a range of liquid products gaining popularity and which have many uses in the garden. These products, which are applied as a soil drench or spray, were first used in the transplant seedling industry and are now employed in transplanting nursery stock and mature trees, allowing them to establish without setback. Moisture loss is reduced by up to 50 per cent, thereby allowing root systems to grow before placing heavy demands on them.

Envy by Agrobest is a liquid polymer that, when mixed with water and applied, dries rapidly to provide a thin, clear film that reduces transpiration, assists with frost protection in moderate frosts and reduces windburn and sunburn in extreme climates. It reduces moisture loss by up to 50 per cent, which greatly decreases the stress on the newly forming roots.

Above: Marching elephants at Old Wesleydale, Tasmania: created from easily propagated *Lonicera nitida*.

PRUNING

Pruning

No matter how low maintenance your garden might be, it is unlikely you will be able to avoid having to master the basic principles of pruning—to keep your plants looking their best, to promote fruiting or flowering, and to maintain the required size and shape.

In most gardens winter is peak pruning time. While the days are short and often cold and damp, there are plenty of jobs that must be completed if you want to reap the joys that spring—the freshest and brightest of seasons—brings. And one of those chores is pruning.

Among several reasons for pruning any plant is the promotion of correct growth and abundant flowering. When considering how to prune, you need to come to terms with the way each species grows and its special needs: whether, for instance, it flowers and fruits on this season's or last season's 'wood' or growth. Put simply, you don't want to prune when and where the flower buds are forming.

Then there are the decorative reasons for pruning. According to Australian botanist Peter Valder, the Chinese are masters at pruning, with a long history of training plants into evocative shapes. In his book, *Gardens in China*, Valder describes a camellia (at the Yufeng Temple near Lijiang, north-west Yunnan) pruned to two dimensions, as a flat plane, which produces 10,000 blooms.

The Chinese, who see the garden as a multi-dimensional landscape painting, have long been expert at pruning plants, from large trees to the smallest shrub, to maintain a size to fit the space for which they are intended. Sensitive pruning creates plants either reminiscent of those depicted by the classical landscape painters or gives them symbolic meaning. And, explains Valder, it was the Chinese who first developed the art of dwarfing trees, pruning the roots as well as the above-ground sections of the plant to create a desired size and shape.

There are various types of pruning to achieve decorative effects in the garden.

Decorative pruning
Espalier

It is perhaps in formal gardens, where geometry is all important, that espalier—the art of pruning a plant to lie flat against an upright support—comes into its own. And if space is your problem, the art of the espalier is a skill you might wish to learn (*see also* Vertical Surfaces). This impressive method of pruning a tree or shrub to grow flush with a wall or fence along a framework (usually of wires) is the small-space gardener's answer to the prayer of wanting it all.

It is not difficult to train apples or pears (if you live in a climate with cold winters) or citrus (for those in warmer areas) into fan shapes, rope-like cordons, or diamonds, which will quickly decorate any surface.

The English seem to espalier almost anything —you've probably seen *Magnolia grandiflora* 'Exmouth' carefully trained flat against the wall of a grand house in any one of their famous gardens. You might well wonder if the growing plant will damage the point work, and in this country we'd be concerned about providing a conduit for possums to scamper up and gain easy access to the roof.

Previous page: At Holker Hall in England, a shaded tunnel is created by pleaching.

Espaliered plants can add interest and definition to any and every surface—fences or walls. If your fence is less than perfect, clad it first, and then lime-wash or render it. And plants espaliered on wired-up frames can provide a beautiful and economic free-standing divider in any garden, large or small.

As well as being decorative, growing fruit as an espalier will also increase yield. Trials in commercial orchards have proved that espaliered fruit trees are easier to care for, more economical to harvest, and allow more trees to be grown in a smaller area. Espalier allows greater protection of the crop, increasing flower and fruit production. Figs, apples and pears also happily comply with this method of training, and even the crab-apple (particularly *Malus ioensis*) is suitable for pruning in this way. Olives, risky planted as a tree in a small space, are kept in check when trained against warm walls (for further cultivation tips, *see* Fruit).

Paradise in Italy's north

On Isola Madre, a glorious garden covering an island in Lake Maggiore in Italy's north, a clutch of *Magnolia grandiflora* is clipped and espaliered onto a summer house with spectacular effect.

HOW TO ESPALIER

When espaliering on a flat surface, the distance between the wall and wires should be no less than 50 mm to aid in air circulation.

If concerned about intrusive roots near precious walls, use a root-control barrier, such as black plastic or corrugated fibreglass. Run it along the wall beneath the soil and plant in front.

When creating your espalier, remove any crossing branches. Look for buds that are sidewards facing, and prune to direct the growth along your supporting wires, which will be strained at about 30 cm apart. As with all pruning, turn your secateurs upside down so the cutting blade is on the side of the plant that will remain on the bush. This ensures you don't bruise the remaining wood, inviting disease.

The desirable qualities of a plant to be bought for this purpose are worth considering. First, choose a young, vigorous plant that is well proportioned. Plants like camellias should be symmetrical; apples and pears should be a one-year-old tree called a 'whip', which can be ordered from your garden centre and which you can then develop in the desired way. When buying plants to espalier, try to select one not planted in the centre of the pot, which may comprise too much root ball, preventing planting almost flush with the wall. If you can't avoid such a specimen, plant in winter, so you can safely remove any unwanted root material.

And among the good news about espalier is that it is warm-weather work, as it is essential to develop a pleasing symmetrical shape as the plant is growing.

Lattice hedges

At Foxglove Spires, a large garden and nursery at Tilba Tilba just inland from the far south coast of New South Wales, the main garden is separated from the potager and the rose garden by an impressive and highly decorative 'Bouche Thomas' lattice hedge of apples: another form of espalier, which is both decorative and practical. Yet again, management of fruit grown in this way encourages a heavier crop, is easier to net and harvest, and is space saving. This method of pruning is a more complicated version of a simple cordon to form a living lattice and can be used to create a fence or divide. Thankfully, it is easier than it looks.

Erect strong, tensioned, horizontal support wires—about 30 to 50 cm apart—between upright posts 2.2 m apart. Choose young trees with well-placed laterals (these will form your lattice) and plant at a 45 degree angle (which will also serve to reduce vigour and increase fruit production). You can attach, at the same angle, a bamboo stake for support over the first few seasons. Cut away shoots that do not contribute to the eventual lattice pattern. Hard-prune in winter (back to fruiting spurs if desired shape and cover has developed) and tip-prune all year round to maintain overall shape and size. Equal spacing ensures a perfect lattice pattern.

Pollarding

Pollarding seems to be a French habit: you see these knobbly-knuckled trees in winter lining village and town squares. While they can look rather sad in winter, come summer they spring to life to form a cool, green, shaded canopy in spaces that may not be large enough to allow them to develop to their full splendour.

You buy or train a tree with a well-branched head at the height you want your canopy to form. In winter, remove the main central stem at that height to encourage a cluster of new branches to shoot from this point. Then, early each winter, just after the leaves have fallen, you cut a little further out from the previous year's scar to create

The topiary gardens of Levens Hall

The most famous of topiary gardens must be Levens Hall, near Kendal, in the very south of the English Lake District. Much photographed, this 2 ha garden has to be seen in person to be believed. Laid out in 1694 as the indulgence of a mysterious Frenchman named Guillaume Beaumont, Levens is a garden of fanciful shapes, sophisticated parterres, an exciting *potager* and innovative and instructive perennial borders.

There, the big daddy of all the hedging and topiary plants, the sombre yew (*Taxus baccata*), grows in splendour. It is slow growing, however, so the various *Cupressus* species of conifer seem more suited to our climate and our 'quick fix' aspirations. Common beech (*Fagus sylvatica*) is another northern hemisphere classic; in Australia, common hornbeam (*Carpinus betulus*) is less fussy and faster.

the instantly recognisable 'knuckles'. Trees most often pruned in this way include plane (*Platanus* spp.), ash (*Fraxinus* spp.), limes (*Tilia* spp.), willow (*Salix* spp.) and even dogwoods (*Cornus* spp.).

Pleaching

Pleaching involves two rows of a single type of tree, often lime or mulberry (*Morus nigra*), planted to create a shaded avenue or green tunnel, 2 to 3 m wide. Wires are strung along the length of the rows at canopy height; branches are pruned and attached—pleached—along the supporting wires to weave into each other. You may want to erect a wooden scaffold to assist in the training in the early years; it can be removed when the pollarded avenue is completely self supporting.

Topiary

'Landscape is what happens when culture meets nature,' writes Columbia University's Professor Simon Schama in *Landscape and Memory*, his 1995 dissertation on just what it is that informs and fires our imagination. There could be no greater demonstration of the manipulation of nature than the art of topiary, the clipping of plant matter into all sorts of shapes.

If you have a fair dose of patience and a healthy irreverence for rules and regulations, then you will no doubt keep an open mind on the ancient art of topiary, which is not to everyone's taste. This form of clipped control has featured in gardens throughout gardening history, from the formal gardens of the wealthy residents of Pompeii to the extravagant detail of Versailles or the great gardens of Japanese noblemen.

Today, some turn up their noses at this clipped form of garden art with its associated animals and nursery rhyme characters. Others laugh at such rules of good taste, housing a veritable zoo in their garden. In some gardens you might see chickens being pursued across the lawn by a fox. Elephants make their way towards the rose garden, or bare-breasted women recline on the lawn—all created from living plants. You could grow

1. Levens Hall, where clipping is king.
2. Well-clipped plants create a calm atmosphere in a small space.
3. In Peter Stubbs' Adelaide garden.
4. Walls beautifully espaliered at Broughton House in England's Cotswolds.
5. The 'Bouche Thomas' lattice at Foxglove Spires.

Two months of rose pruning

Garden activity at Melbourne's Flemington Racecourse heats up in the first week of June, when the first of the hard pruning of the roses occurs. Pruning, which takes place over an eight-week period, is completed in the first week of August, and is timed so that the roses reach their peak on Cup Day in early November. Different varieties are pruned at different times, as some take longer than others to flower. First to be pruned are the majority of the Floribundas, with the exception of the yellow-flowering roses. Along with 'Kagayaki', a scarlet-coloured Floribunda bred in Japan in 1970, the yellows are not pruned until mid-July.

advises that a small bird should be able to fly straight through a camellia. So, prune lightly to improve flowering and open up the bush and remove any lower or crossing branches to improve the shape. The larger growing rhododendron is also pruned to encourage air circulation and the desired shape.

Trees

'Leave well alone,' would be my first comment when asked how to prune a tree. In most western gardens, where trees are grown on several planes or dimensions, they should be pruned as little as possible—prune just to improve the shape or to remove crossing or dead branches, or to encourage flowers or fruit.

Removing lower branches, perhaps to provide easy access for the mower, weakens a tree. A tree growing naturally, with lower branches sweeping the ground and dying when their use to the tree is complete, will live longer and will rarely suffer a break in the crown.

And nothing looks more tragic than a tree pruned badly or inappropriately because the wrong species has been chosen for a site. In many Australian cities, the entire centres of street trees have been removed to allow for power lines—a brutal sight. Better to remove the tree or, better still, choose more carefully in the first place.

Roses

August is the month much of the country prunes its roses. Of paramount importance is to know which of your roses repeat flower. You should not assume that all old-fashioned roses should be pruned after flowering. Those with a big spring flush of blooms flower on last season's wood, so they should be pruned around November, after flowering. Those that are remontant (such as the old-fashioned Bourbons) will generally flower on current season's growth, so should be pruned in winter.

To encourage the greatest flowering from your climbing roses, with blooms all the way along the stems, tie them down flat—as horizontal as possible—to promote stress, and shoots, all the way along the branch. After flowering, cut back to one or two shoots for repeat flowering. Tip-prune the water shoots in the autumn or winter.

Alternatively, plant multiples of the one rose and tie canes in repeating 'S's to encourage dense flowering. And, to stimulate roses to flower right up a pole—particularly useful for people who garden in a small space—prune to encourage each shoot to develop in a different direction.

Use only the parrot beak style of secateurs, rather than pruners with an anvil-type cut, for roses. Ensure the holding arm is the piece gripping the section of the bush that is being removed, otherwise you will bruise the plant and invite dieback. Dip secateurs into a disinfectant bath or spray with metho between rose bushes. For more in-depth information on roses, their uses and care, *see* Part 2, Roses.

Moving Plants

Who was it who said passionate gardeners should plant in wheelbarrows, so that their treasures could be moved about at whim? Obviously another gardener.

Gardening must be the most difficult of art forms: plants grow, often in ways that defy expectation and explanation. Nothing remains static. Gardens are not like sitting-rooms (where sofas, lamps, tables and cushions can be easily rearranged to perfect a scene)—everything in them is volatile, and the unexpected is often the most inspired. When designing a new garden, it is unlikely that you will know exactly where each chosen plant will grow best. And often, depending upon your climate, soil and other environmental conditions, a plant will grow at a different rate and to a different height than your reference book, or the plant label, has indicated.

Sometimes it is not only a change of mind or a struggling plant that necessitates moving it, but a change of address, and a dearly loved plant (with the new owner's full knowledge) moves with you.

When and how to transplant

Trees and shrubs should be moved, where possible, when the plant is dormant: deciduous trees will obviously be transplanted in winter; evergreen trees or shrubs are best moved after flowering and when the weather becomes cool. If you are moving an evergreen, or are forced to move a deciduous tree or shrub in the growing season, help reduce stress to the plant by applying a foliar spray, such as Seasol.

In general, move fruit trees after cropping, but summer-fruiting trees prefer to be moved when the weather has cooled.

Most species of palms and tree ferns indigenous to warmer climates like to be moved in the warmer months, when their roots are growing.

Transplant evergreen perennials after flowering (but cut them back before you do so). Deciduous herbaceous species can be cut back and moved in winter, when they can also be divided (*see also* Propagation).

Some plants, of course, such as Australian native plants, and some herbaceous plants, including peonies, do not respond well to being moved, so think carefully before choosing their place in the garden. Of course, a very large tree will be a job for a professional arborist.

You will want to move plants in the coolest part of the day and, if possible, in the absence of damaging winds.

Weeks in advance, warn your plant that moving day is approaching by digging a trench around it, just outside the perimeter of the drip line. Water

Opposite: A collection of old terracotta pots: beautiful as well as useful. *Above*: Another life for those pots!

well a few days before transplanting to ameliorate any potential shock. When it is time to transplant, prepare a large hole (twice as wide and a little deeper than the root ball). Add a handful of fertiliser, which you will cover with a little soil, so that newly planted roots are not burned. Once you have dug out the root ball, transport the plant to the prepared hole on hessian or plastic. Compensate by trimming off damaged roots and some foliage. Take care to replant to the same depth as before. Water deeply (but don't waterlog) and provide a seaweed conditioner. When mulching, avoid bringing the mulch flush with the trunk of the plant, as this will encourage collar rot. Follow up with a fortnightly tonic of conditioner.

When removing a plant from a pot, you may find that it is pot-bound and that very little soil remains. Tease out the roots and cut away any damaged sections. If re-potting, use new potting mix, to which you have added a few water-saving crystals.

If moving plants from one property to another, always advise prospective buyers of those plants that will not be included in the sale. You can mark these, and other treasured possessions, with brightly coloured ribbon.

Above: Planting in pots: versatile.

Pests

Without exception, pests and diseases comprise my least favourite subject, as it is the peaceful aspects of garden-making that appeal. To be honest with you, it is the dreaming and planning that attract me, closely followed by the harvesting of the garden's bounty.

However, to enjoy the joy and the tranquility of a vigorous and productive garden, we have to face up to some of the less creative activities—and these include keeping the garden healthy. So I will, at least briefly, discuss the main nuisances and challenges you might encounter in the garden.

My main antidote for a plant that becomes sick is to choose another, one that is absolutely suited to its conditions, and is therefore likely to remain strong and pest free. However, I admit that passionate gardeners often covet what they shouldn't, and desire treasures unsuited to their garden situation—from roses in a climate that is too humid to wisteria in a region of late frost.

What I like to call 'good garden-keeping' will also help to keep plants strong, to avoid disease and resist the onslaught of many pests. Clear away fallen and damaged fruit, which may encourage disease. Clean up underneath plants after pruning, particularly if you are pruning away unhealthy foliage: don't leave cuttings and damaged leaves on the ground. Spray the ground with lime sulphur after pruning to kill any lurking spores.

Keep plants strong by growing them in their preferred climate and conditions, and by fertilising, watering and mulching correctly.

However, there are some 'fixes' if your plants succumb to any of the most common of garden ills. If you don't like using chemicals, such problems can be addressed quite happily these days with organic, non-toxic products.

Pests

- **Ants** are a sign that plants are stressed and possibly moisture deprived; they feed off the honeydew exuded by a variety of sap-sucking insects. Keep your plants healthy by feeding. Add water-holding crystals to pots and, if ants do gather, use Mortein Ant Sand on the soil surface. And find the source of the honeydew and rid the plant of this pest.

- **Aphids** are sap-sucking insects that attack a range of plants. Leaves and shoots appear to curl or wilt. Aphids exude a sticky honeydew, which provides a food supply for ants and mould (a fungi that forms a black, sooty coating over flowers, leaves, stems and fruit)—I've even seen it covering a white-painted fence! For small infestations, remove the aphids with your fingers, or spray with a low toxic systemic spray, which will also help with sooty mould. For gardeners of smaller spaces, it's available in an easy-to-use trigger pack.

- **Armyworm** cause large brown patches on lawns—and rising panic in home owners. Along with sod web worm and curl grub, this mainly summer-active caterpillar can quickly ruin a perfect green sward. Hose the lawn (on allowed days, of course) to bring them to the surface and hope the birds will feast on them. They are usually dark brown or green to black in colour, with bodies larger than their heads, and move in armies (hence their name). They can be sprayed with Baythroid.

- **Azalea lace bugs** suck the sap from leaves, creating tell-tale silver trails. Spray with Confidor

Previous page: A healthy 'Ballerina' apple.

or non-toxic, plant-based Eco-Oil, or Natrasoap, when new growth starts after flowering, and then once a month while the plants are still producing growth.

• **Birds** are a constant problem in many country and city gardens. If you despair of birds stripping precious trees of leaves and flower buds and nipping off the nascent red shoots of your Tea roses, there are several deterrents you might try. As these wily creatures, like possums, become accustomed to any deterrent, you should change your methods every few weeks. Try weaving a piece of black 'ag' pipe—or a black rubber snake from a National Geographic shop—through the branches. Or try tying disused CDs to branches: they glint as they turn and catch the sun, and will deter birds for a while. One gardener I know hoists large plastic owls—the sort used on boats to deter seagulls—onto poles, while another uses yellow balloons with blue texta eyes to ward off destructive birds from her roses.

If you become completely desperate, construct rose covers from large sheets of chicken wire wrapped around each rose bush. A circular 'lid' of chicken wire is sewn onto the top.

• **Borers:** Holes in the trunk (with accompanying sawdust) of trees and shrubs point to the presence of this caterpillar, which is often found in plants which are under stress from drought or poor soil. The classic method of eradicating them is to impale them on a wire that you have inserted into the wound of the tree. Most importantly, improve the growing conditions of the plant.

• **Budworms** burrow into the buds of many plants, chewing from the inside, sometimes undetected until the damage becomes obvious. Spray with Dipel, which is non-toxic to humans and has no withholding period, or with Confidor, as the buds are growing.

• **Caterpillars**, which turn into various moths, can be controlled by non-toxic Dipel, or Mavrik, which is also low in toxicity and is harmless to treasured bees and ladybirds.

• **Citrus leafminer:** Silvery lines on leaves are evidence of this pest, which causes leaves to curl

and drop: prevent with regular use of PestOil or Eco-Oil.

• **Codling moth** larvae chew their way into fruit, such as apples and pears. Prevent eggs from hatching by spraying the canopy with 1 part white oil to 50 parts water, fortnightly, from September to November. As well, hessian wrapped around the tree trunk will attract the grubs; this can be regularly checked to dispose of them.

• **Curl grubs** are the white, C-shaped larvae of the African black beetle. They cause dead patches in the lawn by feeding on grass roots. Kill the beetle as it emerges in summer with Baythroid, which is safe for your precious earthworms. Water in well and repeat to eradicate hatching eggs.

• **Cutworms** are infuriating, creamy-grey to green caterpillars and members of the moth group Noctuideae, which chew away at plants at soil level during the night. They hide under clumps of soil during the day, curling up when disturbed. Counter with Dipel.

• **Elm leaf beetle:** This small beetle (*Pyrrhalta luteola*), first seen in Victoria in the late 1980s, has caused the devastation of many revered, established plantings of elm, particularly the English elm (*Ulmus procera*), which has been under stress in many cities in the south of the country through prolonged drought. The yellow and black, or bronze, beetles emerge from beneath the bark of the tree as the weather warms in spring, leaving shot holes in leaves and laying rows of eggs on their undersides. These hatch later in spring and the larvae skeletonise the leaves before pupating in the bark and soil.

Elm leaf beetle hitchhikes

Please take care when travelling that you do not bring home much more than happy memories and great photographs: it is thought that the devastating elm leaf beetle was brought into Australia in the suitcase of a traveller from the USA.

Among treatments tried—which may prolong the life of a much-loved tree—are spraying the canopy, as well as drenching the soil around the tree with a solution of Confidor; it is best to get a professional arborist to undertake either of these treatments.

- **Erinose mites** make themselves at home in new leaves, particularly of some eucalypt species, causing unsightly blisters and lumps and brown, velvety patches on the underside of leaves, which can twist and curl. Grapevines, walnuts and lychee trees are also among a diverse range of plants that can be affected. This microscopic mite is spread by wind or foraging bees, and attacks new shoots, leaves, flower buds and fruit. Prune and destroy damaged parts of the plant. Practise good plant management, such as appropriate site selection, watering and fertilising. In orchard situations, successive sprays with wettable sulphur are recommended.

- **Fruit fly** attacks summer fruits, along with some vegetables. This pest lays its eggs just beneath the fruit's surface; when the eggs hatch, the larvae burrow in towards the centre of the fruit. Infested fruit can be treated with the systemic Lebaycid, which has replaced the more brutal Rogor (now discontinued by its manufacturer). Install Eco traps and lures (see Products, page 316) to ascertain the arrival of this pest. And again, practise good garden-keeping by collecting and destroying fallen fruit.

  You can make fruit-fly traps with empty plastic drink bottles. Pierce medium-sized holes a third of the way down, add a mix of 2 tablespoons of cloudy ammonia, 2 tablespoons of sugar and 1 cup water, re-screw on the lid and hang in the trees. Check the traps for dead flies; recharge.

- **Gall wasps:** Remove the distinctive galls of the citrus gall wasp by late winter, before the adult wasps hatch, usually between early September and November. Prune away weakened or damaged sections of the affected plant. Heavily infested plants will lose leaves and produce little fruit.

- **Hibiscus flower beetles:** These tiny black, shiny beetles will chew into the flower buds, causing neat holes. Control with Confidor spray, PestOil

or Eco-Oil. Alternatively, place containers of soapy water near the plant, or hang cut-outs smeared with Vaseline to commit these small pests to a sticky end.

- **Lady birds:** Of course, the common ladybird with 18 spots and its larvae are not pests at all, as they obligingly eat aphids and scale insects. The 26- or 28-spotted orange to yellow ladybird and its larvae, however, feed on the surface and undersurface of leaves. Spray with Eco-Oil or PestOil.

- **Leaf miners** are the larvae of several insects, including beetles, wasps, sawflies or moths. They leave tell-tale thin, meandering lines or blisters on leaves. If damage is not too widespread, prune and destroy the damaged leaves or branches. If severe, treat with a systemic pesticide, such as Confidor.

- **Mealy bugs** are a common sap-sucking pest, indicated by white fluff on leaves and buds, particularly on plants growing where air circulation is poor. Treat them with a systemic spray such as Confidor, or with Natrasoap, or remove with a cotton bud dipped in methylated spirits.

- **Millipedes** have two pairs of legs per segment, as opposed to the centipede, with has one pair per segment. Millipedes are often harmless—although annoying—creatures; the Portuguese millipede, however, appears in great numbers, invading houses and damaging young roots, seeds and seedlings. Some species also emit a poisonous secretion when crushed, which can irritate the eyes and skin.

  Control can prove extremely difficult, as millipedes live in the organic matter in the soil, and you won't want to be drenching large areas of soil with chemicals. Yates recommends using snail and slug bait, again being careful to protect pets and wildlife.

- **Nematodes** are small organisms—some harmless—that live just beneath the soil surface, feeding on fungi, bacteria and other organisms. Harmful nematodes attach to plant roots, where they feed on root juices. They are most often found in sandy soils and each species attacks a different group of plants. Apart from identifying the species and not growing that plant for some time, the best option is to fumigate the soil. Drench it with 1 litre of molasses dissolved in 3 litres of warm water. Keep up plant health by feeding and mulching and other good garden-keeping practices.

- **Pear and cherry slugs**, which cause heartbreak to gardeners in cold climates where this ugly small black 'slug'—the larvae of the sawfly—infests quince, apple and pear plantings, can quickly defoliate a tree. If left unchecked, this will cause the eventual death of the tree. Spray at leaf-fall and bud burst with Bordeaux or with Yates Success to keep it in check.
- **Possums:** The only real deterrent to this pesky animal is a barrier of shade cloth or wire netting. Products like D-Ter and quassia chips are not effective in my experience. You could try CDs dangling on fishing wire, or aluminum pie cases, or flying hawks, or plastic snakes—but those clever possums soon become accustomed to them (*see also* Birds, page 311).

  You can try to prevent possums accessing trees by placing a tall band of tin around the trunk, about 50 cm from the ground. Also make sure that branches don't overhang the roof, providing easy access into the roof, where they can sound like a football team in training.
- **Psyllid:** Lillypillies and many eucalypts are particularly susceptible to these small, lice-like native insects, which cause pimples on the leaves. Treat them in early spring with Eco-Oil or Confidor before the plant is attacked, or prune off affected foliage, discard it safely and treat the remaining plant. There are also new psyllid-resistant varieties of lillypilly available (*see* Native Plants).
- **Snails:** For those who don't want to use snail bait in the garden (even in milk bottles to protect family pets, but into which blue tongue lizards can still reach), try sinking the bottom half of a narrow plastic milk bottle into the soil. Partly fill with beer and watch as the snails drown happily. A new product, Multiguard, is an iron chelate ingested by, and toxic to, snails, but

harmless to other sections of the environment (including dogs).
- **Two-spotted mites:** Previously called red spider mite, these are the bane of azalea lovers and are just visible on the underside of leaves. They cause yellow mottling on leaves and eventually leaf-fall. They also produce cobwebbing on stems and leaves. Discourage them by misting, as they dislike humidity. If the plant is badly damaged, remove it. The two-spotted mite has many natural enemies, so avoid using chemical sprays to encourage these. You can spray with Eco-Oil, which won't harm such organisms.
- **White fly** is a small, sap-sucking fly that affects a wide range of ornamental plants and vegetables, including brassicas, tomatoes and beans. They can rise in clouds from the vegie patch when disturbed. Use sticky traps to catch them. With regular use, Natrasoap will also reduce numbers.
- **White scale** often grows on plants with poor health or which are growing in an unsuitable environment. Large infestations have the appearance of white powder, which often covers stems and branches, weakening the plant and causing dieback. Scrape off or spray with PestOil or Confidor, and improve the plant's health with better watering and fertilising (or move it to a better growing position).

Diseases

For plant nutrient deficiencies, which can encourage diseases, *see* Fertilisers (page 286). Remember, that a well-fed plant means a healthy, pest-free plant.
- **Anthracnose** is a fruit-rot fungus, which is active towards the end of the growing season and is most common on tomatoes. It also affects avocados, lettuces and mangoes. It appears as sunken brown patches at the base of the fruit. A monthly spray with Bordeaux solution from bud burst to harvest will help protect fruit and vegetables. Practices such as staking tomatoes, to increase air circulation around the plants, and mulching to prevent spores from the soil being splashed on the fruit are also recommended.

1. The fungus *Pholiota spectabilis* at the base of a dead radiata pine.
2. Save netting from supermarket purchases to protect individual clusters of homegrown fruit.

- **Armillaria species:** This is a group of fungi, most commonly called the honey fungi. They should strike fear into the heart of every gardener. Identified by a white, fan-like fungus underneath the bark or a tangle of black, shoelace-like cords (rhizomorphs), it spreads quickly through the soil, under the bark of trees and shrubs and on their roots. The symptoms include wilting, curling and leaf-fall and, quickly, the death of the plant. It is found on a variety of trees and shrubs but also on plants like strawberries and raspberries. Remove and destroy the affected plant as quickly as possible.

- **Black spot** is caused by a variety of fungal diseases. It is one of several problems to afflict roses, particularly in humid climates. Treat the unsightly spots by spraying weekly with a mix of 3 teaspoons of bicarbonate of soda, 2 teaspoons of PestOil and 5 litres of water. Or use Yates Fungus Gun, a systemic fungicide spray.

  More importantly grow roses in full sun. Drip-irrigate to lessen the amount of water on the leaves and water deeply in the morning once or twice a week. Grow roses suited to your climate: those gardening in the warmer parts of the country will have greater success with Tea roses, which come from the warmer southern part of China.

- **Bracket fungi:** The fruiting body of a decaying fungus, bracket or shelf fungi appear like flat mushrooms (or Frisbees), most often embedded on a tree trunk in horizontal layers. Often orange with green markings, these fungi indicate serious decay within the plant. Cut away and burn affected parts of the plant. In extreme cases, the removal of the plant will be the only option.

- **Collar rot** is a soil-borne fungus caused by mulch applied too close to the trunk of a tree or shrub, or by poor drainage. At worst, it will ringbark the plant. Symptoms are yellowing and dying off of the leaves and sap oozing from the trunk. Clear away the mulch from around the base of the plant, then drench the soil with a systemic fungicide like Fongarid.

- **Cypress canker** affects several genera of conifers and can cause branches to die off. The spores of the fungus are spread by wind or water and enter the tree via damaged bark. While you may not be able to save severely damaged trees, if the damage is minor use a phosphorous acid like Yates Anti Rot, which is sprayed on the foliage.

- **Dieback** is a fungus that enters plants through wounds. Sterilise pruning tools between plants to help prevent introduction and spread of disease. Spray or drench soil with a fungicide like Fongarid.

- **Leaf gall** is a fungus that causes swollen leaves on azaleas and some camellias. Cut off affected parts of the plant and destroy.

- **Peach leaf curl** is a fungal disease that causes unsightly, distorted leaves in spring and summer on peaches and nectarines. It causes leaf-fall and fruit loss. It is best prevented by spraying with Bordeaux solution at leaf-fall and again at bud swell.

- **Powdery mildew** is most common on roses and grapevines, but also affects many shrubs and perennials, particularly in humid climates. It should be treated at first occurrence with a fungicide like Yates Fungus Gun. Organic gardeners also swear by milk, diluted in water 1:10, sprayed all over leaves. But it's best to choose plants suited to your climatic conditions.

Rust spots spoil frangipani.

- **Root rot** is a fungus that causes dieback in a range of plants. Among its causes are poor drainage or soil or mulch being applied too close to the trunk of a shrub. Treat the soil by drenching it with a fungicide like Fongarid and spray foliage with Yates Anti Rot (a systemic, low toxic fungicide) and ensure you maintain good gardening practices. In heavier soils, where drainage might be poor, adding a soil conditioner such as a fish- or molasses-based product to enhance the natural, friendly biology will also improve plant health. Improves the soil structure also (*see* Soil).
- **Rose scale** makes its appearance as a small white scale crusted onto the stems and branches of the plant. Spray this sap-sucking pest with PestOil and repeat a few weeks later.
- **Rust** comprises millions of spores that spread infection. The most likely victims are roses, iris, stone fruits, frangipani, climbing plants and even the easygoing pelargoniums. Respond to this problem when you first notice it for, as with most problems in the garden, that old saying 'a stitch in time saves nine' is really pertinent here. First, destroy any affected leaves, or cut away and destroy affected sections of the plant. Spray with Eco-Oil.
- **Sooty mould** is a fungus that forms a black, sooty-like coating over leaves, stems, branches and fruit. It grows on the honeydew excreted by sap-sucking insects, including aphids, scale and mealy bug. Clean it off with a mild detergent, or spray with Eco-Oil or Natrasoap. Alternatively, Confidor, a systemic spray of low toxicity, will also help.
- **Wilt:** This is most often associated, infuriatingly, with tomatoes. It's a disease of the soil and in the stems (which turn brown inside). Destroy the plants. Keep your vegie patch clean of weeds and rubbish to help soil health. Resistant varieties include 'Summertaste' and 'Roma'.

Products for organic and chemical control

It goes without saying that gardeners should read instructions carefully for any product—even organic preparations—respecting safety instructions and any withholding periods that apply for edible plants.

- **Baythroid:** This insecticide is a non-systemic, rapid-knock-down, synthetic pyrethroid for pests including army- and lawn worms, adult African black beetles, lawn grubs, ants, fleas, aphids and thrips, which can damage ornamentals, vegetables and native plants. It is of low toxicity to mammals and birds, and when used in accordance with the directions, is harmless to earthworms.
- **Bordeaux spray**, a mix of copper sulphate and lime, is a low-toxicity spray, used to treat a variety of fungal and mildew diseases (as well as pear and cherry slug), particularly on pome fruits.
- **Confidor** is a low toxic, systemic and long-lasting insecticide that combats a huge range of plant-eating insects, from aphids, lace bugs, hibiscus flower beetles, thrips and mealy bugs to curl grubs. It is not registered for edible citrus.
- **Dipel** from Yates is, according to the website (www.yates.com.au), a pest-control mainstay for organic growers worldwide. It contains *Bacillus thuringiensis* (Bt), which is highly effective and selective against most species of caterpillars of moths and butterflies. This biological control

acts as a bacterial stomach poison and is mixed with water and sprayed onto foliage. It must be ingested by the actively feeding caterpillar, which dies three to five days later. It is totally safe to beneficial insects and mammals, but is broken down by sunlight within a few days, so repeated applications may be necessary.

· **Eco Natra** lure is totally organic and effective in protecting a large range of fruit and vegetables from fruit fly. The lure attracts and kills both male and female fruit fly.

· **Eco-Oil** is an organically certified miticide or insecticide. Its active ingredient is potassium bicarbonate and it is used for the control of green peach aphid, citrus leafminer, scale, two-spotted mite, aphids, whitefly and various other sap-sucking insects in food and ornamental crops. It has no withholding period, no re-entry restrictions and maximum user safety, obviating the need for excessive spray protection gear.

According to the manufacturer, insect pests like mites have a low-level resistance potential to Eco-Oil. This allows more regular application than the chemically active insecticides, and does away with complex insect resistance management strategies.

· **Fongarid** is a systemic fungicide that controls damping off and root diseases caused by *Pythium* species and *Phytophthora* fungi in ornamental flowers, shrubs and trees. For long-lasting disease control (up to 10 weeks), it can be applied as a pre-plant soil mix, as a post-plant soil drench or soil surface spray.

· **Mavrik** is a very low toxic, synthetic pyrethroid, also found in Yates Rose Gun and Rose Shield with a new systemic fungicide, Myclobutanil, which fights against chewing and sap-sucking pests on ornamentals and vegetables. It is not harmful to bees and does not leave an unattractive residue on foliage.

· **Natrasoap** is an organically certified insecticide for the control of aphids, mites, leaf hopper, thrips, scale, whitefly, mealy bug and fungus nats in fruit trees, vegetable crops and ornamental plants. It has maximum user safety (negating the need for excessive spray protection gear) and no withholding period. Natrasoap has several modes of action, which means it has a low-level resistance potential in insect pests, allowing more regular application without worrying about pest management strategies. The product is also soft on non-target predators, such as ladybirds and spiders.

· **PestOil**, a petroleum derivative, has a patented additive that acts like sunscreen and, therefore, is less likely to burn plants in hot weather. It also contains added emulsifiers to ensure that it mixes better with water to provide a superior coverage (all oils work by smothering and deterring pests, so coverage is important). It has registrations for fruit trees and ornamentals—it is most commonly used for controlling citrus leaf-miner—and has a one-day withholding period.

· **Success** from Yates is derived from a naturally occurring soil organism (actinomycete). It is a fast-acting insecticide that controls a wide range of caterpillars on fruit and vegetables, including cabbage white butterfly, diamond back moth, heliothis (budworm), light brown apple moth, and that dreadful scourge, pear and cherry slug. It has a low toxicity to beneficial insects and to birds, earthworms and mammals. It can also be used on ornamentals.

· **Yates Anti Rot Phosacid** is a phosphorous acid (very similar to phosphoric acid, a food additive) that inhibits the growth of fungus and enhances a plant's defence system. It is sprayed over the foliage, where it is absorbed into the plant for the control of collar rot in citrus and ornamentals, root rot in citrus, avocados and exotic and native ornamentals, and downy mildew in grapes. It breaks down in the soil and is harmless to the environment. The product has no withholding period and can be sprayed up to harvest.

· **Yates Fungus Gun** is a systemic fungicide spray against mildews, black spot and rusts on roses, and other ornamental plants like hydrangeas, geraniums, hollyhocks and sweet peas. It is based on the fungicide Myclobutanil, which enters the plant's system and moves to where the damage is being done.

WEEDS IN THE GARDEN

Weeds
IN THE GARDEN

The greatest cliché of all in the gardening world is surely the adage that a weed is nothing more than a plant growing in the wrong place. Like most clichés, however, this is a true and extremely useful thought. A plant that may be a weed to one gardener can also be a saviour to another who gardens in a different climate, but if you do have one that has the potential to be invasive, be extremely careful to contain it.

Those plants that were once confined to the garden (both exotic and native) but have escaped to earn the title of 'weed' are included in the discussion of conservation and environmental concerns in Part 1.

But there are still plenty of weeds that we don't want growing among our precious botanical treasures within the garden—species that will poison, cause pain, trigger allergies, damage paving or buildings, harbour pests or just look unsightly. These are the common garden weeds, and most are easy enough to pull out by hand, best done when they are small and certainly before they have set seed.

These include weeds like spurge, sow thistle, deadly nightshade, common ivy (which can choke trees and shrubs), even some ferns: in fact, anything that pushes aside the plants we wish to nurture. Many more that have not been relegated to the weed category also make themselves too much at home—think of bog sage and some of the crocosmias. These are noted throughout the book in the relevant chapters.

Have you noticed how some of the weeds of the plant kingdom are often the most attractive? There are those, however, that are almost impossible to eradicate once established, no matter how pretty they may be. It is never worth planting them and, if you do find you have inherited any of them, remove them quickly and thoroughly. These are among the worst of them.

- **Asparagus fern** (*Asparagus aethiopicus*): A native of southern Africa, this weed (with its vicious thorns on tough, wiry stems that produce pink flowers and red berries) is difficult to eradicate once established, so don't be fooled by its delicate, feathery fronds; eradicate it the moment you notice it.
- **Asthma weed**, pellitory (*Parietaria judaica*) is a perennial herb from Europe that flourishes in neglected gardens, roadsides and other denuded sites. Its small flowers, which cluster in the leaf axils, produce large amounts of pollen. The dark brown-black seeds are spread by wind, water and attachment: eradicate with a glyphosate, or pull out before seeds form.
- **Bindii** (*Soliva pterosperma*) is an annual weed from South America that flowers with rosettes of spines (these entangle themselves in dogs' coats and torture barefoot children on summer lawns). Control it by spraying in spring before the seed has formed. Keep lawns healthy by keeping the mower blades high (*see* Lawns), so that you don't create bare, scalped patches, which invite weeds. Dig out the rosettes by hand in early spring. Specific products such as Chemspray Bin-Die contain Dicamba, which can harm nearby plants.
- **Onion grass** (*Romulea* spp.): This native herb from southern and eastern Africa and the Mediterranean has linear narrow leaves formed on corms. It causes endless heartache for many

Opposite: The arum lily: too much at home in some climates.

Tip: An easy-to-use solution for many home garden weeds is the new Yates Zero Weeding Brush. It's also great for painting glyphosate onto stubborn onion grass. But the best way to deal with weeds is to eradicate them early in their life cycle. A little a day is, as with most gardening, the most efficient and effective way to go.

gardeners as it's difficult and time-consuming to eradicate. Doing the job properly at the outset, however, is the only way to deal with it. Digging out the corms just creates more. So, if you are starting a new garden, you should spray off the onion grass with glyphosate, and repeat after three months. Repeat again. Most of us can't, or won't, take the time to prepare the soil so thoroughly, or have inherited an established garden. In that case, paint on the glyphosate with a fine paintbrush; repeat. If you have large infestations, you can smother them with thick piles of newspaper, placed around the plants you wish to keep.

- **Running bamboo** (*Bambusa* and *Phyllostachys* spp.): You don't want to buy a house anywhere near this group of weeds; they are almost impossible to remove once established. *Phyllostachys* spreads quickly over great areas as loosely clumped shoots; the spreading clumps of *Bambusa* are more dense. If you find yourself neighbour to a bamboo making itself at home in your garden, apart from digging it up, you can cut it off at ground level and paint with glyphosate. Repeat. And repeat again (*see also* Bamboos)!

- **Wood sorrels** (*Oxalis* spp.): The genus *Oxalis* contains more than 800 species, some of which are well behaved, forming very pretty ground covers. Most species in Australia spread by creeping roots, bulbs or bulbils. If you are unlucky enough to have the weedy species in your garden, apply a glyphosate to kill the clover-like leaves; you will probably have to repeat the application several times. Mulch your garden beds thickly to help prevent plants establishing or reappearing and spreading their seed, which is also dispersed by lawn mowers.

Opposite: *Rhododendron ponticum* can become a nuisance. *Above*: Pretty, perhaps, but poisonous: a field of Patterson's Curse.

Shaping the Garden

PART FIVE

DESIGN

Design

How do you design a garden? This is, of course, too large a question to answer and compress into a single chapter of a gardener's companion—but many readers may want to think about the rudiments of good garden design.

Bare bones revealed

A great deal of garden planning takes place in the depths of winter. It is then, when the garden is bare, that light, vistas and aspect are most easily seen. It is then that the skeleton of the garden—its bones—are most clear. And it's then that good ideas come to mind.

❧ Planting—dreaming, serendipity and mystery

DREAMING

Dreaming has a good deal to do with good garden design! While planning to scale on paper is the most sensible, time-saving and economic method by which to achieve a good garden, many great ideas come to mind while standing at a window, a cup of tea in hand, contemplating. Your favourite time in the garden might be in the early morning light, with no one about but you, the birds, the mists and the dew.

SERENDIPITY

Often the best features in any garden happen by chance. Two plants you would never consider teaming get together without your permission—and the combination works well. It is called serendipity.

In many of the best gardens it is the unexpected and undesigned touch—the happy coincidences—that work well and contribute to success. It might be a maidenhair tree (*Ginkgo biloba*), that has become home to the climbing rose 'Altissimo';

the late summer butter-gold, fan-shaped leaves of the ginkgo look wonderful with the clear red, single blooms of this rose. And have you ever noticed how the lemon tones in that lovely pink-flowering climbing rose 'Souvenir de Madame Léonie Viennot', match the tones in the leaves of the silver birch so well? Or perhaps it's a *Magnolia × soulangeana* flowering pink in one front garden at the same moment as a neighbour's deeper pink, double Japanese cherry—possibly *Prunus* 'Kanzan'—which creates an amazing sight. Such unplanned pictures provide proof of the success of serendipity.

MYSTERY

Mystery is another key element in a good garden. Professor EG Waterhouse, a linguist who became world renowned for his work in camellia hybridisation (which is immortalised in the garden of his Sydney house, Eryldene), was a firm proponent of this adage, writing, 'Not all should be seen at once, but everything should add up to make a complete unit. It should be a place to wander in, to enjoy the foliage and the passing cloud.' His words, written more than half a century ago, remain relevant today. They have been said by gardeners and landscapers before, and since.

Rules to be obeyed—and sometimes broken

Here are just a few:
• Hasten slowly. If you have bought an established property, do nothing for a year. It is then that you will see **what appears in the garden as each**

Opposite: Plant in swathes: *Polygonatum × hybridum*. *Previous page*: *Sedum spectabile* 'Autumn Joy'.

1. A simple, formal parterre at Redding House, Benalla.
2. The Villa Reale, Lucca.
3. Mass planting of the one species adds up to good design: here, the Villa Landriana, near Rome.
4. Paradise in enclosed spaces: Naranjestan garden.

season unfolds and what treasures are held hidden beneath the earth. This is, of course, quite difficult, if you, like many other gardeners, want to rush in with ideas and dreams.

- Whether yours is an established garden just waiting for your personal touch, or a new, pristine piece of land, take a lesson from the designer Kath Carr: **sit outside your property for a while, quietly contemplating its mood and its atmosphere**. You can then start planning from the front gate.

- Next, **go inside the house, and view the garden through the windows**. Ensure that vistas are not being obscured. Is there borrowed landscape that could be included into your garden by the judicious removal of a shrub or tree? What you take out is often more important than what you put in.

- Place star posts in the ground to mark where you imagine your chosen trees might be planted. **Return into the house** to ensure they are in the correct place and that they will, when grown, frame, rather than block, views. You can then move them a little, reconsider, and perhaps move them again, until you are happy that they are 'just right'.

- Try the hose trick! This is particularly useful in a large garden. Mark out garden beds by rolling out a hose or two: this template will give you not only a sense of its finished shape, but its scale and dimensions.

- **Draw a plan**. If you have a small garden, you can measure it up yourself. A larger area will call for a surveyor to draw an accurate and to-scale survey that will show land contours. You can then start committing your design ideas to paper, drawing them to scale. The stiff tracing paper known as butter paper is ideal.

You might even advance to the stage of creating overlays from butter paper, so that you can contemplate 'before' and 'after' visions of your garden, with and without your proposed improvements and additions.

- Hard elements, like paths, steps and planter boxes, should be **drawn to scale**, as should garden beds. Make to-scale cut-outs of your steps and walls, your key trees (at the width the canopy will eventually reach) and your important beds, and move them around on your plan. You can even colour your trees and other key plants. Enjoy the hours of fun!

- And the simple trick of taking lots of photographs of your garden and drawing on them—it is best in Texta—is extremely helpful. This method is made even more accessible in these days of digital photography and home printers. You can draw on your trees—and then think about their placement for a while. You can draw in a sweep of drystone wall—and contemplate its placement. Garden beds, water features and steps can all be drawn on to your pictures.

- **The relationship between void and mass is all-important to the success of the garden.** Japanese designers seek two-thirds passive space and one-third active or planted space for maximum, and the most pleasing, effect.

- Design with large blocks of just a few plants. Draw up a list of the plants you want, delete 75 per cent of them, and multiply each many times over—depending upon the size of your garden. If you find it hard to be disciplined, or difficult to decide what you cannot live without, you might try plants first in pots, to be moved around at whim.

- And don't forget to draw in a space for utilities, such as bins and the washing-line. You can hide them behind hedges, carefully framed-up lattice, or screens of scented climbers.

Garden design has been undergoing something of a revolution in recent years, with the Australian family backyard changing in its use, as working patterns of married couples change. While lawn will always be important for families, as children become older owners are calling for a low-maintenance, minimalist look. Keep hard surfaces consistent with the style and tone of the house, pots and furniture. Strong, clean lines and beautiful natural materials help to create a calm, serene space (*see* Courtyards, page 360; Hardscaping).

COLOUR

Colour

Having coveted, years ago in a country garden, hundreds of pink and pale green, frilled, 'parrot' tulips, blooming in massive drifts under a cloud of bright pink flowering crab-apple, *Malus floribunda*, I decided this clever combination was something every large garden needed. After hours of trawling through catalogues, and a dozen phone calls later, I found the tulip, with its swirls of gentle green splashed across a delicate salmon-pink. At least, that's how it looked in the catalogue, just begging to be planted under my 'grove' of *M. ioensis*, to me the queen of crab-apples. Her apple-green leaves emerge at the end of winter on outstretched arms. The soft leaves are followed by dark pink flower buds, which remain shut for ages, tempting you to daily inspections. Finally, after weeks of teasing, they unfurl to reveal the most restrained and refined of pale pink blossoms.

Well, dozens of the treasured tulip were ordered, and planted—with memories of the cautionary tales of those who, in seventeenth-century Amsterdam, lost their houses over their passion for the tulip, pushed to the far reaches of the mind. There was great excitement as the teale-coloured leaves of the bulbs pushed through the frozen July ground. A garden open-day was even timed to demonstrate this exercise in colour coordination. As the buds of the tulips swelled, however, early suspicion turned to real fear, to be confirmed with horror, as the flowers opened: a bright red to orange, slashed with an acid yellow.

Challenging, adventurous and playful use of colour is exhilarating, however, whether you garden in small or expansive spaces. Experimenting with combinations of texture and form—and of colour—is part of the fun of gardening. You can paint the garden in restrained tones of the one colour, with neighbouring colours from the same section of the colour wheel, or you can shock with contrast and counterpoint.

White

While mixing and combining colours in the garden, and creating planting patterns of different colour schemes to accompany the changing seasons is an engaging challenge, white tones are also important. White provides a clean, calm backdrop into which you might introduce just one key colour. And there is surely nothing more restful than a garden of white-flowering plants set against a background of calm, cool green.

In small gardens, or enclosed spaces, disciplined use of colour is probably wise: white upon white or white upon greens of different shades are calmer, more pleasing and more successful than a paintbox of different hues and tones. And such a scheme surely requires a little less planning and less effort to maintain.

Set fresh greens and crisp whites against a deep green backdrop created by a high hedge of a clipped conifer (*see* Conifers). Create a border that is bursting with the white, scented sweet rocket (*Hesperis matronalis*—a cousin of the stock), the nodding white bells of Solomon's seal, with a dozen different hostas, including the white and green hosta, *H. fortunei* 'Albomarginata'. Edge this scheme with the lime-green of *Alchemilla mollis*. White delphiniums look wonderful towards the back of the picture, along with the bee-attracting

Opposite: The summer colours of 'Gold Bunny'.

Crambe cordifolia with her mass of feathery white panicles in summer, adding height and structure to the design. Cover a black-painted, sturdy tripod in a white-flowering clematis.

You may not have a large enough garden to dedicate an entire 'room' to a white palette, but even a white border will provide a peaceful place into which you can retreat for quiet contemplation. Offset the picture with a lacy, white-painted wirework garden seat placed upon a smooth green lawn.

The possible plant list for a white garden is almost never ending. Whichever plants you choose, try to make sure your selection will provide a steady progression of flower and foliage interest in almost every month.

🌿 Planting

To create a restful white garden, first design a basic structure with a template of hedges in whichever of the many suitable species you love, and which performs well in your climate (*see* Hedges). Create the walls and also a parterre of box as the bones of the room.

Have a scaled-up, simple arbour forged, to create a central focal point. Then, try to discipline yourself to choose between all the marvellous climbing white roses available, with which you will decorate this centrepiece. You could choose the gorgeous *R. brunonnii*, with its elegant, long, apple-green leaves and large trusses of white blossom, or 'Wedding Day', or the luscious 'Albéric Barbier', with its clusters of scented double blooms in clotted cream. The climbing Tea rose 'Devoniensis', blooming with a pink blush in spring, but ageing to cream in autumn, is a delightful alternative.

Underplant this arbour with the so-smart *Astrantia major* and the white bearded iris 'Mesmerizer', bred in 1990 (and rather space-age in appearance, as the beard extends to a highly ruffled flounce held at 45 degrees). Add to the ethereal atmosphere with clouds of white-flowering poppies and give gifts of the seeds to all your neighbours, helping to create a local garden vernacular.

A gardener's Mecca

White gardens have been fashionable since Vita Sackville-West wrote about her elegant 'garden room' of creams, whites, greys and silver at Sissinghurst Castle, Kent, in the UK—the large garden she and her husband, the diplomat and amateur architect Harold Nicolson, created from 1930. Her weekly newspaper column was published for several decades until her death in 1962. Sissinghurst became widely known after it opened to the public in 1938 and today remains influential and a Mecca for many gardeners worldwide.

There would be few gardeners who have not heard or read about Sissinghurst's White Garden. In this small, personal space, several squares of box hedging enclose a profusion of white- and cream-flowering perennials, silver-leaved plants, white roses and magnolias. Its centrepiece is an iron arbour covered in *Rosa mulliganii*, which bursts into clouds of white flowers each July (having replaced earlier plantings of almond trees).

The White Garden continues to be emulated by gardeners throughout the western world, including in Australia and the USA, where it has become a leitmotif for good taste, style and restraint.

You might in-fill a parterre of box (*Buxus* spp.) with the windflower, which blooms with single white flowers at Easter time. Add the white-flowering lupins and the easygoing nicotiana, along with tall- and mid-growing white bearded iris, with its soft, glaucous foliage. If you garden in a climate that won't allow you to enjoy the bearded iris, substitute it with a white-flowering daylily.

Create the borders around the perimeter of the 'room' with permanent plantings of the gloriously scented philadelphus, among them the cultivars 'Beauclerk' and 'Belle Etoile', along with a smaller growing *Deutzia* like 'Nikko,' which you can

1. The white garden at Sissinghurst.
2. *Rosa* 'Wedding Day'.
3. *Narcissus papyraceus*.

plant in the foreground. The white to pale pink flowering *Rhododendron* 'Virginale' will provide a backdrop to perennials such as white lychnis and white species gladioli, which keep visitors enthralled once the first of the roses are over. Fill in any gaps in the borders with a selection of white-flowering bulbs, from the early *Narcissus* 'Paper White' and 'Erlicheer', suitable for humid climates; also add white hyacinths, sheets of white freesias, and the white form of the tiny grape hyacinth. Carpet the ground in a white species geranium and the white-flowering *Lamium* 'White Nancy'.

If you garden in a dry climate, break up the border with plantings of a white-flowering *Cistus*, such as *C. × cyprius*. If in a cool climate, plant the flamboyant Japanese rice-paper plant, *Tetrapanax papyrifer*, with its enormous leaf and bold sprays of cream flowers in summer: it teams adroitly with a swathe of white foxgloves.

You may also want to be contrary from time to time by adding splashes of blue and lilac to this refined planting scheme.

Greys, greens and silvers

These colours work well together and can be employed in the white garden to create the shades and shadows necessary to ensure the garden is not so well mannered that it is bland. Greys also connect different sections of any garden, whatever colour provides its backbone, tying various schemes together perfectly and allowing you to move seamlessly from one area to the next.

Grey-leaved plants can be tricky to grow, however, as many will not tolerate humidity. As with most species, for success look to where your chosen plant grows best when deciding whether it is suitable for your climate.

❧ Planting

In cool climates that don't suffer from humidity, the soft grey-green leaves of the tall-growing *Thalictrum aquilegiifolium* (a clump-forming perennial native to western China) is very useful, as is Russian sage (*Perovskia atriplicifolia*), from the Himalayas, with its lilac summer flowers and felted leaves, reminiscent of lavender.

The curry plant (*Helichrysum italicum*) along with *Teucrium fruticans* (a member of the mint family) can be clipped to form a low, informal hedge. And the lavenders are always useful, if you do not garden in humidity.

The gorgeous wormwoods (*Artemisia* spp.) add delicacy to any border, although you might want to remove the acid-yellow flowers of some species. They come from the dry Mediterranean region and other arid parts of the northern hemisphere. Among the prettiest are *A. ludoviciana* from Mexico and the west of North America; 'Valerie Finnis' and 'Silver Queen' are the two most popular cultivars. 'Powis Castle' is an extremely popular hybrid with feathery, dissected leaves; it needs rigorous cutting back in cool climates, however, to keep it from smothering more fragile treasures. Somewhat similar, and just as hardy, is *A. absinthium* 'Lambrook Silver', which spreads by rhizomes and will root wherever pieces fall. The wormwoods look stunning when threaded through with the metallic grey-blue heads of the thistles, particularly *Eryngium giganteum*, or with the cardoons (*Cynara cardunculus*), which must be the easiest plant to use for making a statement.

Dusty Miller (*Senecio cineraria*), with its attractive grey foliage, is one of 1000 species in a genus native to all corners of the globe. It grows to about 60 cm tall and as wide. It is extremely easy to propagate, which also indicates that it needs taking to with the secateurs to keep it in check; and again, you may want to prune off those acid-yellow flowers which, if allowed to bloom, also create a straggly-looking plant.

The grey-leaved, highly scented *Dianthus* 'Mrs Sinkins' is stunning for her silver-grey foliage alone. She will not bear her scented, pale pink blooms in humid climates but is worth growing, in any case, for her spreading, mat-like foliage.

And, green upon green upon green in all its tones will often carry on through winter, to brighten up those dark days. Think about the euphorbias, and even the somewhat thuggish,

1. The soft grey foliage of *Melianthus major*.
2. The white and silver garden at Benwerren, in the Strathbogie Ranges.
3. The grey border at Wychwood, in northern Tasmania.

A decorator's garden

Across the Pacific Ocean in New Zealand's north island, and just a 20-minute drive from Auckland, is Wood-bridge, a magnificent 5 hectare garden that incorporates rolling lawns, lakes edged with bog garden plants, rose gardens, a beautifully laid out vegetable garden and a virtuoso collection of succulents and dry garden species. This is a garden for the designer, as well as for those who are fascinated with rare and unusual plants. It is also a decorator's garden; Christine Peek, who has developed Woodbridge over the past 12 years with her husband, Tony, has a happy knack of combining colours and tones, textures and shapes in the most effective way.

You enter the garden through an arch (which in summer is resplendent with the large-flowering, deep purple *Clematis* 'Niobe') and walk on to the vegetable garden. Here trellises of broad beans are offset by collectors' plants like the climbing red nasturtium 'Empress of India'. A small door set in a high wall takes you out onto sweeping lawns bound on one side by a high hedge of the silvery toned *Cupressus arizonica* 'Blue Ice', a conifer also recommended for Australian gardens as it is resistant to both drought and borer. On the other side, a croquet lawn is separated

from the garden by a long pergola covered in *Rosa* 'Albéric Barbier', seen growing wild on the roadsides throughout New Zealand and sometimes called the gardenia rose, even though it has the scent of apples.

In front of the long, low homestead is a wide, semi-circular terrace, which provides a home for a collection of waterwise sedums and echeverias in tones of bronze, cerise and pink. Generous steps, centred on the terrace, direct you down to the lake and spring-fed stream, surrounded in November with deep blue *Iris sibirica* 'Caesar's Brother'. Angelica, with its ruffled, glossy leaves, teams with the soft grey of the grass *Miscanthus sinensis* 'Morning Light'. The giant ornamental rhubarb (*Gunnera manicata*) thrives in the shade of tall tree ferns.

Christine is an admirer of the work of English garden designer and author Beth Chatto, who plants in generous blocks of species to create an effective underlying structure to which she adds the stars of the garden world. She also works with big groups of different textures and foliages (flowers are secondary) to create a tapestry effect. She has succeeded admirably.

1. *Kniphofia* 'Winter Cheer'.
2. *Hosta fortunei* 'Aurea'.
3. Timber seat at Lismore Castle.
4. The rich colours of smoke bush
   and sedum.

bright green *E. robbiae,* which looks fantastic planted massed with swathes of senecio; the tones knit together in the most pleasing and restful way. The evergreen euphorbia looks very good with hot pinks, especially in a dedicated section of its own. For spring, plant it with the so-elegant, so-snooty *Rosa* 'Baronne Henriette de Snoy'—her pink blooms held on red stems look terrific with the red 'eye' of the euphorbia. Or back those lime-green bracts with the bright green mopheads of *Heliotropium arborescens*; add something in hot pink like a deep edge of *Dianthus* 'Highland Queen' or 'Napoleon III'. You could opt instead for similar tones that contain lemon: team lime-green with the hot yellow rose 'Gold Bunny', the delicate pink with lemon climbing tea 'Souvenir de Madame Léonie Viennot', or the Australian-bred 'Honeyflow'.

Yellows and golds

In a country of clear blue skies, such as we enjoy for many months of the year in Australia, discreet colours can look insipid. You might want to get a little hotter with a series of plantings in gold and yellow—a difficult colour, however, as it draws the eye immediately towards it, distracting the observer from anything else.

❧ Planting

The thornless honey locust (*Gleditsia triacanthos* 'Sunburst') will spill a broad pool of golden light over any garden, and will light up glowering skies. Illuminate shadows with variegated ivy, and with the lime to yellow *Helichrysum* 'Limeglow', which is also effective clipped into domes or a hedge. Throw in the glorious yellow and red honeysuckle *Lonicera × heckrottii* for even more colour and scent. Include the yellow-flowering mulleins (*Verbascum* spp.), single-flowered dahlias like 'Yellow Hammer' (which have captured the horticultural spotlight in recent years) and the tall coneflower (*Rudbeckia* spp.), and anchor it all by repeat plantings of the cosmos-like *Bidens triplinervia*.

If you garden in a cool climate, tone down a lime to yellow coloured feverfew, set off with

Out of Town

In the rugged foothills of Mount Pilot Forest Park, near the village of Chiltern in north-east Victoria, is an exciting 2 hectare garden and nursery aptly known as Out of Town. Owners Gavin Doherty and Tina Fraser admit to a love affair with colour and a passion for exploring the use of texture and foliage, emotions that are evident the moment you arrive at the brightly painted garden gate. The garden leads the visitor on an inspirational tour through different 'rooms' connected by strong contrasts and successful harmonies.

Gavin and Tina are still discovering all the planting possibilities within their particular environment—hot and dry in summer and winters that drop to minus 5 degrees Celsius. Silver and Mediterranean plants are grown for their hardiness, and the microclimates created by the tougher plants are now used to protect more fragile treasures.

The various sections of the garden are linked by arbours of rich red roses, such as 'Madame Isaac Pereire', 'Cardinal de Richelieu' and 'Reine des Violettes'. The pink, scented 'Constance Spry', the first rose bred by Englishman David Austin, is a favourite throughout this garden.

tripods of the eye-catching golden climbing hop (*Humulus lupulus* 'Aureus') with the black-leaved perennial *Corydalis flexuosa*. Underplant that curious fossil, the maidenhair tree (*Ginkgo biloba*), with its leaves that turn butter-yellow in autumn, with the bright yellow leaves of *Hosta* 'Aurea'. Inject some pizzazz by adding chairs, tables and pots in kingfisher blue to the picture.

For those who live in warmer climates, cordylines are becoming increasingly popular for their structure, their brilliantly marked foliage and the colour they add to a garden. An artist has clearly gone mad with his paintbrush: some are splashed in oranges and yellows, creams, cerise and pink, or reds and browns. Add more heat with a seam of bromeliads, golden aloe, kangaroo paw, kniph-ofias and cannas, all flowering in yellows; cool them down with cream gazanias. Introduce more drama with ribbons of Japanese blood grass, a lurid red kniphofia and a red-flowered canna.

Let your imagination go mad with colour and planting schemes: you will have hours of fun planning combinations using these easygoing show ponies.

Apricots and golds

The more conservative among us, however, might want to substitute hot yellows for gentler shades of apricot.

🌿 Planting

A dense hedge of the apricot-coloured Hybrid Tea rose 'Just Joey' or 'Apricot Nectar' behind a lower hedge of the rose 'Perle d'Or', edged with a toffee-coloured bearded iris like 'Bronzet Star', has always appealed. Add in the generous *Phygelius* 'Salmon Leap' and the apricot *Dahlia* 'Heat Wave'. You might reinforce the glaucous leaves of the iris with another edge of snow-in-summer (*Cerastium tomentosum*), which has delicate grey leaves with a green-grey underside.

Blues and lavenders

Like grey and silver tones, blues help to link the various sections of the garden and can cool down outrageous colour schemes.

🌿 Planting

Use a trellis of wisteria to back a border of the tall-growing sage *Salvia guaranitica* 'Blue Enigma', lavenders, the tall catmint *Nepeta* 'Six Hills Giant' and blue-flowering tulbaghias. Ground covers like the tricky gentians are stunning in cold climates.

The pale blue climber *Petrea volubilis* and clump-forming perennial *Geranium × magnificum* do well in warm temperate to subtropical climates. And always consider the easy-to-please borage,

with its blue flowers so loved by the bees, which are essential for fruit pollination.

Purples, pinks, russets and reds

If you garden with colour in mind, you will not have to wait until autumn to enjoy a kaleidoscope of reds and russets, puces, plums and purples in your garden. With a little thought you can create luscious colourways of burgundies, coppers and rusts to ensure interest all year.

Plants with burgundy and bronze foliage are indispensable: use them as incidental plants all over the garden. You can, of course, team them with plants that flower in all the pinks, from blush to cerise to magenta. They are also invaluable if you want to tone down oranges, reds and yellows. Add them to your whites and sugary or icy pinks to contribute a velvety richness. And they are marvellous picked and added to almost any flower arrangement for the house.

🌿 Planting

Borders of different shades of red, finished off with splashes of lipstick pink, will set you apart from the mainstream. One of the best plants for the cool temperate garden is the smoke bush (*Cotinus* spp.); the crushed red grape coloured leaves of both 'Royal Purple' and 'Purpureus' are textured in a way that reflects light, providing a sumptuous richness. And the foliage of 'Grace' is a coppery brown. In a large garden, multiple plantings of smoke bush, with its faded raspberry, fluffy clouds of blossom, look wonderful with crimson-flowering rhododendron, like 'Earl of Athlone', 'Gibraltar' or 'Fusilier'. For attention getting, add wide threads of the peony 'Sarah Bernhardt': the rhododendron may have finished flowering by the time the peony flowers in early summer, but she will look great with the foliage of the smoke bush.

Use watsonias if your climate will not permit you peonies. Add splashes of an indestructible rugosa rose, such as the pale pink 'Sarah van

Fleet', with its glossy red hips in autumn, and you will never be without branches, berries and blooms to admire and pick. And add a couple of paler pink flowering clematis to further extend the blooming season and excitement. In cool climates weave the cranesbills through clumps of the architectural onion *Allium cristophii* or *A. giganteum*, teamed with that stunning purple flowering poppy, *Papaver* 'Patty's Plum'.

Other magentas include the purple orach *Atriplex hortensis* var. *rubra* (an edible annual that self-seeds) and the dark-leaved form of cow parsley, *Anthriscus sylvestris* 'Ravenswing'—although some say it runs amok in their gardens. Lucky them! There are the sedums, such as 'Autumn Joy', many of which start flowering pink to cerise and fade to a rich russet in late autumn and winter. Do not ignore the black hues of the *Euphorbia dulcis* 'Chameleon' (*see* Succulents) and the smaller growing, black-leaved *Heuchera* 'Plum Pudding'.

Many of the burgundy-flowered roses, such as *Rosa mutabilis* or *R.* 'Reine des Violettes' might be allowed to wander through such a border: they will add bones and structure. Or be outrageous with the candy-coloured daylily, *L.* 'Dragon's Eye'.

Among many new cultivars of cordylines is 'Red Fountain', which forms finely textured clumps some 1.2 m tall and 1 m wide. Plant it in full sun for the best colour; it will also tolerate shade.

In subtropical and tropical climates, the spiderworts (*Tradescantia* spp., also known as *Rhoeo* spp.) make a fast growing and spectacular ground cover, but some are poisonous. The trailing *T. pallida* 'Purple Heart', with its burgundy leaves and pink summer flowers, will quickly cover the ground. Cut spiderworts back ruthlessly when they start to straggle. Many have pink flowers; the upright species have coveted blue flowers and make a perfect companion for hippeastrums.

Beds of rust tones are particularly suited to autumn days: tans, burnt umbers, chocolates and dull reds reflect the mellow mood of the season. You might choose a burgundy-leaved phormium to go with bronze fennel, tone it with a fire-coloured achillea; add texture with a golden carex and depth with an edging of chocolate-leaved *Heuchera*. You could push the boundaries with the orange rose 'Bengali'. For a cool or south-facing border, drop a curtain of *Hydrangea quercifolia*, with its intense wine-coloured autumn leaves.

And imagine backing a rib of daphne with a small-leaved camellia such as the tea-producing species *C. sinensis*. The delicate pale pink flowers of the camellia bloom at the same time as *Daphne odora*, with its delicious scent. Or go mad with tones of cerise and crushed raspberry with *C. japonica* 'Dixie Knight Supreme'. Tone it all down with a choice of edgings from your grey and silver palette.

A taste of paradise in medieval France

In the medieval hilltop town of Cordes sur Ciel, in south-west France, lies Jardin du Paradis, a breathtaking combination of several different small garden areas. Gravel paths and stone steps lead to the picking gardens, divided into three colourways, each separated by a woven willow screen affording enticing glimpses from one area to the next. This garden room, designed as a floral tapestry inspired by a finely woven Persian carpet, employs sequences of perennials and annuals to ensure continual flowering as well as exciting colour, texture and shape.

In the first section, the tall-growing, deep blue to purple *Verbena bonariensis*, the pastel *Nicotiana alata*, and species geraniums, aquilegias and irises wash the garden in blues, greys, creams and whites. Next, the hot garden explodes with yellow or orange kniphofias, yellow and red daylilies, the sprawling, fast growing *Cosmos sulphureus* 'Klondijke' and dill, boasting bright yellow, fluffy flower-heads.

Lilac colours are repeated through the borders: penstemons, statice, sea hollies (*Eryngium giganteum*), cherry pie (*Heliotropium arborescens*) and, towards the front, *Ajuga reptans* 'Bugle Boy'. This is a garden you *must* visit.

SCENT

Scent

'It is a golden maxim to cultivate the garden for the nose, and the eyes will take care of themselves.'—Robert Louis Stevenson, 'The Ideal House', *Essays of Travel* (1905)

One of the many joys of gardening is the scent that each season introduces. Even in winter the garden offers up evocative and exhilarating fragrances, from that of freshly dug soil to the heavy scent of daphne. And have you ever noticed that very particular scent of early spring? There can be few things more exciting than moments when, on that first dawn morning, you notice the fragrance of the warmer months ahead lingering in the soft, milky air.

Fragrant plants are among the simplest of the great pleasures. Daphne's perfume tells you winter is almost over; the fragrance of viburnum might transport you to the garden where you first encountered its heavenly perfume; gardenia carries strong memories of Christmases past. And the smell of freshly cut grass is one of the best of summer. Scent is so evocative: even the whiff of a certain suntan oil can bring back memories of the popular songs of a summer holiday long ago.

I love all scented plants, but here are my favourites.

Bouvardia longiflora

Scented bouvardia is an evergreen shrub that hails from Mexico and is the most widely grown of this genus of 30-odd species from the southern states of the USA to Central America. The glossy leaves are a deep green and the white tubular flowers, appearing from autumn into winter, are wonderfully scented. This species grows to around 1 m high (and as wide) and likes a sheltered position in dappled light, with protection from frost. It enjoys rich, well-drained soil; prune lightly after flowering.

Buddleia

The *Buddleia* genus contains around 100 species and is a group of deciduous, semi-deciduous and evergreen shrubs and small trees (native to Asia, America and South Africa). They attract hordes of fluttering butterflies when their panicles of delicately scented flowers appear in spring and summer. Most are grown as garden shrubs and are generally easygoing and undemanding. They are said to like alkaline soil, but I have found they also flourish in acid soil and cope with heavy frosts. Buddleias make a great loose hedge behind, for instance, a lower hedge of roses. Prune them carefully in early spring or take to them with the hedging shears—they won't mind.

The most frequently grown species is *B. davidii* (butterfly bush), from which hundreds of named varieties have been bred. Originally from central and western China, this flamboyant species is also called summer lilac. Among the many stunning cultivars are the lilac 'Nanho Blue' and the deeper purple 'Black Knight'; there is also the pink-flowering 'Orchid Beauty' and 'White Cloud'.

The fountain buddleia (*B. alternifolia*) looks stunning as a punctuation point in a complicated flowering border and, if grown towards the rear, also provides height. From the north-west of China, it flowers with arching sprays of misty-lilac, heavily scented blooms.

Also good as a fast-growing backdrop to a wide border is the freesia-scented *B. salviifolia* 'Spring Promise', with its felty, grey-green, sage-like leaves.

Opposite: The luscious, scented blooms of *Viburnum × carlcephalum*.

Daphne

Daphne must be my favourite plant. On cold winter days it fills the garden with the most coveted perfume of all. Even one specimen will give you weeks of joy, and its fragrance can be detected from metres away. I like it planted en masse, woven through a border of species glads, salvia and penstemon, and carpeted with violets, which flower at the same time. Or, you can use it as an informal hedge. Allow the low-growing *Clematis integrifolia* to scramble through it; when the flowers of the daphne are over, this brilliant blue clematis will flower against forest-green leaves. In a temperate to cold climate the delicate but intensely blue grape hyacinth (*Muscari* spp.) flowers with the daphne; picked, they look exquisite together in a bowl.

Most daphnes are low growing, reaching only 1.5 m in ideal conditions after several years; many are prostrate and suitable for rock-gardens. The latter also make good ground covers or can disguise an unsightly retaining wall. The colours of the tubular flowers vary from the pink, red and white of *D. odora* to lilac and purple, bluish pink and pure white.

Daphne has a reputation for being a prima donna, pernickety with its demands about performance conditions, and given to tantrums or even to suddenly dying. While it loves a south-east or easterly aspect, I have found it will grow well in even a north-westerly aspect if provided with dappled shade from overhead trees. Daphne will survive in areas of heavy frost, if planted against a protective wall. It copes with a variety of soils, from Sydney sand to rich basalt loam, and the alpine species love a scree; good drainage is its most important demand.

But its intense, distinctive fragrance is so marvellous—just one sprig in a vase can fill a room—that any bad behaviour is worth indulging. It is easy to appreciate that daphne was among the many plants that Australia's early European settlers dearly missed.

Be warned, though: the daphne's milky sap is toxic if ingested. Also, it doesn't need, nor will it

tolerate, much pruning. Just the light prune given as you pick the flowers suits it best but, as with all plants, remove any dead wood or crossing branches to minimise disease. You can propagate daphne by layering: peg down any whippy, low-growing branches and cover with soil. Cut away the rooted branch a year later to pot up.

A genus of around 50 species, the best known—and to me the most superior—is the winter daphne (*D. odora*). This small evergreen shrub is native to Japan and China and was introduced to the western world in 1771.

Another of the loveliest species is the semi-evergreen *D.* × *burkwoodii* (a more open and delicate shrub than *D. odora*), which has masses of pretty, pastel pink flowers in late winter. This can make an informal hedge and is particularly stunning planted against a backdrop of the more dense, deep green *Camellia sasanqua* or *C. japonica*.

The alpine scrambling species such as *D. retusa* and *D. cneorum* flower in late spring; there is a variegated form (*D. cneorum* 'Variegata'), which looks wonderful lighting up a dark area but, like many variegated plants, can be more difficult to grow well.

D. mezereum is covered in sweetly scented purple flowers in late spring. And collectors love *D. genkwa*, introduced from China to a voracious western world by the plant hunter Robert Fortune in 1843; it is a beautiful deciduous shrub that bears lilac flowers along bare branches in spring. This species is difficult to obtain and tricky to grow, demanding summer watering and perfect drainage.

Also a collector's item is *D. pontica*, which will cope with heavier soil. From northern Iran, Turkey and Bulgaria, this is a spreading, evergreen shrub with lightly scented, unusual yellow to lime-green, spidery flowers. The plant hunter Ernest Wilson found *D. tangutica* in China in the early 1900s; it is a dwarf evergreen shrub that bears clusters of purple-tinged, white fragrant flowers in spring.

Gardenia

Did I say that daphne was my favourite scented plant? Well, I am not sure because, when the gardenias start to unfurl their perfect, thick white petals, I start to think of the holiday season and the happiness and friendship that surround the Christmas table.

A genus of around 300 species of small shrubs, gardenias are native to Africa and Asia. Most have highly scented, fleshy white flowers, which appear through summer. Use the different species in different positions and landscape applications. The ground-covering, small-flowered *Gardenia augusta* 'Radicans' is useful for planting at the front of a border. It will mass over, covering any untidy edges or will cascade down a retaining wall. *Gardenia augusta*, native to China and Japan, is probably the most widely grown and has large, glossy, deep green foliage. Its cultivar 'Florida' grows to about 1 m tall and has double flowers from spring to the end of autumn. 'Grandiflora' has larger leaves and glorious white blooms; *G. augusta* 'Magnifica' has the largest flowers of all. The starry gardenia (*Gardenia thunbergia*) from southern Africa can reach almost 4 m in height, and is covered in single white flowers throughout summer.

Gardenias love acid soils but will cope with a range of soils; they will not tolerate frost, however. They are also thirsty, so, if you don't have tank water and do have onerous watering restrictions, you may prefer to buy them in bunches from the florist. They love a warm situation and will even flower well in the westerly sun—given enough water. Lack of water will cause yellow leaves; they also like a good feed, so apply a general garden fertiliser after watering. Yellow leaves with green veins are a sign of iron deficiency, remedied by a feed of iron chelate, while a rim of yellow with an arrow-shaped green centre is indicative of magnesium deficiency, helped by Epsom salts (*see* Fertilisers, page 286).

Syringa

Also way up on my list of flowers that I cannot live without is the lilac, most particularly the common lilac (*Syringa vulgaris*). While gardeners are being forced to look to waterwise plants, and many are depending more upon indigenous species as we address sustainable garden design, some of us would never eschew the lilac, if our garden conditions were sympathetic. You might design a secret area for this genus, perhaps enclosed by a hedge of graceful, arching may (*Spiraea* spp.), for the lilac is resplendent for just a few brief, if brilliant, weeks each year. Apart from those few glory days it is probably better backstage, somewhat like a rose garden out of season.

But the lilac also makes a wonderful walkway, discreetly leading you on to greater things when not in bloom. Or it makes a backdrop for other flamboyant plantings; take care with timing, however, for when those luscious panicles appear, they should take centre stage, without competition from other prima donnas.

Most of the two dozen species of lilac come from the mountainous regions of Asia—from Afghanistan through to China and Japan—although the ancestor of our common lilac (*Syringa vulgaris*) is one of two species from eastern Europe. *Syringa pekinensis* arrived in western gardens from China in the mid-1700s, *S. oblata* in 1856, *S. pubescens* in 1880 and *S. villosa* in 1889. The delicate *S. meyeri* was discovered in a garden near Peking in 1909; *S. × persica* is good for hedging. *S. protolaciniata*, and its offspring, will tolerate much less cold than most species. Many species host delicate blooms and some are probably just for collectors.

It is the 1500-odd cultivars of the common lilac (*S. vulgaris*)—most developed in France in the late 19th and early 20th centuries and often grafted onto its close cousin privet—that fill most gardeners with the greatest admiration.

Among the great lilac breeders is the French Lemoine family, whose gorgeous cultivars, such as the white 'Madame Lemoine', are still popular. The spectacular Rochester varieties, created for the lilac gardens at Highland Park in Rochester, New York, include the famous blue-purple 'President Lincoln'. Other great collections are held in St Petersburg, at the Arnold Arboretum in the USA, and at Kew Gardens in London.

1. Lilac blooms in May in the English village of Chawton.
2. *Syringa* 'Mme Lemoine'.
3. The variegated lilac 'Sensation'.

A little scent with breathtaking beauty

Imagine a long, meandering driveway in a country garden. It is edged with the shrub *Viburnum plicatum* 'Mariesii' as an underplanting to the wedding cake dogwood, *Cornus controversa*. Neither are scented but both share elegantly tiered branches. During spring, the bright green, softly pleated leaves of 'Mariesii' are complemented by flat white lacecap flowers (reminiscent of the lacecap hydrangea). *C. controversa*, a medium to large tree, bursts with broad, flat clusters of cream flowers in early summer. In autumn its black fruits appear as the leaves are turning to purple. You could use the autumn-colouring epimediums as a carpet beneath the 'Mariesii', offset with clumps of the exquisitely scented lily-of-the-valley.

Lilacs flower in panicles of many shades, from the palest mauve to a rich, intense purple, but also in cerise and pink, whites and creams. They all work wonderfully together in a vase; all they require to add sparkle is the fresh, bright green of a few leaves to offset the magnificence of the blooms. While lilac may be a flash in the pan in terms of flowering time, the beauty of the blossom and its fragrance means this old-fashioned favourite is forever popular.

Lilacs are happy in most soils, in sun or light shade, but need around 1000 hours below 10 degrees Celsius to flower well: they struggle in the coastal areas, from Sydney north. Take care, if buying grafted specimens, to remove any suckers that appear from below the graft. You can grow them from cuttings.

Lilacs only really need pruning to remove any dead wood or crossing branches, which increase the risk of disease entering bare or damaged areas. Apart from that, the light prune you do as you pick those gloriously scented bunches will be sufficient.

Lonicera

Often scorned by experienced gardeners as 'weedy', honeysuckle or woodbine is greatly valued by others for its delicious scent. I also love to combine it with other plants: the climbing species with clematis and the shrubby honeysuckles as a no-fuss addition to big borders. You can hedge it, standardise it, add it to tripods or lattice screens, or force it to scramble over banks and retaining walls as a tough and easy-to-please ground cover.

The most widely grown of the shrub-like species is probably *Lonicera fragrantissima*, invaluable as its highly perfumed cream flowers appear through winter. *Lonicera henryi* is a wiry climber from western China that can reach 10 m. It flowers with yellow and maroon blooms, making it a great subject for fun with colour.

The box honeysuckle (*Lonicera nitida*) is not grown for perfume but as a hedge or topiary plant, clipped in the same way as *Buxus* (*see* Hedges).

Grow honeysuckles in rich, well-drained soil, although they will cope well with less than perfect conditions and with frost. Prune to keep to the shape and use required.

Luculia

Luculias are winter-flowering, highly perfumed deciduous or evergreen shrubs that grow to about 4 m. With their deep green, ribbed, glossy foliage and beautiful tumbles of flowers, they are a stunning addition to any garden. A genus of just five species, luculias grow naturally in the high forests of India and China but are happy to grow in the warm temperate parts of Australia; indeed, they hate frost.

L. grandiflora blooms in highly scented, white tubular flowers set in the midst of huge, glossy leaves with fascinating purple markings. It comes from the high forests of Bhutan.

L. gratissima is native to the Himalayas but is happy in the warm coastal areas of Australia. Enrich well-drained soil with compost and enjoy the pink flower heads from autumn through winter.

Philadelphus

This gorgeous shrub, often called mock orange, flowers in spring with elegant, so-refined mostly single white blooms that have one of the richest fragrances found in horticulture. Philadelphus won't flower for you if you garden in a humid climate, as they come from the open, rocky hillsides or woodlands of the Himalayas and east Asia, and Central and North America.

Among the most luscious of the 60 species in the genus is *P. coronarius*, the common mock orange, which is native to southern Europe and western Asia. It has egg-shaped leaves, glamorous peeling bark and scented white flowers. 'Aureus' is a variety with rich yellow leaves, while 'Bowles' Variety' has leaves with a smart white margin. Many of the wonderful cultivars contain this species in their lineage and many were bred by the French Lemoine family in the late nineteenth century and the beginning of the last century. Among the best are 'Belle Etoile', with a purple splotch in the centre of the blossom; 'Beauclerk', an English hybrid with pink-tinged centres and an intense fragrance; and *P. madrensis* 'Manteau d'Hermine', with elegant pink buds that open to a double cream flower.

Employ a rib of this highly scented shrub to weave through a wide border, or use it in several garden beds to tie the entire scheme together. It prefers moist, well-drained soil in sun or light shade. Prune after flowering, of course, by simply removing the oldest canes at the base to retain that lovely weeping habit.

Rosa

Roses, of course, are among the most evocative of scented flowers, but they are so special they deserve an entire chapter (*see* Roses).

Viburnum

The viburnums are a large genus of about 150 species of evergreen, semi-evergreen and deciduous shrubs, from tough and hardy troopers that will perform for any of us, to pernickety treasures for those with the greenest of fingers who garden in the climate such viburnums demand.

Viburnums are native to the North American woodlands, from Korea to Japan and throughout China. Many have blooms that are so richly scented they are the stuff of dreams—or childhood memories.

Many also have wonderful clusters of blue, black, red or yellow berries and in autumn colour to fiery oranges and rich reds that rival any Japanese maple—all extend the aesthetic excitement and picking power.

Among the best are the gloriously scented *V. carlesii*, and *V.* × *carlcephalum*, which that *grande dame* of English garden-writing, Vita Sackville-West, called '… one of the most exciting things I have grown for years past'. She instructed her readers to '… get it at once' if they did not possess one. Both species grow to 4 m in well-drained soil and make perfect specimens for the back of a border or shrubbery. They also make an effective informal hedge, responding well to clipping. And you will want to cut branches of the dense, rounded heads of flowers, which turn from delicate pink in bud to pure white. This will be all the pruning they need. The scent is similar to that of daphne; there is nothing like it on a warm spring evening. The berries are jet black; the ovate leaves are an elegant, velvety, soft apple-green, colouring deeply in autumn.

If you live in a cold climate, *V. farreri,* native to western China, carries its winter flowers all along its slim stems. *V.* × *bodnantense* is gloriously scented and comes in various cultivars for those who cannot get enough of the fragrance. The lovely pink tones of *V.* × *burkwoodii*—from the Yunnan province in southern China—look marvellous with other purple-toned plants. Try it behind a low hedge of the small-growing *Pittosporum* 'Tom Thumb' (*see also* Hedges). *V. macrocephalum* is an evergreen shrub with large white flower heads reminiscent of the mophead hydrangea. It was discovered in China in 1844 by the plant hunter Robert Fortune.

V. odoratissimum is one of the few viburnums to thrive in hot climates, and has highly perfumed white flowers in winter and red berries in late spring.

You can extend excitement and interest right throughout the year by the clever use of the viburnums, for their scent, autumn colour, and winter flowers and berries.

Viburnums are trouble free and tolerate most soils—but, sadly, you must forget the highly scented species if you live in sandy, coastal regions. For the warmer climates, go for the tough, drought tolerant *V. tinus*, which makes an effective dense hedge but has nothing of the glorious scent, fruit or foliage of the cold climate species. Propagation of viburnums is easy, from cuttings taken in spring; some can be multiplied by layering.

SHADE

Shade

Not everyone has a garden that basks in the Australian sun, replete with wisterias, roses and lavenders that like it hot and dry. Many country readers, with gardens featuring mature trees that cast deep shade in summer, or those who garden around city buildings, face the challenge of choosing plants that will thrive with little light (and sometimes little water). Or, if you enjoy a large garden, you might want to create a woodland, full of species that love the low light.

There are lots of plants that like shade and part shade, although not many that will perform in dense, dry shade. The clivia is an evergreen, strappy perennial that will, however (*see* Bulbs). It loves neglect and is perfectly happy to flower reliably under eaves or trees, where not much else will grow. It hates frost, though, so if you live in a cold climate you will have to protect it, or opt for the spider lily (*Lycoris* spp.) instead. Recently I saw a windbreak of dark pines protecting a large

garden. The area beneath them was begging to be lit from beneath by thousands of the golden spider lily (*L. aurea*).

Or you might fancy, in such a situation, a mass planting of the scented yellow and gold ghent azalea, although it would need a backing plant less aggressive than the pine, which robs the ground beneath it of both moisture and nutrients.

❤ Favourite shade plants

AJUGA REPTANS

The bugle is a member of the mint family, so that will tell you something of its habits. This frost-hardy ground cover requires almost no care: given a little shade and a dressing of blood and bone in late winter, it will reward you with a carpet of azure flowers from spring to autumn. It looks great planted with violets, if the invasion of that ground cover doesn't scare you away (*see also* Colour).

CORYDALIS

The shade-loving species of this genus multiply wonderfully in cold-climate gardens—but don't covet this plant if your climate is humid, as it will only break your heart. Native to cool regions of the northern hemisphere, particularly to the mountainous parts of central Asia, most are perennials. With their decorative, dissected leaves and their tolerance of shade they are

Previous page: *Hydrangea macrophylla* 'Blue Wave'. *Above*: A lover of dappled light: *Polygonatum* × *hybridum*.

valuable additions to the woodland or tapestry garden: their tubular flowers, which range from the coveted blue of *Corydalis flexuosa* to the cream to yellow of the promiscuous *C. lutea,* are a bonus. They love humus-rich, damp, but well-drained soil.

CYCLAMEN

The cyclamen is a tuberous perennial that will thrive in part shade or sun and well-drained soil high in organic matter. It bears heart-shaped leaves, often decorated on the upper surface with patterns. It is perfectly content to live with dry conditions in summer (while dormant), but enjoys watering during its growth period. It does not enjoy humidity. Its beautiful small, delicate flowers (from red to pink to white) usually appear in winter to early spring. Some cyclamens are frost tender, while others are extremely frost hardy (*see* Bulbs for greater detail).

DAPHNE

This temperamental star loves a south-facing position in filtered light and will cope with some humidity or plenty of frost (*see* Scent for greater detail).

ERYTHRONIUM

The trout lilies (or dog's tooth violets), particularly *Erythronium californicum,* look fussy, but are, in fact, easy to grow well in part shade in a cool climate. Native to central Asia and North America, these frost-hardy, small perennial lilies are suited to cool climates where, if planted in humus-rich soil, they will happily multiply.

HELLEBORUS

The hellebore is thought of as a cold-climate shade plant, but the orientalis hybrids do well in warmer climates, along with some of the species like *Helleborus × ballardiae,* which generously offers the added bonus of pewter-coloured foliage. The hybrids are easy to grow and give a never-ending variety of different flowers, from purple to wine coloured to white with red dustings (*see* Hellebores for greater detail).

LAMIUM

While most of the lamiums—also known as the aluminium plant (*see* Colour)—prefer full sun, *Lamium galeobdolon* (syn. *Galeobdolon argentatum*) is a groundcover that likes moist shade so much that it can become a nuisance. I like to 'whipper snipper' it into shape and avoid its yellow flowers. Its leaves bear silver markings and it flowers with yellow spikes in summer—perfect for lighting up dark, shaded corners.

POLYGONATUM

Solomon's seal is a genus of 30-odd species, which must be among the most generous of all garden plants. With little or no attention, these forest-floor dwellers push up luscious, bright green shoots each spring. Charming white bells, which are often edged in a fine green line, appear along the arching wands in summer. They love rich, damp soil and protection from sun; if planted in conditions to their liking they will reward you by multiplying to create abundant swathes. Divide the clumps to propagate.

TILLANDSIA USNEOIDES

Spanish moss is an epiphyte seen in old gardens in the deep south of the USA. Part of the bromeliad group, it requires scant attention and seems to survive on little more than air and the occasional raindrop! Allow it to drip in festoons from branches (*see* Bromeliads).

The queen of part shade
HYDRANGEA

The hydrangea is probably the queen of the half-shade lovers and will grow in all but tropical climates. Come December, the florists are full of them: they jostle for space like richly coloured precious stones in a treasure chest. Mopheads in deep cerise snuggle up to those in dusky pink or intense blue. Others, frilly in shell pink, look elegant keeping company with those in creamy white.

With an old-fashioned reputation, the hydrangea is anything but dowdy these days as modern breeding has given us dozens of glamorous and exciting cultivars. The only difficulty is exercising restraint, for their impact is more dramatic if several of the one cultivar are planted en masse, quickly giving a full and voluminous effect.

Belonging to the family Hydrangeaceae, these generous plants were first described in 1784 as *Viburnum macrophylla*, before being reclassified in 1830 as the genus *Hydrangea*.

The different species are most easily distinguished by their flowers. The most common is *H. macrophylla* (the mophead), which is then broken into several subspecies.

The showy lacecaps, also part of the *macrophylla* species, comprise tiny fertile flowers surrounded by clusters of sepals. Among the most popular is the deep blue 'Blue Wave', and 'Beauté Vendômoise', which unfurls a beguiling pale green to pink and deepens to lilac. The new 'Mathilde Gütges' is a rich blue-purple, fabulous as backing to pink-flowering salvias and daylilies, or fore-grounding burgundy-leaved cannas. The serrated edges of the white-flowering 'Nymphe' look wonderful planted as a rib through the garden, edged with, for example, the low-growing white *Agapanthus* 'Snowball'.

The frost-hardy *H. aspera* var. *villosa* makes a big statement with its mauve lacecap flowers, while the deciduous *H. paniculata* (from China and Japan) flowers in cream to pink cone-shaped panicles. As its origins would suggest, it is happiest in dappled shade. The oak-leaf hydrangea (*H. quercifolia*), with its leaves that deepen to wine red in autumn, flowers for weeks with white panicles that turn pale pink with age. The late-blooming *Clematis* 'Gipsy Queen', with its large burgundy flowers, looks marvellous growing through this species, providing a palette of reds, pinks and purples as the hydrangea leaves turn towards autumn.

H. arborescens, also frost hardy, has smart lime-green mopheads, with the cultivar 'Annabelle' a favourite because of its gorgeous leaves and large white flowers: for year-round excitement, edge this with white freesias or (if your climate allows) snowdrops. Try the climbing *H. petiolaris*—which will clothe a tree trunk or decorate a brick wall—as a ground cover as well.

Hydrangeas look wonderful edging paths that wend through woodlands of viburnums, dogwoods, maples and birches; underplant them with massed *Ajuga*. A mass of *H.* 'Blue Wave' looks wonderful planted behind a mass of the oyster plant (*Acanthus mollis*), all reflected in a large dam or a small courtyard pool. Many of the hellebores provide the perfect accompaniment, particularly the easy-to-grow *Helleborus* × *hybridus*, with its crushed-silk blooms that hang on for months past its winter peak.

Jewels—or jelly beans—they may be when fresh, but some hydrangeas fade just as evocatively. Leave the mopheads on the shrub to die gracefully, fading into the muted colours of ancient silk underwear. Picked, hydrangeas last for days if plunged immediately into a deep vase of water.

While they have a reputation for being thirsty, for most of the year the hydrangea demands little attention, apart from winter pruning. Tip all your spare and saved water on them when flowering and they will reward you for weeks. Horticultural wisdom says to plant them on the east or south side of the house; mine, however, thrive on the western side, protected only a little by the dappled shade cast by a lattice screen.

> **Tip:** If your soil is acid, the macrophyllas will flower blue; if alkaline, blooms will be pink. However, the vast range of exciting new cultivars means that there is a range of colours for every garden. You can also apply a hydrangea blueing agent, which contains aluminium sulphate, when the flowers start to form.

PROPAGATING HYDRANGEAS

The hydrangea must be the easiest plant to propagate. Take sections with three sets of nodes from your late-winter prunings. Scrape a little of the outer layer of tissue from the base of each

1. *Hydrangea macrophylla* 'Schneeball'.
2. The hydrangea border at Bruce Rosenberg's garden, Yarrawa, in the New South Wales Southern Highlands.
3. The climbing *Hydrangea petiolaris*.
4. *Hydrangea macrophylla* 'Beauté Vendômoise'.
5. A pink form of the mophead *Hydrangea macrophylla*.
6. *Hydrangea paniculata*.

cutting and plunge the cutting into a pot of propagating mix. Water, cover in plastic and leave in a warm but protected spot. In less than a year you will have flourishing pots to bring inside at Christmas or to give as gifts.

PRUNING HYDRANGEAS

Pruning, in late winter, is pretty simple. First, remove any crossing, untidy or spindly limbs at the base of the plant. Then cut out all stems that flowered this year and prune those that didn't to two fat buds. Don't fret if you don't get time to do this, however: I also prune as I pick the flowers in summer, and in some winters, if feeling energetic, I cut the bushes right back to the base.

Woodland gardens

One of my earliest memories of garden dreaming was drooling over pictures in a glossy book of an English garden in Sussex called High Beeches. It was not just the giant stands of beech that had me dreaming of grand designs, but the extraordinary colour created by thousands of simple bluebells that were flowering beneath them. I couldn't wait to create just such an enchanting, shadowy, cool, secret place in my own garden.

For those gardening with shade and moisture, the North American native *Tellima grandiflora* 'Rubra', with its purple foliage in winter, and *Symphytum grandiflorum,* a dainty relative of the handsome but thuggish herb comfrey, also make effective companions in a woodland setting. Add *Trachystemon orientalis*, with its spikes of blue star flowers, which emerge through bare earth in late August, and light up dark corners with the beautifully variegated *Symphytum* 'Goldsmith'.

You don't need vast acres to create an enchanted woodland: even in a small garden you can encourage easygoing species to mass out. *Ajuga reptans* looks fantastic foregrounding the burgundy-leaved heucheras, which are frost hardy and humidity happy, and will grow in sun or

A shady garden

A cool woodland is central to Beverley McConnell's large garden, Ayrlies, at Whitford, not far from Auckland in New Zealand's north island. Hectares of lakes, wetlands and bog gardens, featuring superb plantings and linked by waterfalls, are balanced by a woodland of foxgloves— the classic woodland plant, as it grows naturally in great swathes on the edges of woods, loving the dappled shade. You reach the woodland through a wildflower meadow that affords views of the surrounding countryside. From there, waterfalls feed into a large lake, where a massive pink-flowering *Rosa cathayensis* (which will flower even in dense shade) clambers over a tea house.

semi-shade. There are cultivars like *H. micrantha* var. *diversifolia* 'Palace Purple' or 'Plum Pudding' to plant, with an edge of black mondo grass (*Ophiopogon planiscapus* 'Nigrescens'). Add a backing of the purple-flowering hellebores, like the cultivar 'Burgundy', and for toned perfection a rib of the shade-loving blue hostas, such as *H. tokudama* or *H.* 'Halcyon'.

The windflower (*Anemone* × *hybrida*), among the easiest flowers to grow in a cool climate, naturalises wonderfully in the dappled light at the edge of a woodland. *Anemone nemorosa*, with its pale lilac flower, and the graceful *Vancouveria* also spread out beautifully in woodland conditions.

Paths that wind through a woodland area might be of gravel, tamped earth or sawdust, and edged with massed gentians, a temperamental plant with wonderful cobalt-blue flowers, happy at altitude and in a rich, free-draining volcanic soil. Or plant any of the easygoing bulbs to ensure scented excitement each year.

1. Foxgloves flourish on the edges of the woodland garden at Ayrlies, in New Zealand's North Island.
2. A shady glen in a mountain garden.
3. Variegated box lights of a corner at Hillview, in the New South Wales Southern Highlands.
4. In the North American state of Maine, The McLaughlin Gardens rely on a soothing tapestry of greens.

The Built Garden

PART SIX

GARDEN BUILDINGS

Garden Buildings

In October 1928 the English novelist Virginia Woolf (1882–1941) presented a paper to a group of young women at Newnham College, Cambridge. 'A woman must have money and a room of her own,' she told her audience—original and brave words, surely, at a time when women had only just started receiving a full degree from the university. Woolf was musing upon the circumstances needed to write fiction, but with the publication the following year of her novella, *A Room of One's Own* (a satire on male society), her words became something of a feminist motif.

The garden shed

But men, as well as women, need a calm, private, personal place to decompress and restore mind and body. Painters, sculptors, writers—and the rest of us—all need a space of our own for thinking and reading. And gardeners need a shed for designing and dreaming, tinkering and making a mess—or just pottering about. Such a shed does not fall into the same category as the utilitarian buildings that house pool equipment, firewood or the spill-over of detritus from the house or garage. This is a space where you can be close to nature, surrounded by, but protected from, the elements.

Garden sheds come in many forms and in a huge range of styles and materials, from simple to deluxe; they can be bought in kit form or can be custom made. Create them from galvanised iron, pine, or recycled timbers which bring their own fascinating provenance to their setting. Your shed might be simple or elaborate; your budget and your imagination—and the style of your garden—are your only constraints.

Sheds need to relate to the garden and house and reflect your taste and mood; they will be low key in an informal garden, while a formal garden calls for balance, restraint and discretion. Think of the Renaissance architect Andreas Palladio and his refined, simple lines.

A plain shed could be set unobtrusively at one corner of a 'garden room', under a spreading tree or in a vegetable garden, for instance. Conversely, you could create a focal point with a white-painted structure to attract the eye. And for durability your shed needs to be set on footings or a concrete slab; the path that directs you there should be wide and made of material compatible with other hard landscaping in the garden.

Whatever you choose to call your 'shed' (greenhouse or glasshouse; cabana or log cabin; summer house, pavilion or gazebo; garden or potting shed), such rooms are cubbies for grown-ups, who also need, I believe, the magical escape into play enjoyed by children.

The glasshouse

The glasshouse (also known, of course, as the conservatory or hothouse), is among the most useful and decorative of garden sheds.

The repeal of the glass tax in Britain in 1845 (which caused the price of glass to fall dramatically) and the invention of sheet glass a couple of years later (coupled with the invention of heating from the 1820s) meant that hothouses, and thus horticulture, became more readily available in the nineteenth century to many more than an elite few.

Opposite: Wouldn't we all love a rustic shed like this? *Previous page*: *Paeonia lactiflora* 'White Wings'.

> **Tip:** Care needs to be taken in Australia when designing and orientating a conservatory as, contrary to the UK, we do not want to trap the heat. We want the light and, often, protection from wind. Glass in any roof needs to be installed in a way that it can be controlled to influence heat, light and cleaning. You might consider a compromise by installing an opaque roof, with glass skylights that open. Some skylights come with blinds between the double glazing, which are electrically operated.

The exotic plants of the Far East and the Americas, eagerly collected by British plant hunters, were no longer confined to the greenhouses of the aristocracy, filling, by the end of the century, 200 large nurseries in Britain. With standard structures offered by several manufacturers, glasshouse production of fruit, vegetables and other tender plants expanded rapidly.

In no garden have glasshouses been used more enthusiastically and to greater effect than at Chatsworth, the Derbyshire estate of the Dukes of Devonshire, and arguably the most influential of all the great British gardens since the royal gardeners, Wise and London, laid out formal gardens for the first Duke in the 1690s.

The Great Conservatory, built by gardener, architect and garden designer Sir Joseph Paxton for the sixth Duke of Devonshire between 1836 and 1841, housed rare plants collected from throughout the Empire. Kings and queens, scientists, politicians and the general public marvelled at it. Charles Darwin said of it, 'Art beats nature altogether here.'

Another of the Paxton monuments, The Conservative Wall, some 200 m in length and enclosed with glass, protects (among other treasures that descend from exotic plants collected more than a hundred years ago) two extraordinary specimens of the camellia *C. reticulata* 'Captain Rawes'. The base of each is almost 1 m in diameter.

The use of glass to house botanical collections continued, with work on the still-famous Palm House at Kew starting in 1844; in London's Hyde Park, Paxton's Crystal Palace was purpose built in 1851 to house the London Exhibition. With the opening of Sydney's Garden Palace in 1879, the fashion for showing off agricultural, artistic and industrial prowess was launched in the colonies.

Above: The tea house at Nindooinbah, at Beaudesert, west of Brisbane, reflects the Edwardian fascination with things oriental.
Opposite: The seed house at Mount Vernon.

Iconic garden buildings

There are certain garden buildings around the world that are recognised by most garden tourists as iconic. These include the seed houses in the kitchen garden at George Washington's Mount Vernon, sited just south of Washington DC, on the banks of the Potomac River. There are also the much-photographed twin pavilions at Hidcote Manor in England's Cotswolds. At Nooroo, at Mt Wilson in New South Wales the pristine, white-painted, filigreed summer house, off-set at the top of a winding flight of stone steps, was afforded what is surely the ultimate honour—that of gracing a postage stamp. In autumn, the summer house is lit by a mass of white nerines, and in spring it is framed by scented mollis azaleas and the early-season greens on the outstretched ballerina-arms of Japanese maples.

The advice of a nineteenth-century garden writer

Scottish author John Claudius Loudon (1783–1843), the most prolific garden writer of the nineteenth century, greatly influenced early settlers in the Australian colonies, where his books were widely available. Two tomes, *The Encyclopedia of Cottage, Farm, and Villa Architecture and Furniture* (1833) and *The Suburban Gardener and Villa Companion* (1838) provide pages of advice on garden structures, from malt-houses and poultry-houses, grottoes and moss-houses to model cottages, and his detailed patterns were much copied in England, where he lived from the age of twenty. Loudon believed that expensive garden buildings (such as classical temples, porticoes and colonnades) should rarely be used in small places and were better adapted for the grounds of 'hereditary residences'.

A place of taste, elegance and beauty

Eryldene, on Sydney's upper North Shore, was designed in 1913 by William Hardy Wilson (1881–1955) for his friend, Professor EG Waterhouse (1881–1977), a linguist and Sydney University professor, who became internationally renowned for his work in camellia propagation and hybridisation.

Hardy Wilson was an architect, artist and author who promoted what he called 'The Rule of Taste'. He advocated simplicity, writing that he designed 'nothing grand, nothing ornate; just whitewash, red China roses and common olive trees'. Variously described as an Australian version of the Georgian Revival and Colonial Revival, Eryldene was typical of Hardy Wilson's work—an unpretentious low building with colonnaded verandahs, offset by pavilions. The interest in Oriental culture of both the architect and his client is reflected throughout the garden and house.

Much photographed by the legendary Harold Cazneaux (1878–1953), the garden at Eryldene was planned as a series of spaces which emphasise form and balance and, most importantly, accommodate Waterhouse's precious camellias. Hardy Wilson designed the architectural structures throughout the garden—the fountain, dovecote, garden study, Oriental Tea House, garden furniture and planting tubs—between 1913 and 1936, ensuring that each area flowed harmoniously to the next.

Commissioned to restore Eryldene in 1981, architect Clive Lucas believes that it is a magical place—the house and wonderful Waterhouse garden with Chinese pavilion and pigeon house remain essentially unaltered since Hardy Wilson's time. 'It is a place of taste, elegance and beauty.'

1. The summer house at Nooroo, a garden created by Peter Valder and his family and today owned by Anthony and Lorraine Barrett.
2. The setting sun illuminates this charming shed at Black Springs Bakery, Beechworth.

Gardening in Small Spaces

Gardening in confined spaces is a challenge many of us face as we turn our backs on large gardens in city suburbs or country towns. City life today often means that gardeners reside in apartments or terrace houses, where the maximisation of small spaces is crucial and gardens are made on balconies, rooftops and in courtyards. Smaller, simplified garden spaces are part of a changing demographic and lifestyle—the increase in the number of women entering the workforce, a surge in holiday travel and a different use of outdoor space are all factors that have led to the rise of the small garden.

Downsizing need not mean a life without plants, however; discipline—a difficult concept for the truly passionate gardener—is probably the key.

Courtyards and garden rooms

Busy lives and changing life circumstances don't mean that we wish to forgo good design and with careful planning and a little knowledge, small spaces can provide as much excitement as a wider expanse. Even a large garden can benefit from the creation of a series of smaller, more secluded, protected spaces or 'garden rooms'.

Many good gardeners consider the term 'garden rooms' to be overused. Even if true, it is a useful term and—as is most often the case with a cliché—has become one for a good reason. Most gardens, whatever their size, benefit from division into spaces or garden rooms. Larger areas are made more manageable, from both a design and maintenance point of view. You might think about keeping one room at a time in the condition you want—pristine perfect or in 'gentle chaos'. And some areas, like a rose garden or area devoted to the quick thrill of the lilac season, can be happily shut down when they are not at their best. After all, everyone needs an occasional rest.

Small gardens appear larger by providing a sense that there are areas to explore beyond those immediately apparent. Excitement, along with a sense of enclosure, mystery and surprise, is introduced and different moods created as you move from one garden room to another. You might create a special entry area, different places for sitting (in sun or shade), a children's play area or spaces for dining.

The division of a garden space into rooms will also contribute to the structure of a garden, essential in the middle of winter, when its strengths and weaknesses are revealed for all to see.

How you create or divide space in your small garden or courtyard will dictate not only its use but also its mood. Courtyards that are enclosed on two or more sides by city buildings can be cleverly designed to form contemplative spaces during daylight hours: turn them into atmospheric retreats with subtle lighting as night falls (*see* Lighting, page 364). And often the line between indoors and outdoors is deliberately blurred.

Internal courtyards

Glass walls not only allow more light into small indoor garden rooms but can slide open completely onto a side passage to create internal courtyard gardens, again cleverly making use of every inch of available space. Again, create additional

Previous page: A 'living pot' created from box.

Courtyard of marble, cast glass and steel

English designer Philip Nash won gold at the Royal Horticultural Society's 2004 Chelsea Flower Show for his elegant, restrained courtyard of marble, glass and steel. A glass walkway covering a sheet of still water led to an elevated, 'floating' steel-edged terrace. Benches on the perimeter were of cast glass. The use of mature plants enhanced the minimalist, contemporary design.

Palm paradise on a rooftop

In a Brisbane roof garden, more than a dozen of the elegant Alexandra palm (*Archontophoenix alexandrae*) grow contentedly and, after almost three decades in place, have reached more than 15 m. These palms, which can be seen for kilometres and are something of a city landmark, were lifted (almost fully grown) to the roof of this twenty-storey building by helicopter.

depth in a shallow garden space with the judicious placement of mirrors. Such moveable glass walls, feeding onto a rear garden, allow the house to wrap around a space, and contribute to a seamless indoor-outdoor flow of the house. (And think about high windows to draw the eye up to views of tree canopies, creating a further sense of space and height.)

Balconies

Creating a pleasing garden in the small space of a balcony is a big challenge. This is where gardening in pots comes into its own: even in a space of 4 x 3 m, you can grow vegetables and fruit. The question of aspect is crucial: check that you receive enough light—few plants will thrive on less than four to five hours of light each day.

Roof gardens

What do you do when you live in a high-rise apartment in the city but still want to enjoy the scents of a garden and the sound of birdsong? If the only space available to you is on the roof, that is where you create your oasis (I am told roof gardens are mandatory in some 30 per cent of buildings in Japan).

The challenges facing those who garden above the rest of the world are many: questions of drain-

age, wind and access must be addressed before design begins. Plants that are able to withstand the onslaught of the elements, such as fierce winds and relentless heat, must be selected. Perfect drainage and the prevention of leakage are also imperative, as is, in most cases, permission from your body corporate.

Aspect

Understanding the aspect of a courtyard or balcony is extremely important. West-facing spaces (which will become hot in the afternoon) need different treatment from east-facing spaces, which only enjoy the sun for a short time each morning.

The study of the needs of each plant on your must-have list is critical in a small space, where a microclimate is often created by its boundaries. And as each plant needs to work double time, several criteria must be considered when creating a plant palette.

Scale

Scale is an important consideration in a small space: think large in small spaces for maximum effect. One beautiful tree, planted off-centre, will look smarter than a clutch of shrubs. (But take pity on your drains; think about the root system and steer clear of heavy drinkers.) As walls around courtyards, and between properties, are often high, up-scale planting is often appropriate.

Lines in courtyards are often severe and simplified, which often means architectural plants make the most pleasing choice (*see* page 366). A restricted palette of mass-planted species is, as always, the key to good looks.

Hard surfaces

Crucial to the look and amenity of your courtyard or roof garden is your choice of hard surfaces. Try to use only one material and style—for fences, walls, paths, pots, steps or seats. Simple materials, employing neutral tones and clean lines, of the best quality you can afford, will be the most successful.

Because pavers will dominate the space, be careful in your selection. There is a vast choice available, from slate, sandstone or concrete to almost anything reconstituted (*see* Hardscaping). Simple is best in smaller spaces, while in a larger space you may want to soften the look with plantings between pavers of native violet, matting thyme or the shade-loving pratia. In one Adelaide courtyard, bluestone paving has been laid in a random pattern and teamed with the blue-flowering ground cover *Vinca minor*—a living contrast to soften the hardscaping.

Loose stones or gravel may look chic, but quickly make for high maintenance as they scatter across hard surfaces and are walked inside, scratching polished floors. For easier care, set washed river stones in cement.

Courtyards are one square you should 'think outside'—or above. And that means commandeering the vertical space. Think of your boundaries as a further surface to plant. Again, it is worth investing in good quality boundaries. Go for capped brick walls, the most solid palings you can afford, or well-framed lattice. If you must retain an unsightly fence, paint it, cover it with inexpensive chicken wire and let a quick-growing creeper romp away (*see* Vertical Surfaces for a discussion of living fences). Of course, space can be broken up with plants rather than walls, screens or fences (*see* Hedging, page 366).

Drainage

Drainage is all-important: water must not sit. Run-off should be collected in channels and filtered into a drainage pit to be removed by the main drainage of the building.

Structures

Except, perhaps, in a very small space, a pergola will add not only height, but also *gravitas* to a courtyard by emphasising scale and directing the eye upwards. Add a grapevine for summer protection and atmosphere—think bucolic luncheons under a shady canopy—or in winter to welcome the sun. You might choose an ornamental grape or a white-skinned variety of fruiting grape (such as sultana) instead of a red-skinned grape, to prevent the courtyard tiles becoming stained. Use large-scale, well-framed, painted lattice to hide rubbish bins, the clothes-line or the compost bin (*see* Supports and Structures).

Furniture and planter boxes

Raised planter boxes, along one or more sides of your courtyard or roof garden, are an economic use of space. Scale them up, so that plantings can be generous. And build them in double brick: you could cover them with a tile in the colour of a nearby water feature, or bag and paint them to tone with the house.

Planter boxes must be waterproof, particularly if you are gardening on the roof of an apartment building. One rooftop gardener lines planter boxes with three different materials: a silicon jelly, polyurethane or rubber lining. The bricks in the retaining walls in his garden are 'shot through' with rods travelling both horizontally and vertically (to the base). Any cavity is filled with cement and bitumen. This way, the bricks cannot move sideways or collapse forward.

Designer John Sullivan advises treating planter boxes as you would a pool. He asks the builder or architect to design them as a water feature or pond, so that they are properly sealed.

Opposite top: In Peter Stubbs' Adelaide courtyard, a mirror reflects plantings to provide a sense of space.
Opposite bottom: Stefan Ackerie's rooftop garden overlooks the Brisbane River.

However, drainage for planter boxes needs to be considered carefully: place 'ag' pipes, surrounded with blue metal or coarse river sand, at their base. Excess water needs to drain—via a pipe protected with geo-tech fabric to prevent fine soil escaping—to a safely sited pit.

Built-in benches and tables are also space-saving. If a conventional free-standing table will occupy too much space, think about installing a bench the length of the boundary or retaining wall and attaching a table to the flooring. Free-standing chairs on the other side of the table can be stacked away when not in use, opening up the area.

Water

Consider the cooling effect of the sound of moving water, even in a small space. A simple and inexpensive fountain can be created with bricks, bagged and painted with a colour to blend with the house.

A basic wall fountain can have a catchment tank or tray at its base, with stones placed in different arrangements to create different sounds. A beautiful pot filled with water will also add calm in restricted spaces (*see also* Water Features).

Lighting

Whatever style of courtyard suits your situation, good lighting is essential for night-time atmosphere: you want to create the subtle effect of a clear moonlit night. Up-light trees, or hang lights in branches to create a dappled effect on the pavement. Use capped lights to attach to walls and fences to create soft down-lighting. Less is more, so choose the very best quality fittings available.

Or, if you are determined to be outrageous, use coloured lights to create moods: red lights add pizzazz; blue lights look ethereal and mysterious (*see also* Lighting).

Design tricks

Illusion is useful in small spaces. Clever effects can trick the eye and mind into seeing a space that is much larger than it actually is. To create this sense of greater space, you might consider painting a lattice—a *trompe-l'œil*—on one wall. Mirrors reflect plantings and extend vistas. Use a smart framed-up mirror, or tuck an unframed mirror, flush with a wall or boundary, among creepers or vines—but test it out first with an inexpensive mirror to ensure that you like what you see reflected.

Plant palette

When space is limited, hard-to-control monsters won't be welcome, so try some small-growing varieties. Here are the plants that I find work best for maximum impact in courtyards, balconies or rooftop gardens.

GROUND COVERS AND EDGING PLANTS

Effective and easy-care ground covers include *Ajuga reptans*, with its short spires of azure-blue flowers, and the tough but deceptively delicate looking *Liriope muscari* (also with small, blue, hyacinth-like flowers), which looks smart with black mondo grass (*Ophiopogon planiscapus* 'Nigrescens') or the soft grey of *Festuca glauca*. Try also *L. m.* 'Variegata' to highlight gloomy corners.

Native violets (*Viola hederacea*) and matting thyme (*Thymus serpyllum*) are among the most easygoing ground covers or fillers between pavers. If the site is shaded, *Pratia perpusilla* is soft and attractive, while *Pratia angulata* tolerates sun. Mini mondo is also good for the difficult shady spot.

Clivia will also thrive in dense, dry shade, while miniature agapanthus are useful for massing in small spaces or as edging plants. The tiny echeveria, an attractive grey to silver succulent, will mass out effectively in a dry, sunny spot. The ground covering gardenia (*Gardenia augusta* 'Radicans') works double time with scent and good looks but needs plenty of water in summer.

An excellent ground cover for small (or large) spaces is the tough, pink-tipped, variegated jasmine (*Trachelospermum jasminoides* 'Variegatum'), which also looks impressive tumbling from planter boxes.

PERENNIALS AND SHRUBS
FOR PLANTER BOXES AND POTS

Many species love being grown in planter boxes and pots, from clivias and fuchsias to magnolias, gordonias, Japanese maples and, of course, citrus.

Team *Iris* 'Black Knight' with the purple-black leaves of the sweetly scented cherry pie (*Heliotropium arborescens*) and black mondo grass. Provide definition and structure with voluptuous plantings of sacred bamboo (*Nandina domestica*).

Plant gardenias in the sun, but not in a west-facing position. Daphne makes a perfect courtyard plant for those in cool climates; they love an easterly spot. The oyster plant (*Acanthus mollis*), with its large leaves and spires of purple and white flowers, loves dry shade, as does the Kaffir lily (*Clivea* spp.). The dwarf *Brugmansia*, growing to about a metre, and providing flowers from November to April, is another that is perfectly happy in a pot. Take care, however, as all parts of this plant are poisonous.

Think also standards in pots: wisteria, roses and lillypilly (*Syzigium paniculatum*), which is more sun tolerant than *Ficus* spp., are all suitable.

Your house might be painted in a green-grey limewash to tone perfectly with a pair of tall charcoal-grey pots, each holding an architectural *Agave attenuata*. Or be brave with a pair of dragon's-blood trees (*Dracaena draco*) to help add vertical accent to the scene: they will grow to some 9 m.

Dark and shady corners can be lit by the grey *Melianthus major*, which is also prized for its bird-attracting tubular flowers.

And don't forget vegetables. Tomatoes (summer favourites) are easily grown in small spaces; just ensure they get full sun and lots of food. You don't need planter boxes or pots—you can grow them in simple polystyrene boxes or even garbage bags; discard the lot when they are past their best. Or, you can make effective *faux* stone troughs.

Yates has released an excellent range of seeds for those gardening in pots. There is Balcony Instant Colour, a pack that includes chrysanthemum, alyssum and dwarf marigold. In the series there is also Yates Balcony Instant Salad—great for creating salad bowls as Christmas presents. Explore Yates Balcony Instant Flavour and Yates Balcony Instant Stirfry, a pack containing spring onion, celery and capsicum. Also try the Yates seed strips for those who dream of trouble-free gardening in confined circumstances.

PLANTS FOR SCENT

Scent is particularly important in a small space, where every plant has to work hard to earn its keep. The heavily perfumed *Mandevilla boliviensis*, the hardier *M. laxa* and the compact *Trachelospermum asiaticum* are just a few of many climbers that will provide scent and a cooling green cover. The Californian jasmine, *Gelsemium sempervirens*, will cover balcony railings with yellow flowers in autumn. You might also want to try the wonderfully scented evergreen shrub *Cestrum nocturnum*, scrupulously clipped to keep it neat (*see also* Scent).

HERBS

If you are not seeking a maintenance-free courtyard or rooftop, nor looking to entertain a crowd or provide uninterrupted space for children's ride-on toys, you might consider a herb garden in the midst of your courtyard. Place a bird-bath or sundial in the centre for height and surround it with tall-growing herbs, like English lavender and tarragon. Clumps of rosemary are a must, along with varieties of parsley and basil; edge with strawberries or allow thyme to spill over the pavers. Perimeter planting should be soft rather than severe. Try the wonderfully scented lemon verbena (which also makes a delicious tea) and soft-coloured grevilleas to entice the birds.

PLANTS FOR TOPIARY

Again, many evergreen plants love being clipped into globes, domes, cones, pyramids and obelisks; they contribute to the successful and supremely restful theme of green upon green upon green, which you might lift a little with splashes of white. Standards of the bay laurel (*Laurus nobilis*) will also provide leaves for cooking. Try also clipped spheres of Japanese box and globes of the small-leaved *Pittosporum tenuifolium* 'Green Pillar'. And clipped and 'clouded' shrubs, which emulate larger trees, will add dimension to the small garden.

HEDGING

Hedges are, of course, essential in the creation of garden rooms, along with walls and screens. And walls covered in a climber like *Parthenocisus tricuspidata* will break the space into several useful areas that will fit together like a meccano set, and will hide the clothes-line and vegetable garden, and create a spot for the chooks.

A beautiful screen from the street or boundary hedge can be created with a well-clipped coral bark maple (*Acer palmatum* 'Sango-kaku'). With its brilliant red stems, it makes a stunning hedge against a black-painted boundary fence. It is also perfect as a small tree for a restricted space.

The Japanese privet (*Ligustrum japonicum*)—kept well clipped so that it doesn't flower to create seed that can be spread by wind or birds—is also effective in small spaces. And low hedges of the quick-growing *Ligustrum vulgare buxifolium* 'Tuscany' look smart backed with a second hedge of gardenias or port wine magnolia. For a third layer of planting in a narrow space, cover walls or fences with boston ivy, *Parthenocissus tricuspidata*. A hedge of *Ficus microcarpa* var. *hillii* will also provide wind protection. Prune it hard to ensure it behaves.

Try the Japanese box, *Buxus microphylla* var. *japonica*), which is faster growing, hardier and more waterwise than common box, *Buxus sempervirens*.

It tolerates full sun or semi-shade and doesn't have the unpleasant smell of the common box (*see also* Hedges; Vertical Surfaces).

ARCHITECTURAL PLANTS

The bright orange flowers of the bird of paradise (*Strelitzia reginae*) are striking against an ochre-painted wall.

Massed plantings of bromeliads, aeoniums and agaves and cycads are popular as focal points or as an easy-care, but effective, understorey to a 'stilt hedge' of, for instance, golden robinia. While cycads are pretty tough, they like protection from the worst of the westerly sun and need some water in summer.

FEATURE TREES FOR COURTYARDS

Top of my must-have list for good-looking trees suitable for small spaces is the evergreen *Magnolia grandiflora* 'Little Gem', which will provide you with months of big, cream, lusciously scented flowers without muscling in on the house. This cultivar of the bull bay magnolia is surely the plant of the decade—the one future garden historians will single out as exemplifying the early years of this century. It is hardly without a flower and grows to about

> **Tip:** There are several golden rules for gardening in small spaces:
> - Go vertical (*see* Vertical Surfaces).
> - When choosing pots, less will always be more (*see* Pots).
> - Fertilise rooftop gardens monthly with composted chicken manure. Seasol has a new seaweed fertiliser in a spray, which (they note) is ideal for patios, courtyards, balconies and potted plants (spray it on the foliage for instant uptake of nutrients).
> - It's a mistake to think that small spaces call for small features. Scale up plants, garden ornaments and furniture to endow substance and body.
> - Take care with plants like agaves and strelitzias if you have small children: beware of damage to the eyes.

Opposite: A Jardin des Paradis water feature.

Paradise in contained spaces

A 20 minute drive from Albi, in the Tarn region of south-west France, and some 70 km north of Toulouse, stands the fortified town of Cordes-sur-Ciel. It perches atop a rocky hill, little changed since its establishment in 1222. This part of the country seems to have escaped the worst of the tourist-born scourges of appalling traffic, sky-high prices and disappointing coffee that afflict some of the more well-known areas—at least in summer. It's a farming region, rich in gourmet traditions, replete with villages built of mellow local stone and, once you know where to look, some fascinating gardens. One, in particular, is well worth a visit for its series of contained spaces, each with a distinct mood.

The Jardin des Paradis was laid out in 1998 on a steep hillside in the old section of Cordes by two plantsmen, Eric Ossat and Arnaud Maurières. Like other Paradise gardens, with their origins in ancient Persia, the Jardin des Paradis comprises a series of enclosures, some large and some small, and each designed for a different purpose; it covers some 3500 square metres over three terraces. It is a garden of surprise, excitement and inspiration. A cloister filled with blue-flowering plants arranged around a large square bed of thyme, and from which a water sculpture erupts, leads you into the garden. The walls are clothed in a deep blue clematis, and paths are of broken slate, adding colour and sound to the space.

On the middle level, a cool enclave of lush bananas, protected by a tall box hedge, provides another surprise. Although they will withstand temperatures to minus 15 degrees Celsius, the bananas are protected from frosts during winter by hessian shrouds. Paulownias, annually coppiced into a living pergola, provide summer shade.

A garden of themed rooms

Sissinghurst, in the English county of Kent, is arguably the world's most visited garden. It was a run-down property when bought by the garden writer Vita Sackville-West (1892–1962) and her husband, Harold Nicolson (an amateur architect and diplomat) in 1930. Together they created a garden based around the division of a large space into smaller, manageable areas of themed rooms, walks and wild areas that, for many, epitomises English gardening. The linear severity, perspectives and structure of Sissinghurst were Nicolson's work (and are most evident from the roof of the tower), while the flamboyant planting schemes highlighting colour, form and texture demonstrated his wife's artistic skill and energy.

The garden opened to the public in 1938 and became widely known and influential through Sackville-West's garden columns, which first appeared in the *Evening Standard* in 1924.

Part of the appeal of Sissinghurst is that it holds something for everyone, and there is plenty for the everyday gardener to learn. The enclosed herb garden, with its chamomile-cushioned seat carved of local stone, provides lessons for those who garden in city spaces. Low-growing thymes of different species, flowering in a glittering array of tiny white, pink and cerise stars, edge brick and stone paths, and compete with grey santolina, golden oregano, marjoram, sorrel, tarragon and basil for summer. Borage, with its blue flowers attracting the bees essential for fruit pollination, rises above a selection of the never-fail salvia.

Clipped yew hedges lead to the nuttery, an area that typifies Sackville-West's exuberant enthusiasm, a romantic and somewhat unruly grove of suckering hazelnuts stuffed full of blue-flowering ground covers, such as gentians and hostas. It is a mysterious and romantic area, which speaks volumes about its creator (an at times impractical but ever passionate plantswoman). This leads to a more restrained walk of limes (*Tilia platyphyllos* 'Rubra') which are pleached onto horizontal wires and cut and tied twice a year—and on to the formal rooms.

In the formal spaces, walls are covered in a mix of roses and clematis and form the background for deep beds, where shrubs like ceanothus, berberis and smoke bush are colour-teamed with liliums, peonies, lupins and hollyhocks among a vast array of spring- and summer-flowering perennials. There are purple borders of lavenders, lilacs, magentas and burgundies; the hot borders are filled with cannas, daylilies, wallflowers, dahlias and kniphofias. There are also romantic rose gardens, and walks and walls edged in superbly trained wisterias.

While the garden you see today is, to a large extent, the work of Sybylle Kreutzberger and Pam Schwerdt (head gardeners since 1959), Vita Sackville-West continues to influence gardeners around the world, long after her death in 1962.

---

4 m. As it is evergreen, however, think about whether you want winter light in your house.

Other magnolias suitable for small spaces include *M. stellata* and *M.* × *soulangeana*. *Michelia* 'Emerald Green' is a small tree related to the magnolia, with the same wonderfully scented flowers. *Gordonia axillaris* with its crepe-paper, camellia-like white blooms, makes a wonderful shade tree for small gardens in temperate zones.

The frangipani is a good tree for a courtyard in a subtropical to tropical climate, and when bare, in winter, provides a coat hanger for an evergreen climber that is not too strident.

In cool climates, any of the medium-sized crab-apples are a perfect choice: not only do they provide shade for summer luncheons but they allow you to appreciate the changing seasons.

The ornamental cherry, such as *Prunus serrulata* 'Mt Fuji', is wonderful spreading its elegant arms in a courtyard. The judas tree (*Cercis siliquastrum*), also with pink blossom, and any of the dwarf crepe myrtle, *Lagerstroemia indica* 'Indian Summer' series, are suitable, too.

If your space is not too small, trees like the maidenhair tree (*Ginkgo biloba*), with leaves that turn a rich butter-yellow in autumn, also work double time: choose a male tree, as the female bears fruit that has an unpleasant smell.

There are some excellent indigenous small trees available for confined spaces (with several new grafted varieties bred to grow to just a few metres), flowering in showy reds, pinks and apricots (*see* Native Plants).

Hardscaping

Hardscaping or, more correctly, hard landscaping (as opposed to 'soft-scaping' through planting) provides much of the structure that is essential to good garden design (*see also* Design). These are the elements that remain during winter, when many trees and shrubs—and even some hedges—are bare. The hard surfaces also help set the mood and tone of your garden and contribute to its distinct style. It's the steps, walls and paving that will set the great garden apart from the less pleasing; they are the bones that will remain, long after creators of the garden have departed.

Because it is the hard surfaces that will dictate much of the success of a garden, and consume a substantial part of any budget, it is worth taking the time to get it right: proportions, scale and materials. Less is most definitely more when it comes to choosing materials for hard surfaces: use the very best materials you can to ensure that the essential elements of your garden are appropriate and pleasing from the beginning.

This may be the time to share some advice I read recently: 'Think about each job three times, measure it up twice, but do it only once, properly.' There is no better advice when planning paving, paths, steps and other expensive and crucial aspects of your garden's infrastructure.

A word about materials

When building the hard surfaces of your garden, it is always more successful to employ only one material and style, whether the decision concerns fences, walls, paths, pots, steps or seats. This is particularly relevant in a small garden.

Stone

Stone is often the best and most beautiful material from which to make hard surfaces; if you are lucky enough to have local stone and it suits the style of your house, use it. Although it can be expensive, it will provide the unique vernacular for your garden. The landscape designer Ellis Stones (1895–1975) knew this when he wrote in his *Australian Garden Design* (1971), 'The reason ... old English villages were so lovely was that man had to manage with the materials available and although the result was achieved from necessity, it demonstrates that planning around existing contours and where possible, taking advantage of local materials, always gives the best result.' His mentor, Edna Walling, would have agreed. Ellis Stones left a legacy of numerous beautiful gardens, created around dignified stone work, many of which endure half a century later (*see also* Drystone walls, page 382).

Paving

The selection of paving materials is vast, but remember: less is more. Use local stone if possible, saw or split. Bricks (try to match those used in your house) can be laid in different patterns. Create chequerboard effects with precast pavers. Leave spaces between precast pavers for plantings of matting thyme, native violets or mondo grass for a softer look. This is not maintenance free, however, and, at least initially, will take weeding and watering to achieve the look you want.

Previous page: Flexible edging keeps gravel paths in their place.

As an alternative, insert other finishes such as brick edging for a formal look. Or set smooth stones in concrete between pavers for easy care: use different sizes and shapes of stones and pebbles to achieve texture and a more natural effect. As always, observe how nature creates: you never find stones the same size.

Alternatively, choose pavers of different sizes and mix rectangular with square for a less formal design.

POLISHED CONCRETE

Among the variety of finishes for paving is polished concrete. You can create fabulous effects with patterns and borders of stone in small or large areas of concrete by using a template of polystyrene to make shapes within the setting concrete. Once the concrete is hard, the polystyrene is melted with diesel and the stones are set into the remaining void.

To set stones in concrete, mix a mortar base of 3:1 sand and cement (if desired, add in a chosen colour). A grout additive makes the mortar more flexible, preventing cracking. Trowel the mortar into the spaces left by the dissolved polystyrene template. As it starts to set—not too wet, not too dry—tap in pebbles. With a wooden float, tap in stones to finish flush and, as you go, sponge off the residue.

PREPARING THE SITE

Laying any expanse of paving is quite complex and this book does not intend to go into any detail. If you are not familiar with the process, consult the appropriate specialist for this extremely important component of your garden.

Some of the considerations that will need to be addressed include levelling the area, ensuring that drainage is adequate and installing underground piping or conduit to allow for lighting or irrigation.

Paths

It is likely that your garden (whether large or small) will employ a range of paths, from simple to sophisticated. Paths are practical, allowing you to maintain the various areas of the garden, or to move from one area to another; they protect areas or surfaces that may be more fragile, or that you want to keep clear of mud and other garden detritus. They also allow enjoyment, providing a platform from which you can appreciate your work. A well-planned path—a mix of common sense, utility and aesthetics—can even make a trip to the clothes-line an adventure.

It's always wise not to rush into the process of creating a garden—and often budgets dictate careful thought before decisions are made. It's equally important to hold back when it comes to siting paths.

Garden paths should always lead somewhere. They should have a purpose, most obviously taking the garden visitor from one point to another, inviting them to explore. Paths need not proceed directly, however. They are more exciting if they meander, leading you on a journey of intrigue and surprise. Paths should wend their way through the garden so that you cannot always see your ultimate destination. And create an indirect approach to a front door: it takes longer but, by creating a sense of expectation, is much more interesting.

Paths should be wide enough to allow two people to walk comfortably arm in arm: 120 to 150 cm. Subsidiary paths (or those in a small garden) can be narrower—about 90 cm—so that they don't dominate the scene.

Stepping-stones placed to entice you through a cottage garden have an intimate feel, suggesting that this is a place to be shared only with close friends. And stones placed further apart will cause you to pause and appreciate your surroundings, while stones or pavers close together will increase the pace of your journey.

In a large garden you might sweep visitors around the perimeter of the property before bringing them to the house. In this way, the garden is revealed slowly. I like to conjure up the image of the designer Kath Carr, who would jump in a country client's 'ute' to 'swoop around' the property to achieve a natural, curving drive. Similarly, I have had great fun marking out paths in clients' country gardens with the help of the ride-on mower.

Goat tracks

Landscape gardener Tim Hays, who designs tropical gardens in northern New South Wales, calls them desire lines. They're the goat tracks in a garden that people—particularly children—will make, no matter what else is provided, to access a certain point.

Hays finds that the placement of paths becomes obvious as a job evolves. He often begins a commission without a complete vision of where every single plant, rock or path will eventually be placed. He may place one rock first, then another, followed by the main planting and the strong focal points. He sees it as 'a painterly way'.

1. In Zaragoza, in Spain, bricks laid in different ways create a stunning courtyard.
2. A path of local gravel winds through this garden on Victoria's Mornington Peninsula.
3. Use plantings to soften courtyard pavers.

Materials for paths

Create natural-looking 'organic' paths by using gravel, eucalypt litter or local woodchip or, for something very different, crushed apricot kernels from a local factory. If you live near the seaside, a path of crushed shells will place the garden in its coastal context.

Expense will always be a consideration in path construction: a 'path within a path' can be a way of using the very best materials without ruining the budget. Feature the more expensive material in the central section of the path; along the sides use broken pieces of the same material (which are cheaper), or another material that complements that material.

You can create a brick path in a variety of patterns: there is basket weave, herringbone (square or diagonal) or stretcher bond, to name a few. A path of bricks laid in a herringbone pattern looks particularly effective when edged with rectangles of weathered stone, or cleverly aged concrete. Or, use a header course of bricks to decorate and contain a gravel path.

Garden boardwalk

The Saltings, a garden in New Zealand's north island, overlooks the clear blue expanse of Kawau Bay. A boardwalk along one side of the house directs you above and through mass plantings of the local renga renga lily (*Arthropodium cirratum* 'Matapouri Bay'), strongly reminding you that this is a coastal garden.

Laying a path

Laying a path need not be an exercise in advanced engineering. After you've marked out the path by mowing it (or by string and pegs), dig out the soil to a depth of 20 to 30 cm. Ideally, add a layer of gravel and top that with course sand. Pack that down and use a spirit level to ensure the surface is level. Place in your paving material and tamp down firmly. If laying a path on concrete, you will need to insert boards, along your string line and held in place with pegs, to allow you to run a plank across: you kneel on this as you lay your material onto the setting cement.

Path edging

A low, clipped hedge can skirt a path, but if allowed to grow too high it might divide the garden into seemingly inaccessible spaces. And clipped perfection needs to be just that: perfect, if it is to continue to look effective. You can also edge the path with lower, natural-looking plantings—matting thyme, snow-in-summer (*Cerastium tomentosum*) and the delightfully scented dianthus, which will creep out across gravel in a relaxed manner. Or, you could decorate your path edge with herbs and vegetables. Alternatively, edge it with box spheres, placed at varying distances apart, along each side of the path.

If, however, you want a path to blend unobtrusively with the garden, fill the spaces between slabs with sand and the seed of matting plants such as pratias and thymes—charming if you don't want everything manicured. If flower borders are to line the path, lay the paving stones or bricks higher than the beds, so that soil doesn't spill onto the path. If lawn is to edge the path, mowing will be easier if the path is slightly lower.

Steps

The use of steps in gardens dates back to the Renaissance architect Donato Bramante (1444–1514), who used them to connect different levels in a grand landscape designed next to the Vatican in Rome for Pope Julius II.

Steps should always be wide enough for two people to walk arm in arm. As well, like all hard surfaces, they should be of the best materials you can afford. Local stone will always be a favourite of mine, but cured or aged sleepers can make fine steps, with treads of grass or pine

Designer brief: Tim Hays

Landscape designer Tim Hays enjoys creating gardens around houses built from simple, basic materials such as weatherboards that have been left to grey and fibro left unpainted. 'Truth to materials', is how he puts it. This way the house sits happily within the landscape.

Hays admits that creating pictures with plants is among the most difficult of artistic pursuits. Trained in painting at the National Art School and the Julian Ashton School of Art in Sydney, he joins other acclaimed artists in applying his training to garden design: Brazilian landscaper and painter Roberto Burle Marx (1909–1994); Russell Page (1906–1985), who studied painting in London and Paris and through his book *The Education of a Gardener* has influenced generations of garden-makers; and American artist and landscaper Martha Schwartz. Hays once considered gardening a trade, rather than an art. But after accepting a traineeship with Sydney's Royal Botanic Gardens, he soon realised that he was creating three-dimensional living sculptures.

Almost a decade ago, he retreated to the hills behind the far north coast of New South Wales, where he creates exciting gardens of vibrantly coloured flowers and up-scale foliage plants that provide immediate structure and impact.

Hays often employs massive boulders as terrific natural-looking steps, succeeding in that most difficult design trick of all—making the garden look as if it has just happened, with nature alone involved. He is an advocate of letting the site dictate design. In a steeply sloping garden belonging to Sydney-based clients overlooking the sea, he has created a series of tropical courtyards within a house, built as several pavilions in several stages. In the rear courtyard, very large rocks are used as stepping-stones to lead up to the verandahs. It was a difficult site due to the steep terrain and a base of pure white sand—it was even impossible to drive a bobcat up the slope. Tonnes of topsoil were brought in to enrich the site and to make it stable enough to bring in the rocks.

A great deal of thought went into the choice of rocks—their role was structural (to retain the soil) but also aesthetic (to be pieces of sculpture). Watching the client's children walking on builders' planks up to their bedroom was the turning point for this section of the garden: Hays recognised this as the first area to place a rock.

Dwarf mondo grass creeps between the stepping stones, along with a variegated *Acorus* and *Gardenia augusta* 'Radicans'. There is a tall backdrop of *Dracaena marginata* teamed with banks of multi-coloured cordylines, the blue ginger (*Dichorisandra thyrsiflora*) and plantings of miniature canna.

Tip: The overall tone of a garden will be more harmonious if steps and paths are built from the same materials.

bark. Well-aged bricks, when carefully laid on a prepared surface, also look good, particularly when softened on the edge with plant material. Think of ground-covering conifers, lavenders and herbs, which release their scent when brushed against or trodden upon; succulents like *Sempervivum* spp. are undemanding and take no watering. *Erigeron karvinskianus*, or baby's tears, looks marvellous when left to self-seed at the base of each riser.

Consider a pair of special trees at the top or base of a set of steps: a pair of almond trees might frame a more distant view. If you live in a cold climate, you could make a statement with the sculptural weeping Japanese maple (*Acer palmatum* 'Dissectum Atropurpureum') planted on either side at the base of the steps, also enjoying the leaves as they change with the seasons.

Steps closer to the house would usually be more formal and become more natural further into the

In league with La Notre

A few years ago one of my readers, Bert Tukian of Mystery Bay in New South Wales, sent calculations for the construction of garden steps that don't force you to break your stride. The formula is two times the riser plus the tread, all to equal 650 mm. So if you use his preferred riser of no higher than 130 mm, the tread would be 390 mm.

'If you use the proper formula,' he wrote 'you'll be in the same league with he who designed the Spanish Steps in Rome and La Notre, who was knighted for his work at Versailles all those hundreds of years ago.'

garden. 'A feeling of distance is created in a narrow garden by the proper placing of stones,' wrote landscape designer Ellis Stones.

You should be able to walk up steps without breaking your stride. Ensure that treads incorporate a slight fall so that water does not collect, that plantings have not encroached onto the treads making them slippery, and that stones have not lifted.

Garden edging

If ground covers spilling in a relaxed fashion from a garden bed onto a path or lawn are not your style or you are not prepared to regularly maintain a deep, spaded edge to a garden bed, there are various options for keeping the surfaces separate or preventing material from one spilling onto the other. Here are a few:

- A metal strip laid against the soil profile of a spaded edge facilitates mowing and keeps the edges neat; it is most often seen in large public gardens, however.
- A wide mowing edge of stone looks beautiful. If this is between the garden bed and grass, it should be flush with the grass to facilitate mowing.
- Flexible ply (avoid using Western Australia's much-depleted jarrah) can be bought from major nurseries and curves easily. Small slashes in wooden edgings will make curving easier. If you have invasive grass, use 5 cm thick edging; this needs wetting to gently curve it. Repeat over the next few days, increasing the curve gradually to the desired shape. Alternatively, good-looking, dark plastic flexible edging can be bought from hardware stores: it can serve to prevent grass runners entering garden beds and can be disguised by spreading plants.
- Edging tiles with plain or decorative details are often made of terracotta and are suitable for a cottage garden look or in a garden around a Victorian or Federation house.
- Wire edgings were also popular in Victorian-style gardens and can still be purchased by the roll. I have not found them practical, however, as they always trip me up!

Opposite: The Fletcher Steele–designed steps in the village of Camden on the east coast of the USA.

Garden seating

Many gardens aren't large enough to boast a generous low wall of the kind that Edna Walling often advocated for the gardens she designed (*see also* Design; Vertical Surfaces). Nor do most gardeners have time to sit still in their own creations, as Walling promoted, but it's certainly pleasant, when visiting the gardens of others, to find a well-placed seat from which to contemplate the beauty around you.

All gardens, large or small, need a seat, at least to convey the idea that it is a place of rest and contemplation. And a well-placed seat, apart from being beautiful in itself, anchors the entire design.

The seat also conveys information—about the garden, its owners, their aspirations and what gardening means to them. There are grand and important seats, made decades ago from stone or galvanised iron; there are scaled-up wooden seats that, if made with aged woods that have enjoyed a former life, are vested with palimpsests of someone else's memories. There are quirky seats that reflect the owners' joy in the exploration of garden-making: I once saw a seat in New Zealand made from bullock cart wheels teamed with recycled timbers from a local wharf.

As with most things, in garden design less is more: it is more effective to buy fewer of the very best you can buy than to go for lots of cheaper options. Whatever your choice, some restraint is in order—but restraint is perhaps the factor most often absent from the lexicon of the passionate gardener. In a large garden, seating that is uniform ties the entire scheme together, rather like key planting that is repeated throughout. In one of the most successful country gardens I know, all the seats are of heavy, aged railway sleepers reclining on two squat pieces of wood. The look is simple and the outcome effective in this extremely smart, sophisticated garden.

If you buy seats manufactured in plantation-grown hardwood, choose one style, whether you choose a design based around vertical slats, cross-hatching or diamond-webbing. If you must have a few different styles, because you just can't resist something beautiful, try to be disciplined about colour. If the material is wood, either leave it unpainted or paint it a colour that will pick up on your pool, the garden foliage or the predominant flower. And colour is one way of adding your own signature to off-the-rack garden furniture.

If you like the rustic look, you can make seats from prunings of still-green willow, hazel or pear; get even more individual by weaving bark, leaves or glass beads into your design.

> **Tip:** Protect seats made of willow or fruitwood with a dressing of a mix of linseed oil, turps and floor wax.

In a small garden or courtyard, it is likely there will be pavers or flagstones on which to place the seat. In a larger garden, consider placing the seat within, but at the edge of, the flower border. A seat resting on gravel instead of grass and backed with a border burgeoning with sweet peas, roses, lavenders and edgings of herbs is a seat placed in heaven.

In a meadow garden or on a wide lawn, a seat needs to be 'earthed' by being placed under or near a tree. (You would treat a piece of sculpture in the same way; a large pot, for example, will look more centred, more connected, if sited near a tree.)

The dictionary definition of a bower is 'a shady retreat with sides and roof covered in climbing plants'. This description conjures up images of mysterious places in cool English gardens, often a subject for the Romantic poets. Such retreats are even more appropriate in the sometimes ruthless Australian climate. Think of a cleverly designed seat of red gum (*Eucalyptus camaldulensis*) shaded by a dome of galvanised mesh shaped over poles of treated pine supporting a dense canopy of evergreen climbers (choose from the selection in the Climbers chapter).

1. An elegant, woven wire seat looks wonderful on a perfect green lawn, backed with a tapestry of green and white hostas.
2. A rustic seat is perfect in this garden on Kangaroo Island.
3. At Asticou Gardens, on the east coast of the USA, a simple seat of local granite.

Seats can be effectively incorporated into retaining walls: a ground cover, such as the grey-leaved, blue-flowered *Convolvulus sabatius*, tumbling down the walls will soften the entire scene.

As in other aspects of your garden, any seat or arbour needs to suit the overall design; materials need to take their cue from what is used in the garden: rock walling calls for a seat from rock or stone.

Seats can be tucked into garden corners, doubling as pieces of sculpture, like the stone seat at the Asticou Azalea Garden in Northeast Harbor, Maine (USA), which is created from the vernacular stone of the area. Leftover pieces of the material used for hard landscaping—such as off-cuts of sandstone—provide a uniform look throughout the garden and prevent a confused, busy appearance.

Woven wire seats, popular in Victorian times, are works of art in themselves. While sturdier than they look, they are more suited to an enclosed, intimate garden space. They look best hosted by a swathe of green lawn, set before a deep border of flowering perennials. If choosing wrought iron, always buy the best you can manage. If you can't afford the coveted, antique Colebrookdale, go for top-quality galvanised cast iron. Flimsy aluminium imitations will rarely satisfy—somewhat like breakfasting on an all-egg-white omelette.

In city courtyard gardens where space is at a premium, built-in timber seats with hinged tops serve a double purpose. They can be boxed in to provide storage for cushions and outdoor games (*see also* Gardening in Small Spaces).

And a seat can provide a focal point. It can be placed at the end of an avenue of trees, which, after all, should lead somewhere—perhaps to a point of rest from where you can contemplate your horticultural success.

VERTICAL SURFACES

Vertical Surfaces

Walls and fences—any upright surface, in fact—play a crucial role in dividing and defining space, apart from their obvious role in outlining boundaries and providing privacy.

The range of fences, front or side boundary, you might erect is as diverse as your imagination. They can be paling, paling and stone, wire, brick or a hedge, depending upon your budget and the style of your house and garden. Your choice will also be dictated by practical as well as aesthetic concerns: paling fences, for instance, while less expensive than brick walls, will require ongoing maintenance. A barbed-wire fence looks appropriate in a country setting, but a more formal fence, in keeping with the era of the building, suits an urban house.

But for those of us who have small gardens, upright surfaces also give us another indispensable gardening dimension—vertical space. They provide us with the use of free space: the air. They can provide a backdrop—perhaps in a rich green—to more flamboyant colour schemes, allowing us to further indulge our imagination, hopes and dreams for our garden.

Hedges and living screens (*see also* Hedges; Climbers) add yet another dimension to the design choices, although they also add to the list of garden chores.

Let's discuss a few possibilities.

The fence

Think about it. The fence is not an innocent bystander in the meanings a garden carries. Fences convey information about the aspirations, taste and circumstances of the owner.

Drive around the suburbs of any Australian town or city and you can date a garden even before you open the gate. And not only can the front fence identify the age of the property it graces, but it can also describe a culture.

The style of the front fence has changed over the decades in keeping with architectural fashion. The earliest paintings and photographs of town and country gardens in Australian colonies depict a wooden picket fence as the favoured means of enclosure. The level of detail of the fence was an indicator of the position and affluence of the occupants within. (And, along with the style of the fence, the front garden—neat or otherwise—carried messages about the homemaker beyond.)

Around the turn of the nineteenth century, with the building of Federation or Queen Anne Revival houses, complementary decorative fretwork was seen in fencing. Woven wire fences also became popular, allowing passers-by glimpses of the front garden.

High walls to ensure greater privacy became common in the late twentieth century, as smaller spaces meant that outdoor courtyards became extensions of living spaces. In a city garden side fences are sometimes kept low to afford views into neighbours' gardens, creating a sense of space and 'borrowing' their landscape.

But the front fence, which clearly marks out the owner's territory is, in some circles, considered somewhat impolite. Consider Michael Pollan's *Second Nature,* his charming and thought-provoking account of the creation of a garden around his Connecticut farm house in north-eastern USA. Pollan recounts the defining elements of his created landscape, grounded in the experiences of his childhood and the quest for the great American dream where, he writes, ' lawn steps right up to the street in a gesture of openness and welcome'.

Opposite: With age, a wall becomes even more beautiful.

In Pollan's memory, a front fence meant that the family who lived behind it was 'anti-social, perhaps even had something to hide'. In some Australian garden suburbs—where the population doesn't seem to fear being overlooked, and dogs are more polite—the front fence is also frowned upon as exclusionist.

The living fence

If it is a living screen you are erecting, you can build a top-end structure, of solid timber trellising in a diagonal or straight square pattern—or a combination of both—nicely encased in a scaled-up frame. It must be well made, a solid feature in itself, and must not fight with the architectural detail of the house. Paint it a colour that picks up, for instance, nearby swimming pool tiles, or outdoor soft furnishings, and then allow the climbing plants to romp away. Combinations of roses work wonderfully as screens, and in tricky climates where humidity is the enemy of good rose growing, this is by far the least heartbreaking way to enjoy them; they can reach for the sun and avoid the diseases caused by damp heat at ground level. Try the so-elegant, pale pink Bourbon 'Kathleen Harrop' with her aunt, the cerise 'Zéphirine Drouhin'. Both have the additional advantage of being thornless (see also Roses).

Country gardens

In country gardens, fences of galvanised iron, mesh or barbed wire might surround the home paddock. Here, the fence often serves as a support for climbers. At Ruston Roses, in South Australia's Riverland, the fragrant, repeat-flowering, pale pink *R.* 'Madame Abel Chatenay' (bred in 1897 and one of the earliest Hybrid Teas) waltzes with the cerise-coloured *R.* 'Peter Frankenfeld'. In some outback Queensland gardens, a simple wire fence is covered in *R. laevigata*, which grows so densely that she forms an impenetrable hedge for stock control (see also Hedges; Roses).

In a well-known Canberra garden, a parterre of *Buxus*, containing four weeping cherries (*Prunus* 'Mount Fuji') underplanted with periwinkle, is enclosed by a fence supporting ivy, which is trained in a fascinating method dating to Roman times. This wonderfully effective pruning technique involves attaching wires to the fence in a diamond pattern and planting the ivy at the base. Just one strand of each ivy plant is allowed to grow and is twisted around the wire. When the ivy reaches the desired height, it is allowed to spread to become a hedge along the top of the fence (see Climbers for decorating plain walls or fences; see also Hedges).

Rabbit-proof your garden with a fence of wire mesh. Bury the lower section of mesh several centimetres into the ground and help secure it in place by positioning rocks around its base.

Walls
Stone walls

Australian garden designer Edna Walling (1895–1973) loved low walls, advising that a wall should be just the right height for sitting. 'For casual seating they are most useful—one always likes to perch in unexpected places about the garden, rarely in the spots where seats have been carefully provided. Here, too, we are glad to rest the tea tray,' she wrote in *Cottage and Garden in Australia*, published in 1947.

Quaint words today, perhaps (and it's not often that the gardener has time to sit with a cup of tea to contemplate his or her own creation), but no designer has bettered Walling's understanding of scale and space, of mass and void. Her big, strong, sweeping stone walls with their wonderful languid curves—a Walling signature—were the bones of her distinctive gardens, ensuring that they have endured to this day.

Walling understood perfectly that it was the integrity of simple, natural materials that adds greatly to a design. The rugged walls throughout her gardens were built without the use of mortar and with local stone, often by her trusted colleague, Eric Hammond, and his team.

1. Thyme makes itself at home in this granite wall.
2. The vernacular fence at Mission House, Stockbridge, Massachusetts, USA.
3. The ha-ha wall is said to have been invented for Levens Hall, in England's Lake District.
4. Ha-ha wall under construction at Old Wesleydale, northern Tasmania.
5. A beautiful wall at Johnniefields on the Southern Tablelands of New South Wales.

The prince of walls

The prince of walls is perhaps the ha-ha (the boundary you don't see), first built at Levens Hall at the southern end of England's Lake District to facilitate an eighteenth-century Arcadian ideal. Created by William Kent—the first of that triumvirate of great English landscapers—the ha-ha is a ditch built along a perimeter of a garden, retained with a wall on its inner side below ground level, and is invisible from the house. An extremely useful invention to exclude stock from a country garden, the ha-ha affords a view across the landscape uninterrupted by a wire or paling fence, while the stock appear to be grazing in bucolic peace within the garden picture.

Scott Wilson has built a 100 m ha-ha at his Old Wesleydale at Chudleigh in northern Tasmania, and points out that the ha-ha is essentially the same as a free-standing stone wall, with the advantage of only requiring one face. His ha-ha is almost a metre thick with a batter of 110 cm in 1.25 m; that is, lying back from the vertical. It is also built in a sweeping concave, which also adds strength like a dam wall.

Edna Walling understood that the beauty of the ha-ha was that there was nothing to stop the eye from travelling across the land-scape into the distance. According to some of her clients, Walling sometimes insisted on its construction, impervious to the cost.

Gordon Ford was a colleague of Walling who shared her vision for a natural style of garden. In *The Natural Australian Garden*, published in 1999, he, too, applauded the use of local rocks to add dignity to both the landscape and the constructed garden.

And Paul Sorensen, who designed gardens in New South Wales almost until his death in 1983, had his own idiosyncratic way of constructing his elegant 'bookleaf' walls of local stone. With a flat rock on the top and on the bottom restraining smaller upright stones, his walls still stand in many gardens in the Blue Mountains, testament to his skill.

Drystone walls

'Two stones over one; one stone over two.' That's the golden rule by which those constructing drystone walls work. Of great value for their dignified beauty and quiet strength, such walls also relate an important social history, often indicating the heritage of their maker. And they are useful: they are the result of stones being cleared from the land, they provide shelter from wind and fire and keep stock in place.

Drystone walling was practised in the UK from the mid-1700s, when the Enclosures Act changed the way common land was used and resulted in the building of over 120,000 km of walls in England alone. The art was brought to the colonies by settlers from England, Ireland, Scotland and Wales—although in Victoria some stone walls were built by Italian migrants. Just as in the UK, each region in South Australia, Victoria and Tasmania employs a unique form of walling, to a certain extent dictated by the stone found in the area. In the Chudleigh Valley in northern Tasmania, for instance, the stone is the very hard, heavy dolerite; a few hours away in the Midlands, the walls are of softer sandstone. In a garden setting today, drystone walling is used decoratively, to divide areas or as retaining walls.

Drystone walls can harbour snakes in this country, so take care!

> **Tip:** Fill gaps and crevices of your drystone wall with matting thyme and small succulents, which can exist in almost no soil and with little water.

BUILDING A DRYSTONE WALL

Use whatever stone is in close proximity to your garden, whether it is the local granite, dolerite or sandstone. Sort through your stones according to size and intended use: for foundation, filling or feature stones, for instance. As there is a great deal of weight in any wall (between 1 and 2 tonnes per lineal metre), and no mortar is used, the placement of each stone is of the greatest importance. Foundation stones are laid on a shallow layer of blue metal gravel in a trench about 0.5 m deep, and two stones deep at the foundation will allow for a higher wall of up to 3 m.

Once the foundation is in place, the wall is built up, with the largest stones placed nearest the base. To avoid creating any weak 'running joints' being incorporated into the wall, the rule of one stone placed above two, and two over one, must be scrupulously respected. Thus, the wall gains strength as it increases in height. Each side of the wall—the skin—is built up in this way, with rubble—the heart—tightly packed between the skins. 'Through-stones', which span the entire width of the wall, are included at various heights. They are left either protruding or flush, to add strength, as a signature of the craftsman, or to be used as stiles. The coping finishes off the wall: stones laid on end are known as 'coping stones', while those laid flat are called 'capping stones'.

To ensure strength, drystone walls are built to incorporate a 'batter': the sides taper in. The standard batter is 1:12—for every rise of 30 cm in height, the wall narrows 2.5 cm on each side. To provide a guide for a consistent slope, wooden frames are built on each end of a section, joined by string lines.

Entrances

Just as your front garden mediates between the space inside your house and the outside world, and gives the passer-by information about you, so too the entrance to your property tells a tale. And your front gate, most often the focal point of your boundary, is also where the story of you and your garden begins. It can be inviting or excluding, mysterious or minimalist, hardly noticed at all, or shouting your message.

The erstwhile Australian garden designer Kath Carr stipulated that the entrance to any garden was the most important part of the overall design. She would start painting her garden picture from the front gate, where she would often sit in her car for lengthy periods, contemplating the mood of the garden beyond, before she would enter. Carr, mostly working on gardens in the country, did not approve of grand gates and entrances, particularly in an Australian setting: simple, workmanlike gates and fences were what she stipulated for her designs.

Grand gates and gate houses, and grand entrances, have their place in grand settings, of course—like at Cottesbrooke Hall in Northamptonshire, a part of England whose glorious gardens remain relatively unknown. There, hand-forged iron gates incorporate family crests that relate a history dating back to the early eighteenth century. Cottesbrooke Hall's lovely entrance—which then leads you on a journey of anticipation, winding through parkland and across a bridge and a lake until you reach a point where you can perfectly appreciate the house, resting peacefully, promisingly, on its wide stone terrace—sets you up for the treat to come. And, within the 250 ha of parkland, wildflower meadows and formal gardens, there are many other simple gates directing the visitor into secret walled gardens.

Your front gate is, most often, the first element of your property that the visitor experiences: which-

ever style you choose, it will set the tone for what is to follow. There are almost countless styles of gate to choose from, and your choice will depend on the architecture and period of your house, as well as on the statement you wish to make.

In a city garden, if the front door is visible from the front gate, the two should probably complement each other—both in design and colour. Suburban cottages may employ the Victorian wire gate; Federation houses are suited to sturdy wooden gates decorated with fretwork that matches verandah woodwork. Fences can be picket, paling, iron or Colorbond. Futuristic gates of heavy, polished, galvanised uprights suit the home architecture of the twenty-first century, which is often pared back and of scaled-up, rendered brick, a nod to Mediterranean climates similar to ours in Australia. The design of your gate also depends on its function: is it simply for decoration, or for security and perhaps also to prevent children from escaping onto a busy road? If gates are to be automated for additional security, a simple design will be called for.

Lychgates, particularly suited to Victorian, Queen Anne Revival and Federation houses, allow the visitor to pause and contemplate the garden before them, adding a further sense of anticipation to the visit. Lychgates can also have a practical purpose in the city, allowing access from the outside for deliveries, but, through the addition of a second, locked gate, denying immediate entry into the property.

Previous page: A beautiful country gate.

Your entrance should match the style and period of your property.

Simple arches or pergolas can lead to the front garden or can link different spaces and 'rooms' within the garden—and, of course, they provide us with another structure on which to grow a climber! Within your garden, simple wooden gates set within fences can create an inexpensive diversion when painted a vibrant and surprising colour. They can create the illusion that much more lies beyond: you can even 'borrow' your neighbour's land. There may not even be garden beyond the gate; by employing a version of a *trompe-l'oeil*, you further increase a sense of space.

Blue-painted gates will make the garden appear larger, leading the eye on, while a white gate will 'stop' the eye and bring the gate in closer. But then, Kath Carr would never allow anything in the garden to be painted white. 'Too stark', she would have said, or 'It's not what nature would have intended.' This may not be relevant in the city garden, with its different light, or in smaller spaces, where the white-painted gate can look über-smart.

If I lived in a tropical or subtropical climate, on lots of land, I would have an entrance of poinciana trees, *Delonix regia*. They would follow a long, curving drive, their delicate, fern-like, mid-green foliage forming an elegant and somewhat mysterious canopy across the track. A second avenue of jacaranda would roughly mirror the first, a row on each side. On either side of the front at the gate would be a silky oak, *Grevillea robusta*. The umber-coloured flowers of this tallest of the grevilleas appear at the same time as the flame-red, orchid-like flowers of the poinciana and, in a lucky season, the azure flowers of the jacaranda. For good measure—and to avoid any risk of a design cliché—I would 'throw out' a third *Grevillea robusta* off to one side and a little back, into the garden, just as if the wind had planted it there; I wouldn't want my entrance to appear too predictable. I might even add a clutch or two of frangipanis nearby. With their twisted fleshy branches, similar, spreading form and scented summer flowers in sunrise and sunset colours, they would ensure that excitement continued for months.

In my imaginary subtropical garden, I would have a boundary gate of wood, simple but very solid, and the drive would curve away, making the garden secret, so that the visitor could not see everything at once and would want to explore what was beyond the trees. Creating this sense of mystery is important in the gardens designed by Carr. Her philosophy was to create mystery by bringing the visitor through the front gate and, where possible, right around the perimeter of the garden, to catch glimpses of the house, through groups of trees, before entering the more formal sections of the garden. But Carr did not approve of grand entrances or driveways lined with trees, cautioning against creating a tunnel effect.

And yet, an avenue of lemon-scented gums (*Corymbia citriodora*) lines the curving entrance into one of Australia's most admired—and successful—country gardens. There, ghostly, smooth trunks and silvery-green leaves tone beautifully with the iris-leaf-green wooden fences around the property, creating a calm and soothing effect. And the entrance to Beleura, the Italianate mansion built in the late nineteenth century by the theatrical entrepreneur Sir George Tallis at Mornington on Victoria's Mornington Peninsula, is also lined successfully with lemon-scented gums, planted in about 1920.

Pairs of trees have long provided a smart entrance to any garden, whether large and relaxed or small and formal. You might choose *Malus floribunda,* the first of the crab-apples to flower, or, in a cool climate, the tall-growing, columnar *Liriodendron tulipifera*, which turns butter-yellow in autumn and in late spring is covered in magnificent, large tulip-like yellow blooms. In small gardens, entrances can be marked by smart pots of topiary in a range of plant species.

Designer brief: Michael Bligh

The garden that landscaper Michael Bligh has created for his family is a perfect example of his design philosophy, fine-tuned over almost three decades of advising on gardens from Longreach and Cunnamulla in north-western Queensland to beyond Bourke and to his home country, the Southern Tablelands of New South Wales. 'We always begin at the front entrance,' he says of his approach to a client's garden. 'I pretend I am a guest arriving for the first time. Then you walk towards the front door and assess what you see. As you go, there are nearly always opportunities: just taking that shrub out there, to open up a view into the garden. Or the shape of that bed could be improved, or we need a bench seat over there to draw the eye into that corner.'

The approach to his own property, Summerhill, where he lives with his wife, Annie, and three children, exemplifies his design ideas. The drive leading up to the 1880s stone house takes visitors around the garden: guests are unobtrusively directed to park in a special area that is well screened from the house and shaded by several Chinese elms.

An early task after the Blighs bought the property in the mid-1990s was to augment an existing windbreak of three rows of *Pinus radiata* that ran the full length of the western boundary with hardy photinia to create an in-fill between the ground and the canopy of the trees. A low hedge of may along a distant boundary screened passing cars without interrupting the vistas into the surrounding countryside. The garden is now 2.5 ha of parkland housing a mix of evergreen and deciduous trees, some flowering, some chosen for their foliage. The philosophy is to maintain simple plantings towards the perimeter, with detail becoming important nearer the house.

Crab-apples are a favourite in this garden; the first to flower in early spring is *Malus floribunda*. A pair of the delicate-flowered *M. ioensis* directs visitors to the front door, while a group of burgundy-leaved *M. eyelii* contrasts with the yellow of an inherited golden cypress.

Conditions can be tough in the gardens of many country clients, with frost, heat, drought or the availability of artesian water to consider. However, by choosing the right plants, judiciously removing certain shrubs or adding a pergola of local materials, Bligh has been able to create or improve gardens while keeping within budgets and other limitations.

'The responsibility of the designer is to design a garden that is affordable to the client and that the client can maintain,' he says. 'The last thing we ever want to do is create a garden that will become a monster, or a burden to the client. That is not good design. You can show ways of improving the garden to the next level, but you are not looking for a Chatsworth.'

Supports and Structures

Many Australians will feel that English gardens don't have too many answers for those of us who dwell in a land of climatic vicissitudes, and that we can't keep harking back to those lush green meadows, pining for wide perennial borders made possible by regular, soft rain. There are, however, some lessons that can be learned from that nation of passionate landscapers and plants-people. One of those lessons is that nothing from the garden need be wasted.

Supports

In English gardens—from the grandest to the most discreet and simple—good use is made of every garden cutting. Winter prunings that might otherwise be discarded make marvellous supports for tall-growing perennials in every English border. After winter pruning or coppicing, slender branches, or stems, are stripped of foliage and positioned in a variety of garden beds. Cuttings and prunings are used to create baskets which, upturned, become rose supports and trellises, to make obelisks, tripods and simple-but-clever low, woven fences.

In deep borders of perennials that are bare in winter, and that magically come to life with voluptuous layers of flowering plants for the short summer season, 'nests' of twiggy prunings are put in place before the first shoots emerge. Then, in spring, as plants grow, their lush foliage hides the sticks and twigs. Even before the border is at its peak they are covered and the tall plants supported from any sudden onslaught of damaging winds. While the plants are growing the supports look rustic, in harmony with nature—and so much smarter than wooden stakes.

Supports can be extremely decorative, even when not covered in plant material. Whether rustic or rather more formal—of metal or brightly painted wood—they lend height to, and a focus for, the garden bed. In winter, when not much else is happening, they provide body and scale.

While wooden or metal obelisks in a variety of simple or complicated patterns look good in a small, clipped town garden, in a less formal setting rustic supports may look more appropriate.

Any type of woody plant can be used to make supports: many of the fruit trees, including mulberry, plum and apple, provide excellent, flexible prunings that won't break when bent. Trees grown specifically for this purpose may be coppiced, so that the long, slender canes are produced each spring. Or dropped branches might be collected during walks in the bush. In country gardens, supports from melaleuca, willow or hazel prunings blur the line between the gardened landscape and the surrounding environment. (And whippy prunings from pear or hazelnut trees turn, in a few minutes, into scalloped edges to stop the mower from cutting the corner—or, at least, that's the theory.)

Create a minimalist support—or, for a more organic look, incorporate wool clippings, wattle, bark, leaves or reeds into the weaving. Make clever supports for tall-stemmed summer flowers like delphiniums by arranging pea sticks or willow, hazelnut or fruit-tree prunings like a wigwam, and strapping all together with raffia from a craft shop.

Screens and hurdles

Hurdles, or panels—traditionally used in the northern hemisphere as portable stockyards for

Previous page: The clematis 'Niobe'.

1. Rustic iron arbours support climbing roses at Jardin des Paradis.
2. A black-painted arbour covered in *Rosa* 'Zéphirine Drouhin' provides height and scale to the large vegetable garden at Rowandale on the Southern Highlands of New South Wales.
3. Simple supports for beans and peas.
4. Supports of prunings are attractive, even when not yet hidden by tall-growing summer perennials.

sheep—make interesting, rustic edges in herb gardens or to divide the vegetable garden. They look charming in a medieval-inspired parterre: think great tubs of lemons in the centre, with edges of box or lavender and willow hurdles along paths. Living screens woven from prunings can also be moved about to change the mood and feel of a border or can hide the 'housekeeping' areas like the garbage bins and compost heap.

Common garden plants like nasturtium and violets look anything but common when clambering over a low panel of woven willow. Panels can be fixed to a wall to support roses, in an interesting twist on the trellis.

Hurdles are woven between half a dozen or so (depending on the length you want) sharpened stakes that you've pruned from a tree. And half the fun in creating such structures lies in collecting your own materials, exploring new ground, out in the countryside, among nature.

Frames and pergolas

Free-standing, decorative frames constructed in a vase shape from steel piping, in as simple or detailed a design as takes your fancy, can support espaliered apple or pear trees. These are particularly effective in a vegetable garden or can divide a large garden without creating a sense of enclosure.

Structures, no matter how beautiful, should be useful. Pergolas must have a purpose, most often to provide shade and a support for climbing plants. An arbour also provides a framework for climbers—often roses, wisteria or espaliered fruit trees. It should also lead the visitor somewhere.

You might clothe a steel arbour—perhaps some 50 m in length for the ultimate effect—in carefully pruned and clipped Manchurian pear. It will be a mass of white blossom in late winter: continue the excitement with underplantings of spring-flowering bluebells and hellebores. This could also form part of a walk along part of a perimeter

of a garden and create the setting for bucolic outdoor dining.

An inexpensive disguise for an unsightly cement water tank can be created with galvanised steel fence posts—or more elegant frames—erected in a semi-circle and on which wires are strained. Discipline wisteria to grow only on the wires if you have plenty of time, or just let it go mad, but keep it strictly pruned back to the structure, and enjoy a mass of scented lilac-coloured blooms in late spring.

Tip: When collecting material, search out the supple and compliant. The versatile willow is perfect for tripods, hurdles, wigwams and tepees as it can be bent, almost like a piece of string. Very reedy material is used for baskets. It is best to let the material age for at least two weeks after pruning, to allow for shrinkage. Use it while it is still flexible, though, to allow tighter packing (for hurdles) and to achieve a firmer structure.

Balcony gardeners can twist whippy cuttings into an attractive structure to support tomatoes and climbers.

A long walk

At the Southbank Parklands on the south side of the Brisbane River, a Grand Arbour constructed from zinc covered with steel runs the 500 m length of the gardens. Galvanised wires are tensioned to support the brilliant cerise-flowering bougainvillea 'Mrs Butt', known for its climbing ability, rapid growth and prolific flowering.

LIGHTING

Lighting

Less is definitely more when it comes to lighting your garden. If the interplay of light and shadow adds depth and feeling to the daytime garden, it is the quality of night-time light that can turn the most ordinary space into an enchanted, magical forest. In summer, clever, subtle lighting can lengthen the day even further, and there is nothing more likely to brighten up a cold winter evening than looking out onto a beautifully lit garden.

Good lighting transforms any garden to create a new and different composition at night, providing an extra dimension and extending living area. Subtlety and discretion is the key to creating a gentle, enveloping mood in the after-dark garden—you don't want to be lit up like a Christmas tree or the car park of the local pub. The easy option of flooding the area with light from a single source may prevent you from tripping over the dog's bone, but will not impart any sense of intrigue or mystery. A change in mood can be created by using different lights in a variety of ways. Trees can be lit from the base. Or hanging lights high in a tree creates a 'moonlight' effect, with the tracery of branches forming breathtaking patterns upon bare surfaces below. Lights set on a flat, upright surface cast a soft glow, which 'grazes' a wall. Directional lights stabbed into the ground can bring a hedge to life.

Highlight features with dramatic shapes: select key elements within the garden, such as a special tree or sculpture. Create darting shadows. Extraneous elements—an adjoining property, for instance—can be deleted with selective and directional lighting easily inserted into the ground on spikes.

Gently illuminate steps and paths with capped lights, installed and wired in during construction. The key to creating the right mood, however, is that you should hardly be conscious of the lighting.

Reno Rizzo and Christopher Hansson of Inarc Architects pay great attention to the detail of the outdoor lighting in their commissions. Because their projects employ expanses of glass they place great importance on the connection between the outside and the inside. The landscape is not shut out with the use of curtains; double glazing is preferred.

The Inarc philosophy is evident in a recent commission for clients who had relocated to an inner Melbourne suburb from a large country garden. The interior of the terrace house was gutted and the spaces re-organised. The house was opened up completely, with clear glass walls at the rear to provide views onto a beautiful back garden of hedges and roses. A long reflecting pool, lined with dark river stones, is the central feature and is visible from the moment you open the front door. At night it looks magnificent, softly illuminated with marine-grade, stainless-steel lights beneath the surface.

At the rear of the garden a dense green background—against which a row of pear trees turns red and gold in May—is created by well-clipped

> **Tip:** Quality is crucial in garden lighting. Buy heavy cast-iron, copper or black fittings that disappear into the plant material.

Previous page: At the Hotel Cipriani, on the Guidecca in Venice, the vineyard where Casanova is said to have courted the young novice Caterina Capretta still thrives in the rear garden.

conifers. In front, a pair of weeping cherries is underplanted with the small-flowering periwinkle, *Vinca minor*. These, and a stand of trident maples, are lit from beneath with multiple recessed up-lights, set low to the ground and protected by a grill. The whitest light possible is used to lend the best tone to foliage.

For a very large tree in a large back yard, commercial space or country garden, Inarc uses a more powerful sunken accent light. Brick lights, recessed flush into the walls (normally with a directional baffle), are employed in functional areas.

Garden lighting doesn't have to be permanent, however, and can change with the weather, the season or the event. One of the most effective ways of creating atmosphere for a party is to place tea lights, anchored in sand, in brown-paper bags: line the driveway or the path to the buffet with them. This looks moody and effective. Place short,

Safety first: never leave candles unattended.

stumpy candles in flower pots or in clear glass vases on the steps. Or even string some subtle—never gaudy—white fairy lights through a widely branched tree to create your own starry, starry night.

Switches for garden lighting should be easily accessible: integrate them with house lighting so that illuminating the garden becomes part of the evening routine. But don't leave lighting—inside or out—on for long periods of time without a thought for saving energy and respecting the environment. And consider the use of energy-efficient light sources, such as compact fluorescents or LED fittings in lieu of those using halogen or incandescent lamps.

Simple and solid is often most pleasing for garden lighting.

Pots

Moving your horticultural treasures from a large garden to a small courtyard—or worse, to a balcony—must be somewhat like fitting the possessions of a lifetime into an apartment after the children have left home. One solution is to cultivate your favourite plants in pots that can be arranged in groups, or tiered on shelving and stands, or hung from vertical surfaces; or as baskets that can be hung from overhead beams. There would be few gardens, whether a small city courtyard or a country spread, that wouldn't benefit from the addition of a handsome pot or a collection of potted plants.

Pot plants also allow the hopelessly undisciplined among us to indulge our love of plant hunting by changing pots of flowering plants with season or fashion while maintaining any underlying design. Thus, you can create different looks and moods, and, by changing your pots, can reflect the seasons—rather like changing sofa covers with the weather, a phenomenon of 'good housekeeping' that seems most prevalent in American decorating magazines.

You can also reflect botanical fashion with your choice of plants. Create the prairie look—so popular at present—with pots of grasses, or create a metaphor for an Australian meadow with pots of flannel flowers (*Actinotus helianthi*) or kangaroo paw, *Anigozanthos* spp. Ring in Christmas with containers stuffed with red and white petunias; they are simple to grow and delicately scented. So, you don't have to own acreage to boast a beautiful garden or a collection of treasures.

Style

Success with container gardening depends on several factors. Groups of identical or similar pots will always look smarter than a random collection of containers gathered over the years. Versailles-style planter boxes painted in an appropriate colour are classically elegant, or go for a clutch in terracotta.

There are a few rules to consider, however, if your pots are to add glamour to your garden, rather than looking like an untidy collection of afterthoughts. The style, colour and material of your pots should marry with the architecture and finish of the building. Glazed pots suit Santa Fe, coastal or modern architectural styles, while the more traditional terracotta and sandstone pots suit older-style houses with formal, 'English' or cottage gardens. Severe plants call for severe pots with clean lines.

Less is usually more when choosing pots and the key to success is to avoid mixing styles. And a special pot may stand alone as a work of art in itself, providing a focal point at the end of a walk or border, or to highlight a secluded, quiet corner.

Don't make the mistake of thinking that a small space calls for a small pot (or a small plant): scale up any container planting for a more effective result.

Living pots are an extremely clever, if not entirely maintenance-free, addition to any space. A outside 'pot' formed by clipped box, or by the hardy native wire vine (*Muehlenbeckia axillaris*) trained on a wire frame, can contain a simple plastic pot of flowering plants that can be changed regularly.

The English designer Gertrude Jekyll used this principle in gardens like the Manor House at Upton Grey when she created raised containers

Opposite: A mass of 'hen and chicken' cascades from its pot.

of stone to fill with a changing display. They also provided the bare winter garden with all-important structure.

New Zealand gardener Bernie Hawkings admits that she never throws anything away: an old pair of men's work boots is filled with annuals; discarded pots are made smart with painted finishes; planters are created from massive metal crushers—once used to make different grades of road base—from a nearby disused quarry. Annuals such as the brilliant blue lobelia, white daisies and red petunias fill these pots and baskets while about a dozen more are 'growing on', hidden away to replace plants that become stressed over summer.

Then there are hanging baskets: did you know that the city of Bath employs three full-time gardeners just to take care of the glorious hanging baskets? Excess is the way to go with hanging baskets, so cram in lots of seedlings and liquid-feed every fortnight. Succulents are a good choice for baskets, but for me nothing beats a basket jam-packed with softly scented petunias. Lobelia and pansies are also effective: poke small plants in the sides of the baskets for a full and rich effect. The sought-after clear-red *Tropaeolum speciosum* looks wonderful cascading from a black filigree basket.

Line your basket with green or black shade cloth, perhaps disguised with sphagnum moss, which also holds water. Use a dried compressed liner that expands once dunked in water; as hanging baskets dry out quickly, add wetting crystals to your potting mix.

Potting mix

Second only to the style of the pot is the importance of the potting mix you choose. Always buy a mix that carries the Australian Standards tick of approval, to ensure a good-quality planting medium and a suitable balance of nutrients

The air porosity of the mix is crucial, as air enables the roots of your plants to breathe and function. The new soil-less potting mixes are an excellent alternative as they are based on recycled materials and resist breaking down, thus retaining structure and holding greater amounts of available water.

A note of caution: potting mix can contain harmful bacteria. Keep your face away from the bag, particularly when opening it, and take care not to breathe in any 'dust' given off. When handling the potting mix, wear gloves and a face mask, and make sure it stays moist.

Plants suitable for pots

The contribution made by each plant in a tiny garden is virtually doubled, so focus, perhaps, on scented plants; and ensure year-round interest by choosing deciduous plants. There is a vast range of plants that are perfectly happy in pots. Among those particularly suited to container growing are clivias, orchids, camellias and begonias. I also love to see clematis, wisteria or even the common jasmine—that harbinger of spring—cascading from pots.

Tip: Simple black plastic or fibreglass pots can be made to look like treasured antiques by applying an antique rust and/or a verdigris effect. First, apply a real cast-iron paint, then apply a real copper paint as a highlight. Finally, apply an oxidising patina to turn the iron paint to rust and the copper paint to verdigris. Go for different-sized containers decorated with the one design, finish or glaze for maximum effect. Drying times (depending on the weather) are approximately 30 minutes for the paint and 1 to 2 hours for the oxidising patina.

Add tripods or scaled-up obelisks, in either a brightly painted wood or galvanised iron, to support climbing star jasmine, honeysuckle or clematis. Use beautifully made structures to support climbers such as clematis, if your climate will allow such delicacies, to add height and chutzpah to the garden. These can be pushed into planter boxes and pots.

1. A collection of pots and plants is offered for sale on a Paris footpath.
2. 'Stone look' pots are easy to make.
3. Geraniums and nasturtiums cascade from a window box in the French hill town of St Paul de Vence.

Creating 'stone' troughs

Stone tubs and troughs are hard to find these days and, if available, often impossibly expensive. Edna Walling made her own antique stone–looking troughs in which clients could create a miniature landscape or plant a collection of precious bulbs. Here's how:

Take 2 buckets of coarse sand and 2 buckets of composted pine bark. Mix with 1 bucket of cement and 1 cup of oxide. Mix dry ingredients—a cement mixer is ideal—and slowly start adding water. Consistency should be firm with just a little water dripping out when the mix is squeezed into a ball in the palm of the hand. Cover a pile of sand, or a polystyrene box—the desired size and shape of the finished trough—with the mixture to the required thickness. Use a hose to punch drainage holes in the base.

'Patience is the chief thing in making pots with cement,' advised Walling, in *Cottage and Garden in Australia*, published in 1947. 'The colours are best kept faint if they are not to compete with the plants.'

SMALL-GROWING SPECIES

Clivias, which like their roots restricted and undisturbed, are among the species most suited to container growing. They don't need fertiliser, although they'll thank you for an annual application of a folar feed. They don't need much water: wet feet will cause them to rot. They need good drainage so will thrive in a scoria mixture. Provide shelter in frost-prone areas, perhaps under awnings, which will also keep them dry. And they tolerate hot afternoon sun (*see also* Bulbs).

Cyclamens are a perfect choice for small pots, particularly as they like being placed outside during the night. Don't water too much in summer, but do apply a seaweed-based liquid fertiliser monthly from autumn. Remove spent leaves and flowers.

Hydrangeas, which make perfect flowering indoor plants, can be easily grown in plastic tubs (which, indoors, you would disguise, of course). After flowering take the pot outside to a cool spot and virtually forget it until the following Christmas, when the flowering plant can again decorate your house.

Orchids, like clivias, thrive in the microclimate of a tiny garden, but all varieties need sun, most particularly in the morning.

SHRUBS AND TREES

The cut-leaf maples (*Acer palmatum* var. *dissectum*), which grow particularly well in a pot, represent great value for money, providing a constantly changing landscape and signalling each changing season.

Camellias also earn their keep in a small space. The *sasanqua* camellias, some of which are scented, and the miniature japonicas are particularly hard working. A dark corner of a courtyard might be lit by the variegated *Camellia japonica* 'Benten' or *C. j.* 'Autumn Glory'. The elegant *japonica* 'Nuccio's Gem'—surely the most perfect of all—is suited to container growing. *Camellia sasanqua*, so good for hedging, lends itself to clipping into obelisks and orbs. If you are lucky, you might find the tiny pink miniature *Camellia japonica* 'Rosiflora Cascade', perfectly suited for growing in a pot or a small space. The Sydney-bred *sasanqua* hybrid 'Marge Miller' looks terrific cascading from a pot. The large white camellia 'Elegans Champagne' looks stunning in a white-painted, wooden Versailles-style tub.

Standards of white-flowering roses, planted in up-scale pots in a luscious cream glaze, also look wonderful.

Think green upon green for a supremely restful effect in a small space. An entrance flanked by a pair of standardised lillypillies (*Syzigium paniculatum*), bays or clipped figs (*Ficus hillii*) looks smart. Topiary, planted in pots, looks good in a small space: ligustrum, box and hebe all clip successfully. Globes, obelisks or pyramids of the small-leaved pittosporum (*Pittosporum tenuifolium* 'Green Pillar'), of buxus, or of the dwarf euonymus (*Euonymus japonicus* 'Microphyllus') make impressive statements. Again, use the best pots you can manage and keep pots uniform; either contrast, or team, them with the pavers you have chosen.

Citrus are well suited to pots: 'Meyer' lemon, which is cold tolerant, is an excellent potted, scented choice.

Figs, which have aggressive, invasive root systems that make them dangerous to plant out in the garden, look great in pots, often clipped into spheres. *Ficus hillii* and *F. benjamina* love water, so keep them moist.

Poinsettias, which in this country often decorate the Christmas table—although they are really winter flowering—do well in pots. They traditionally flower with brilliant red bracts but now also come in cream, pink and salmon. Place in a sunny, protected spot. They will cope with a heavy prune after flowering and then tip pruning to encourage thick growth.

The slow-growing indigenous grass trees, *Xanthorrhoea* spp., are an arresting sight when growing in an open, sunny position. (*See also* Native Plants.)

Among the conifers, the dwarf *Juniperis communis* 'Pyramidalis' and *Thuja orientalis* 'Aurea Nana' are slow growing and don't need clipping to retain their smart shape.

And why not pot up a Wollemi pine? We've all heard the exciting story of the discovery of this unique pine, a dinosaur of the botanical world, by ranger David Noble in a national park some 150 km north-west of Sydney in 1994. Think of it as a Christmas tree, to be taken out into your courtyard afterwards.

Planting

Experiment with different types of potting mix. Add rice hulls or peanut shells to create perfect drainage. Carefully 'spoon' into pots that have been lined with heavy black plastic or painted with a sealer to prevent moisture loss through porous containers.

Add a small amount of water-storage crystals to the soil mix, two-thirds of the way down the pot, to best utilise every drop of moisture you, or the heavens, provide. Don't be heavy handed, as the crystals swell considerably and you don't want the pot bulging, unable to catch any rain that may fall. Water the plant to settle it into its new soil, and allow it to drain well. Repeat over the next few days to allow the water crystals to swell to their full capacity.

Re-pot plants into fresh potting mix every few years, usually into a pot one size larger. If pots are root bound, tease out and trim roots before re-potting, most often best done in winter, when many plants are dormant. A plant drying out and suffering disease is a sure indication that it is pot-bound.

Mulch well.

Care

To produce healthy plants that can resist pests and diseases it's important to fertilise pots. Slow-release fertiliser is the most convenient way to add nutrients, or try the liquid plant foods based on seaweed, fish emulsion and other trace elements.

Most pots will benefit from a good soaking twice each week. Make sure drainage is good, and air must be allowed to circulate beneath the pot, so hoist pots up on 'feet'. Add a fine mesh or a large-weave shade cloth at the base of the pot, above drainage holes, to ensure that potting mix doesn't leak over paving—but make sure drainage holes don't become clogged.

ABSENTEE WATERING

The garden you grow in containers needs special attention if you are about to leave it to go on holiday. You won't want to return to pot plants dried to a brown crisp, with roots cooked in the baking sun. I like to re-pot all my pot plants in early summer if I am leaving town for any extended summer break. As I won't be home to appreciate the foliage, I cut it back to help the roots cope with the stress of summer heat; water well and mulch thickly.

Before heading off, move those pots that are not too large to the coolest corner of the garden, placing them close together and in a position to catch any rain that does fall.

Food for pots

Bernie Hawkings 'force feeds' her pots of flowering plants. A 2000 litre tank is installed at the top of her garden; each time it is filled from the spring-fed weir on the property, a 1 kg bag of all-purpose fertiliser is added and allowed to dissolve. The pots are then fertilised as they are watered.

Some gardeners like to stand pots on slabs of wet newspaper, hoping that by the time the paper has dried out it will have rained, renewing this osmotic 'watering' system. I stand my pots close together in a series of huge plastic saucers, then fill the saucers with water. While normally I would ensure that pots can drain well, this method is acceptable for the purposes of keeping your plants alive for the short period in which you are away.

Some gardeners scatter around a few plastic bottles of water in which tiny holes have been made, allowing drip-feed watering over an extended period of time. And remember to move all pots off verandas, as they can't walk out to sing in the rain!

Sculpture

As in many things—including flavours on a plate, decorations for the Christmas tree and garden lighting—less is more when it comes to garden art. A few beautiful, carefully selected pieces of sculpture that you cannot live without will always make you more content than lots of items of questionable beauty. And, when choosing sculpture for your garden, the natural environment is a good starting point: watch and learn from the way in which the soil supports life forms.

The size of both your property and your budget is most relevant when choosing a piece of sculpture for your garden. Other considerations are the location, style and age of the garden.

Sculpture is presented to us, both by artists and nature, in myriad styles and a variety of mediums—from concrete to stone and clay, bronze, steel, marble or wood. Whether your taste and available funds run to classical sculpture of museum quality, or a piece of wood collected from a field, the work needs to sit easily in its location, connected to the surrounding landscape.

The grand sculptures favoured by large, historic gardens in the English countryside, or found in Italian or French gardens, rely on a formal garden design. Massive, intricately carved stone urns resting upon a stone plinth look perfect as the focal point at the end of a long avenue of pleached limes, or a double hedge of hawthorn or beech. A statue in marble of a figure drawn from the classics is given additional importance when set in a niche cut into a dense, severely clipped hedge.

The massive arches of glowing pink stone that Andy Goldsworthy creates call for a landscaped parkland of 'Capability' Brown scale and consequence. A few years ago I visited one in a field that was part of a grand English garden; it stood strong and solid, but, somehow, also rested lightly upon the landscape. In the late-afternoon light of early autumn, the tapestry of golds, russets and reds of the turning leaves of the surrounding forest provided a perfect foil. There, the skill of the artist matched the art of the landscape to provide an extraordinary experience of both aesthetic stimulation and tranquillity.

The less ambitious amongst us might place a single, scaled-up, urn on a smooth green sheet of lawn for immediate impact. A stone finial on a plinth or a hand-made terracotta pot tucked into a corner of the garden, or around a turn in a woodland walk, will also provide an exciting element of surprise.

I love the idea of a bronze heron fossicking for food among a planting of *Iris pseudocorus* on the edge of a pond or lake. To make it work, think about how that bird might naturally have come to rest in that spot. Again, try to replicate nature for success in design.

In a vegetable garden, woven cloches for covering young plants are a work of art in themselves, and their functionality and relevance to their siting impart an additional importance. At the end of a walk through a wild meadow, or to one corner of an orchard, a scaled-up apple or pear, carved in a vernacular material—local stone perhaps—anchors and contextualises the garden and emphasises its changing moods.

Whatever you choose, each piece of sculpture should be carefully positioned to relate it to the texture of the plants or to the skyline beyond. Think of the lines of the house and garden when choosing sculpture: a stand of pencil pines might

Opposite: An upturned stone toadstool: a simple garden sculpture favoured by landscapers Edna Walling and Kath Carr.

1. Bronwyn Berman's *Ring of Fire*.
2. *Rising* by Bronwyn Berman.
3. An eagle skims the water at Crisp Gallery.
4. Beautifully placed bronzes at Yengo garden, Mt Wilson, New South Wales.
5. A sculpture is perfectly placed at the end of an important avenue at Cottisbrooke Hall.

be echoed in a vertical piece of sculpture, while a horizontal work may reflect the lawn on which it is set. A work on a verandah will connect the house and its garden.

Most artists advise that you don't fret too much over where a work will be placed. One says that it is much more pleasing to 'just happen upon' something, rather than find a work in an obvious position. You want to round a corner to discover a piece nestled against a tree or lightening up a dark corner—perhaps a conifer—or a bronze figure sitting among some irises, she says. Sculpture is a very individual thing: if you love it, you will find a place for it.

Scale and size

The scale of the piece should relate to both the size of the garden and the height and scale of the house. The sculpture might also relate to a specific part of the house—for example, a piece on a wall might invest the background with its own importance.

You don't need large spaces to successfully display art in the garden: you might use the side of your house or a wall of a courtyard to feature a relief sculpture—just a leaf or a flower, perhaps. Be careful, though, if you can only have one piece: choose something with which you have fallen in love. In a small space a single, carefully selected piece—one you feel you cannot live without—will be more effective than a potentially disparate collection. Or if you simply cannot decide between a few works, choose several: you can always put one or two away, to be brought out as your mood and the seasons change.

Sculpture gardens: a few of the best
Maroochy Bushland Botanic Gardens

Several works, created from sandstone, marble or granite, now rest permanently in the 82 ha Maroochy Bushland Botanic Gardens following a staging, a few years ago, of a symposium titled 'Harmony between man and the living earth'.

The artists invited to the symposium created works in a wide range of styles: Silvio Apponyi carved Australian animals—from large, reclining kangaroos to goannas lazing on polished rocks—that were very tactile and a favourite with children. Seung-Woo Hwang, from South Korea, hollowed out stone to create the sound of wind or water.

Curator Craig Medson's pieces—most often in marble—were abstract in nature, usually related to the natural elements of earth, fire, wind and water. 'For me, stone carries connotations of eternity, solidity and strength,' he explains. 'The concept of taking material straight from the earth and creating something totally new appeals immensely.'

'The art of the sculptor is to match the piece to its surroundings,' he says. 'Sometimes people have a site in mind, or an artist will design something specific to a particular garden. Many parks all over

the world mix styles, from figurative, to abstract—as long as each area is suited to each piece.'

Stone was chosen because of its integrity, ensuring survival long into the future. The sandstone, from the Brisbane hinterland, can be seen in many of the buildings that have contributed so much to the character of the city; the marble is a rare, pure white from Chillagoe, 200 km west of Cairns, and was formed 300 million years ago, when Chillagoe was on the coast. Some of the artists used the pink granite from Brisbane's Mount Cootha area and a grey granite from Gympie.

The works have found a home among the giant stands of Queensland blue gum (*Eucalyptus tereticornis*) in the gardens, which shelter some 400 plant species native to subtropical coastal Australia; there are a fern glade, a contemplation garden and wetlands.

Berman Garden

The sculptor Bronwyn Berman wakes each dawn to the song of a thousand birds: they have come to feast on the flowering gums, banksias and persoonias that have burst into bloom with the advent of spring in her garden. On misty mornings her house, which protrudes from a western escarpment of the Great Dividing Range hundreds of metres above the Wingecarribee River, appears to be hovering above clouds.

Berman is inspired by the geography and geology of the landscape and by the timeline, dating from Gondwana, described by the escarpment. Her work is also influenced by the house. She planted the garden, to blend seamlessly into its bush setting, with species indigenous to the area. 'The Australian bush is chaotic,' concedes Berman. Often using found materials—fencing wire, aluminium, stone and glass—her work seeks to understand her environment, simplifying it.

Just outside her front door is a mound garden, created from the local conglomerate, with its jewel-like quartz pebbles and chips of ironstone, in a palette of whites, greys, browns and blacks. 'This is about the moon,' she explains. 'And the wholeness of life here in the wilderness.' Grasses and sisyrinchiums thrive in the tough conditions.

Her work *The Journey*, set under a canopy of the local stringybark, reflects the glass that is central to the house, and the patterns of life and of the river. 'The two streams of glass wind around each other,' she explains. The canoe section of the work is carved from a tree that had to be removed and which Berman wanted to reinstate in the landscape. *Rising*, inspired by the work of British artist Andy Goldsworthy, is created from aluminium wire and fencing wire. It rests on a plinth of stone that was taken from the ground in perfect, geometric shapes. There is *Sphere*, which transforms rubble into a shape present in the landscape in many forms, among them seed pods and the curve of the tree branch. The work rests comfortably, on a natural stone platform, in a bend in the drive. 'The whole gesture of the landscape is this swirl. You can imagine that, as the river came down, it turned. As you go through the bands of rock, you can sense the movement on the river.'

It is not surprising that Berman admits to 'spending a lot of time just looking, and being, and breathing in' her surroundings. And to many cups of tea; just dreaming.

Crisp Gallery and Garden

Peter Crisp's 3 ha garden—located just near the New South Wales town of Yass—is laid out around his world-renowned glass gallery in the midst of a large sheep station.

Crisp, an internationally recognised glass artist, opened his studio in 1992 and—with his brother, horticulturalist Sandy, and his mother, Helen— started laying out the garden as a series of large spaces. Fanning out from the studio and gallery is a shady avenue of New Zealand hybrid willows, under which a winter carpet of jonquils and daffodils is followed by bluebells. Green-flowering and purple-flowering hellebores, the strikingly

Whimsy

Tugurium, the Mount Macedon garden of plantsman Stephen Ryan, houses several very individual garden ornaments. 'If you are going to have statuary or sculpture in the garden it's silly to import something,' he says. 'You don't want your diaphanously draped Dianas; you want something that is Australian in theme without having a koala letterbox. So I've got my metal bull ants and my topiary spider and those bits of whimsy.'

'I used to pass this dead tree on the road,' says New Zealand gardener Bernie Hawkings of a large piece of driftwood in a section of her garden. One day she brought it home, to become a 'coat hanger' for the white-flowering *Clematis montana* 'Alba' that is covered in starry white blossom in spring. In December, decked out with small lights, the driftwood becomes a Christmas tree.

blue, tall ajuga *A. reptans* 'Caitlin's Giant' and white hydrangeas bloom through summer. At the end of the avenue, a planting of white arum lilies and pale blue *Iris japonica* leads to the rill garden with its charming sculpture in mild steel by the late Michael Murphy of a water bird in flight, followed by the expected splashes.

Pathways lead you off in different directions in this garden. From the rill garden a turn to your right will take you to a hillside of clipped *Teucrium fruticans*, overshadowed by a combination of Persian lilac and white lilac. To your left lies the formal lavender garden. Arranged as a parterre of squares, rectangles and diamonds, this is a garden of different lavenders enclosed by hedges of *Lonicera nitida*. Although the lavender is at its most intense during December, the range of species grown ensures that this garden is in bloom from October to January. Each section is marked with a metal cone over which honeysuckle has been trained.

To one side a sculpture by Wagga-based artist John Woods, *Suddenly*, comprises a collection of violins and reflects the performances that take place in the garden during summer. The tulip trees (*Liriodendron tulipifera*), with their butter-yellow, goblet-shaped flowers in spring, which mark the corners of the lavender parterre, were a gift to the garden from Crisp's first piano teacher. At the centre a stone cairn is encircled by a shadowy grove of Manchurian pears. Avenues of quince and of *Prunus serrulata* and *P.* 'Mt Fuji', with its double, pale pink blossom, link this area with an adjacent orchard.

You step down from this plateau to the Waterfall Garden, where a lake is edged with a palette of blue-flowering iris, westringia and periwinkle—the latter a nuisance if allowed to run riot but a most effective ground cover if kept under strict control. The steep sides of the lake are stabilised with cascading wisteria and the prostrate rosemary 'Blue Lagoon'. An eagle dragging a European carp from the water, also by Michael Murphy, testifies to the artist's work as a conservationist. 'He chose the carp as a fish that must be eradicated,' explains Crisp. For evening events in summer the lake is lit from beneath the water. That will be something to see.

Our National Gallery

Even in the depths of a bitter Canberra winter the sculpture garden at the National Gallery in Canberra is an uplifting place. In summer, the soft and dappled light provided by the plantings of Australian natives is in absolute counterpoint to the severe lines of the gallery building. Designed in 1981, the secluded sculpture garden stretches over 3 ha, from the northern face of the gallery to Lake Burley Griffin.

The garden is designed as a series of spaces revolving around the four seasons; each space offers textures, colours and light, which reflect, and are unique to, each sculpture. The first 'room' you enter is the Winter Garden, paved in slate, which complements the white trunks and grey foliage of the *Eucalyptus mannifera*. In this space, *The Burghers of Calais* by Auguste Rodin contrasts with the voluptuous *Floating Figure* by Gaston Lachaise, poised above a large, hard-edged rectangular pool. You walk to the Summer Garden through dense stands of *Casuarina cunninghamiana*, cool and shadowy in mid-summer.

Sculptures are hidden amid the foliage or sited on grassy knolls. Each has been carefully positioned to relate to the texture of the plants or to the skyline beyond. The garden is a place where the art of the landscape is matched to the art of the sculptor to provide an experience that is both calming and exhilarating.

Sculpture by the Sea

There could perhaps be no better setting for a sculpture exhibition than the coastal walk between Bondi Beach and Tamarama, surely the quintessential Sydney experience. The salt- and wind-ravaged cliffs, the blue sea and that somewhat unique collection of ageing plus new buildings that hug the strip resonate perfectly with what it means to be a Sydneysider. This is where the annual 'Sculpture by the Sea' exhibition is held.

One of the most exciting works one year was the floating woman. There she lolled, no longer the svelte beach babe, her generous breasts bobbing on the gentle swell. A lone snorkeller was diving close-by, oblivious to the work of art sharing his space. For anyone who has trodden through French gardens where inviting green swathes of lawn are intercepted by 'Keep off the Grass' signs, the insouciance of the diver summed up much that makes our country unique.

Above: *Cones* by Bert Flugelman, in the sculpture garden at the National Gallery in Canberra.

WATER FEATURES

Water Features

Water is part of the imagination and the iconography of Australia; it is just one detail in a shared set of ideas, memories and feelings that binds us together as a culture. Clear blue waves pounding Bondi Beach, the aqua waters that surround the Great Barrier Reef, even the mysterious ebb and flow of Lake Eyre or the secret life of Kakadu: these are images that come to mind when, homesick abroad, we think of our country.

No Australian needs to be reminded that water is the essence of life. There may be other factors that contribute to the quality of our existence, but it's water that is the defining element. Just as the vast spaces of this country outline our sense of ourselves as Australians, the availability of water sets the possibilities. There is perhaps no other country in the world where water—or the lack of it—so controls development. No farmer need be told that it is water that will determine his success.

And you have only to consider how Australians crowd the narrow coastal strip to know that we love water—the sight, the sound, the feel and even the smell of it.

While city folk may think at first that water is simply what comes out of a tap, the value of water in creating a different dimension in a garden, once understood, becomes crucial to the enjoyment of that garden. Every garden, no matter how small, is improved by the addition of water. You don't have to swim in it, or even dip your toe in it: just looking upon water has a soothing effect. And it needn't be an expanse of water that would make 'Capability' Brown proud, or even a so-smart Edwin Lutyens–style reflecting pool. A lap pool, a small rill just a few bricks wide and not much longer, set in the paving of a courtyard, or even a water-filled ceramic pot, will do. And if the water in your feature moves, all the better: the sound of splashing or trickling water is particularly calming.

The health-giving properties of water—either still or moving—are well documented. The feel, sight and sound of water—whether in a public space, along our coastline or in a garden—refresh the spirit, soothe the soul and calm the mind. Water doesn't just add interest to a garden: it brings it to life.

In the ancient gardens of the Middle East, water spilled from fountains and flowed through the various spaces in narrow canals, irrigating flower beds and citrus trees and cooling plants and people in the process. The water cascades of the stepped Moghul gardens of northern India have inspired modern examples such as that at Chatsworth House in Derbyshire, England; at Holker Hall in England's Lake District; and at the Fletcher Steele–designed Naumkeag in Massachusetts.

Fountains can be found in the earliest histories of the ancient Greeks, who protected their precious springs with marble covers to ensure the purity of the water. Fountains are used today across cultures, but many we see in modern gardens have been inspired by Greek mythology.

The importance of water in any garden was acknowledged centuries before landscaper Sylvia Crowe wrote, in 1956, 'No element of landscape design is more potent than a stretch of water giving serenity to a scene. It has the same simplifying effect on the landscape that is given by a covering of snow; the trivialities are smoothed away. All objects are enhanced by their reflection ... by their repetition in the water.'

Opposite: Water: just the sight of it is soothing.

Fortunately, you don't have to own the space, nor have the budget to install a vast watery expanse, to enjoy water in your garden. A birdbath is a happy and simple solution for those of us without the luxury of gardening on the scale of an historic property. A small dish or ceramic pot partly filled with water can be home to water iris, or a simple and inexpensive pump sunk into a rubber-lined pond can provide the sound of running water to sooth the nerves and divert your attention from the city traffic humming past your front gate. For a variety of tones or harmonies use different water-flow rates. Place rocks or stones of various sizes so that the water can fall onto them. Change the stones and their arrangement to vary the sounds created.

The water in your garden needs to complement its style and tone. Small, restrained courtyards call for formal water arrangements; an historic garden will suit a grander feature; while a large, more informal, country garden provides the opportunity to design an expanse of water that mirrors nature. Low boggy areas can be turned into lagoons; dams can be shaped to form large lakes.

The ideas and opportunities for your water feature are unlimited. You can create a break in a wall and direct water to cascade over it, dropping onto gravel or rocks below. Water can cascade behind long, thin panels of wall-mounted glass; elevated platforms of hardened plastic or cast glass, washed by a film of water, could hover above still water. A wall-mounted fountain, feeding into a trough or bowl, can be bought as a total unit from a nursery centre and installed with little fuss. A vast range of pump-driven fountains, bubblers and multi-head jets is also available.

If your garden is made up of a series of 'rooms', you could build a more formal, raised reflecting pool, widening the stone or brick coping to accommodate flat cushions for sitting. Construct shelves to house a revolving display of flowering plants such as water iris.

In a country garden, water can bubble through a collection of large and small stones set in a gravelled area, as if a spring is welling up from beneath the ground. You could enhance a steeply sloping site with a waterfall and a series of rock pools. Consider the musicality of water: break the flow of water with stones to create different sound patterns. Ensure your pump has different flow rates so that you can adjust the force of any fountain.

And if all that sounds like too much trouble, even a simple stone basin, filled with water and resting on a rock or among the garden foliage, will attract birdlife and add serenity to a garden design.

Some designs

Personalised fountains like that in the delightful Anne's Garden at Mount Stewart in Northern Ireland, where water tinkles from bells held by one of the children of the house—all sculpted in bronze—and set on a bronze lily leaf, are beyond the means of most of us. And in the centre of Kalamunda, a small town in the hills behind Perth, in Western Australia, water weeps from the huge gumnuts that hang from a bronze eucalypt branch.

Less ambitious fountains are created by a single water jet erupting from a pool; you can set the pressure low for a more restrained, calming effect, or turn up the energy for greater impact. Water can bubble from an antique olive jar, or from a simple bowl or tub. A large basin can brim with water, perhaps spilling over, splashing onto a pebble bed—from where, of course, it can be recycled. Basin fountains can feature important antique lead statues of angels, or even frogs, spouting water.

Tip: Take care, when planning a water feature, that you are not about to excavate over power or phone lines. In consultation with your electrician, ensure that power for your pump and lights is accessible. And obviously, with all water features, the safety of children is the first consideration.

Tip: Ponds, which attract frogs, insects and birds, are not difficult to install. First, find your piece of flat land. Mark out a shape with a garden hose and cut around with a sharp spade to remove soil to about 1 m, leaving a shallow shelf around the perimeter. Spread a 50 mm layer of sand on the base; rake flat, checking with a spirit level. Add a protective sheet of polyester, and cover with heavy-duty flexible lining, leaving a good overlap. Weigh the edge down with stones, and trim. Cover the liner with sand and then another 50 mm of soil.

Fill the pond with water and, once the liner has settled, remove the stones. You can make a 'beach' of pebbles on one side to allow birds to wade; dapple the other edges with damp-loving plants. Alternatively, you can install a rigid pool unit, which is easily disguised with perimeter planting.

Fixing a leaking lake

At Ampelon, a large garden near Mildura, owner Margot Mills has seeded a rye lawn in the base of her generously proportioned lake. It has become thick and matted, preventing leakage.

Fixing a leaking pond

At Bruce Rosenberg's Southern Highlands garden Yarrawa, rotary hoeing of his leaking pond was followed by an application of the flocculent Sodium tripolyphosphate, which was tamped in with a Traxcavator. This did the trick and the porous, volcanic, basalt soil no longer leaks.

Wall-mounted fountains, of masks, lions' heads or cherubs—in marble, stone, bronze, painted concrete or even plastic—are perfect for the smallest of spaces and can be found, as a package, complete with the necessary pump, at good nurseries. Fountains, from bronze water birds and copper strelitzias to grand fountains that are affordable replicas of the famous Colebrookdale tiered extravaganzas of the nineteenth century, can be purchased 'ready to go'. For modern settings, there are many different self-contained water features on the market. Made from a wide range of materials, they are generally easy to install, affordable and low maintenance. But always ask to see a fountain or water feature in operation before you buy.

Among the most successful ideas for water features are those inspired by nature. Water flowing over a large, smooth rock set in a gravel garden, or in a shallow collection pool, strikes me as supremely restful and endlessly fascinating. The smooth rock creates different water patterns and reflections, the gravel or decorative stones below different sounds. The rock becomes the best form of garden art, appearing as if nature had placed it there.

In a warm-climate garden plant native orchids around a small rock pool, which might be lined with a large sheet of black rubber. Plant in orchid mix and set into the ground; strap other orchids to the rocks with black netting. Allow a waterfall to course over the rocks, fed from the irrigation system for the garden which might emanate from a main pump at another level.

Create a fountain from a 220 litre drum—cut in half and burnt to give it a rustic look—in which a submersible pump has been sunk.

Bog gardens

Damp areas in any garden are a godsend—particularly in these days of drought, climate change and water restrictions—and are an opportunity to use an exciting and evocative range of water-loving plants. I've coveted a boggy area ever since seeing, at a coastal garden in Cornwall in

1. Twin fishing lodges stand at the waterfall exit from a lake at Studley Royal.
2. Still in Yorkshire, the landscape at Harewood House was largely created by 'Capability' Brown in the late eighteenth century. Here, the cascades that feed from the 15 ha lake include water plants such as the giant rhubarb, *Gunnera manicata*.
3. A simple concrete birdbath also looks effective.
4. At Villa Reale, near Lucca, in Italy.

Studley Royal

At Studley Royal, an extraordinary landscape constructed in Yorkshire in the north of England in the early eighteenth century, water is central. This great garden was laid out along the valley of the river Skell by John Aislabie, who was Chancellor of the Exchequer from 1714 to 1718. Wooded hills rise steeply on either side and are set with banqueting houses, temples and grottoes. As you marvel at the massive expanses of water, guarded by great allegorical statues, and twin fishing lodges, you round a bend in the river to come upon what must be the ultimate backdrop—the ruins of the Cistercian Fountains Abbey, destroyed by Henry VIII in the Dissolution. There could surely be no greater example of bringing the landscape into your garden picture.

England, an enormous swathe of that prehistoric-looking plant *Gunnera manicata*, which, as if by some miracle, seems to appear from nowhere each spring to grow to many metres in height. This extraordinary stand was backed with more than a hectare of the brilliantly blue lace-cap Hydrangea 'Blue Wave': it was breathtaking, although you don't need a bog garden to successfully grow hydrangeas.

That most delicate of irises, *Iris ensata*—once known as *I. kaempferi*, loves damp feet. I have adored it since spending a year in Japan in the 1970s; my hosts often took me to gardens, often in the ancient city of Kyoto where great swathes of these irises,

with their flat, delicate flowers like resting butterflies, were revered and respected by the crowds.

If you don't have a naturally badly drained area in your garden, you can create your own bog garden by lining an area with black plastic.

Bog-loving plants

Louisana iris and *Iris pseudacorus* love wet feet and acid soil. A frost-tolerant choice is *Iris sibirica*, which enjoys damp soil but doesn't like standing in water (*see also* Irises).

The arum lily (*Zantedeschia childsiana*) loves damp soils. (And it loves Western Australia so much it has been declared a garden escape in that state.)

Meadowsweet, properly called *Filipendula ulmaria*, flowers in clouds of cream-coloured, almond-scented froth. I love it en masse, in ribbons and swathes. If planted in the distance it will draw your eye to the end of the garden.

Take care not to plant rampant species of papyrus such as *Cyperus papyrus* unless carefully contained in a strong pot.

Plant water lilies (*Nymphaea* spp.) in a container as, like most water plants, they spread very rapidly and can become a nuisance. They thrive in still ponds, so, if possible, avoid planting them in a

> **Tip:** Submerged plants oxygenate the water and prevent it from becoming cloudy; aquatic plants that collect, filter and dissolve nutrients are called macrophytes. In the tropics emergent plants such as taro (*Colocasia esculenta*) and its black-leaved cultivar *Colocasia esculenta* 'Fontanesii' are planted to clear the water; gardeners further south might use water iris.

Above: In Helen Dillon's Dublin garden.

Designer brief: Dean Herald

Many of the gardens that landscape designer Dean Herald creates celebrate life in the harbour city of Sydney. As many are gardens where space is limited, each item in the plan is required to work hard. Dining tables double as water features, planter boxes become seats, seats hide storage space.

When designing for clients, Herald's first task is to inquire about lifestyle. 'From there I can tailor a space that is suited to their needs and introduce a selection of plant material and other feature items that complement the space,' he explains.

Plant material is carefully chosen with long-term growth habits in mind. Favourites include formiums and dianellas, appreciated for their foliage, and the succulents for shape. Clumping bamboos are used for their beautifully patterned stems and soft, moving foliage and, with their upright growth, for screening.

Whether designing large or small gardens, Herald concentrates on achieving the correct scale. 'Size and proportion are critical to the end result,' he explains. 'I design items that are larger than needed.'

Central to his design for a recent 'Sydney in Bloom' exhibition was an outdoor dining area with an enviable cooking space and a stunning water-feature dining table made from structural steel which was cantilevered from a wall. Two layers of toughened glass were installed on steel arms and water was pumped between the layers to create a beautiful falling sheath. Stones placed, and occasionally rearranged, in the collection trough below contributed to the musicality of the falling water. 'Inspirational and humorous quotes were inscribed on the table as a conversation starter,' Herald explains, 'whilst also being a statement of the life we are privileged to enjoy in this country.'

feature with trickling water. Fertilise by wrapping the water lilies, with a handful of blood and bone, tightly in newspaper and pushing them down firmly into a snugly fitting pot. Over 12 months the fertiliser will be released as the newspaper breaks down. Or plant species like water lilies in compost in hessian-lined aquatic baskets: top with pebbles and place on the base of the pond.

Among the trees that love damp feet and boggy conditions is the fast-growing Italian alder (*Alnus cordata*). With my usual gift for exaggeration, I say 'Throw a bucket of water on them each time you look at them.' These are trees for large spaces, not for the city garden—where, if planted too close, they will quickly push over fences or walls.

Lighting

Lighting is essential to fully appreciate your carefully considered water feature as it will enable you to create a different mood by night. Subtle lighting is always best: choose several low-wattage lights rather than one floodlight. Use simple submersible spotlights and make sure they are not directed at the viewing point, but rather focused on a sculpted feature, on cascading water, up into the water jets, diffused onto foliage or softly washing a wall from beneath a fountain head.

POND HEALTH

Excessive light entering a pond introduces nutrients to the water, so that plants that float on the surface are best if you want to introduce fish to your pond—these plants provide shade, preventing algal bloom. Garden designer John Sullivan advises using shade cloth to imitate a complete plant cover if you don't want to purchase a large quantity of floating plants. 'Or look at some sort of filtration system that keeps the nutrients at a lower level so you don't get the algae growing. With algal bloom happening you will lose a lot of oxygen, so you will have less fish,' he explains.

Use a bubbler filter system to oxygenate the water and to counteract algal bloom. You can also help to keep your pond oxygenated by circulating water over rocks to ensure circulation.

Flower Arranging

'Everyone loves flowers,' says Janet Bourke, owner, with Nelson Pringle, of Bloomey's Florist in Sydney's Elizabeth Bay, renowned for more than two decades for stunning, up-to-the-minute flower arrangements. 'They employ all the senses,' she explains, when seeking to explain why an engagement with flowers can be so therapeutic. 'You can eat them, you can smell them, you can touch them, they are tactile, they are beautiful, they are sculptured, original, authentic; they have integrity.'

A large posy of flowers could be made up from your garden, creating what Janet and Nelson call 'garden pick with a little bit of lyricism'. Try combining peppermint geranium, creamy 'Erlicheer' narcissus, white roses and artemisia. 'It's much more romantic, more natural, [to have] a little bit of air in between and not always the symmetrical perfect posie.' The Bloomey's team call these arrangements 'at home' flowers, room accessory flowers, rather than the 'the main event' flowers for which they are so applauded. They suit interiors from traditional to contemporary to 'shabby chic'.

Janet and Nelson's arrangements are anything but predictable. The pair admit to becoming bored quickly, so they make a determined effort to constantly experiment. 'Look at new colours, clash the things,' they advise. They re-think materials and combinations and watch trends in interior design, conscious that colours and textures are often dictated by the fabric and fashion houses.

An economical way of keeping a vase of florist flowers full is to add foliage from your own garden: pittosporum, prunus or stems of magnolia. 'Find your rangy bits,' advises Janet. 'That piece there is balancing that piece there. Relax it off,' she says, teaming the old-fashioned succulent, *Kalanchoe tubiflora,* with a bunch of stiff-stemmed apricot roses, deep maroon calla lilies, anthurium leaves and artemisia.

The rosarian David Ruston, in demand around the world for his lectures and flower-arranging demonstrations, agrees that a loose, natural look is popular at present. 'I use only flowers I grow myself, no soft glasshouse flowers,' he says. The roses most popular at present, says David, are the apricots, peaches, browns and hot pinks. He nominates the David Austin pale pink 'Clair Rose' as one of the most requested. 'It's got beautiful foliage; it outlasts everything else. People are looking for long-lasting quality.'

The work of another Sydney floral artist, Tracy Deep, is inspired by landscapes, particularly the coastline—especially untouched, undeveloped places. 'Nature feeds your soul. Tiny bird prints in the sand. And the rocks: watch their patterns, shapes, textures and colours,' she muses. And she loves masses of the one beautiful thing.

Tracy selects elements that provide an architectural focus and that have a long life: perhaps sections of wild bamboo that will be hung against a white wall, every movement recorded in changing shadow patterns. Starting off a fresh green, the bamboo will slowly age. Another work, *Desert,* is a shimmering work of dusty pinks, reds and pale ochres, all created with swirls of the discarded caps that protected the flower of the eucalypt and set against a coconut fibre-base. Her aim is to suggest to the viewer a fresh way of observing

Previous page: The gorgeous, rich tones of sweet peas.

nature. She advises creating a table of living sculptures from unusual vegetables that relied upon texture and colour.

Or choose leaves, dried and curled, a branch mis-shapen, gumnuts slowly splitting to reveal the blossom beneath, the flower that is less than perfect. Her works each focus on one element. She might promote the bizarre flower heads of the Banksia men (*Banksia serrata*), or the red stems of *Acer senkaki* might be central to a piece. Horizontal branches have a softer, more natural movement. Bromeliads, with their hot-pink, jelly-bean flowers, appeal.

To create such arrangements Tracy advises we look for strong shapes and textures—and keep it simple. She maintains that the material directs her aesthetic. 'In a piece I will choose one predominant colour,' she explains. 'The textures will bring out that colour more. Look at the shapes. Cluster things.' She searches out the patterns in nature. 'Look up through the branches of a tree to the sky.' She suggests looking deeply into a pod, for instance. 'It looks like a piece of architecture. I feed off that, really.'

Me, I like to tone colours and to use just one species of flower: I find that leads more easily to an arrangement that looks artistic and stylish! Think pots of sweet peas in different shades of pink, cerise and red, or a bucket of lilac in all its glorious tones of lilac, purple and purplish-pink. And there is perhaps nothing lovelier than a vase of David Austin roses: with their romantic, old-fashioned, blowsy form and gentle colours, a selection of several different varieties look perfect together. 'Yellow Charles Austin', peach 'Evelyn', 'Jayne Austin' and apricot 'Abraham Derby' all tone together beautifully. I love to use my collection of china—vases, cache pots, huge cups bought in French markets, sauce jugs and even teapots that can no longer be used for tea—to hold my flowers.

For Janet and Nelson, anything that holds water is a container. 'Please re-think containers,' says Janet. Use an old jam tin, a silver chaffing dish no longer in use, a teapot that is chipped, a brandy balloon with a camellia or rose head in it at every setting on the dinner table. 'In the country, on Christmas Day, take a gumboot, fill it with christmas bush and use it to hold open the swing door,' she says. 'Why not? Have fun with it.'

Why not, indeed.

To achieve the most from your flowers

Pick flowers early in the morning, before the day warms up; or late in the afternoon, when the sun is no longer on the plants. I always strip off leaves in the garden as I pick and plunge the cut stems straight into a waiting vase of water. Re-cut a stem after you take the flowers home from the florist, or after you have walked around the garden.

Rinse out vases in bleach and change water daily. And never re-use your oasis. Bacteria will lodge in an oasis and diminish flower life.

Dahlias: Cut blooms in the cool of the early morning, with as many buds as possible to allow for days of flowers. Dip cut stalks in hot water and then plunge into cool water to prevent drooping.

Hellebores: If you have plenty of time on your hands, hellebores will not hang their heads if you pinprick the base of each flower. The blooms are charming in old-fashioned posies or table arrangements. Or pick flowers with about 10 mm stems to float in a bowl to appreciate the delicate and diverse markings on their upturned faces.

Hydrangeas: Cut stems on a slant to assist in water uptake; fill the laundry sink and immerse the whole thing, head and all, in water. And like violets, hydrangeas absorb water through their petals, so extend the flowering life of the bloom in the vase by misting.

Roses: Leave foliage and thorns off below the water; on above the water. David Ruston advises cutting of a little of the stem of roses after they are picked and placing them in tepid to warm water, in a cool place, for a few hours before you arrange them. This prevents the bud opening too soon.

Plants and Places that Inspire

PART SEVEN

CHINA

China

Did you know that China is home to one-eighth of the world's plants? And that it's from this huge and diverse country that many of the ornamental plants we know so well hail? Many of the plants essential to the daily lives of Australians—tea, oranges, peaches—come from China, where plants have been cultivated for many thousands of years.

The western provinces of Yunnan and Sichuan, home to more than half of China's 31,000 species, have provided many of these garden plants. Yunnan, which translates as 'south of colourful clouds', is a mountainous province in south-west China bordering Vietnam, Laos and Myanmar. High mountains and deep valleys result in a great complexity of landforms and a vastly diverse climate—from tropical to subtropical, temperate and frigid temperature zones. And, happily for us, the species from the lower-altitude areas, where the climate is tropical to subtropical to temperate, have been perfectly content in Australian gardens.

Many Chinese plants are used medicinally and many more are imbued with special significance and meaning. Bamboo is considered hollow, depicting humility and gentleness. The Chinese assign a flower to every month and every season of the year. Plum blossom, pine and bamboo traditionally signify the mood of winter—plum blossom because it flowers, on bare branches, in the dark depths of winter; pine because of its longevity; and bamboo because of its evergreen state in the winter and because it bends in the wind to rise again when the storm has abated. Camellia is one of the flowers that suggests spring; the chrysanthemum represents autumn; and the lotus is associated with summer.

Tracing the route by which plants such as the Tea rose, peony, daphne, viburnum, philadelphus and magnolia arrived in Australia from China makes a fascinating study, just as the movement of plants into China from states close by, and from Manchuria, Korea and Japan to the north, reflect the sometimes turbulent history of the region. In his book *The Garden Plants of China*, Australian botanist Peter Valder relates how plants arrived from the Middle East, probably through Iran, and how Portuguese and Spanish ships, particularly after the sixteenth century, called at ports in Guangdong and Fujian provinces, bringing with them species from the Americas. No doubt decorative Chinese plants, along with tea, spices and other commodities, found their way onto these ships for the return journey. The greatest movement of plants from China occurred after the last decades of the eighteenth century, largely through the efforts of plant hunters, most from the United Kingdom.

Many of the botanical treasures that had reached Great Britain arrived in the colony of New South Wales with John Macarthur, who brought plants, seeds and cuttings with him on his return after both of his periods of exile, first returning from England in late 1804 on his own ship, the *Argo*. From 1807 the Macarthurs enjoyed a direct contact in Canton, Walter Stevenson Davidson, who undoubtedly sent many precious botanical treasures to Parramatta. On his second return from England in March 1817, on board the *Lord Eldon*, Macarthur brought vines, olives, and fruit trees as well as camellias, roses and peonies, all protected in a greenhouse that he had had specially built on the deck.

Opposite: *Magnolia delavayi*. *Previous page*: The soft grey leaves of *Stachys lanata*.

A hotspot

The Hengduan Mountain Range in south-central China is one of the unique biological regions of the world. Lying at the eastern end of the Himalayas between the Tibetan plateau and the central plain of China, these spectacular ridges, which run from north to south, are home to many endangered animal species, including the giant panda and the red panda, the snow leopard and the golden monkey.

The Hengduan also contains the most diverse vascular plant flora of any region of comparable size in the temperate zone. Identified as one of 25 biodiversity 'hotspots' on earth, this vast region, covering an area of 500,000 square kilometres, contains over 12,000 species of vascular plants, with almost 3500 endemic species and at least 20 endemic genera.

The term *hotspot*, coined by British ecologist Norman Myers, is used to designate areas that are home to a high number of endemic species—those whose distribution is limited to a single region—and that are under severe threat of destruction because of human activities. These threatened regions cover less than 2 per cent of the earth's land but are home to more than 65 per cent of all vascular plant species. Twenty-five designated hotspots remain, most of them in the tropics; others are found in the Hengduan Mountains, south-western Australia, California Floristic Province, central Chile and the Cape Province of South Africa.

Source: Virginia Morell, *China's Hengduan Mountains*, National Geographic, April 2002.

In addition, a vigorous intellectual discourse, and plant exchange, was taking place between the leading families in the colony, those interested in botany and scientific advancement, the colonial government, and other sites of learning, particularly botanic gardens, around the world. These included Lachlan Macquarie (governor 1810–21), who founded the botanic gardens in Sydney in 1816, and Alexander Macleay (1767–1848), who arrived in January 1826 to take up the post of Colonial Secretary under Governor Darling. Macleay's 2.2 ha gardens at Elizabeth Bay House, which took 10 years and more than 20 men employed full-time to create, became the repository for species from around the globe, including China.

Many thousands of the beautiful plants native to China are now an essential part of many Australian gardens and of gardens around the globe. Many more are not so well known.

❤ My favourites

• *Boehmeria nivea*, commonly called China grass, is a member of the nettle family. But don't panic: it doesn't have the stinging hairs that cause so much discomfort. A gentle breeze reveals the elegant silvery underside to the leaves, and the flowers are long tassels.

Tip: In China *Boehmeria nivea* was once used for making paper money—its stems are still harvested for their strong white fibre, supposedly the toughest and most silky of all known vegetative fibres. Consequently, it is also used to produce rope and fabric.

• *Metapanax delavayi* bears pale-green to white blooms in spring and summer and grows to about 5 m. This elegant evergreen shrub, a member of the Araliaceae family, is native to the Yunnan province.

Opposite: In the southern China plant collection at the Royal Botanic Gardens, Melbourne.

Where to find them

There is a fascinating collection of southern China species at the Royal Botanic Gardens, Melbourne: all are plants significant to the Chinese—for fibre, medicine or festivals. Rather than being arranged as a traditional Chinese garden, the collection is spread throughout the gardens: paths meander through, in traditional style, as evil spirits always travel in straight lines.

In the gardens you'll find the highly aromatic *Acorus gramineus*, which, with its liriope-like flower spike, is traditionally used as matting, and hung on doors to keep troubles away. Also in the collection is the rare *Amorphophallus yunnanensis* with its somewhat bizarre, hooded flower, which has been grown by the Chinese for food for 1500 years. The leaves and the tubers, which are rich in starch and amino acids, are important as food and medicine for ethnic groups in various parts of China. With their feathery leaves, they look particularly effective planted with Solomon's Seal.

The giant hyssop (*Agastache rugosa*) is used in traditional Chinese medicine as an antibacterial herb that stimulates the digestive system, and is employed in treating the common cold and abdominal pain. The collection also holds the beautiful heavenly bamboo (*Nandina domestica*), easy to grow in most parts of Australia, adding delicacy, as well as a lacy form and height, to any garden. Every part of this plant, a symbol for good fortune and endurance, is used in Chinese medicine.

Camptotheca acuminata, similar in appearance to the beautiful, autumn-colouring tupelo (*Nyssa sylvatica*) is used in subtropical and warm temperate parts of China as a street tree. Work is continuing to harness its reputed anti-cancer properties. And the Royal Botanic Gardens' Western Lawn is home to an excellent specimen of the conifer *Taiwania cryptomerioides* native to Yunnan, Burma and Taiwan, which bears stunning green cones stained a deep red.

- *Osmanthus delavayi* is gloriously scented and one of around 30 species of the genus, most of which are native to the Himalayas, China and Japan. It reaches about 2 m and its arching branches are decorated throughout summer with profuse bunches of tubular white flowers.
- *Reineckea carnea*, a one-species genus from the lily family, is a non-invasive evergreen, rhizomatous perennial that grows to 25 cm. It is rather like the liriope or mondo grass but has broader, glossy, lime-green leaves and bears spikes of scented pink flowers in summer. A ground cover or edging plant, it will handle dry shade; in Chinese it is called 'ji xiang cao', which means lucky grass.
- Species of the sweet box (*Sarcococca* spp.), from the Buxaceae, or box, family, are evergreen shrubs with glossy, pointed leaves, growing to 2 m. In late autumn or early winter they produce highly scented, tiny, starry blooms which are followed by ornamental fruits. *Sarcococca confusa* bears black berries in autumn and winter, and *S. ruscifolia*, native to central China, has scarlet berries. They are hardy shrubs for shade, can withstand periods of drought, and do not require clipping to look good 365 days of the year! *S. ruscifolia* var. *chinensis*, with finer leaves and a daintier arching form, was collected by Bob Cherry and Terry Smyth in 1994, on Jizu Shan (Chicken Foot Mountain), in Yunnan province.
- The Chinese wax shrub, or Chinese allspice (*Sinocalycanthus chinensis*), discovered in the late 1980s west of Shanghai, is rare in the wild, surviving only on a few wooded slopes in eastern China. This large, deciduous shrub, with its gorgeous blooms like those of the gordonia—and closely related to species in the genus *Calycanthus*, the allspices of North America—has slightly aromatic wood and striking, white, waxy flowers, produced in spring.
- *Sorbaria* spp., false spirea, is a small genus of deciduous shrubs and trees native to eastern Asia, belonging to the rose family. They have soft, pinnate foliage with serrated leaflets, and blooms with fluffy white panicles. *S. kirilowii*, which is native to Jong Jai Go in the northern Sichuan province (according to some, the most beautiful place in the world), bears fluffy cream flowers from among bright-green, pinnate leaves. Take care: false spireas can sucker.
- *Taiwania cryptomerioides* var. *flousiana* is a conifer rare in the wild and rare in cultivation. (It can be found at Bob Cherry's Paradise Plants.) Related to *Cryptomeria*, *Taiwania* is a genus of just a few species from China and Taiwan.

Above: *Camellia japonica* 'Thomsonii'

Japanese Gardens

Green is a colour, isn't it? It's perhaps the best colour of all—surely the most calming, the most restful. Nowhere is the value of green more evident than in Japanese gardens, where it is central to the peaceful atmosphere that is so keenly sought.

The underlying principles of Japanese garden design derive from the observation of nature. A garden may be the literal interpretation, in miniature, of a landscape, or a symbolic recreation of it through the placement of just three rocks; the garden becomes an allegorical journey from the mountains to the sea.

Japanese gardens fall into several different categories, among them the tea garden and the stroll garden—restrained, quiet and tasteful. Katsura, in the old capital of Kyoto, is the greatest example of a stroll garden: the visitor travels through hills and mountains, crosses bridges and lakes and visits tea houses. Temple gardens—of which the best example is perhaps Kyoto's Silver Pavilion, Jishoji, once the retirement villa of an emperor—were intended to be more striking, many built by shoguns as a display of wealth and power. Another style of temple garden comprises dry stones and employs pebbles raked into patterns, with rocks carefully placed to represent islands; famous among this style are Ryoanji and Daisenin, both in Kyoto.

Ken Lamb, a director of the International Association of Japanese Gardeners, has been creating Japanese-style gardens for private homes and corporate clients in Australia for more than 20 years. His work is exemplified at his Imperial Gardens, in Sydney's Terrey Hills, from where he runs his landscape design and supply business.

Designed as a small stroll garden, Imperial Gardens demonstrates several different styles. Traditional plants are used: there are the small-leaved kurume azaleas, severely clipped into domes to reflect hillsides. Ken explains that they are always in a state of transition, finally growing to join together to form rolling hills. When smaller, they represent low hills; as you climb the stone stairs to the highest part of the garden, they have grown to represent mountains and clouds. And, contrary to popular belief, flowers are important in Japanese gardens as they reflect the changing of the seasons.

Also central to the garden are the Japanese black pine (*Pinus thunbergii*) and the Japanese red pine (*Pinus densiflora*), pruned and shaped over two decades to create layers of elegant, horizontal limbs that drape long needles over the lake. The outstretched arms of a Japanese weeping maple, with its fine, filigreed leaves, are reflected in the water, and slow-growing Buddhist pines (*Podocarpus macrophyllus*) are also pruned into clouds. *Osmanthus fragrans*, native to Japan, is greatly prized for its scent, along with gardenias and daphne.

Ground covers include *Juniperus procumbens*, backed with a swathe of architectural cycads. Winding paths set with stepping stones, carefully placed to temper the pace of your journey, are softened with kidney weed, *Dichondra micrantha*. Paths that flank a watercourse and lake are edged with small-leaved Korean box (*Buxus microphylla* var. *koreana*) and mondo grass.

A special rake is created specifically for each garden that Ken Lamb designs; at Imperial

Previous page: The rich hue of a Japanese maple.

Gardens the gravel is raked each morning to reflect the weather and the change of the seasons. 'If it is very windy, as it often is in August in Sydney, we can create a swirling pattern,' he explains. On inclement days a raindrop pattern features ripples moving out from a central point. Rocks are chosen for colour, shape and character, and with each garden in mind. 'Even in the field, when you are choosing, you know exactly where that rock will go in a garden.'

Scale is also important in the creation of a restful garden, with a balance of one-third active (that is, planted) space and two-thirds passive space considered ideal to ensure a sense of peacefulness and calm. The relationship of the garden to its environment is always considered: borrowed scenery—*shakkei* (perhaps trees in the background in a neighbouring garden)—will make the garden appear larger than it is.

Among Ken Lamb's favourite gardens in Japan is the popular Daisenin, a small garden with dramatic rock work, built in the fifteenth century at the Daitokuji Temple. 'The abbot of the temple, Soen Oseki, is a very good ambassador for Zen teaching and Japanese garden teaching. He brings into Japanese gardening the relationship with the Buddhist teaching tradition and he brings it to life for the visitors,' Ken explains. 'It contains all the elements of mountain and sea within an area that is only 3 m deep by 10 long.'

An hour south of Melbourne, a feeling of peace descends upon you as you enter the studio garden of potter Paul Davis. You walk through a copse of pines, casting dark, cool, scented shadows, to emerge into the dappled light of his Japanese-style garden. A teacher of ceramics for 30 years, Paul studied during 1995 with the great Japanese potter Saka Koraizaemon, whose family has worked for over 900 years in the artisan town of Hagi in the southern prefecture of Yamaguchi. The garden around Paul's studio was designed in collaboration with Melbourne's Mark Denavon, who trained in Japan as a landscape gardener. 'I wanted people who came to the property to have some sense of respect for what the workshop is about,' he says. 'In Japan when you visit a potter it is a whole experience. You would walk through a beautiful garden; you are brought a cup of tea. You talk to the artist, and you go into the showroom to look at the work, and then, if the artist feels comfortable about your presence, he will invite you into the workshop.'

In Paul Davis's garden each element has a particular meaning. Set off to one side of the garden are three large rocks representing mountains. Euonymus are clipped to form a rolling hedge alongside the solid stone steps; some 300 small-leaved 'Kirin' azaleas rise behind like clouds. The garden is designed to change constantly throughout the year. Once the mass of pink azaleas has flowered, the rhododendrons that surround the water basin bloom. Then the michelias are covered in their goblet-like, scented flowers. In autumn, the maples provide a mass of colour: in winter all the leaves drop and the maples are pruned for a sculptured look. And so, the garden stays in balance.

Guests are invited to sit on the expansive wooden sitting deck at the long redgum table, looking out at the garden across the mossy lawn to the perimeter, where several beech trees are left to grow to their natural size. There are also several varieties of clumping, non-invasive bamboo.

Each item in this spiritual garden may be symbolic in its own right, but the total gives a sense of seamless peace and tranquillity.

Planting and care

To create an antiqued look throughout Paul Davis's garden, moss was removed from the shaded grass areas and placed in a vitamiser. A growth hormone was added and the mixture watered onto the rocks.

Paul insists that the maintenance of a Japanese garden is easy, providing you tend it for one or two hours each day. 'When I first go down to the workshop each morning I walk around the garden and water, and weed.'

FOLIAGE GARDENS

Foliage Gardens

Foliage gardens—to my mind the most soothing of all types of garden—rely upon what is evocatively known, in the gardener's lexicon, as 'tapestry'. Tapestry might refer to a hedge made up of several different deciduous species that colours like an intricately woven Persian carpet in autumn before dropping its leaves to reveal a fascinating winter skeleton. Or it might refer to the pattern of green upon cool green: it might refer to the markings on many foliage plants, or to the combinations of their textures and shapes.

The importance of foliage—its shape, texture and shade of green—is often overlooked when the design of a garden is being considered. While all plants, en masse, create a pleasing pattern of form and texture, there are some that lend themselves particularly well to forming a lush, decorative and detailed tapestry carpet.

A garden that concentrates on foliage and its tones of green is sure to be among the most restful, and successful. Think of the peacefulness of Japanese gardens, which concentrate on green. It is the most restful colour on the eyes; the human iris, which closes when it sees bright colours and opens when it encounters dark, is not obliged to work hard when the eye looks at deep green.

If a trouble-free garden appeals, one well clothed with foliage is likely to provide the most satisfaction. Of course, following the first rule of good garden design, it is crucial to buy enough of each plant: more is more in this case, and the discipline to select many of just a few species is still essential for success.

My top 20

COOL CLIMATE

Alchemilla

This genus, which goes by the common name of lady's mantle, includes around 300 species of herbaceous perennials most prized for their attractive palmate, lime-green leaf. Some come from alpine regions of Australia and New Zealand, but the most widely cultivated, with the best foliage, is *Alchemilla mollis*, which has tiny yellow flowers in cool climates, and masses out to cover the ground.

Arisaemas

I love the aroids—more often known as cobra lilies—which, despite the mysterious spathe-like form of their flowers, are not just for the plant collector. Part of the Arum family, there are around 150 species in the genus, most useful for their foliage, but also prized for their weird flowers. Tolerant of frost, they are mostly found in temperate climates, in woodland conditions, where their flowers push through humus-rich, damp soil. With their deep green leaves, usually made up of three leaflets, they are a perfect companion for the hellebores. Among my favourites is the very desirable *Arisaema candidissimum*, from China, which flowers in a delicate shell pink with white stripes. It multiplies easily, which is also why I love it. The exquisite *A. sikokianum*, native to Japan, is trouble free, with a 15 cm-long purple-brown flower spathe that has fascinating green and cream stripes.

Astilbes

Astilbes are wonderful plants for cool-climate gardens if you can supply plenty of water. They

Opposite: Hostas: the perfect foliage plant. Here, 'June'.

are perfect when massing out by the side of a lake or at the edges of a bog garden, where plentiful, frothy, plume-like flowers will emerge from lush foliage.

Cimicifuga

Now answering to the much less evocative name of *Actaea*, this is a plant just made to be married, mixed and matched with other foliage colours and textures. Part of the Ranunculaceae family and native to the northern hemisphere, the plants have beautiful, complex, toothed leaves, the perfect accompaniment for astilbes, for example. *Actaea simplex* 'Brunette' provides interest for months throughout summer to finish with a big finale of striking spires of cream to pink starry flowers held on stiff maroon stems, like elegant blush-pink pokers. Providing an end-of-summer display that will distract attention from areas of the garden that are past their prime, they would look gorgeous towering above *Hydrangea macrophylla* blooms that have been allowed to remain on the bush to fade to the colours of old silk.

Geraniums

There would hardly be a genus more useful to tapestry gardens than *Geranium* spp., the species geranium, which all mass out quickly to create a beautiful carpet in warm temperate, or cool temperate to cold climates. Succumb to the blue and purple tones with a mass of the never-fail *Geranium* × *magnificum*, which is covered for months with small, true-blue flowers. (*See also* Geraniums.)

Hosta

Plantain lilies, native to Japan and China and introduced to the West from the Far East in the late eighteenth century, are among the most effective of all foliage plants, and the easiest to grow; you could create a tranquil garden using almost no other genus. The Empress Josephine was one of the first European gardeners to fall in love with hostas, growing them at her house, Malmaison, just outside Paris. I wonder if she too noticed how the rain or dew collects in the leaves and creates an imaginary jewel.

Hostas love shade and, while they are not too thirsty, they are certainly not drought tolerant. The leaves of the hosta come in all sizes and almost all shapes and in a range of colours from bright lime-green to yellow (perfect for illuminating dark areas), through to greens and blues, to be laced into a border or to grace a courtyard. Then there are the fancy ones with splashes of colour in varying arrangements—to match with, and add dash and genius to, other plantings.

Among the largest is *Hosta plantaginea* 'Grandiflora', which grows to 60 cm tall and has clear green, heart-shaped leaves and huge white trumpet flowers with a scent of gardenia.

Hostas come in all tones of green, from the deep green of *H. ventricosa* to the mid-green of *H. fortunei*, the blue-green of *H. tokudama* and the yellow-green of the cultivar *H. fortunei* 'Aurea'. *H. undulata* has cream-coloured leaves edged in green, while 'Antioch' has green leaves with a creamy white edge.

Background *H.* 'GroundMaster' with the larger leaved *H. fortunei* 'Aureomarginata'; both are edged in yellow. Team them with *H. fortunei* var. *albopicta* (syn. 'Aureomaculata'), where the placement of the colours is reversed, with the yellow splashed down the middle of the leaf. 'Great Expectations' has large leaves with gold centres and a thin green edge.

H. 'Sum and Substance' and 'Gold Standard' are bright yellow and would look irresistible planted in front of a backbone of *Euphorbia characias* subsp. *wulfenii*. 'June' is yellow-green splashed with an intense blue. *H.* 'Honeybells', a miniature, reaches just 25 cm.

The spires of hosta flowers, ranging from whites to creams and from lilac to purple, are, to my mind, incidental—simply a lovely bonus; it's the foliage that captivates. Team them with plantings of shrubs, or use them as ground covers; or select several species for a beautiful green carpet.

Hostas enjoy deep, rich, moist but well-drained soil: grow them also in pots so that they can be given extra, saved water in summer. Divide them in spring, when new growth is appearing. Lift out the clump and divide, or simply cut off wedges with a sharp knife. They are caviar to snails: once

1. A tapestry of rich foliage in Pat and Judy Bowley's garden.
2. Fascinating blooms are a bonus to excellent foliage when you plant arisaemas: here *Arisaema candidissimum*.
3. A matrix of large groups of a few species is most effective: here the strident markings on a begonia.

these creatures find your hostas, the damage remains for the entire season. Surround with gravel to deter snails and slugs. Try a ring of copper (from plumbing suppliers) placed around hostas as a kind deterrent. Or put snail pellets in plastic milk bottles or cartons to attract snails but keep household animals and wildlife safe.

Hydrangeas

Hydrangeas, of course—particularly species like the oak-leaved hydrangea (*Hydrangea quercifolia*)—are prized for their foliage, which takes on rich russet tones towards autumn. Back them with cimicifuga and tetrapanax, and mass-plant hostas at their feet to create the mood and feel of a rich tapestry carpet (*see also* Shade).

Tellima

Ideal for woodland gardens, *Tellima grandiflora*, native to North America, forms a ground cover with palmate leaves, similar to both astilbe and cimicifuga. These plants flower with cream to lemon blooms in spring. 'Rubra' is a stunning, burgundy-leaved cultivar with pink flowers.

Tetrapanax

The rice-paper plant (*Tetrapanax papyrifer*), with its enormous leaf, which is grey underneath, and its bold sprays of cream flowers in summer, mixes wonderfully with shrubs like *Hydrangea paniculata* 'Grandiflora' and with other cool-climate foliage plants discussed here. Prune it hard each year to keep it fresh and at 2 m, instead of its natural 5 m.

Trilliums

Woodland plants like the trillium—which is, in fact, a member of the lily family—make an early start in a deciduous forest to catch the light and the sun before the canopy comes to life and creates a play of dappled shadow. Native to the forests of North America, Japan and northern Asia, these elegant, three-leaved foliage plants flower with upright funnels which remind me of a pirouetting ballerina with an overly generous, ruffed skirt. The easiest to grow of the 30-odd species is *Trillium grandiflorum*, which will reward you with a mass of white flowers in spring if you can provide it with a cool climate and the rich environment of the forest floor.

WARM CLIMATE

The zebra plant (*Aphelandra squarrosa*) is a stunning foliage species for subtropical and tropical climates or for cultivating as indoor plants. 'Louisae' is a well-known cultivar, with arresting cream veins and midrib.

For tropical and subtropical climates, the flamboyantly marked gold dust plant (*Aucuba* spp.) will light up dark corners. From east Asia, this genus contains just three species; they love shade and are valued for their mottled and speckled leaves and their berries in autumn.

Calatheas

The calatheas, a large genus of some 300 species from the West Indies and Central and South America, with their endlessly interesting and intricate markings, are wonderful en masse but do love humidity, so they struggle south of Coffs Harbour. They also like plenty of water. The lilac-coloured *Calathea burle-marxii*, named in honour of the great Brazilian designer Roberto Burle Marx, is a dwarf species with stunning pale lilac flowers somewhat like torches. *Calathea lutea*, reaching some 3 m, has paddle-shaped leaves, perfect for creating a lush tropical look around a swimming pool. *C. zebrina* and *C. veitchiana* are small-growing species with stunning cream markings.

Clerodendrum

The colourful *Clerodendrum quadriloculare* is a striking, colourful foliage plant for warm climates. Some have foliage with burgundy undersides; others are splashed in cream, yellow and pink, while others are rimmed in different colours. Clip them into a hedge and team them with hibiscus and tropical, flowering trees and shrubs. Its cousin, the less outrageous *C. bungei*, flowers with clusters of scented pink blossom from large, heart-shaped, mid-green leaves. They like full sun or dappled light.

Opposite: Hostas form a carpet of green at the McLaughlin Gardens, in the North American state of Maine.

Cycads

Stories told by Peter Heirbloom, who owns Eudlo Cycad Gardens in the hinterland behind Noosa, of photographing and studying the prehistoric cycads in some of the world's more remote and dangerous countries bring to mind the feats of the intrepid plant hunters and botanists of the last century who braved unthinkable conditions to give us the thousands of plants we now take for granted. (And did you know that Queen Hatshepsut of Egypt was the first ruler documented to have sent out plant hunters?)

During his travels through Africa, Heirbloom made friends with the Swahili-speaking pygmies of Zaire (now properly called the Democratic Republic of Congo), ignoring their poisoned arrows; he cut through unexplored jungles, and dealt with truculent officials at border crossings. In Mozambique, he went in search of the obscure *Encephalartos turneri*; in South Africa, the endangered *E. lebomboensis*.

In South Africa, where all cycads in the wild are microchipped, you need a permit just to move a cycad, even in your own garden. Peter Heirbloom has 80 species available, some the only examples for sale in the world. All come with permits.

There is a place for cycads in the home garden: they mix well with other plants but are also good used massed as a single species. I have seen the Japanese sago cycad (*Cycas revoluta*) used to great effect as an edge to a garden in Port Douglas that seemed to step off into the impossibly blue Coral Sea. And for those who have indigenous gardens, there are many Australian species, native to areas from Far North Queensland to the south coast of New South Wales: some, however, are tricky to grow. Cycads are tough but they do like protection from hot sun—and don't let them dry out in summer.

Plectranthus

Plectranthus is a large genus of some 350 species of frost-tender shrubs, perennials and annuals that are native to South Africa, Australia and Asia. They are most useful for their foliage. They like dappled light and good soil; some can become weedy, often suckering much too easily. The vigorous *Plectranthus argentatus* will sucker wherever you leave a cutting—although a light frost would keep it in check. The blue to grey, soft, felty, oval-shaped leaves are very attractive.

COMMUNITY GARDENS

Community Gardens

There are not too many thrills greater than that of serving friends and loved ones with a meal prepared from produce you have grown. The joy derived from the planning, the preparation of the soil and the nurturing of the vegetables, herbs and fruits, and the pleasure of knowing that what you are using is pure and free of chemicals, far outweigh the expenditure of time.

However, while clever things can be done with small spaces, the production of enough food for a family can take a little more land than the average backyard will allow. Community gardens, long the tradition in Europe and the United States, are one answer. Many of us have observed, from the windows of moving trains, hectares of small plots in the outer suburbs of cities like Rome and Paris. In Boston, skirting the 'Emerald Necklace'—a series of green spaces that the nineteenth-century landscape architect Frederick Law Olmsted (1822–1903) created as an essential lung for the city—is a kilometre of community gardens that provides more than just apples and oranges, fragrance and flowers.

Some of the plots are smart and well designed; some a bit of a hotchpotch, a jumble of decorative and edible species. Many seem to be a home away from home for their owners, with small sheds replete with the tools of tea making, and with chairs and umbrellas ready for when the garden work is done. Regardless of style, you would probably agree that the social interaction and the sense of sharing and cooperation most often engendered by these schemes are as important as what is raised from the soil.

A sense of belonging and essential communication with friends and neighbours is central to the community garden ethos. Throughout Australia, community gardens are gaining popularity, increasingly recognised by councils as playing an important role in bringing together people of different backgrounds, all united in their love of gardening. Australia is now a country of many diverse cultures, beliefs and religions: the exchange of plants can overcome many a language gap, just as the sharing of food can bridge the widest communication chasm.

The Australian Community Gardens Network (www.communitygarden.org), started in 1996, is one of several informal organisations linking people interested in community gardening across Australia. Through a website and national community harvest newsletter, the network aims to promote the benefits of community gardening and urban agriculture in cities of changing work, economic and social environments, and to make practical information available Australia-wide.

Opposite: Community gardens: green spaces amidst Boston's city skyscrapers.
Above: A place for community consultation: more than flowers and fruit.

A community garden thrives between city apartment blocks.

CERES

Just 5 km from Melbourne's GPO is a community garden that will make many of us who raise our vegetables in pots on the balcony very envious. It is difficult to believe that the Centre for Education and Research in Environmental Strategies (CERES—also the name of the Roman goddess of agriculture), an organic garden, farm and park, was a tip just 25 years ago.

Today the 4 ha site that once featured car bodies and old boots, and which was leased to the community by Brunswick Council in 1982, boasts terraced food gardens, an orchard of 62 fruit and nut trees and 15 varieties of vines. Further, there is a wood-fired oven producing 300 loaves of bread each week and a farm of Rhode Island red chooks, ducks, geese, Dexter cows, goats, pigs and bees. Vegetable plots can be rented there for $30 a week and the farm and garden produce is sold at the CERES Saturday and Wednesday markets, which are held from 9 am to 1 pm.

The vegetable and herb gardens are arranged in raised rectangular beds, terraced down the hillside, and were built by 13 women and two men over a six-month period as part of the work-for-the-dole scheme. With companion planting, intensive hands-on work and the help of ducks foraging for snails among the plants, the garden is completely biodynamic and is under certification with the National Association for Sustainable Agriculture (NASA).

One of the purposes of CERES is to demonstrate that organics and biodynamics do not have to be untidy: that a garden can look attractive while remaining sustainable.

Rotation planting is practised at CERES. Root vegetables are rotated with leaf vegetables and flowers; a green manure crop such as white clover or lupins is then grown, slashed and worked into the soil; and, finally, the rotation process starts again.

In summer the orchard of peaches, nectarines, apples, apricots and pears—different varieties are planted for maximum pollination— all but disappears beneath a sea of pumpkin vines, which provides a protective ground cover for the soil. No non-organic sprays are used. A biodynamic tree paste—a mixture of cow manure, chamomile, dandelion, tansy and clay—is applied to the trunks of the fruit trees over winter. This feeds the outer layer during the cold months, and any pests hiding inside the bark are suffocated.

One of the mottos at CERES is 'Healthy soil, healthy plants', and a homemade, biodynamic compost is regularly incorporated into the soil. Herbal preparations are added, and cow manure to heat and break down the composition is another essential ingredient.

Also important is the worm farm, which is made from a built-up bed of sleepers filled with layers of newspaper or straw between kitchen and garden scraps. The whole area is sealed off with thick layers of straw to enable the worms to process the waste material in complete darkness.

All water used is collected and purified via an aquaculture grey-water system. A series of old baths arranged to cascade down the sloping garden collects and filters water from the roofs of the buildings. Water plants in the baths take up the heavy metals and process them, and the purified water ends up in a pond at the bottom of the garden. There are frogs and fish in that pond, and the water has been tested by the CSIRO and deemed fit for human consumption.

If all this seems daunting, beyond the abilities of even the best-intentioned gardener, consider attending one of CERES's workshops. You won't regret it!

VEGETABLE GARDENING

Vegetable Gardening

It is interesting that, at the beginning of the twenty-first century, although we Australians may no longer be churning our own butter or growing hops for our beer, we are increasingly producing our own food—growing vegetables and keeping chooks. This is, perhaps, a response to an increasingly busy, urbanised and motorised lifestyle, reflecting a need to connect with the soil and an increasing understanding of the benefits of sustainable living.

While it is most often easier to buy your 'veg' from the fruit shop—and even, at times, probably more economical—it's just not the same as picking and serving your own produce. And the size of your garden need not be a deterrent to producing your own fruit and vegetables.

There are vegetables suitable for planting in every season of the year, even in the depths of winter. Some vegies are planted in autumn for winter or early spring harvesting, and many more go into the ground when it has warmed, in spring. In Sydney you might plant summer-maturing vegetables in the first week of September. In Brisbane planting is much earlier, of course, and in Tasmania friends are still covering their tomatoes, to protect them against frost, each night up until Christmas Day. After planting, success in the vegie garden comes from doing a little, often.

All the senses—sight, sound, taste, smell and touch—are fully engaged in a vegetable garden, from the crunch of terracotta, slate or gravel paths to the scent of crushed leaves, the perfumes of the flowers you might weave into the design and the visual excitement of their brilliant colours. A vegetable garden is high maintenance but also high reward. Experience it.

A great deal has been written about vegetable gardens, about their design, about the rotation of crops and the benefits of raising green manure. It all sounds complicated but I am going to reduce vegetable gardening to its most basic and most simple.

First, draw up a list of what you would like to grow: the vegies you can't live without. Then get out pencils, a ruler, a rubber and some sheets of inexpensive butchers paper. Sketch out a rough plan, not worrying about scale.

If you have the space available for a good-sized vegie plot, create a main area in which you will grow the three groups of vegetables—brassicas, root vegetables and other crops—each in their own section. If you are following the rules you will want to rotate each crop, each year, so any soil-borne diseases unique to one group of plants won't multiply to become a problem. You might divide your large section into four, both for symmetry and, more importantly, to allow you to grow a green manure crop each year that you will turn into the soil to add essential nutrients and structure (*see* Soil).

Next draw in an area for your perennial, or permanent, vegetables or fruit—for things like asparagus or artichokes or strawberries; these might be grown in rectangular beds around the perimeter of the vegetable garden. You might create a boundary fence of trellises of raspberries: just be prepared to share them with the birds. Step-over hedges—or walls—will support decorative and delicious espaliers of pears or apples (*see also* Fruit).

If you have room, a hedge—perhaps edible or tapestry—or a picket fence makes your potager a destination, a place to be entered with anticipation and excitement, and helps to protect it from marauding wildlife. Along one side a high trellis,

Previous page: Poultry: good for the vegie garden.

perhaps for privacy or for wind protection, might be covered with an old scented red rose to add to the cooking pot of strawberry jam.

You may want to include a central fruit cage—as decorative as budget will allow—in which to grow soft berry fruits. Or a central iron arbour, covered in a thornless climbing rose or in espaliered fruit trees, looks fantastic in the centre of the garden.

Look at the chapter on hardscaping and on edges and hedges to plan the borders of each section. Or you might 'finish' beds with herbs like basil or chives, or with strawberries, as colonial gardeners did, before box hedging became affordable. But remember to think about ease of maintenance; you don't want to create huge amounts of additional work to which you will become a slave.

Beds that are about a metre wide and edged in a material such as aged sleepers, to stand on when harvesting (or weeding) without compressing soil and damaging precious produce, help with maintenance. (And sleepers allow you to build your bed up without digging, if you prefer.) And if you wish to be kind to your back, grow vegetables in raised beds.

Mulch well, of course, to prevent weeds and retain moisture. One gardener applies a decorative 'lattice' of folded newspaper—not too thickly—around the plants; you could add a mulch of straw on top of this for camouflage.

Now that you have roughly sketched these thoughts and designs on scrap or butchers paper, you can draw up your vegetable garden to scale, allowing your imagination and design talent free rein. You can even create overlays of tracing paper to show the vegetable garden and its sections burgeoning with produce in the different seasons, in the manner of the eighteenth-century designer Humphry Repton when he created his Red Books to demonstrate to clients the possible appearance of their landscape after he had woven his magic.

❧ Planting and care

Plant your crops progressively through the summer to ensure a constant supply of your favourite vegetables, including tomatoes, lettuces, eggplant and capsicums. For instance, plant one punnet of tomatoes and then, a month later, plant another.

Plant winter vegetables—cauliflowers, broccoli, Brussels sprouts, spinach, bok choy, beetroot—just before Easter when the soil is still warm but, hopefully, the hot days are over.

Good news for all of us who have no luck with seeds are commercially produced seed strips, which are perfect for all who hanker for a French potager but who can't draw a straight line. The seeds are impregnated into a composting tape: you just lay out the tape in a 1 cm deep groove, cover with soil and keep moist. They may need some thinning if too many germinate. Available in this form are Red Rubin Radish, Baby Carrot, Beetroot Detroit Red—the most popular line in Queensland—and Spring Onion Straight Leaf, the gardener's choice in Western Australia.

Slugs, snails, possums and rodents are an international problem: you might need to be creative and clever, employing a variety of ruses to deceive the heartbreaking predators. Beer traps—an open plastic container sunk into the ground and filled with beer—will attract slugs. You might raise seedlings in cut-off and upturned plastic bottles until they are big enough to be unattractive to nibbling mice (*see also* Pests and Diseases).

A potager that is a happy mix of herbs, vegetables, flowers and foliage is an art and a joy. Espalier 'Jonathon' and 'Granny Smith' apples against a garage wall to provide an impressive, decorative and productive backdrop. Divide the space into several sections with gravel or brick paths which also surround a central bed housing standard roses or a fruit tree. Clipped hedges of English box—or of lavender—can edge each section to encase your selection. Each year plant lettuce, bok choy, beans, basil, carrots, leeks and eggplant: add borage and love-in-the-mist to flower blue throughout much of the year and to attract the bees to assist in pollination. English spinach and ruby chard might jostle with wallflowers and with extensive plantings of herbs. If the sections are large enough, add height with tripods, perhaps painted in brilliant colours, supporting peas and beans; artichokes and well-staked tomatoes will add a second layer of height.

Gravetye Manor

Each morning, when you wake at Gravetye Manor, the glorious house and gardens created by William Robinson in England's south that are today a country house hotel, the water you pour from the jug on your bedside table will have been drawn from the spring that has been in use since a well was sunk in the garden in 1598, the year the house was built. Today it is in the midst of the 1 ha walled vegetable garden, resplendent with produce in high summer. Laid out in 1898, the vegetable garden today supplies the wood-panelled restaurant with 70 per cent of its needs.

The ancient well provides limitless spring water, which undergoes a rigorous process of screening through ultraviolet light and multiple chalk filters to ensure its purity. Unlike most Victorian vegetable gardens, which are square, this south-facing garden is elliptical, to provide even light and, nineteenth-century gardeners thought, to deny pests and diseases corners in which to multiply. Kiwifruit, grapes, currants and teaberries are espaliered against the stone walls, which are set on foundations that sink 2.5 m below the surface.

Laid out in the style of a potager, with flowers for the house planted between the rows of vegetables and edgings of herbs and strawberries, the garden is three degrees warmer than any other section of the grounds.

Bamboo tripods that support sweet peas, sugar-snap peas, broad beans and French climbing beans form a spine down several sections of the garden. There are gooseberries, white, black and redcurrants, and the raspberry 'Autumn Bliss', to be made into jams for breakfast and for afternoon tea.

Beds of lilies, irises and yarrow (*Achillea* spp.) are interspersed with a variety of potatoes, including 'Ratte', 'Charlotte', 'Pink Fir Apple' and 'Desiree', which are rotated each year. Beds of fennel, with their clouds of lacy green-and-burgundy foliage, are planted with species gladioli and with purple-headed alliums, and are edged with thyme, purple basil and nasturtiums. Wedge-shaped beds house countless varieties of lettuce, edged with spicy rocket and highlighted with horseradish, celeriac, and with blue-flowering borage, also loved by the bees.

There is an ancient, very productive, asparagus bed, and another of globe artichokes for early summer. A section is devoted to rhubarb, which is forced in the dark microclimate created by ceramic Cretan jars; the rhubarb grows quickly, becoming sweet and deeply coloured.

William Robinson's peach house (a hothouse for raising peach trees) was restored four years ago at a cost of £20,000. The sole peach harvested in the first year—surely the most valuable in Britain— was presented to former owner Peter Herbert in a silk-lined box. The following year, 1500 were harvested.

The seasons experienced in this glorious vegetable garden are reflected in the menus offered in the restaurant. Produce is used when nature intended it to be used: the English asparagus is on the menu when it is in season in late spring, globe artichokes in early summer. In July the zucchinis will flower, ready to be filled with salmon or lobster mousse.

Watercress soup (serves 4)

6 bunches watercress (stalks removed)

200 g potatoes (boil until the potatoes are totally cooked)

1 L water

50 ml cream

Method

Place a large pan on the stove and let it get very hot. Toss the watercress in the pan with a little oil. Sauté very quickly until it is a deep green colour. Pour over the boiling potato and its water. Cook for two minutes. Take off the heat and liquidise immediately. Pass into a bowl over iced water. Season whilst still hot and leave to chill. (From Mark Raffan, Executive Chef & Co-Proprietor, Gravetye Manor)

Note: I have sometimes substituted six leeks for the watercress. Finely slice the white sections of the leeks, wash well, then sauté till clear. Continue as above.

Traditional summer pudding

1 loaf white bread

500 g mixed summer berries

2 leaves gelatine

100 g sugar

Method

Prepare the fruits by removing all the stalks. Gently wash and drain.

Put the fruit into a saucepan with the sugar and warm very gently. Avoid stirring the mixture as the fruit will break up.

Melt the gelatine and very gently mix with the warm fruit.

Slice the bread approximately ½ cm thick and line individual pudding moulds with it.

Then press in fruit with plenty of the juice, as it will all soak into the bread.

Seal the top with another piece of bread and place onto a tray. Place another tray across the top of the puddings and add a heavy weight.

The puddings must be left for at least 24 hours before being turned out.

Simply serve the pudding with clotted cream and summer berry coulis.

(From Mark Raffan, Executive Chef & Co-Proprietor, Gravetye Manor)

Above left and right: In the elliptical walled vegetable garden at Gravetye Manor.

An easy-care vegie garden

In a suburban garden in New Zealand, 13 cement-edged squares, brightly painted in purple, are set into a courtyard of pebbles. Each square is packed with brilliantly coloured vegetables. Lettuces and herbs grow most of the year; cabbages are planted in late winter, tomatoes in October. Marigolds, planted to keep garden pests at bay, are also valued for their happy colours.

At one end of this space is a shallow pool, its clear water reflecting the luminous Paua (abalone) shells with which it is lined. Each year the squares are repainted in a colour selected from the Paua shells. The owner insists that hers is a very easy garden in which the gardener can just potter—wandering in the early morning with a cup of tea and perhaps weeding one or two squares. Cabbage, beetroot, rainbow chard and colourful lettuces are all rotated among the squares.

1. Small squares allow for easy-care vegetable gardening in Auckland.
2. Water is an important part of this city vegetable garden.

If space is further limited, think about a strip garden along one end of, perhaps, a swimming pool. You will be surprised at just how much you can produce in a small space.

Asparagus and goat's cheese tart

This is an easy tart as an entrée, or a main course if served with a salad of rocket and other greens and a fresh tomato and basil salad. Make sure your shortcrust pastry is very fine.

225 g shortcrust or puff pastry (I prefer shortcrust)

3 tbsp Reggiano parmesan cheese, finely grated

1 tbsp olive oil

110 g goat's cheese

One bunch asparagus, with the tough ends trimmed off

Method

Roll out pastry onto a sheet of baking paper, to a rectangle into which the asparagus will fit side by side with a border of pastry left.

Fry the asparagus briefly in the olive oil to coat; cool and arrange on the pastry. Scatter crumbled goat's cheese over, cover with clingwrap and chill for at least 30 minutes (up to five hours). Lift, together with the baking paper, onto a heated baking tray and bake in a preheated 220 degree oven until the tart is browned and, if puff pastry is used, puffed up. Serve warm.

My dozen

ASPARAGUS

I must confess that I have always found the growing and harvesting of this vegetable slightly confusing, and the fact that I have visited several country gardens that boast century-old asparagus beds only adds to its mystery and intrigue. I am told that asparagus (*Asparagus officinalis*) is a heavy feeder and loves the sun, although Peter Bennett, in *Organic Gardening*, writes, 'Edible asparagus is hardy and will do well in almost any soil.' Plant crowns in early winter in a spot where they will receive perfect drainage and can remain undisturbed for decades.

The spears that we all love so much—*just* poached and served with butter, pepper and salt and a shaving of best-quality parmesan—are the emerging shoots of the ferny leaves. Therefore, don't be too greedy too soon: it is important to allow your asparagus to grow fully in the first year, after which you should leave some spears to develop the feathery heads to support the following year's fruit. They grow best in cool and cold climates, where they will die down over winter. Grow two plants for each consumer in your family.

BEETROOT

Rich, sweet and coloured burgundy, beetroot are among the most versatile, but perhaps the most under-utilised, of vegetables. Boil them or roast them and slice or dice them. Toss them with cubes of goat's cheese, then add a few of the best fresh walnuts and a drizzle of olive oil. Delicious, nutritious and different.

Beetroot, which can be planted in any month, is also among the easiest of vegetables to grow, and, with its green and burgundy leaves, looks extremely decorative in the potager. The leaves, which are high in iron and in vitamin A, can be used in salads, or poached as a green vegetable and served with a knob of cold butter, salt, pepper and a grating of nutmeg. The beetroots themselves can be wrapped in foil and baked in a medium oven: I then wear rubber gloves to wipe off the skin, which comes away easily.

Grow them, and harvest them, quickly: you want them sweet, not old and woody!

They should be ready to pull 25 to 35 days from planting as seedlings. They demand good drainage and plenty of sunshine (*see also* Soil for a discussion of boron deficiency, which can sometimes cause a problem with beetroot).

BROCCOLI

Well-grown broccoli, picked when they have just formed tightly packed sweet, mid-green heads, are extremely nutritious, and delicious chopped into smaller pieces and tossed and lightly sautéed

An exquisite potager

There is a potager—of the sort you might expect to see only in the most luxurious of garden books—at Kennerton Green on the Southern Highlands of New South Wales. It is reminiscent of a bountiful Eden, where, dreamlike, everything flowers together. Lime-green lettuces, which tone perfectly with yellow, fringed 'Hamilton' tulips for spring, are planted in June. Cerise-coloured lettuces are at their best when the pink tulips are in bloom. Winter vegetables at Kennerton Green include kale, leeks, cabbages and parsnips. The climbing purple-podded pea and the purple runner bean are planted in early September. Summer vegetables go out once all hint of frost has passed and the soil is warming up. Preparation of the soil is perhaps the most important part of vegie gardening, and at Kennerton Green the sandy soil is bulked out with a compost of leaves, some lawn clippings and blood and bone. The soil is dug over to a depth of two spades.

The exquisite potager at Kennerton Green, on the Southern Highlands of New South Wales.

in olive oil, with a knob of butter, a finely chopped chilli, crushed garlic. Jazz it all up with some anchovy fillets added at the last minute.

Classed as a leaf vegetable, broccoli is planted in late summer for early winter harvesting; small heads will continue to appear for several months if you don't allow flowers to form. You will pull them out by the end of August to prepare the bed for summer vegetables.

CAPSICUM (CAPSICUM ANNUUM)

From the Solanaceae family, the capsicum, or bell pepper, is rich in vitamin C. I grow capsicums because they look vibrant in the vegie garden, but also because the large yellow variety looks wonderful baked in a slow oven and sliced, then tossed with baked beetroot. Together with the chilli (*Capsicum frutescens*)—among the hottest of which is the 'Jalapeno' variety—they are native to South America, and it is thought that Christopher Columbus took seeds back to Spain and Portugal. Capsicum was grown in domestic gardens in Mexico more than 2000 years ago.

Plant in warm soil, in early to mid-summer, after which they will bear fruit quickly and for a long period. Stake capsicums as you would eggplants and tomatoes.

CARROTS

Small and sweet, carrots are delicious, but all too often they are woody and even bitter.

Rich, friable clay loams are the best environment, and, as with most vegetables—indeed, with most plants—good drainage is the key. Carrots are usually sown as seed and in a mix of sand, so you can see where you are planting (the seeds are dark in colour). Sow seed in almost every month of the year, once the soil has warmed up. Thin seedlings after about 10 days so that those remaining can achieve a decent size. You'll grow good quantities in a small space and you will be pulling them right through winter.

EGGPLANT

Native to India, eggplant, or aubergines (*Solanum melongena*), are ripe when the skin is glossy and purple: don't let them become overripe as the seeds will be bitter. A tropical fruit, they should be planted when risk of frost is over; they like flood irrigation, so plant in east–west troughs, each plant half a metre apart.

GARLIC

I know it is cheap enough to buy at the green-grocer, but, because I like to bake garlic whole, I prefer to grow my own as it is a little milder. Garlic can be easily grown by taking a clove and pushing it into the soil in winter, traditionally on the shortest day of the year. Use a soluble fertiliser though spring and summer. Harvest in late summer when the leaves die down: hang bulbs in an airy position.

ONIONS

Weave these luscious, decorative plants, with their rich green tops, through flower borders; they don't need to be confined to the potager, although, arranged in straight rows, or as an edging plant, they also look smart there. You can harvest them progressively as they grow and use the chopped tops in salads before they become too thick. Peter Bennett advises that they are a time- and ground-consuming crop, taking up space for about 10 months of the year. Plant in a weed-free environment, as they don't like competition. Sow—not too deep—when the ground is still warm in autumn so that they will grow through winter for final harvesting in the warm months. But again, try growing them in polystyrene boxes which can be moved out of sight if you have visitors!

POTATOES

Hundreds of varieties of this delicious vegetable are available, but until recently most Australians had tried but a few. There are white-fleshed varieties, including 'Pontiac', yellow-fleshed ('Kipfler', 'Desiree' and 'Nicola') and 'Toolangi Delight', which has purple skin and white flesh. Experiment with the different types for your soil and climate conditions, and for different culinary uses.

Potatoes are full of nutrients—vitamins C and B, folate, niacin, iodine, thiamine and more—and, if you resist the butter, few kilojoules. Fertilise tuber vegetables, including potatoes and kumera,

1. In a large potager in a country garden an iron arbour provides a central focus.
2. Soft fruits are espaliered on a warm brick wall.
3. In the author's small city vegetable garden.

with a potassium-rich product. Nitrogen-rich fertilisers will produce leaves at the expense of tubers.

In warm climates sow potatoes in autumn and winter for spring harvest. In cold, frost-prone areas, plant your potatoes from early spring to summer. You can grow them in poly boxes on your balcony in a sunny spot. Add compost, old manure and some slow-release fertiliser to a good potting mix. Plant seed potatoes, bought from your nursery, at a depth of about 10 cm; as the leaves emerge, add more compost and straw to ensure the plant develops tubers up the stem.

The leaves will flower and die back, telling you your spuds are ready to harvest. Harvest new potatoes a month after the flowers die, old potatoes when the leaves have died.

PUMPKINS

Plant the seeds of these easy-growing but delicious and decorative vegetables when the soil is still warm but any risk of frost has passed. They will happily help themselves to spare space and bare ground, and will flower in mid-summer, then develop those large golden globes. Harvest some when the first frost hits and causes the stems to wither. Leave the remainder of the vine to die off, then harvest the rest of the crop. Cube them, roast them or make a delicious soup which is served in the whole pumpkin.

Spaghetti squash is a pumpkin-like vine that basks in the sun and can be used as a low-kilojoule base for sauces, and as an alternative to pasta for those who are gluten intolerant. The spaghetti squash (*Curcubita pepo*) is a long, seed-bearing squash that is high in many vitamins and minerals. Plant in all but the coldest months and cultivate as you would pumpkin.

SALAD GREENS

What could be easier than planting punnets of those 'cut and come again' lettuce combinations, allowing you to go out into the garden each evening to cut fresh lettuce for your daily salad. As with all salad greens, grow them—and harvest them—quickly so that you can enjoy sweet young leaves.

Leaf or cos lettuces are sweeter and more flavoursome than the traditional head lettuce. 'Buttercrunch' is one of the best for the home gardener with limited space. Plant with rocket, and chicory—which will add spice to your leaf salad—for your health. Allow the rocket to make itself at home, so that it just goes on and on.

TOMATOES

Many of you will have visited Heronswood, at Dromana, on Victoria's Mornington Peninsula, and marvelled at its wonderful vegetable garden. Owned by Clive and Penny Blazey, who have long been advocates of preserving old varieties of vegetables, the garden is also home to Diggers Seeds, through which Australian gardeners have access to heirloom varieties. 'Seed banks are terribly important in preserving old varieties,' says Clive. 'If we don't preserve the old, our best garden varieties will disappear. Everyone presumes the new varieties are much better, but we've done tests in every single vegetable category and found the older pre-hybrid varieties are better in yield, earliness and length of harvest, and flavour, than the hybrids.'

Clive nominates six varieties of tomato (*Lycopersicon esculentum*), like the sweet pepper originating in South America, as his all-time favourites. First is the orange and yellow flecked 'Tigerella', which yields 20 kg of fruit per plant: it fruits early and late, and continuously. The winner of the taste test is 'Tommy Toe'; it yields 10 kilos per plant. Also recommended are 'Amish Paste' and 'Green Zebra', good for storing. 'Broad Ripple Yellow Currant' is currant-size and prolific; for something very different try 'Black Krim'.

Most tomatoes need staking and will benefit from the removal of the side shoots to encourage a stronger-growing plant. In colder climates tomatoes will fruit until January; in Perth, Sydney and Brisbane, the last harvest would be during April or May.

Companion plantings

Companion plantings can be beneficial to the general health of herb, fruit and vegetable gardens. Foxgloves are grown as an old-fashioned perennial companion plant for apples and pears. Basil is planted with tomatoes, along with marigolds, which are also said to help in the prevention of white fly. Sage, rosemary and the mints are often sown in rose gardens.

Tip: I can't think of a more delicious lunch than a plate of home-grown tomatoes, sliced and dressed, with a half or a quarter of creamy, fresh buffalo mozzarella and a leaf of fresh basil. The quickest grind of salt and pepper and a drizzle of the best olive oil finishes it perfectly. The first meal my daughter and I had on a recent trip to Rome—her first to that gorgeous city—was just this, at an outdoor restaurant in the Piazza Navona. The square may have been humming with tourists, but that simple dish was the real thing!

Mazes, Parterres and Knot Gardens

In November 1997, after some five years in the planning, a garden of extraordinary vision and ambition opened to the public on Victoria's Mornington Peninsula. Then called the Arthur's Seat Maze, and since renamed the Enchanted Maze, the brainchild of Michael Savage and his medical practitioner wife Sally, it comprises 20 different themed 'rooms' and living puzzles, all created within some 6 ha of land.

Mazes

A maze, also commonly called a labyrinth, is a series of paths and passages created by a complex arrangement of hedges or walls. For thousands of years the maze symbolised entertainment, mystery and paths to wisdom. The concept is thought to have derived from the ancient mythology of the minotaur who terrorised maidens in the winding tunnels beneath the Palace of Knossos, seat of King Minos. In the middle ages labyrinths and mazes signified the difficult path Christians were often forced to follow, and represented a journey to the Holy Land. At first mazes were marked out in masonry or stone—with one of the earliest known mazes being recorded at Woodstock, in England, where, in the twelfth century, King Henry II courted Rosamund. Later they were delineated with rock or turf, and then with hedges and other plant material.

Today mazes are created either in box (*Buxus* spp.), from hedges of roses or from mown sections of turf. Sometimes they are created from patterns planted in corn, and kept only for a season.

At the Enchanted Maze a traditional cypress hedge maze, covering 1000 square metres, is just one of the beautifully maintained garden 'rooms'. There is also a turf maze, and a paving maze that is unicursal: it is 450 m long and keeps winding back on itself. A Maize Maze has been created annually over the past decade, with a different design each year, and remains in place from late February to the end of April.

There is a peaceful 'Japanese' garden of stone and water and a fragrant garden displaying roses and lavenders, as well as shrubs such as mock orange, *Murraya paniculata*. An African savannah garden demonstrates most effectively the use of different grasses and ground covers; there are poas and festucas as well as the sea daisy, *Erigeron karvinskianus*. At the bottom of the garden is the children's area, complete with chooks, a playhouse and a fairy garden. There is also a series of six-minute mazes, including a hay bale maze, a tyre maze and a rope maze.

Planting and care

In the past mazes were traditionally created of cypress or yew (*see* Conifers) although today *Buxus* spp. and roses are also employed. The traditional maze at the Enchanted Maze is of × *Cupressocyparis leylandii* 'Leighton Green'.

At 'Le Labyrinthe des Roses' plants were nursed, when young, with a carefully laid out irrigation system fed from a spring on the property which has flowed continuously since Roman times, even through the driest years. Watering is now needed only occasionally and a thick mulch of gravel keeps the roots cool, even in the midst of summer, when temperatures can reach almost 40 degrees Celsius. One handful of a slow-release fertiliser in pellet form is given each year in early spring to each plant. Serious pruning takes place—with the hedge trimmer—after flowering in autumn or spring.

Opposite: This effective turf maze at Wychwood is simply mown grass.

The ladies' garden

At Broughton Castle, the fourteenth-century moated and fortified manor house set in the charming village of Saye and Sele in Oxfordshire, and home to Lord and Lady Sele, the exquisite knot garden, known as 'the ladies' garden', is, again, best viewed from above—from the roof and parapets of the castle. High walls of soft grey Cotswold stone, clothed in large-flowered hybrid clematis and old-fashioned roses, enclose this secluded 'garden room'. Open windows built into the walls allow glimpses to the exuberant tapestry-like planting, tempting the visitor from outside. Within the ladies' garden, a parterre in the shape of the *fleur de lis* (installed after World War II on the advice of the American garden designer Lanning Roper, who made England his home) is edged in clipped box. Voluptuous plantings of old-fashioned roses and perennials spill over the hedges onto the gravel paths. The 'Rose de Rescht', a very double, scented old Damask rose with purple-red flowers and purple-grey foliage, creates a focal point in the centre of the arrangement.

Above: The exquisite 'ladies' garden' at Broughton Castle, in England.

Meadow Gardens

The meadow—the space between a formal garden and the woodland beyond—has long been part of large English gardens. Meadow gardens, also known as wild gardens, were popularised by the renowned gardener and writer William Robinson in the late nineteenth century. It was he who also advocated throwing out bulbs from a bucket, as if tossing out potatoes, to achieve a natural look. In this spirit, meadow gardening appears very easy, but the wildflower meadow is, in fact, among the most difficult of garden styles, despite its appearance of nonchalance.

The Fellow's Garden, part of St John's College in Cambridge, is a wildflower meadow of martagon lilies, designed by Lancelot 'Capability' Brown in 1773. In Oxford the famous Magdalen Meadow is a sea of snake's head fritillaries (*Fritillaria meleagris*) in May. At Newnham College, Cambridge, the covetable wild meadow is packed with nerines and crocus for autumn, with *Iris stylosa* for winter and with daffodils, tulips, fritillaries and bluebells for spring. These are followed in early summer by species gladioli, by the frothy, cream heads of Queen Anne's lace, and by Dutch iris. At Studley Royal in Yorkshire there is a vast expanse of the true primula (*Primula veris*) growing among the soft grasses in front of the folly, the banqueting house.

It can be done in Australia, but some compromises must be made—unless you are prepared to re-plant annually, to employ a team of gardeners to weed and hold our grasses at bay and, as at the village of Cricklade in Wiltshire, to hire a guard to watch over your fritillaries in spring. Our tough and rampant grasses and long growing season make this form of gardening difficult if not heartbreaking, rather than maintenance free. And the everlasting daisies that form a finely detailed tapestry of pinks, whites, yellows and blues after winter rains in Western Australia need very specific conditions that are difficult to replicate for the home gardener.

As one who made several attempts at this supposed low-maintenance style of gardening, I am living proof that gardeners are always optimistic. In a large country garden I planted a wildflower meadow of half a hectare. After repeated sowing of large and extravagant packets of wildflower meadow seed mix, I learnt to achieve a pleasing, natural effect with grasses and spring bulbs.

Anyone who has tried to cultivate a traditional wildflower meadow would no doubt agree with Horace Walpole who, more than two centuries ago, said of the designer William Kent, 'His genius is so great that people will think it is the work of nature.'

Planting and care

If you've nominated an area for a meadow, the first job—in late winter to early spring—is to spray off, and then rotary hoe, the area to be planted out. Scatter your selection of grass and flower seed, along with the bulbs. For an easy and pleasing Australian meadow garden, plant smaller growing bulbs on the edges and near the central path, taller towards the middle, and plant a variety of early, mid-season and late-flowering bulbs. Bluebells, which some gardeners eschew as weeds, will multiply wonderfully and flower till the end of November. Invasive plants, like Chinese

Opposite: Everlasting daisies bloom in the Western Australian desert after good winter rains.

Tip: If you are serious about more traditional meadow flowers you will paint each emerging weed with a brush dipped in a glyphosate poison, perhaps using a cut-down plastic drink bottle as an additional guard to ensure you don't get a drop on any of your treasures. Or you can ignore all but the worst weeds, and proclaim those remaining to be rare and special grasses.

1. At Studley Royal, in England's north, the real primrose, *Primula vernis*, flowers in front of the ancient banqueting hall.
2. After winter rains, the everlasting daisies form a carpet at the Coal Seam Gully, a few hours drive north of Perth.
3. At Rowandale in the Southern Highlands of New South Wales, a swooping, mown path leads through the wildflower meadow towards a walk of apples.
4. The meadow at Sissinghurst plays host to fruit trees.

The father of wildflower gardening

Some readers will know that the Elizabethan house Gravetye Manor was home to William Robinson (1838–1935) from 1885 until he died, well into his nineties. At the centre of many of England's best gardens—Sissinghurst, High Beeches, Nymans, Great Dixter and The Manor House at Upton Grey—Gravetye provides the perfect focus for a horticultural pilgrimage.

Some 40 years ago the property was restored by Peter Herbert to create a marvellous country house hotel. Herbert has now retired, having sold to two key staff, general manager Andrew Russell and executive chef Mark Raffan, and today the gardens comprise 18 ha, with a further 500 ha managed by the forestry commission.

It doesn't matter which month you choose for your visit to Gravetye, as Robinson planned the garden to be memorable in each season. In April the magnolias unfurl and bluebells and fritillaries push through the cold earth. In May the scent of the azaleas, and of wisteria, is overwhelming and in high summer the borders burst with luscious roses, fat delphiniums and voluptuous peonies. And it is in summer that Robinson's famous wild garden, which rolls down to the lakes and the forest, blooming with cowslips, wild orchids and buttercups, is at its very best.

1. An easy-care meadow of spring bulbs.
2. A effective expanse of spring daffodils provides a no-fuss meadow.

forget-me-knot or comfrey, that you wouldn't put near your fragile treasures, nor in your detailed borders, come into their own in this situation. You can also plant kangaroo paw, gaura, yarrow (*Achillea millefolium*—so tough you can't kill it) and even, on the edge of your path, *Fritillaria meleagris*, one of the genus that will grow easily in this country, at least in the cool temperate to cold areas.

Swoop through the centre of the meadow on the ride-on mower to create a looping, wide path to lead the visitor from the very maintained sec-tion of the garden through the meadow, towards another section of the garden—perhaps to an orchard or a pear walk. A carefully placed, scaled-up piece of sculpture might lead your eye from one area to the next. (A large, smooth apple, carved in local stone, seems perfect if your mown path leads towards an apple orchard.)

In early summer, after the bulbs have died down, rough-cut the meadow with the mower blades as high as possible. Then a mow once a month will do—until Easter, when the bulbs will again emerge.

ROSE GARDENS

Rose Gardens

Who does not adore roses? The form of the blooms, either fragile and elegant or overblown and voluptuous, their myriad colours, whether delicate or rich, and their different fragrances all contribute to ensuring that roses remain greatly loved plants of extraordinary complexity.

There are countless marvellous rose gardens around Australia that showcase the story of the rose; here are a dozen or so that are among the best.

New South Wales

BALADONGA

There surely could be no greater treat for a garden tourist than to stay in the midst of a glorious garden. There is the joy of waking up with the early-morning mists and dew to the sounds and scents of an unfamiliar garden, the thrill of discovering new plants used in new ways, and the comfort of garden chat with another like-minded soul. This is your chance to enjoy the fruits of someone else's hard labour and creative talent—with relief, perhaps, that you need feel no guilt in avoiding the spade or lawnmower. The garden homestay is an easy choice over the motel on the highway where the lorries roar past at four in the morning.

You don't have to be a garden enthusiast, though, to check into Rossie and Gayford Thompson's Baladonga homestay, set within a working 1620 ha farm in the Coolah district of western New South Wales, close to the Mudgee vineyards and the attractions of the Warrumbungle Ranges.

Roses feature in this garden, designed over the past two decades to complement the 1880s sandstone homestead. In summer, when the paddocks are dry and the wheat is a golden, aestivating sheet ready to be harvested, the roses are bursting with health and vigour. If you arrive at the back door, as is often the country custom, you enter a lush garden through a gate set into a fence awash with the clotted-cream blooms of *Rosa* 'Buff Beauty', and with the coconut-ice colours of 'Pierre de Ronsard' bred by the French rosarian Alain Meilland (who also raised the rose 'Peace', so named to mark the end of World War II).

Close by is the tennis court, covered in the climbing rose 'Souvenir de Mme Léonie Viennot'. With her apricot-pink blooms bearing just a hint of lemon, she tones beautifully with the new-green leaves of deciduous trees, such as the nearby silver birch. 'We mostly have pink roses,' says Rossie, 'with a splash of yellow, some white and a couple of red. I think you have to be careful not to overdo red.' Colour combinations are clever at Baladonga. A golden ash teams with the purple leaves of a berberis; the yellow climbing Tea rose 'Lady Hillingdon', with her distinctive red stems, along with swathes of pale yellow iris, adds extra drama. Golden oregano accentuates the cerise rose 'Complicata', which directs the eye inexorably towards the deep burgundy colours of a prunus, set against the emerald-green lawn that unfolds from the red-roofed homestead.

One of the first projects that the Thompsons undertook when they arrived at Baladonga in 1983 was the restoration of the courtyard around which the house is built. In its centre a pond and fountain now provide the cooling sound of falling water. The Bourbon rose 'Souvenir de la Malmaison' happily covers the sunny courtyard wall. With her quartered, old-fashioned blooms, her

Previous page: The clear lemon tones of the climbing rose 'Mermaid'.

scent and the fact that she keeps on flowering well into the winter, she is a favourite.

Victoria

SEVEN CREEKS ESTATE

Imagine this: the year is 1827 and a woman is walking, unchaperoned, through the villages of Saxony and Prussia, two young boys in tow. She is selecting the finest specimens of Saxon merino sheep from local farms, paying £30 for each and attaching to each a sealed collar. Sometimes her papers are seized by suspicious authorities; she fears for her safety on many occasions.

The woman is Eliza Forlonge, the wife of a Glasgow wine merchant. She is purchasing sheep to enable her to emigrate, with her sons, to the colony of New South Wales, where she has been told the weather will be kinder to their health.

Eliza is to make several more, similar, journeys to Saxony. She sells the first flock at profit, and despatches her 18-year-old son William to Australia with the second, while she returns to Saxony for more. William arrives in Tasmania in 1831, where he founds the Kenilworth merino stud. Those bloodlines now extend through many of the great studs producing superfine merino wool, both in Australia and around the world.

David Austin

David Austin roses are bred to be repeat flowering, disease resistant and with the rich scent of the old-fashioned roses. Austin's first rose, in 1961, was 'Constance Spry', commemorating the English florist of the same name.

Reunited in Tasmania, Eliza and William left the island colony to settle, eventually, at Seven Creeks Estate at Euroa in north-east Victoria, their holdings soon extending to tens of thousands of hectares.

Today Seven Creeks Estate is owned by Dennis and Margaret Marks and is the home of the great race horse Ustinov, the progeny of another famous bloodline, Mr Prospector, and son of 1991 Melbourne Cup winner Let's Elope.

The garden that Margaret Marks has restored was first laid out—on an Italianate plan—by Mr and Mrs Ian Currie, who bought the property in 1912 and subsequently brought several gardeners from England to maintain the parkland, the flower borders and the rose gardens. The imprint of a design for a section of the garden, drawn up by landscape gardener Edna Walling in 1928, is also evident.

It is said that from the second storey of the house Eliza pointed out where she wanted to be buried, at the foot of the Garden Range Spur, part of the Strathbogie Ranges that surround the property. Local mythology also says that the second storey was added to enable a watch to be kept for the bushranger Ned Kelly.

An avenue of cedars—*Cedrus deodara* and *C. atlantica* 'Glauca'—leads across wide lawns towards the heritage rose garden that Margaret has designed to relate the history of the rose. The early Heritage, or Old, roses, including the Damasks, the Alba roses and the Moss roses, are housed in semi-circular beds. Another bed houses the Bourbon roses, including the highly perfumed 'Kronprinzessin Viktoria'; another is home to the early Hybrid Perpetuals such as the repeat-flowering 'Baronne Prevost' and the striped 'Roger Lambelin'.

To the south of the homestead is the new orchard, part of which has been propagated by Margaret from the remnants of Eliza's original orchard, down by Seven Creeks. This is protected from prevailing winds by a fence covered in roses, including the stunning rose 'Crimson Glory', raised by the German breeder Reimer Kordes, whose successes also include the disease-resistant, deep pink 'Esmeralda'.

On another side, the orchard is bound by a red and burgundy iris border, dominated by brown and burgundy blooms in October, followed by reds and apricots as summer progresses. The collection includes the ruby-red iris 'Chief Quin-aby', the mulberry-coloured 'Venus Butterfly', a wisteria-blue 'Ascent of Angels' and the blackest of all irises, 'Hello Darkness'.

A winding path edged with the rose 'Penelope' divides the orchard from the cream and white beds. Here, the single-flowered cream rose 'Wind-rush', raised by English breeder David Austin, and hardy species roses mix with bird-attracting Australian natives.

A little further on, tough Rugosa roses and massed daylilies mix with grevilleas that are grafted onto rootstock to suit local conditions—all part of Margaret Marks's restoration plan, where the best of exotic plants blend with indig-enous species.

THE ROSE GARDEN AT THE INLAND BOTANIC GARDEN, MILDURA

The rose garden at the Australian Inland Botanic Garden in Mildura is something of a hidden treasure. Set within 100 ha that display the genera of many of the horticultural regions of the world—including Africa, Asia, New Zealand, the Americas and, of course, Australia—the rose garden com-prises 3 ha holding 1624 rose bushes.

The beds within the rose garden are arranged as a fan, with colours coordinated from a central pav-ilion out to the boundaries. The plants are arranged also to travel across the colour spectrum. Each bed contains just one cultivar, with the yellow-flower-ing roses planted on the north side, graduating to the pinks to the south. And, so that the visitor can stand in the middle and view them all, the lower-growing varieties are planted in the centre.

The northern boundary is formed by arches covered in climbing yellow roses—there is 'Sutter's Gold', 'Souvenir de Mme Boullet', 'Bettina', 'Casino' and 'Royal Gold'. 'Limelight', bred by Kordes, masses out at the base.

As you walk among the bush roses you pass the orange 'Las Vegas', a Kordes rose of 1981; the large-flowered, yellow 'Helmut Schmidt', bred by Kordes in 1979, competes with the apricot Hybrid Tea 'Just Joey' in the race to be the first to flower in this garden.

The southern end of the rose garden is bound by a series of complete circles onto which climbers in shades of red and pink are trained. The colours move from the double, red 'Excelsa' to 'American Pillar', to the cerise 'Maria Callas' and the beautiful pink 'Mme Abel Chatenay'. Then there are the lilacs to pinks: 'Hannah Gordon', 'Viol-ette', 'Blossomtime' and 'Blue Moon'. From the outside and across a hedge of the dainty 'Ferdy', these ellipses provide windows into the garden.

Close by, the beds of red Hybrid Teas move through shades of deep lilac, with 'Vol de Nuit' and 'Angel Face', to the clear red of 'Mr Lincoln' and the black-reds of 'Norita' and 'Black Beauty'. Then you arrive at the orange beds, with 'Angelique' and the very orange 'Corso'; the entire scene is backed by a hedge of the repeat-flowering deep apricot 'Crépuscule'.

The western side of the garden is bound by a 30 m long sturdy pergola that supports the elegant, pale pink climber 'Royal Highness'. Around her feet is a mass of the pink 'Flamingo'; nearby an entire bed is devoted to the cream Hybrid Tea 'Pascali'.

Every rose in this garden enjoys an individual dripper, which comes to life early in the morning. Each of the beds includes a rose that is susceptible to disease, an advance warning when defensive action is needed. Pruning starts in the first week-end in July, and the roses are deadheaded weekly.

Along with the 350 Friends and volunteers, these beautiful gardens are maintained by six full-time gardeners, including three apprentices. Go see for yourself.

COPE-WILLIAMS WINERY GARDENS

On a summer's day, in the extensive gardens of Judy and Gordon Cope-Williams' winery and conference centre, the scent of hundreds of roses hangs in the air. The Cope-Williams' gardens are set 700 m above sea level, near the village of Romsey in the foothills of the Macedon ranges, but just 25 minutes from Melbourne's Tullamarine airport.

A driveway of roses by the Australian breeders Alister Clark and Frank Reithmuller leads you

1. Circles covered in roses become windows into the Rose Garden at the Inland Botanic Garden, Mildura.
2. The roses 'Pierre de Ronsard' and 'Buff Beauty' adorn the gate that leads into Baladonga.
3. The Rose Garden at the Inland Botanic Garden, Mildura.

1. The walled rose garden at Cope-Williams Winery.
2. A perfect place for a wedding: the Wedding Garden at Cope-Williams Winery.
3. The Alister Clark Memorial Garden.

into the property. To the south of the house is a double border marked out by chains supporting rose swags of 'Leverkusen', flowering a soft yellow and with particularly attractive leaves; of 'Clair Matin', the frothy pink 'Albertine', 'American Pillar', 'Wedding Day', 'Souvenir de la Malmaison' and 'Constance Spry'.

A certain amount of serendipity was responsible for the glorious walled rose garden that is central to these gardens. An English gardening friend who was relocating from a large country garden to a small London space sent the elaborate iron gates that now form the entrance. Accompanying the gates was a plan for a quintessentially English walled rose garden, to be arranged, traditionally, around a cruciform shape.

In the centre is an arbour of 'Climbing Iceberg' roses, from which brick paths radiate. Sentinels of clipped juniper (*Juniperus communis* 'Compressa') stand to attention at flower beds where delphiniums, hollyhocks, the Chinese forget-me-not (*Cynoglossum amabile*) and the architectural onion (*Allium cristophii*) flower with Floribunda and Tea roses.

The double brick walls of soft apricot Bendigo bricks enclose a Roman Square 1.6 times the width of the length—in this case 20 m by 13.3 m. These beautiful walls now support the luscious cream rose 'Lamarque' and the shell-pink 'Madame Gregoire Staechelin', a must-have (though only once flowering), as well as climbing hydrangea, *Hydrangea anomala* spp. *petiolaris*.

Close by is the reflection garden, a quiet, calm space that focuses on a small, stone-edged pool enclosed by a hedge of the single deep-cream Rugosa rose 'Nevada' and shaded by a variegated tulip tree. Deep-blue Japanese irises flower profusely in pots standing in the water.

A new garden, the Wedding Garden, has been created to house roses flowering in pastels: lemons, creams and pale pinks. An entrance arch covered in the climbing rose 'Pinkie' is set into a fast-growing boundary hedge of box honeysuckle, *Lonicera nitida*. This garden is divided into four beds, with a tripod supporting climbing roses in the midst of each. Yellow and cream roses bloom in one quarter, apricots in the second, pinks in another and whites and creams in the fourth. There is the elegant, lemon 'Golden Ophelia' and the deep-yellow 'Mrs Oakley Fisher'. The rich copper rambler 'Aviateur Blériot', which came as a cutting from the tennis court at the acclaimed Southern Highlands garden Milton Park, takes pride of place among the apricots. There is 'Pierre de Ronsard' as well as the repeat-flowering deep pink 'Mary Rose'. The white 'Mme Hardy' flowers alongside 'Seafoam'. A mass of old-fashioned perennials, including sweet peas, lupins and hollyhocks, along with an abundance of plants in soft greys, completes the romantic scene. There could surely be no place more heavenly for a wedding.

THE ALISTER CLARK MEMORIAL GARDEN

When you think of rose breeding, you think of France and Italy, and, of course, of Britain's David Austin—who produces those gorgeous, blowsy roses that are old-fashioned in appearance but repeat flower with modern reliability.

Australia also boasts rose breeders, but, perhaps due to our small market, they do not become world renowned. One was Alister Clark (1864–1949). Born at Glenara, the family property near

Bulla, just north of where Tullamarine airport sits today, Clark spent many of his school years in Britain and studied law at Cambridge. After he returned to Australia, he further developed a 10 ha garden at Glenara, breeding hundreds of new roses.

The Alister Clark Memorial Garden was established almost a decade ago, at Bulla, by a group of volunteers, with help from the local council, who assigned an historian and a designer to the project. The volunteer group, including Tid Alston, whose parents were close friends of Clark, has created a charming garden that displays 70 of his favourites.

Tid feels that Clark's work has not been well enough recognised. 'The [Second World] war interrupted his production and he lost his gardeners at Glenara,' she explains. 'And after the war, when you could import things again, the big blowsy Hybrid Teas became fashionable, and he got pushed aside.' Clark's roses are wonderful, though—bred to be tough and disease resistant, with a good perfume and repeat flowering.

The garden is protected by a cream-painted picket fence resplendent from early summer with the thorny 'Milkmaid', a luscious creamy-yellow rose, bred in 1925 from 'Crépuscule', and the red 'Billy Boiler'. A beautiful bluestone church, moved to the site from what is now Tullamarine's north–south runway, was re-opened in 1974.

Laid out as a semi-circle, the garden is divided into sections, with pergolas and arches displaying the climbers and pillar roses at their best. Colours have been kept together: the four beds in the middle of the garden house yellow and buff-flowering roses, then there is a bed of soft pinks and of bright pinks. Lavender and catmint edge the beds, pruned into round shapes, in keeping with the style that Clark employed at Glenara— 'And so that if we have one that does not do so well, it is not so obvious,' says Tid.

Laminated signs tell the story of each rose and its namesake. There is 'Amy Johnson', bred in 1931 and named after the aviator; there is 'Cicily Lascelles', named for the golfer, and the cerise 'Mrs Harold Alston', named for Tid Alston's mother. The red-flowering 'Nancy Hayward', named after a rose lover from Adelaide, blooms in winter, along with the constantly flowering, apricot to pink coloured 'Lorraine Lee'.

Tid's favourite rose is 'Mrs Fred Danks', in honour of one of Alister Clark's gardening friends. 'She was a keen gardener, skilled in garden design and flower arranging,' says Tid. 'Her husband was a plant breeder, specialising in delphiniums, polyanthas, freesias and iris.' Another of Tid's favourites is 'Daydream', which, like many others in the memorial garden, has been propagated from her own garden. 'She is really tough, and repeat flowers.' 'Golden Vision', with a beautiful, very double, lemon bloom, is another favourite, along with 'Lady Huntingfield'. 'She goes with all the modern roses like 'Just Joey' and 'Apricot Nectar'. She has a beaut perfume, and she's self-deadheading, which is very useful.' Then there is 'Squatter's Dream', bred in 1923. 'She flowers the whole year and makes a perfect hedge rose.'

The prime time to visit is for the Gala over the first weekend in November, but the garden performs throughout summer and autumn. And, as the Alister Clarks repeat flower, there is much to enjoy all year round.

THE PERFUMED GARDEN AND ROSERAIE

You enter Sophie Adamson's display garden and nursery, the Perfumed Garden and Roseraie, on Victoria's Mornington Peninsula, through a vivid blue pergola bedecked with a colour range of climbing roses; walk on to the Perfumed Garden, which houses the David Austin roses, and continue to the terraces describing the history of the rose.

Once through the pergola you come to the pink garden, protected by high walls painted an earth-coloured wash, providing an ideal foil for the species rose *Rosa glauca* (syn. *R. rubrifolia*), perfectly placed to display her grey leaves on the plum stems so favoured by florists. Her delicate single flower intermingles with the old Portland rose 'Comte de Chambord'. This garden is reached beyond a hedge of the Wingthorn rose (*R. sericea f. pteracantha*) with its spectacular translucent thorns and stems. 'The trick is to prune it mid-summer, as well as in winter, to encourage the regrowth not usually seen in this species rose,' Sophie explains.

The next section, the Perfumed Garden, contains the David Austin collection, held for the Ornamental Plant Conservation Association of Australia and arranged in colours in circular beds. First are the creams, then the salmons, then pale pink, deeper pink and lilac colours, and, last, the red beds. Recent releases include 'The Endeavour', 'Teasing Georgia' and 'William Morris'.

This garden is edged in the box-leaved privet (*Ligustrum undulatum*). 'Never let it get berries,' Sophie cautions. 'Keep it pruned. It's very quick growing so it needs more frequent cutting, but it gives a soft and gentle look around the rose, and very good protection.'

Further on is half a hectare that tells the story of old roses. First, there are the species roses, showing how roses grew naturally in the wild. Then come the old roses developed from the species: the Gallicas, the Damask roses, the Moss roses, the Albas and then the China roses. Finally, at the top of the hill are two beds of the best of the modern Hybrid Tea roses. There, a hedge of the early David Austin rose 'Chianti' divides the garden from an adjoining vineyard.

VICTORIAN STATE ROSE GARDEN

The Victorian State Rose Garden, sited at Werribee, about an hour from Melbourne, opened in 1986 and is maintained by a group of volunteers who meet each Wednesday to tend some 5000 plants of 600 different roses.

The garden is designed in the shape of a Tudor rose. At the centre of the design is a rotunda surrounded by 'Pink Iceberg' roses. Avenues edged with standard roses, including the apricot 'Brass Band', 'Victoria Gold' (produced for the centenary of the Victoria Rose Society) and 'Bridal Pink' fan out from this central point.

Arches covered in climbing roses direct the visitor to beds of Hybrid Tea and Floribunda roses, arranged in colour groups but with consideration as to height and size as well as type and timing of flowering. There is 'Double Delight',

then the shell-pink 'Ophelia', giving way to 'Big Chief', a fantastic deep-red show rose. Another star is the huge, pale lemon-flowering 'Elina'.

Around the outside of the design are festoons of roses supported by two wires suspended between posts. One colour adorns each festoon; single and double flowering roses, small and large flowerers are mixed. The climbing roses are trained on the top wire and the ramblers, which flower facing downwards, grow on the lower wire. There is the clear red, single 'Altissimo' on top, and 'Bloomfield Courage', the rambler, on the bottom. This is teamed with 'Sympathy' and 'Doctor Huey', then 'Dublin Bay', the big double red, with 'Bloomfield Courage'.

The Australian garden, in the shape of a leaf, and where a collection of Australian-bred roses from every state grows, was created to mark the centenary of Federation. In the centre, five callistemons, planted to represent the stars of the Southern Cross, provide height as well as shade for visitors. There are Alister Clarks, including 'Lorraine Lee' and 'Lady Huntingfield'; there is 'Carabella', released in 1960 by Frank Riethmuller, a breeder from New South Wales. *Rosa* 'Wildfire', very orange, was released in 2000 for the South Australian Country Fire Association. 'Paheka', white with a blush of pink, was released in 1980; the so-elegant 'Iced Parfait' was bred by Tasmania's Sister Mary Xavier in 1972. There is 'Valerie June', a pale, pale apricot, bred by Victorian Bill Allender in 1982.

You could visit this garden weekly, especially to catch the once-only flowering old-fashioned roses in the new heritage walk. All the famous groups, from the early species roses to the Moss roses, the Bourbons and the autumn-flowering Noisettes, are represented here. There is the species rose, *R. sericea* f. *pteracantha*, with its terrifying thorns, and the gorgeous lilac-pink 1835 'Bourbon Queen', bred in France by Mauget of Orléans; there is the 1842 Noisette 'Céline Forrestier' as well as 'Claire Jacquier', a peachy-yellow vigorous climber bred in 1888. There are 'Kathleen' and 'Francesca', bred by England's Reverend Joseph Pemberton at the beginning of the twentieth century.

While a million visitors enjoy the garden each year, it remains supremely peaceful.

South Australia

GADEN'S OLD PLACE

If it is November in Queensland the jacarandas are flowering their unique shade of blue against a cloudless sky; November throughout New South Wales sees the golden flowers of the *Grevillea robusta* and the pink blossom of the mugga ironbark (*Eucalyptus sideroxylon* 'Rosea'), and in South Australia the roses will be at their glorious best.

The parade—which starts with the Cherokee rose (*Rosa laevigata*) in early spring, closely followed by the vigorous, yellow-flowered 'Mermaid'—reaches the main act with the David Austin-bred roses and the old-fashioned roses. The finale is much later, with the rich cream climbing Tea rose 'Devoniensis' performing until Easter. Then, there are many encores, and 'Lorraine Lee' blooms on, into winter.

Gaden's Old Place, one of the most sumptuous rose gardens in a state that can easily justify its claim to being the rose centre of the world, lies close to the South Australian wine-growing district of Coonawarra.

Established as Moruya in 1904 by Otto Gaden as a 25 ha farm, the property, now half a hectare in size, was bought by the present owners, Margaret and Grant Harrington, in 1978. The original two-storey barn, complete with a loft that served as single men's quarters, including stables, tack rooms and the space for two buggies, now forms the backdrop to the Harringtons' beautiful rose garden.

The Harringtons' first priority was to build a series of hedges to provide protection from wind and frost. A hedge of *Pittosporum tenuifolium* 'Stirling Mist' forms an understorey among mature gums and conifers, and protection for the collection of Heritage, David Austin and Hybrid Tea roses, as well as roses by Alister Clark.

You enter the garden by the original drive, planted with almond trees in the 1920s; this leads to a rear courtyard constructed on a piece of solid limestone and to the old stables. The garden is divided by pergolas into several sections housing both formal and informal rose gardens. Grant Harrington built all the structures that, as well as directing the visitor from one area to the next, support climbing roses.

In one garden room 'Pierre de Ronsard' is planted with the cluster-flowered 'Carabella', the lipstick-pink tones stunning together. Planted behind is a clutch of 'Heritage', bred by David Austin. One of the best standard roses, 'Sea Foam', a mass of small, cream and pink flowers, adds further glamour.

Clever colour combinations are a feature of this garden. One section is edged with the *Euphorbia dulcis* 'Chameleon'; its bronze leaves, which turn burgundy in spring, are marvellous with the colours of the Hybrid Tea rose 'Apricot Nectar' and with the oregano 'Kent Beauty', which forms a generous ground cover.

The Harringtons are looking for the elusive black red rose, as the beautifully scented 'Mister Lincoln' is not deep enough in colour—nor, even, is the Alister Clark–bred 'Black Boy'. When they find it, it will team beautifully with Margaret's plantings of burgundies and greys: the blue-flowered, grey-leaved catmint, the perennial *Heuchera* 'Amethyst' and the new species geranium *G.* × *oxonianum* 'Walters Gift'.

CAMAWALD

Sue Zwar also has a passion for roses, and the greater part of her 3.5 ha garden in the Coonawarra district, created from 1976, is dedicated to this most beautiful member of the botanical world. The Tripod Garden is dominated by several sturdy structures in treated pine, which are covered in climbing roses. The repeat-flowering, modern, rich-pink climber 'Bantry Bay' flourishes with the deeper pink 'Titian'. Close by is the soft apricot 'Abraham Darby', growing with the apricot-coloured 'Westerland'. Growing at their feet are multiples of pink David Austin roses, including 'Cottage Rose', 'The Nun' and the very remontant 'Lilian Austin'.

The rose garden around the tennis court was built in 1994 and contains a mixture of Sue's

1. A tripod covered in 'Bantry Bay' and 'Titian' in Sue and John Zwar's garden.
2. The Victorian State Rose Garden.
3. Tripods of climbing roses add height to Sue and John Zwar's rose garden.
4. The repeat-flowering climbing rose 'Westerland'.

1. The rose growing fields at
   Ruston Roses, at Renmark
   in South Australia.
2. The much-loved rosarian
   David Ruston.
3. Pillars of 'Blossomtime' and
   'Fugue'.
4. A fence is dressed in the
   climbing rose 'Mme Abel de
   Chatenay', an early Hybrid Tea
   bred in 1897, and the deeper
   pink 'Peter Frankenfeld'.

favourites. There is 'Cornelia', raised by Pemberton, along with her cousin 'Penelope' and the delicate, single 'Sally Holmes'. Then there are the David Austin roses again: 'LD Braithwaite', named after the grower's father-in-law, along with 'Emanuel' and the crimson 'Prospero'. Climbing happily over the tennis court pavilion is the apricot-pink 'Phyllis Bide' (bred from 'Perle d'Or' and 'Gloire de Dijon'), which is rarely without a flower.

A garden of shade houses and pergolas, built by John Zwar to commemorate a milestone wedding anniversary, is also devoted to roses. Here the scene is all pinks and creams, with 'Lamarque', 'Renae' and 'New Dawn' competing for sun and space. With more than 600 roses planted throughout, Camawald is, Sue admits, a high-maintenance garden.

RUSTON ROSES

As the dawn light creeps over tall stands of century-old trees, a milky wash illuminates fields of roses in every colour and of every type. Some do not exist anywhere else in the world and all are at their peak at the end of October.

This is Ruston Roses, at Renmark, in South Australia's Riverland, home to David Ruston and more than 50,000 rose bushes of over 4000 varieties. David's father arrived from the United Kingdom in 1911 and planted grapes for the dried-fruit industry. But the young David, who started growing roses at the age of eight, eventually planted 11 ha, all of old varieties. He started selling commercially in 1968 and the company, now owned by his niece, Anne, supplies florists all over Australia with field-grown roses, and nurseries with budwood for grafting.

The roses are arranged in large paddocks. The most ancient in the garden are the wild species roses: *Rosa gallica* var. *officinalis*, or the apothecary's rose, along with *R. × damascena* and *R. rubiginosa*—roses that have been grown throughout Europe for centuries.

In one area, the delicate, tiny blooms of 'Cecile Brunner' clamber over a pergola, next to the double-white *Rosa banksiae* var. *banksiae*, with its strong perfume redolent of violets. On three separate pillars are 'Blossomtime', the red-bloomed 'Fugue' and the very pink 'Baronne Edmond de Rothschild'. An arch covered in the deep cerise, single-flowered 'Bloomfield Courage' leads the eye to the end of this paddock, across a field of the salmon-pink 'Violet Carson', bred in 1964 by the Irish Sam McCredy, now a resident of New Zealand.

'It's very, very difficult,' David Rustin replies when asked which is his favourite rose. 'Probably 'Mr Lincoln'. The scent, the substance of the petals, the way the bush goes straight up and you don't have to disbud it: you have one flower to a stem. Of the old roses I still love *Rosa laevigata*, first to flower and six weeks of beauty; no flowers afterwards but who cares. It's in full flower before some of the Damasks have even shot.'

David likes to team his roses with irises, particularly blue-flowering varieties. There are 700 varieties at Ruston Roses, from bearded irises to Louisianas and the largest collection of spuria irises in Australia.

URRBRAE ROSE GARDEN

One of the many gardens heavy with scented blooms for months each year is the Urrbrae Rose Garden at Urrbrae House, which was built in 1891 by one of the state's leading pastoralists, Peter Waite, in the Adelaide foothills. Waite died in 1922, leaving his estate to the University of Adelaide to further the teaching and research of agriculture and related disciplines.

The rose garden was created at the suggestion of the late rosarian Deane Ross, to mark the centenary of this historic property and to trace the development of the rose from the turn of the century. The garden includes almost 200 different varieties, ranging from Hybrid Teas and Floribundas to Hybrid Musks, Polyanthas, miniatures and an avenue of climbers.

The search for roses that had bloomed in Waite's garden in the late nineteenth and early twentieth centuries, some of which were long gone, began. Budwood was sourced from growers around the world and, with the help of noted Australian rose growers David Ruston and Walter Duncan, and members of the Heritage Rose Society, roses no longer readily available were sourced and have been saved. 'Climbing Hadley', a Hybrid Tea of 1914, along with the 1929 'Talisman' and 'Irish Elegance' of 1905, are among the much-loved but almost forgotten roses that are flowering again.

In the restored gardens in the grounds of the elaborate nineteenth-century house, disciplined planting is very effective. Around the grand carriage loop are generous plantings of just one rose, 'Red Meidiland'; from there a long walk is hedged with 'Cécile Brunner' and the bright pink 'Ferdy'.

Along one entire side of the house is a low hedge of 'White Meidiland', backed with a deep border of Hybrid Musk roses, 'Penelope' and 'Cornelia'; a walkway edged with 'Bonica' leads from the house.

Height and scale are ensured by a series of arbours supporting a collection of climbing roses bred during the last century. There is 'Crépuscule', 'Black Boy' and the pink Bourbon rose 'Kathleen Harrop'.

A mass of the coral pink 'Simply Magic' decorates the Fountain Garden.

In the Waite Arboretum, established in 1928, 2500 trees represent 850 native and exotic species. Many trees are on the National Trust Register of Significant Trees, including an avenue of 70 mature English elms, *Ulmus procera*.

Western Australia

QUATRE SAISONS HERITAGE ROSE GARDEN

You would expect roses to flourish in the hot and dry climate of Western Australia. At Quatre Saisons, a 1 ha rose garden created over some 20 years and sited atop the Darling Scarp, 30 minutes east of Perth, they certainly do.

The garden, which is surrounded by a forest of the indigenous jarrah (*Eucalyptus marginata*), is among the country's largest private collections of Heritage roses. Named for the glorious old-fashioned rose of the same name, Quatre Saisons houses more

than 800 roses, including collections of species roses, as well as of Alba, Damask, Moss, Centifolia and Gallica roses.

There was no easy journey to the beautiful garden that is Quatre Saisons today, built as it is on laterite ironstone gravel soil, deficient in nitrogen and phosphorus as well as the trace elements of copper, zinc and magnesium. Fourteen semi-trailer loads of a landscaping mix provided the base for the garden, and hours were spent each evening after work and under floodlight, drawing out and preparing the beds.

After the preparation came the treat of choosing which roses to plant. The first shortlist of roses, chosen over a six-month period of dreaming, reading and planning in the early days of the garden, were 'Pink Grootendorst', 'Scabrosa', 'Reine des Violettes', 'Alba Maxima', 'Cardinal de Richelieu', 'Madame Isaac Pereire', 'Cornelia' and 'Duchesse de Brabant'.

The garden is designed in several distinct sections. A formal rose garden, influenced by European traditions, is a feature of the southern side of the property. Around the main lawn the style is more relaxed, with roses in a cottage garden setting. Another section focuses on roses bred in Australia by Alister Clark.

The apothecary's rose or *Rosa gallica* var. *officinalis*, used since ancient times for medicinal and cosmetic purposes, can be found in another section, along with the ancient Damasks, used by the Roman emperors. The Autumn Garden features Hybrid Tea roses.

Like most things horticultural in Australia, success also depends on water, and a bore sunk to 60 m provided for the expanding orchard, as well as for the vegetables and roses.

Lavenders and grey-foliaged plants, along with cascades of bougainvillea, including the white *B.* 'Penelope', team well with the roses and are most appropriate in this difficult gardening country, where gardeners cope with searing winds and high evaporation rates, along with the low rainfall. And Quatre Saisons is home to an abundance of birdlife, as the garden is managed organically.

THE ROSE GARDEN AT ARALUEN BOTANIC PARK

In the Darling Range, just behind Perth, set amongst tall gums—mainly jarrah (*Eucalyptus marginata*) and marri (*Corymbia calophylla*)—a large garden flourishes, welcoming thousands of visitors each year.

Araluen Botanic Park was the inspiration of a young Perth businessman, John Joseph Simons, who bought the 60-odd hectares in the early 1930s as a place for the city's youth to participate in outdoor activities. Simons chose the site for its rich soils, its streams and its forests of eucalypts, casuarinas and tall banksias, with their complex understorey of grass trees, native ferns, orchids and other wildflowers.

Picturesque walking trails constructed down the sloping landscape and culminating in a series of waterfalls and rock pools were created. Roses popular at the time were also planted, both in garden beds and at the base of each of 38 massive cylindrical stone pillars built to support a magnificent 50 m long, curving pergola. Wisteria was also planted to decorate great hardwood logs that formed the overhead cross-beams.

After Simons' death in 1948, the garden fell into disrepair until it was rescued in the early 1990s by a group of Western Australian garden lovers. Araluen is now owned by the state government and leased and managed by these volunteers, who formed the Araluen Botanic Park Foundation.

One of the early restoration projects was the stone pergola, which once supported 80 climbing roses. The few that survived to 1990 included the lovely peach to apricot coloured 'Climbing Lorraine Lee'. There was also the blush-pink 'Climbing Lady Sylvia', a sort of 'Ophelia', and the climbing Hybrid Tea 'Souvenir de Mme Boullet'. Mud-spattered notes in Simons' handwriting had been discovered, listing the names of the roses planted in the garden in August 1938. The position of each rose, and the nursery from which each was obtained, had been carefully recorded, invaluable in the restoration: only three of the original varieties proved unobtainable.

Over the past decade a new garden of old roses, including Tea roses, China roses and Alister Clarks, has been created by the Western Australian branch of the Heritage Rose Society, on a series of wide terraces at the top of the Araluen gardens.

Challenges in the new rose garden included coping with the ravages of wildlife, which feasted on the new growth as if it were caviar, providing constant hard pruning! In addition, volunteers had to hand-water using buckets. Fencing, and other improvements that included a reticulated watering system, have meant that the roses, now numbering more than a thousand, have since thrived.

The little-known Polyantha rose 'Mme Jules Thibaud' seems to always be in bloom, and many largely evergreen and constantly blooming Tea roses, with their heritage in the warmer southern provinces of China and which love the Western Australian climate, provide a succession of colour throughout the year. Garden stars include the soft-pink 'Mrs BR Cant', the very fragrant, pink 'Mme Antoine Mari', the cerise 'Papa Gontier', the salmon pink to gold 'Mme Berkeley', 'Isabella Sprunt' with a rich yellow double bloom, and the cream 'William R Smith'.

The roses in the beds devoted to the work of Alister Clark, and which attract the most attention from garden visitors, include the very fragrant, deep, velvety-red 'Restless', the very pink 'Mrs Fred Danks', the golden 'Lady Huntingfield', 'Sunlit' and 'Marjorie Palmer'. There is also a hedge of 'Sunny South'. Plans are under way to expand the Araluen Tea roses into a national collection to ensure their continuing survival and to provide a study resource.

Over time this magnificent garden has become a valued venue for recreation, including for concerts, festivals and horticultural shows—from the Chilli Festival in March to Tulip Time in spring, through to early November, when the once-flowering Heritage roses are at their best.

Tasmania

THE NATIONAL ROSE GARDEN, WOOLMERS

Designed at the turn of the twentieth century, the National Rose Garden, set in the historic

Woolmers estate close to Launceston in northern Tasmania, was the brainchild of a group of friends, including Pam Hutchins, today head rosarian. The garden has been established with joint funding from government, council and industry, assisted by labour from a work-for-the-dole scheme.

The entrance to the 3 ha rose garden, beyond the outbuildings and homestead of the Woolmers estate, home to the Thomas Archer family from 1817 to 1994, is through an 80 m arbour of the German-bred climbing rose 'Westerland', which bears orange and apricot blooms that tie the garden to the ochre-washed buildings behind.

'Westerland' was selected for several additional reasons: it has a good perfume, is a repeat and prolific bloomer, and is disease resistant. As well, it has good foliage and drops its petals, so does not require deadheading. Along the length of the arbour the white-flowering *Viburnum plicatum* 'Newzam', growing to just over a metre, hides the bare legs of the climbing rose and is bounded by a second hedge of clipped box.

Hedges, including *Pittosporum* 'Silver Song', are a feature of the garden. They combat the winds that accompany the fabulous views over the Longford Valley and the South Esk River, divide the garden into manageable spaces, and ensure that all is not visible at once.

A central rill, running perpendicular to the 'Westerland' arbour, and set in a 120 m by 35 m parterre, dissects the garden. Metal birds and water plants, including reeds and lily pads to disguise the mechanics of the water feature, have been crafted by the sculptor Folko Kooper. The modern Hybrid Tea roses, a cross between the earliest English roses and the Chinese roses that arrived in the United Kingdom on the tea clippers, are arranged in this central bed.

The first European roses are set out in chronological order on one side of the garden. Opposite are the wild species roses and the ancient Chinese roses, including the Rugosas, and Pimpinellifolias.

Smaller parterres of the different groups are laid out on either side of the central section. The pink standard 'Mary Rose', bred by David Austin, surrounds a mass of the soft pink 'Bonica', from the Meilland family.

In another bed is the Hybrid Musk rose 'Sally Holmes', covered in pale yellow blooms, with the single yellow 'Nevada' and the minute flowers of 'Canary Bird' close by. There is a bed of *Rosa* 'Falklands', its foliage turning a fiery red in autumn.

Tasmanian gardens are at constant risk of damage from late spring frost: volunteers wait until after the chance of another severe, late frost has passed before trimming away the burnt foliage. 'But as far as I'm concerned you can't have a war with mother nature,' says Pam Hutchins. 'You won't win it, so you just come to terms with it. In 30 days they will all be great again.'

Above: The National Rose Garden at Woolmers, northern Tasmania.

Native Gardens

The 'hoo-whip' of the whipbird wakes you. That piping sound is the king-parrot. There is the mellow call of the grey butcher bird, the 'peep' of the spotted pardalote. There is the wonker bird, which loves the wild tobacco bush; there are crimson rosellas, bellbirds, cat birds, the pretty yellow robin, the rufus fantail, the paradise rifle bird, the eastern spine bill and the golden whistler. The warbles, whips and bells of the early morning birdsong truly do create an orchestra.

Queensland

The rising sun slowly lights the scene to reveal the forest-clad mountains of the McPherson Ranges, folding out before you as the mists swirl through the ravines and gullies of this section of the Great Dividing Range. You are literally on top of the clouds, in the World Heritage–listed Lamington National Park—more than 20,000 ha of pristine subtropical rainforest and 160 km of walking tracks. You are just 20 minutes from the Gold Coast, but a world away.

Holidays over almost two decades have been spent walking through the 2000-year-old forests of Antarctic beech: swimming in deep-blue, ice-cold rock pools; listening to the bush tales of the cunjevoi lily, the antidote to the stinging tree that grows above it; and watching, hushed, for that great mimic, the lyrebird.

There are tales of human adventure and great bravery, too, in these mountains. In 1937 Bernard O'Reilly trekked from his O'Reilly's Guesthouse, now called O'Reilly's Rainforest Retreat, through rugged mountainous bush, to find the wreck of a Stinson plane, thus saving the lives of two men. Nearby, pioneering conservationists Romeo Lahey and Arthur Groom fell in love with those mountains in the 1920s and invited a group of friends to join them on a camp, hoping they would invest in a 25 ha site that would make the mountains more accessible to others. They all took up the challenge, and in 1933 the Binna Burra Mountain

Lodge was born and was brought up in pieces, by flying fox, from the bottom of the mountain.

The gardens around the lodge were first laid out in the 1960s and utilise species indigenous to Lamington. The wide lawns that roll out from the main building form viewing decks that are shaded by the New England blackbutts (*Eucalyptus andrewsii*), which also play host to cascades of yellow-flowering king orchids, *Dendrobium speciosum*. The rockeries around the perimeter house the two species of mint bush native to the region: *Prostanthera ovalifolia*, a mass of purple flowers in early spring, and *P. phylicifolia*. Their scented leaves make both of them attractive to butterflies. Ground covers include prostrate grevilleas and the native sarsaparilla, *Hardenbergia violacea*.

The walk through the lower section of the gardens has been planted for the butterflies: there is the lemon myrtle (*Backhousia citriodora*), a Queensland rainforest tree, greatly loved by butterflies and providing a protective upper storey for blue-flowered flax lily (*Dianella caerulea*), and the native daphne (*Philotheca myoporoides*), with its tiny white flowers. There are clumps of mat rush grass (*Lomandra longifolia*), a butterfly magnet; and the wild cotton bush, food for the brown and black wanderer, or Monarch, butterfly.

The native wisteria, now called *Callerya megasperma* (syn. *Millettia megasperma*), which grows throughout the rainforest, romps through the four banksias that are native to the area—*Banksia obtusifolia*, *B. integrifolia*, *B. conferta* and *B. spinulosa*.

Previous page: Verticordia grandis.

1. The native wisteria, or native sarsaparilla, *Hardenbergia violacea*.
2. The tough and waterwise flax lily, *Dianella revoluta*.
3. The white cedar, *Melia azedarach*.
4. Native daphne, re-classified *Philotheca myoporoides* (syn. *Erisotemon myoporoides*).

There is the white cedar (*Melia azedarach*), indigenous to the dryer edges of the plateau, which is mostly of deep red volcanic soils that are slightly acidic. Also growing on the edge of the rainforest is the local *Allocasuarina torulosa*, the rose she-oak, providing food for the long-lived glossy black cockatoo, now rare.

The plantings around the two tiers of guest cabins—the earliest were constructed from sawn tallowwood (*Eucalyptus microcorys*) and topped with shingles of stringybark (*E. eugenioides*)—are also indigenous to the Lamington Plateau. There is the rare native cycad (*Lepidozamia peroffskyana*), along with the local *Cordyline petiolaris*. The delicately scented native gardenia (*Randia chartacea*) is a favourite of the pencilled blue and large banded awl butterflies, and is also happy in more temperate climates.

New South Wales

The garden at Buronga Hill Winery—today the second-largest winery in Australia, crushing 120,000 tonnes each year—was established on a bald sand hill in 1984 at Buronga, on the Silver City Highway, in the far south-west of New South Wales, just across the river from Mildura on windswept mallee country.

The surrounding landscape is home to two species of mallee indigenous to these salty, red, sandy loam soils, which receive just 250 mm of rain in a good year: *Eucalyptus gracilis*, the common mallee gum, distinguished by its dark-green leaves, and *E. foecunda*, which bears lime-green leaves.

Along with these, some 8000 trees were planted, at 2.5 m apart, to create a woodland of eucalypt species that would tolerate the salty soils and provide some protection to the western side of the complex of winery buildings. Lemon-scented gums (*Corymbia citriodora*), with their shining, smooth white trunks and pendulous branches, thrive along with the local river red gum (*Eucalyptus camaldulensis*) and with the river she-oak, *Casuarina cunninghamiana*. Geraldton wax, from the sands of the south of Western Australia, was also planted but refused to flourish in the local soil.

This woodland area is irrigated by recycled water from wash-downs and general run-off, which is gathered in underground sumps fed by drains running under the winery. The water is filtered and settles in large ponds situated among the stands of mallee before being pumped onto the gardens. The bird life—plovers, lorikeets, galahs and magpies—that flourishes among these native plantings is magnificent.

Groups of the local mallee pine (*Callitris verrucosa*), along with *Callistemon* 'Queen's Park', protect the administration buildings from the road. There are also plantings of the black-trunked mugga ironbark (*Eucalyptus sideroxylon* 'Rosea'), its highly perfumed pink blossom greatly loved by the birds. These lovely gardens demonstrate perfectly how exotic plants can team effectively with local species and how, by good garden practices such as water recycling, a lush garden need not be at odds with the environment.

THREDBO

Even for Australians who have not been there, the Australian Alps are part of our imagination; their stories and characters form part of the mythology that makes up our culture. And nowhere is the sense of place greater than atop the main range above Thredbo Village in the New South Wales Snowy Mountains. From there you can look out across folds of silent mountains, shimmering blue with their cover of eucalypts, to Dead Horse Gap and into Victoria, and reflect upon your engagement with the subtle beauty of this landscape.

Above the tree line, at about 1850 m, on the walk to Mount Kosciuszko (at 2228 m, Australia's highest peak), the alpine meadows flower in a kaleidoscope of delicate pastel blooms throughout summer. Carpets of snow daisies, billy buttons, heaths and other alpine flora form meadows of delicate colour among the bare, imposing rocky peaks and the brutal granite outcrops. First to flower in spring are the marsh marigolds, which push through as soon as enough light penetrates the melting snows. Then, fields of eye bright bloom in purple and white, finishing by Christmas to make way for the billy buttons, silver snow daisies and alpine celery that will all continue to flower throughout January.

The flowers of the high country, like those of most Australian native plants, are not as flamboyant as the exotics we may prefer for the gardens we construct, but they impart a sense of peace to those who take the time to contemplate and appreciate them. There is a quiet spiritualism about this place that is addictive; it will have you returning again, and again.

Victoria

HESKET HOUSE

It is 6 am and the sun is rising, casting pale-yellow first-light shafts onto the still lake. There has been rain overnight and the scent of eucalyptus is hanging softly in the morning air. Black swans glide silently on the lake, past watery beds of Japanese iris, sparkling blue as the morning sun lights the raindrops lingering on their flat petals. A huge black kangaroo bounds away. The koalas are barking and the white cockatoos screeching, but for all this noise it is supremely peaceful.

Hesket House is sited between the villages of Hesket and Romsey on the north-western side of Victoria's Mount Macedon, amidst manna gums (*Eucalyptus viminalis*—the preferred food of Victoria's koalas), messmate, swamp gum and peppermint; its garden pays homage to the 80 ha of pristine bushland in which it rests. The property is a wildlife shelter, and ring-tail possums, kangaroos and wombats seem to co-habit happily in the planted landscape.

Designed predominantly with native plants, the garden is laid out around a 1 ha lake, with its jetty perfect for sitting on, or jumping from, in summer. The path around the lake—among 7 km of walking tracks on the property—leads you past plantings of Geraldton wax, flowering in a mass of white and pale pink in early summer, past westringias and native mint bush (*Prostanthera* spp.) before it bends to hug the edge of the lake, where a seat is placed to allow you to sit in restorative contemplation. Three species of the tough, rush-like *Lomandra* genus are a favourite around the lake.

1. The Grevillea Park at Woolongong, New South Wales.
2. The smooth, cream trunk of the lemon-scented gum, *Corymbia citriodora*.
3. Dawn lights the lake at Hesket House.

1. *Grevillea georgeana*.
2. Lawns have been replaced by ground covering native species in Diana and Brian Snape's garden.
3. Low growing native species edge paths in the Snape garden.

Hugging the very edge of the lake is the small-flowered *Grevillea* 'White Wings', a great favourite with the birds. There is also a white-flowering tea tree (*Leptospermum juniperinum*), which occurs naturally on the property and grows to about 2 m high; the 'Horizontalis' cultivar is a stunning, spreading plant. Among the damp soil are clumps of blue-flowering Japanese iris—*Iris ensata*, formerly known as *I. kaempheri*.

Also in the garden is the blood-red flowering cinnamon wattle (*Acacia leprosa* 'Scarlet Blaze'), recently chanced upon in a forest north-east of Melbourne, Victoria, and propagated from cuttings. There is a large silver wattle (*Acacia dealbata*), with its grey bark and shimmering silver foliage. The native *Clematis aristata*, which has made itself at home in the trees, spreads its scent throughout the garden at dusk. Rocks are integrated throughout the garden to provide unobtrusive seating.

A series of well-planted, wide terraces leads you from the house to the water's edge. Plantings of burnt-orange daylilies and kangaroo paw team with an Easter daisy that flowers in great clouds of yellow and blue. The blue-flowering catmint and rosemary tie the scheme together. The ground cover is the prostrate *Grevillea* 'Poorinda Royal Mantle'.

Hesket House is not just a beautiful setting; in this perfect environment workshops are conducted to teach participants about environmental sustainability and responsibility.

SNAPE GARDEN

Drought and climate change have forced many Australian gardeners over recent years to re-think their 'garden keeping' practices along with their choice of plants. However, waterwise plants from countries with a similar climate to our own don't always provide the solution. Many South African plants—for instance, the freesia, the watsonia, the cape daisy and the white arum lily—are so happy here that they have become garden escapes. There is no simple answer to good garden design for Australia, but one solution is to garden with plants that are indigenous, and appropriate, to the area in which you live.

Diana Snape's garden, created with her husband Brian over the past 30 years, is testament to the expertise and experience evident in her book *The Australian Garden: Designing with Australian Plants*. The majority of plants in this garden, which is on a classic Australian quarter acre (0.1 ha) block and is 9 km from the centre of Melbourne, are Victorian, although the Snapes have welcomed some plants native to other states, especially Western Australia. All lawns were replaced with mulched, ground-covering plants, or with hardscaping. This has saved water and maintenance.

Winter is never bleak in this garden, where collections of grevilleas, banksias and correas continue to flower throughout the cold months. The front garden is a combination of different native daisies and grasses, which attract butterflies and other insects. The small shrubs like the crowea, epacris and darwinia, with their subtle, delicately coloured flowers, provide the under-storey. Ground covers include a prostrate form of the mounded *Melaleuca hypericifolia* and a lilac form of *Scaevola aemula*. There is *Zieria prostrata*, a well-behaved plant with attractive foliage. There is also the white-flowering *Platysace lanceolata*, greatly appreciated over summer.

A deck at the rear of the house extends the living space into the garden and is protected by a red spotted gum (*Eucalyptus mannifera* subsp. *maculosa*). 'In summer it stops high sun from getting into the house, and in winter the sun can get underneath it,' Diana explains. Edging the brick path that meanders through the back garden are the prostrate *Banksia petiolaris* and *B. blechnifolia*, greatly loved by the wattle birds. There is also the prostrate *Grevillea* 'Old Gold' with its deep-orange flower. The native jasmine (*Jasminum suavissimum*) fills the air with the scent of vanilla on a summer evening.

For those who do not consider themselves purists, many Australian plants team well with exotics, particularly some from South Africa (take care, of course, not to plant those that love our similar climate so much that they have become weeds). Matching or toning leaf shape, texture and colour is probably one of the keys to successfully combining exotic with native. Diana advises that glossy-leaved native plants team well with glossy-leaved exotics, for instance. She finds that plants like the chef's cap correa (*Correa baeuerlenii*), with its rich green leaves and attractive form, along with the native gardenia, frangipani and hibiscus, seem at home with exotics.

Among the many bonuses of using local plants in the garden is that of being woken by the birds: Brian Snape would like to see more gardens with at least a few indigenous plants so that a wildlife corridor is created. 'It would give the area a little of its distinctiveness back, a sense of place,' he says. And the cacophony created by the more than 60 species of native birds that are found in the Snape garden would be reward enough.

South Australia

Kangaroo Island, discovered by Matthew Flinders in 1802, circumnavigated by Nicholas Baudin in 1803 and populated by American whalers in 1804, has since become a much-loved holiday destination for South Australians but remains something of a secret to the rest of us. Some 4500 square kilometres of rolling green hills and sometimes savage, occasionally mild, coastline, this island, just a 20 minute flight from Adelaide, is completely unspoiled; the developers' dollar and the creeping rash of subdivision has, thankfully, passed it by. Like the proverbial jewel, the island floats on a cerulean bed of ocean.

And the island holds many secrets. Home to the famous Ligurian honey bee, one of the last pure strains in the world, and to koalas, platypus, rosenberg sand goannas and New Zealand fur seals, Kangaroo Island also protects the sea lions that colonise its beaches hugging the Southern Ocean. The locals produce wine, make cheese, grow free-range poultry in a fox- and rabbit-free environment and extract pure eucalyptus oil from the indigenous narrow-leaved mallee. One-third of the island, home to 920 indigenous plants, of which 46 are endemic, remains uncleared, and there are 23 national parks. And there are some marvellous gardens.

One of these is Little Riccorang, on the outskirts of Kingscote, where Helen and Bill Richards have gardened since 1996. A howling wind in the first winter after they moved to the property prompted them to create banks of protective plant material around their house. They had come from the high rainfall part of the island, so the low rainfall of just 400 mm in their first year forced them to rethink how they would garden and, in the sandy soil, to rely heavily on mulch. The Richardses feed their plants with a slow-release pelletised fertiliser for natives, and an organic fertiliser for others. They leave weeds on the ground, then add compost and a mulch of well-aged pine bark, obtained free of charge from the local mill. The result is a beautiful and protected garden of waterwise lawns and sweeping beds reliant on Australian native plants, full of birdsong.

A long, winding drive planted with eucalypts, allocasuarinas and acacias leads you into the garden. The Richardses, volunteers for the Trees for Life programme started in South Australia 20 years ago, grow thousands of native trees each year for distribution to Landcare groups, local farmers and gardeners. They grow over 20 different species of eucalyptus, including the sugar gum (*Eucalyptus cladocalyx*), the Sydney blue gum (*E. saligna*), *E. leucoxylon* and the small *E. forrestiana* with its beautiful red, bell-like flowers and seed pods, all suited to the sandy soil in this part of the island.

Helen admits to a passion for *Eucalyptus caesia*, the gorgeous silver princess from Western Australia. 'I grow a box full every year and dot them around: I absolutely adore them.' On propagating the trees from seed she says, 'It's not really that difficult. Just plant the seeds and water them. And they grow.'

Winding paths lead through deep plantings of tea tree, grevilleas and banksias, mixed with buddleia, tecoma and smokebush. The emu bush, an *Eremophila* species, lends its soft grey foliage to plantings of Geraldton wax and purple statice. Close by is a long, sweeping bed, mass-planted with *Leucospermum patersonii,* flowering a brilliant red in late spring.

In the back garden is the elegant *Agonis flexuosa*—the variegated variety 'Pied Piper'—along with *Leptospermum* 'Copper Glow' and the rare *Grevillea petrophiloides* subsp. *magnifica,* with its pink toothbrush flowers.

Little Riccorang is a mix of natives and exotic plants. 'I go looking for things that are relatively hardy, that take less water rather than more and I like different colours of foliage,' says Helen, who doesn't grow annuals.

When planting out seedlings the Richardses add to the soil a generous quantity of compost, organic fertiliser, a wetting agent and, in areas where the soil is a light sand, some clay soil. Trees are not drip-irrigated. Plants are well weeded and watered for the first 12 months, after which they look after themselves.

Another virtuoso garden on Kangaroo Island is John and Carol Stanton's Stokes Bay Bush Garden, on the north side of the island. This 3 ha, 23-year-old, native plant garden has been divided into several walks, including the Blue Boronia Walk, the Grass Trigger-Plant Walk and the Hakea Walk. Numbers and colour-coded markers match plants to names in the guide-book published for each trail.

The Stantons wanted to show what style of garden could be created on the soil, which is a slightly acid, well-drained sand and gravel over clay. Rainfall averages 450 mm a year.

The plants have dictated the layout of the garden. 'Like most gardening it was trial and error,' says John. 'The soil changes in certain parts of the garden. We tried to match plant needs.' The Stantons found that a distance of just 5 m can determine whether or not a native plant thrives in their garden.

There are 1000 different species in the Stokes Bay Bush Garden, including a large selection of plants indigenous to Western Australia that thrive in the soil and climatic conditions.

The Blue Boronia Walk follows the ridge where this rare plant (*Boronia coerulescens*) occurs naturally. There is also the endemic *Pimelea macrostegia* with its cream, pendulous, pompom-like flowers. *Adenanthos macropodianus*, with silver foliage and small red flowers, also grows naturally only on Kangaroo Island.

Gravel paths take you past 90 different terrestrial orchids, 75 of which were introduced from other areas of Australia. There is an orchid in flower every month of the year. Among the many grevillea species is *Grevillea petrophiloides* with its beautiful, large salmon-pink flowers. *G. tenuiloba*, the amber grevillea from Western Australia, is a spreading shrub that grows to about 1.5 m in height and is used in this garden as a ground cover: its toothbrush-like inflorescences range from cream to orange.

The garden houses almost all the 70 species of banksia. From Western Australia there is the stunning, red-flowered *Banksia coccinea*, *B. hookeriana* and the rare *B. cuneata*, the matchstick banksia, with flower heads resembling a matchstick—cream with a red tip. There is also *B. laevigata* with its startling flowers that look somewhat like green stress balls. There are the two banksias indigenous to Kangaroo Island: the low, branching *B. ornata* and the silver banksia *B. marginata*.

The collection of darwinia, a genus of around 45 species, all of which are endemic to Australia, includes *Darwinia oxylepis* with its tiny red bell-like bracts that hang from the branches. There is the rare *D. carnea*, a spreading shrub with greenish bell flowers, from Western Australia.

You will also find *Boronia molloyae*, named after the early settler Georgiana Molloy, who filled her lonely days by collecting the plant material of the south-west for the English botanist Captain James Mangles. Georgiana's carefully pressed and numbered plants and seeds were a valuable contribution to the world's understanding of the species of Western Australia, and many are now housed at Kew Gardens.

At the Stokes Bay Bush Garden plants are nursed for two years, then must look after themselves. Seed is often sown directly into the ground.

Among the birds that abound there are the beautiful yellow New Holland honeyeater and the golden whistler, with its deep-gold chest. It is not just for their melodious song that the birds are so valued. 'Birds let you know if there are any snakes by a loud chattering noise just above [the snakes] and a shrill noise if a hawk is around,' says John Stanton.

Western Australia
GINGIN

Just an hour and a bit north of Perth is an area that the locals consider their own Garden of Eden. Gingin, first opened up in 1831, just two years after the birth of the new colony of Western Australia, lies along several lush valleys that rise gently from Breera, Lennard's and Gingin Brooks. You can grow almost anything in the area, say its residents. There are stone fruit, passionfruit and mangoes—the district being the most southerly point at which the latter are grown commercially. The valley is becoming an important centre for olives, and a local wine industry is developing. Wildflowers bloom throughout the year, including the firewood banksia and the very pretty rose-bloomed *Banksia menziesii*, as well as the candle banksias, *B. attenuata* and *B. hookeriana*.

Gingin was first settled in 1831 and, with its Mediterranean climate, is considered today one of the three best places in the world for the cultivation of the chenin blanc grapes. Sally and Greg Page also grow over 200 species of Western Australian wildflowers on their Breera Brook Farm. There is the local *Chamelaucium* sp. *gingin*, a waxflower endemic to the area and some 50 species of verticordia, including the brilliant orange featherflower, *Verticordia nitens*, which grows naturally on the local sandplains with the Christmas tree, *Nuytsia floribunda*, both flowering in early summer.

While summer temperatures can reach 40 degrees Celsius, the average temperature during February is a comfortable 25 degrees Celsius; while rainfall is 800 mm per annum, water is plentiful in the area due to the presence of aquifers, large natural water storage areas underground. Soils vary enormously, from silver-white sand to a heavy red loam.

Seaside Gardening

The scent of salt in the air, whales making themselves at home just beyond your front verandah, and a sea that is a constantly changing canvas: these are among the many joys of coastal living. If there has to be a drawback to living in paradise it is that gardening can be a challenge. Perhaps the most difficult situation in which to garden is one where the sea breezes, welcome as they may be, constantly dump salt. You have to be a resourceful gardener to create a calm oasis in these conditions.

Of course, no two coastal situations are the same. With the Australian coastline extending some 60,000 km and enjoying the full gamut of compass aspects, it's not practical for a book to provide all the answers. You need to explore what will best suit not only your region, but indeed your own microclimate. Local plant growers or nurseries will be a good resource; also observe the undisturbed natural environment to see what has always grown there, and look around your immediate neighbourhood to see what other gardeners have grown with greatest success. In the end you will benefit most from your own experimentation—and your inevitable disappointments will be counterbalanced, and hopefully outnumbered, by hard-won triumphs. In seaside gardening more than any other, perseverance is the key.

The most important element in a garden that has to cope with the mean-spirited lash of salt-laden winds is the construction of a series of hedges, or windbreaks, that will present several lines of defence. Preferably of plants indigenous to the local area, these hedges will create a micro-climate for what is planted in their protective 'shadow'.

Hedges of salt tolerant plants

When creating wind breaks take care to install a series of barriers that will sift and filter the wind:

if you create a single impenetrable wall you will only direct the wind up and over, to continue on its destructive path. For this reason, two lines of defence are recommended.

FIRST LINE PLANTINGS

The first line of defence should incorporate a variety of tough trees and shrubs. These might include the paperbarks *Melaleuca bracteata*, *M. linariifolia* and *M. quinquenervia*. Again, your choice will be dictated by the climate in which you garden.

You could create clever 'living screens' with the South Pacific *Metrosideros excelsa*, with its red 'powder puff' flowers. The genus *Calliandra*, of some 200 species of evergreen shrubs and trees, bears similar flowers in reds, pinks or creams. These trees look superb with the white flowers of the tough-leaved, evergreen *Rhaphiolepis indica*, commonly known as Indian hawthorn—although, in fact, it hails from China. It bears white to pink flowers in late winter and spring and has leathery leaves that withstand the onslaught of the salt wind. Escallonia is another valuable plant for an exposed site and forms a useful hedge.

One of the best plants for front line defence against salt winds is the oleander (*Nerium oleander*), which will also tolerate a hot western position and little water. Among the cultivars are

Previous page: The tough *Rhaphiolepis indica* will cope with salt winds; it can become a problem in warm temperate climates.
Opposite above: Swathes of the renga renga lily edge a boardwalk at The Saltings in New Zealand's North Island.
Opposite below: Bernie Hawkings' New Zealand garden overlooks the blue waters of the Matakana estuary and the Pacific Ocean.

'Mrs Fred Roeding', which grows to about 1 m, and 'Petite Pink' and 'Petite Salmon', lower growing varieties.

More choice is provided by the grey-leaved coastal rosemary (*Westringia fruticosa*), with its lilac flowers, which can be clipped into a hedge or left as a shrub.

Eriostemon, now mostly re-classified as *Philotheca* spp., is a tough but beautiful indigenous genus of some 45 species. The most common is probably *P. myoporoides*, hardy, adaptable, with a long flowering period, and easy to propagate from cuttings. It loves sandy soil, but keep its roots cool.

SECOND LINE PLANTINGS

The lillypilly (*Syzygium* spp.), with its pink tips on new growth, makes an excellent hedge, and is more suited to a humid climate than the traditional box. A loose hedge of a selection of the grevilleas is another alternative for the second line of planting: the pretty cultivars like *Grevillea* 'Moonlight' attract wattle birds, lorikeets and kookaburras (*see also* Native Plants).

The large genus *Hebe*, tough and waterwise, makes an excellent low hedge or second line of defence; these plants tolerate humidity better than the traditional box. For late summer colour, choose 'Purple Queen' or 'Alicia Amherst', stunning with *Hebe albicans*, or 'White Gem', perhaps embracing a mass of the special varieties of agapanthus that won't go mad and become garden escapes (*see* Agapanthus). Or a collection of the rock rose (*Cistus* spp.), with its tissue paper flowers, would look effective planted behind a hedge of hebe. Native to the Mediterranean climates, these evergreen shrubs will cope with dry conditions and poor soil, but don't enjoy humidity.

For seaside gardens the coast daisy (*Olearia axilaris*) performs well, as does the versatile native *Correa reflexa*.

SPECIAL PLANTINGS

Once the layers of protection are in place it is time to add repeat plantings of a selection of softer plants. The Norfolk Island hibiscus will

tolerate salt on its leaves; or try the small-leaved camellias, which will cope well in the shadow of several layers of tough plants. A selection of the candy to pastel-flowering *Pentas*, suited to tropical to warm temperate climates, will look stunning behind a protective hedge.

Add grey-leaved succulents or the silver-foliaged New Zealand native *Astelia banksii*. The renga renga lily (*Arthropodium cirratum*), also native to New Zealand, can create a beautiful, soft grey to green ribbon of foliage when planted in multiples.

You can play with colour combinations provided by showmen such as the bird of paradise (*Strelitzia reginae*) and the flamboyant *Canna* 'Tropicana', the orange, apricot and pink stripes of its foliage adding drama to this previously overlooked performer.

GROUND COVERS

Among the ground covers that will now cope with a coastal position are the grey-leaved, blue-flowered convolvulus, which will also cascade down retaining walls. And that tough, scented friend *Trachelospermum jasminoides* will thrive as either a ground cover or a climber.

Festuca glauca, with its grey–green tufts, is a stunning seaside plant, particularly effective if growing among a mulch of shells. Replace lawn with waterwise ground covers such as aluminum plant, massed pelargoniums and the spreading lippia (*Phyla nodiflora*), instead of thirsty grasses.

Tip: Use *Phyla nodiflora* when planting lippia as some members of the genus can invade waterways and wetlands.

Trees for coastal gardens

Apart from the majestic paperbarks already mentioned in this chapter, it is hard to go past the feathery-leaved poinciana (*Delonix regia*) as a shade and avenue tree for a coastal position. With

1. Use the tough renga renga lily to create ribbons of soft blue-green.
2. The red powder puff flowers of *Metrosideros excelsus*.
3. The nautical theme starts on the footpath outside Bernie Hawkings' garden.
4. *Nerium oleander*.

its gracious, spreading canopy, the poinciana is redolent of lazy days in tropical gardens. What could be more relaxing than to look out across a deep green lawn, as you sip your drink from the shade of a wide verandah, looking at the sea beyond. For cooler climates, the deciduous silk tree (*Albizia julibrissin*) provides a similar atmosphere.

Of course accent trees don't come much better than the frangipani, flowering in a fruit salad of colours, to bend and twist over the entire arrangement and to remind you when summer has arrived. The dragon's-blood tree (*Dracaena draco*), not a tree you might covet for your own piece of paradise, looks terrific when planted singly or en masse in a beachfront garden: there is something very special about that arresting architectural form when silhouetted against a cobalt blue, cloudless Queensland sky.

WATERWISE GARDENING

Waterwise Gardening

As Australia continues to struggle with the vicissitudes of climate change, cities and towns are suffering increasingly rigorous water restrictions. It is essential, therefore, that we all address the issue of waterwise gardening and consider using a palette of plants that are not too thirsty. The message being conveyed by garden writers, landscapers and much of the nursery industry is that that the time has passed when we should struggle to replicate gardens that flourish in countries with dramatically different climates, even though many of our ancestors have come from those regions.

However, respect for the scarcity of water doesn't mean that gardeners must eschew exotic species—many of which we have all enjoyed since the earliest plant hunters risked their lives trekking through the high mountain passes of the sub-continent, seeking treasure to satisfy an increasingly insatiable gardening appetite in the western world. Through good garden keeping and with a little commonsense, you can enjoy the species of the northern hemisphere—along with Australian native species—without wasting water.

Top of the list of 'must-do's is mulching, using just about anything non-toxic that you can lay your hands on (*see* Mulch). Then you need to choose species that are suited to your climate and soil type. Think about the climate and soil conditions that prevail in the country in which your plants grow naturally; the yellow species rose *Rosa foetida*, for example, is native to the dry plains of Iran. Most importantly, annuals, which not only take up unthinkable amounts of time and energy, but also consume bucket-loads of precious water, are best avoided.

Experiment with a combination of xerophytic plants (those needing very little water), such as the aeoniums and agaves, with hardy exotics like daylilies, iris, plumbago, the sterile varieties of agapanthus (one species of this South African plant is so hardy it has been declared noxious in some states), jasmine or ceanothus. Take care, though, as many of the dry-climate plants such as the sedums, lavenders, artemisias and echiums love the heat but will rot if subjected to humidity.

Herbs make effective ground covers, as do edging plants like liriope and the native wisteria (*Hardenbergia violacea*). And don't forget the grasses, which, when chosen with care, are user friendly, creating an up-to-the-minute look that is perfectly happy in drought conditions (*see* Grasses).

❤ Some favourites

ARTHROPODIUM

The lovely, easy-going renga renga lily (*Arthropodium cirratum*) is native to New Zealand, where you see it flowering in dry shade beneath spreading street trees, so it must be as tough as boots. It looks delicate, however, flowering each summer in generous fluffy white panicles, which emerge on wiry stems from within rosettes of grey-green foliage. The plant has a use in Maori medicine. There are several cultivars available from nurserymen in New Zealand: all love warm temperate climates and well-drained soil.

Opposite: *Echium thyrsiflora*.

BULBS

Grape hyacinths, sparaxis, babianas, freesias, and most of the bulbs from South Africa and many from Mediterranean countries will also thrive in the warmer climates in drought conditions. The spring-flowering bulbs, which won't thank you for water during summer—their dormant season—are the perfect choice for waterwise gardens (*see also* Bulbs).

CISTUS

The hardy rock roses, which hail from the Mediterranean and the Canary Islands, are another smart choice for a dry garden: they require very little water and their delicate, crêpey blooms—which are reminiscent of fully open single roses—flower for months. They don't like humidity, love heat, will tolerate frost and demand a well-drained, gravelly soil. They flower in a range of colours, from white to pink and purple. Tip-prune to prevent the plant growing rangy, and use the cuttings to propagate more. Plant them in drifts, in dry-garden borders, or to cascade down banks and retaining walls.

CLIVIAS

Clivias, of course, are a favourite and are one of the most useful, easy-to-please plants for dry shade (*see* Shade).

ECHIUM

Echiums, native to regions around the Mediterranean, are an excellent choice for the water-conscious gardener who doesn't have to cope with severe frost. They team well with agapanthus, which I love so much that I have given them a section of their own. Although there are around 40 species in the Echium genus, we grow two main species in this country, both of which prefer frost-free climates, or at least some protection from late spring frosts.

Pride of Madeira, *Echium candicans* (syn. *Echium fastuosum*), has tall blue to lilac rounded flower spikes which emerge in late spring from grey-green, felt-like whorls of leaves. The flowers last through summer, sometimes causing the bush to collapse over the ground; prune by cutting off spent flowers. They are happy with poor, sandy soil and just a little water.

Echium pininana is a biennial and bears a taller and sharper funnel-like flower spike which erupts from a basal rosette of sharp leaves. The plant dies after flowering, so take a series of cuttings to keep propagating new plants.

LAVENDER

Humidity is the enemy of the evocative lavender: they like hot, dry summers and thrive in full sun, in well drained, sandy soil. Think Mediterranean climate and poor, rocky soils, as in the south of France—although lavenders also occur naturally into the Middle East and India. I love lavender as a hedge: you may not want to clip it to perfection, though—then, if one plant dies, you are not left with a glaring gap! (And in a garden in country Victoria, a long hedge of English lavender is clipped into a wave pattern to emulate the blue, undulating hills and mountains in the near distance.) Lavenders make the perfect accompaniment to roses as the two like similar conditions.

Lavandula angustifolia, English lavender, is the best known and most common species. It is from the oil glands at the base of the flowers of this species, and *L. stoechas*, that the pungent lavender oil is distilled. There are several cultivated varieties of the *L. angustifolia*: the variety we now know as 'Hidcote' was found by Lawrence Johnston in the hills in the south of France and brought back as seed to his garden, Hidcote, in England's Cotswolds district. An Australian selection, *L. angustifolia* 'Egerton Blue', is valued for its oil; 'Munstead', 'Twickel Purple' and 'Hidcote' are excellent for dried flowers. The later-flowering *L. angustifolia*. 'Rosea' and 'Folgate' will extend the flowering season.

Lavandula × intermedia 'Seal' is a tall-growing variety of the hybrid between *L. angustifolia* and *L. latifolia* species, and is used for dried flowers. *L. × intermedia* 'Miss Donnington' (syn. 'Bogong') has a sweet, camphorous perfume for stripped, dried flowers, while *L. × intermedia* 'Yuulong' and 'Grosso', along with *L. allardii* and *L. dentata*, var. *candicans*, are planted for cut bunches of fresh lavender.

Opposite: The waterwise garden at the Royal Botanic Gardens, Melbourne.

Waterwise gardens: Royal Botanic Gardens, Melbourne

Staff at the Royal Botanic Gardens, Melbourne, have been working towards water wisdom for more than a decade. In that period the gardens have reduced water consumption by over 40 per cent through careful monitoring of the use and needs of species planted and through management of the irrigation system.

Eighty per cent of the gardens—which comprise 35 ha just a 20 minute walk from the heart of the business district—is watered by an irrigation system that is carefully managed according to the needs of each plant. An automatic weather station gives accurate data on evaporation and precipitation, allowing the horticultural staff to control the computer that regulates the system.

In the Water Conservation Garden, sited in an exposed, north-facing section of the gardens, plants with similar horticultural needs have been grouped together. In the first of four elliptical beds are the brightly coloured phormiums, or flaxes, from New Zealand, along with an intensely blue catmint, mixing with the grey-leaved, yellow-flowered senecios. There is *Phlomis fruticosa*, from the Mediterranean, and cycads, which hate too much water, from Africa. Adding form and pizzazz is *Agave geminiflora*, with its striking, tall-flowering stalks, indigenous to Madagascar. The red flowers of the African daisy (*Arctotis* spp.) team with a little yellow native everlasting daisy, *Chrysocephalum apiculatum*. From Western Australia comes the beautiful weeping eucalypt known as the silver princess, *Eucalyptus caesia*. The bed is edged with the drought-loving *Echeveria secunda*, which quickly multiplies to form a water-conserving, dense ground cover.

Another bed is devoted to mass plantings of Mediterranean grasses, predominantly the soft grey-blue *Miscanthus sinensis* 'Gracillimus'. Drama is added by the bright orange flowers of the bird of paradise (*Strelitzia reginae*) and cerise flowering alliums.

The different masses of plants create a layering effect and the soft form of the grey grasses contrasts perfectly with the upright structure of the flowers.

A collection of trees with gnarled and twisted forms is housed in yet another bed. There is the tortured form of the tree aloe (*Aloe bainesii*), found in South Africa, which bears extraordinary, hot-pink flowers in spring and summer, and *Echium candicans*, with its 60 cm spires of lilac-blue flowers throughout summer. There is the native hibiscus (*Alyogyne huegelii* 'West Coast Gem'), from Western Australia, along with *Banksia integrifolia*, tolerant of a variety of conditions. The purple flowers of *Teucrium marum*, from the Mediterranean and a member of the mint family, team perfectly with the textured leaves and pale lemon flowers of *Stachys thirkei*.

It's not just these beautifully planted dry-garden beds at the Botanic Gardens that are waterwise, however. Many of the plantings throughout the Gardens rely on the strong statements made by textural plants with architectural forms: the aloes, yuccas, agaves and phormiums, plants from New Zealand, Madagascar and Western Australia, so loved by the landscape architect and early gardens director William Guilfoyle.

Lavandula stoechas, French lavender, is classed as a weed in some parts of Australia—easy to believe when you realise the lavenders belong to the mint family. Two mid-winter flowering varieties recently made available are the compact and very pretty *L. pedunculata* cultivars 'Winter Lace', which flowers in a soft to deep lavender, and 'Violet Lace', with masses of purple flowers.

RUSSELIA

The drought-tolerant *Russelia equisetiformis*, from a genus of around 50 species from Mexico and South America, flowers in vibrant red on soft cascades of green, needle-like foliage. Plant it in great swathes to cover the ground or to cascade down a bank or retaining wall.

SUCCULENTS

The many genera that we call succulents are, of course, perfect for the hot and dry garden and have a section of their own (*see* Succulents; Seaside Gardening).

Planting and care

Lavenders love an alkaline soil: add sand and lime to acidic clay soil.

Prune lavenders back to the beginning of the season's growth after flowering. If you cut too drastically into old wood you might lose the plant. As with hedges, it is best to prune from the beginning of the plant's life to encourage thick growth from the base.

Useful Contact Details

ART IN THE GARDEN
Bronwyn Berman
Tel: 02 4878 5069
bronwyn.berman@pol.net.au

'Botanica' and 'Art in the Gardens'
Exhibitions organised annually
by the Friends of the Royal
Botanic Gardens, Sydney.
www.rbgsyd.nsw.gov.au/friends

The Crisp Galleries
Tel: 02 6227 6073
www.petercrisp.com.au

Maroochy Bushland Botanic
Gardens, near Buderim.
Friends of the Maroochy
Bushland Botanic Gardens
Tel: 07 5445 5525

The Sculpture Garden
National Gallery, Canberra
Tel: 02 6240 6411
www.nga.gov.au/sculpturegarden

Sculpture by the Sea
www.sculpturebythesea.com

Yengo Sculpture Garden
Tel: 02 4756 2002

**CONSERVATION, ENVIRONMENT
AND WATER ISSUES**
Banrock Station Wine
and Wetland Centre
Tel: 08 8583 0299
www.banrockstation.com.au

Centre for Education and
Research in Environmental
Strategies (CERES)
Tel: 03 9387 2609
www.ceres.org.au

Peach Flat Community
Wetland Project
Tel/Fax: 03 9853 1152
www.adland.com.au

Wendy Van Dok
Water Efficient Gardenscapes
Tel: 03 9802 7211; 0408 550 876
http://home.nemesis.com.au/water

DESIGNERS
David Baptiste Design
Tel: 08 8346 9626;

0418 845 054
dbdesign@adam.com.au

Michael Bligh Landscape Design
Tel: 02 4821 8462
www.michaelbligh.com.au

Tim Hays
Tel: 02 6677 1116
timhays@mullum.com.au

Dean Herald
Tel: 02 9651 5002
www.rollingstonelandscapes.com

Michael McCoy
Tel: 0411 514 982

Peter Stubbs City Gardens
Tel: 08 8231 2945; 0411 454 855

John Sullivan, Hortulus Landscaping
Tel: 07 4099 5856; 0412 944 793

**FLOWERS AND
FLOWER ARRANGING**
Bloomey's Florists
Tel: 02 9360 1788

Tracey Deep Installations
Tel: 02 9328 7321

**GARDENS MENTIONED
THAT WELCOME VISITORS**
Some of these gardens open by
appointment only, while others
offer accommodation. To find out
more, visit this website for garden
tourists: www.gardensopen.com.au

Ayrlies, near Auckland,
New Zealand
Tel: 00 11 64 9 530 8706

Camden Park, Camden
This house and garden is open
annually, for one weekend
in September.
Tel: 02 4655 8466

Culzean, Tasmania
Tel: 03 6393 1132

Experiment Farm Cottage,
Parramatta
Tel: 02 9635 5655
www.nsw.nationaltrust.org

Foxglove Spires, Tilba Tilba
Tel: 02 44737 375
foxglovespires@hotmail.com

Gravetye Manor Country House Hotel,
West Sussex, England
Tel: 0011 44 1342 810567
www.gravetyemanor.co.uk

Imperial Gardens, Terrey Hills
Tel: 02 9450 2455
www.imperialgardens.com.au

Isola Madre and Isola Bella,
Lake Maggiore, Italy
www.borromeoturismo.it

Jardin des Paradis, France
cordes.development@wanadoo.fr

Levens Hall, Lake District, England
www.nationaltrust.org.uk

McLaughlin Garden and
Horticultural Centre,
Maine, USA
Tel: 00 111 207 743 8820
www.mclaughlingarden.org

Mount Vernon, USA
www.mountvernon.org
For more information on Virginia,
see www.virginia.org

Mount Stewart, Northern Ireland
www.nationaltrust.org.uk
Follow the links to historic
properties, and then Mount Stewart.
See also www.tourismireland.com.au

Naumkeag,
Massachussetts, USA
Tel: 00 111 413 298 8146
westregion@ttor.org

Nooroo, Mt Wilson
www.mtwilson.com.au

Old Wesleydale, Tasmania
tassiedevil76@hotmail.com

Royal Botanic Gardens, Melbourne
www.rbg.vic.gov.au

Royal Botanic Gardens, Sydney
www.rbgsyd.nsw.gov.au/friends

Sissinghurst, Kent, England
www.nationaltrust.org.uk

Studley Royal, England
www.nationaltrust.org.uk

The Saltings, north of Auckland,
New Zealand
www.saltings.co.nz

Thuya and Asticou Gardens,
Maine, USA
www.asticou.com/gardens

Woodbridge, near Auckland,
New Zealand
Tel: 0011 64 9 415 7525
woodbridgegardens@xtra.co.nz

HEDGES, MAZES, PARTERRES AND WALLS

Broughton Castle, Banbury,
Oxfordshire, OX15 5EB
Tel/fax: 0011 44 1295 276070
admin@broughtoncastle.
demon.co.uk

Great Fosters
Tel: 0011 44 1784 433822
www.greatfosters.co.uk

Drystone walls
Andrew Garner
andezandliza@aapt.net.au
Visit also Dry Stone Walls Association
of Australia www.dswaa.org.au

National Hedgelaying Society,
Britain
www.hedgelaying.org.uk

LIGHTING

Inarc Architects
Tel: 03 9819 0677
rr@inarc.com.au

NATIVE PLANTS AND GARDENS

Association of Societies
for Growing Australian Plants
http://asgap.org.edu

Binna Burra Mountain Lodge,
Beechmont, Queensland
Tel: 07 5533 3622
www.binnaburralodge.com.au

Hesket House, Romsey
Tel: 03 5427 0608
www.heskethouse.com.au

Illawarra Grevillea Park
Tel: 02 4284 9216
www.grevilleapark.org

Thredbo
www.thredbo.com.au
To take part in a guided walk with
the Discovery Ranger Program of
the National Parks and Wildlife
Service, find the link on
www.nationalparks.nsw.gov.au
Tel: 02 6450 5600

NURSERIES, AND PLACES TO FIND MY FAVOURITE PLANTS

Agapanthus
Nobbies View Drought
Tolerant Plant Farm
Tel: 03 5989 0745
nobbies_view_plant_farm@
bigpond.com

Bamboo
Bamboo Society of Australia
www.bamboo.org.au

Mr Bamboo
Tel: 02 9486 3604; 0412 379 898
www.mrbamboo.com.au

Bulbs
Blue Dandenongs Bulb Farm
Tel: 03 9751 9555
admin@bluebulbs.com.au

Hancocks Bulbs
Tel: 03 9754 3328
www.daffodilbulbs.com.au

Hill View Rare Plants
Tel: 03 6224 0770

Garry and Sue Reid
Tel: 02 6027 1514

Tesselaars Bulb Farm
Tel: 03 9737 9811
enquiries@tesselaar.net.au
www.tesselaar.net.au

Van Diemen Quality Bulbs
Tel: 03 6442 2012
www.vdqbulbs.com.au

Camellias
Eryldene
Tel: 02 9498 2271

Paradise Plants
Tel: 02 4376 1330
admin@paradiseplants.com.au

Conifers
www.wollemipine.com

Cycads
Eudlo Cycad Gardens
Tel: 07 5445 0496

Eucalypts
Toowoomba Wildflowers
Tel: 07 4630 9410

Ferns
Mt Waverley Fern Society
Tel: 03 9306 5570

Fruit
Flemings Nurseries
Tel: 03 9756 6105
www.flemings.com.au
(also stock many trees and
shrubs)

Horticultural Research and
Advisory Station, Department
of Primary Industries
www.ricecrc.org/reader/
res-stations/ars-cowra.htm

International Olive Oil Council
www.internationaloliveoil.org

Olives Australia
www.oliveaustralia.com.au

The Wagga Olive Centre,
Charles Sturt University
Tel: 02 6933 2773
Joint venture with the
Agricultural Research Institute,
part of NSW Agriculture
Tel: 02 6938 1999

Hellebores
Elizabeth Town Nursery
Tel: 03 6368 1192
hortus@southcom.com.au

Post Office Farm Nursery
www.postofficefarmnursery.com.au
(mail order and sale days)

Lavenders
Nedlands Lavender Farm
Mornington Peninsula
Tel: 03 5974 4160

Orchids
Wonga Belle Tropical Gardens
Tel: 07 4098 7173; 0427 987 173
csacolin@bigpond.com

Peonies
Romswood Peony Farm
Tel: 03 54 270 260
romswood@optusnet.com.au

Perennials
Visit www.nurseriesonline.com.au

Out of Town Nursery
and Humming Garden,
near Beechworth
Tel: 03 5726 1554

Stephen Ryan's
Dicksonia Rare Plants
Tel: 03 5426 3075

Wychwood
Tel: 03 6363 1210
enquiries@wychwoodtasmania.com

Rhododendron
Australian Rhododendron
Society, Mt Waverley
Tel: 03 9756 6327

Ilnacullin Garden, Ireland
www.toursimireland.com.au

National Rhododendron
Gardens, Victoria
Tel: 03 9751 1980

Roses
Alister Clark Memorial Garden
(visitors welcome at any time)
Tel: Tid Alston, 03 9333 1514

Araluen Botanic Park,
near Perth
Tel: 08 9496 1171
www.araluenbotanicpark.com.au

Baladonga Homestay
Tel: 02 6377 1390

Cope-Williams
Winery Gardens
Tel: 03 5429 5428
enquiries@cope-williams.com.au

National Rose Gardens
at Woolmers
Tel: 03 6391 2230
www.nationalrosegarden.org.au

Perfumed Garden and Roseaie
Tel: 03 5974 4833
www.theperfumedgarden.net.au

Quatre Saisons Heritage
Rose Garden, near Perth
Tel: 08 9299 7555
www.quatresaisons.com.au

Rose Garden at the Inland Botanic
Garden, Mildura, open daily except
Christmas Day and Good Friday,
weekdays from 7.30 am to 4.30 pm,
weekends and public holidays
from 10 am to 4.30 pm.

Ross Roses
Tel: 08 8556 2555
www.rossroses.com.au

Ruston Roses
Tel: 08 8586 6191
rustrose@riverland.net.au

Urrbrae Rose Garden,
Waite Campus,
Urrbrae, South Australia
Open dawn to dusk, daily.

Victorian State Rose Garden
Tel: 03 9742 6717; 03 9742 4291
roses@werple.net.au

Salvias
Sue Templeton Salvias,
near Albury, NSW
templeton@albury.net.au

Trees
Vintage Tree Nursery
Tel: 0417 229 658
www.vintagetree.com.au

Tropical
Botanical Ark,
north of Port Douglas
Tel: 07 4098 8174
www.botanicalark.com

PESTS, DISEASES AND WEEDS
Department of Natural Resources
www.dnr.qld.gov.au

A report on horticultural
dangers to our environment
www.wwf.org.au

The South Australian
Government's research
site is extremely useful:
www.bugsforbugs.com.au
www.sardi.sa.gov.au
www.tpp.uq.edu.au

Yates information line
and consumer advice
Tel: 1800 224 428

POTS
Purchase antiquing paints
from Haymes Paint Pty Ltd
Tel: 1300 033 431

TOURIST BUREAUX
AND FESTIVALS
Autumn Garden Festival, Bright
Bright Information Centre
Tel: 1800 500 117
www.brightautumnfestival.org.au

Dunedin Tourist Office
www.DunedinNZ.com

Irish Tourism
www.tourismireland.com.au

Kangaroo Island Tourism
www.kangarooisland.com.au

Lake Maggiore, Italian Lakes
Visit www.distrettolaghi.it
or Tourism Italia at www.enit.it

Larnach Castle, Dunedin
Tel: 0011 64 3476 1616
www.larnachcastle.co.nz

Mount Macedon Horticultural
Society's autumn and spring fairs
www.mountmacedon.org.au

Visit Mount Wilson gardens
in autumn and spring
www.pnc.com.au/~galelect/
gardens.htm

New Zealand
www.newzealand.com

Renmark Rose Festival
(October)
Tel: 08 8586 6094

Renmark Tourist Centre
Tel: 08 8586 6704

South Australia
www.tourismsouthaustralia.
com.au

Southern Highlands, NSW,
Tourist Bureau
Tel: 02 4871 2888

Bibliography

Works Cited and Sources Consulted

Banks, David P and Perkins, Andrew, *Flora's Orchids*, ABC Books, Sydney, 2005.

Baxter, Paul and Tankard, Glen, *Growing Fruit in Australia*, Macmillan, Melbourne, 1990.

Beales, P, *Classic Roses*, HarperCollins, London, 1997.

Bennett, Jennifer, *Lilacs for the Garden*, Firefly Books, Ontario, 2002.

Bennett, Peter, *Organic Gardening*, New Holland, Sydney, 2006.

Bisgrove, Richard, *The English Garden*, Viking, London, 1990.

Brooker, Ian and Kleinig, David, *The Field Guide to Eucalypts*, vol. 1, Blooming Books, Melbourne, 1999.

Brown, Deni, *The Royal Horticultural Society New Encyclopedia of Herbs and Their Uses*, Dorling Kindersley, London, 2002.

Callaway, Dorothy, *The World of Magnolias*, Timber Press, Portland, 1999 (first published 1994).

Cave, Yvonne, *Succulents for the Contemporary Garden*, Florilegium, Sydney, 2002.

Chatto, Beth, *The Dry Garden*, Orion, London, 1998 (first published 1978).

Clebsch, Betsy, *The New Book of Salvias*, Florilegium, Sydney, 2003.

Cox, Peter, *Australian Roses*, Blooming Books, Melbourne, 1999.

Cuffley, Peter, *Traditional Gardens in Australia*, Five Mile Press, Melbourne, 1991.

Cunningham, Peter and Surgeon, RN, edited by David S Macmillan, *Two Years in New South Wales*, Angus & Robertson, Sydney, 1966 (first published 1827).

Dirr, Michael A, *Hydrangeas for American Gardens*, Timber Press, Portland, 2004.

Etherington, Kate, *Flora's Trees and Shrubs*, ABC Books, Sydney, 2005.

Fiala, Father John, *Flowering Crabapples: The Genus Malus*, Timber Press, Portland, 1994.

Ford, Gordon, *The Natural Australian Garden*, Blooming Books, Melbourne, 1999.

Fullerton, Ticky, *Watershed: Deciding Our Water Future*, ABC Books, Sydney, 2001.

Gardiner, Jim, *A Gardener's Guide to Magnolias*, Timber Press, Portland, 1989.

Garnett, TR, *Man of Roses: Alister Clark of Glenara and His Family*, Kangaroo Press, Sydney, 1990.

Gerritsen, Henk and Oudolf, Piet, *Dream Plants for the Natural Garden*, Frances Lincoln Limited, London, 2000.

Glowinski, Louis, *Complete Book of Fruit Growing in Australia*, New Holland, Sydney, 2006.

Handreck, K and Black, N, *Growing Media for Ornamental Plants and Turf*, UNSW Press, Sydney, 1991.

Harris, James GS, *The Gardener's Guide to Growing Maples*, Blooming Books, Melbourne, 2000.

Hibbert, Margaret, *The Aussie Plant Finder*, Florilegeum, Sydney, 2006.

Jekyll, Gertrude, *Colour in the Flower Garden*, Mitchell Beazley, London, 1995 (first published 1908).

Jellicoe, G, Jellicoe, S, Goode, P and Lancaster, M, *The Oxford Companion to Gardens*, Oxford University Press, Oxford, 1991.

Jones, David L, *A Complete Guide to Native Orchids of Australia*, New Holland, Sydney, 2006.

Kelly, J Hillier, *Gardener's Guide to Trees and Shrubs*, David & Charles Devon, Devon, 1995.

Kerr Forsyth, Holly, *The Garden Lover's Guide to Australia*, Random House, Sydney, 1998 (first published 1996).

—*Gardens in My Year*, New Holland, Sydney, 2000.

—*Remembered Gardens: Eight Women and Their Visions of an Australian Landscape*, Miegunyah Press, Melbourne, 2006.

Latreille, Anne, *The Natural Garden Ellis Stones*, Viking O'Neil, Melbourne, 1990.

Leonard, G, *Eucalypts: A Bushwalker's Guide*, UNSW Press, Sydney, 1993.

Mathew, Brian and Swindells, Philip, *The Complete Book of Bulbs*, Mitchell Beazley, Sydney, 1995.

McMaugh, Judy, *What Garden Pest or Disease is That?* Weldon, Sydney, 1990.

Morris, Colleen et al., *Interwar Gardens: A Guide to the History, Conservation and Management of Gardens of 1915–1940*, The National Trust of Australia (NSW) Parks and Gardens Conservation Committee, Sydney, 2003.

Norrington, Leonie, *Tropical Food Gardens*, Bloomings Books, Melbourne, 2001.

Pollan, Michael, *Second Nature*, Bloomsbury, London, 2002 (first published 1996).

Ratcliffe, R, *Australia's Master Gardener: Paul Sorensen and His Gardens*, Kangaroo Press, Sydney, 1990.

Riffle, Robert Lee, *The Tropical Look: An Encycopaedia of Landscape Plants*, Thames and Hudson, London, 1998.

Ross, Graham et al., *Botanica*, Random House, Sydney, 1997.

Royal Horticultural Society, *Encyclopedia of Plants and Flowers*, Dorling Kindersley, London, 1994.

Short, Philip, *In Pursuit of Plants*, University of Western Australia Press, Perth, 2003.

Snape, Diana, *The Australian Garden: Designing with*

Australian Plants, Bloomings Books, Melbourne, 2003.

Steen, Andrew, *Bromeliads for the Contemporary Garden*, Florilegium, Sydney, 2003.

Stewart, Angus, *Gardening on the Wildside: The New Australian Bush Garden*, ABC Books, Sydney, 1999 (first published 1990).

—*Let's Propagate! A Plant Propagation Manual for Australia*, ABC Books, Sydney, 1999.

Stones, Ellis, *Australian Garden Design*, Macmillan, Melbourne, 1971.

Thompson, Ken, *Compost*, Dorling Kindersley, London, 2007.

Timms, Peter, *Australia's Quarter Acre*, Miegunyah Press, Melbourne, 2006.

Valder, Peter, *The Garden Plants of China*, Florilegium, Sydney, 1999.

Walling, Edna, *Gardens in Australia: Their Design and Care*, Oxford University Press, Melbourne, 1946 (first published 1943).

—*Cottage and Garden in Australia*, Oxford University Press, Melbourne, 1947.

Warren, William, *Tropical Garden Plants*, Thames and Hudson, London, 1997.

Watts, Peter, *Edna Walling and Her Gardens*, Florilegium, Melbourne, 1991.

Woodward, Penny and Vardy, Pam, *Community Gardens*, Hyland House, Melbourne, 2005.

Young, Helen, *Balcony: Gardening in Small Spaces*, Lothian Books, Sydney, 2005.

Plant Index

General Index